EXERCISE AND SPORT SCIENCES REVIEWS

Volume 16, 1988

Edited by KENT B. PANDOLF, Ph.D.

Director, Military Ergonomics Division
US Army Research Institute of Environmental Medicine
Natick, Massachusetts

Adjunct Professor of Health Sciences
Sargent College of Allied Health Professions
Boston University
Boston, Massachusetts

Adjunct Professor of Environmental Medicine
Springfield College
Springfield, Massachusetts

American College of Sports Medicine Series

MACMILLAN PUBLISHING COMPANY
NEW YORK
COLLIER MACMILLAN CANADA, INC.
TORONTO
COLLIER MACMILLAN PUBLISHERS
LONDON

Guest Referee Editors

The Editor of *Exercise and Sport Sciences Reviews* gratefully acknowledges the services of the following Guest Referee Editors who assisted the Editorial Board in the review of these chapters.

Anne E. Allan

F. Wayne Askew

Elsworth R. Buskirk

Victor A. Convertino

Bradley D. Hatfield

Robert S. Hutton

Bruce H. Jones

Kiernan J. Killian

Edward McAuley

John Olerud

Vern Seefeldt

John R. Sutton

Macmillan Publishing Company
866 Third Avenue, New York, New York 10022

Collier Macmillan Canada, Inc.

Collier Macmillan Publishers • London

International Standard Book Number: 0-02-390570-0

Library of Congress Catalog Card Number: 72-12187

Printing: 1 2 3 4 5 6 7 8   Year: 8 9 0 1 2 3 4 5 6

Preface

Exercise and Sport Sciences Reviews is an annual publication sponsored by the American College of Sports Medicine that reviews current research concerning behavioral, biochemical, biomechanical, clinical, physiological, and rehabilitational topics involving exercise science. The Editorial Board for this series currently consists of ten recognized authorities who have assumed the responsibility for one of the following general topics: Biochemistry, Exercise Physiology, Psychology, Motor Control, Athletic Medicine, Rehabilitation, Sociology of Sport, Environmental Physiology, Biomechanics, and Growth and Development. The organization of the Editorial Board should help foster the commitment of the American College of Sports Medicine to publish timely reviews in broad areas of interest to clinicians, educators, exercise scientists, and students. The goal for this Editorial Board is to provide at least one review in each of these ten areas for each issue of *Exercise and Sport Sciences Reviews*. Further, the Editor shall select three or four additional topics to be developed into chapters based on current interest, timeliness, and importance to the above audience.

The contributors for each volume are selected by the Editorial Board members and the Editor. Although the majority of these reviews are invited, unsolicited manuscripts or other potential chapter topics will be received by the Editor and reviewed by him and/or various members of the Editorial Board for possible inclusion in future volumes. Correspondence should be directed to Kent B. Pandolf, Ph.D., U.S. Army Research Institute of Environmental Medicine, Natick, MA 01760-5007, who assumed the role as Editor of *Exercise and Sport Sciences Reviews* beginning with Volume 14.

Kent B. Pandolf, Ph.D.
Editor

iv

Contributors

James A. Ashton-Miller, Ph.D.
Department of Mechanical
Engineering and Applied
  Mathematics
College of Engineering
The University of Michigan
Ann Arbor, Michigan

Wilma F. Bergfeld, M.D.
Section of Dermatopathology
The Cleveland Clinic Foundation
Cleveland, Ohio

Gaston Beunen, Ph.D.
Institute of Physical Education
Catholic University of Leuven
Leuven, Belgium

Susan J. Birrell, Ph.D.
Department of Physical
Education and Sports Studies
The University of Iowa
Iowa City, Iowa

E. Cafarelli, Ph.D., F.A.S.C.M.
Department of Physical
  Education and Athletics
Bethune College
York University
Downsview, Ontario
Canada

Ronald D. Fell, Ph.D.
Exercise Physiology Laboratory
University of Louisville
Louisville, Kentucky

Deborah L. Feltz, Ph.D.
School of Health Education,
  Counseling Psychology and
  Human Performance
Michigan State University
East Lansing, Michigan

Ralph P. Francesconi, Ph.D.
Heat Research Division
U.S. Army Research Institute of
  Environmental Medicine
Natick, Massachusetts

C. Zvi Fuchs, Ed.D.
Department of Research and
  Sports Medicine
Wingate Institute
Natanya, Israel

Charles E. Henning, M.D.
Mid-America Center for Sports
  Medicine
Wichita, Kansas

Gary R. Kantor, M.D.
10151 Bustleton Avenue
Philadelphia, Pennsylvania

Gary A. Klug, Ph.D., F.A.S.C.M.
College of Human Development
and Performance
Institute of Neuroscience
University of Oregon
Eugene, Oregon

Robert M. Malina, Ph.D.,
F.A.C.S.M.
Department of Anthropology
University of Texas
Austin, Texas

X. J. Musacchia, Ph.D.
Department of Physiology
University of Louisville
Louisville, Kentucky

E. Otten, Ph.D.
Orofacial Research Group
Laboratory of Physiology
University of Groningen
Groningen, The Netherlands

Patricia L. Painter, Ph.D.,
F.A.S.C.M.
Satellite Dialysis Centers, Inc.
Redwood City, California

Neil B. Ruderman, M.D.
University Hospital
Boston University School of
Medicine
Boston, Massachusetts

Stephen H. Schneider, M.D.
Division of Endocrinology,
Metabolism and Nutrition
University of Medicine and
Dentistry of New Jersey
Robert Wood Johnson Medical
School
New Brunswick, New Jersey

Albert B. Schultz, Ph.D.
Department of Mechanical
Engineering and Applied
Mathematics
College of Engineering
The University of Michigan
Ann Arbor, Michigan

Bryant A. Stamford, Ph.D.,
F.A.C.S.M.
Health Promotion and Wellness
Center
Division of Allied Health Sciences
University of Louisville
Louisville, Kentucky

Joseph M. Steffen, Ph.D.
Department of Biology
University of Louisville
Louisville, Kentucky

Glen F. Tibbits, Ph.D.
Schrum Science Center
Simon Fraser University
Burnaby, British Columbia
Canada

Angelica Vitug, M.D.
Division of Endocrinology,
Metabolism and Nutrition
University of Medicine and
Dentistry of New Jersey
Robert Wood Johnson Medical
School
New Brunswick, New Jersey

Leonard D. Zaichkowsky, Ph.D.
Division of Instructional
Development and Administration
School of Education
Boston University
Boston, Massachusetts

Contents

1
The Effect of Activity on Calcium-Mediated Events in Striated Muscle

GARY A. KLUG, Ph.D.
GLEN F. TIBBITS, Ph.D.

INTRODUCTION

For several decades, a growing body of research has described the extraordinary capacity of striated muscle to adapt to the physiological demands imposed by exercise. Although this work has established the basic framework of exercise biology, it is apparent that continual progress in this area depends on a better understanding of the mechanisms responsible for exercise-induced adaptations, as well as the identification of potential intracellular signals that could modulate cell function in response to activity. To this end, this review will focus on the role of Ca^{2+} in mediating the response of skeletal and cardiac muscle to acute and chronic exercise.

The crucial role that Ca^{2+} plays in muscle function was demonstrated over 100 years ago in the classic experiments of Sidney Ringer on the heart [199]. The universality of Ca^{2+} as a signal to initiate or modulate cellular events is now well documented across species (from single-celled eukaryotes to humans) and across tissues. It is difficult to overestimate the importance of Ca^{2+}, and nowhere is this statement truer than in regard to muscle. Because of the importance of the topic, there have been numerous recent reviews on particular aspects of this issue, and the reader will be directed to these if more information is required. Although skeletal and cardiac muscle have many Ca^{2+} regulatory systems in common, the differences in these tissues are important. These differences are related, in part, to the mechanisms by which these two types of muscles regulate tension production. In skeletal muscle, this is accomplished by recruitment of motor units and regulation of firing frequency, whereas cardiac muscle can neither recruit nor tetanize and Ca^{2+} concentration ($[Ca^{2+}]$) is the major means of varying tension output. Furthermore, it has been demonstrated that different mechanisms exist within fibers types of skeletal muscles for Ca^{2+} regulation, and undoubtedly more will be unveiled with time.

It is clear that, in addition to the role that Ca^{2+} plays in the contractile response, muscle energy metabolism, and structure are also influenced

1

by cytosolic $[Ca^{2+}]$. For example, phosphorylase, the enzyme responsible for activation of glycogenolysis, is activated by Ca^{2+} due to the presence of the Ca^{2+}-dependent activator protein calmodulin as a constituent of the enzyme complex. Ca^{2+} also influences the activity of pyruvate dehydrogenase, a critical enzyme linking glycolysis with the citric acid cycle. Furthermore, the capacity of the mitochondria to sequester large amounts of Ca^{2+} may influence oxidative metabolism as well as the intracellular $[Ca^{2+}]$ itself. In addition, hormones such as catecholamines, insulin, and thyroxine, which have a profound effect on muscle metabolism, have release mechanisms that involve Ca^{2+}. Muscle structure is also directly affected in some cases and indirectly in others by Ca^{2+}. For example, the glycocalyx requires a minimum $[Ca^{2+}]$ in the extracellular compartment to maintain structural integrity. The turnover of many muscle structural proteins, including myosin, is regulated by Ca^{2+}-activated proteases. Clearly, Ca^{2+} is significant in the regulation of so many aspects of muscle function that it is impossible to discuss all of these roles in this chapter.

Therefore, this chapter will focus on the mechanisms by which Ca^{2+} regulates muscle contractile function and the evidence for plasticity of these systems in response to activity. The decision not to discuss other Ca^{2+}-dependent systems in depth should not be construed as a failure to appreciate their significance. Rather, it reflects the enormity of the topic and the experience of the authors.

REGULATION OF $[Ca^{2+}]_i$

Although the cytoplasmic Ca^{2+} content of muscle is on the order of 1–2 mmol per liter of sarcoplasm, the majority is sequestered in intracellular organelles and the cytosolic free Ca^{2+} concentration ($[Ca^{2+}]_i$) is maintained at around 200 nM under quiescent conditions. Because of the low $[Ca^{2+}]_i$, it is convenient to express these values in terms of pCa [-log Ca^{2+}]. However, it should be pointed out (see section on Experimental Considerations in Ca^{2+} Transport Studies for more details) that although pH is an expression of H^+ activity, pCa is normally used as $[Ca^{2+}]$. Thus, pCa in resting muscle is maintained at around 6.8. Since an expression of $[Ca^{2+}]$ concentration is on the order of 1.5 mM, the transsarcolemmal gradient is approximately 10^4 and the large, inwardly directed gradient is reflected in a Ca^{2+} equilibrium potential of about + 120 mV. The ability of Ca^{2+} to serve as a signal, or second messenger, depends on the capacity of muscle fibers to maintain this large gradient during quiescence. Because of this, elaborate control systems are in place and failure to maintain the high pCa during rest results in cell dysfunction and imminent death. The efficacy of these systems in resisting changes in pCa is illustrated by the fact that the addition of 20 μmol

Ca^{2+} per liter of cell water over a period of minutes may raise $[Ca^{2+}]_i$ by less than 1 μM [192].

On the other hand, depolarization of the sarcolemma in both cardiac and skeletal muscles results in a rapid increase in the cytosolic $[Ca^{2+}]_i$ by one to two orders of magnitude. Thus, following depolarization, pCa falls from about 6.8 to values that may approach 5 under certain conditions.

The precise regulation of pCa is maintained in two general ways: (a) Ca^{2+} transport mechanisms, as outlined below, and (b) intracellular Ca^{2+} buffers, which include Ca^{2+} binding proteins (see section on Mechanisms of Mediation of $[Ca^{2+}]$) and a variety of intracellular binding sites (including lipid bilayers) and ligands.

Sarcolemma—Efflux

NA^+/CA^{2+} EXCHANGE. Na^+/Ca^{2+} exchange was demonstrated less than two decades ago independently by two groups using guinea pig atria [196] and squid axons [3]. The process is electrogenic and sensitive to the membrane potential, as the probable stoichiometry of the antiporter involves the exchange of three Na^+ for one Ca^{2+} [187]. The exchanger also transports Sr^{2+} and Ba^{2+}, with stoichiometries comparable to that of Ca^{2+} [239]. The exchanger is able to pump Ca^{2+} out of the cell against a large electrochemical gradient by using the energy from the Na^+ electrochemical gradient. Conversely, under certain conditions (see the section on Influx), it may drive Na^+ out of the cell with energy derived from the Ca^{2+} electrochemical potential. Although the exchanger does not use ATP per se, in order to be an effective Ca^{2+} efflux transporter, it requires $[Na^+]_i$ to be maintained at low levels. The maintenance of $[Na^+]_i$ at around 8 mM involves ATP expenditure by the Na^+/K^+ ATPase to pump Na^+ ions uphill. The antiporter, as of this writing, has not been isolated and fully characterized, although it has been reconstituted into proteoliposomes [155, 216].

Cardiac muscle. Na^+/Ca^{2+} exchange was first demonstrated in cardiac sarcolemmal (SL) vesicles by Reeves and Sutko [193] and has since been studied in great detail using this preparation [187, 194]. It has been proposed that Na^+/Ca^{2+} exchange is an important phenomenon in the regulation of myocardial contractility [126, 160]. This suggestion comes, in part, from the demonstration of high rates of activity of the exchanger in vitro (30 nmol × mg prot^{-1} × s^{-1}), which are comparable to Ca^{2+} uptake rates by cardiac sarcoplasmic reticulum (SR). Na^+/Ca^{2+} exchange activity exhibits Michaelis-Menton characteristics with respect to $[Ca^{2+}]_i$ in SL vesicles, cultured myocytes, and intact tissue [193]. The apparent K_m for Ca^{2+} has been reported to range from 1 to 30 μM. The range reflects, in part, the fact that the apparent K_m is subject to modulation by a wide variety of experimental [187, 189] and physiological interventions [240] that potentially could be mediated by lipid composition or exchanger phosphorylation [32].

Skeletal muscle. Unlike cardiac muscle, there is a paucity of literature on Na^+/Ca^{2+} exchange in skeletal muscle. Although the transsarcolemmal flux of Ca^{2+} during contraction is much lower in skeletal than in cardiac muscle, maintaining pCa during quiescence is just as critical. It has been estimated that resting skeletal muscle uses about 1% of the total energy to maintain the transsarcolemmal Ca^{2+} gradient [74]. Na^+/Ca^{2+} exchange has been demonstrated in intact frog skeletal muscle [29], guinea pig diaphragm [258], and SL vesicles isolated from rabbit skeletal muscle [75]. Although relatively little is known about the exchanger in skeletal compared to cardiac muscle, its K_m for Ca^{2+} and Na^+ (28 μM and 10 mM, respectively) are comparable to that for heart but the maximum velocity of exchange is an order of magnitude lower [75]. It is not known whether the latter is due to an inherent property of the exchanger, lower sarcolemmal density, or greater cross-contamination (see section on Experimental Considerations in Ca^{2+} Transport Studies) of the sarcolemmal vesicles studied in comparison to cardiac muscle.

CA^{2+} ATPASE. Common to most living cells is the presence of a Ca^{2+} ATPase on the plasma membrane that extrudes Ca^{2+} to the extracellular space and maintains high pCa under resting conditions. The pump, in general, is characterized by relatively low apparent K_m values for Ca^{2+} and ATP and is stimulated directly by calmodulin [205]. In muscle, the confirmation of the presence of this protein has been confounded by cross-contamination with the Ca^{2+} ATPase of the sarcoplasmic reticulum (see section on Experimental Considerations in Ca^{2+} Transport Studies).

Cardiac muscle. The SL Ca^{2+} ATPase contributes only to the extrusion of Ca^{2+} and its maximum Ca^{2+} transport capacity (0.5 nmol × mg prot^{-1} × s^{-1}) is 30 to 60 times less than that of the exchanger [30]. However, in the heart this system has been characterized as having an apparent K_m for Ca^{2+} and ATP of 0.3 and 30 μM, respectively [31]. These data suggest that the Ca^{2+} pump functions continuously in cardiac myocytes. In nanomolar concentrations, calmodulin stimulates the pump directly in the heart. It has been suggested that the SL Ca^{2+} ATPase can be distinguished experimentally from that on the SR (see section on Uptake) by several criteria. These include sensitivity to vanadate, molecular weight, substrate preference reference, and antigenicity [30].

Skeletal muscle. The presence of a Ca^{2+} ATPase has also been identified in SL from skeletal muscle. This protein appears to be found primarily in the transverse tubule component of the plasma membrane [21]. As in cardiac muscle, the Ca^{2+} ATPase is characterized by relatively low apparent K_m values for Ca^{2+} (5 μM) and ATP (10 μM) and yet is clearly distinguished from the SR Ca^{2+} ATPase.

Sarcolemma—Influx

CA^{2+} CHANNELS. A considerable amount of information concerning the properties of Ca^{2+} channels in muscle has recently been accumulated using the patch clamp technique. At least three different types of Ca^{2+} channels have been observed in excitable tissues. These have been identified as L, T, and N based on their electrophysiological and pharmacological characteristics. The terminology implies the following: L—longlasting or type II, according to the designation of Hagiwara and Byerly [87]; T—transient or type I; and N—neither T nor L types. Although all three types are voltage dependent and, under physiological conditions, contribute only to Ca^{2+} influx, they play different roles in the function of excitable tissues.

Cardiac muscle. Undoubtedly in cardiac ventricles, the main mechanism of transsarcolemmal Ca^{2+} influx is through voltage-dependent Ca^{2+} channels [197, 242]. The L type is the major (if not the only) Ca^{2+} current carrier in both mammalian and amphibian ventricles [148, 198]. These channels are dihydropyridine sensitive, generate long-lasting Ca^{2+} currents (slowly inactivating), and are modulated by cyclic AMP. Cyclic AMP-dependent protein kinases phosphorylate the subunits of the channel protein [44] that modifies the probability of any given channel opening in response to depolarization [198]. This effect is probably the main mechanism by which myocardial contractility increases acutely with exercise or catecholamine infusion (see section on Role of Ca^{2+} in the Adaptation to Activity). The importance of this inward current in the regulation of cardiac muscle contractility is illustrated further by the extreme sensitivity of muscle tension production to a variety of Ca^{2+} antagonists (which block the current) and variations in $[Ca^{2+}]_o$. As dihydropyridines are thought to bind specifically to L-type channels, these compounds have been used in the partial purification of the channel [42, 231] and in estimation of channel density in SL preparations [41, 240]. Using this technique, changes in ventricular L-type Ca^{2+} channel density have been observed in response to cardiomyopathy [246] and exercise [253]. These studies suggest that the regulation of ventricular L-type Ca^{2+} channels represents an important strategy of adaptation to stressors in the heart (see section on Role of Ca^{2+} in the Adaptation to Activity).

Skeletal muscle. Based on the dihydropyridine binding criterion, skeletal muscle transverse tubules are the richest source of the L-type Ca^{2+} channel found in any tissue [82]. However, measurements of the Ca^{2+} current during a normal action potential indicate that it is small and would result in an insignificant amount of Ca^{2+} permeating the SL [221].

More recently, this discrepancy in skeletal muscle was related to the fact that only a small fraction of the dihydropyridine binding sites are functional Ca^{2+} channels [207]. This is in contrast to cardiac muscle, where the predicted Ca^{2+} channel densities from electrophysiological measurements of Ca^{2+} current and dihydropyridine binding are quite similar [240]. The differences are highlighted further by the dissociation constant (K_d) for dihydropyridine binding, which is an order of magnitude greater in skeletal muscle than it is in the myocardium or other tissues in which the transsarcolemmal Ca^{2+} current is significant [53]. This suggests that the dihydropyridine binding site is qualitatively different in skeletal muscle. In spite of the small transsarcolemmal current in skeletal muscle, it appears to be important for two reasons; (a) during sustained tetanus a considerable amount of Ca^{2+} may enter the sarcoplasm from this source [221], and (b) blocking this current under certain conditions can inhibit the ability of the muscle to contract [60, 70]. Some investigators have used this binding to support the notion of calcium-induced calcium release as a means of excitation-contraction coupling in skeletal muscle [70]. However, this mechanism is far from being universally accepted (see section on SR Ca^{2+} Release).

NA$^+$/CA^{2+} EXCHANGE. *Cardiac muscle.* Although the antiporter apparently makes a significant contribution to Ca^{2+} efflux, the possibility that it also contributes to Ca^{2+} influx during the action potential has been raised. There are several lines of evidence to support the concept that the exchanger can contribute to Ca^{2+} influx as well as efflux in heart muscle: (a) in vitro experiments with isolated cardiac SL vesicles clearly and unequivocally demonstrate the ability of Ca^{2+} uptake via Na^+/Ca^{2+} exchange in both right-side and inside-out vesicles, as well as Na^+ dependent efflux in both vesicular populations [184, 187, 194]; (b) it is well established that the Ca^{2+} movement by the exchanger is driven by the Na^+ electrochemical gradient [187, 194]. Therefore, the direction of Ca^{2+} flux depends on the direction of the Na^+ electrochemical gradient and influx of Ca^{2+} is expected when

$$nzF(E_{Na} + -E_m) < zF (E_{Ca}{}^{2+} - E_m)$$

where n is the stoichiometry [160]. Thus, there appears to be a "reversal" potential, and using reasonable values for the above parameters, one might predict that the exchanger contributes to Ca^{2+} influx during the plateau phase of the action potential; (c) some experiments have demonstrated that inhibition of the exchanger has a negative inotropic effect and stimulation of the exchanger augments contractility. An amiloride derivative (dichlorobenzamil), a potent inhibitor of the exchanger, also impairs the strength of myocardial contraction [212]. Recently, it was demonstrated that sodium dodecyl sulfate (SDS) (an anionic acyl chain) dramatically stimulates both the activity of the exchanger [185] and papillary muscle contractility [188]. The specificity of the effect on the exchanger by dichlorobenzamil and SDS is questionable, however and these data should be interpreted cautiously.

Skeletal muscle. The relatively low V_{max} of the exchanger in skeletal muscle, and the short period that skeletal muscle is depolarized during a twitch as compared to cardiac tissue, argue against a significant role of the exchanger in Ca^{2+} influx in this tissue. Perhaps under periods of prolonged rapid stimulation, the role may become more substantial, but this is unknown at present.

Sarcoplasmic Reticulum

STRUCTURE. Skeletal muscle SR is a membranous compartment, closed to the cytosol, that is in close proximity and parallel to the individual myofibrils [71]. Although numerous terms have been used to describe the structure of SR, classically it has been divided into two separate regions referred to as the "longitudinal tubules (LT)" and the "terminal cisternae (TC)." More recently, the terms "junctional SR" and "nonjunctional SR" have been used. Junctional SR represents the area associated with the SL or transverse tubules (TT), specialized invaginations of the SL running perpendicular to the long axis of the muscle fiber. Conversely, nonjunctional SR is the structure that is continuous with the junctional SR but not connected to the other membrane systems. The TT and SR are structurally discontinuous, but they are linked in some manner by dense material that appears as bridging structures or "feet" [71]. Release of Ca^{2+} is initiated by communication of the action potential from the SL via the TT to the SR. The precise mechanism of this communication is unknown (see section on Ca^{2+} release); however, it may involve the feet and may be either electrical, ionic, or enzymatic in nature.

Phospholipids account for up to 80% of the lipid content of SR, with the residual 20% being cholesterol. This composition is somewhat unique to this membrane system, as the plasma membrane normally has a much higher concentration of cholesterol [63]. The phospholipids phosphatidylinositol, phosphatidylethanolamine, and phosphatidylserine are distributed asymmetrically in the outer and inner monolayers of the SR membrane bilayer. This distribution is complementary with the asymmetric arrangement of proteins within the membrane, where 50–60% of the total protein is outside of the bilayer [101]. The unique protein/lipid relationship may be significant in regulating the "vectorial" flux of Ca^{2+} across the membrane from the cytosol to the lumen of the SR [101]. In addition, the phospholipid structure of the SR membrane is critical for the maintenance of Ca^{2+}-pumping activity [165], although the cholesterol and neutral lipids can be removed without appreciable effect on function [56].

The major protein associated with the SR membrane is the Ca^{2+} ATPase pump protein (Mr 100,000), which accounts for 30–90% of the protein. The Ca^{2+} ATPase protein has three distinct binding sites on the exterior of the protein facing the cytoplasm. Two of these sites bind Ca^{2+} with high affinity [107] and Mg^{2+} with much lower affinity, and the third is a phosphorylation site that is covalently phosphorylated by ATP [142].

In addition to the Ca^{2+} ATPase, two Ca^{2+} binding proteins are associated with the SR. Calsequestrin (Mr 63,000 [see 143] or 44,000 [137], depending on the pH of the identifying electrophoresis system) is located in the lumen of the SR and has extremely high binding and storage capacities but a low Ca^{2+} affinity (for review see [138]). Recently, the molecular weight of calsequestrin was determined to be approximately 42,000 by amino acid sequence [69]. Storage of Ca^{2+} can reach 130–150 μmol $\times$ g SR protein^{-1}, with most of this bound to calsequestrin, a fact that is important both in the function of the Ca^{2+} ATPase (see below) and in the ability to concentrate the Ca^{2+} in the TC that is required for release during excitation.

Campbell and MacLennan [26, 27] reported the existence of a SR glycoprotein (Mr 53,000) whose concentration appears to be linearly related to the extent of coupling between the hydrolysis of ATP and Ca^{2+} transport by the ATPase [132]. In addition, a high-affinity Ca^{2+}-binding protein (Mr 55,000) of unknown function was thought to be present in the lumen of the SR, but at low concentrations [152, 172]. Later, it was suggested that this protein band, isolated electrophoretically, actually consisted of three separate proteins of molecular weight 53,000, 55,000, and 56,000. The major component of this fraction is the 53,000-dalton glycoprotein, with the 56,000-dalton high-affinity binding protein being present in small amounts [25, 152]. The Ca^{2+} ATPase is uniformly distributed throughout the SR, whereas calsequestrin is found primarily in the fraction containing the TC [201]. In cardiac and slow-twitch skeletal muscle the Ca^{2+} ATPase is associated with phospholamban (Mr 22,000), a protein that can be phosphorylated by catecholamine-stimulated activation of cyclic AMP-dependent protein kinase [115, 229], as well as a calmodulin-dependent kinase [133]. Phosphorylation of phospholamban stimulates Ca^{2+} uptake [114].

UPTAKE. Relaxation in striated muscle following the cessation of stimulation involves uptake of Ca^{2+} by SR by the action of Ca^{2+} pump protein present in the membrane that is driven by ATP hydrolysis. Maximum ATPase activity requires the presence of both Ca^{2+} and Mg^{2+}. SR vesicles demonstrate a low level of ATP consumption in the absence of Ca^{2+} and in the presence of Mg^{2+}, which is the "basal" activity [93]. This activity is normally measured in the presence of an EGTA buffering system so that the free Ca^{2+} concentration does not exceed 10^{-9} M. Ca^{2+}-stimulated or "extra" ATPase activity is calculated from the difference between the maximum and basal activities.

Presently, there is considerable debate about the origin and significance of the basal activity. Both the Ca^{2+}- and Mg^{2+}-stimulated activities may be derived from the same enzyme, and the basal ATPase may represent an inhibited form that does not support Ca^{2+} uptake [109]. The basal activity may be converted to Ca^{2+}-stimulated activity [109]. Conversely, failure of Mg^{2+} to cause formation of the phosphorylated form of the ATPase protein associated with Ca^{2+}/Mg^{2+} stimulation (see below) suggests that the two activities are independent [49, 230]. It is also possible that the basal activity is due to contamination by TT membranes that display a very high Mg^{2+}-stimulated ATPase activity [171]. The TT-Mg^{2+}ATPase has been identified as a 102,000-dalton glycoprotein with structural similarity to the SR Ca^{2+}ATPase [46].

The exact molecular mechanism of the transport of cytoplasmic Ca^{2+} has been the subject of exhaustive experimentation in the last several decades [for review 79, 94, 138, 141, 144, 145, 230]. When the cytosolic [Ca^{2+}] reaches a threshold of approximately 10^{-7} M, 1 mol of Mg-ATP and 2 mols of Ca^{2+} are bound to the appropriate binding sites of the ATPase on the cytoplasmic side of the SR membrane. Ca^{2+} binding is random and cooperative, and there is no evidence for an allosteric interaction between the Mg-ATP and the Ca^{2+} sites [111] (for schematic, see Figure 1). Occupation of these sites is followed by the formation of a phosphorylated intermediate of the enzyme, and subsequently ADP is released into the medium [72]. This phosphorylation occurs only in the presence of Ca^{2+} and is obligatory for completion of Ca^{2+} transport. This high-energy form is said to be "ADP-sensitive," as the process can be reversed by high levels of intravesicular Ca^{2+} in the presence of ADP and Pi, resulting in the synthesis of ATP [232]. Phosphorylation is followed by a confirmational change in the phosphorylated enzyme complex, and the ATPase is transported through the membrane [110]. The binding sites are no longer accessible to the extravesicular medium, and a dramatic reduction in their affinity for Ca^{2+} occurs until it is equivalent to that for Mg^{2+} [257]. There is concomitant formation of a new "ADP-insensitive" form of the phosphorylated ATPase that is no longer capable of phosphorylating ADP [94]. As a consequence of the low affinity of the binding sites, Ca^{2+} is released into the intravesicular space. Following the release of Ca^{2+}, the enzyme is dephosphorylated, with Pi liberated on the cytoplasmic side of the membrane. Release of Ca^{2+} and the presence of Mg^{2+} are obligatory for this step, and the process is inhibited by increases in intravesicular Ca^{2+}, which inhibit the entire process of Ca^{2+} transport [94]. Calsequestrin may play a significant role in maintaining the necessary low Ca^{2+} levels *in vivo*. In isolated SR the absence of this Ca^{2+} binding protein causes inhibition of Ca^{2+} uptake to begin after only a few cycles of the pump. The return of the outwardly oriented transport of ATPase occurs upon the release of Mg^{2+}. One complete

FIGURE 1

Schematic representation of the mechanism of Ca^{2+} uptake by SR, modified from the model proposed by De Meis, 1980 (In Sarcoplasmic Reticulum, *John Wiley & Sons, New York). Ca^{2+} uptake is initiated by the binding of two Ca^{2+} ions to the Ca^{2+}ATPase and phosphorylation of the enzyme. Subsequently, the phosphenzyme undergoes a series of confirmational changes described in the text, resulting in transport of the ATPase through the membrane and a decrease in its affinity for Ca^{2+}. Completion of the uptake cycle occurs with the release of Ca^{2+} into the lumen of the SR and inorganic phosphate to the cytoplasmic side of the membrane. The process can be reversed under conditions of high intravesicular concentrations of Ca^{2+}, ADP, and inorganic phosphate, resulting in the synthesis of ATP (see text).*

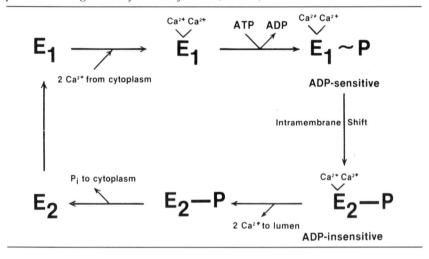

cycle of the system results in the transport of 2 Ca^{2+} and the hydrolysis of 1 ATP [49]. Recently, the Ca^{2+}ATPase has been cloned and a hypothesis explaining the mechanism of Ca^{2+} translocation across the SR membrane has been proposed based on its amino acid sequence. [19].

FIBER-TYPE SPECIFIC CHARACTERISTICS OF SARCOPLASMIC RETICULUM. The major differences that exist between the rate of relaxation of muscle contraction in different muscles suggest that their SR may vary with regard to its capacity to sequester Ca^{2+}. A discussion of these differences, as well as comparisons of any fiber type-specific characteristics, first requires comment concerning the classification of fiber types.

It is well known that there are numerous histochemical and biochemical methodologies by which muscle fibers can be classified [see 81]. Unfortunately, the use of such classifications, although necessary for the purpose of discussion, has led to the simplistic impression that fibers can be assigned to discrete categories. Numerous studies [for review see 81,

181, 182] indicate that not only are these classifications dependent to a large extent on experimental protocol, but also that the characteristics upon which they are based are dynamic and can be modified substantially by interventions such as activity and/or hormonal status. Gollnick and Hodgson [81] suggest that application of a classification scheme should be based upon how it will be put to use. For example, the simple categories "red and white" might be sufficient for some circumstances, whereas others might demand more rigid categories that include a number of characteristics. The important point is that any discussion of fiber-type specific characteristics must be considered in light of the methodology utilized to classify the fibers. This is necessary to avoid misunderstanding that might arise from the casual extrapolation of results obtained in studies that use one classification scheme to those from experiments that have employed a different system to separate fibers. An example would be the common assumption of the interchangeability of type IIB, IIA, and I fibers with fast glycolytic (FG), fast oxidative glycolytic (FOG), and slow oxidative (SO), respectively, which has been shown to be erroneous [80, 83]. While it is true that types IIB, IIA, FG, and FOG can all be considered "fast" and type I and SO fibers "slow," any further assumptions made about the correlation between fibers typed by these two methodologies is tenuous. This is simply because the classification systems employ different criteria for separation. When applied to SR, such confusion creates the impression that histochemical determination of the pH stability of the myofibrillar ATPase of a fiber or levels of mitochondrial enzymes can provide an accurate assessment of the structure and capacity for Ca^{2+} sequestration by the SR of that fiber. This is not the case, and this type of thinking should be avoided.

It has been established that both Ca^{2+} uptake and Ca^{2+}-stimulated ATPase activity are greater in SR isolated from fast-twitch mammalian muscle compared to those of slow-twitch muscle [96, 113, 201, 218, 254]. The maximal Ca^{2+} uptake is 3–11 times greater and the storage capacity 2–4 times greater in fast- than in slow-twitch muscle [79]. Comparisons of the SR Ca^{2+}ATPase activities of these two types of muscle also demonstrate that the Mg^{2+}-stimulated basal activity is substantially higher in slow-twitch muscle [201, 219]. The ratio of Ca^{2+}-stimulated extra activity to basal activity is elevated with increased temperature in SR from fast-twitch muscle but is unaffected in slow-twitch muscle SR [109]. Recently, Brandl et al. [20] demonstrated that two separate genes encode for the Ca^{2+}ATPase in fast-twitch and slow-twitch muscle and that the cardiac Ca^{2+}ATPase is encoded by the slow-twitch gene. These observations are in agreement with the suggestion of the existence of ATPase isoforms in fast and slow muscle [45, 128]. Further separation of fibers into fast white and fast red, using a combination of visual appearance and contractile speed, indicates that no major differences exist between their Ca^{2+} uptake capacity [66].

In addition to pump activity, there are differences in the structural components of the SR from fast and slow muscle. The fractional volume of SR is greater in fast-twitch muscle due primarily to a 50% lower TC area [59] in the slow muscle. Slight differences were found between the volume density of the LT in FG and FOG fibers, but the volume of the TC was the same in these two fiber types [243]. Wiehrer and Pette [254], using electrophoretic analysis, demonstrated that SR isolated from IIB fibers has the greatest relative concentration of the 115,000-molecular weight Ca^{2+}ATPase protein, followed in descending order by isolated SR fractions from type IIA and type I fibers. These results have recently been confirmed by Leberer and Pette [128] in muscle homogenates using an enzyme-linked immunosensitive adsorbent assay (ELISA) that eliminates problems with differential recovery of SR protein from the muscle types. These investigators demonstrated that the concentration of Ca^{2+} ATPase varies in type IIB fibers taken from various muscles. The difference in the concentration of calsequestrin between fast and slow muscles is not as great as expected from examination of the Ca^{2+}ATPase protein [128]. Despite the large discrepancies in the amount of this pump protein, calsequestrin in type I fibers from rabbit muscle is approximately 50–75% of that in type IIA and IIB fibers, and no differences exist between the type II subclassifications. These discrepancies may be attributed to variations in the volume of the TC [243], as this is the location of calsequestrin. Similar fiber type-specific distributions of Ca^{2+}ATPase and calsequestrin were found by immunofluorescence microscopy [112, 139].

Integration of Ca^{2+} Transport Systems
Although a clearer picture of the biochemical properties of each Ca^{2+} transport system is emerging, little is known about how they function *in vivo*. Attempts have been made, based upon *in vitro* experiments, to identify the specific roles and establish the relative contributions of each of these systems in the total process of regulation of $[Ca^{2+}]$ [30]. Physiologically, however, the systems have a high degree of complexity, which is just beginning to unfold. For example, simply stretching muscle fibres is known to affect the sensitivity of the myofibrils to Ca^{2+}, as well as Ca^{2+} delivery [2]. Clearly, our understanding will be improved by the integration of experimental data from both intact fibers and subcellular fractions.

Ca^{2+} RELEASE. *Cardiac muscle.* Fabiato has put forth an interesting hypothesis to explain Ca^{2+} release in heart muscle that is described as "calcium-induced calcium release (CICR)" [64]. The magnitude of the SR Ca^{2+} release is envisaged as being regulated by the rate of Ca^{2+} influx ($d[Ca^{2+}]_i/dt$), not the total amount of influx. However, experiments indicate that the maximum amount of Ca^{2+} released by the SR of skinned fibers is sufficient to generate only one-half of the tension when the pCa of the perfusate is reduced to 5.0 or less [65]. This finding has important ramifications for the control of contractility. The measurement of V_{max} of actomyosin or myofibrillar ATPase is, perhaps, of less significance compared to the importance of the pCa–ATPase relationship (or the pCa tension generation in skinned fibers) in the regulation of contractility.

Skeletal muscle. Propagation of the action potential down the transverse (T) tubules precedes the large release of calcium from the terminal cisternae of the SR by about 2 ms. The mechanism of coupling of T-tubule depolarization with SR calcium release has been a major obstacle to the understanding of muscle function. It may involve the feet and may be either electrical, ionic, or enzymatic in nature (see below). Support for the involvement of the feet structures in Ca^{2+} release comes from the observation that a receptor for the neutral plant alkaloid ryanodine is isolated together with the proteins that compose the feet in preparations of rabbit skeletal muscle [124]. This ryanodine receptor is a component of the Ca^{2+} release channel [149].

The outward movement of Ca^{2+} from the SR into the cytoplasm occurs primarily in the TC through "Ca^{2+}-release channels" [38]. Agents such as caffeine that can trigger Ca^{2+} release produce rapid conformational changes in the Ca^{2+}ATPase protein, suggesting that this enzyme functions in some capacity in the release mechanism [151]. However, there is evidence that argues against the possibility that Ca^{2+} release *in vivo* occurs as a result of reversal of the uptake process and that Ca^{2+} uptake and release involve a common carrier [210]. In any case, release of Ca^{2+} from SR is extremely rapid, as the amount required to initiate activity in fast muscle is between 4 and 8 $\mu mol \times mg\ SR^{-1} \times s^{-1}$ [251].

The identity of the signal that passes between the TT and the SR, leading to the explosive release of Ca^{2+}, is the subject of considerable research [for review see 54, 61, 62, 145, 191, 222]. Several mechanisms have been proposed to account for the transmission of the signal, as well as the instantaneous permeability changes in the SR that are required for release.

CICR has been studied using isolated SR and skinned muscle fibers to determine its feasibility as an *in vivo* link in the excitation of the TT to skeletal muscle contraction. It is postulated that stimulation of the TT induces release of Ca^{2+} from TT membranes, perhaps from the cytoplasmic surface [70], triggering the opening of Ca^{2+} SR channel gates. Endo [61] questioned this hypothesis on the basis of problems concerning the amount of Ca^{2+} required to induce release. However, Fabiato [64] has provided evidence that the concentration of Ca^{2+} required for release may be lower than was originally believed. Others have also argued against dismissal of this hypothesis [222]. However, McCleskey [147] demonstrated that blocking of the Ca^{2+} channels on the cell membrane with selective blocking agents did not result in inhibition of Ca^{2+} release from the SR or tension development, which is inconsistent with the existence of such a mechanism. It is clear that much remains to be done before the existence of CICR in skeletal muscle can be supported or refuted. However, it can be said that there is more support for this mechanism in cardiac than skeletal muscle.

An alternative hypothesis to CICR in skeletal muscle was proposed by Mathias et al. [146]. They suggest that current flow from the TT results in depolarization of the SR membrane, which opens voltage-dependent channels, permitting Ca^{2+} release. There is evidence that SR is indeed depolarized during muscle activation [145]. The observation [11] of a transient increase in fluorescence of the voltage-sensitive dye Nile blue that precedes tension development supports this hypothesis. To date, however, it has been difficult to establish a correlation between the magnitude of the depolarization of the SR membrane and the rate of Ca^{2+} release [7]. Furthermore, Baylor et al. [5] reported that Ca^{2+} release occurs earlier than depolarization of the SR membrane, which argues against such a mechanism. Thus, as in CICR, the physiological significance of the involvement of a depolarization signal in the coupling of the TT signal to SR Ca^{2+} release remains equivocal.

D-Myo-inositol 1,4,5-triphosphate (IP$_3$) is a molecule that is formed by the enzymatically catalyzed decomposition of a form of the membrane phospholipid, phosphatidylinostitol, by a mechanism outlined below. A mechanism for communication between the TT and the SR has been proposed involving the formation of this messenger molecule [167, 244, 245]. Vegara et al. [244] presented four lines of support for this hypothesis: (a) electrical stimulation of skeletal muscle generates IP$_3$; (b) IP$_3$ can release Ca^{2+} from skinned muscle fibers; (c) manipulations of Mg^{2+} concentration and/or the addition of 2,3 bisphosphoglycerate or Cd^{2+}, all of which act to inhibit the phosphatase that breaks down IP$_3$, potentiate the mechanical response in muscle resulting from IP$_3$ application; (d) neomycin, a drug that binds phosphatidylinostitol phosphates, preventing their degradation while blocking the release of IP$_3$ in red blood cells, inhibits the Ca^{2+} transients elicited by the skeletal muscle action potential. Thus, it is conceivable that the voltage-induced changes in the TT induce the formation of IP$_3$, which acts to increase SR membrane permeability and to elicit Ca^{2+} release. Although feasible, this hypothesis has been questioned in recent experiments using a photolabile but biologically active precursor of IP$_3$ called "caged IP$_3$" [247]. Results of these studies indicated that both the concentration of IP$_3$ required for activation and the rate of activation were not compatible with a physiological role for this mechanism in fast skeletal muscle. However, this evidence does not completely rule out a role for IP_3 in TT–SR coupling, as it may serve as one of the key elements in a complex series of events [217, 245].

Duggan and Martinosi [57] suggested that pH changes can trigger Ca^{2+} release from isolated SR vesicles. Increasing the pH of the bathing medium of skinned fibers enhanced tension development [211] independent of the initial pH (pH range, 6.5–7.5), suggesting that activation of Ca^{2+} release is due to perturbation of the normal H^+ gradient across the membrane and not to a specific change in pH. Attempts to validate the suggestion that pH and/or H^+ gradients may be significant in E–C coupling by determination of the actual pH change during a muscle twitch have shown that the increases are too small to trigger release [4]. This, coupled with data concerning difficulties in establishing and maintaining the necessary gradients, have led to questions regarding the physiological role of this mechanism [145].

MECHANISMS OF MEDIATION

Ca^{2+} flux across the SL and the SR are not the only factors that influence the $[Ca^{2+}]_i$ and the characteristics of contraction. A number of proteins exist that regulate the free Ca^{2+} concentration and the activity of various enzymes and other Ca^{2+}-mediated events either by directly binding Ca^{2+} or indirectly through the activation of specific protein kinases. Although it is not possible to comment on all of these systems in a chapter of this size, several that are pertinent to the regulation of muscle contraction will be discussed, along with some recent theories regarding the mechanisms by which they may exert their influence.

Troponin C

The ability of the contractile proteins actin and myosin to generate tension in response to variations in $[Ca^{2+}]_i$ over the physiological range for pCa comes about by the presence of Troponin C (TnC), a thin-filament calcium-binding protein, discovered over 20 years ago by Ebashi and co-workers [58]. The magnitude of muscle tension generation is determined by the number and cycling rate of actin and myosin interactions, which in turn reflect the amount of Ca^{2+} bound to TnC. Thus, tension production is regulated primarily by pCa. TnC from both skeletal and cardiac muscle contains two classes of Ca^{2+}-binding sites: low-affinity Ca^{2+} specific sites and high-affinity Ca^{2+}-Mg^{2+} sites. The binding of Ca^{2+} to TnC shows cooperativity and is responsible for the sigmoidal relationship between myofibrillar ATPase and pCa. Skeletal muscle TnC contains two low-affinity sites with a binding constant of 5×10^5 M^{-1} and two high-affinity binding sites with a higher binding constant (2×10^7 M^{-1})

but that also bind Mg^{2+} competitively. Thus, at maximal steady state Ca^{2+} activation, skeletal muscle TnC contains 4 mol of calcium per mol of TnC. Cardiac TnC also has two high-affinity sites with binding constants that are similar to those found in skeletal muscle. On the other hand, cardiac TnC has only one low-affinity site, presumably because region I (residues 28–40) of the protein has several substitutions in amino acid composition compared to skeletal muscle. This suggests that in cardiac muscle the maximum binding is 3 mol of calcium per mol of TnC.

As stated previously, the correlation of myofibrillar ATPase activity and/or tension generation is correlated to the mole fraction of calcium bound to TnC. Thus, Ca^{2+} regulation of contraction comes about primarily by (a) controlling pCa and the rate of change of pCa during each contraction and (b) controlling the sensitivity of the contractile element to Ca^{2+}.

FIBER-TYPE DIFFERENCES AND THE EFFECT OF ACTIVITY ON TNC. Isoforms of TnC exist in skeletal muscle, with slow-switch muscle containing a distinct type of all three subunits of the troponin complex compared to fast-twitch muscle. No differences exist between TnC isolated from IIA and IIB fibers [50, 202]. However, both types of TnC have been identified in the same cells in developing muscles [51]. Despite the structural differences mentioned in the preceding paragraph, antibodies against rabbit TnC from slow muscle have been reported to react with cardiac TnC. This is consistent with the early observation that the primary structural sequences of the TnC from the two muscle types are very similar.

It is apparent that the activity pattern of the muscle is important in regulating the type of TnC that is expressed in skeletal muscle. An alteration in the normal activity of skeletal muscle produced by cross-reinnervation results in the replacement of the slow form of TnC with the fast form in the soleus muscle and the reverse effect in the fast-twitch tibialis anterior and extensor digitorum longus muscles [50].

Calmodulin

Calmodulin is a ubiquitous Ca^{2+}-binding protein first discovered as a regulator of the activity of phosphodiesterase in bovine brain [36]. Since that time, it has been shown that this protein assists in the regulation of such diverse processes as neurotransmitter release, microtubule assembly/disassembly, membrane phosphorylation, glycogen metabolism, secretion, and smooth muscle contraction [see 117, 154, 248 and references therein]. A role for calmodulin-mediated activation of myosin light chain kinase has also been proposed in the regulation of contraction in skeletal and cardiac muscle (see below). Teo and Wang [233] demonstrated that calmodulin is a Ca^{2+}-binding protein, and it is now recognized as the most important element in biological functions where Ca^{2+} serves as a second messenger.

In general, activation of calmodulin-mediated events is triggered by an increase in the intracellular free $[Ca^{2+}]$ from approximately 10^{-7} to 10^{-5} M [35]. Therefore, in striated muscle, activation of processes that are calmodulin dependent occur simultaneously with the onset of contraction. Normally the regulatory calmodulin involved is not bound to the target protein at low $[Ca^{2+}]$. However, in some instances, such as the activation of the phosphorylase kinase, an enzyme involved in the activation of glycogenolysis, the protein can exist as a component of the enzyme complex [40].

Ca^{2+} sensitivity to calmodulin-mediated events is due to the presence of four binding sites on this protein whose Ca^{2+} affinities vary depending upon the presence or absence of monovalent and divalent cations in the assay medium. Questions still persist as to whether there is a single class of binding sites or two separate classes with different affinities [89, 116, 250]. Binding of Ca^{2+} results in the formation of a Ca^{2+}-calmodulin complex. Subsequently, various structural changes occur in this complex that result in the formation of the operative form, which is capable of enzyme activation. Some enzymes, such as myosin light chain kinase, appear to require the occupation of all four binding sites by Ca^{2+} for activation [17], whereas others, such as phosphorylase kinase, may require only three Ca^{2+} per calmodulin [23].

Activity is initiated by binding of the Ca^{2+}-calmodulin complex to the target enzymes, but, surprisingly, there appears to be no calmodulin binding domain that is common to all these proteins. In addition, the nature of binding of calmodulin to the target varies for different enzymes. In some (e.g., phosphorylase kinase), activation can occur as a result of the binding of a single calmodulin fragment that exists near the C-terminus of the protein, whereas others (e.g., myosin light chain kinase) require interaction with two separate sites on calmodulin [117]. Thus, despite the capacity of calmodulin to affect a multitude of biological processes, no single activation mechanism can explain this ability under all circumstances. Inactivation of most calmodulin-dependent processes is thought to occur first by the dissociation of Ca^{2+} from the Ca^{2+}-calmodulin complex [23, 35].

The concentration of calmodulin varies greatly between smooth and skeletal muscle, with the values being 400–600 mg $\times$ kg^{-1} and approximately 70 mg $\times$ kg^{-1}, respectively. It should be noted that these values represent both free calmodulin and that bound to membranes and enzymes such as phosphorylase kinase. The importance of calmodulin with regard to muscle contraction and metabolism is not limited to its role as an activator protein. The computer model of Robertson et al. [200], representing the binding response to Ca^{2+} transients in skeletal muscle, indicates that greater than 94% of the Ca^{2+} released during a single transient is bound to calmodulin and TnC. Thus, it is apparent that calmodulin and TnC influence the regulation of the intracellular free $[Ca^{2+}]$ during muscle activity. This capability suggests that the concentration of these proteins may even indirectly influence other cellular Ca^{2+}-activated processes that they do not directly regulate.

The effect of activity on the concentration of calmodulin has not been elucidated. However, in light of the large number of cellular processes that are dependent on its presence, it may be an important area of research in the future. Furthermore, if muscle activity does affect calmodulin concentration, knowledge concerning such a response may help to clarify the physiological significance in striated muscle of Ca^{2+}/calmodulin-dependent processes such as myosin phosphorylation.

Myosin Light Chain Kinase
In the last decade, considerable experimentation has been conducted regarding a Ca^{2+}/calmodulin-mediated event in skeletal and cardiac muscle that may be significant in the regulation of contraction in both of these muscle types. Myosin light chain kinase (MLCK) is an enzyme, identified in skeletal, cardiac, and smooth muscle, that catalyzes the phosphorylation of the 18.5 kDA (LC_2 or DTNB) light chain of myosin [177]. Phosphorylation of the "P-light" chain has been studied in these different muscle types [1, 190, 249], and it is now established that this event is obligatory for initiation of contraction in smooth muscle [90]. However, its role in cardiac and skeletal muscle is related to the regulation of contractile strength as opposed to the initial activation of the contractile process (see below).

In resting muscle, when intracellular free $[Ca^{2+}]$ is low, MLCK exists in an inactive form. An elevation of the myoplasmic free Ca^{2+} concentration of the magnitude that initiates active tension development also activates the enzyme [17] by the multistep mechanism involving calmodulin that has been previously described. Inactivation, accompanying the cessation of stimulation, although not uniquely described for MLCK, is thought to occur in a manner similar to that of other calmodulin-dependent processes such as the activation of phosphodiesterase.

Dephosphorylation of the P-light chain, a process that is slower than phosphorylation [140], is catalyzed by myosin light chain phosphatase (MLCP), an enzyme thought to be unregulated. Recent biochemical and immunochemical experiments have established that MLCK exists in a number of different molecular weight isoforms [226]. However, no functional significance has been attached to the variations in its structure observed in different species and tissues.

Evidence for phosphorylation of myosin *in vivo* has been obtained using tetanic [140] and repetitive stimulation in animal models [118,

156], as well as with voluntary contractions in humans [105]. The amounts of MLCK and MLCP present in specific muscle types appear to dictate the ability of the P-light chains of myosins of different muscle fiber types to be phosphorylated *in vivo* (see below).

FIBER-TYPE DIFFERENCES IN MYOSIN LIGHT CHAIN KINASE AND MYOSIN PHOSPHORYLATION. The concentrations of MLCK and MLCP vary considerably in different muscle types. When histochemically classified by the method of Peter et al. [180], FG muscle fibers have the highest kinase activity, followed in order by FOG, SO, and heart muscle [156, 226]. This hierarchy is altered with respect to the MLCP, as slow-twitch muscle has the highest concentration, followed in descending order by fast-twitch and heart muscle [226]. Thus, the MLCK/MLCP ratio in fast muscle would favor rapid phosphorylation and slow dephosphorylation, whereas in slow muscle, the effect would be the opposite.

This suggested control of phosphorylation *in vivo* by differences in enzyme concentration is supported by the observations that low-frequency stimulation for short periods of time produces phosphorylation of about 60% of the P-light chains in the white portion of rat gastrocnemius, whereas the value is less in red gastrocnemius [156]. Conversely, no phosphorylation occurs under similar stimulation conditions in the slow-twitch soleus (20-kD P-light chain), and significant elevation in phosphate content is observed only when higher stimulation frequencies are applied (30–100 Hz) for longer periods of time. The maximum initial rate of phosphorylation in fast muscle exceeds that measured in slow muscle. The observation that dephosphorylation of the light chains is four times slower in white gastrocnemius ($t_{1/2} = 1.7$ minutes [140]) than in soleus supports this hypothesis for control of phosphorylation.

In vivo phosphorylation of the P-light chain is frequency dependent [156]. Stimulation of rat gastrocnemius at 0.5 Hz elevates P-light chain phosphate content, whereas stimulation at 5 or 10 Hz produces an additional 50% increase in the maximum value and a 2.6- and 12.3-fold increase in the initial rate of phosphorylation, respectively.

A qualitatively similar frequency dependence has also been observed in the electrically paced rabbit ventricular septae preparation [213]. Preparations paced at frequencies between 0 and 126 beats per minute varied in P-light chain phosphate content from 0.1 to 0.4 mol phos × mol P – light chain^{-1}. As can be predicted from the low levels of MLCK present in cardiac muscle [225], these frequency-dependent increases in phosphorylation were smaller and required 30–90 minutes as opposed to less than 1 minute in skeletal muscle.

These observations led to the development of a model for the regulation of MLCK activity and phosphorylation during repetitive stimulation [156, 226] *in vivo*. This model is based on the premise that the amount of Ca^{2+} released in a single Ca^{2+} transient activates only a small portion of the total available MLCK and that, once activated, the rate of inactivation of MLCK is very slow ($t_{1/2}$ = 0.9 second) relative to the contractile cycle [226]. Under these constraints, the amount of active MLCK formed during repetitive stimulation at a given frequency would be determined by the equilibrium established between the processes of activation and inactivation. An increase in stimulus frequency would cause the formation of a greater amount of active kinase, since more Ca^{2+} transients would be delivered per unit time and the inactivation period between twitches would be reduced. This mechanism could then explain why an increase in stimulation frequency results in greater P-light chain phosphorylation. It could also explain the absence of phosphorylation in slow muscle, as the total amount of kinase activated during a transient would be trivial due to the low concentration of the enzyme. This, coupled with the higher concentration of the phosphatase, would allow MLCP to rapidly reverse the small amount of phosphorylation that occurs under these conditions. Thus, for appreciable phosphorylation to occur in this muscle type, high stimulation frequencies and long periods would be required for a sufficient amount of available MLCK to be activated to overcome the MLCP activity. This model for kinase activation is supported by the observations that the amount of phosphorylation predicted by the model agrees with the experimentally measured amounts [226].

THE POSSIBLE ROLE OF MYOSIN PHOSPHORYLATION IN THE REGULATION OF CONTRACTION. Despite the data concerning the effect of muscle activity on P-light chain phosphorylation, questions remain with regard to the physiological role of this phenomenon in skeletal and cardiac muscle. Although no evidence exists for the obligatory phosphorylation of myosin for contraction in striated muscle, MLCK activity and phosphorylation are regulated *in vivo* in a manner consistent with their participation in the contractile process.

The potentiation of isometric twitch tension following a brief tetany or repetitive low-frequency stimulation is a well-known phenomenon that occurs in fast but rarely, if ever, in slow muscle [39]. In the past several years, it has been demonstrated that close temporal- and frequency-dependent correlations exist between phosphorylation and twitch potentiation [118, 140, 156] in isolated and *in situ* skeletal muscle preparations. These correlations have been challenged by Westwood et al. [252], but the discrepancies appear to be related to the methodology used in determining P-light chain phosphorylation in these latter experiments [157]. This relationship has been extended to electrical stimulation of human muscle following a single maximal voluntary contraction [105].

The existence of a correlation between myosin phosphorylation and twitch potentiation does not necessarily establish a causal relationship between these two events. Crow and Kushmerick [43] reported a reduction in shortening velocity of intact muscle following a brief tetanus when myosin phosphorylation was elevated, an observation inconsistent with twitch potentiation. However, this down regulation was unique to the specific methodology employed, and the decrease in velocity may be related to conditions other than P-light chain phosphorylation, such as pH or metabolite accumulation [24, 227]. It is now accepted that maximal isometric tension [179, 227] and maximal shortening velocity [24, 227] are unaffected by P-light chain phosphorylation.

A mechanism that could provide a link between P-light chain phosphorylation and potentiation comes from *in vitro* data regarding the effect of phosphorylation on actin-activated myosin ATPase activity [226]. Phosphorylation reduces the K_m of myosin for actin, with no effect on V_{max} in skeletal [178] and cardiac [159] muscle. The character of the phosphorylation-enhanced ATPase activity is dependent on the experimental conditions under which measurements are made, with ionic strength, Mg-ATP concentration, and the presence or absence of regulatory proteins being important factors [108, 223].

Addition of exogenous MLCK to skinned muscle fibers has demonstrated that phosphorylation increases tension development in cardiac and skeletal muscle fibers at nonsaturating levels of Ca^{2+} but not at concentrations that produce maximum tension [159, 179, 228]. This effect is characterized by a leftward shift of the pCa-tension curve below 50% maximum activation [228]. Several mechanisms have been suggested to explain the effect of phosphorylation on tension development [228].

If the kinetics of the myosin/actin crossbridge cycle were altered in a manner that would prolong their time of attachment, tension would be enhanced. However, the data regarding phosphorylation and maximum shortening velocity (see above) appear to eliminate this possibility. Conversely, if phosphorylation is accompanied by an increase in the affinity of myosin for actin, more crossbridges might be formed during a single Ca^{2+} transient, resulting in an enhanced tension generation and explaining the potentiation observed in intact muscle. Sweeney and Stull [228] noted that for such a mechanism to be operative, Ca^{2+} must be present during the twitch at levels that would not maximally activate troponin. Support for this possibility comes from modeling experiments that show that frog muscle troponin is probably not saturated with Ca^{2+} during a single muscle twitch [28].

Qualitative similarities of the phosphorylation in skeletal and cardiac muscle do exist. Despite these findings and the evidence supporting a possible link between phosphorylation and twitch potentiation in skeletal muscle, a similar relationship in heart cannot be inferred from the data from skeletal muscle. Clearly, phosphorylation of the P-light chain is not obligatory for contraction in cardiac muscle [213]. However, a rapid increase in phosphorylation has been reported to accompany beta-adrenergic stimulation [195]. On the basis of the rapid rates of phosphorylation compared to the small amount of MLCK present in this tissue, these results have been challenged by Silver et al. [213]. In the septal preparation, no significant increase in P-light chain phosphate content was observed when the tissues were frozen at the peak of the contractile response produced by isoproterenol. These data suggest that it is unwise to assume that the effects of myosin phosphorylation on contraction are similar in all striated muscles and point to the necessity for continued, specific investigation involving the significance of phosphorylation in cardiac muscle.

Parvalbumin

STRUCTURE. TnC and calmodulin are not the only Ca^{2+}-binding proteins that have the capacity to influence muscle contractile characteristics. Parvalbumin (PA) is a low molecular weight (Mr 11,000–12,000) cytosolic Ca^{2+}-binding protein first discovered in the muscle of lower vertebrates. Numerous isoforms of this protein have been isolated from mammalian muscle, as well as a large number of other eukaryotic cell types [for review, see 98, 99, 256]. The existence of PA in muscle is fiber type specific, as it is present in fast-twitch skeletal muscle but detectable in slow-twitch muscle only with very sensitive techniques [16, 119, 127]. Generally, PA exists in the largest concentrations in type IIb fibers, shows a high degree of variability in IIa fibers, and is virtually undetectable in type I fibers [33, 127]. However, it has been shown that the PA concentration ([PA]) of a specific fiber type can vary when the fibers are taken from different muscles or different mammals [127]. A close correlation exists between [PA] and the Ca^{2+}ATPase of SR in fast-twitch muscles, but this relationship is not apparent in slow-twitch muscle [128].

PA can bind approximately 2 moles of Ca^{2+} per mole of protein, due to the existence of two high-affinity Ca^{2+} binding sites [200]. These sites are not Ca^{2+} specific and also competitively bind Mg^{2+}, but with a lower affinity. This affinity for Ca^{2+}, coupled with the high [PA] in fast-twitch muscle, suggests that, in this type of muscle, it could have some regulatory significance in the myriad Ca^{2+}-mediated events in muscle metabolism and/or contraction, perhaps by serving as a Ca^{2+} sink.

POSSIBLE REGULATORY ROLE OF PARVALBUMIN IN MUSCLE CONTRACTION. The similarity with respect to molecular weight and Ca^{2+} binding between PA and calmodulin has suggested a role for PA in enzyme regulation. However, studies have failed to substantiate any role for this protein in the control of enzyme activity [131, 175]. A relationship between relaxation time and [PA] in various muscles [97] has supported the hypothesis that PA serves as a soluble factor that may influence muscle relaxation [22, 73, 78, 79, 176].

Pechere et al. [176] proposed a model for Ca^{2+} binding involving PA, SR, and the myofibrils that attempts to explain the potential role of PA in the relaxation process in fast muscle. They suggested that the Ca^{2+} released from the SR concomitant with excitation of the muscle immediately binds to the myofibrils, resulting in the activation of tension development. The preferential binding to the myofibrils over that of PA is related to the fact that, at rest, the Ca^{2+}/Mg^{2+} sites of PA are occupied by Mg^{2+}. This means that an exchange must take place at these sites, which is not the case for the Ca^{2+} sites on troponin. Upon cessation of stimulation, Ca^{2+} is first removed from the myofibrils by PA and then is resequestered by the SR. This process of resequestration from PA to the SR may extend beyond the cessation of active tension development. This regulatory scheme was supported by the observations that SR was able to remove Ca^{2+} bound to PA [16] and that, after contraction, most of the Ca^{2+} released from the SR was localized in the cytoplasm possibly bound to PA [77]. The existence of a Ca^{2+} for Mg^{2+} exchange required by this model is supported by experiments suggesting an increase in Mg^{2+} concentration following muscle activity [4]. The magnitude of this exchange may be significant; Smith and Woledge [215] have calculated that if the exchange is complete, it could account for 50% of the labile heat produced by frog muscle during isometric tetanus. The extremely low concentration of PA in slow muscle would preclude this mechanism in this muscle type. Thus, variations in the concentration of PA may contribute, along with a lower capacity for Ca^{2+} uptake by SR, to the observed slower relaxation rate in these muscles.

Heizmann et al. [97] suggested that for PA to serve as a relaxing factor, its distribution among fiber types and the variations in its concentration within a defined fiber type must meet four criteria: (a) within a single species [PA] should be higher in those muscles with the highest relaxation time; (b) within a single species [PA] should be related to fiber composition, as described above; (c) a positive correlation should exist between speed of relaxation and [PA] in muscles of the same type in different animals and; (d) within a single species, muscles with similar fiber compositions but different relaxation speeds should have different [PA]. These criteria were satisfied in muscles taken from different species, ranging from mice to man, where [PA] varied between 4.9 and 0.001 $g \times kg^{-1}$ wet weight. In addition, this correlation can be observed in the muscles of the C57BL/6J (dy2J/dy2J) dystrophic mouse, where PA is decreased [121] and one-half relaxation time is prolonged [174] when compared to normal mouse muscle.

Despite the close relationships between [PA] and relaxation, its role as a soluble relaxing factor has been questioned [170, 200]. This skepticism is based, in part, upon experiments using computer modeling of the time courses for Ca^{2+} binding to calmodulin, troponin, PA, and myosin in response to transient increases in intracellular free Ca^{2+} of the magnitude thought to occur during a muscle twitch. This work suggests that, at rest, when free Ca^{2+} is low, the majority of the Ca^{2+}/Mg^{2+} sites of PA are occupied by Mg^{2+}, thus supporting the previously mentioned requirement for Ca^{2+}/Mg^{2+} exchange. The model indicates that the only Ca^{2+} binding that occurs with sufficient rapidity to permit involvement in a single contractile cycle is that involving the Ca^{2+}-specific sites of troponin and calmodulin. If so, the magnitude of the exchange of Ca^{2+} for Mg^{2+} at the PA binding sites during a single twitch is trivial in comparison to the Ca^{2+} bound to these other proteins. Thus, for any appreciable Ca^{2+}/Mg^{2+} exchange to occur in a time frame affecting relaxation, a train of repetitive twitches would be required. The possible involvement of PA in relaxation is further questioned by the observation that the dissociation of bound Ca^{2+} from the Ca^{2+}/Mg^{2+} binding sites is so slow that this process can be of no significance on a twitch-by-twitch basis.

Collectively, these data illustrate that if PA has a role in relaxation, it must be in the later stages of a train of stimuli. This possibility is supported by studies with the "adr" neuromuscular mouse mutant [224]. This mutant, which has abnormally low muscle [PA], displays near-normal twitch relaxation times but long-lasting after-contractions in response to repetitive stimulations.

The *in vitro* Ca^{2+} binding measurements made on isolated proteins may not accurately reflect the critical relationships between the Ca^{2+}-binding proteins that are relevant in any evaluation of the physiological role of PA *in vivo*. Many of the Ca^{2+} binding measurements etc. made in the development of models for PA function were devised using measurements made on lower vertebrate proteins. It can be argued that possible differences in the metal-binding characteristics of PA isolated from these species [88] may cast doubt on the validity of the models previously constructed that have used such data to examine questions regarding mammalian PA.

Simple correlations between [PA] and relaxation time in different muscle types used to determine the physiological role of PA suffer from significant limitations. It is known that other elements of the Ca^{2+} regulatory system, such as the SR, also differ between muscle fiber types [for review, see 181]. Thus, such comparisons make it difficult to differentiate between the contributions of SR and PA to the relaxation process.

Transduction of Ca^{2+} Signals by IP_3
Although the calcium-binding proteins allow a rapid response to intracellular $[Ca^{2+}]_i$ transients, sustained responses may also be initiated by

the same signal. One means of transduction involves an elegant hypothesis first proposed by Michell more than 10 years ago [153]. Ca^{2+} activation of phospholipase C catalyzes the hydrolysis of the SL phospholipid polyphosphatidylinositol, creating inositol triphosphate (IP_3) and diacylglycerol (DAG), both of which can serve as intracellular signals. IP_3 has been suggested (as described earlier) as a putative signal for SR Ca^{2+} release by Vergara et al. [244] and others [167]. DAG can potentially stimulate protein kinase C, resulting in phosphorylation in several proteins. The reader is directed to several recent reviews for more information [166, 192]. The full implication of these systems in striated muscle is not yet known.

EXPERIMENTAL CONSIDERATIONS IN Ca^{2+} TRANSPORT STUDIES

Measurement of $[Ca^{2+}]_i$

The accurate determination of $[Ca^{2+}]_i$ is of fundamental importance in studies concerning its influence on striated muscle. Unfortunately, these measurements are difficult and complicated by potential artifacts. The problems include, but are not limited to (a) the difficulties associated with determining low concentrations of one alkaline earth metal (Ca^{2+}) in the presence of another (Mg^{2+}) of which the concentration is four orders of magnitude higher; (b) a pronounced affect of pH in the physiological range of pCa; (c) and a physiological range of $[Ca^{2+}]$ that spans more than two orders of magnitude. Despite these problems, techniques exist that, when used judiciously, give satisfactory results. A survey of the literature in the study of exercise-induced adaptations, unfortunately, suggests that the application of these techniques has been poor. As a result of these and other problems discussed below, progress in understanding the effect of exercise-induced adaptations on Ca^{2+} transport systems has been limited. For several excellent, comprehensive reviews on the pitfalls of the measurement of $[Ca^{2+}]_i$, the reader is directed to the work of Blinks and Blinks et al. [14, 15].

Ca^{2+} Buffers

As the physiological range for $[Ca^{2+}]_i$ is 0.1 to 10 μmol/L, the *in vitro* characterization of Ca^{2+} transport is hampered by the fact that contaminating $[Ca^{2+}]$ of solutions made from distilled and deionized water is in the range of 2–5 μM. Clearly, without some form of Ca^{2+} buffering, this may cause problems. The most commonly used Ca^{2+} buffer is EGTA, primarily because of its high selectivity of Ca^{2+} over Mg^{2+} and because the apparent stability constant of EGTA for Ca^{2+} is on the order of 2×10^6 M^{-1} under physiological conditions. Thus, if one considers that a buffer, in general, will function adequately $\pm$ 0.5 unit on either side of the pK, it should serve as an effective Ca^{2+} buffer between pCa 5.9

and 6.9. There are several difficulties, however, that need to be addressed. First, the stability constant is sensitive to ionic strength, temperature, and pH in the physiological range. Second, the nominal concentrations of Ca^{2+} and EGTA should not be inferred to be the actual concentrations. For example, the hydration state of $CaCl_2$ and EGTA can vary, and the presence of contaminants results in purities that are seldom as high as the labeled specifications [13]. Third, it is frequently useful to study the effects of Ca^{2+} outside the range of pCa in which EGTA is an efficient buffer (i.e., approximately >6.9 or <5.9, but which varies with the experimental conditions). Thus, one should be aware of the range for the given conditions and either restrict the range or use an additional Ca^{2+} buffer. Fourth, it has been shown that EGTA has a direct effect (independent of the Ca^{2+} buffering) on some Ca^{2+} transport systems, including SR Ca^{2+}-ATPase [12] and Na^+/Ca^{2+} exchange [241].

The calculation of the apparent stability constant under the experimental conditions used is critical, and there are two main approaches to this question. One is theoretical, in which all of the "absolute" stability constants of EGTA and the other competing ligands in solution (e.g., ATP, CP) for the cations involved (Mg^{2+}, Ca^{2+}, and H^+) and the total concentrations of all species are used to calculate the apparent stability constants and the free and bound concentration of each species at equilibrium. One error that exists in the literature with regard to these calculations is the use of 10^{-pH} as the proton concentration when it clearly represents activity. Activity is the product of the concentration and the activity coefficient. Under physiological conditions, the activity coefficient for H^+ is approximately 0.7 and, therefore, 10^{-pH} underestimates the H^+ concentration by about 30%. This error can result in a significant miscalculation of pCa. The activity coefficient of Ca^{2+} under intracellular conditions is thought to be about 0.32; thus, there is a large discrepancy between $[Ca^{2+}]$ and Ca^{2+} activity. Activity is, of course, the critical determinant of the chemical potential of the ion solution.

A second method for determining the apparent stability constant is empirical. Of the methods used, perhaps the least complicated and most useful is that of Bers [13]. The technique involves the use of Ca^{2+}-selective electrodes (see below) and allows one to determine accurately the [EGTA], as well as the apparent stability constant of EGTA for Ca^{2+} under the chosen experimental conditions.

Ca^{2+}-Sensitive Electrodes

Although Ca^{2+}-selective electrodes measure Ca^{2+} activity (as do all the other techniques described below), they are normally calibrated with solutions of known Ca^{2+} concentration, and thus the results are often expressed as such. This type of electrode can either be purchased from commercial sources or made in the laboratory using neutral-carrier ion-selective membranes [214]. One advantage of these electrodes is their broad range of sensitivity and their ability to determine pCa to 7 or greater [214]. They are easily calibrated, can be used as macro- or microelectrodes (and therefore are useful for both intracellular and small-sample volume recording), and can continuously monitor Ca^{2+} activity over time. The most serious limitation is their slow speed of response. The time constant is dependent on the $[Ca^{2+}]$ and ranges from slightly less than 0.1 seconds at high $[Ca^{2+}]$ to several minutes at low concentrations [14]. The response time, therefore, precludes the use of electrodes for the detection of the rapid Ca^{2+} transients that occur during muscle contraction or fast Ca^{2+} uptake kinetics *in vitro*.

[Ca^{2+}] Indicators
In the past two decades, useful Ca^{2+} indicators have been developed and popularized for the study of Ca^{2+} transport. These substances include the metallochromic dyes, the fluorescent dyes, and the photoproteins. One of the advantages of these compounds is their relatively fast reaction kinetics. Thus, under the appropriate conditions, these indicators are amenable to the study of Ca^{2+} transport, with a time resolution in the millisecond range.

Although the kinetics are favorable, several other difficulties may confound the results. Theoretically, a useful indicator should have (a) high sensitivity, (b) good selectivity over other cations such as magnesium, (c) a minimal Ca^{2+} buffering effect on the milieu to avoid artifactually altering physiological function, and (d) homogeneous distribution in the cytosol. Each type of dye has its own set of problems.

METALLOCHROMIC DYES. Murexide and its derivative, tetramethyl-murexide, have a Ca^{2+} sensitivity that is rather low and that restricts their usage to higher $[Ca^{2+}]$. However, they have been used effectively to monitor $[Ca^{2+}]_o$ in the millimolar range [102]. Arsenazo III has been used more extensively than any other Ca^{2+}-sensitive dye and thus has been characterized to a greater degree [15]. Both antipyrylazo III and arsenazo III may bind to muscle proteins, decreasing sensitivity and introducing spatial heterogeneity. Arsenazo III in low concentrations inhibits SR Ca^{2+} uptake in frog muscle [169]. Antipyrylazo III has a number of advantages over arsenazo III, including a more rapid response to alterations in $[Ca^{2+}]$. Its absorption spectrum is the same *in vitro* and *in vivo*, and it binds to Ca^{2+} with a stoichiometry of 1:1 [5]. Arsenazo III has been effectively used in *in vitro* experiments by a number of investigators [173, 216] to monitor changes in $[Ca^{2+}]$ in the extravesicular space.

FLUORESCENT DYES. Many of the problems associated with the earlier fluorescent dyes, such as chlorotetracycline and quin2, have been circumvented with a new generation of dyes, including fura-2 and indo-1, produced by Tsien and co-workers [85]. Fura-2 is an improvement over quin2, as it gives a 30-fold brighter fluorescence, has better selectivity, gives a higher quantum yield, and shifts its wavelength with Ca^{2+} binding (not simply increasing in fluorescence). A major advantage of these dyes over the metallochromic dyes and the photoproteins is their relative ease of introduction into intact cells using the acetomethoxy derivatives. These dyes have already been used extensively, and it is hoped that they can be employed effectively in the study of exercise biology.

PHOTOPROTEINS. The photoprotein, aequorin, offers another important means of monitoring $[Ca^{2+}]$ in various environments. Photoproteins are extracts from marine organisms that luminesce upon reacting with Ca^{2+}. Although aequoerin has been extensively and effectively used in the measurements of Ca^{2+} transients during muscle contraction, the difficulty of its introduction into the cell and other technical problems may not make it as practical as some of the dyes for routine measurements of Ca^{2+} uptake.

CA^{2+} ISOTOPES. Most studies addressing Ca^{2+} transport in exercise-induced adaptation have used $^{45}Ca^{2+}$ to monitor uptake into vesicles. Another isotope, $^{47}Ca^{2+}$, offers much higher specific activity; however, its expense and short half-life make it impractical. Although $^{45}Ca^{2+}$ offers high sensitivity, it is virtually impossible to follow the uptake as a continuous function of time. Normally, the uptake is terminated by harvesting the vesicles on cellulose nitrate or glass fiber filters. Unless rapid quenching techniques are used in conjunction with filtration, it is unlikely (without some intervention) that one can measure initial rates (see section on Kinetics of Transport) with this procedure. It should be pointed out that one is actually measuring vesicular content, and that calculating uptake from this value is predicated on vesicular characteristics that may change with the adaptation to activity.

Preparations Used in the Study of Ca^{2+} Transport
In all of the preparations outlined below, the fiber composition of muscles examined is an issue that needs to be addressed. It is apparent from the discussion above that heterogeneity in fiber composition can significantly affect the measured rates of Ca^{2+} transport.

SUBCELLULAR FRACTIONATION. Subcellular fractionation has been used in the study of a variety of problems in exercise biology, some of which are outlined in the section on the Role of Ca^{2+} in the Adaptation To Activity. The technique normally involves homogenization, which fragments the plasma membrane and subcellular organelles, and then separation of the organelle vesicles that are formed based on differential density, using differential and/or gradient centrifugation. The technique has the potential to offer significant insight into the mechanisms of adaptation to exercise, but the following potential artifacts should be addressed in each experiment; (a) degree of cross-contamination, (b) vesicular orientation, and (c) passive permeability.

In all isolations, a finite and often substantial cross-contamination exists in which the presence of vesicles from other organelles may affect the measurement of the transport process in question. Some investigators have addressed this issue by determining the yield (mg protein $\times$ g^{-1} wet weight) in both groups. Although a step in the right direction, by itself it is inadequate. It is clear that if a differential contamination exists, it may lead to invalid assumptions concerning the absolute amount of protein in the isolated fractions. This may be particularly true in training studies when disproportionate increases in mitochondrial protein, compared to that in other organelles, may affect the degree of cross-contamination. Therefore, marker enzymes for a variety of potential contaminating vesicles should be routinely assayed. These assays and/or other techniques, such as electron microscopy, electrophoresis, or quantification of the concentration of the transporter in question by immunoprecipitation, may help to ensure that differential contamination does not contribute to the observed effects.

A second problem that has often been ignored is an assessment of the vesicular orientation and perhaps volume. Asymmetry of membrane proteins and phospholipids can mask the substrate binding sites if the distribution of right-side-out vesicles is not the same in the groups being studied. An elegant way to approach this problem has been developed by Caroni and Carafoli [32] for SL, but it may be applied, in principle, to other membranes as well. This technique relies on the known orientation of the Na^+/K^+ATPase in the membrane. It is known that the K^+ site on the enzyme is accessible from the extracellular space and that both the Na^+ and ATP sites face the intracellular milieu. Based on this premise, it is clear (but seldom appreciated) that the measurement of this enzyme in homogenates or subcellular fractions represents only those vesicles that are leaky, because both right-side-out vesicles (ROV) and inside-out vesicles (IOV) preclude access to one or more extravesicular substrates. Addition of a K^+ ionophore should stimulate the activity by the recruitment of the IOV, as K^+ now has access to its binding site. Prudent use of detergents may allow both Na^+ and ATP access to the appropriate sites and allow expression of the ROV, thus stimulating activity further. Thus, two points can be made. First, vesicular orientation can be quantitated biochemically. Second, researchers in this field should be aware that simply following an assay may determine the activity in only a limited population of vesicles.

Passive permeability constitutes the third pitfall. Measurements of the true initial rates may circumvent the problems associated with this and vesicular volume. In the case of Ca^{2+} transport studies, it is not difficult to load vesicles with high concentrations of $^{45}Ca^{2+}$ and establish conditions under which the efflux can be monitored in the absence of influx [239]. Thus, one can compare directly passive Ca^{2+} permeability of the vesicles derived from muscles of animals from different experimental groups.

The large number of possible errors in the preparation of membrane vesicles indicate that prior to any evaluation of transport function, extensive vesicular characterization is necessary. These evaluations are helpful in understanding the variability that has plagued this field. In the absence of such controls, any conclusions are tenuous at best.

CRUDE HOMOGENATES. Crude homogenates offer the advantage of simple preparation, less harsh treatment, and less time for isolation, which in the case of subcellular fractionation may take 30 hours or more. This preparation can offer a good control for experiments with highly purified subcellular fractions. Although issues such as yields and recoveries are minimized, one problem that is not widely appreciated is that the process of homogenization results in the formation of vesicles. Thus, the problems of vesicular orientation, volume, and passive permiability still exist. Of course, the biggest difficulty is attempting to follow one Ca^{2+} transport system independently of others that may be functional in the homogenate. Under certain conditions, this may not be significant. Leberer et al. [130], for example, found that the addition of ruthenium red and sodium azide, inhibitors of mitochondrial Ca^{2+} transport, did not reduce the measured rate of SR Ca^{2+} uptake in muscle homogenates. However, antibodies against the SR Ca^{2+} ATPase completely abolished Ca^{2+} uptake. This problem, of course, must be addressed with each set of experimental conditions.

SKINNED FIBERS. Skinning of muscle fibers involves either removing the SL mechanically or rendering it permeable by treatment with EGTA or saponin. In this preparation, various substances can be introduced to the interior of the cell, but some small cytoplasmic Ca^{2+}-binding proteins such as PA may be lost in this process. Thus, extrapolation of *in vitro* results to the regulation of $[Ca^{2+}]$ *in vivo* must be done with caution, as several of these proteins have been implicated in the relaxation process (see above). Glycerol treatment and the use of detergents such as Triton X-100 are often employed to skin fibers. However, care must be taken, as these techniques also cause an increase in the permeability of intracellular membranes, which could be a problem with Ca^{2+} uptake measurements [79].

SECTIONS. Ca^{2+} uptake has been measured in thin cryosections of skeletal muscle by addition of an appropriate reaction medium containing oxalate and $^{45}Ca^{2+}$ [135]. This technique has two advantages: (a) it can be performed on small muscle samples and (b) histochemical determination of muscle fiber types can be simultaneously performed on samples of the same cross section. Not surprisingly, however, this technique suffers from considerable variability [79].

Kinetics of Transport

One of the major problems associated with the study of Ca^{2+} transport systems in response to exercise is that of kinetics. Presumably, the studies are conducted to make inferences about a specific Ca^{2+} transport system. The measurement of initial rates is critical because direct inferences about the transporter often can be drawn only under these conditions. The vesicles derived from subcellular fractionation typically have relatively small volumes (5 μl $\times$ mg prot^{-1}). After short periods of time, the vesicles can develop high $[Ca^{2+}]$ or other conditions that can impede uptake independent of the transporter per se. Furthermore, when the transport rates are measured by vesicular content, high passive permeabilities grossly underestimate rates of transport. Therefore, noninitial rates do not allow one to draw any conclusions about the transporter. One important, but not infallible, test is to ensure that the reaction rate is a linear function of time for a finite period. All subsequent measurements should then be made within this time frame. Two possible solutions include (a) following the uptake with rapid kinetics or techniques with an appropriate time constant or (b) extending the time frame of linearity by experimental intervention. Such strategies may include, for example, using lower temperatures or, as in the case of SR Ca^{2+} uptake, Ca^{2+}-precipitating ions [92]. The most commonly used anion is oxalate, which is freely permeable to the SR membrane and thus can enter the vesicles, precipitate Ca^{2+}, and maintain a low free $[Ca^{2+}]$. It is not always known, however, what effect these experimental interventions have on the measured rates.

ROLE OF Ca^{2+} IN THE ADAPTATION TO ACTIVITY

Response to Acute Exercise and Fatigue

   Cardiac muscle. Although the increase in myocardial contractility observed in response to inotropic stimulants as well as exercise is brought about by extremely complex alterations in the Ca^{2+} regulatory systems, a discussion of these changes is beyond the scope of this chapter [34, 125, 198]. Little is known about these processes in the heart in response to exhaustive exercise [238].

   Skeletal muscle. In the past decade, the role of alterations in Ca^{2+} handling following exhaustive exercise has been studied in an attempt to explain the alterations of contractile properties under these conditions. Because of the significance of SR in muscle contractile function, a decline in the rate or magnitude of Ca^{2+} release could reduce tension generation, whereas a decrement in the rate of SR Ca^{2+} uptake could be the basis for a reduced rate of relaxation. The first point has not been addressed experimentally under conditions associated with exhaustive work and thus is not discussed. It is unfortunate that this problem has not been studied, as techniques exist for testing this hypothesis. The second issue, however, merits further attention. Several hypotheses relating to a reduction of crossbridge cycling and/or SR Ca^{2+} sequestration have been proposed to explain the slower relaxation rate that is observed under fatiguing conditions [48]. These proposals include an elevated free ADP concentration which would reduce the free energy resulting from hydrolysis of ATP by the various ATPases associated with the contractile proteins [255]. In the case of the actinomyosin ATPase, this could affect crossbridge cycling, whereas with the SR Ca^{2+}ATPase, it could impair the rate of Ca^{2+} uptake. A second possibility is a local reduction of ATP content in the immediate vicinity of either of these ATPases or a reduced rate of ATP production [106]. Thirdly, acidosis, which is known to reduce the activities of these enzymes, could affect relaxation, as could the production of some inhibitor of enzyme function.

Bonner et al. [18] reported a depression in maximal Ca^{2+} uptake but no change in ATPase activity following 8 minutes of high-intensity exercise in untrained rats. Sembrowich and Gollnick [208] demonstrated that the ATP-supported Ca^{2+} accumulation by SR vesicles isolated from gastrocnemius muscles of rats run to exhaustion (mean duration, 200 minutes) was reduced as a function of exercise time, with the nadir corresponding to exhaustion. One hour of recovery was sufficient to return Ca^{2+} uptake by SR vesicles to control or above-control values. A similar finding was observed with crude homogenates [91], suggesting that this effect on SR is not an artifact of the isolation procedure. Later, these results were confirmed [10, 67, 68] and expanded to demonstrate that the reduction in SR Ca^{2+} uptake was fiber-type specific and limited to muscles that were composed predominantly of type I and type IIA fibers [67, 68]. Phillips [183] demonstrated a similar depression of SR Ca^{2+} accumulation, using an *in situ* gastrocnemius muscle model where all fibers were activated, indicating that the cause of the fiber type differences may not be related to the intrinsic properties of the SR but rather to the fiber recruitment pattern. A further fractionation of isolated SR, by sucrose density gradient centrifugation into light and heavy components corresponding to longitudinal and terminal cisternal SR, demonstrated that the greatest depression occurred in the light SR fraction. This coincided with increases in the one-half relaxation time and decreases in the peak -dP/dt of muscle contraction. Gilchrist et al. [76] challenged these early findings and reported that acute exercise does not impair Ca^{2+} transport. Issues raised earlier in this chapter associated with vesicular purification, orientation, and the rate constants for passive Ca^{2+} efflux have not been addressed under these conditions. Despite these caveats, it is apparent that prolonged work alters SR function *in vitro* in a manner that is rapidly reversed during recovery.

Considerable disparity exists with regard to the effect of acute exercise on the ATPase activity of SR following exhaustive exercise. Some investigators have reported that decreases in ATPase activity are accompanied by a reduction in Ca^{2+} uptake [9, 208], whereas others found depressed uptake with no apparent effect on ATPase activity [18, 68]. Another combination of results is seen from a comparison of two studies from the same laboratory [76, 136], where a decrease in ATPase activity was observed in the absence of any effect in Ca^{2+} uptake. Thus, exercise seems to produce effects that are varied and inconsistent, particularly in light of the high reproducibility of the data from chronic stimulation studies (see below). It can be argued that exercise is more difficult to regulate than electrical stimulation and that the varied responses depend on the mode and intensity of exercise and other factors, such as circulating hormones, that are not altered by stimulation. However, a comparison of a number of these conflicting reports indicates that the exercise protocols employed are not sufficiently different to account for all of the large divergence of the results. It may be that a failure to standardize and validate the isolation and measurement protocols (see section on Experimental Considerations in Ca^{2+} Transport Studies) may have contributed to these discrepancies between the reported results.

Despite the large number of conflicting conclusions regarding exercise and SR function, the weight of these data support the conclusion that physical activity modifies this system. If future experimentation supports the conclusion that the actual rate of ATP-dependent SR Ca^{2+} uptake is impaired during prolonged work, the ramifications of this conclusion for muscle structure and function are important. This presents an interesting possibility, as it is independent of the acute effects of low [ATP], elevated [ADP] (and, as a correlate, independent of changes in the free energy of ATP hydrolysis), and lower pH. However, one cannot rule out the possibility that these adaptations occuring *in vivo* have an impact on the *in vitro* membrane characteristics that affect SR Ca^{2+} accumulation. Furthermore, possible effects on PA [97] and SL function [209] should not be ignored in the study of the effect of activity on the regulation of $[Ca^{2+}]$.

One question that has not been addressed concerns the underlying cause of such an effect. Most studies that report changes with SR function and exercise have observed that the effects are correlated with low muscle glycogen [68, 208]. Horl et al. [104] suggested that phosphorylase kinase stimulates SR activity, whereas phosphorylase phosphatase inhibits it. Thus, it may be that some coordinated relationship exists between the glycogen energy supply and the ATP requirements of the SR. An alternative possibility may be related to the increase in free fatty acids that accompanies long-term exercise. Incubation of SR with oleic acid attenuates Ca^{2+} uptake [150], possibly by disrupting the membrane structure. Since the plasma free fatty acid concentration is elevated substantially during prolonged exercise, a link may exist between fatty acids and SR function. Support for this hypothesis comes from the work of Szarzala et al. [204], who demonstrated increases in lysophosphatides and non-esterified fatty acids in SR from chronically stimulated muscle. Davies et al. [47] have reported an accumulation of free radicals and a decline in intracellular antioxidants following exhaustive exercise. Free radicals that are formed from partial reduction of oxygen in the electron transport chain, as well as other oxygenation reactions are highly reactive. A link between exercise and SR function may be an oxidation of critical elements of the SR membrane or pump such as sulfhydryl groups, which are known to decrease the formation of the phosphoprotein intermediate [206]. Finally, an elevation of muscle temperature is another possible mechanism, as SR Ca^{2+} uptake is temperature dependent, being reduced as these values exceed body temperature [219]. Temperatures following exhaustive exercise may exceed 41°C, a level that depresses SR function *in vitro*. However, it cannot be assumed that the temperature dependence of Ca^{2+} sequestration measured in isolated SR vesicles *in vitro* represents that which exists *in vivo*. This is due to the possible protective effect on membrane and/or protein structure provided by the large number of other cellular proteins that are not present in isolated vesicles.

Adaptation to Training and Chronic Stimulation
  Cardiac muscle. Although it is well documented that exercise training can increase myocardial stroke volume [55], the mechanisms have proven to be controversial. In animal models, it has frequently been observed that training results in an intrinsic adaptation of the myocardium that may result in increased contractility [55]. Several hypotheses have been proposed to explain the enhancement of contractility in response to training. The postulates fall into two groups: (a) alteration in the contractile element due to shifts in myosin isoforms and (b) enhanced Ca^{2+} delivery to the contractile element by means of adaptation(s) in Ca^{2+} transport processes. Since this chapter focuses on the role of Ca^{2+} in muscle adaptation, the latter notion will be explored in some detail. An excellent synopsis of the earlier work on the role of Ca^{2+} in cardiac adaptation can be found in Dowell [55] and will not be reiterated here. As detailed in the section on Regulation of Ca^{2+}, augmentation of Ca^{2+} delivery would most likely be brought about by changes in the sarcolemma and/or sarcoplasmic reticulum.
  Unfortunately, we have very little knowledge about the possible adaptation of SR Ca^{2+} release mechanisms in response to training, yet this

may prove to be an important and fruitful avenue of research. An increased Ca^{2+} flux in response to exercise training is attractive in that it may serve to (a) directly activate the myofibrillar ATPase to a greater degree, resulting in greater force production, (b) result in a greater release of SR Ca^{2+}, as predicted by the CICR hypothesis [64], (c) concomitantly stimulate metabolism by the impact of $[Ca^{2+}]_i$ on several metabolic steps, and (d) activate MLCK and other calcium-dependent modulators that may affect contractile activity. It was proposed 10 years ago [235] that adaptation(s) in myocardial SL Ca^{2+} transport systems in response to training augment contractility. This hypothesis is supported by the fact that hearts from trained animals have exhibited (a) lowered sensitivity to La^{3+} [235], a cation that acts on the SL to uncouple excitation from contraction; (b) prolongation of the plateau phase of the action potential [236]; and (c) substantial alterations in the lipid composition of the SL [237]. As stated in the section on Regulation of $[Ca^{2+}]_i$, the dihydropyridines are a potent class of calcium antagonists thought to block specifically the L-type Ca^{2+} channel [148], and in low micromolar concentrations they can completely inhibit tension production [158] in the heart. By using the dihydropyridine [^{3}H] PN200-110 over a wide range of ligand concentrations, it was found that the specific binding in both the homogenate and the SL-enriched fractions was statistically greater in the trained animals compared to the control [253]. As outlined in the section on Experimental Considerations in Ca^{2+} Transport Studies, one must be cautious in comparing subcellular fractions from two different groups. First, one should consider the possibility of differential purification. This problem was addressed in several ways: (a) SL marker enzyme-specific activities did not differ between the groups, (b) linear regression of [^{3}H]PN200-110 specific binding as a function of SL marker activity generated a significantly greater slope in vesicles from the trained hearts, and (c) the differences were also observed in the crude homogenates. Second, the vesicles derived from the isolation procedure are of mixed orientation. Differential vesicular sidedness, however, does not appear to account for the group differences for two reasons: (a) the vesicles were loaded with an isotonic medium and then diluted into an optimal hypotonic solution [Tibbits, Weymann, and Diffee, unpublished observations], causing the vesicles to rupture and allowing access to both sides of the vesicle, and (b) previous pilot studies using an evaluation of membrane orientation by monensin and SDS stimulation suggest that there is no difference between the groups with respect to the percentage of ROV. Third, it is conceivable that these observations could be explained by an adaptation distinct from the binding site that modulates binding. Calmodulin, for example, has been shown to modify DHP binding [Tibbits, Weymann, and Diffee, unpublished observations] and may be required for full activation of the Ca^{2+}

channel. The similar dissociation constants of ligand binding that were found could be used as arguments against that notion. The increased [3H] PN200-110 binding induced by exercise is qualitatively similar to that of a previous study using another dihydropyridine, nitrendipine [52]. From these data, it was calculated that exercise training increases the Ca^{2+} channel density from 3.6 to approximately 5.7 channels per μm^2 of SL surface area. There is some evidence to suggest that there may be a parallel in the nature of the adaptation of the heart to a variety of stressors. Wagner et al. [246] observed a substantial increase in the number of nitrendipine binding sites in the hearts of cardiomyopathic hamsters. Although the physiological effects of these stressors are substantially different, there may be some similarity in the adaptation strategies and/or the signals that induce the myocardial response.

The apparent increase in Ca^{2+} channel density is consistent with the enhanced myocardial contractility observed in the rat in response to this exercise regimen [236]. These findings, however, may also represent an important strategy to simply maintain contractility in the face of myocyte hypertrophy that may be induced by more strenuous regimens or pathology. If, as expected with hypertrophy, the surface/volume ratio decreases, one would predict that the transsarcolemmal Ca^{2+} current density and the Ca^{2+} delivery to the myofilaments would decrease. This could result in decreased contractility if there was no concomitant adaptation in the Ca^{2+} delivery systems.

Na^+/Ca^{2+} Exchange. As outlined in the section on Regulation of $[Ca^{2+}]_i$, the high activity of the cardiac Na^+/Ca^{2+} exchanger and other physiological evidence has led to the suggestion that it plays an important role in the regulation of myocardial contractility. The potential for this antiporter to contribute to both the efflux and influx of Ca^{2+}, coupled with the fact that it is profoundly affected by membrane lipid composition, makes it an interesting candidate for study in exercise-induced adaptations. In general, anionic amphiphiles stimulate the initial rate by a reduction in the apparent K_m of the exchanger of Ca^{2+}. The converse is true for cationic amphiphiles [188]. The effect of training on Na^+/Ca^{2+} exchange was studied in highly purified SL vesicles using rapid-quenching techniques [239]. Over a range of Ca^{2+} concentrations from 10 to 80 μM, the absolute initial rate of uptake (quenched at 1 second) was significantly higher in SL vesicles from trained hearts. From Eadie-Hofstee plots of the initial rates, the derived V_{max} values were not significantly different between the groups. The apparent K_m of the myocardial Na^+/Ca^{2+} exchanger for Ca^{2+} was significantly lower as a result of the exercise regimen. The observed increase in the affinity of the exchanger for Ca^{2+} was not attributed to group differences in vesicular purity, cross-

contamination, or passive Ca^{2+} efflux. This observation is consistent with observed alterations in SL composition in response to exercise training [237]. Vesicular orientation does not appear to explain the findings for several reasons. *In vitro* experiments have demonstrated that both sides of the membrane have similar apparent K_m values for Ca^{2+}, as well as the same response to pH and valinomycin. Although there is some controversy as to the symmetry of the Na^+ binding site, in these experiments the intravesicular Na^+ concentration (140 mM) exceeded the reported apparent K_m values for both sides of the membrane by a factor greater than four, and hence was not likely to account for the differences in initial rates between the groups. It would appear, therefore, that stimulation of the exchanger resulting from exercise training in these experiments is not an artifact of the vesicular isolation procedure. An attractive hypothesis, requiring closer examination, is that the stimulation of Na^+/Ca^{2+} exchange is the result of the substantial increase in SL phosphatidylserine content found to occur in response to this perturbation.

Although these experiments may offer insight into the nature of the adaptation of the heart to exercise, one should also bear in mind that other species need to be examined. Also, the findings would be strengthened by corroboration with electrophysiological and $[Ca^{2+}]_i$ measurements.

Skeletal Muscle

SR. The synthesis of SR during embryonic and postnatal development occurs as a result of the insertion of ATPase molecules into rough endoplasmic reticulum and concomitant changes in phospholipid composition [138, 143]. Both presumptive fast- and slow-twitch muscle fibers express Ca^{2+}ATPase and calsequestrin during embryonic development [129, 203]. Their concentrations, which are different early in the development of these two muscle types [129], increase with age, but the rate of increase is greater for calsequestrin [103]. Synthesis of both proteins occurs more rapidly in fast muscle, which is consistent with their concentrations in adult muscles. Recently, Brandl et al. [19] demonstrated that neonatal skeletal muscle expresses a form of the Ca^{2+} ATPase that is identical with adult slow-twitch and cardiac muscle. This form, which is the predominant species in late fetal and early neonatal skeletal muscle, disappears as the muscle differentiates into the adult fast type. Denervation of muscle during development attenuates this normal pattern of development in the SR but does not abolish the fiber-type specific differences for Ca^{2+}ATPase [129]. Thus, both specific neural factors (e.g., activity) and some type of intrinsic control that is unrelated to activity influence the development of these two proteins [129].

Chronic electrical stimulation of fast muscle reduces the Ca^{2+} pumping capacity and Ca^{2+}-stimulated ATPase activity of SR isolated from fast-twitch muscle [95]. These time-dependent decreases were reported to be accompanied by reductions in the concentration of the Ca^{2+}ATPase protein and formation of the Ca^{2+}-dependent phospho-rylated intermediate [95, 130], as well as alterations in the phospho-lipid matrix [204]. These events occur within 1–2 days of the onset of altered activity and are among the earliest changes in muscle fibers produced by stimulation [120]. Leberer et al. [130], using an ELISA with muscle homogenates, have demonstrated that stimulation does not decrease the actual tissue content of the ATPase protein. They sug-gest that the previous reports of decreases in the ATPase protein con-centration in isolated SR from stimulated muscle [120, 254] resulted from increases in contamination with non-SR membranes, which translated into a lower amount of ATPase protein relative to the total amount of protein in the isolated membrane fraction. This conclusion was supported by experiments in which the relative amounts of ATP-ase were measured in calcium oxalate–loaded SR vesicles. Using this technique, which reduces contamination by non-SR proteins, it was found that the relative amount of SR was equal in both stimulated and control muscle.

Despite the questions regarding the structural basis for the effect of chronic stimulation, it is now established that SR Ca^{2+} uptake is atten-uated by up to 50% in stimulated muscle. Since this is not the result of a reduction in the Ca^{2+}ATPase protein, the question arises as to the locus of the effect. Leberer et al. [130] demonstrated that reduc-tions in Ca^{2+} uptake were accompanied by concomitant decreases in the formation of the phosphoprotein intermediate. Disruption of the obligatory process of phosphorylation is suggested by a reduction in the magnitude of binding of fluorescein isothiocyanate (FITC), a com-pound that associates with the ATP binding site. In contrast, the affin-ity for ATP is unaltered. One explanation of these results is that chronic activity creates two populations of Ca^{2+}ATPase molecules, one capa-ble of Ca^{2+} transport and a second, inactive form. The reversal of the effects of stimulation on Ca^{2+} uptake within 6 days suggests that the inactive ATPase proteins can be reactivated. An alternative explana-tion is the synthesis in stimulated muscle of an ATPase inhibitor pro-tein [163] or conversion from a fast-type ATPase isozyme to a slow type with lower ATPase activity. However, neither of these changes has been found [130]. When functional, the active ATPase molecules are normal, as illustrated by normal Ca^{2+} and ATP dependence of

Ca^{2+} ATPase activity and an unaltered relationship between the Ca^{2+} transported and ATP hydrolyzed.

Recent work suggests that the stimulation-induced effects on SR may alter the intracellular milieu and the function of the muscle fibers. Sreter et al. [220], using Ca^{2+}-sensitive microelectrodes, reported a fivefold increase in intracellular free Ca^{2+} in single muscle fibers in the first few days of chronic stimulation. In addition, a prolongation of one-half relaxation time existed in the rabbit tibialis anterior muscle after 1 day of stimulation [123]. This is consistent with a reduction in the Ca^{2+}-sequestering capacity of SR.

The high sensitivity of the Ca^{2+} uptake characteristics of SR to alterations in normal activity points to the possibility that chronic endurance exercise may be capable of producing qualitatively similar results. Unfortunately, there is a paucity of data in the literature dealing with this question.

Belcastro et al. [8] did report an increase in the Ca^{2+}-binding capacity of SR vesicles isolated from endurance-trained rats compared to age-matched controls. However, Ca^{2+} uptake was not enhanced by training. Conversely, Kim et al. [113] reported, that 1 hour of treadmill exercise per day for up to 16 weeks reduced the maximum rate of Ca^{2+} uptake and the K_m for Ca^{2+} in crude muscle homogenates of the rat superficial vastus lateralis (SVL) muscle, an effect that was not apparent in the deep vastus (DVL). It is of interest to note that the SVL (100% type IIB fibers) was the only portion of the muscle affected by training, despite the fact that type IIA fibers are preferentially activated over type IIB fibers in endurance exercise [234]. Furthermore, SR measured on vesicles isolated from SVL was unaffected by a single bout of swimming, whereas SR from types I and IIA was altered [67, 68] (see above). It is surprising that the training did not affect the latter, since there are only minimal structural and functional differences between SR of IIB and IIA fibers. It may be that swimming and running do not produce the same effect on the SR. Green et al. [84], using a severe endurance training program of treadmill exercise, have supported the concept of the fiber type-specific effects of endurance exercise on SR. Electrophoretic determination of the concentration of the Ca^{2+} ATPase in isolated SR vesicles indicated substantial reductions in both SVL and DVL. These results probably reflect decreases in the relative percentage of the Ca^{2+} ATPase compared to the total protein in the isolated SR membrane fraction as opposed to reductions in the actual amount of the ATPase [129, 130]. These results indicate that fiber type-specific differences should not be attributed to a heightened sensitivity to activity by some fiber types over others. Instead, as previously stated, such results may be strictly a function of fiber recruitment patterns common to a given type of exercise.

It is clear that many molecular mechanisms related to the capacity of SR to sequester Ca^{2+} could be influenced by exercise; however, none has been adequately addressed. Past investigations have concentrated on the role of altered SR function in the development of muscle fatigue. Although this is certainly a working hypothesis, there are a number of other cellular processes that could be influenced by increases or decreases in intracellular Ca^{2+}. A role for Ca^{2+} in protein synthesis and degradation has been recognized for some time [134]. Based on the decrease in Ca^{2+} uptake capacity and concomitant elevation in intracellular free Ca^{2+} [220], Pette [182] proposed that alterations in Ca^{2+} metabolism serve as a signal for the response of skeletal muscle structure and function to increased activity. Furthermore, activity-induced decreases in SR function, coupled with a reduced concentration of the Ca^{2+}-binding protein PA (see below), may alter the tension development characteristics of muscle.

The process of relaxation in skeletal muscle is presently being reexamined. The role played by SR in this process may not be to simply remove Ca^{2+} from TnC, but to interact with a number of other Ca^{2+}-binding systems in a more complex process (see above). Robertson et al. [200] suggested that substantial Ca^{2+} sequestration occurs by SR at low intracellular concentrations long after force has subsided. If true, this argues against the suggestion that the only meaningful measurements of SR Ca^{2+} uptake are those in the millisecond range and thereby adds credibility to the experiments that have used techniques with slower time resolution. These investigations suggest that the amount of Ca^{2+} handled by the SR during a twitch is lower than expected. If this is true, the decrease in Ca^{2+} sequestration that accompanies exercise is an interesting observation of little physiological significance to the regulation of muscle contraction. With all of the methodological considerations and the number of possible unanswered questions concerning the ramifications of altered SR function, much remains to be accomplished in this field.

Myosin Light Chain Kinase and Myosin Phosphorylation
As stated previously, the activities of MLCK and MLCP vary in different muscle fiber types. The evidence that these variations are important regulators of myosin P-light chain phosphorylation and twitch potentiation in skeletal muscle presents the possibility that any intervention that produces changes in the concentration of these enzymes might be significant in the long-term regulation of muscle contraction.

Resink et al. [195] reported that in isolated perfused hearts, the incorporation of phosphate into the P-light chain of myosin in response to isoproterenol stimulation was greater in the hearts of treadmill-trained animals compared to control animals. They suggested that this difference resulted from an increased susceptibility to phosphorylation of the light chain, increased MLCK, decreased MLCP, or increased availability of Ca^{2+} in the hearts of the trained animals. However, no measurements were made to support or refute these hypotheses. As with virtually all of the type-specific muscle characteristics [181, 182], chronic, low-frequency stimulation of fast-twitch muscle alters the concentration of MLCK in a manner indicating a fast-to-slow type conversion. Stimulation produces a rapid reduction in MLCK activity that persists with prolonged stimulation until the concentration is similar to that of slow muscle [122]. The magnitude and time course of these decreases produced by stimulation are different from the alterations observed for the myosin isozyme pattern. Thus, activity may alter the normal relationship between the concentration of the enzyme and the myosin isoform. This illustrates that all components of a given system need not show the same degree of sensitivity to altered activity. Preliminary experiments suggest that 1–2 days of chronic stimulation of tibialis anterior muscle attenuates the ability to phosphorylate the light chains in response to a 25-second, 5-Hz stimulus train [Klug, Houston, Mumby, Stull, and Pette, unpublished observations].

Numerous experiments have been performed to assess the ability of exercise to alter the structural and functional characteristics of muscle. Quite naturally, because of their importance in the process of tension development, many of these studies have focused on the contractile proteins. Chronic stimulation studies have demonstrated that these proteins are more resistant to change than those involved with Ca^{2+} binding and sequestering (see above) and, as shown here, MLCK and P-light chain phosphorylation. Due to sensitivity of MLCK and phosphorylation to activity, and the proposed role of P-light chain phosphorylation in the regulation of tension development, it may be useful to examine this process closely. If exercise training mimics the effects of chronic electrical stimulation, such work might provide a new approach to an old question and prove important with regard to a greater understanding of the adaptive capabilities of skeletal muscle.

Parvalbumin

A progressive decrease in PA begins within 4–5 days of chronic, low-frequency stimulation of fast-twitch muscle at 10 Hz [119, 120] and continues until after 21 days, when the PA concentration is reduced 5–10% of its original value [119, 127]. A similar reduction in PA was also observed in denervated tibialis anterior (TA) muscle and in denervated extensor digitorum longus (EDL) reinnervated by the nerve of the slow soleus muscle [161]. Conversely, an increase in PA in soleus muscle accompanies cross-reinnervation by the EDL nerve [162]. Interestingly, chronic electrical stimulation produces a more rapid reduction in PA than does dennervation [127]. Thus, regulation of PA synthesis depends not only on the presence or absence of activity, but on the frequency and duration of the activity pattern. Although an effect of neurotrophic factors cannot be ruled out, Gunderson et al. [86] showed that direct electrical stimulation of fast muscle with a slow, continuous stimulus paradigm also reduced [PA].

The effects of activity on [PA] are not limited to nonphysiological alterations in the normal pattern of activity. Exercise training reduces PA in the deep portion of the vastis lateralis muscle of treadmill-trained rats [84], but not in the superficial portion of this muscle. Clarification of the ability of exercise to mimic the effects of electrical stimulation on [PA] awaits experiments that incorporate different training protocols and an examination of a variety of muscle types.

Activity also influences [PA] during development. In the early stages, PA appears in presumptive fast-twitch muscle at 1–4 days after birth but is undetectable in presumptive slow-twitch muscle [127]. The initiation of synthesis correlates with the transition from neonatal to high-frequency phasic adult motor activity [164] and the loss of polyneural innervation [168]. If the muscles are denervated during development, there is a rapid reduction of PA until the concentration is similar to that of slow muscles [127]. The cause of stimulation-induced decreases in PA appears to be related to altered transcription, as mRNA for PA is reduced by 50% approximately 5 days prior to a loss of similar magnitude in the actual concentration of the protein [127].

Chronic electrical stimulation produces decreases in the Ca^{2+}-sequestering capacity of SR [120, 129, 130] that precede any reduction in PA by 3–4 days. This experimental model of electrical stimulation has been used to study the role of PA in muscle relaxation [123]. One-half relaxation time and [PA] were examined at various time points in stimulated and contralateral TA muscles of rabbits that underwent chronic 10-Hz stimulation for 1–21 days. Stimulation produced a small increase in one-half relaxation time but failed to alter [PA] (Figure 2). Thus, in the early days of stimulation, attenuation of relaxation is clearly not related to a decrease in [PA]. A comparison of the data regarding one-half relaxation time with studies by Leberer et al. [130] indicates that the early decrease in one-half relaxation time is temporally correlated to a 50% reduction in SR Ca^{2+} uptake, which is maintained at this level even after 50 days of stimulation. Prolongation of the stimulation for periods of 5–12 days did not potentiate the original effect on one-half relaxation time, whereas [PA] was reduced by 50%. Thus, no clear relationship exists between [PA] and one-half relaxation time in rabbit TA muscle under conditions where the PA content is reduced to as much as one-half of its normal value.

Between 5 and 21 days, [PA] fell to approximately 10% of normal

FIGURE 2

Time course of changes in one-half relaxation time, PA content, and Ca^{2+} uptake by the SR in chronically stimulated fast-twitch muscle. Data regarding one-half relaxation time and PA are taken from Klug et al. Pflügus Arch. *(In press), and the Ca^{2+} uptake data are those of Leberer et al. (Eur. J. Biochem. 162:555–561, 1987; reprinted by permission of D. Pette). Values are expressed as ratios of the data from experimental versus contralateral muscles. Curves a and b, representing one-half relaxation time, are measurements taken before and immediately after a 25-second, 5-Hz stimulus train, respectively.*

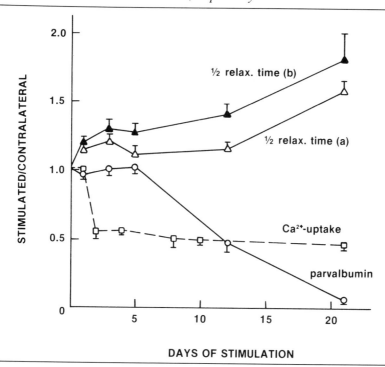

DAYS OF STIMULATION

and one-half relaxation time was prolonged by 60%. These changes, coupled with the fact that SR function is not altered during this period, support a role for PA in relaxation once its concentration is reduced to a critical level. This is supported by regression analysis of the relationship between these two variables from day 5 to day 21, which yielded a correlation coefficient of −0.72.

The reduction of [PA] by 90% but one-half relaxation time by only 60% at 21 days of stimulation is evidence that the role of PA in relaxation is more complex than can be explained by a simple linear relationship. Such departures from linearity have been observed with adr mutants [224], with cross-reinnervation [162], and in denervated muscle [86].

Interestingly, the effect of stimulation on one-half relaxation time was potentiated if the relaxation measurements were made on a twitch immediately following a 25-second, 5-Hz train of stimuli. This indicates that PA may be more critical with regard to relaxation after a series of Ca^{2+} transients that accompany repetitive stimulation (see above).

Although most investigations concerning PA have concentrated on its role in muscle relaxation, the experiments discussed here indicate that this is not the only muscle characteristic that is altered when the capacities for Ca^{2+} binding and sequestration are reduced. When PA was reduced to 50% of normal (12 days), isometric twitch tension was 34% above the value in the contralateral muscle. At 21 days when [PA] was only 10% of normal, twitch tension increased by nearly 80%, whereas tetanic tension was reduced by more than 30%. As a consequence, stimulation produced an increase in the twitch tetanus ratio from 0.22 to 0.49. Thus, it appears that a loss of PA and a decrease in SR function may result in the prolongation of the active state of contraction so that a greater percentage of the maximal tetanic force can be expressed in a single twitch.

[PA] is a muscle fiber type-specific characteristic that is mutable by activity, and these changes may affect the contractile characteristics of fast skeletal muscle. However, even if it is determined that PA does not function as a soluble relaxing factor, its sensitivity to activity, coupled with its variability between fiber types and its capacity to bind a large amount of Ca^{2+}, suggest that it may also serve other functions in muscle that are not related to the contractile process. One possible alternative arises from studies concerning the pattern of changes in muscle fiber type-specific characteristics (for a complete review, see [181, 182]).

As stated previously, permutations of muscle fiber characteristics by chronic stimulation occur sequentially [120]. An early event in the transformation process is a decrease in Ca^{2+} uptake of the SR, which may result in a fivefold increase in intracellular free $[Ca^{2+}]$ [220] during this time period. [PA] then decreases, which, because of the loss of its capacity to bind Ca^{2+}, could produce a permanent elevation in intracellular free $[Ca^{2+}]$. This possibility is supported by observations that the initial increase in intracellular $[Ca^{2+}]$ is sustained, albeit at a lower magnitude, for 30 days [220]. Thus, SR and PA changes may contribute to the regulation of protein synthesis, as suggested above. Furthermore, the greater sensitivity of SR and PA to activity, compared to myosin light and heavy chains [181, 182], presents the possibility of the existence of muscle fibers that have the Ca^{2+}-binding and -sequestering characteristics of a slow muscle coupled with fast contractile proteins.

A great deal is known about the biochemical characteristics of PA from modeling and *in vitro* studies. However, to date, the physiological role of this protein remains unclear. It is conceivable that fluctuations in its concentration could be a link between altered activity patterns and an intracellular regulator like Ca^{2+}. Therefore, it may be prudent for future experiments to examine the effect of activity on PA from the perspective of its role as a regulator of muscle structure and function, as opposed to limiting its significance to its effect on contractile behavior on a twitch-by-twitch basis.

CONCLUSION

We have attempted to present an overview of some of the Ca^{2+}-dependent events in striated muscle and to discuss the adaptive capacities of these systems. In spite of the limited scope of this presentation, it illustrates the incompleteness of the work in these areas and suggests research in this field that may extend current understanding in exercise biology. The number of events in striated muscle that are directly or indirectly mediated by Ca^{2+} represent a large percentage of the total number of regulatory processes generic to these tissues. These include the beat-to-beat regulation of cardiac muscle contraction, the control of twitch tension in skeletal muscle, glycolytic and oxidative energy metabolism, and protein synthesis and degradation. In light of these myriad influences, experimentation in this area should prove valuable in answering fundamental questions ranging from identification of the causes for the exercise-induced augmentation of cardiac function to possible loci for skeletal muscle fatigue.

The value of such experiments is not limited solely to the study of the responses of SL, SR, and Ca^{2+}-binding proteins to acute exercise. The ability of chronic activity to modify these important Ca^{2+}-regulatory systems in a controlled, predictable manner provides models whereby hypotheses concerning the relationship between the structure and function of striated muscle, as well as its capacity for adaptation, can be carefully tested. For example, if the Ca^{2+}-regulatory systems in skeletal muscle are indeed more sensitive to activity than enzymes and/or contractile proteins, alterations in Ca^{2+} metabolism may be a link between activity and modifications of muscle structure and function. This differential sensitivity to activity also suggests that training could produce a continuum of hybrid muscle fibers containing a mixture of type-specific characteristics common to fast and slow muscle rather than the several discrete categories that are commonly thought to exist. In addition, a better understanding of the adaptive capacities of Na^+/Ca^{2+} exchange, and the mechanisms by which the Ca^{2+} flux across the SL is regulated, may assist in elucidating the mechanism(s) for the enhancement of cardiac output that accompanies training. Such knowledge may also be valuable in the treatment and/or prevention of cardiovascular disease.

The study of the effect of activity on the components of the Ca^{2+}-regulatory mechanisms requires careful consideration of several issues. First, their structure and function vary considerably among muscle types. Thus, it is important that conclusions derived from experiments on one type of muscle be limited only to that tissue and not automatically extrapolated to other types. Second, there are a large number of methodological considerations that must be addressed, which are critical in determining the validity of data derived from experiments where alterations in normal activity are employed. Finally, although research in this area is facilitated by the availability of a large number of techniques, each has distinct advantages and disadvantages with regard to issues such as sensitivity, linearity, and response time. Accurate extrapolation of the results of experiments conducted *in vitro* to the function of these systems *in vivo* demands that these factors be considered.

Despite the potential significance of activity-induced alterations in Ca^{2+}-mediated cellular events, numerous questions remain unanswered. Data concerning the effect of acute and chronic exercise on Ca^{2+} release from SR are absent from the literature, as are measurements of Ca^{2+} uptake on well-characterized vesicles or skinned fibers. In addition, no experiments exist regarding these measurements where techniques were used that are capable of assessing rapid Ca^{2+} fluxes. Very few reports have examined how structural changes in Ca^{2+}-binding proteins, membrane lipid composition, channels, and/or pumps affect the contractile function of muscles that are exposed to alterations in their normal activity pattern.

The study of adaptations of the components of the Ca^{2+}-regulatory systems to alterations in activity provides those researchers who have an understanding of exercise with a unique opportunity to contribute to this important area of muscle research. As in other areas such as cardiovascular physiology, much can be added to our understanding of the metabolic and mechanical functions of striated muscle by studying how it responds to the stresses imposed by dynamic exercise.

ACKNOWLEDGMENTS

The authors thank Drs. P.D. Gollnick, J.T. Stull, R.L. Moore, and E. Leberer for their comments and advice during the preparation of this manuscript. G.A.K. was supported by the Alexander Von Humboldt Stiftung, Deutsche Forschungsgemeinschaft, Sonderforschungsbereiche 138, the American Heart Association (Colorado Affiliate), and the Medical Research Foundation of Oregon. G.F.T. gratefully acknowledges the support of Natural Sciences and Engineering Research Council (NSERC) of Canada and the British Columbia Heart Foundation.

REFERENCES

1. Adelstein, R.S., and C.B. Klee. Purification and characterization of smooth muscle myosin light chain kinase. *J. Biol. Chem.* 256:7501–7509, 1981.
2. Allen, D.G., and J.C. Kentish. The cellular basis of the length–tension relation in cardiac muscle. *J. Mol. Cell. Cardiol.* 17:821–840, 1985.
3. Baker, P.F., M.P. Blaustein, A.L. Hodgkin, and R.A. Steinhardt. The influence of calcium ions on sodium efflux in squid axons. *J. Physiol. (Lond.)* 200:451–458, 1969.
4. Baylor, S.M., W.K. Chandler, and M.W. Marshall. Optical measurements of intracellular pH and magnesium in frog muscle fibers. *J. Physiol. (Lond.)* 331:139–177, 1982.
5. Baylor, S.M., M.E. Quinta-Ferreria, and C.S. Hui. Comparison of isotropic calcium signals from intact frog muscle fibers injected with arsenazo III and antipyrylazo. *Biophys. J.* 44:107–112, 1983.
6. Baylor, S.M., W.K. Chandler, and M.W. Marshall. Calcium release and sarcoplasmic reticulum membrane potential in frog muscle fibers. *J. Physiol. (Lond.)* 348:209–238, 1984.
7. Beeler, T., J.T. Russell, and A. Martinosi. Optical probe responses on sarcoplasmic reticulum: Oxacarbocyanides as probes of membrane potential. *Eur. J. Biochem.* 95:579–571, 1979.
8. Belcastro, A.N., H. Wenger, T. Nihei, D. Secord, and A. Bonen. Functional overload of rat fast-twitch skeletal muscle during development. *J. Appl. Physiol.* 49:583–588, 1980.
9. Belcastro, A.N., M. Rossiter, M.P. Low, and M.M. Sopper. Calcium activation of sarcoplasmic reticulum ATPase following strenuous exercise. *Can. J. Physiol. Pharmacol.* 59:1214–1218, 1981.
10. Belcastro, A.N., I. MacLean, and J. Gilchrist. Biochemical basis of muscular fatigue associated with repetitious contractions of skeletal muscle. *Int. J. Biochem.* 17:447–453, 1985.
11. Benzanilla, F., and P. Horowicz. Fluorescence intensity changes associated with contractile activation in frog muscle stained with Nile Blue. *Am. J. Physiol.* 246:709–735, 1975.
12. Berman, M.C. Stimulation of calcium transport of sarcoplasmic reticulum vesicles by the calcium complex of ethylene glycol bis(B-aminoethyl ether)-N,N',tetraacetic acid. *J. Biol. Chem.* 257:1953–1957, 1982.
13. Bers, D.M. A simple method for the accurate determination of free [Ca] in Ca-EGTA solutions. *Am. J. Physiol.* 242:C404–C408, 1982.
14. Blinks, J.R., W.G. Wier, P. Hess, and F.R. Prendergast. Measurement of Ca^{2+} concentrations in living cells. *Prog. Biophys. Mol. Biol.* 40:1–114, 1982.
15. Blinks, J.R. Determination of intracellular $[Ca^{2+}]$. In Bader, H., K. Gietzen, J. Rosenthal, R. Ruedel, and H.U. Wolf. (eds.). *Intracellular* Ca^{2+} *Regulation.* Oxford: Manchester, 1986, p. 1–14.
16. Blum, H.E., P. Lehky, L. Kohler, E.A. Stein, and E.H. Fischer. Comparative properties of vertebrate paravalbumins. *J. Biol. Chem.* 252:2834–2838, 1977.
17. Blumenthal, D.K., and J.T. Stull. Activation of skeletal muscle myosin light chain kinase by Ca (2 +) and calmodulin. *Biochemistry.* 19:5608–5614, 1980.
18. Bonner, H.W., S.W. Leslie, A.B. Combs, and C.A. Tate. Effects of exercise training and exhaustion on $^{45}Ca^{2+}$-uptake by rat skeletal muscle mitochondria and sarcoplasmic reticulum. *Res. Commun. Chem. Pathol. Pharmacol.* 14:767–770, 1976.
19. Brandl, C.J., N.M. Green, B. Korczak, and D.H. MacLennan. Two Ca^{2+} ATPase genes: Homologies and mechanistic implications of deduced amino acid sequences. *Cell* 44:596–607, 1986.
20. Brandl, C.J., S. deLeon, D.R. Martin, and D.H. MacLennan. Adult forms of the

Ca^{2+}-ATPase of sarcoplasmic reticulum. Expression in developing muscles. *J. Biol. Chem.* 262:3768–3774, 1987.

21. Brandt, N.R., A.H. Caswell and J.P. Brunschwig. ATP-energized Ca^{2+} pump in isolated transverse tubules of skeletal muscles. *J. Biol. Chem.* 255:6290–6298, 1980.

22. Briggs, N. Identification of the soluble relaxing factor as parvalbumin. *Fed. Proc.* 34:540, 1975. (Abstract)

23. Burger, D., E.A. Stein, and J.A. Cox. Free energy coupling in the interaction between Ca^{2+}, calmodulin and phosphorylase kinase. *J. Biol. Chem.* 258:14733–14739, 1983.

24. Butler, T.M., M.J. Siegmann, S.U. Mooers, and R.J. Barsotti. Myosin light chain phosphorylation does not modulate cross bridge cycling rate in mouse skeletal muscle. *Science* 220:1167–1169, 1983.

25. Campbell, K.P., C. Franzini-Armstrong, and A.E. Shamoo. Further characterization of light and heavy sarcoplasmic reticulum vesicles. Identification of the "sarcoplasmic reticulum feet" associated with heavy sarcoplasmic reticulum vesicles. *Biochim. Biophys. Acta* 602:97–116, 1980.

26. Campbell, K.P., and D.H. MacLennan. Purification and characterization of the 53,000-dalton glycoprotein from the sarcoplasmic reticulum. *J. Biol. Chem.* 256:4626–4632, 1981.

27. Campbell, K.P., and D.H. MacLennan. Labeling of the high affinity ATP-binding sites on the 53,000 and 160,000 glycoproteins of the sarcoplasmic gamma-^{32}P-ATP. *J. Biol. Chem.* 258:1391–1394, 1983.

28. Cannell, M.B., and D.G. Allen. Model of calcium movements during activation in the sarcomere of frog skeletal muscle. *Biophys. J.* 45:913–925, 1984.

29. Caputo, C., and P. Bolanos. Effect of external sodium and calcium on calcium efflux in frog striated muscle. *J. Membr. Biol.* 41:1–14, 1978.

30. Carafoli, E. The homeostasis of calcium in heart cells. *J. Mol. Cell. Cardiol.* 17:203–212, 1985.

31. Caroni, P., and E. Carafoli. The Ca^{2+}-pumping ATPase of heart sarcolemma. *J. Biol. Chem.* 256:3263–3270, 1981.

32. Caroni, P., and E. Carafoli. The regulation of the Na$^+$-Ca^{2+} exchanger of heart sarcolemma. *Eur. J. Biochem.* 132:451–460, 1983.

33. Celio, M.R., and C.W. Heizmann. Calcium-binding protein parvalbumin is associated with fast contracting fibers. *Nature* 297:504–506, 1982.

34. Chapman, R. Control of cardiac contractility at the cellular level. *Am. J. Physiol.* 245:H535–H552, 1983.

35. Chau, V., C.Y. Huang, P.B. Chock, J.H. Wang, and R.K. Sharma. Kinetic properties of the activation of cyclic nucleotide phosphodiesterase by Ca^{++} and calmodulin. In Kakiuchi S., H. Hiaka, and A.R. Means (eds.). *Calmodulin and Intracellular Ca^{2+}-Receptors.* New York: Plenum Press, 1982, pp. 199–217.

36. Cheung, W.Y. Cyclic 3',5'-nucleotide phosphodiesterase. Evidence for and properties of a protein activator. *J. Biol. Chem.* 246:2859–2869, 1971.

37. Cheung, W.Y. *Calcium and Cell Function: Calmodulin.* New York: Academic Press, 1980.

38. Chu, A., P. Volpe, B. Costello, and S. Fleischer. Functional characterization of the junctional cisternae from mammalian fast skeletal sarcoplasmic reticulum. *Biochemistry* 25:8315–8324, 1986.

39. Close, R., and J.F.Y. Hoh. The after-effects of repetitive stimulation of the isometric twitch contraction of rat fast twitch muscle. *J. Physiol. (Lond.)* 197:461–467, 1968.

40. Cohen, P., A. Burchell, J.G. Foulkes, P.T.W. Cohen, T.C. Vanaman, and A.L. Nairn. Identification of the Ca^{2+}-dependent modulator protein as the fourth subunit of rabbit skeletal muscle phosphorylase kinase. *FEBS Lett.* 92:287–293, 1978.

41. Colvin, R.A., T.F. Ashavaid, and L.G. Herbette. Structure-function of canine cardiac

sarcolemma membranes. Estimation of receptor densities. *Biochim. Biophys. Acta* 812:601–608, 1985.

42. Cooper, C.L., S. Vandaele, J. Barhanin, M. Fosset, M. Lazdunski, and M.M. Hosey. Purification and characterization of the dihydropyridine-sensitive voltage-dependent calcium channel from cardiac muscle. *J. Biol. Chem.* 262:509–512, 1987.

43. Crow, M.T., and M.J. Kushmerick. Correlated reduction of velocity of shortening and the rate of energy utilization in mouse fast-twitch muscle during continuous tetanus. *Biochim. Biophys. Acta* 82:703–720, 1983.

44. Curtis, B.M., and W.A. Catterall. Purification of the calcium antagonist receptor of the voltage-sensitive calcium channel from skeletal muscle transverse tubules. *Biochemistry* 23:2113–2118, 1984.

45. Damiani, E., R. Betto, S. Salvatori, P. Volpe, G. Salviati, and M. Margreth. Polymorphism of sarcoplasmic reticulum adenosine triphosphate of rabbit skeletal muscle. *Biochem. J.* 197:245–248, 1981.

46. Damiani, E., A. Magreth, A. Furlan, A.S. Dahms, J. Arnn, and R.A. Sabbadini. Common structural domains in the sarcoplasmic reticulum Ca-ATPase and the transverse tubule Mg^{2+}-ATPase. *J. Cell. Biol.* 104:461–472, 1987.

47. Davies, K.J.A., A.T. Quintanilha, G.A. Brooks, and L. Packer. Free radicals and tissue damage produced by exercise. *Biochem. Biophys. Res. Commun.* 107:1198–1205, 1982.

48. Dawson, M.J., D.G. Gadian, and D.R. Wilkie. Mechanical relaxation rate and metabolism studied in fatiguing muscle by phosphorus nuclear magnetic resonance. *J. Physiol. (Lond.)* 299:465–484, 1980.

49. DeMeis, L., and A.L. Vianna. Energy conversion by the Ca^{2+}-dependent ATPase of the sarcoplasmic reticulum. *Ann. Rev. Biochem.* 48:275–292, 1979.

50. Dhoot, G.K., G. Vrbová, and S.V. Perry. Changes in the distribution of the components of the troponin complex in muscle fibres after cross reinnervation. *Exp. Neurol.* 72:513–530, 1981.

51. Dhoot, G.K., and S.V. Perry. Distribution of polymorphic forms of troponin components and tropomyosin in skeletal muscle. *Nature* 278:714–718, 1979.

52. Diffee, G.M., and G.F. Tibbits. Dihydropyridine binding to myocardial sarcolemma: Adaptation to exercise. *Clin. Physiol.* 5:29, 1985. (Abstract)

53. Dompert, W.U., and J. Traber. Binding sites for dihydropyridine calcium antagonists. In Opie, L.H. (ed.). *Calcium Antagonists and Cardiovascular Disease.* New York: Raven Press, 1984, pp. 175–179.

54. Donaldson, S.K. Mammalian muscle fiber types: Comparison of excitation-contraction coupling mechanisms. *Acta Physiol. Scand.* 128(suppl.556):157–166, 1986.

55. Dowell, R. Cardiac adaptations to exercise. *Exercise Sports Sci. Rev.* 11:99–117, 1983.

56. Drabikowski, W., M.G. Sarzala, and A. Wroniszewska. Role of cholesterol in Ca-uptake and ATPase activity of fragmented sarcoplasmic reticulum. *Biochim. Biophys. Acta* 274:158–170, 1974.

57. Duggan, P.F., and A. Martinosi. Sarcoplasmic reticulum. IX. The permeability of sarcoplasmic reticulum membranes. *J. Gen. Physiol.* 56:147–167, 1970.

58. Ebashi, S., and M. Endo. Calcium ions and muscle contraction. *Prog. Biophys.* 18:123–183, 1968.

59. Eisenberg, B.R. Quantitative ultrastructure of mammalian skeletal muscle. In Peachey, L.D., R.H. Adrian, and S.R. Geiger (eds.). *Handbook of Physiology: Skeletal Muscle,* Baltimore: Williams & Wilkins, 1983, pp. 73–112.

60. Eisenberg, R., R.T. McCarthy, and R.L. Milton. Paralysis of frog skeletal muscle fibres by the calcium antagonist D-600. *J. Physiol. (Lond.)* 341:495–505, 1983.

61. Endo, M. Calcium release from the sarcoplasmic reticulum. *Physiol. Rev.* 57:71–108, 1977.

62. Endo, M. Mechanism of calcium induced calcium release in the SR membrane. In Ohnishi, S.T., and M. Endo (eds.). *The Mechanism of Gated Calcium Transport Across Biological Membranes*, New York: Academic Press, 1981, pp. 257–264.

63. Endo, M., and M. Iino. Specific perforations of muscle cell membranes with preserved SR functions by saponin treatment. *J. Muscle Cell Res. Motil.* 1:89–100, 1980.

64. Fabiato, A. Calcium-induced release of Ca^{2+} from the cardiac sarcoplasmic reticulum. *Am. J. Physiol* 245:C1–C14, 1985.

65. Fabiato, A. Rapid ionic modifications during the aequorin-detected calcium transient in a skinned canine cardiac Purkinje cell. *Biochim. Biophys. Acta* 85:189–246, 1985.

66. Fiehn, W., and J.B. Peter. Properties of the fragmented sarcoplasmic reticulum from fast and slow muscle. *J. Clin. Invest.* 50:570–573, 1971.

67. Fitts, R.H., D.H. Kim, and F.A. Witzmann. The effect of prolonged activity on the sarcoplasmic reticulum and myofibrils of fast and slow muscle. *Physiologist* 22:38, 1979. (Abstract)

68. Fitts, R.H., J.B. Courtwright, D.H. Kim, and F.A. Witzmann. The effect of prolonged exercise: Contractile and biochemical alterations. *Am. J. Physiol.* 242:C65–C73, 1982.

69. Fliegel, L., M. Ohnishi, M.R. Carpenter, V.J. Khanna, R.A.F. Reithmeier, and D.H. MacLennan. Amino acid sequence of rabbit fast-twitch muscle calsequestrin deduced from cDNA and peptide sequence. *PNAS (USA)* 84:1167–1171, 1987.

70. Frank, G.B. Roles of intracellular and trigger calcium ions in excitation-contraction coupling in skeletal muscle. *Can J. Physiol. Pharmacol.* 60:427–439, 1982.

71. Franzini-Armstrong, C. Structure of the sarcoplasmic reticulum. *Fed. Proc.* 39:2403–2409, 1980.

72. Froehlich, J.P., and E.W. Taylor. Transient state kinetics studies of sarcoplasmic reticulum adenosine triphosphate. *J. Biol. Chem.* 250:2013–2021, 1975.

73. Gerday, C., and J.M. Gillis. The possible role of parvalbumins in the control of contraction. *J. Physiol. (Lond.)* 258:96P, 1976. (Abstract)

74. Gilbert, D.L., and W.O. Fenn. Calcium equilibrium in muscle. *Biochim. Biophys. Acta* 40:393–408, 1957.

75. Gilbert, J.R., and G. Meissner. Sodium-calcium ion exchange in skeletal muscle sarcolemmal vesicles. *J. Membr. Biol.* 69:77–84, 1982.

76. Gilchrist, J., I.M. Maclean, R.A. Turcotte, and A.N. Belcastro. Calcium fluxes in the sarcoplasmic reticulum of male and female rats after a prolonged run to exhaustion. *Clin. Physiol.* 5 (suppl 4.):145, 1985. (Abstract)

77. Gillis, J.M., A. Piront, and C. Gosselin-Rey. Parvalbumins: Distribution and physical state inside the muscle cell. *Biochim. Biophys. Acta* 585:444–450, 1979.

78. Gillis, J.M., D. Thomason, J. Lefevre, and R.H. Kretsinger. Parvalalbumins and muscle relaxation: A computer study. *J. Muscle. Res. Cell Motil.* 3:377–398, 1982.

79. Gillis, J.M. Relaxation of vertebrate skeletal muscle. A synthesis of biochemical and physiological approaches. *Biochim. Biophys. Acta* 811:97–145, 1985.

80. Gollnick, P.D., D.B. Parsons, and C.R. Oakley. Differentiation of fiber types in skeletal muscle from the sequential inactivation of myofibrillar actomyosin ATPase during acid preincubation. *Histochemistry* 77:543–555, 1983.

81. Gollnick, P.D., and D.R. Hodgson. The identification of muscle fiber types in skeletal muscle: A continual dilemma. *Exercise Sports Sci. Rev.* 14:81–104, 1986.

82. Gould, R.J., K.M. Murphy, and S. Snyder. Tissue heterogeneity of calcium channel antagonist binding sites labeled by [^{3}H] NTP. *Mol. Pharmacol* 25:235–241, 1983.

83. Green, H.J., H. Reichmann, and D. Pette. A comparison of two ATPase based schemes for histochemical muscle fiber typing in various mammals. *Histochemistry* 76:21–31, 1982.

84. Green, H.J., G.A. Klug, H. Reichmann, U. Seedorf, W. Wiehrer, and D. Pette. Exercise-induced fiber type transitions with regard to myosin, parvalbumin, and sarcoplasmic reticulum in muscles of the rat. *Pflugers Arch.* 400:432–438, 1984.

85. Grynkiewicz, G., M. Poenie, and R.Y. Tsien. A new generation of Ca^{2+} indicators with greatly improved fluorescence properties. *J. Biol. Chem.* 260:3440–3450, 1985.

86. Gunderson, K., E. Leberer, T. Lomo, D. Pette, and R.S. Staron. Ca^{2+}-sequestering proteins and metabolic enzymes in denervated and chronically stimulated muscles of the rat. *J. Physiol. (Lond.)* (in press), 1987.
87. Hagiwara, S., and L. Byerly. Calcium channel. *Ann. Rev. Neurosci.* 4:69–125, 1981.
88. Haiech, J., J. Derancourt, J-F. Perchere, and J.G. DeMaille. Magnesium and calcium binding to parvalbumins: Evidence for differences between parvalbumins and an explanation of their relaxing function. *Biochemistry* 18:2752–2758, 1979.
89. Haiech, J., C.B. Klee, and J.G. DeMaille. Effects of cations on affinity of calmodulin for calcium. Ordered binding of calcium ions allows the specific activation of calmodulin-stimulated enzymes. *Biochemistry* 20:3890–3897, 1981.
90. Hartshorne, D., and R.F. Siemankowski. Regulation of smooth muscle actomyosin. *Ann. Rev. Physiol.* 43:519–530, 1981.
91. Hashimoto, I., W.L. Sembrowich, and P.D. Gollnick. Calcium uptake by isolated sarcoplasmic reticulum and homogenates in different fiber types following exhaustive exercise. *Med. Sci. Sports Exerc.* 10:42, 1978. (Abstract)
92. Hasselbach, W., and M. Makinose. The calcium pump of the relaxing granules of muscle and its dependence on ATP splitting. *Biochem. Z.* 333:518–528, 1961.
93. Hasselbach, W. The kinetic response of sarcoplasmic reticulum during Ca^{2+} sequestration. *Prog. Biophys. Mol. Biol.* 14:169–222, 1964.
94. Hayes, D.H. Mechanism of calcium transport by the Ca^{2+}-Mg^{2+}-ATPase pump: Analysis of major states and pathways. *Am. J. Physiol.* 244:G3–G12, 1983.
95. Heilmann, C., and D. Pette. Molecular transformation in sarcoplasmic reticulum of fast-twitch muscle by electrostimulation. *Eur. J. Biochem.* 93:437–446, 1979.
96. Heilmann, C., D. Bridiczka, E. Kickel, and D. Pette. ATPase activities, Ca^{2+}-transport and phosphoprotein formation in the sarcoplasmic reticulum subfractions of fast and slow rabbit muscle. *Eur. J. Biochem.* 81:211–222, 1977.
97. Heizmann, C.W., M.W. Berchtold, and A.M. Rowlerson. Correlation of parvalbumin concentration with relaxation speed in mammalian muscles. *PNAS (USA)* 79:7243–7247, 1982.
98. Heizmann, C.W., and M.R. Celio. Immunolocalization of parvalbumin. *Methods Enzymol.* 139:552–550, 1987.
99. Heizmann, C.W. Parvalbumin, an intracellular calcium-binding protein; distribution, properties and possible roles in mammalian cells. *Experientia* 40:910–921, 1984.
100. Heizmann, C.W., and M.W. Berchtold. Expression of parvalbumin and other Ca^{2+}-binding proteins in normal and tumor cells: A topical review. *Cell Calcium* 8:1–41, 1987.
101. Herbette, L., J.K. Blasie, P. DeFoor, S. Fleischer, R.J. Bick, W.B. Van Winkle, C.A. Tate, and M.L. Entman. Phospholipid asymmetry in the isolated sarcoplasmic reticulum membrane. *Arch. Biochem. Biophys.* 234:235–242, 1984.
102. Hilgemann, D.W. Extracellular calcium transients at single excitations in rabbit atrium measured with tetramethylmurexide. *Biochim. Biophys. Acta* 87:707–735, 1986.
103. Holland, P.C., and D.H. MacLennan. Assembly of sarcoplasmic reticulum. Biosynthesis of the adenosine triphosphatase in rat skeletal muscle cell culture. *J. Biol. Chem.* 251:2030–2036, 1976.
104. Horl, W.H., H.P. Jennison, and L.M. Heilmayer. Evidence for the participation of a Ca^{2+}-dependent protein kinase and a protein phosphatase in the regulation of the Ca^{2+}-transport of the sarcoplasmic reticulum. 1. Effects of inhibition of the Ca^{2+}-dependent protein kinase and protein phosphatase. *Biochemistry* 17:759–765, 1978.
105. Houston, M.E., H.J. Green, and J.T. Stull. Myosin light chain phosphorylation and twitch potentiation in intact human muscle. *Pflugers Arch.* 403:348–352, 1985.
106. Hultman, E., H. Sjoholm, K. Sahlin, and L. Edstrom. Glycolytic and oxidative energy metabolism and contraction characteristics of intact human muscle. In Porter, R. and J. Whelan (eds.). *Human Muscle Fatigue: Physiological Mechanisms*. London: Pitman Medical, Ciba Foundation Symposium. 1981, pp. 19–35.

107. Ikemoto, N. Transport and inhibition of the Ca^{2+}-binding sites on the ATPase enzyme isolated from the sarcoplasmic reticulum. *J. Biol. Chem.* 250:7219–7224, 1975.

108. Ikeuchi, I. Phosphorylation in skeletal myosin light chain modulates the actin–myosin interaction in the presence of regulatory proteins in vitro. *Int. J. Biochem.* 18:251–255, 1986.

109. Inesi, G., J.A. Cohen, and C.R. Coan. Two functional states of the sarcoplasmic reticulum ATPase. *Biochemistry* 15:5293–5298, 1976.

110. Inesi, G., C. Coan, S. Verjovski-Almeida, M. Kurzmack, and D.E. Lewis. Mechanism of free energy utilization for active transport of Ca^{2+} ions. In *Frontiers of Biological Energetics*. New York: Academic Press, 1979, pp. 1212–1217.

111. Inesi, G., M. Kurzmack, C. Coan, and D.E. Lewis. Cooperative calcium binding and ATPase activation in sarcoplasmic reticulum vesicles. *J. Biol. Chem.* 255:3025–3031, 1980.

112. Jorgensen, A.O., V. Kalnins, and D.H. MacLennan. Localization of sarcoplasmic reticulum proteins in rat skeletal muscle by immunofluorescence. *J. Cell. Biol.* 80:372–374, 1979.

113. Kim, D.H., G.S. Wible, F.A. Witzman, and R.H. Fitts. A comparison of sarcoplasmic reticulum function in fast and slow muscle using crude homogenates and isolated vesicles. *Life Sci.* 28:2761–2677, 1981.

114. Kirchberger, M.A., M. Tada, and A.M. Katz. Adenosine 3',5,-monophosphate-dependent protein kinase-catalyzed phosphorylation reaction and its relationship to calcium transport in cardiac sarcoplasmic reticulum. *J. Biol. Chem.* 249:6166–6173, 1974.

115. Kirchberger, M.A., and M. Tada. Effects of adenosine 3',5'-monophosphate-dependent protein kinase on sarcoplasmic reticulum isolated from cardiac and fast and slow contracting skeletal muscle. *J. Biol. Chem.* 251:725–729, 1976.

116. Klee, C.B., and T.C. Vanaman. Calmodulin. *Adv. Prot. Chem.* 35:213–321, 1982.

117. Klee, C.B., D.L. Newton, W-C. Ni, and J. Haiech. Regulation of the calcium signal by calmodulin. In Baker, P.F. (ed.). *Calcium and the Cell.* Ciba Foundation 122. Chichester: Wiley & Sons, 1986, pp. 164–182.

118. Klug, G.A., B.R. Botterman, and J.T. Stull. The effect of low frequency stimulation on myosin light chain phosphorylation in skeletal muscle. *J. Biol. Chem.* 257:4688–4690, 1982.

119. Klug, G.A., H. Reichmann, and D. Pette. Rapid reduction in parvalbumin concentration during chronic stimulation of fast muscle. *FEBS Lett.* 152:180–182, 1983.

120. Klug, G.A., W. Wiehrer, H. Reichmann, E. Leberer, and D. Pette. Relationships between early alterations in parvalbumin, sarcoplasmic reticulum, and metabolic enzymes in chronically stimulated fast twitch muscle. *Pflugers Arch.* 399:280–284, 1983.

121. Klug, G.A., H. Reichmann, and D. Pette. Decreased parvalbumin contents in skeletal muscles of C57BL/6J (dy^{2J}/dy^{2J}) dystrophic mice. *Muscle Nerve* 8:576–579, 1985.

122. Klug, G.A., M.E. Houston, J.T. Stull, and D. Pette. Decreased myosin light chain kinase activity of rabbit fast muscle by chronic stimulation. *FEBS Lett.* 200:352–354, 1986.

123. Klug, G.A., E. Leberer, E. Leisner, and D. Pette. Relationship between parvalbumin content and the speed of relaxation in chronically stimulated rabbit-fast twitch muscle. *Pflugers Arch.* (In press)

124. Lai, F.A., H. Erickson, B.A. Block, and G. Meissner. Evidence for a junctional feet-ryanodine receptor complex from sarcoplasmic reticulum. *Biochem. Biophys. Res. Commun.* 143:704–709, 1987.

125. Langer, G.A. The role of calcium in the control of myocardial contractility: An update. *J. Mol. Cell. Cardiol.* 12:231–239, 1980.

126. Langer, G.A. Sodium–calcium exchange in the heart. *Ann. Rev. Physiol.* 44:435–449, 1982.
127. Leberer, E., and D. Pette. Neural regulation of parvalbumin expression in mammalian skeletal muscle. *Biochem. J.* 235:67–73, 1986.
128. Leberer, E., and D. Pette. Immunochemical quantitation of sarcoplasmic reticulum ATPase, of calsequestrin and of parvalbumin in rabbit skeletal muscles of defined fiber composition. *Eur. J. Biochem.* 156:489–496, 1986.
129. Leberer, E., U. Seedorf, and D. Pette. Neural control of gene expression in skeletal muscle. Ca-sequestering proteins in developing and chronically stimulated rabbit skeletal muscles. *Biochem. J.* 239:295–300, 1986.
130. Leberer, E., K.-T. Haertner, and D. Pette. Reversible inhibition of sarcoplasmic reticulum Ca-ATPase by altered neuromuscular activity in rabbit fast twitch muscle. *Eur. J. Biochem.* 162:555–561, 1987.
131. LeDonne, N.C. Jr., and J.C. Coffee. Inability of parvalbumin to function as a calcium-dependent activator of cyclic nucleotide phosphodiesterase activity. *J. Biol. Chem.* 254:4317–4320, 1979.
132. Leonards, K.S., and H. Kutchai. Coupling of Ca^{2+}-transport to ATP hydrolysis by the Ca-ATPase of sarcoplasmic reticulum: Potential of the 53-kilodalton glycoprotein. *Biochemistry* 24:4876–4884, 1985.
133. LePeuch, C.J., J. Haiech, and J.G. Demaille. Concerted regulation of cardiac sarcoplasmic reticulum calcium transport by cyclic adenosine monophosphate-dependent and calcium-calmodulin-dependent phosphorylations. *Biochemistry* 18:5150–5157, 1979.
134. Lewis, S.E., P. Anderson, and D.F. Goldspink. The effects of calcium on protein turnover in skeletal muscles of the rat. *Biochem. J.* 204:257–264, 1982.
135. Mabuchi, K. and F.A. Sreter. Use of cryostat sections for measurement of Ca^{2+}-uptake by sarcoplasmic reticulum. *Anal. Biochem.* 86:733–742, 1978.
136. Maclean, I.M., J. Gilchrist, R.A. Turcotte, and A.N. Belcastro. Kinetics of sarcoplasmic reticulum ATPase following exhaustive treadmill exercise in male and female rats. *Clin. Physiol.* 5 (suppl. 4):149, 1985. (Abstract)
137. MacLennan, D.H., and P.T.S. Wong. Isolation of a calcium-sequestering protein from sarcoplasmic reticulum. *PNAS (USA)* 68:1231–1235, 1971.
138. MacLennan, D.H., E. Zubrzycka-Gaarn, and A.O. Jorgensen. Assembly of sarcoplasmic reticulum during muscle development. *Cur. Topics Mem. Trans.* 24:338–368, 1985.
139. Maier, A., E. Leberer, and D. Pette. Distribution of sarcoplasmic reticulum Ca-ATPase and calsequestrin in rabbit and rat skeletal muscle. *Histochemistry* 86:63–69, 1986.
140. Manning, D.R., and J.T. Stull. Myosin light chain phosphorylation-dephosphorylation in mammalian skeletal muscle. *Am. J. Physiol.* 242:C234–C241, 1982.
141. Martinosi, A.N., and R. Ferretos. Sarcoplasmic reticulum. I. The uptake of Ca^{2+} by sarcoplasmic reticulum fragments. *J. Biol. Chem.* 239:648–658, 1964.
142. Martinosi, A.N. The protein composition of sarcoplasmic reticulum membranes. *Biochem. Biophys. Res. Commun.* 36:1039–1044, 1969.
143. Martinosi, A.N. The development of sarcoplasmic reticulum membranes. *Ann Rev. Physiol.* 44:337–355, 1982.
144. Martinosi, A.N. Transport of calcium by sarcoplasmic reticulum. In Cheung W.Y. (ed.). *Calcium and Cell Function.* New York: Academic Press, 1982, pp. 38–77.
145. Martinosi, A.N. Mechanisms of calcium release from sarcoplasmic reticulum of skeletal muscle. *Physiol. Rev.* 64:1240–1320, 1984.
146. Mathias, R.T., R.A. Levis, and R.S. Eisenberg. Electrical models of excitation-con-

traction coupling and charge movement in skeletal muscle. *Biochim. Biophys. Acta* 76:1–31, 1980.

147. McCleskey, E.W. Calcium channels and intracellular calcium release are pharmacologically different in frog muscle. *J. Physiol. (Lond.)* 361:231–249, 1985.

148. McCleskey, E.W., A.P. Fox, D. Feldman, and R.W. Tsien. Different types of calcium channels. *J. Exp. Biol.* 124:177–190, 1986.

149. Meissner, G. Ryanodine activation and inhibition of the Ca^{2+}-release channel of sarcoplasmic reticulum. *J. Biol. Chem.* 261:6300–6306, 1986.

150. Messineo, F.C., M. Rathier, C. Favreau, J. Watras, and H. Takenaka. Mechanisms of fatty acid effects on sarcoplasmic reticulum. III. The effects of palmitic and oleic acids on sarcoplasmic reticulum function—a model for fatty acid membrane interactions. *J. Biol. Chem.* 259:1336–1343, 1984.

151. Meszaros, L.G., and N. Ikemoto. Confirmational changes in the Ca^{2+}-ATPase as early events in the Ca^{2+}-release from sarcoplasmic reticulum. *J. Biol. Chem.* 260:16076–16079, 1985.

152. Michalak, M., K.P. Campbell, and D.H. MacLennan. Localization of the high affinity calcium-binding protein and intrinsic glycoprotein in sarcoplasmic reticulum membranes. *J. Biol. Chem.* 255:1317–1326, 1980.

153. Michell, R.H. Inositol phospholipids and cell surface receptor function. *Biochim. Biophys. Acta* 415:81–147, 1975.

154. Michiel, D.F., and J.H. Wang. Calcium-binding proteins. In Bader, H., K. Gietzen, J. Rosenthal, R. Ruedel, and H.U. Wolf (eds.). *Intracellular Calcium Regulation.* Manchester: Manchester Press, 1986, pp. 121–138.

155. Miyamoto, H., and E. Racker. Solubilization and partial purification of the Ca^{2+}/Na^+ antiporter from the plasma membrane of bovine heart. *J. Biol. Chem.* 255:2656–2658, 1980.

156. Moore, R.L., and J.T. Stull. Myosin light chain phosphorylation in fast and slow skeletal muscles in situ. *Am. J. Physiol.* 247:C462–471, 1984.

157. Moore, R.L., M.E. Houston, G.A. Iwamoto, and J.T. Stull. Phosphorylation of rabbit skeletal muscle in situ. *J. Cell. Physiol.* 125:301–305, 1985.

158. Morad, M., Y.E. Goldman, and D.R. Trentham. Rapid photochemical inactivation of Ca^{2+}-antagonists shows that Ca^{2+} entry directly activates contraction in frog heart. *Nature* 304:635–638, 1983.

159. Morano, I., H. Arndt, C. Baechle-Syolz, and J.C. Ruegg. Further studies of the effect of myosin phosphorylation on contractile properties of skinned cardiac fibers. *Basic Res. Cardiol.* 81:611–619, 1986.

160. Mullins, L.J. The generation of electrical currents in cardiac fibers by Na/Ca exchange. *Am. J. Physiol.* 236:C103–C110, 1979.

161. Muntener, C.M., M.W. Berchtold, and C.W. Heizmann. Parvalbumin in cross-reinnerverated and denervated muscles. *Muscle Nerve* 8:132–137, 1985.

162. Muntener, C.M., A.M. Rowlerson, M.W. Berchtold, and C.W. Heizmann. Changes in concentration of the calcium-binding parvalbumin in cross-reinnervated rat muscles. Comparison of biochemical with physiological and histochemical parameters. *J. Biol. Chem.* 262:465–469, 1987.

163. Narayanan, N., M. Newman, and D. Neudorf. Inhibition of sarcoplasmic reticulum calcium pumping by cytosolic protein(s) endogenous to heart and slow skeletal muscle but not fast skeletal muscle. *Biochim. Biophys. Acta* 735:53–66, 1983.

164. Navarette, R., and G. Vrbova. Changes in activity patterns in slow and fast muscles during development. *Dev. Brain Res.* 8:11–19, 1983.

165. Navarro, J., M. Tovio-Kinnucan, and M. Racher. Effect of lipid composition of the calcium/adenosine triphosphate coupling ratio of the Ca^{2+}-ATPase of sarcoplasmic reticulum. *Biochemistry* 23:130–135, 1984.

166. Nishizuka, Y. Calcium, phospholipid turnover and transmembrane signaling. *Phil. Trans. R. Soc. Lond.* 302:101–112, 1983.
167. Nosek, T.M., M.F. Williams, S.T. Zeigler, and R.E. Godt. Inositol triphosphate enhances calcium release in skinned cardiac and skeletal muscle. *Am. J. Physiol.* 250:C807–811, 1986.
168. O'Brien, R.A.D., A.J.C. Ostberg, and G. Vrbova. Observations on the elimination of polyneural innervation in developing mammalian skeletal muscle. *J. Physiol. (Lond.)* 282:571–582, 1978.
169. Ogawa, Y., H. Harafuji, and N. Kurebayashi. Comparison of the characteristics of four metallochromic dyes as potential calcium indicators for biological experiments. *J. Biochem. (Tokyo)* 87:1293–1303, 1980.
170. Ogawa, Y., and M. Tanokura. Kinetic studies of calcium binding to parvalbumin from bullfrog skeletal muscle. *J. Biochem.* 99:81–89, 1986.
171. Okamoto, V.R., M.P. Moulton, E.M. Runte, C.D. Kent, H.G. Lebherz, A.S. Dahms, and R.A. Sabbadini. Characterization of transverse tubule membrane proteins: Tentative identification of the Mg^{2+}-ATPase. *Arch. Biochem. Biophys.* 237:43–54, 1985.
172. Ostwald, T.J., and D.H. MacLennan. Isolation of a high affinity calcium-binding protein from sarcoplasmic reticulum. *J. Biol. Chem.* 249:974–979, 1974.
173. Palade, P., and J. Vergara. Arsenazo III and antipyryllazo III calcium transients in single skeletal muscle fibers. *Biochim. Biophys. Acta* 79:679–707, 1982.
174. Parslow, H.G., and D.J. Parry. Slowing of fast-twitch muscle in the dystrophic mouse. *Exp. Neurol.* 73:686–699, 1981.
175. Pechere, J.-F., and B. Focant. Carp myogens of white and red muscle. Gross isolation on sephadex columns of the low-molecular-weight components and examination of their participation in anaerobic glycolysis. *Biochem. J.* 96:113–118, 1965.
176. Pechere, J.-F., J. Derancourt, and J. Haiech. The participation of parvalbumins in the activation-relaxation cycle of vertebrate fast skeletal muscle. *FEBS Lett.* 75:111–114, 1977.
177. Perrie, W.T., L.B. Smillie, and S.V. Perry. A phosphorylated light chain component from skeletal muscle. *Biochem. J.* 135:151–156, 1973.
178. Persechini, A., and J.T. Stull. Phosphorylation kinetics of skeletal muscle myosin and the effect of phosphorylation on actomyosin adenosine triphosphatase activity. *Biochemistry* 23:4144–4150, 1984.
179. Persechini, A., J.T. Stull, and R. Cooke. The effect of myosin phosphorylation on the contractile properties of skinned rabbit skeletal muscle fibers. *J. Biol. Chem.* 260:7951–7954, 1985.
180. Peter, J.B., R.J. Barnhard, V.R. Edgerton, C.A. Gillespie, and K.E. Stempel. Metabolic profiles of three fiber types of skeletal muscles in guinea pigs and rabbits. *Biochemistry* 11:2627–2633, 1972.
181. Pette, D., and G. Vrbova. Invited review: Neural control of phenotypic expression in mammalian muscle. *Muscle Nerve* 8:676–689, 1985.
182. Pette, D. Regulation of phenotypic expression in skeletal muscle fibers by increased contractile activity. In Saltin, B. (ed.). *Biochemistry of Exercise,* Vol. VI. Champaign, Ill.: Human Kinetics, 1986, pp. 3–27.
183. Phillips, G.I. Calcium uptake in the sarcoplasmic reticulum from fatigued skeletal muscles. Master's thesis, University of Washington, Seattle, 1982.
184. Philipson, K.D., and A.Y. Nishimoto. Na–Ca exchange in inside-out cardiac sarcolemmal vesicles. *J. Biol. Chem.* 257:5111–5117, 1982.
185. Philipson, K.D. Interaction of charged amphiphiles with Na^+-Ca^{2+} exchange in cardiac sarcolemmal vesicles. *J. Biol. Chem.* 259:13999–14002, 1984.

186. Philipson, K.D., and A.Y. Nishimoto. Stimulation of Na-Ca exchange in cardiac sarcolemmal vesicles by phospholipase D. *J. Biol. Chem.* 259:16–19, 1984.
187. Philipson, K.D. Sodium-calcium exchange in plasma membrane vesicles. *Ann. Rev. Physiol.* 47:561–571, 1985.
188. Philipson, K.D., G.A. Langer, and T.L. Rich. Charged amphiphiles regulate heart contractility and sarcolemma-Ca^{2+} interactions. *Am. J. Physiol.* 248:H147–H150, 1985.
189. Philipson, K.D., and R. Ward. Modulation of Na^+-Ca^{2+} exchange and Ca^{2+} permeability in cardiac sarcolemmal vesicles by doxylstearic acids. *Biochim. Biophys. Acta* 897:152–158, 1987.
190. Pires, E.M.V., and S.V. Perry. Purification and properties of myosin light chain kinase from fast skeletal muscle. *Biochem. J.* 167:137–146, 1977.
191. Rasmussen, H., and P.Q. Barrett. Calcium messenger system: An integrated review. *Physiol. Rev.* 64:938–984, 1984.
192. Rasmussen, H. The calcium messenger system. *N. Engl. J. Med.* 314:1094–1101, 1987.
193. Reeves, J., and J. Sutko. Sodium-calcium ion exchange in cardiac membrane vesicles. *PNAS (USA)* 76:590–594, 1979.
194. Reeves, J. The sarcolemmal sodium-calcium exchange system. *Curr. Topics Membr. Trans.* 25:77–127, 1985.
195. Resink, T.J., W. Gevers, T.D. Noakes, and L.H. Opie. Increased myosin ATPase as a biochemical adaptation to running training: Enhanced response to catecholamines and a role for myosin phosphorylation. *J. Mol. Cell. Cardiol.* 13:679–694, 1981.
196. Reuter, H., and N. Seitz. The dependence of calcium efflux from cardiac muscle on temperature and external ion composition. *J. Physiol. (Lond.)* 195:451–470, 1969.
197. Reuter, H. Properties of two inward membrane currents in the heart. *Ann. Rev. Physiol.* 41:413–424, 1979.
198. Reuter, H., S. Kokubun, and B. Prodhom. Properties and modulation of cardiac calcium channels. *J. Exp. Biol.* 124:191–201, 1986.
199. Ringer, S. A further contribution regarding the influence of the blood on the contraction of the heart. *J. Physiol. (Lond.)* 4:29–42, 1883.
200. Robertson, S.P., J.D. Johnson, and J.D. Potter. The time course of calcium exchange with calmodulin, troponin, parvalbumin, and myosin in response to transient increases in Ca. *Biophys. J.* 34:559–569, 1982.
201. Salviatti, P., P. Volpe, S. Salvatori, R. Betto, E. Damiani, A. Margreth, and Y. Pasqual-Ronchetti. Biochemical heterogeneity of skeletal muscle microsomal membranes. *Biochem. J.* 202:289–301, 1982.
202. Salviatti, G., R. Betto, and D. Danieli Betto. Polymorphism of myofibrillar proteins of rabbit skeletal-muscle fibres. *Biochem. J.* 207:261–272, 1982.
203. Sarzala, M., M. Pilarska, E. Zubrzycka, and M. Michalak. Changes in the structure, composition, and function of sarcoplasmic reticulum membrane during development. *Eur. J. Biochem.* 57:25–34, 1975.
204. Sarzala, M.G., G. Szymanska, W. Wiehrer, and D. Pette. Effects of chronic stimulation at low frequency on the lipid phase of sarcoplasmic reticulum in rabbit fast twitch muscle. *Eur. J. Biochem.* 123:241–245, 1982.
205. Schatzmann, H.J. The red cell calcium pump. *Ann. Rev. Physiol.* 45:303–312, 1983.
206. Scherer, N.M., and E.W. Deamer. Oxidative stress impairs the function of sarcoplasmic reticulum by oxidation of sulfhydryl groups in the Ca^{2+}-ATPase. *Arch. Biochem. Biophys.* 246:589–601, 1986.
207. Schwartz, L.M., E.W. McCleskey, and W. Almers. Dihydropyridine receptors in muscle are voltage-dependent but most are not functional calcium channels. *Nature* 14:747–751, 1985.
208. Sembrowich, W.L., and P.D. Gollnick. Calcium uptake by heart and skeletal muscle sarcoplasmic reticulum from exercised rats. *Med. Sci. Sports. Exerc.* 9:64, 1977. (Abstract)

209. Shaw, A., F. Nagao, V. Sahgal, and H. Singh. Effect of nerve stimulation on rat skeletal muscle. A study of plasma membrane. *Experientia* 41:1396–1398, 1985.

210. Shoshan, V., K.P. Campbell, D.H. MacLennan, W. Frodis, and B.A. Britt. Quercetin inhibits Ca^{2+}-uptake but not Ca^{2+}-release by sarcoplasmic reticulum in skinned muscle fibers. *PNAS (USA)* 77:4435–4438, 1980.

211. Shoshan, V., D.H. MacLennan, and D.S. Wood. A proton gradient controls a calcium-release channel in sarcoplasmic reticulum. *PNAS (USA)* 78:4828–4832, 1981.

212. Siegl, P.K.S., E.J. Cragoe, M.J. Trumble, and G.J. Kaczorowski. Inhibition of Na^+/Ca^{2+} exchange in membrane vesicles and papillary muscle preparations from guinea pig heart by analogs of amiloride. *PNAS (USA)* 81:3238–3242, 1984.

213. Silver, P.J., L.M. Buja, and J.T. Stull. Frequency-dependent myosin light chain phosphorylation in isolated myocardium. *J. Mol. Cell Cardiol.* 18:31–37, 1986.

214. Simon, N., D. Ammann, M. Oehme, and W.E. Morf. Calcium-sensitive electrodes. *Ann. N.Y. Acad. Sci.* 307:52–70, 1978.

215. Smith, S.J., and R.C. Woledge. Thermodynamic analysis of calcium binding to frog parvalbumin. *J. Mus. Res. Cell. Motil.* 6:757–768, 1985.

216. Soldati, L. The Na^2/Ca^{2+} exchanger of the heart sarcolemma: Reconstitution and partial purification Ph.D. thesis, Swiss Federal Institute of Technology, Zurich, 1985.

217. Somlyo, A.P. The message across the gap. *Nature* 316:298–299, 1985.

218. Sreter, F.A., and J. Gergely. Comparative studies of the Mg-activated ATPase activity and the Ca^{2+}-uptake of fractions of white and red muscle homogenates. *Biochem. Biophys. Res. Commun.* 16:438–443, 1964.

219. Sreter, F.A. Temperature, pH, and seasonal dependence of Ca^{2+}-uptake and ATPase activity of white and red muscle macrosomes. *Arch. Biochem. Biophys.* 134:25–33, 1969.

220. Sreter, F.A., L. Lopez, L. Alamo, K. Papp, K. Macbuchi, and J. Gergeley. Changes in the ionized calcium concentration in stimulated muscle. *Biophys. J.* 47:314a, 1985. (Abstract)

221. Stefani, E., and D.J. Chiarandini. Ionic channels in skeletal muscles. *Ann. Rev. Physiol.* 44:357–372, 1982.

222. Stephenson, E. Activation of fast skeletal muscle: Contributions of studies on skinned fibers. *Am. J. Physiol.* 240:C1–C19, 1981.

223. Stepkowski, D., D. Szczesna, M. Wrotek, and I. Kakol. Factors influencing interaction of phosphorylated and dephosphorylated myosin with actin. *Biochim. Biophys. Acta* 831:321–329, 1985.

224. Stuhlfauth I., J. Reininghouse, J. Jockusch, and C.W. Heizmann. Calcium-binding protein, parvalbumin, is reduced in mutant mammalian muscle with abnormal contractile properties. *PNAS (USA)* 81:4814–4818, 1984.

225. Stull, J.T., D.K. Blumenthal, J.R. Miller, and J. DiSalvo. Regulation of myosin phosphorylation. *J. Mol. Cell. Cardiol.* 14 (suppl 3):105–110, 1982.

226. Stull, J.T., M.H. Nunnaly, R.L. Moore, and D.K. Blumenthal. Myosin light chain kinases and phosphorylation in skeletal muscle. In G. Weber (ed.). *Advances in Enzyme Regulation*. New York: Pergamon, 1985, pp. 123–140.

227. Sweeney, H.L., and M.J. Kushmerick. Myosin phosphorylation in permeabilized rabbit psoas fibers. *Am. J. Physiol.* 249:C362–C365, 1985.

228. Sweeney, H.L., and J.T. Stull. Phosphorylation of myosin in permeabilized mammalian and cardiac muscle cells. *Am. J. Physiol.* 250:C657–C660, 1986.

229. Tada, M., M.A. Kirchberger, and A.M. Katz. Phosphorylation of a 22,000 dalton component of cardiac sarcoplasmic reticulum by adenosine 3',5,-monophosphate-dependent protein kinase. *J. Cyclic Nucleotide Res.* 1:329–338, 1975.

230. Tada, M., T. Yamamoto, and Y. Tonomura. Molecular mechanism of active Ca^{2+}-transport. *Physiol. Rev.* 58:1–79, 1978.

231. Takahashi, M., and W.A. Catterall. Identification of an alpha subunit of dihydropyridine-sensitive brain calcium channels. *Science* 236:88–91, 1987.

232. Takisawa, H., and Y. Tonomura. ADP-sensitive and -insensitive phosphorylated

intermediates of solubilized Ca^{2+}, Mg^{2+}-dependent ATPase of the sarcoplasmic reticulum from skeletal muscle. *J. Biochem. (Tokyo)* 86:425–441, 1979.

233. Teo, T.S., and J.H. Wang. Mechanism of activation of a cyclic adenosine 3′,5′-monophosphate phosphodiesterase from bovine heart by calcium ions. *J. Biol. Chem.* 248:5950–5955, 1973.

234. Terjung, R.L. Muscle fiber involvement during training of different training intensities and durations. *Am. J. Physiol.* 230:946–950, 1976.

235. Tibbits, G.F., B.J. Koziol, N.K. Roberts, K.M. Baldwin, and R.J. Barnard. Adaptation of the rat myocardium to endurance training. *J. Appl. Physiol.* 44:85–89, 1978.

236. Tibbits, G.F., R.J. Barnard, K.M. Baldwin, N. Cugalj, and N.K. Roberts. Influence of exercise on excitation-contraction coupling in rat myocardium. *Am. J. Physiol.* 240:H472–H480, 1981.

237. Tibbits, G.F., M. Sasaki, T. Nagatomo, and R.J. Barnard. Cardiac sarcolemma: Compositional adaptation to exercise. *Science* 213:1271–1273, 1981.

238. Tibbits, G.F. Regulation of myocardial contractility in exhaustive exercise. *Med. Sci. Sports. Exerc.* 17:529–537, 1985.

239. Tibbits, G.F., and K.D. Philipson. Na^+-dependent alkaline earth metal uptake in cardiac sarcolemmal vesicles. *Biochim. Biophys. Acta* 817:327–332, 1985.

240. Tibbits, G.F., and H. Kashihara. Adaptation of myocardial Na/Ca exchange. *Med. Sci. Sports. Exerc.* 19:S27, 1987. (Abstract)

241. Trosper, T., and K.D. Philipson. Stimulatory effect of calcium chelators on Na^+-Ca^{2+} exchange in cardiac sarcolemmal vesicles. *Cell Calcium* 5:211–222, 1984.

242. Tsien, R.W. Calcium channels in excitable membranes. *Ann. Rev. Physiol.* 45:341–358, 1983.

243. Van Winkle, W.B., and A. Schwartz. Morphological and biochemical correlates of skeletal muscle contractility in cats. I. Histochemical and electron microscope studies. *J. Cell Physiol.* 97:99–120, 1978.

244. Vegara, J., R.Y. Tsien, and M. Delay. Inositol 1,4,5-triphosphate: A possible chemical link in the excitation-contraction coupling in muscle. *PNAS (USA)* 82:6352–6356, 1985.

245. Volpe, P., G. Salviati, F. Di Virgilio, and T. Pozzan. Inositol 1,4,5-triphosphate induces calcium release from sarcoplasmic reticulum of skeletal muscle. *Nature* 316:347–349, 1985.

246. Wagner, J., I. Reynolds, H. Weisman, P. Dudeck, M. Weisfeldt, and S. Snyder. Calcium antagonist receptors in cardiomyopathic hamster: Selective increases in heart, muscle, and brain. *Science* 232:515–518, 1986.

247. Walker, J.A., A.V. Somlyo, Y.E. Goldman, A.P. Somlyo, and D.R. Trentham. Kinetics of smooth and skeletal muscle by laser photolysis of caged inositol 1,4,5 triphosphate. *Nature* 327:249–252, 1987.

248. Wallace, R.W., E.A. Tallant, and W.Y. Cheung. Assay and preparation of calmodulin. In Cheung, W.Y. (ed.). *Calcium and Cell Function: Calmodulin.* New York: Academic Press, 1980, pp. 13–40.

249. Walsh, M.P., B. Valet, F. Autric, and J.G. de Maille. Purification and characterization of bovine cardiac calmodulin-dependent myosin light chain kinase. *J. Biol. Chem.* 254:12136–12144, 1979.

250. Wang, C.L.A. A note on the Ca^{2+}-binding to calmodulin. *Biochem. Biophys. Res. Commun.* 130:426–430, 1985.

251. Weber, A., and R. Herz. The binding of calcium to actomyosin systems in relation to their biological activity. *J. Biol. Chem.* 238:599–605, 1963.

252. Westwood, S.A., O. Hudlicka, and S.V. Perry. Phosphorylation in vivo of the P-light chain of myosin in rabbit fast and slow muscles. *Biochem. J.* 218:841–847, 1984.

253. Weymann, M., and G.F. Tibbits. Cardiac Ca-antagonist binding alterations with exercise training. *Med. Sci. Sports. Exerc.* 19:S82, 1987. (Abstract)

254. Wiehrer, W., and D. Pette. The ratio of intrinsic 115 kDa and 30 kDa peptides as a

marker of fibre type-specific sarcoplasmic reticulum in mammalian muscles. *FEBS Lett.* 158:317–320, 1983.

255. Wilkie, D. Shortage of chemical fuel as a cause of fatigue: Studies by nuclear magnetic resonance and bicycle ergometry. In Porter, R. and J. Whelan (eds.). *Human Muscle Fatigue: Physiological Mechanisms.* (Ciba Foundation Symposium). London: Pitman Medical, 1981, pp. 102–114.

256. Wnuk, W., J.A. Cox, and E.A. Stein. Parvalbumins and other soluble high affinity calcium-binding proteins from muscle. In Cheung. W.Y. (ed.). *Calcium and Cell Function.* New York: Academic Press, 1982, pp. 243–278.

257. Yamada, S., and Y. Tonomura. Reaction mechanism of the Ca-dependent ATPase of sarcoplasmic reticulum from skeletal muscle. VII. Recognition and release of Ca^{2+}-ions. *J. Biochem. (Tokyo)* 72:417–425, 1972.

258. Yamamoto, S., and K. Greef. Effect of intracellular sodium on calcium uptake in isolated guinea pig diaphragm and atria. *Biochim. Biophys. Acta* 646:348–352, 1981.

2
Disuse Atrophy of Skeletal Muscle: Animal Models

X.J. MUSACCHIA, Ph.D.
JOSEPH M. STEFFEN, Ph.D.
RONALD D. FELL, Ph.D.

INTRODUCTION

A basic description of muscle atrophy is a decrease in cell size. Atrophy has variously been interpreted to include decreased muscle mass; reduced growth rate, protein content, and/or protein DNA ratios; loss of strength; and decreased fiber numbers. In our view, a basic definition of muscle atrophy must include, at least, a decrease in fiber size, whether of longitudinal dimension or cross-sectional area.

This chapter will focus on the type of atrophy produced by muscle disuse—specifically, on animal models designed to produce various conditions of disuse and to simulate specific responses seen in human muscle atrophy. Because disuse is a relative concept, we define it as a reduced level of contractile activity. Reduced contractile activity has two characteristic components: hypokinesia and hypodynamia. Hypokinesia describes the reduced level of contractile activity, i.e., reduction of limb movements, whereas hypodynamia pertains to a reduction in mechanical loading, i.e., weight-bearing function.

The major thrust of this chapter is a consideration of conditions in which disuse is the principal stimulus for muscle atrophy. Among the more commonly encountered clinical forms of disuse are the conditions of bed rest, limb casting, and denervation (e.g., spinal cord injury). Prolonged exposure to a weightless environment has recently been identified as a unique form of muscle disuse. Despite the limited preliminary evidence from both human and animal studies, it is clear that conditions of weightlessness result in significant changes in limb skeletal muscles in response to both hypokinesia and hypodynamia. Occupational settings may also be characterized by hypokinesia and hypodynamia when individuals exist under prolonged sedentary or stationary conditions. Clinical entities such as various neuromuscular diseases (e.g., muscular dystrophy, myasthenia gravis, multiple sclerosis, poliomyolitis) also exhibit varying degrees of disuse associated with skeletal muscle atrophy. However, the extent to which disuse contributes to this atrophy, over and

61

above the primary pathology of these muscular diseases, is not well understood.

In the human subject placed under conditions of hypokinesia and/or hypodynamia, as in bed rest or limb casting, and more recently with exposure to weightlessness, there is indirect evidence of loss of muscle mass through measurements of leg girth and volume [43, 129, 138]. One aspect of measuring leg girth and assessing loss in muscle mass is the potential artifact due to decreases in leg volume from redistribution of interstitial fluid [47]. This anatomical change illustrates some of the limitations of noninvasive experimentation in the human subject.

The atrophic response of skeletal muscle to disuse has been examined in relation to functional, morphological, and metabolic parameters. Altered contractile properties, and decrements in muscle strength and exercise tolerance, clearly indicate the impact of disuse on muscle function [14, 138]. These functional changes can be accounted for at the cellular level. Morphometric observations suggest that both slow- and fast-twitch fibers are affected by disuse atrophy, with significant decreases in fiber cross-sectional area in both types of fibers [71]. Studies of VO_2max have been reported in humans to illustrate the metabolic consequences of muscle disuse [43, 44]. Reduction in VO_2max has been credited to changes in stroke volume and cardiac output [109]. However, such studies do not define specific metabolic responses of muscle to disuse. In addition, relatively few studies have provided data to assess mechanisms relevant to the regulation of disuse atrophy. In recent years, an increased number of animal studies have begun to provide the data necessary to address the mechanisms underlying the atrophic process and associated physiologic and biochemical alterations.

ANIMAL MODELS OF DISUSE ATROPHY

To understand the underlying causes and mechanisms of skeletal muscle disuse atrophy, a variety of animal models have been developed, varying from invasive techniques such as denervation and tenotomy to noninvasive techniques such as limb casting and body suspension. Historically, invasive techniques such as denervation, tenotomy, and joint pinning provided the base of knowledge in the area of disuse atrophy. Subsequently this data base was expanded with the advent of noninvasive procedures. This expansion of animal models has been aided by the interest of the National Aeronautics and Space Administration in determining the mechanisms of and appropriate countermeasures for the disuse atrophy associated with exposure to weightlessness.

Since many readers may not be familiar with the variety of animal models currently being used, a brief description of generalized procedures for the more common techniques is presented. Denervation has been achieved through mechanical (sectioning or crushing) or chemical blocking (curare, tetrodotoxin, etc.) means. In effect, elimination of nerve-muscle communication is the objective of these techniques. However, denervation also interrupts neural input to nonskeletal muscle tissue (i.e., vascular tissue); the results must be interpreted cautiously because of the possible contribution of altered blood flow to the atrophic process. Tenotomy, in contrast, leaves neurons intact but severs the tendinous connection of muscle to bone. As a result, muscle length is reduced below resting length (L_o) and contractile activity becomes fully isotonic. Tenotomy has two principal effects; a direct effect on the tenotomized muscle (i.e., atrophy) and an indirect effect on synergistic muscles that undergo a compensatory hypertrophy.

In contrast to the above procedures, in which muscles are not held at a fixed length, limb casting and joint pinning provide alternative methods for the study of disuse atrophy. Joint pinning is a technique for limb immobilization in which the junction of two long bones is fixed at a set angle by the implantation of metal rods. The angle at which the joint is immobilized determines the degree of passive stretch or shortening in a given muscle and subsequent muscle responses. Limb casting immobilization is achieved by fixing the limb with orthopedic plaster or plastic cast materials. These approaches result in atrophy and hypertrophy of various anterior and posterior compartment hind limb muscles, depending upon the angle of the immobilized joint. In many respects, this is comparable to joint pinning in that muscles are fixed in lengthened or shortened positions. These models have been highly productive in studies of disuse. However, in both procedures, one must take into account the possibility of isometric contractions inside the cast or against the pinning device. This could limit the extent of hypodynamia. Immobilization by cage restraint has also been utilized as a noninvasive technique for induction of muscle disuse. It has been of limited interest, perhaps because it results chiefly in hypokinesia with little or no hypodynamia, and therefore will not be discussed further.

Suspension with hind limb unloading is a more recent technique, and several variations are currently being utilized. The original impetus for the development of this model was an attempt to simulate more realistically the unloading effects associated with the conditions of weightlessness in space flight, including the retention of freedom of voluntary limb movements. Whole body suspension (Figure 1, top) utilizes a cloth suit that attaches the subject to a back brace [86]. The dorsal brace provides whole body support of the suspended animal, thus avoiding potential problems of lordosis. This whole body suspension model affords the flexibility of positioning the animal in a horizontal, head-down, or head-up position. Also, a range of animal sizes from young to adult rats can be accommodated. Recent modifications of the whole body technique

FIGURE 1

Top: *Rat whole body suspension system illustrating capability for head-down tilt and horizontal suspension positions. In each case, hind limbs are unloaded to produce hypokinetic and hypodynamic responses. (From Musacchia, X.J., D.R. Deavers, G.A. Meininger, and T.P. Davis. A model for hypokinesia: Effects on muscle atrophy in the rat.* J. Appl. Physiol. *48:479–486, 1980.)*

Bottom: *Rat tail-cast suspension with head-down tilt. Hind limbs are unloaded to produce hypokinetic and hypodynamic responses. (From Jaspers, S.R., and M.E. Tischler. Atrophy and growth failure of rat hindlimb muscles in tail-cast suspension.* J. Appl. Physiol. *57:1472–1479, 1984.)*

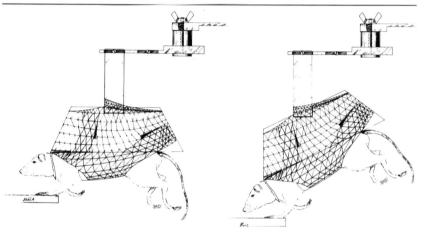

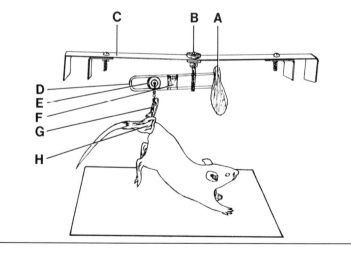

employ either a plexiglass tube [62] or a cloth, sock-like suit for support [31]. In each of these approaches, the hind limbs are unloaded but free to contract voluntarily in a full range of motion. Another variation of the suspension technique involves tail casting to lift the hindquarters to an unloaded position (Figure 1, bottom). This method was initially described by Ilyin and Novikov [56] and later popularized by Morey-Holton and reviewed by Morey-Holton and Wronski [84]. Additional modifications of these suspension procedures have been reported, but they require surgical interventions [69, 127].

ANIMAL STUDIES OF MUSCLE DISUSE

Morphological Aspects
A primary characteristic of muscle disuse atrophy is a reduction in fiber size. In a recent review of atrophic myopathies, Edwards and Jones [21] stated that when atrophy is present, it is observed more often in fast-twitch fibers. In contrast, Edstrom [20] examined the vastus medialis in subjects with knee injuries resulting in long-term disuse, and reported selective type I atrophy but no change in type II fibers. Interpretations of these observations are complicated by findings in humans of reductions in the size of both fiber types [71]. These authors examined biopsy specimens from the medial head (vastus medialis) of the quadriceps femoris in humans who had unilateral knee joint lesions of long duration. They found that there were no differences in the number of type I and type II fibers, but there was a definite reduction (about 20%) in the size of both fiber types. Such discrepancies continue to trouble investigators of disuse muscle atrophy and highlight the variability in different methods of morphometric approaches.

A variety of animal species (e.g., rat, cat, guinea pig, rabbit) have been used under different conditions to elucidate the microscopic alterations resulting from muscle disuse. In response to either invasive or noninvasive procedures, muscle disuse atrophy may result in reduced cross-sectional area of both slow-twitch and fast-twitch fibers. Such changes at the cellular microscopic level correlate with the gross observations of muscle mass and protein decreases.

Tomanek and Cooper [130] reported that following tenotomy in adult guinea pigs, there was more rapid and marked degeneration in slow-twitch fibers in the soleus than in fast-twitch red and white fibers of the vastus lateralis. As early as 5 days after unilateral tenotomy, the mean fiber diameter in slow-twitch soleus decreased by about 8%; at 21 days the decrease was as much as 18%, but the mean fiber diameter had returned to control values. Despite this marked effect, there was no significant conversion of fiber types following tenotomy with extended observation (90 days). Herbison et al. [52] compared muscle atrophy in response to tenotomy, denervation, and cast immobilization. The slow-twitch soleus appeared to be most responsive to all of these atrophic conditions when compared with fast-twitch muscles such as the gastrocnemius and plantaris. A primary effect of cast immobilization and tenotomy was a decrease in type I fiber diameter, whereas with denervation there was a marked effect on the type II fibers. Thus, caution must be exercised in evaluating morphometric results when comparing different types of disuse atrophy.

Booth and Kelso [8] reported that after 4 weeks of cast immobilization, the rat soleus showed an increase in fast-twitch oxidative (FO) fibers and a decrease in the total number of fibers, suggesting the occurrence of a shift in fiber types. Their observations of speed-related contractile properties correlated positively with the histochemical data. They noted that these results differed from previous observations of Nelson [90] using the cat and those of Wells [137] using the rat in which only the ankle joint was immobilized. In such cases, there may not have been a significant reduction in muscular activity.

Cardenas et al. [11] examined rats (10 to 12 weeks of age) in which the entire hind limb was cast immobilized for 4 weeks with full ankle plantar flexion. They counted the soleus muscle fibers and reported no significant differences between control and immobilized subjects. They contrasted their results with those of Booth and Kelso [8], who also cast immobilized hind limbs of (10- to 11-week-old) rats and reported that after 4 weeks there was a 24% loss in soleus muscle fibers. Cardenas et al. attempted to resolve the problem by suggesting the presence of a "deficiency in technique" related to the location of cross sections taken within the muscle for microscopic examination.

Templeton et al. [128] examined responses of the gastrocnemius from rats suspended for 1 and 2 weeks to unload the hind limbs. Although the responses of the different fiber types were not uniform, it is clear that atrophy occurred in both type I and II fibers in rats suspended for 2 weeks. These authors also reported that with suspension hypokinesia after 2 and 4 weeks, there was atrophy of type I fibers in the soleus. In addition, they reported "major shifts" of the type I and type II distributions. Where initially in the soleus there was a 70–90% type I fiber content, following suspension this was reduced to about 50%. This type of fiber shift is in agreement with preferential atrophy of slow-twitch fibers previously reported by Booth and Kelso [8]. However, questions about fiber type conversions should not be based on histochemistry alone. While these data [8, 127, 128] may support the altered contractile properties discussed below (page 70), the question remains of whether this magnitude of shift in fiber types correlates with smaller changes in metabolic capacity.

Recently we compared soleus muscles from 1-week whole-body-suspended adult rats with 1-week microgravity (SL-3 flight) exposed adult rats and reported a significant decrease (-15 to -35%) in type I fiber cross-sectional areas [89]. This correlates with the increase in density (fibers/mm^2) of the same fibers ($+15$ to $+30\%$). Type II fibers in the same muscle also evidenced a significant decrease in cross-sectional area and an increase in density. Rats exposed to weightlessness for a week also showed significantly decreased cross-sectional areas and increased fiber densities. While the magnitude of these morphological responses differed, these findings have been of particular interest since the soleus, a principal gravity-responsive muscle, responded in a comparable manner in both the whole-body-suspended and flight-exposed subjects. We, as well as others [29], have maintained that suspension models more accurately reflect and simulate space flight responses.

In any consideration of skeletal muscle fiber morphometrics, the distribution of capillaries is essential to assessments of functional changes. The techniques used to visualize fiber morphology are readily adapted to the identification of capillaries. Using the same frozen sections and an ATPase stain with carefully regulated preincubation pH, both fibers (slow and fast) and capillaries can be visualized [18, 111].

During normal muscle growth there are characteristic changes in fiber size and capillary distribution. During normal maturation, as fibers grow in length and circumference, capillaries are "pushed apart" [104]. The result of such displacement is that in a microscopic field one sees a decrease in the number of capillaries per cross-sectional area of muscle. In contrast to the changes that occur during normal growth, fiber size was reduced and capillaries became more concentrated with disuse atrophy in the soleus of rats after 7 days of space flight and in ground-based, suspended animals [88]. However, when one calculates a capillary/fiber ratio using capillary and fiber densities in the soleus of adult rats, there was no difference between the disuse of flight or suspension compared to controls. It may be concluded that the relationship of number of fibers to numbers of capillaries does not change.

In the suspended and flight rats, the constancy of the capillary/fiber ratio and the increase in capillary density raise some interesting questions in terms of blood distribution and blood flow. Our studies suggest that there is a potential for change in blood flow per fiber area. However, the presence of an altered capillary bed per se does not provide information about the amount of blood flow within a tissue. In a recent study of hind limb–unloaded rats, Joyner et al. [62] reported a decrease in blood flow to the hind limb. Coupling their findings with our measures of increased capillary density, one is led to a tentative conclusion that there may be an increase in peripheral resistance. Additional evidence for a change in circulatory characteristics may be taken from an earlier report from our laboratory. We showed that with suspension in head-down tilted rats, there was a significant increase in arterial blood pressures [87]. Indirectly, this suggested a cardiovascular effort to improve blood flow. The functional role of altered circulation in animal models of disuse atrophy and recovery requires further investigation. There is no information concerning blood pressure, blood flow, and/or blood distribution in experimental animals under conditions of weightlessness. Such information will be forthcoming only when space flight opportunities are improved.

Physiology

A common observation associated with muscle disuse is differential atrophy, suggesting differences in susceptibility to disuse among fiber types. However, the differential response may be specific to the procedures utilized to induce atrophy. For instance, the degree of atrophy during limb immobilization is highly dependent upon the fixed length of the muscle [7]. Even when soleus (slow-twitch) and extensor digitorum longus (EDL, fast-twitch) muscles are fixed in maximally shortened positions, the soleus atrophies to a greater extent [142]. Witzmann et al. [142] suggested that during maximal plantar flexion the soleus is shortened to a greater extent than when the EDL muscle is maximally shortened by dorsal flexion. Such factors must be considered when attempting to explain the mechanisms for differential responses. As pointed out by Appell [1], the susceptibility of specific fiber types to immobilization atrophy remains in question. Additional evidence for differential responses was reported by Booth and Kelso [8]. However, they showed that when muscles were fixed at neutral lengths in experimental animals, greater atrophy of the slow-twitch soleus fibers remained evident. During suspension disuse, in which the hind limbs are free to contract in a full range of motion, the predominantly slow-twitch soleus muscle is also the most susceptible to atrophy. Finally, it appears logical to suggest that the slow-twitch fibers should be most affected by disuse. It is these fibers that receive continual neural input to maintain their tonic weight-bearing, postural functions, unlike the fast-twitch fibers, which are recruited only during more prolonged contractile activity or a more intense type of activity [108].

Muscle Strength

A common finding in animal models of skeletal muscle disuse has been a loss in muscle strength. This has been shown with denervation [73, 117], limb immobilization [30, 32, 65, 73, 75, 107, 112, 117, 141, 142], hind limb unloading by suspension [13, 28, 29, 127], and during weightlessness [95, 99]. Loss of absolute tension-generating capacity of disused muscle is related to the extent of atrophy. Witzmann et al. [142] found that when both slow-twitch soleus and fast-twitch EDL muscles were immobilized in the shortest possible positions, the soleus but not the EDL became significantly shorter through a reduction in the number of sarcomeres per fiber. When these authors corrected the absolute tension developed for muscle cross-sectional area by dividing muscle mass by L_o [12], a significant reduction in peak twitch tension was demonstrated but not a significant decline in peak tetanic tension.

Using a suspension system, Templeton et al. [127] also reported a significant reduction in peak twitch tension in soleus. In their study, muscle force was not corrected for either muscle mass or muscle cross-sectional area. If such a correction were made, it appears that reduced contractile strength would still exist in the atrophied muscles. Similarly, we have reported a reduced absolute peak isometric strength in the soleus of suspended young rats, as measured by twitch, tetanic, and train contractions [28]. When lower absolute soleus tension was expressed per gram of muscle, there were no differences between the atrophied and control muscles. However, gastrocnemius muscles from suspended rats generated the same amount of absolute tension (twitch, tetanic, and train) as their control counterparts. When gastrocnemius muscle tension was expressed per gram of muscle, there was a greater twitch strength compared to controls.

Muscle strength has been associated with cross-sectional area [66]. In the case of disuse atrophy, where fiber cross-sectional areas are reduced (see section on Morphological Aspects above), there are no apparent differences between making tension corrections on a mass or cross-sectional-area basis. In both cases, the smaller muscles generate lower tensions but an equal amount of tension per unit muscle. From a functional standpoint, the disused muscle tissue is still capable of generating tension at a control level on a relative basis (i.e., per gram or per square centimeter). On the other hand, extrapolation of these results to a work environment suggests that with smaller atrophied muscles, absolute muscle strength and potential endurance work capacity may be reduced. The mechanism for such a loss of strength in disuse-atrophied muscles remains unclear; however, it does not appear to be related to a disproportionate loss of contractile protein compared to other cell components. Such considerations may ultimately affect long-duration space flights, but even more immediately the construction of near-earth space stations.

Lastly, the clinical treatment of musculoskeletal injury has primarily involved immobilization. A major concern in clinical conditions is the associated loss of muscle strength and the increased fatigability. Strength loss can result in prolonged recovery time and the need for more extensive rehabilitative procedures. Perhaps the restoration of normal contractile function can be accelerated through less use of immobilization as a treatment.

The speed-related contractile properties of an entire muscle result from a collective integration of all of the characteristics in the individual fibers making up that muscle. Isotonic shortening velocity has been correlated with myosin ATPase activity [4]. The higher the ATPase activity, the greater the velocity of shortening. In contrast, the isometric contraction time, composed of time to peak tension (TPT) and one-half relaxation time (1/2 RT), has been related to calcium cycling by the sarcotubular network (see [3]).

Witzmann et al. [142] cast immobilized the hind limbs of 200- to 260-g female rats for 1–42 days. Despite significant atrophy in the soleus and EDL muscles, they reported that isometric twitch duration (TPT + 1/2 RT) decreased only in the soleus, while both TPT and 1/2 RT were prolonged in the EDL. The effect occurred early in the disuse period and was suggested to be related to alterations in sarcoplasmic reticulum function. However, other work from their laboratory indicates that changes in calcium uptake by sarcoplasmic reticulum were not responsible [65]. Witzmann et al. [142] also reported an increase in the maximal isotonic shortening velocity in both slow-twitch soleus and fast-twitch EDL muscles. The time course of this change was slower than those of the altered isometric properties and was suggested to be due to a delayed rise in myosin ATPase activity.

Using a modified hind limb suspension system, Templeton et al. [127] reported that in 160-g male rats exposed to suspension for 2 weeks, 1/2 RT and TPT of the soleus muscle decreased by an average of 25%. These authors used polyacrylamide gel electrophoresis to examine total myosin as well as myosin from type I (low-ATPase) and type II (high-ATPase) fibers. Total myosin, as well as type I fiber myosin, was found to be reduced in soleus muscles after 2 weeks of disuse, while no change was observed in the content of type II fiber myosin. The authors reported that the myosin type changes supported the preferential loss of type I fibers and was responsible for the speeding of the soleus.

In our studies [28], using 7 days of suspension in young (180-g) rats, we were unable to document changes in soleus or gastrocnemius isometric twitch contraction times (TPT and 1/2 RT). However, 1 week may not be sufficient for such contractile property changes to occur when using younger animals in this disuse model. In a study comparing 1 and 2 weeks of suspension and limb immobilization in older rats, Fitts et al. [29] reported a decreased soleus isometric twitch duration in both disuse procedures. The decrease in twitch duration was greater with suspension disuse than with immobilization because of an additional shortening of the TPT during the second week. The decrease in twitch duration that occurred with limb immobilization was due to reductions in both TPT and 1/2 RT. The mechanisms for such a change in twitch duration are unknown. The maximal isotonic speed of shortening was also compared in the two disuse models in this study [29]. The speed of isotonic shortening was increased after 1 and 2 weeks of suspension, whereas it increased only after 28 days of immobilization. The authors suggested that a rapid increase in shortening velocity following suspension was due to the expression of a new myosin isozyme, with an electrophoretic mobility similar to that of fast myosin.

Pette [96] suggested that fiber type conversions may be related to the amount of contractile activity rather than to the frequency at which the activity is elicited. This suggestion was supported by the finding that both increased contractile activity (endurance exercise) and chronic nerve stimulation induced qualitatively similar fast to slow transitions in the calcium cycling system (release and uptake) and the myofibrillar apparatus [42]. Therefore, with the hypokinesia of disuse, it seems logical to suggest that the lack of contractile activity imposed on muscle may induce the opposite fiber transformations (i.e., slow to fast).

Relatively few investigations have examined the effects of muscle disuse atrophy on the endurance work capacity or fatigability of skeletal muscle. In a study by Witzmann et al. [141], soleus and EDL muscles were stimulated to contract *in situ* following 6 weeks of limb immobilization. These investigators observed significant fatigue, as measured by a loss of muscle tetanic contractile tension, over a 30-minute stimulation period. However, there were no differences in fatigability between muscles from control and limb-casted animals. Atrophied muscles exhibited a greater reduction in ATP concentrations compared to control muscles during the stimulation period. In addition, these atrophied muscles exhibited a greater dependence on anaerobic energy production, as suggested by a greater rate of glycogen disappearance and increased lactate production. The work load placed on these muscles was an intense tetanic stimulation protocol (110 trains/minute at 100 Hz for soleus; 30 trains/minute at 200 Hz for EDL) and may have masked any subtle fatigability differences.

Similarly, Maier et al. [75] reported no fatigue differences between atrophied and contralateral control soleus muscles from 16-week limb-immobilized guinea pigs when stimulated *in situ* for 10 minutes at 2 Hz. This observation may be explained by the lack of sufficient stimulus intensity, since fatigue of the control muscles did not occur. In this study the gastrocnemius was stimulated at 5 Hz, and after 10 minutes the atrophied muscle had fatigued to 22% of the initial value. Again, there were no differences between the fatigue of atrophied and contralateral control gastrocnemius muscles.

Using a moderate electrically stimulated work intensity (100-ms trains, 45/minute, 50 Hz), Fell et al. [28] reported a greater rate of fatigue in gastrocnemius muscles (*in situ*) from 7-day whole-body-suspended rats. In contrast, soleus muscles from experimental and control subjects were not fatigued by this protocol, as evidenced by only a 6% reduction from initial tension after the 16-minute stimulation period. The reasons for differences in gastrocnemius fatigability between the work of Fell et al. [28], Maier et al. [75], and Witzmann et al. [142] are unknown. *In situ* technique differences, methods of inducing disuse atrophy, and electrical stimulation parameters used to induce fatigue could explain such differences.

The mechanisms regulating the rate of fatigue in disused muscles remain unclear. However, it seems reasonable to suggest that the combination of decreased muscle strength, shifts in contractile protein content, and altered metabolic capacities (discussed below) may all play a role. These altered parameters may act in combination to explain the common complaint from astronauts about fatigue during and after space flight.

Biochemistry
Regardless of the techniques utilized to induce muscle disuse in animals, the consequent atrophy is routinely associated with reductions in total protein content (in milligrams) without decrements in protein concentration, i.e., milligrams of protein per gram of muscle weight [38, 39, 59, 119]. Whereas protein concentrations are, in general, unaltered by muscle disuse, individual proteins such as cytochrome c [27] can exhibit significant reductions in concentration. Herbison et al. [52] and Jaspers et al. [57] have noted that myofibrillar (contractile) proteins appear to be more susceptible to disuse effects following tenotomy, denervation, cast immobilization, and suspension. These observations are consistent with recent determinations made on muscles from rats exposed to weightlessness [120] aboard the space shuttle for 7 days. They are in contrast to observations of equal reductions in myofibrillar and sarcoplasmic protein fractions following hypogravity exposure for 21 days during COSMOS biosatellite experiments [33]. These differences may be accounted for by the longer duration of the COSMOS 690 flight.

Numbers of muscle fibers have been reported to increase following denervation [63] and to decrease during immobilization by restraint [24] or casting [8]. However, the variability associated with the indirect method of cell number estimation used in several of these investigations (i.e., counting fibers in small areas and multiplying by the total cross-sectional area) and the use of single-muscle cross sections have been questioned by Cardenas et al. [11]. These authors, counting total numbers of cells in complete muscle cross sections of the cast-immobilized soleus, could detect no alteration in fiber numbers. Steffen and Musacchia [119] reported that absolute levels of muscle DNA are unaffected by suspension of rats for up to 14 days. DNA content relative to muscle mass, however, was observed to increase markedly in atrophic muscles, with a subsequent reversal toward presuspension levels during a period of recovery. These findings are consistent with the observations of Cardenas et al. [11], with morphological parameters indicating decrements in cross-sectional areas of fibers from disused muscles (see section on Morphological Aspects above), and are in substantial agreement with results of space flight experiments [120]. Goldspink et al. [40], in a more recent study of suspended rats, reported significant decreases in absolute muscle DNA content following as little as 5 days of suspension.

Disuse effects on muscle protein synthesis and degradation have been assessed in several animal models. Muscle atrophy resulting from denervation or tenotomy has generally been found to be associated with marked enhancement of protein breakdown and with lesser effects on protein synthesis [35, 39]. Alterations in protein turnover following limb casting are effected primarily by a marked and rapid (e.g., within 6 hours) inhibition of protein synthesis, with a smaller, more latent effect on protein breakdown [6, 38, 132]. These alterations can not only be demonstrated for rates of total protein synthesis, but can be extended to synthesis rates of specific proteins such as actin [136] and cytochrome c [85]. Muscle atrophy induced by suspension has been ascribed to an inhibition of muscle protein synthesis in concert with an enhanced rate of protein degradation [40, 57, 74]. In contrast to limb casting, however, suspension induces more prominent effects on protein degradation than on muscle protein synthesis.

Aside from potential limitations imposed by inadequate levels of precursors or a reduced capacity for energy production, depressed rates of protein synthesis in disused muscles can ultimately be traced to the translational or transcriptional levels. Because 80% or more of muscle RNA is ribosomal, assessment of total muscle RNA content provides a reliable estimate of maximal protein synthetic capacity. Reduced absolute levels of RNA have been documented following tenotomy [39], denervation [37], limb casting [38, 85, 136], and suspension [37, 38, 74]. Among these authors, however, there is no consensus as to whether RNA concentrations (i.e., RNA per gram of tissue) are decreased during muscle disuse. The decline in absolute muscle RNA content can be accounted for, at least in part, by a sharp depression of RNA synthesis [25]. In addition to this fall in maximal protein synthetic capacity during disuse, the efficiency of the remaining ribosomes may also be altered, as suggested by reductions in synthesis expressed relative to muscle RNA content [37, 38, 74]. Metafora et al. [82] have reported a marked decline of the polysome/monosome ratio in the gastrocnemius following denervation. In this context, Booth and Seider [6] and Watson et al. [136] have suggested that the levels or phosphorylation status of protein synthesis initiation factors (especially initiation factor 2) may play a critical regulatory role in transducing the effects of reduced contractile activity at the cellular level. Despite the clear relevance of this suggestion, there is a notable absence of information in the literature on this question.

The role of transcriptional control in the regulation of protein synthesis during muscle disuse has recently received attention. Denervation clearly alters the composition of the mRNA pool in skeletal muscle [83] and produces a discoordinate regulation of myofibrillar protein synthesis [78]. Watson et al. [136] determined the rate of α-actin synthesis concurrently with levels of α-actin mRNA at time points ranging from 6 hours to 7 days following cast immobilization (with shortening) of the gastrocnemius muscle. Whereas α-actin synthesis was reduced by 66% within the first 6 hours of immobilization, α-actin mRNA levels were reduced significantly only after 7 days of disuse. This would suggest that transcriptional control is exercised following more chronic periods of muscle disuse. This same conclusion was reached by Morrison et al. [85] in a comparable study of cytochrome c synthesis rates and mRNA levels. In that study, a nearly 30% decrease in cytochrome c synthesis within 6 hours of cast immobilization was not accompanied by significant decrements in cytochrome c mRNA levels. In contrast, using a suspension model, Howard et al. [54] have documented significant reductions in soleus α-actin mRNA and messages for several other unidentified soleus-specific proteins within 24 hours and following 7 days of unloading. Babij and Booth [2] have also observed reduced actin mRNA levels with 7 days of suspension.

Both lysosomal and nonlysosomal systems could be implicated in the mechanism of intracellular degradative processes in muscle and have been reviewed in depth [64, 139]. Increased levels of lysosomal proteases have been observed following denervation and tenotomy [34], joint pinning [80], and limb casting [140]. The time course of the increased activities of several hydrolytic enzymes appears to correlate well with rates of muscle mass loss. In addition, the effects of denervation on protein breakdown can be partially ameliorated by inhibitors (e.g., leupeptin, chymostatin) of lysosomal enzymes [70]. It has been reported [94] that the activity of lysosomal endopeptidases (specifically, cathepsins B and D) was markedly increased in skeletal muscles of rats following a 22-day exposure to weightlessness (COSMOS 605). Similarly, lysosomal tripeptidylaminopeptidase activity was found to be elevated by 60% following the 7-day SL-3 space shuttle flight [103]. However, in tissues such as muscle with a relatively low content of lysosomes, the nonlysosomal system of protein degradation may play a particularly important role. The principal nonlysosomal enzymes involved in catabolic processes are the alkaline serine protease, which is probably of mast cell origin [143], and the neutral Ca^{2+}-activated protease. There appears to have been little attention directed to the activities of these enzymes in animal models of disuse, although Riley et al. [103] have reported a 26% increase in Ca^{2+}-activated protease activity following 7 days of space flight.

Eichelberger et al. [22] and Booth and Gianetta [9], using limb casting, and Joffe et al. [60], using denervation, have reported that total muscle calcium levels are elevated during disuse. A number of investigators have reported decreased sarcoplasmic reticulum calcium uptake and/or Ca^{2+}-ATPase activity following denervation [118, 125] and limb casting [65]. This could result in an increased cytosolic calcium concentration and the potential activation of proteolytic activity. Cytosolic calcium concentration is buffered by a variety of binding proteins such as parvalbumin and calsequestrin. Levels of parvalbumin are clearly under neural regulation and decrease markedly in fast-twitch muscle following denervation [68], but the levels of these proteins have not been determined in other models of disuse. The ability of calcium to regulate muscle proteolysis does not require activation of neutral proteases but may be mediated by prostaglandin levels, especially PGE_2 [105]. Phospholipase A, the rate-limiting enzyme in the synthesis of this class of prostaglandins, is calcium dependent, and the increased levels of PGE_2 could activate lysosomal proteolytic activity. Templeton et al. [126] have provided some indirect evidence for the potential involvement of prostaglandins in the atrophic response to suspension. Turinsky [133] has observed a marked (300%) increase in PGE_2 release following *in vitro* incubation of the denervated soleus, but inhibition of PGE_2 synthesis did not eliminate the increased proteolysis. Therefore, it appears that both the lysosomal and nonlysosomal systems may play significant roles in proteolysis during muscle disuse.

Several aspects of endocrine involvement in disuse atrophy of skeletal muscle have been documented in a variety of animal models. The areas that have received the most extensive inquiry include the potential role of glucocorticoids in the mechanism(s) underlying disuse atrophy and the altered insulin responsiveness of disused skeletal muscle. Recent developments in these areas will be highlighted, in addition to several topics that have received less attention.

The specific signals at the cellular level that initiate the loss of muscle mass and protein in response to disuse have not been thoroughly elucidated. The potential involvement of prostaglandins has been mentioned previously. Results of recent studies suggest that steroids (glucocorticoids and androgens) may play a role in disuse effects on muscle protein turnover. Glucocorticoids have a pronounced catabolic effect on skeletal muscle [98]. Elevated levels of circulating glucocorticoids have been documented in response to limb casting [110] and suspension [97, 121], although the effect appears to be acute rather than chronic. Based upon the lack of significant effects of immobilization on contralateral control limbs, Nicholson et al. [92] have discounted the importance of systemic circulating factors in the initiation of disuse muscle atrophy. Similarly, Jaspers and Tischler [58] have reported that adrenalectomy did not prevent muscle atrophy in the suspended rat.

Glucocorticoid responses at the cellular level are mediated by specific receptor proteins [115]. Skeletal muscle could potentially demonstrate catabolic responses to normal levels of glucocorticoids should the concentration of receptor sites be increased. Markedly elevated skeletal muscle glucocorticoid receptor concentrations have been observed in several animal models of disuse, including joint immobilization [16], denervation [17, 131], limb casting [92], and suspension [121]. In support of the hypothesis that such receptor alterations produce hypersensitivity of disused muscles to the catabolic effects of glucocorticoids, denervated [35] and cast-immobilized [81] muscles are more responsive to administration of exogenous hormone. Nicholson et al. [92], however, have argued that changes in receptor concentration do not initiate muscle responses to disuse, since they do not precede effects of disuse on protein synthesis.

It has been postulated that decreased responsiveness to the anabolic effects of androgens could also be involved in the etiology of skeletal muscle disuse atrophy [5]. However, those authors and others [46] have reported increased androgen receptor levels in disused muscles. In contrast, Hughes and Krieg [55] have more recently reported significant decreases in androgen receptor concentrations following denervation. They postulated that a better correlation between steroid binding and muscle atrophy could be established by the use of glucocorticoid/androgen receptor ratios, which would better signal the overall catabolic or anabolic state of the tissue. Testosterone propionate administration to hind limb-immobilized rats had a statistically significant but relatively minor overall effect on muscle mass retention and metabolic properties [23].

The role of other growth-promoting factors, either as causative agents in disuse atrophy through reductions in normal circulating or cellular levels, or as potential agents for ameliorating atrophic responses, seems a significant area of further research. Growth hormone attenuates the atrophic effects of denervation, tenotomy, and joint pinning [15, 36]. Grindeland et al. [45] have reported that space flight is associated with significant reductions in the *in vitro* release of growth hormone from rat pituitary somatotrophs. The relationship between decreased growth hormone secretion and muscle atrophy in response to weightlessness has not been elucidated. It is known that passive muscle stretch induces the generation of soluble growth-promoting factors [123]. Immobilization or other forms of muscle disuse could result in deficits of such factors, with subsequent catabolic effects, but there appears to have been a lack of research effort in this direction. Recently, attention has turned to the effects of clenbuterol on retardation and reversal of denervation-induced atrophy [76, 144]. This β_2-adrenergic agonist appears to exert its growth-promoting effects by inhibiting muscle protein degradation [100], with the most prominent effect noted in type I fibers. Further research on the ability of this and similar compounds to attenuate and/or reverse the effects of other forms of muscle disuse are necessary.

The effects of decreased physical activity on the reduced responsiveness of skeletal muscle to insulin have been clearly documented in the human [72]. Denervation [114], casting [93], and suspension [50] reduce the activation of glycogen synthase by insulin. Despite this reduced enzymatic activity, most reports document elevated concentrations of muscle glycogen following disuse, possibly due to a concentration effect resulting from reduced muscle size [27, 50, 110]. Denervation [114] reduced insulin stimulation of glucose incorporation into glycogen, and both denervation [134] and cast immobilization [110] significantly decreased insulin stimulation of glucose uptake. Neither effect could be accounted for by decreased numbers of insulin receptors [93, 114], suggesting a postreceptor defect in insulin action [10]. The insulin insensitivity in cast-immobilized muscle is particularly rapid, with significant depression in insulin responses noted within 3 hours. Fell et al. [27] have reported that suspension produces a marked insulin insensitivity across the entire hind limb, using a perfusion technique. In contrast, Henriksen et al. [50], using an *in vitro* incubation system, reported that suspension produced insulin hypersensitivity in the atrophic soleus concomitant with a greater density of insulin receptors. It is apparent that there is general agreement about the occurrence of insulin insensitivity following muscle disuse.

The majority of studies that have examined metabolic capacity in disused muscles have utilized indirect measures of metabolic capacity (i.e., oxidative or glycolytic enzyme markers). These measures have been accepted by a majority of investigators as useful for qualitative analysis of the maximum capacity to use carbohydrate or fat to produce energy. Skeletal muscle is highly adaptable to its metabolic needs. For example, if muscle tissue is very active for prolonged periods of time, the oxidative enzyme content increases. On the other hand, when the level of muscle activity decreases, the oxidative capacity has been shown to be reduced. Commonly associated with a reduced oxidative or glycolytic enzyme level is a reduced capability for energy production. This appears to be the general case in disused skeletal muscle regardless of the method by which disuse of the muscle has been brought about.

Reductions in muscle oxidative capacity have been observed in denervated muscles [49, 51, 53, 91, 124], in muscles from immobilized hind limbs [7, 19, 77, 79, 102], and in those muscles exposed to suspension disuse [26, 27, 31, 113]. Decreased oxidative capacity has also been reported in rats exposed to conditions of weightlessness during the Spacelab 3 flight [103]. In addition, decreases in glycolytic capacity have been reported in muscle disuse resulting from denervation [49, 51, 53] and limb immobilization [19, 116, 135]. In contrast, more recent studies of denervation and suspension indicated that there was no decrease in oxidative capacity, as measured by citrate synthase [106] or succinate dehydrogenase activities [41, 48]. In these studies, glycolytic capacity was determined by measuring α-glycerophosphate and lactate dehydrogenase activities, and was found to increase in both conditions. An explanation for the discrepancies between these and previous studies may be the use of histochemical staining properties, which must be uniform within the individual fibers, as opposed to direct measurements of enzyme activities in whole muscle homogenates. The latter technique would take into account necrotic fibers. Decreased oxidative capacity of disused muscles has also been shown to reduce the ability of the muscle to oxidize energy-providing substrates [101, 102]. Similarly, reductions in oxidative capacity are reflected in observations of decreased state 3 respiration of mitochondrial preparations from both immobilized and denervated hind limb muscles [61, 67].

In our opinion, neither enzyme capacities nor histochemistry can provide information about the more subtle interactions of lipid and carbohydrate metabolism. It is these interactions that regulate substrate utilization at rest and during contractile activity. Through the examination of these metabolic relationships, a greater understanding of energy provision to both normal and disused muscles may be obtained.

Muscles in experimental animals respond differentially to various disuse procedures relative to their fiber composition and metabolic characteristics. It has been reported that denervation decreased succinate dehydrogenase activity significantly in the soleus but not in the gastrocnemius [51]. Sohár et al. [116] concluded from their results that the primary metabolic system (either oxidative or glycolytic) of the muscle fiber will evidence the greatest effect from disuse. These authors suggested that during disuse atrophy, a dedifferentiation of the muscle cell occurs due to increased protein catabolism. This hypothesis is supported by the finding that lysosomal enzyme activities have been shown to be elevated during periods of muscle disuse (see above). More recent information suggests that both elevations in proteolysis and (genetically controlled) reductions in synthesis rates at the level of gene expression [85] may be involved in the decreased metabolic capacity seen with muscle disuse.

There is limited information concerning many other aspects of metabolism that could be influenced by disuse and that could exert potential effects on muscle function. For instance, as reviewed above, there is disuse, namely, altered insulin sensitivity. Despite a loss in the ability of disused muscles to take up glucose and synthesize glycogen, there are elevated glycogen concentrations in disused muscles following suspension [27, 50]. Whether or not the increase in muscle glycogen is a beneficial adaptation to compensate for decreased oxidative capacity remains to be determined. The possibility exists that the elevated glycogen concentrations are a secondary response associated with multiple aspects of substrate supply and enzymatic activity (e.g., insulin sensitivity and/or phosphorylase and synthase activities, respectively). Changes in substrate availability could play a major role in regulating energy production in disused muscles and may be a contributing factor to the increased fatigability in gastrocnemius muscles from suspended rats [28].

FUTURE DIRECTIONS

It is clear that in all of the models reviewed, muscle disuse is characterized by reduced muscle mass and contractile activity. What are the cellular mechanisms that initiate these biologically appropriate but fundamentally detrimental adaptations? This primary question requires input from a variety of scientific disciplines. Although such a complex question may be approached directly by utilization of animal models of muscle disuse, parallel investigations aimed at identifying regulatory factors during normal growth and aging would be highly beneficial. Limited experimental attention has been directed toward the comparative aspects of disuse effects on growing and adult animals. Furthermore, potential age effects should be considered when results are extrapolated from appropriate animal models to the human subject.

A review of the subject of animal models of muscle disuse and their varying responses suggests caution in the selection of the appropriate model to answer specific questions. While disuse through suspension and casting may be appropriate for situations where neural input is maintained, denervation produces a model for clinical conditions in which muscle atrophy is accompanied by the absence of neural input. On the other hand, cast immobilization may be more appropriate to simulate clinical conditions in which muscle length is fixed, but that permit isometric contractile activity. Since exposure to weightlessness is associated with both hypokinesia and hypodynamia, the suspension model realistically simulates the conditions encountered in a microgravity environment. Disuse atrophy is a complex process, and significant differences are associated with the results of the techniques utilized to bring about the disuse.

In the area of endocrine regulation, there are major questions concerning the mechanisms underlying defects of insulin responsiveness, as well as muscle sensitivity to both catabolic and anabolic steroids. Regulation of genetic expression and the subsequent translational activities by the endocrine system during disuse may be major points of control for muscle adaptations at the cellular and molecular levels. In addition, there is need for further study of the interactive role of the endocrine system in both producing and maintaining metabolic alterations. The impact of these metabolic adaptations on energy production is not well understood and may underlie the altered functional responses of disused muscles. There are numerous other cellular adaptations to muscle disuse that have not been fully explored. Questions involving fiber type conversions, modifications of membrane and organelle function, and differentiation of morphological and functional properties are merely a few examples. To better understand metabolic and functional adaptations to disuse, cellular alterations must be investigated.

Conditions of muscle disuse such as bed rest and weightlessness may be influenced by accompanying cephalad fluid shifts and introduce changes in circulation dynamics. Cardiovascular parameters such as blood pressure, peripheral resistance, and microcirculatory functions may be altered. The fluid volume shift during head-down suspension, and its potential effect on blood flow during muscle disuse, may be pertinent to understanding the conditions imposed during bed rest and weightlessness. Associated with these potential circulatory modifications would be the related delivery and removal of substrate and metabolic by-products that may influence the processes involved in muscle atrophy.

An important area for future research is the role of exercise in preservation and rehabilitation, as well as its use as a countermeasure during disuse muscle atrophy. The use of animal models to examine the relationship between exercise and disuse adaptation has only recently been explored [26, 48, 106, 122]. The use of electrical stimulation has received clinical application as both a countermeasure and a rehabilitative procedure. As clinically applied, electrical stimulation has been used primarily for reeducating nerve–muscle connection, but very little attention has been given to its potential involvement in preventing specific functional and metabolic effects of disuse.

REFERENCES

1. Appell, H.J. Skeletal muscle atrophy during immobilization. *Int. J. Sports Med.* 7:1–5, 1986.
2. Babij, P., and F.W. Booth, Cytochrome c mRNA in suspended adult rat soleus muscle. *Med. Sci. Sports Exer.* 19:42, 1987. (Abstract)
3. Baldwin, K.M. Muscle development: Neonatal to adult. In Terjung, R.L. (ed.). *Exercise and Sport Sciences Reviews.* Lexington, Mass.: Collamore Press, 1984, pp. 1–19.
4. Barany, M. ATPase activity of myosin correlated with speed of muscle shortening. *J. Gen. Physiol.* 50:197–218, 1967.

5. Bernard, P.A., N.E. Rance, P.S. Fishman, and S.R. Max. Increased cytosolic androgen receptor binding in rat striated muscle following denervation and disuse. *J. Neurochem.* 43:1479–1483, 1984.

6. Booth, F.W., and M.J. Seider. Early change in skeletal muscle protein synthesis after limb immobilization of rats. *J. Appl. Physiol.* 47:974–977, 1979.

7. Booth, F.W. Time course of muscular atrophy during immobilization of hindlimb in rats. *J. Appl. Physiol.* 43:656–661, 1977.

8. Booth, F.W., and J.R. Kelso. Effect of hind-limb immobilization on contractile and histochemical properties of skeletal muscle. *Pflugers Arch.* 342:231–238, 1973.

9. Booth, F.W., and C.L. Gianneta. Effect of hindlimb immobilization upon skeletal muscle calcium in rat. *Calc. Tiss. Res.* 13:327–330, 1973.

10. Burant, C.F., S.K. Lemmon, M.K. Treutelaar, and M.G. Buse. Insulin resistance of denervated rat muscle: A model for impaired receptor-function coupling. *Am. J. Physiol.* 247:E657–E666, 1984.

11. Cardenas, D.D., W.C. Stolov, and R. Hardy. Muscle fiber number in immobilization atrophy. *Arch. Phys. Med. Rehabil.* 58:423–426, 1977.

12. Close, R.I. Dynamic properties of mammalian skeletal muscles. *Physiol. Rev.* 52:129–197, 1972.

13. Corley, K., N. Kowalchuk, and A.J. McComas. Contrasting effects of suspension on hind limb muscles in the hamster. *Exp. Neurol.* 85:30–40, 1984.

14. Deitrick, J.E., G.D. Whedon, E. Shorr, V. Toscani, and V.B. Davis. Effects of immobilization upon various metabolic and physiologic functions of normal men. *Am. J. Med.* 4:3–35, 1948.

15. Deligiannis, A., M. Apostolakis, and M. Madena-Pyrgaki. The functional effects of growth hormone on experimentally induced muscle atrophy. *Acta Endocrinol.* 244:45–47, 1981.

16. DuBois, D.C., and R.R. Almon. Disuse atrophy of skeletal muscle is associated with an increase in number of glucocorticoid receptors. *Endocrinology* 107:1649–1651, 1980.

17. DuBois, D.C., and R.R. Almon. A possible role for glucocorticoids in denervation atrophy. *Muscle Nerve* 4:370–373, 1981.

18. Dubowitz, V., and M.H. Brooke. *Muscle Biopsy: A Modern Approach.* Toronto: W.B. Saunders Co., 1973.

19. Edes, I., I. Sohár, H. Mazarean, O. Takács, and F. Guba. Immobilization effects upon aerobic and anaerobic metabolism of the skeletal muscles. *Physiologist* 23:S103–S104, 1980.

20. Edstrom, L. Selective atrophy of red muscle fibers in the quadriceps in long-standing knee-joint dysfunction. Injuries to the anterior cruciate ligament. *J. Neurol. Sci.* 11:551–558, 1970.

21. Edwards, R.H.T., and D.A. Jones. Diseases of skeletal muscle. In Peachey, L.D. (ed.). *Handbook of Physiology*, Section 10: *Skeletal Muscle*. Bethesda, Md.: American Physiological Society, 1983, pp. 633–672.

22. Eichelberger, L., M. Roma, and P.V. Moulder. Effects of immobilization atrophy on the histochemical characterization of skeletal muscle. *J. Appl. Physiol.* 12:42–50, 1958.

23. Evans, W.J., and J.L. Ivy. Effects of testosterone propionate on hindlimb immobilized rats. *J. Appl. Physiol.* 52:1643–1647, 1982.

24. Faulkner, J.A., L.C. Maxwell, D.A. Brook, and D.A. Lieberman. Adaptation of guinea pig plantaris muscle fiber to endurance training. *Am. J. Physiol.* 221:291–297, 1971.

25. Fedorov, I.V., G.S. Komolova, and A.V. Chernyy. DNA and RNA synthesis in isolated nuclei of rat skeletal muscles during hypodynamia. *Fiziol. Zhurnal SSSR* 67:1521–1524, 1981.

26. Fell, R.D., J.M. Steffen, K.A. Mook, and X.J. Musacchia. Effect of exercise on rat skeletal muscle exposed to disuse. *Med. Sci. Sports Exerc.* 19:550, 1987. (Abstract)

27. Fell, R.D., J.M. Steffen, and X.J. Musacchia. Effect of hypokinesia-hypodynamia on rat muscle oxidative capacity and glucose uptake. *Am. J. Physiol.* 249:R308–R312, 1985.

28. Fell, R.D., L.B. Gladden, J.M. Steffen, and X.J. Musacchia. Fatigue and contraction of slow and fast muscles in hypokinetic/hypodynamic rats. *J. Appl. Physiol.* 58:65–69, 1985.

29. Fitts, R.H., J.M. Metzger, D.A. Riley, and B.R. Unsworth. Models of disuse: A comparison of hindlimb suspension and immobilization. *J. Appl. Physiol.* 60:1946–1953, 1986.

30. Fitts, R.H., and C.J. Brimmer. Recovery in skeletal muscle contractile function after prolonged hindlimb immobilization. *J. Appl. Physiol.* 59:916–923, 1985.

31. Flynn, D.E., and S.R. Max. Effects of suspension hypokinesia/hypodynamia on rat skeletal muscle. *Aviat. Space Environ. Med.* 56:1065–1069, 1985.

32. Gardiner, P.F., and M.A. LaPointe. Daily in vivo neuromuscular stimulation effects on immobilized rat hindlimb muscles. *J. Appl. Physiol.* 53:960–966, 1982.

33. Gayevskaya, M.S., N.A. Veresotskaya, N.S. Kolganova, Y.V. Kolchina, L.M. Kurkina, and Y.A. Nosova. Changes in metabolism of soleus muscle tissue in rats following flight aboard the COSMOS-690 biosatellite. *Space Biol. Aerosp. Med.* 13:16–19, 1979.

34. Goldberg, A.L., and A.C. St. John. Intracellular protein degradation in mammalian and bacterial cells: Part 2. *Ann. Rev. Biochem.* 45:747–803, 1976.

35. Goldberg, A.L. Protein turnover in skeletal muscle. II. Effects of denervation and cortisone on protein catabolism in skeletal muscle. *J. Biol. Chem.* 244:3223–3229, 1969.

36. Goldberg, A.L., and M.M. Goodman. Relationship between growth hormone and muscular work in determining muscle size. *J. Physiol.* 200:655–666, 1969.

37. Goldspink, D.F. The effects of denervation on protein turnover of rat skeletal muscle. *Biochem. J.* 156:71–80, 1976.

38. Goldspink, D.F. The influence of immobilization and stretch on protein turnover of rat skeletal muscle. *J. Physiol.* 264:267–282, 1977.

39. Goldspink, D.F., P.J. Garlick, and M.A. McNurlan. Protein turnover measured *in vivo* and *in vitro* in muscles undergoing compensatory growth and subsequent denervation atrophy. *Biochem. J.* 210:89–98, 1983.

40. Goldspink, D.F., A.J. Morton, P. Loughna, and G. Goldspink. The effect of hypokinesia and hypodynamia on protein turnover and the growth of four selected muscles of the rat. *Pflugers Arch.* 407:333–340, 1986.

41. Graham, S.C., R.R. Roy, S.P. West, D. Thomason, and K.M. Baldwin. Exercise effects on the size and metabolic properties of fibers in the soleus muscles of hindlimb suspended rats. *Med. Sci. Sports Exerc.* 19:550, 1987. (Abstract)

42. Green, H.J., G.A. Klug, H. Reichmann, U. Seedorf, W. Wiehrer, and D. Pette. Exercise-induced fiber type transitions with regard to myosin, parvalbumin, and sarcoplasmic reticulum in muscles of the rat. *Pflugers Arch.* 400:432–438, 1984.

43. Greenleaf, J.E., C.H. Greenleaf, D. Van Derveer, and K.J. Dorchak. *Adaptation to Prolonged Bedrest In Man: A Compendium of Research.* NASA Technical Memorandum X-3307. Washington, D.C.: NASA, 1976.

44. Greenleaf, J.E., L. Silverstein, J. Bliss, V. Langenheim, H. Rossow, and C. Chao. *Physiological Responses to Prolonged Bedrest and Fluid Immersion in Man: A Compendium of Research (1974–1980).* NASA Technical Memorandum 81324. Washington, D.C.: NASA, 1982.

45. Grindeland, R., W.C. Hymer, M. Farrington, T. Fast, C. Hayes, K. Motter, L. Patil,

and M. Vasques. Changes in pituitary growth hormone cells prepared from rats flown on Spacelab 3. *Am. J. Physiol.* 252:R209–R221, 1987.

46. Gustafsson, J.A., T. Saartok, E. Dahlberg, M. Snochowski, T. Haggmark, and E. Eriksson. Studies on steroid receptors in human and rabbit skeletal muscle—clues to understanding of the mechanism of action of anabolic steroids. *Proc. Clin. Biol. Res.* 142:261–290, 1984.

47. Hargens, A.R., C.M. Tipton, P.D. Gollnick, S.J. Mubarak, B.J. Tucker, and W.H. Akeson. Fluid shifts and muscle function in humans during acute simulated weightlessness. *J. Appl. Physiol.* 54:1003–1009, 1983.

48. Hauschka, E.O., R.R. Roy, and V.R. Edgerton. Size and succinate dehydrogenase activity of rat soleus fiber in hindlimb suspension with periodic weight support. *Med. Sci. Sports Exerc.* 19:550, 1987. (Abstract)

49. Hearn, G.R. Succinate-cytochrome c reductase, cytochrome oxidase, and aldolase activities of denervated rat skeletal muscle. *Am. J. Physiol.* 196:465–466, 1959.

50. Henriksen, E.J., M.E. Tischler, and D.G. Johnson. Increased response to insulin of glucose metabolism in the 6-day unloaded rat soleus muscle. *J. Biol. Chem.* 261:10707–10712, 1986.

51. Henriksson, J., H. Galbo, and E. Blomstrand. Role of the motor nerve in activity-induced enzymatic adaptation in skeletal muscles. *Am. J. Physiol.* 242:C272–C277, 1982.

52. Herbison, G.J., M.M. Jaweed, and J.F. Ditunno. Muscle atrophy in rats following denervation, casting, inflammation and tenotomy. *Arch. Phys. Med. Rehabil.* 60:401–404, 1979.

53. Hogan, E.L., D.M. Dawson, and F.C.A. Romanul. Enzymatic changes in denervated muscle. *Arch. Neurol.* 13:274–282, 1965.

54. Howard, G., J.M. Steffen, and T.E. Geoghegan. Evaluation of protein synthesis regulation in skeletal muscle atrophy. *Fed. Proc.* 45:645, 1986.

55. Hughes, B.J., and M. Krieg. Increased glucocorticoid/androgen receptor ratios in denervated striated muscle. *J. Steroid Biochem.* 25:695–699, 1986.

56. Ilyin, Y.A., and V.Y. Novikov. A stand for simulation of physiological effects of weightlessness in laboratory experiments on rats. *Kosm. Biol. Aviakosmich. Med.* 3:79–80, 1980.

57. Jaspers, S.R., J.M. Fagan, and M.E. Tischler. Biochemical responses to chronic shortening in unloaded soleus muscles. *J. Appl. Physiol.* 59:1159–1163, 1985.

58. Jaspers, S.R., and M.E. Tischler. Role of glucocorticoids in the response of rat leg muscles to reduced activity. *Muscle Nerve* 9:554–561, 1986.

59. Jaspers, S.R., and M.E. Tischler. Atrophy and growth failure of rat hindlimb muscles in tail-cast suspension. *J. Appl. Physiol.* 57:1472–1479, 1984.

60. Joffe, M., N. Savage, and H. Isaacs. Increased muscle calcium. *Biochem. J.* 196:663–667, 1981.

61. Joffe, M., N. Savage, and H. Isaacs. Respiratory activities of subsarcolemmal and intermyofibrillar mitochondrial populations isolated from denervated and control rat soleus muscles. *Comp. Biochem. Physiol.* 76:783–787, 1983.

62. Joyner, M.J., C.M. Tipton, and J.M. Overton. Influence of simulated weightlessness on select cardiovascular parameters: Preliminary results. *Fed. Proc.* 46:1243, 1987. (Abstract)

63. Karpati, G., and W.K. Engel. Histochemical investigation of fiber type ratios with myofibrillar ATPase reaction in normal and denervated skeletal muscles of guinea pig. *Am. J. Anat.* 122:145–155, 1968.

64. Khairdallah, E.A., J.S. Bond, and J.W.C. Bird (eds.). *Intracellular Protein Catabolism.* New York: Alan R. Liss, 1985.

65. Kim, D.H., F.A. Witzmann, and R.H. Fitts. Effect of disuse on sarcoplasmic reticulum in fast and slow skeletal muscle. *Am. J. Physiol.* 243:C156–C160, 1982.

66. Knowlton, G.C., and H.M. Hines. The effects of growth and atrophy upon the strength of skeletal muscle. *Am. J. Physiol.* 128:521–525, 1939–40.

67. Krieger, D.A., C.A. Tate, J. McMillin-Wood, and F.W. Booth. Populations of rat skeletal muscle mitochondria after exercise and immobilization. *J. Appl. Physiol.* 48:23–28, 1980.

68. Leberer, E., and D. Pette. Neural regulation of parvalbumin expression in mammalian skeletal muscle. *Biochem. J.* 235:67–73, 1986.

69. LeBlanc, A., C. Marsh, H. Evans, P. Johnson, V. Schneider, and S. Jhingran. Bone and muscle atrophy with suspension of the rat. *J. Appl. Physiol.* 58:1669–1675, 1985.

70. Libby, P., and A.L. Goldberg. The control and mechanism of protein breakdown in striated muscle: Studies with selective inhibitors. In K. Wildenthal (ed.). *Degradative Processes in Heart and Skeletal Muscle.* Amsterdam: Elsevier North-Holland, 1980, pp. 201–222.

71. Lindboe, C.F., and C.S. Platou. Disuse atrophy of human skeletal muscle. *Acta Neuropathol.* 56:241–244, 1982.

72. Lipman, R.L., P. Raskin, T. Love, J. Triebuvasser, F.R. Lecocq, and L.L. Schnure. Glucose intolerance during decreased physical activity in man. *Diabetes* 21:101–107, 1972.

73. Lomo, T. Neural regulation of membrane and contractile properties of rat skeletal muscle. In B. Saltin (ed.). *Biochemistry of Exercise,* Vol. 6. Champaign, Ill: Human Kinetics, 1986, pp. 27–47.

74. Loughna, P., G. Goldspink, and D.F. Goldspink. Effect of inactivity and passive stretch on protein turnover in phasic and postural rat muscles. *J. Appl. Physiol.* 61:173–179, 1986.

75. Maier, A., J.L. Crockett, D.R. Simpson, C.W. Saubert IV, and V.R. Edgerton. Properties of immobilized guinea pig hindlimb muscles. *Am. J. Physiol.* 231:1520–1526, 1976.

76. Maltin, C.A., P.J. Reeds, M.I. Deldoy, S.M. Hay, F.G. Smith, and G.E. Lobley. Inhibition and reversal of denervation-induced atrophy by the β-agonist growth promoter, *Clenbuterol. Biosci. Rep.* 6:811–818, 1986.

77. Mann, W.S., and B. Salafsky. Enzyme and physiological studies of normal and disused developing fast and slow cat muscles. *J. Physiol.* 208:33–47, 1970.

78. Matsuda, R., D. Spector, and R.C. Strohman. Denervated skeletal muscle displays discoordinate regulation for the synthesis of several myofibrillar proteins. *Proc. Natl. Acad. Sci. U.S.A.* 81:1122–1125, 1984.

79. Max, S.R. Disuse atrophy of skeletal muscle: Loss of functional activity of mitochondria. *Biochem. Biophys. Res. Commun.* 46:1394–1398, 1972.

80. Max, S.R., R.F. Mayer, and L. Vogelsang. Lysosomes and disuse atrophy of skeletal muscle. *Arch. Biochem. Biophys.* 146:227–232, 1971.

81. McGrath, J.A., and D.F. Goldspink. The effects of cortisone treatment on the protein turnover of the soleus muscle after immobilization. *Biochem. Soc. Trans.* 6:1017–1019, 1978.

82. Metafora, S., A. Felsani, R. Cotrufo, G.F. Tajana, G. DiIorio, A. Del Rio, and P.P. De Prisco. Neural control of gene expression in skeletal muscle fibres: The nature of the lesion in the muscular protein-synthesizing machinery following denervation. *Proc. R. Soc. Lond.* 209:239–255, 1980.

83. Metafora, S., A. Felsani, R. Cotrufo, G.F. Tajana, A. Del Rio, P.P. de Prisco, B. Rutigliano, and V. Esposito. Neural control of gene expression in the skeletal muscle fiber: Changes in the muscular mRNA population following denervation. *Proc. R. Soc. Lond.* 209:257–273, 1980.

84. Morey-Holton, E., and T.J. Wronski. Animal models for simulating weightlessness. *Physiologist* 24:S45–S48, 1981.

85. Morrison, P.R., J.A. Montgomery, T.S. Wong, and F.W. Booth. Cytochrome c protein-synthesis rates and mRNA contents during atrophy and recovery in skeletal muscles. *Biochem. J.* 241:257–263, 1987.

86. Musacchia, X.J., D.R. Deavers, G.A. Meininger, and T.P. Davis. A model for hypokinesia: Effects on muscle atrophy in the rat. *J. Appl. Physiol.* 48:479–486, 1980.

87. Musacchia, X.J., and J.M. Steffen. Cardiovascular and hormonal (aldosterone) responses in a rat model which mimics conditions of weightlessness. *Physiologist* 27:S41–S42, 1984.

88. Musacchia, X.J., J.M. Steffen, and R.D. Fell. Response of muscle fibers and capillarity to weightlessness (SL-3 flight) and ground controls. *Fed. Proc.* 45:645, 1986. (Abstract)

89. Musacchia, X.J., J.M. Steffen, R.D. Fell, and J. Dombrowski. Physiological comparison of rat muscle in body suspension and weightlessness. *Physiologist* 30:S102–S105, 1987.

90. Nelson, P.G. Functional consequences of tenotomy in hind limb muscles of cat. *J. Physiol.* 201:321–333, 1969.

91. Nemeth, P.M. Electrical stimulation of denervated muscle prevents decreases in oxidative enzymes. *Muscle Nerve* 5:134–139, 1982.

92. Nicholson, W.F., P.A. Watson, and F.W. Booth. Levels of blood-borne factors and cytosol glucocorticoid receptors during the initiation of muscle atrophy in rodent hindlimbs. *Pflugers Arch.* 401:321–323, 1984.

93. Nicholson, W.F., P.A. Watson, and F.W. Booth. Glucose uptake and glycogen synthesis in muscles from immobilized limbs. *J. Appl. Physiol.* 56:431–435, 1984.

94. Oganesyan, S.S., and M.A. Eloyan. Cathepsin activity of skeletal muscle and myocardial myofibrils after exposure to weightlessness and accelerations. *Kosm. Biol. Aviak. Med.* 15:38–42, 1981.

95. Oganov, V.S., and A.N. Potapov. On the mechanisms of changes in skeletal muscles in the weightless environment. *Life Sci. Space Res.* 14:136–143, 1976.

96. Pette, D. Regulation of phenotype expression in skeletal muscle fibers by increased contractile activity. In B. Saltin (ed.). *Biochemistry of Exercise*, Vol. 6. Champaign, Ill.: Human Kinetics, 1986, pp. 3–26.

97. Popovic, V., P. Popovic, and C. Honeycutt. Hormonal changes in antiorthostatic rats. *Physiologist* 25:S77–S78, 1982.

98. Ramey, E.R. Corticosteroids and skeletal muscle. In H. Blaschko, G. Soyers, and A.D. Smith (eds.). *Handbook of Physiology*, Vol. 6, Section F. Washington, D.C.: American Physiological Society, 1975, pp. 245–261.

99. Rapcsak, M., V.S. Oganov, A. Szoor, S.A. Skuratova, T. Szilagyi, and O. Takacs. Effect of weightlessness on the function of rat skeletal muscles on the biosatellite "COSMOS 1129." *Acta Physiol. Hung.* 62:225–228, 1983.

100. Reeds, P., S. Hay, P. Dorwood, and R. Palmer. Stimulation of muscle growth by clenbuterol: Lack of effect on muscle protein biosynthesis. *Br. J. Nutr.* 56:249–258, 1986.

101. Rifenberick, D.H., J.G. Gamble, and S.R. Max. Response of mitochondrial enzymes to decreased muscular activity. *Am. J. Physiol.* 225:1295–1299, 1973.

102. Rifenberick, D.H., and S.R. Max. Substrate utilization by disused rat skeletal muscle. *Am. J. Physiol.* 226:295–297, 1974.

103. Riley, D.A., S. Ellis, G.R. Slocum, T. Satyanarayana, J.L.W. Bain, and F.R. Sedlak. Morphological and biochemical changes in soleus and extensor digitorum longus muscles of rats orbited in Spacelab 3. *Physiologist* 28:S207–S208, 1985.

104. Ripoll, E., A.H. Sillau, and N. Banchero. Changes in the capillarity of skeletal muscle in the growing rat. *Pflugers Arch.* 380:153–158, 1979.

105. Rodemann, H.P., L. Waxman, and A.L. Goldberg. The stimulation of protein deg-

radation in muscle by Ca^{++} is mediated by prostaglandin E_2 and does not require the calcium-activated protease. *J. Biol. Chem.* 257:8716–8723, 1982.

106. Roy, R.R., K.M. Baldwin, R.D. Sacks, L. Eldridge, and V.R. Edgerton. Mechanical and metabolic properties after prolonged inactivation and/or cross-reinnervation of cat soleus. *Med. Sci. Sports Exerc.* 19:550, 1987. (Abstract)

107. Sale, D.G., A.J. McComas, J.D. MacDougall, and A.R.M. Upton. Neuromuscular adaptation in human thenar muscles following strength training and immobilization. *J. Appl. Physiol.* 53:419–424, 1982.

108. Saltin, B., and P.D. Gollnick. Skeletal muscle adaptability: significance for metabolism and performance. In L.D. Peachey, R.H. Adrian, and S.R. Geiger (eds.). *Handbook of Physiology*, Section 10: *Skeletal Muscle*. Bethesda, Md.: American Physiological Society, 1983, pp. 555–631.

109. Saltin, B., G. Blomqvist, J.H. Mitchell, R.L. Johnson, Jr., K. Wildenthal, and C.B. Chapman. Response to exercise after bedrest and after training. A longitudinal study of adaptive changes in oxygen transport and body composition. *Circulation* (Supplement) 7:38-VII-1 to VII-78, 1968.

110. Seider, M.J., W.F. Nicholson, and F.W. Booth. Insulin resistance to glucose metabolism in disused soleus muscle of mice. *Am. J. Physiol.* 242:E12–E18, 1982.

111. Sillau, A.H., and N. Banchero. Visualization of capillaries in skeletal muscle by the ATPase reaction. *Pflugers Arch.* 369:269–271, 1977.

112. Simard, C.P., S.A. Spector, and V.R. Edgerton. Contractile properties of rat hindlimb muscles immobilized at different lengths. *Exp. Neurol.* 77:467–482, 1982.

113. Simard, C., M. Lacaille, and J. Valliéres. Enzymatic adaptations to suspension hypokinesia in skeletal muscle of young and old rats. *Mech. Aging Dev.* 33:1–9, 1985.

114. Smith, R.L., and J.C. Lawrence, Jr. Insulin action in denervated skeletal muscle. *J. Biol. Chem.* 260:273–278, 1985.

115. Snochowski, M., E. Dahlberg, and J.A. Gustafsson. Characterization and quantification of the androgen and glucocorticoid receptors in cytosol from rat skeletal muscle. *Eur. J. Biochem.* 3:603–606, 1980.

116. Sohár, I., O. Takács, F. Guba, I. Sziklai, and T. Szilágyi. Experimental studies on hypokinesis of skeletal muscle with different functions. VI. Studies on some of the key enzymes of muscle metabolism. *Acta Biol. Acad. Sci. Hung.* 33:385–390, 1982.

117. Spector, S.A. Effects of elimination of activity on contractile and histochemical properties of rat soleus muscle. *J. Neurosci.* 5:2177–2188, 1985.

118. Sreter, F.A. Effect of denervation on fragmented sarcoplasmic reticulum of white and red muscle. *Exp. Neurol.* 29:52–64, 1970.

119. Steffen, J.M., and X.J. Musacchia. Effect of hypokinesia and hypodynamia on protein, RNA and DNA in rat hindlimb muscles. *Am. J. Physiol.* 247:R728–R732, 1984.

120. Steffen, J.M., and X.J. Musacchia. Spaceflight effects on adult rat muscle protein, nucleic acids and amino acids. *Am. J. Physiol.* 251:R1059–R1063, 1986.

121. Steffen, J.M., and X.J. Musacchia. Disuse atrophy, plasma corticosterone and muscle glucocorticoid receptor levels. *Aviat. Space Environ. Med.* 58:996–1000, 1987.

122. Sullenger, S.L., and T.P. White. Chronic hypodynamia interrupted by exercise; attenuation of soleus muscle atrophy. *Med. Sci. Sports Exerc.* 19:550, 1987. (Abstract)

123. Summers, P.J., C.R. Ashmore, Y.B. Lee, and S. Ellis. Stretch-induced growth in chicken wing muscles: Role of soluble growth promoting factors. *J. Cell. Physiol.* 125:288–294, 1985.

124. Takács, O., I. Sahár, T. Pelle, F. Guba, and T. Szilágyi. Experimental investigations on hypokinesis of skeletal muscles with different functions. III. Changes in protein fractions of subcellular components. *Acta Biol. Acad. Sci. Hung.* 28:213–219, 1977.

125. Tate, C.A., R.J. Bick, T.D. Myers, B.J.R. Pitts, W.B. Von Winkle, and M.L. Entman.

Alteration of sarcoplasmic reticulum after denervation of chicken pectoralis muscle. *Biochem. J.* 210:339–344, 1983.

126. Templeton, G.H., M. Padalino, and R. Moss. Influences of inactivity and indomethacin on soleus phosphatidylethanolamine and size. *Prostaglandins* 31:545–559, 1986.

127. Templeton, G.H., M. Padalino, J. Manton, M. Glasberg, C.J. Silver, P. Silver, G. DeMartino, T. Leconey, G. Klug, H. Hagler, and J.L. Sutko. Influence of suspension hypokinesia on rat soleus muscle. *J. Appl. Physiol.* 56:278–286, 1984.

128. Templeton, G.H., M. Padalino, J. Manton, T. Leconey, H. Hagler, and M. Glasberg. The influence of rat suspension-hypokinesia on the gastrocnemius muscle. *Aviat. Space Environ. Med.* 55:381–386, 1984.

129. Thornton, W.E., and J.A. Rummel. Muscular deconditioning and its prevention in space flight. In R.S. Johnston and L.F. Dietlein (eds.). *Biomedical Results from Skylab*. Washington, D.C.: NASA, 1977, pp. 191–197.

130. Tomanek, R.J., and R.R. Cooper. Ultrastructural changes in tenotomized fast- and slow-twitch muscle fibres. *J. Anat.* 113:409–424, 1972.

131. Tremblay, R.R., M.A. Ho-Kim, C. Champagne, J. Gagnon, and J.Y. Dube. Variations of glucocorticoid receptors in intact or denervated muscles: Lack of cause-effect relationship with muscle atrophy in the rat. *J. Recept. Res.* 6:183–193, 1986.

132. Tucker, K.R., M.J. Seider, and F.W. Booth. Protein synthesis rates in atrophied gastrocnemius muscles after limb immobilization. *J. Appl. Physiol.* 51:73–77, 1981.

133. Turinsky, J. Phospholipids, prostaglandin E_2, and proteolysis in denervated muscle. *Am. J. Physiol.* 251:R165–R173, 1986.

134. Turinsky, J. Dynamics of insulin resistance in denervated slow and fast muscles *in vivo*. *Am. J. Physiol.* 252:R531–R537, 1987.

135. Vereb, Gy., Gy. Bot, K. Szücs, E. Kovács, F. Erdödi, I. Kalapos, A. Szöör, M. Rapcsák, and T. Szilágyi. Effect of immobilization on some glycolytic enzymes of skeletal muscle. *Acta Physiol. Hung.* 63:55–61, 1984.

136. Watson, P.A., J.P. Stein, and F.W. Booth. Changes in actin synthesis and α-actin-mRNA content in rat muscle during immobilization. *Am. J. Physiol.* 247:C39–C44, 1984.

137. Wells, J.B. Functional integrity of rat muscle after isometric immobilization. *Exp. Neurol.* 24:514–522, 1969.

138. White, M.J., and C.T.M. Davies. The effects of immobilization, after lower leg fracture, on the contractile properties of human triceps surae. *Clin. Sci.* 66:277–282, 1984.

139. Wildenthal, K. (ed.). *Degradative Processes in Heart and Skeletal Muscle*. Amsterdam: Elsevier North-Holland, 1980.

140. Witzmann, F.A., J.P. Troup, and R.H. Fitts. Acid phosphatase and protease activities in immobilized rat skeletal muscles. *Can. J. Physiol. Pharmacol.* 60:1732–1736, 1982.

141. Witzmann, F.A., D.H. Kim, and R.H. Fitts. Effect of hindlimb immobilization on the fatigability of skeletal muscle. *J. Appl. Physiol.* 54:1242–1248, 1983.

142. Witzmann, F.H., D.H. Kim, and R.H. Fitts. Hindlimb immobilization: Length-tension and contractile properties of skeletal muscle. *J. Appl. Physiol.* 53:335–345, 1982.

143. Woodbury, R.G., M. Everitt, Y. Sanada, N. Katunuma, D. Langunoff, and H. Neurath. A major serine protease in rat skeletal muscle: evidence for mast cell origin. *Proc. Natl. Acad. Sci. U.S.A.* 75:5311–5313, 1978.

144. Zeman, R.J., R. Ludemann, and J.D. Etlinger. Clenbuterol, a β_2-agonist retards atrophy in denervated muscles. *Am. J. Physiol.* 252:E152–E155, 1987.

3
Concepts and Models of Functional Architecture in Skeletal Muscle

E. OTTEN, Ph.D.

INTRODUCTION

Functional models and concepts of skeletal muscle architecture are not abundant, although their history goes back to 1664, when the Danish scientist Stensen published a monograph with "anatomical observations," among which were schematic drawings of pinnate muscles resembling the ones given in the present review [27]. A strikingly high percentage of the subsequent literature is German and Dutch. Probably this is due to the philosophic tradition of these countries, based on idealistic descriptions of nature by Plato and Goethe. The idea that in the functional design of organisms one should look for the *Bauplan* (blueprint or scheme of design) comes from these philosophers and has influenced Dutch and German functional morphology. The advantage of this history is the detail in which authors tended to look at the architecture of muscles. The disadvantage is that authors looked mainly for principles in architecture and changes in geometry during contraction, disregarding their functional effects in terms of force-length diagrams, force-velocity diagrams, and the distribution of internal muscle pressure.

The somewhat neglected subject of this chapter stands between the detailed knowledge of muscle fiber contraction and that of the function of whole bone-muscle-ligament systems (kinesiology). It is perhaps difficult to formulate general concepts on the functional meaning of muscle architecture, given the great variety of such architectural forms. Moreover, muscles do not behave like water-filled balloons or thick rubber bands because of their remarkable contractile properties, and muscle fibers and tendinous tissue are far from isotropic.

This chapter offers an analysis of a dozen publications on functional models of skeletal muscle architecture and proposes revisions of a number of concepts and models. These concern in particular:

a. Principles of the change of shape of muscles during shortening and lengthening.

b. The relation between muscle architecture and force-length diagrams.

c. The relation between muscle architecture and intramuscular pressure.

NOTE

Rather than using the original notation of the reviewed papers, I have chosen symbols representing the various quantities in this chapter to be consistent with each other. All mathematical derivations, proofs, and formulas have been separated from the main text and accumulated in appendices, so that the main arguments are not interrupted by technical details. Nevertheless, a formal approach to this subject is essential, because of its strong geometrical nature and a misleading intuition we may have about that nature.

MUSCLE VOLUME

A number of authors base their functional considerations of muscle architecture on the constraint that muscles retain their volume throughout the contraction process. This is correct according to measurements down to only marginal changes in volume. For instance, Baskin and Paolini measured changes in volume during twitches of the gastrocnemius muscle of the frog of about 3×10^{-5} ml/mg [4], which is a change of only 0.03% of the initial volume.

Pfuhl gave an account of pinnate muscles and their force output [24]. He kept the distance between the planes of insertion of the muscle fibers constant. Because of this, and because no fiber curvature was taken into account, the volume of the modeled muscle was kept constant. The author arrived at the peculiar conclusion that the angle of the fibers relative to the direction of the tendon is unimportant for the "effective total force" output. See Appendix A for his proof. However, the proof is a circular argument, based on the fact that a vector can always be decomposed into two components that can be recombined to produce the original vector. The author does not give any functional definition of "effective total force," other than that it consists of shortening force (*Verkürzungskraft*) and swelling force (*Verdickungskraft*). It is clear, however, that the fact that muscle fibers retain their volume helps a muscle not to collapse when it is producing force. The author also compares the work produced by pinnate muscles and parallel fibered muscles. He shows that the work produced is independent of the fiber angle. This is an early account of the independence of work from muscle architecture, and apart from the effects of work performed by series elastic elements in the muscle, this is still an acceptable rule.

Benninghoff and Rollhäuser produced a paper that is to be considered a classic in muscle architecture literature [5]. They kept constant the volume of the model pinnate muscle by leaving the distance between the surfaces of insertion of the fibers unchanged. They do not explicitly mention volume, but from their drawings and formulas, it becomes clear

FIGURE 1

Diagram illustrating that the volume of a unipinnate muscle remains the same if the distance between the tendinous sheets remains unchanged during shortening.

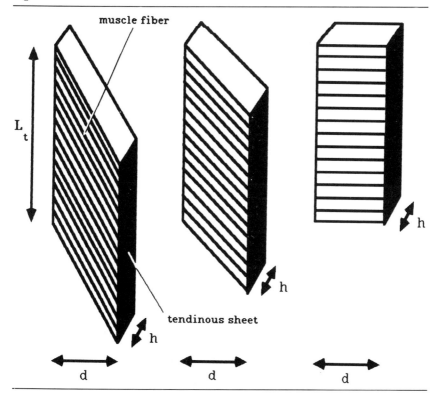

that it is kept constant. Their assumption is vital for the theoretical relations they found, which will be dealt with in the section on Shortening of Muscles and Fibers.

Alexander [2] keeps the volume of a modeled bipinnate muscle constant during contraction by keeping the distances between the insertion surfaces of the fibers constant (see Figure 1, in which, for all three states of shortening, the volume is $dL_t h$). However, he does not keep the volume of a modeled parallel-fibered muscle constant to avoid modeling fiber curvature, which would make his model unpleasantly complex, given the scope of his analysis. His aim is to show that the force produced by a bipinnate muscle compared to the force produced by a parallel-fibered one with equal volume depends on the muscle fiber angle relative to the pulling direction of the tendon, muscle length, and muscle width.

Gans and Bock [9] gave an account of muscle architecture in which

FIGURE 2
Unipinnate muscle model with kite-shaped tendinous sheets. (Modified from Woittiez, R.D., P.A. Huijing, H.B.K. Boom, and R.H. Rozendal. A three-dimensional model: A quantified relation between form and function of skeletal muscles. J. Morphol. *182:95–113, 1984.)*

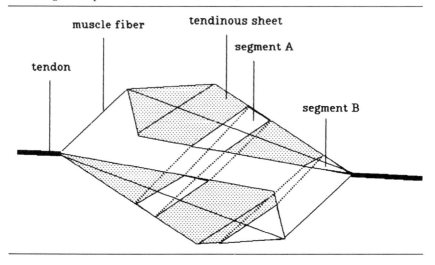

volume considerations also played a central role. They recapitulate the paper by Benninghoff and Rollhäuser [5] and use their formulas as a basis for further theoretical considerations.

Gans [10] shows a figure from which it can be concluded that constant volume is used throughout the range of contraction.

Hatze [13] also models muscles with constant volume by keeping the distance between the areas of insertion of the fibers uniform.

Heukelom et al. wrote a paper on muscle pressure [14]. One of the constraints they use is constancy of muscle volume. The radius of curvature of muscle fibers is adapted such that the muscle retains its volume. This produces a difference in work output of fibers and muscle, which the authors use to calculate the pressure inside the muscle. That procedure will be discussed in the section on Muscle Pressure.

Woittiez et al. [31] also keep the volume of their modeled unipinnate muscle constant. Since their model does not have parallel tendinous sheets, they do not keep the volume constant by keeping the distance between the sheets constant, but rather by using least square parameter estimation on a number of muscle segments together (see Figure 2). This allows volume to move from one segment to another when the modeled muscle is shortening, which in reality could only be brought about by movement of the extracellular fluid between the fibers, since the segments contain whole fibers only. Another peculiar property of the model of Woittiez et al. [31] is that the areas of insertion for muscle fibers in each segment are not the same on the proximal and distal tendinous sheets because of their kite shape. The areas of insertion of fibers in segment A in Figure 2 are the same on both tendinous sheets, but this is not the case in segment B. The latter can only be reconciled by introducing tapered fibers or fibers that do not extend across the entire segment. Apart from a rather abrupt tapering at the tip of muscle fibers, where they merge into the tendinous sheet, tapering of fibers is not observed in muscle histological studies. The functional reason for this is that the force produced by a given part of a muscle fiber needs to be matched by the force in another part of that fiber in order to avoid mechanical instability, resulting in shortening of one part of the fiber at the cost of lengthening of another part. Since the force of a muscle fiber depends on its cross-sectional area, muscle fibers should not taper if this kind of instability is to be avoided. Therefore, the chosen kite shape of the tendinous sheets is not realistic. An elliptic sheet does not create the need for tapered fibers [19]. Extensive tapering of muscle fibers is found in some muscles [18], but here the force is transmitted by series elastic connective tissue, breaking up long fibers into short series interdigitated muscle fibers.

SHORTENING OF MUSCLES AND FIBERS

Benninghoff and Rollhäuser [5] gave a mathematical account of the contraction of oblique pinnate muscles, in which fibers have different lengths and different angles. Their implicit assumption was that the volume of a muscle remains constant because the distance between the planes of insertion of the fibers remains constant (see Figure 1). They stated the following law: The length of muscle fibers should be related to their angle with the tendon such that they all move the tendon over the same distance at equal shortening distances of the fibers relative to their original length. They produced a formula giving the relation between fiber angle and length (see Appendix C). A graph of the relation between the angle and length of fibers, according to their formula, is given for the lifting height and relative fiber shortening found in human flexor hallucis longus muscle. Together with this curve, measurements of fiber length and angle are given for which the curve appears to be a close fit. If this fit were as good for most muscles, the authors would have identified a major determinant of muscle architecture, namely, constancy in percentage shortening of the fibers throughout the muscle. However, if we look at other reports of the length and angle of muscle fibers [6, 30], they do not relate in this way. For instance, in the claw of the edible crab *Cancer pagurus*, the adductor dactylopoditis muscle has increasing fiber angle with increasing fiber length [30], while the formula derived by Benninghoff and Rollhäuser gives the opposite relationship. The same holds for the vastus internus muscle of the frog [6].

A muscle model formulated by Gaspard [11] has a single functional constraint: All muscle fibers should contract equal percentages of their initial length. This model will be discussed in the section on Curvature of Fibers and Stretch of Tendinous Sheets.

It is useful to make some comparisons of different muscle designs in order to understand why the human flexor hallucis longus muscle does not represent oblique muscles in general. If one considers this muscle type, it becomes obvious that spaces between the fibers should be present, since the fibers have different angles relative to the tendinous sheet and do not taper (see Figure 3). Since total fiber volume is a major determinant of the work and power output of a muscle, and since the space inside an organism always seems to be scarce, it is important to use space well. Consequently, neighboring fibers should have only small differences in fiber angle. This is exactly what we see in oblique muscles. Compare, for instance, the drawings by Willemse [30] and Beritoff [6]. In mathematical terms, the fibers form an almost continuous vector field of forces. If this type of muscle is considered to be a linked system of nonoblique muscles (see Figure 3b), the demands that volume be constant and that muscle work output equal fiber work can be satisfied by letting each muscle shorten with constant distances between their planes of insertion. If, then, the tendinous sheet has to maintain its length, it should not change its direction (see Figure 3b,c). The total fiber volume does not change in this way, but the total muscle volume does. This has to do with a change in the amount of space between the fibers. If the planes of insertion of muscle fibers are not parallel, there are several ways to arrange the fibers in between. One could arrange them parallel (see Figure 3d). This would imply different fiber lengths and different relative shortening of the fibers, since the tendinous sheet moves parallel to itself (see Figure 3a–d). This difference can be decreased by introducing differences in fiber angle (see Figure 3e). The extreme form of this condition is the muscle drawn in Figure 3f, in which there is no longer space for the fibers to attach. Here, however, there is almost uniform percentage fiber shortening with a given displacement of the tendinous sheet; consequently, the muscle can shorten more.

Between this extreme and the one shown in Figure 3d, we encounter the compromise between the demand of fiber attachment space and that of uniform percentage fiber shortening, to keep all muscle fibers producing force throughout the contraction range. This compromise is depicted in Figure 3e. Such a compromise is unnecessary in nonoblique muscles, so there must be a good spatial reason for the muscle to be oblique, as in the adductor muscle of the claw of the crab [30]. The

FIGURE 3
Diagram illustrating that oblique muscles (muscles without uniform fiber length) can be interpreted as a set of normal unipinnate submuscles with the same shortening characteristics: In each submuscle, the distance between tendinous sheets remains constant. Oblique muscles show a compromise in architecture between distance of shortening and amount of insertion area for the muscle fibers. Oblique bipinnate muscles can be interpreted to be double oblique unipinnate muscles with the same shortening characteristics.

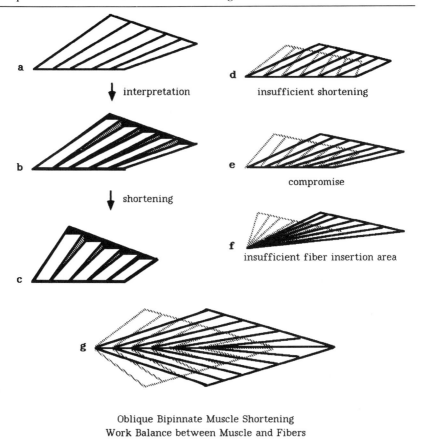

Oblique Bipinnate Muscle Shortening
Work Balance between Muscle and Fibers

competition for space of organs is found everywhere in the organism, and in the case of oblique muscles, that competition may have to be taken into account when explaining their design. If we look back at the muscle analyzed by Benninghoff and Rollhaüser [5], the human flexor hallucis longus muscle, in which fibers are longest at the smallest fiber angle, a solution is found somewhere between Figures 3e and 3f. This may in-

FIGURE 4
The geometrical parameters of a unipinnate muscle.

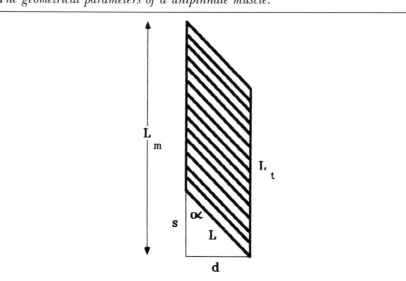

dicate that in this muscle the amount of shortening is more critical than the optimal use of available space. The muscles described by Willemse [30] and Beritoff [5] are more like Figure 3e.

Bipinnate oblique muscles are found frequently in animals and in man. They can be described in the same way as unipinnate oblique muscles (see Figure 3g) in terms of volume retention, work characteristics, and shortening distances.

WORK OF MUSCLES AND FIBERS

Benninghoff and Rollhäuser claimed that fibers with a large angle relative to the direction of the tendon produce less work than those with a small angle, because the former lose more force [5]. They illustrate this point by calculating the work of fibers in a pinnate muscle with different angles. To calculate the work, they derived a formula by integrating over the domain of fiber angle, which is incorrect. Appendix D gives their formula and a suggested correction showing that work is independent of fiber angle. The geometrical arrangement is given in Figure 4. The authors are correct, however, in pointing out that the lifting force of a muscle depends strongly on the fiber angle. The ratio of displacement of the tendon to the shortening distance of the fibers also depends on the fiber angle. This dependence exactly counterbalances the loss of force in terms of the work produced by the

FIGURE 5

Changes of relative fiber length and angle in the dactylopoditis muscle of the edible crab.

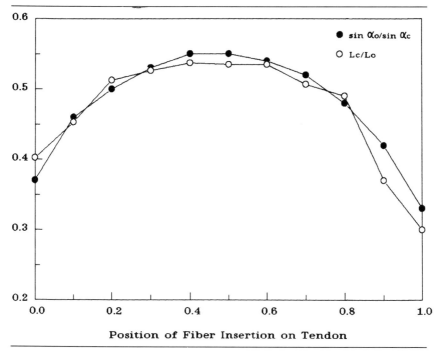

Position of Fiber Insertion on Tendon

muscle, so that the work is completely independent of the fiber angle (see also Otten [20] versus Huijing and Woittiez [16]; see also [24]). It is interesting that authors have often looked for advantages [16] and disadvantages [5] in the architecture of pinnate muscles regarding the production of work. Although fiber architecture determines many characteristics of muscle, it does not determine the work output, unless one includes elasticity and damping of tendinous elements or losses in the muscle due to friction.

Willemse [30] dealt with one pinnate muscle in some detail: the adductor dactylopoditis muscle closing the claw of the crab. He measured the fiber angles for opened and closed claw and fiber shortening ratio (closed-claw fiber length divided by opened-claw fiber length). If the volume of the muscle is not to be changed, the ratio of the sines of the fiber angles in opened and closed positions of the claw should be the same as the inverse of the ratio of the fiber lengths in those positions. The proof of this is given in Appendix E, resulting in formula [22]. In Figure 5, both ratios are plotted as derived from the data of Willemse [30]. The discrepancies between the two graphs fall within the variations found by Willemse in fiber angle and length in various parts of the muscle. Thus there is no reason to abandon the idea that fiber length and fiber angle are related during shortening such that the volume of the muscle remains constant. Willemse set out to test two hypotheses:

a. The hypothesis formulated by Benninghoff and Rollhäuser [5] that fiber angle and fiber length are related such that the fibers always shorten equal percentages of their initial length (see Appendix C, formula [8]).

b. The hypothesis formulated by Fick [8] that all fibers should produce the same amount of work (fiber length linearly related to the cosine of the fiber angle).

Willemse found that neither of these hypotheses agree with the anatomy of the muscle that closes the claw of the edible crab. He argues that this lack of agreement has to do with "room factors": Given that the claw has a tapered shape, there is only room for short muscle fibers at the distal end of the tendinous sheet. These short fibers need to have small angles when the claw is opened in order to be able to move the tendon over the desired distance. The angles are therefore smaller than expected from the two hypotheses mentioned above.

However, we can also look at this problem from two other perspectives, namely, the demand for constancy of volume and the demand for muscle work that equals total muscle fiber work. The latter demand is important in keeping a muscle model from producing more work than the muscle fibers produce together [16, 20]. If it is assumed that no work is lost in the muscle (which implies that friction and viscosity are negligible and that connective tissue is perfectly elastic), then such work balance is an important principle for evaluating simple muscle models. Let us first consider a unipinnate muscle with equal fiber length throughout and with a tendon that has the same direction as the attaching tendinous sheet (see Figures 1 and 6a), which is the most popular form for theoretical investigations [2, 5, 9, 10, 24]. If its volume is to remain constant, the muscle should shorten while keeping the distances of the planes of insertion of the fibers constant. In Appendix E this is shown mathematically. Appendix F shows that this geometrical requirement agrees with the work balance between muscle fibers and whole muscle.

Up to now, investigators have dealt with unipinnate muscles that have a tendon in the same direction as the tendinous sheet (Figure 6a), but wherever a unipinnate muscle has two tendinous sheets, each with point-like attachments to bone or tendons, the configuration is as shown in Figure 6b. The latter muscle cannot produce a couple, whereas a unipinnate muscle with a bony connection as in Figure 6a generates the coupled forces F_c. The direction of the force produced by the muscle relative to the fiber direction is different in the two cases. This difference, in turn, influences the magnitude of the force and the displacement of

FIGURE 6

Two types of unipinnate muscles: one that produces couples (a) and has force transmission to the tendon in the plane of the tendinous sheet and one that does not produce couples (b) with force transmission at an angle to the tendinous sheets.

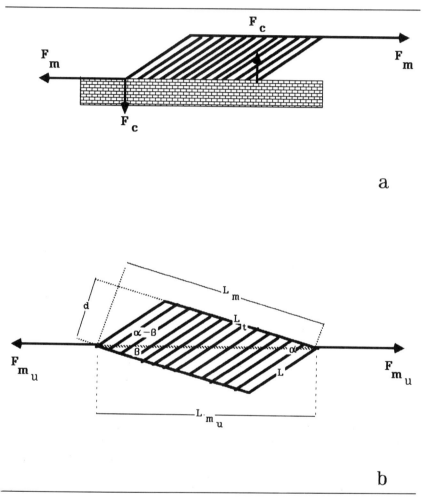

a

b

the tendon. The relations between muscle shortening and fiber shortening are shown in Appendix G. To indicate the difference in amount of muscle shortening and change in volume in the two types, muscle length and volume have been calculated with a muscle optimal length of 5, a muscle fiber optimal length of 2.6, a tendinous sheet length of 2.6, and fiber shortening of 40%. It appears that the type of unipinnate muscle shown in Figure 6a shortens 7% more than the one shown in Figure 6b. However, the volume of the latter would have to decrease by 30% at maximal shortening, while the volume of the former would remain constant. This indicates that a unipinnate muscle of the type shown in Figure 6b with two tendinous sheets should have bulging of curved fibers.

MUSCLE PRESSURE

A number of authors have calculated muscle pressure from measurements of changes in the volume of a muscle during contraction [4, 15]. This method has two drawbacks. First, the calculated pressure can only be the average pressure in the muscle, since only total volume change is measured. Second, the method uses the compressibility of water to derive pressure from volume change, using the argument that a muscle consists mainly of water. The compressibility of water, however, is usually measured in boiled water to remove the dissolved gases. In order to function, it is vital that muscles have gases dissolved in their circulating blood. Moreover, a muscle consists of components that have almost no free water content, like the collagen, actin, and myosin filaments. Their compressibility may be quite different from that of water. Furthermore, muscles expel venous blood during contraction, reducing their total volume. Another problem is that muscle compressibility is so low that a small error in the measurement of volume change translates into large errors in the calculated pressure. Measuring the volume changes of a muscle may be a poor method to determine muscle pressure.

A better method was employed by Petrofsky and Hendershot [23], who fitted a small rubber balloon at the top of a 25-gauge cut needle. The balloon was filled partially with saline. The needle was connected to a low-displacement semiconductor bridge pressure transducer. Both in the belly and in the end of the muscle, the needle was inserted, producing a pressure at maximal stimulation in the former location up to about 23 kPa in the medial gastrocnemius muscle of the cat and up to about 18 kPa in the soleus muscle of the cat. The authors did not indicate whether the muscle was stimulated at its optimal length. Skeletal muscle tissue can produce a stress of about 230 kPa at optimal sarcomere length, which is on the order of a factor of 10 above the pressure found in the muscles by these authors. They mention the

FIGURE 7

Internal muscle pressure in percentage of fiber stress, as measured during te-
tanic contraction of the gastrocnemius muscle of the toad.

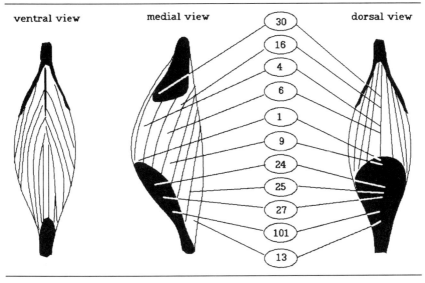

variability in pressure measurements in the literature and attribute this
to differences in muscle thickness and fiber stress. This explanation is
correct, but incomplete. As will be shown in this section, fiber curvature, and in the next section, tendinous sheet curvature also influence
muscle pressure.

Kahabuka and Otten [unpublished results] measured pressure in the
gastrocnemius muscle of the toad (muscle weight, 3.4 g) by means of a
microtip pressure transducer (Millar) with a tip diameter of 1.3 mm.
This transducer was inserted into the muscle after a small incision was
made in the epimysium. The small cavity produced by the transducer
between the muscle fibers was filled by letting a small drop of saline slide
along the catheter of the transducer into the muscle. This ensured that
pressure built up when the muscle contracted. Figure 7 shows the pressure as a percentage of the fiber stress when the muscle was stimulated
supramaximally with intramuscular electrodes, reaching tetanic contraction. The absolute pressure amounts to 133 kPa in the case of the
101% location near the tendon, which is about 1.3 atm. In some places
in the muscle, the pressure was less than 1 kPa at the same total force
output, indicating the variability of pressure in one single muscle. In the
next section, a model will be presented to explain this phenomenon.

The only paper that modeled muscle pressure is the one by Heukelom
et al. [14]. A cylindrical muscle was modeled with parallel fibers (see
Figure 8b, top). A linear force-length diagram of the fibers was used.

FIGURE 8

a. Pressure under a single muscle fiber with stress, T, *thickness,* b, *and radius of curvature,* R. *b. Pressure inside a muscle due to fiber curvature. Layers of fibers with decreasing curvature from periphery to center together produce an increasing pressure.*

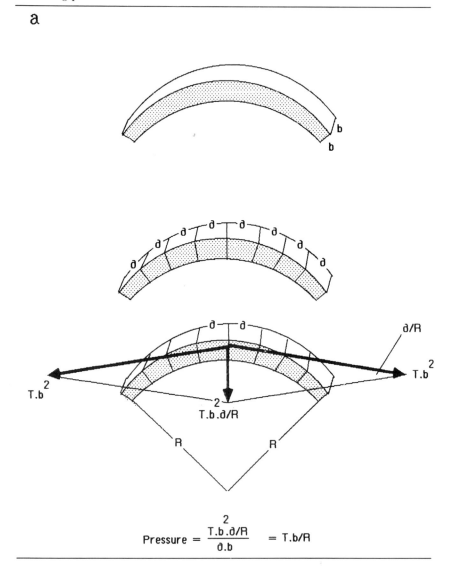

$$\text{Pressure} = \frac{\text{T.b.}\partial/\text{R}}{\partial.\text{b}} = \text{T.b/R}$$

FIGURE 8 *Continued.*

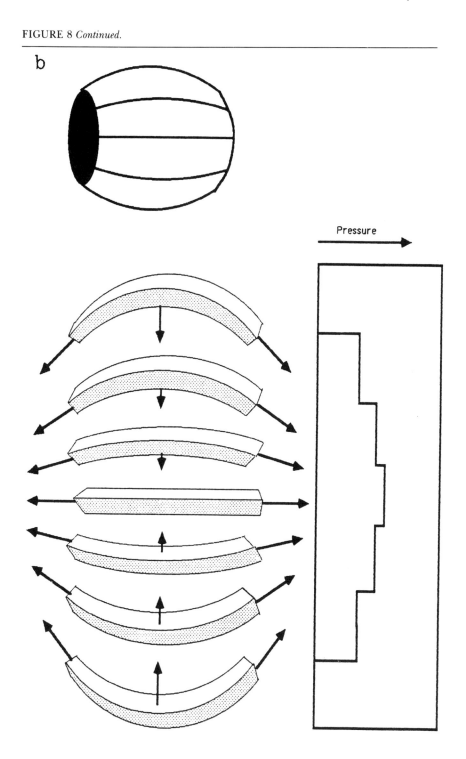

The starting configuration of the muscle was one with straight fibers. When the circular tendon plates were brought together, the volume of the muscle was kept constant by letting the fibers curve and bulge outward (see Figure 8b, top). The shortening of the muscle was performed in small steps (1% of the initial length), and each time the curvature of the fibers was adjusted. At every step, the length of muscle fibers arranged in concentric jackets was calculated. The superficial fibers stay a bit longer when the muscle is shortening because of their higher curvature than central fibers. Appendix H gives the mathematical steps in this model.

The law used by the authors is that the work done by a system equals the pressure times the change in volume. As the volume changed, they took the surface of the circular tendon plate multiplied by its displacement. The total muscle volume was kept constant, however. Since there is no change in the volume of the muscle, the law used by the authors cannot be effective and the pressure that was calculated cannot be reliable. Clearly, the work of the fibers should be the same as that of the muscle (see also the section on Work of Muscles and Fibers).

There is a better way to calculate pressure in a muscle with curved fibers. Appendix H shows the derivation of a simple formula from which internal muscle pressure, generated by the curvature of fibers, can be calculated. Figure 8a shows the pressure under a single muscle fiber and Figure 8b illustrates the pressure inside a barrel-shaped muscle as it is built up by layers of muscle fibers.

There is another source of internal muscle pressure, namely, the orientation of the tendinous sheet. This effect also influences the force that a muscle produces. Figure 9 illustrates this point, while Appendix I derives the necessary relations and shows that if muscle pressure is taken into account, the geometrical transitions that various types of unipinnate muscles go through are the same, regardless of their production of couples (see Figure 6). This effect of tendinous sheet orientation on muscle pressure cannot easily be reconciled with the data of Figure 7, since additional factors, such as tendinous sheet curvature and fiber curvature, need to be taken into account. This will be done in the next section.

CURVATURE OF FIBERS AND STRETCH OF TENDINOUS SHEETS

One publication showed modeling of curved fibers [14], which is discussed in the section on Muscle Pressure.

As shown above in the sections on Muscle Pressure and Work of

FIGURE 9

A unipinnate muscle produces intramuscular pressure when producing force. This pressure is brought about by the orientation of the tendinous sheet and the resistance of the muscle fibers against a decrease in volume. The formulas deriving the forces F_p (producing pressure) and F_{mu} (the muscle force) are produced by setting up a free body diagram of the tendinous sheet.

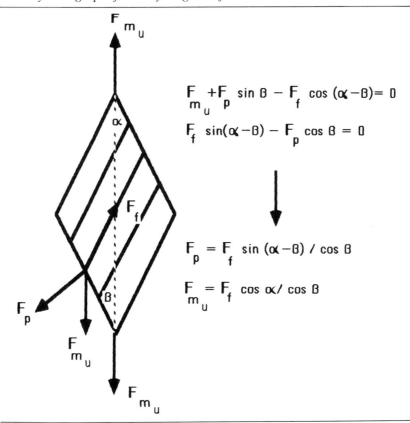

$$F_{m_u} + F_p \sin \beta - F_f \cos (\alpha - \beta) = 0$$

$$F_f \sin(\alpha - \beta) - F_p \cos \beta = 0$$

$$F_p = F_f \sin (\alpha - \beta) / \cos \beta$$

$$F_{m_u} = F_f \cos \alpha / \cos \beta$$

Muscles and Fibers, all types of muscles can be described with the constant volume rule and the "work of fibers equals work of muscle" rule or work balance rule, because both rules dictate the same geometric changes of a muscle. However, this is true only under the condition that the tendinous sheets do not stretch. If muscle fibers are not curved in the geometric configuration of the muscle in which it produces the highest active force, and the tendinous sheets do not stretch, the fibers will not curve during shortening, because both volume and work rules dictate the same geometric transitions. However, if the tendinous sheets do stretch, the fibers may have to start curving in order to comply with the volume and work rules.

To test this hypothesis, I produced a muscle model describing a unipinnate muscle with elliptic planar tendinous sheets and a fiber length-active force diagram as given by Otten [21], while the fiber length-passive force diagram was obtained from measurements by Julian and Moss [17]. A Gaussian distribution in sarcomere length throughout the muscle was chosen with a standard deviation of 0.4 μm and a mean of 2.1 μm, based on measurements of Stephens et al. [29] in the cat medial gastrocnemius. They found a standard deviation in motor unit optimal length of 3 mm in fibers of 18-mm length, which is 0.4 μm at sarcomere level. As a test muscle, the vastus lateralis muscle of the cat was chosen, of which measurements exist of the length-force diagrams [25]. The muscle has a fairly simple unipinnate architecture with two tendinous sheets. The stretch of these sheets was calculated from the results published by Rack and Westbury [26]. They measured tendon stiffness in the soleus muscle of the cat, using the muscle spindle null method, separating tendon strain from muscle fiber strain. In this elegant method, the signal from a muscle spindle is used to determine the frequency of imposed length change on a muscle, for which no length change in the muscle fiber is produced. It is possible to change the length of a muscle sinusoidally without changing the fiber length if the frequency is chosen correctly, due to the mechanical impedances of tendinous material and muscle fibers. All length change imposed is taken up by the tendinous components of the muscle at that frequency. The force is measured simultaneously with the length change, resulting in dynamic stiffness of the tendinous components. Extrapolation of this stiffness to the maximum output force of soleus muscle, as measured by Poliacu [25] in equally sized cats, and integration of the inverse of the stiffness over the force yielded a strain of 0.026 for the entire tendinous component. This indicates that tendinous sheets stretch about 2.6% of their rest length at optimal length of the muscle and maximum recruitment. It should be stressed, however, that this value may be too low due to the fact that dynamic stiffness is usually higher than passive stiffness, because of damping characteristics of material.

The shape of the length-tension curve of the sheets was chosen to be exponential, with a linear part above half of the maximal tension. This linear part, following an exponential part at increasing length, has been observed in tendinous tissue [1, 3]. In fact, Decreamer et al. [7] proposed a mathematical model to account for this linear component following an exponential one. Their model describes a population of linear elastic collagen fibers that have their zero tension at lengths that show a Gaussian distribution. As more fibers are recruited when the whole population is stretched, the tension develops exponentially, while the rise in force becomes linear with length when all fibers are recruited.

The present muscle model keeps muscle volume constant while accounting for work balance: Work produced by the muscle fibers is equal to the sum of the work taken up by the tendinous sheet and the work produced by the muscle. The model was run twice, using the geometry as measured from a fresh vastus lateralis muscle. The first run was without tendinous sheet stretch, the second with a maximum stretch of 2.6%. The geometric configurations are shown in Figure 10a and b. The resulting length-force diagrams, together with the experimental results (fitted average of four muscles; standard deviation 4% of the force after correction for the size of the cats), are given in Figure 10c. A number of comments may be made about these results:

1. There is good agreement between the model results and the experimental ones, especially in terms of the absolute force. The model and experimental active force curves differ slightly in width, which may be an indication that the range of sarcomere lengths at optimal length is more than 0.4 μm in this muscle. The skewness of the model curve with stretch of the tendinous sheet is more like that of the experimental one than the model curve without stretch.

2. Both the model and experimental active curves are almost symmetrical, while the sarcomere length-active force diagram is very skew [12, 21], with an ascending part that is steeper than the descending part. There are three causes of the change in skewness from fiber to whole muscle:

   a. Variation in sarcomere length diminishes the skewness (the convolution of a skew curve with a symmetric one produces a curve with less skewness).

   b. Stretching of series elastic elements shifts the maximum of the length-active force diagram to higher muscle lengths. At high force levels the series elastic element is stretched, adding to the effective length of the muscle.

   c. The fiber angle increases when the muscle shortens so that the muscle force drops. Because of the work balance rule, the shortening distance of the muscle will increase at a given amount of fiber shortening, making the ascending limb of the curve less steep and diminishing the skewness.

3. The shape changes through which the muscle goes are very much the same when the model is run without stretch and with stretch of the tendinous components (see Figure 10a and b). In the stretched case, the muscle fibers curve out somewhat, but this effect does not build up as the muscle is shortening, indicating that there is still good agreement between the rules of constant volume and work balance, with the need for only a small amount of fiber curvature.

With the same model, shortening of the anterior sartorius muscle of the cat was simulated. Fiber curvature and tendinous sheet stretch were included. Here we have an interesting muscle architecture. This muscle appears to have short interdigitated muscle fibers connected by elastic tissue [18]. When the model is run without these interfiber series elastic elements, interpreting the fibers to run from one tendinous sheet to the other, the prediction of the length-force diagrams is not as good as the one with interfiber series elastic elements, with a total length of 12% of the optimal length of the muscle fibers and a maximal stretch of up to 24% of the optimal fiber length (see Figure 11). Width and skewness of the length-active force diagram improve when the series elastic elements are taken into account.

FIGURE 10

Changes in shape during shortening of a unipinnate muscle, the vastus lateralis muscle of the cat, as calculated by a model outlined in the text. The arrows indicate the total muscle force, scaled to the 10-N bar. Panel a. Shows shortening without stretch of tendinous components (no fiber curvature needed). Panel b. Shows shortening with stretch of tendinous components and consequently fiber curvature. Panel c. Length–force diagrams of the vastus lateralis muscle of the cat. Experimental results are given (fitted average of four muscles, corrected for the size of the cats) and two sets of model results with and without stretch of tendinous components.

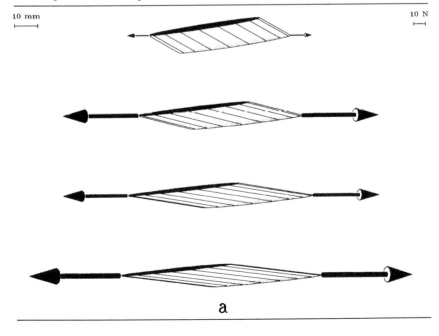

10 mm

10 N

a

FIGURE 10 *Continued.*

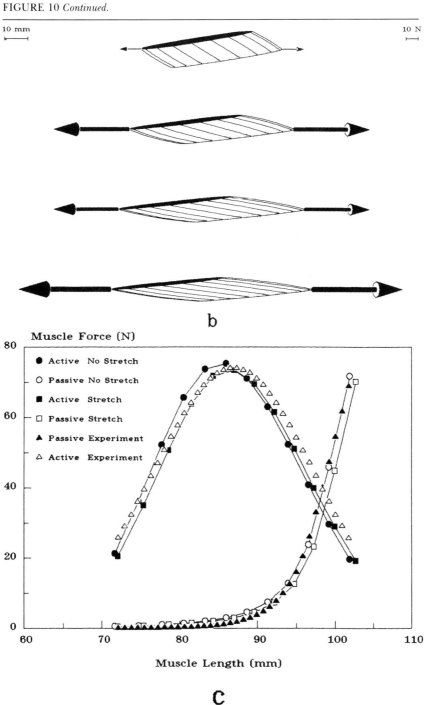

b

c

FIGURE 11

Length–force diagrams of the sartorius anterior muscle of the cat. Experimental results are given (fitted average of six muscles, corrected for the size of the cats) and two sets of model results. Both sets of diagrams are produced by simulating the stretch of tendinous components. One set is produced by simulating the stretch of interfiber series elastic elements that link the short interdigitated muscle fibers [18].

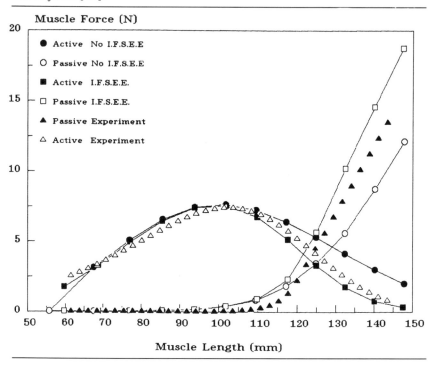

The simulation of the shortening of the anterior sartorius muscle of the cat clearly shows the functional effect of its peculiar architecture on the length-force diagrams. Loeb et al. [18] indicated some other functional implications—for instance, the synchronous activation of the in-series fibers by the motor neurons. If the presence of short interdigitated muscle fibers in parallel-fibered muscles is widespread, it should be taken into account whenever length-force diagrams need to be calculated and understood.

SHAPE OF TENDINOUS SHEETS

Tendinous sheets are represented in a number of models. In most of them, these sheets are planar [2, 5, 9, 10, 13, 14, 31]. I encountered only

FIGURE 12

Muscle model with curved tendinous sheets in the shape of a cissoid of Diocles. The figure is produced from formulas given by Gaspard [11].

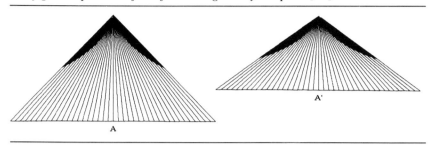

two publications in which curved tendinous sheets are represented in muscle models.

A thesis by van der Stelt [28] offers a myotome model of fish loco-motory musculature. Under the assumption of equal amounts of fiber shortening in the whole body and equal bending moments, a differential equation is formulated that produces two sets of curved myosepts. Some groups of fish have myosepts that are similar to those indicated by these solutions.

The second publication dealing with curved tendinous sheets is a lengthy and highly theoretical monograph by Gaspard [11]. Only one functional criterion is used in this work: Muscle fibers should always contract by equal percentages of their length. A more peculiar assumption in the model is that muscle fibers converge to one single point. Close to this point they insert on tendinous tissue, which has the shape of a cissoid of Diocles (see Appendix J).

Figure 12 shows such an arrangement. This shape makes it possible for the muscle to lift straight edge A with equal percentage fiber short-ening throughout the muscle to the level of A'. This is correct, but is probably interesting only from a theoretical point of view because the authors cite no particular muscle with comparable fiber convergence. No other mechanical constraint is used apart from fiber shortening, which makes the model appear somewhat unrealistic. However, this is one of the few publications that predicts form from functional demands. Most research strategies operate in the reverse direction.

When muscles are observed with tendinous sheets on their outer sur-face, i.e., with fibers inserting on one side only, it is manifest that these sheets are always curved: They are nonplanar. If one looks more closely at the curvature of these sheets, it appears to be highest at the edge away from the tendon and lowest close to the tendon. In order to demonstrate the mechanical basis for this shape, consider the following:

A tendinous sheet consists of strands of collagen fibers, mainly in the direction of force transmission from fibers to tendon. This arrangement makes the sheet fairly strain resistant and, at the same time, flexible to bend in all directions. Therefore, it is reasonable to model the curved sheet by means of small, solid bodies that are connected to each other with ball-and-socket joints (Figure 13a). This description simulates the flexibility of the sheet and its strain resistance. If we select one chain of elements that transmits the force from fibers to tendon (Figure 13b), and from this chain select one single element, the ith element, we can analyze the conditions for mechanical equilibrium of this element, of the chain, and of the sheet. This analysis leads to one formula giving the shape of tendinous sheets and another giving the pressure under them. These formulas are derived in Appendix K.

They are immediately testable, since they give clear predictions about intramuscular pressure and the shape of tendinous sheets. It is important to note that the formula derived ([87]) gives a description of tendinous sheet shape that is independent of fiber stress. This indicates that if gravitational effects, pressure from surrounding muscles, and stretch of tendinous sheets are neglected (as in Figure 13a), the shape of tendinous sheets is independent of the recruitment of a muscle, provided this recruitment is homogeneous. If we look at formula [90] of Appendix K, we see that the relative intramuscular pressure depends only on the angle between the fibers and sheet and a constant. Since the local angle of the tendinous sheet with the line of pull of the muscle adjusts itself according to formula [87] of Appendix K, tendinous sheet shape and relative muscle pressure are completely linked.

For a unipinnate muscle, the shape of two external tendinous sheets was calculated, using a tendinous sheet strength of 300 times muscle fiber strength, sheet edge thickness of 0.01 mm, tendinous sheet length of 20 mm, fiber angle relative to line of pull of 20°, and fiber length of 25 mm. Furthermore, the fiber curvature of peripheral fibers was chosen to be the same as the curvature of the sheet at the edge. Since there is the extra geometrical constraint that fibers and sheets should be attached to each other, this set of parameter values produces a unique configuration, shown in Figure 14a. The relation between peripheral fiber curvature and pressure is known (see Figure 8a and b and formula [52] of Appendix H). The pressure under the sheets can be calculated with formula [90] of Appendix K. Together this gives the estimated isobars of Figure 14b. If we compare these isobars with the estimated ones from the gastrocnemius muscle of the toad (see Figure 14c) from the measurements given in Figure 7, there appears to be some resemblance, especially in the area of the large external tendinous sheet of the muscle. The suggestion is that the differences in intramuscular pressure measured can be explained by the combined effects of muscle fiber curvature

FIGURE 13

a. Elements descriptive of a tendinous sheet. Rigid bodies (the blocks) are inter-connected by ball-and-socket joints (the black balls), producing a structure that resists strain and is flexible at the same time. b. One single chain of elements is selected from the finite element description of the sheet. c. One single element is selected from the chain of elements, of which the static equilibrium of moments and forces can be analyzed. The symbols are used in deriving equations for the shape of the tendinous sheet and the pressure under it.

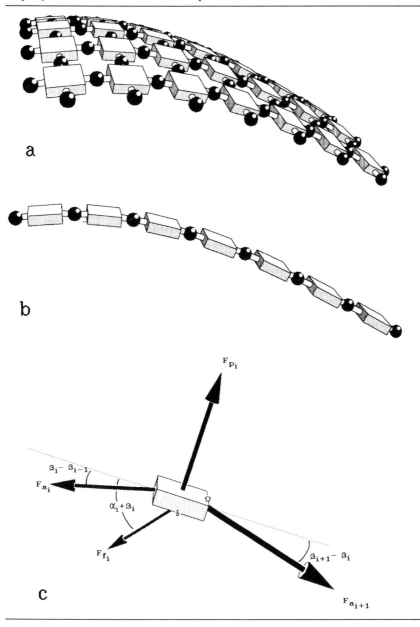

and the shape of the external tendinous sheet, which is due to the buildup of force along the sheet. Figure 15 shows a simulation of the shortening of the lateral gastrocnemius muscle of the cat, using the model employed earlier in this chapter for simulations of the anterior sartorius muscle and vastus lateralis muscles, but now extended with curved tendinous sheets based on formulas from Appendix K.

CONCLUSIONS

Muscles can be modeled in two ways:

Firstly, one can produce some device or algorithm that simulates the

FIGURE 14

a. Model configuration of a unipinnate muscle with curved tendinous sheets and fibers. b. Isobars in percentage of fiber stress derived from pressure measurements in the gastrocnemius muscle of the toad (compare with Figure 7).

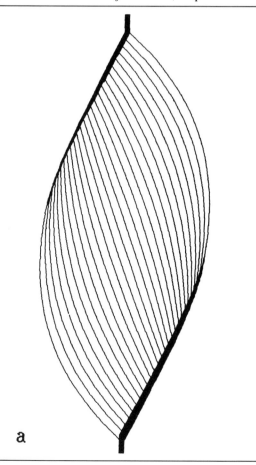

a

FIGURE 14 *Continued.*

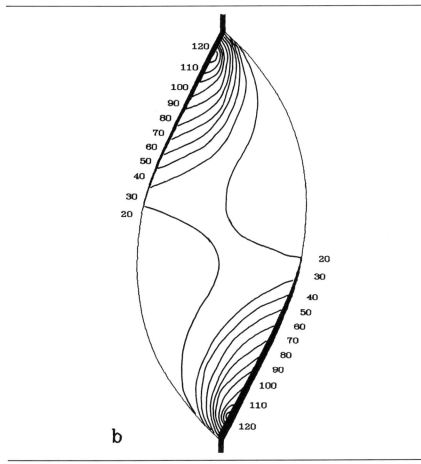

b

behavior of a skeletal muscle. Usually that implies the use of springs and dampers with adjustable, nonlinear characteristics. By tuning these properties carefully, a wide range of functional behavior can be simulated, including force-length and force-velocity characteristics, depending on the stimulation rate. This approach does not give the opportunity to explain the architecture of a muscle from a functional point of view and does not explain the origin of functional characteristics of skeletal muscles. Such models can be useful in evaluating muscular function in a muscle-bone-connective tissue system.

Secondly, one can start with the architecture of a skeletal muscle and the mechanical properties of its constituent components, and find an

FIGURE 14 *Continued.*

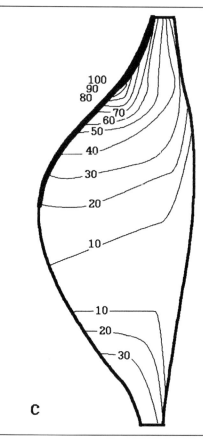

c

algorithm that simulates the spatial process of contraction and force development of a whole muscle. If one succeeds, insight is gained into the relation between the architecture and the functional properties of skeletal muscles. As shown in this chapter, if the model is sufficiently realistic, one also obtains insight into the pressure development within a muscle as a function of the location and the architectural parameters of the muscle. The explanation of the curvature of external tendinous sheets is part of that insight.

Clearly, the second approach offers much more than the first one, but it also demands more computation time and requires many more parameters to be measured.

FIGURE 15

Simulation of shortening of the lateral part of the gastrocnemius muscle of the cat with curved tendinous sheets and fibers. Muscle volume is retained. A balance in the work of shortening fibers, stretching tendinous sheets, and displacing tendons is kept throughout the shortening process.

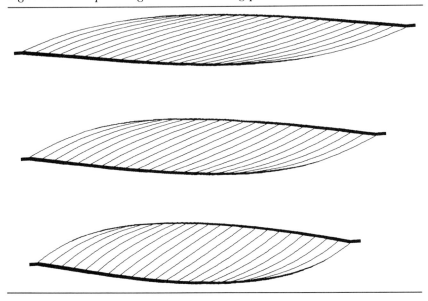

What should one do if one is only interested in the functional characteristics of a number of muscles, which are part of a muscle-bone-connective tissue system, in order to investigate the mechanical properties and control problems of that system? One could measure muscle properties individually, but that takes a lot of work and sophisticated experimental equipment. From the literature, we have some very good measurements of individual muscles of specimens from a number of species. If one has a good architectural model of skeletal muscle and some muscle fiber properties of the species at hand, it is not too difficult to calculate the functional properties of a number of muscles from their architecture rather than measuring them.

The amount of detail to be included in a model depends on the purpose of its output. If one feels that the explanation of motor control lies mainly in the timing of muscle recruitment, a simple model may suffice. In fact, one could learn from a complex model which architectural parameters determine most of the functional characteristics. For instance, to include fiber curvature in a model is important only when one is interested in muscle pressure; it is hardly of importance, in most muscles, for the force-length and force-velocity relations. Fiber length, however, is very important, as is fiber angle. It is often important to include stretch of tendinous components, especially when these components are long compared to the muscle fibers.

One last comment on the detail of architectural models of skeletal muscles: Naturally, the accuracy of the physiological data of muscle fibers, which have been used to test a fiber model or serve as direct input for a muscle model, determines the useful detail of an architectural model of skeletal muscle. The same holds for the accuracy of the morphometric data that serve as inputs for the model.

DISCUSSION

If one takes any skeletal muscle from any organism, divides it into anatomical units, each with its own muscle fiber orientation and structure of insertion; performs some measurements of morphometric characteristics, like muscle length, fiber length and angle, length and width of tendinous sheets, and bony insertions; and if one weighs the muscle units, a number of functional traits can be expressed numerically of each unit:

a. The change in shape during contraction can be calculated. Formulas [22], [23], [31], [42], [43], and [62] express essential relations in a simple description.

b. The length-force diagrams can be calculated using the formulas given by Otten [21] and formulas [5] and [56], plus the parameter values used in this chapter on variation in sarcomere length, stretch of tendinous sheets, and maximal stress produced by muscle fibers.

c. The pressure in the middle of the muscle unit due to fiber curvature can be calculated using formula [52].

d. The pressure under a flat tendinous sheet can be calculated using formula [55], and the pressure under a curved tendinous sheet using formula [90].

e. The shape of an external tendinous sheet can be calculated using formula [87].

These calculations produce predictions that are all testable, as has often been shown in this chapter. This leads to the reasons why one would want to develop any architectural models on muscle contraction.

First, such models produce functional characteristics of muscles that are sometimes hard to measure. Once these models are tested in conditions where measurements can be made, they are open for use in other conditions. Moreover, the models can and should be integrated in models of whole muscle-bone-connective tissue systems, so that the functions of these systems can be simulated and the presence and recruitment of the driving muscles understood [22].

Second, the models offer functional explanations of muscle design, which is important when trying to understand the use of space in an organism.

Muscle models show that muscle force depends on recruitment, average sarcomere length, and muscle volume divided by average fiber length multiplied by correction factors given in formulas [5] or [56]. The maximal distance over which a muscle can displace its point of insertion depends on absolute fiber length and fiber angle and on the variation in sarcomere length in a muscle at optimal length and sarcomere design [21]. The work a muscle can produce in one full shortening movement can be calculated from the force produced and the displacement of the point of insertion (integral of force over displacement), and depends on the volume of the muscle. The power a muscle can produce depends on the volume of the muscle and the fiber type. The maximum contraction velocity of a muscle depends on the fiber type and the formula [31] or [62] (depending on the type of architecture). The stiffness of a muscle is the first derivative of total force (see above) as a function of muscle length (see above). The damping characteristic of a muscle depends on the force-velocity curve [22], which depends on maximal contraction velocity (see above), recruitment, and isometric force (see above). The inertia of a muscle depends on its volume. The whole muscle moves when its origin is fixed and its insertion is free at an average of roughly half the velocity of the point of insertion. (Compare a stretching rubber band on which dots have been drawn.) This gives an estimate of the forces of inertia produced by a muscle when the point of insertion is moving at a changing velocity.

A number of unsolved problems are the following:

a. Nonhomogeneous recruitment of subvolumes of muscle is very hard to model. It may cause sheer in muscles, and produce dimples in tendinous sheets and local changes in pressure. These matters influence overall muscle behavior in complex ways. However, nonhomogeneous recruitment among anatomically divisible parts of a muscle can be simulated by interpreting such parts as separate muscles with mutual mechanical constraints [22].

b. Muscles whose fibers are attached on one side to a tendinous sheet and on the other side to periosteum (like the soleus muscle of the cat) may produce differences in sarcomere length and fiber angle as the muscle is recruited, due to differences in the length of elastic material to which muscle fibers are linked. Those muscles are not so hard to model, but this has not been done yet. Only when these muscles have been modeled can an estimate be given on the importance of these types of insertions.

Knowledge of the physiology of single muscle fibers and that of whole bone-muscle-connective tissue systems can be linked by adequate models simulating the functional architecture of muscles. Thereafter it is possible to start understanding the mechanical implications of control signals going to the muscles [22]. It is clear that muscle function can be evaluated only within the function of the system to which the muscle belongs. Consequently, models of functional architecture of skeletal muscles are not ends, but rather important means in understanding motor control.

APPENDIX A

Pfuhl's Proof That the "Total Effective Force" of a Muscle Is Dependent of Its Fiber Angle
The pulling force F_f of the fibers is reduced to

$$F_m = F_f \cos \alpha \qquad [1]$$

in the direction of the tendon, because of the fiber angle α. The fibers resist deformation of their thickness, which produces a force component

$$F_d = F_f \sin \alpha \qquad [2]$$

in the direction of the tendon. Since the pressure force and the pulling force of the fibers are directed perpendicular to each other, their effects in the direction of the tendon can be added vectorally, resulting in

$$F_s^2 = F_m^2 + F_d^2 = F_f^2 \cos^2 \alpha + F_f^2 \sin^2 \alpha = F_f^2 \qquad [3]$$

$$F_s = F_f \qquad [4]$$

Here's F_s is the effective total force (*wirksame Gesarntkraft*) of the muscle. This indicates that the "total effective force" of a parallel-fibered muscle is the same as that of a pinnate muscle with the same number of fibers.

APPENDIX B

Pfuhl's Proof That Work Produced by a Muscle Is Independent of Its Fiber Angle
The force of the fibers in the direction of the tendon is given as

$$F_t = F_f \cos \alpha \qquad [5]$$

The displacement of the tendon s for given amount of fiber shortening ΔL is

$$s = \frac{\Delta L}{\cos \alpha} \tag{6}$$

The product of force and tendon displacement is work and is therefore

$$W = F_s s = \frac{F_f \cos \alpha \; \Delta L}{\cos \alpha} = F_f \Delta L \tag{7}$$

which is the same as that of a parallel fibered muscle with the same fiber force.

APPENDIX C

Formula from Benninghoff and Rollhaüser [5] Relating Fiber Angle and Fiber Length

$$L = \frac{s}{\cos \alpha - \sqrt{(\cos^2 \alpha + n^2 - 1)}}, \tag{8}$$

in which L is the muscle fiber length, s is the distance over which the tendon is to be moved, α is the angle of pinnation and $n = L/L_0$ is the shortening factor (actual fiber length divided by length at rest).

APPENDIX D

Formula from Benninghoff and Rollhaüser [5] Calculating Work of Pinnate Muscles and a Suggested Alternative
Benninghoff and Rollhaüser [5] calculated the work produced by a muscle by integrating the cosine of the fiber angle $\cos(\alpha)$ over the angle range occupied by a fiber when contracting.

$$W = \frac{\sin(\alpha_2) - \sin(\alpha_1)}{\alpha_2 - \alpha_1} F_f s \tag{9}$$

where W is the muscle work, α_1 and α_2 are the angles of the fiber before and after shortening, respectively, F_f is the force of the fiber, and s is the lifting height of the tendon.

This is, however, not correct: To calculate work, one should integrate force over displacement, not over angle of force.

Looking at Figure 4, we can see that for one particular fiber:

$$\cos(\alpha) = \frac{s}{L} \tag{10}$$

where s is the position of the end of the tendinous sheet and L is the fiber length. If we integrate the force over the displacement of this point, we find:

$$W_m = \int_{s_1}^{s_2} F_f \cdot \cos(\alpha)ds \tag{11}$$

$$d = L\sin(\alpha) \tag{12}$$

$$L = \sqrt{(d^2 + s^2)} \tag{13}$$

From [10], [11], [12], and [13] we obtain

$$W_m = F_f \int_{s_1}^{s_2} \frac{s}{\sqrt{(d^2 + s^2)}}ds \tag{14}$$

$$W_m = F_f\left(\sqrt{(s_2^2 + d^2)} - \sqrt{(s_1^2 + d^2)}\right) \tag{15}$$

which is exactly the same as the work produced by the muscle fibers W_f:

$$W_f = F_f(L_2 - L_1) = W \tag{16}$$

This shows that the work produced by a muscle is independent of muscle fiber angle (versus Benninghoff and Rollhaüser [5]).

APPENDIX E

The Volume of a Pinnate Muscle Does Not Change When Shortening, If the Distance Between the Planes of Insertion of Its Fibers Is Kept Constant
Looking at Figure 4, we see that the distance between the tendinous sheets is

$$d = L \sin (\alpha) \qquad [17]$$

The volume of the muscle is

$$V = hdL_t \qquad [18]$$

in which h is the thickness of the muscle and L_t is the length of the tendinous sheet (see Figure 1). Substituting [17] in [18] we obtain

$$V = hL \sin (\alpha)L_t \qquad [19]$$

The volume of the muscle at start length is

$$V_0 = hL_0 \sin (\alpha_0)L_t \qquad [20]$$

If the volume is to be kept constant, the following relation should hold:

$$hL \sin (\alpha)L_t = hL_0 \sin (\alpha_0)L_t \qquad [21]$$

which can be reduced to

$$L \sin (\alpha) = L_0 \sin (\alpha_0) \qquad [22]$$

Looking at formula [17] we get

$$d = d_0 \qquad [23]$$

indicating that the distance between the planes of insertion needs to remain constant if the volume of the muscle is to remain constant.

APPENDIX F

Proof that Constant Muscle Volume Requires the Same Geometrical
Transitions of a Muscle When Shortening as the One Required by Work
Balance Between Fibers and Muscle

The work produced by the muscle is the integral of force over tendon displacement. The work of the muscle for a small amount of shortening is

$$W_m = \Delta L_m F_f \cos(\alpha) \qquad [24]$$

which should be the same as the work of the fibers:

$$W_f = \Delta L \, F_f \qquad [25]$$

where F_f is the force produced by the fibers together. This work balance is a good assumption when no work is lost in stretch of tendinous sheets or internal friction.

When [24] is equated with [25], the following emerges:

$$\Delta L_m \cos(\alpha) = \Delta L \qquad [26]$$

or

$$\partial L_m / \partial L = \frac{1}{\cos(\alpha)} \qquad [27]$$

for the infinitesimal case. So if [27] holds, the amount of work produced by the fibers is the same as that produced by the muscle. If we start with equations [22] and [23], based on constancy of volume, we can rewrite the muscle length

$$L_m = L_t + L \cos(\alpha) \qquad [28]$$

in which L_t is the length of the tendinous sheet, into

$$L_m = L_t + L \sqrt{\left(1 - \left(\frac{d}{L}\right)^2\right)}, \qquad [29]$$

differentiating L_m with respect to L results in

$$\frac{\partial L_m}{\partial L} = \sqrt{\left(1 - \left(\frac{d}{L}\right)^2\right)} + \frac{d^2}{L^2\sqrt{(1 - (d/L)^2)}} \qquad [30]$$

$$\partial L_m / \partial L = \cos(\alpha) + \frac{\sin^2(\alpha)}{\cos(\alpha)} = \frac{1}{\cos(\alpha)} \qquad [31]$$

which is the same as formula [27], which is derived from the demand of work balance (the work of the muscle is the same as the work produced by the muscle fibers together). This means that both demands, those for constant volume and work balance, are compatible in the same geometrical relation, namely, formula [22]. This is the only formula on which most authors agree because of volume considerations. Here it is shown that it agrees with the concept of work balance.

APPENDIX G

Deriving a Formula Relating Muscle Shortening to Fiber Shortening in Unipinnate Muscles That Do Not Produce Couples
If we define β as the angle between the tendinous sheet and the tendon or force vector, while α is still the angle between the muscle fibers and tendinous sheet and F_f is the total fiber force, then for an amount of fiber shortening ΔL, the amount of work of the fibers is

$$W_f = F_f \Delta L \qquad [32]$$

while the force of the muscle is

$$F_{m_u} = F_f \cos (\alpha - \beta) \qquad [33]$$

in which the extra subscript u refers to this particular type of unipinnate muscle (see Figure 6b). The work produced by the muscle is

$$W_{m_u} = F_f \cos (\alpha - \beta)\Delta L_{m_u} \qquad [34]$$

Work of muscle and fibers should be equal, resulting in

$$F_f \Delta L = F_f \cos (\alpha - \beta)\Delta L_{m_u} \qquad [35]$$

which is

$$\Delta L = \cos (\alpha - \beta)\Delta L_{m_u} \qquad [36]$$

The cosine rule of the triangle muscle length, tendinous sheet length, and fiber length (see Figure 6b) gives us

$$\cos(\alpha - \beta) = (L^2 + L_{m_u}^2 - L_t^2)/(2 L L_{m_u}) \quad [37]$$

Combining [36] and [37] produces

$$\Delta L(2 L L_{m_u}) = \Delta L_{m_u}(L^2 + L_{m_u}^2 - L_t^2) \quad [38]$$

Writing this in infinitesimal form yields

$$\partial L(2L L_{m_u}) = \partial L_{m_u}(L^2 + L_{m_u}^2 - L_t^2) \quad [39]$$

which has the following solution:

$$L_{m_u} = c + \sqrt{(c^2 + L^2 - L_t^2)} \quad [40]$$

with

$$c = (L_t^2 - L_0^2 + L_{m_{uo}}^2)/(2 L_{m_{uo}}) \quad [41]$$

in which the parameters with subscript o are the lengths at optimal length of the muscle.

Formulas [40] and [41] were successfully applied in correcting the simple planimetric muscle model of Huijing and Woittiez [20], producing curves that fit their experimental results better than the curves from their own formulas. This is another relation between muscle length L_{m_u} and fiber length L, in addition to the one based on constancy of volume: As was shown above in that case, the distance between the tendinous sheets should remain constant, and the muscle length is then

$$L_{m_u} = \sqrt{(d^2 + (L_t + \sqrt{(L^2 - d^2)})^2)} \quad [42]$$

$$d = L_0 \sin \alpha_0 \quad [43]$$

APPENDIX H

Internal Muscle Pressure Calculated by Heukelom et al. [14] and a Suggested Alternative

Heukelom et al. [14] used the following argument. Of a cylindrical muscle (see Figure 8b, top), the volume is kept constant by letting the fibers bulge outward when the muscle is shortening in small steps, producing a barrel-shaped muscle. The total work produced by the muscle fibers together is calculated and is called W'_n. The subscript n indicates the step number of shortening. The work performed by the moving tendon plate is calculated in each step by summing the forces of the fibers multiplied by the cosine of their angles by the direction of pull and multiplied by the displacement of the tendon. The resulting quantity is called W_n, the external work done by the muscle. W_n and W'_n appear not to be the same. The authors argue that the difference between these quantities is used to build up pressure. Therefore, they let the pressure accumulate by the difference between W'_n and W_n divided by the product of tendon plate displacement and its surface:

$$P_n = \sum_{i=1}^{n} \frac{W'_i - W_i}{s(V/L_{mo})} \qquad \text{gram cm}^{-2} \qquad [44]$$

in which P_n is the pressure at the nth step, W'_i and W_i are the amounts of work as defined above at the ith step, s is the distance traveled by the tendon plate in each step, V is the volume of the muscle, and L_{mo} is the initial length of the muscle, so V/L_{mo} is the surface of the tendon plate. The authors gave all of the formulas needed to simulate the model, which I did. It appeared that W'_i is always smaller than W_i. That is, the muscle fibers produce less work than the muscle. According to formula [44], this should result in a negative pressure, but the pressure graphs as functions of shortening distance published by Heukelom et al. show only positive values. There is, however, a stronger objection against the argument used by the authors: There is no change in volume, so the law that pressure equals work divided by the change in volume cannot be used. The denominator of [44] is not the change in the volume of the muscle but the volume of external space traversed by the moving tendon plate. This exact volume is used in the bulging of the fibers. The numerator of [44] is net work that is produced by imposing muscle shortening and fiber shortening on the model. If work balance applies, this net work should be zero.

An alternative to the above model is the following: Consider a single muscle fiber with a square cross section of dimension $b \times b$ mm^2, length L mm, radius of curvature of R mm, and stress T N/mm^2 (see Figure 8a). The fiber carries a tensile force of

$$F = Tb^2 \qquad [45]$$

When this fiber is considered to consist of a great number of small, linked, rigid bodies of length ∂ (see Figure 8a), it can be seen that this tensile force produces a pressure on the concave side of the fiber with a magnitude of

$$P = \frac{T \, b^2 \, L \, \partial}{R \, b \, L \, \partial} = \frac{T \, b}{R} \qquad [46]$$

because of the curvature of the fiber. At every point of connection of the rigid bodies, the tensile forces make an angle of ∂/R with each other. Adding the two vectors in a direction perpendicular to the fiber locally produces the force drawn in Figure 8a, resulting in the pressure given above. When R is infinitely long (no fiber curvature), the pressure is zero.

Now consider a cylindrical muscle consisting of N curved fiber layers on top of each other, with decreasing fiber curvature from the periphery, where the curvature is $1/R$, to the center, where the curvature is zero. Let the fiber curvature decrease linearly with depth of the fiber in the muscle and let each fiber layer have thickness b (see Figure 8b). The layers are counted from 0 to N. The pressure in the center of the muscle is the sum of the contributions of the layers. Since the radius of curvature of the ith layer is

$$R_i = \frac{N}{N - i} \cdot R \qquad [47]$$

the pressure in the center of the muscle is

$$P = \sum_{i=0}^{i=N} T \, b \, \frac{(N - i)}{R \, N} \qquad [48]$$

$$= ((Tb)/(RN)) \cdot (N + (N + 1) + \ldots + 2 + 1 + 0) \qquad [49]$$

$$= ((Tb)/(RN)) \cdot (N(N + 1)/2) = T(N + 1)b/(2R) \qquad [50]$$

If we call the distance from the center of the muscle to the periphery

$$H = (N + 1)b, \qquad [51]$$

then

$$P = \frac{T \, H}{(2R)} \qquad [52]$$

which is a simple expression for the pressure inside a cylindrical muscle with peripheral fiber curvature, $1/R$, a half-thickness of H, and muscle fiber stress, T. In order to estimate the kind of pressure this may produce, given an extreme in muscle geometry, consider the following: An extreme in peripheral fiber curvature of a cylindrical muscle is

$$\frac{1}{R} = \frac{1}{H} \qquad [53]$$

Substituting this in [52] results in

$$P = \frac{T}{2} \qquad [54]$$

Since T is about 0.23 N/mm^2 maximally, the pressure can be about 0.115 N/mm^2, which is about 115 kPa, being more than 1 atm over pressure. Interestingly enough, formula [52] is scale independent because H/R is scale independent: If one increases all dimensions of a muscle, for instance, by a factor of two, both R and H will be twice as big, resulting in the same internal muscle pressure. This implies that the circulation in muscles of large animals is not more problematic than that in small animals, given the above considerations.

APPENDIX I

A Formula Giving Pressure Under a Flat Tendinous Sheet of a Unipinnate Muscle and Its Consequences for the Muscle Force Produced and the Muscle Geometry Required by Work Balance and Constancy in Volume
Consider Figure 9. If the tendinous sheet is described as a rigid body, a free body diagram can be drawn, resulting in the force equilibria and expressions of muscle force and a force producing pressure on the tendinous sheet, as shown in Figure 9. Since the total fiber force acts on the same surface as the force producing pressure, one can also write

$$P = \frac{T \sin (\alpha - \beta)}{\cos \beta} \qquad [55]$$

This is the pressure acting on the tendinous sheet produced by the muscle fibers, in which T is the muscle stress, α is the fiber angle, and β is the angle between the tendinous sheet and the tendon. The muscle force produced is

$$F_{m_u} = F_f \frac{\cos (\alpha)}{\cos (\beta)} \qquad [56]$$

which is different from the expression found above in formula [33]. Revisiting the problem of muscle work versus fiber work, the unipinnate muscle described here should have the following work balance:

$$F_f \Delta L = F_{m_u} \Delta L_{m_u} = F_f \frac{\cos (\alpha)}{\cos (\beta)} \Delta L_{m_u} \qquad [57]$$

so

$$\frac{\partial L_{m_u}}{\partial L} = \frac{\cos (\beta)}{\cos (\alpha)} \qquad [58]$$

From formula [31], which was based on constancy of volume, we know that in unipinnate muscles with force transmission in the direction of the tendinous sheet

$$\frac{\partial L_m}{\partial L} = \frac{1}{\cos (\alpha)} \qquad [59]$$

From Figure 6b we can see that

$$L_{m_u} = \sqrt{(L_m^2 + d^2)} \qquad [60]$$

and since

$$\frac{\partial L_{m_u}}{\partial L} = \frac{\partial L_{m_u}}{\partial L_m} \frac{\partial L_m}{\partial L} \qquad \text{(chainrule)} \qquad [61]$$

we obtain

$$\frac{\partial L_{m_u}}{\partial L} = \frac{(L_m / \sqrt{(L_m^2 + d^2)})}{\cos (\alpha)} = \frac{\cos (\beta)}{\cos (\alpha)} \qquad [62]$$

which is the same as formula [58], indicating that volume constancy in unipinnate muscles of the type in Figure 6b demands the same change in geometry during shortening as the one for work balance. This makes formulas [40] and [41] redundant, and formulas [42] and [43] can be used instead.

Besides this advantage, the extra piece of knowledge gained here is that the muscle force produced corresponds to formula [56], taking muscle pressure into account. This formula can produce some quite different results from those that occur simply by correcting the fiber force with the cosine of the fiber angle. For instance, if the angle between fibers and tendinous sheet α is $40°$ and the angle between tendon and tendinous sheet β is $20°$, then the ratio of muscle force to total fiber force is $\cos(40°)/\cos(20°) = 0.815$, according to formula [56], and $\cos(40° - 20°) = 0.940$, according to a direct correction of the force for the angle between fibers and tendon.

APPENDIX J

The Cissoid of Diocles Used by Gaspard Describing the Shape of Tendinous Sheets

If L is the fiber length of a muscle with fibers converging to one point (see Figure 12) and the muscle is positioned in a Cartesian coordinate system with its line of symmetry along the y-axis and the point to which the fibers converge on the origin, the following relation describes the necessary shape of the tendinous sheets that allow the muscle fibers to shorten equal percentages of their initial length.

$$y = \sqrt{\frac{x^3}{L - x}} \qquad [63]$$

This formula is that of a curve known as the "cissoid of Diocles." Figure 12 shows this curve in the shape of tendinous sheets.

APPENDIX K

The Shape of a Tendinous Sheet and the Pressure Under It

Figure 13a is a description of a tendinous sheet. It consists of a number of chains of elements connected by ball-and-socket joints. If the end elements of the chains are connected to some fixed point, like a tendon, the number of mechanical degrees of freedom of the sheet is

$$J = 3N_e \qquad [64]$$

in which N_e is the number of elements per chain. So this number is independent of the number of chains. These degrees of freedom are bending of the sheet perpendicular to the chains and two directions of torsion of the sheet. Bending of the sheet will be analyzed here.

Four forces acting on one element can be distinguished (Figure 13c): F_{p_i} is the force acting perpendicular on the element, directed outward; it is the force resulting from the intramuscular pressure. F_{f_i} is the force from the attached muscle fibers. F_{a_i} is the pulling force acting on the element from the $i - 1$th element, which originates in the tension in the sheet. F_{a_i+1} is the pulling force acting on the element from the $i + 1$th element. The angle between the line of pull of the muscle and the muscle fibers attaching to the ith element is called α_i and the angle between the ith element of the tendinous sheet and the line of pull is called β_i. The length of an element is ∂, while the width is Ω (see Figure 13c). If the ith element is in static equilibrium, the four forces cancel in terms of total force and moment, resulting in the following equations:

$$F_{f_i} \sin(\alpha_i + \beta_i) + F_{a_i} \sin(\beta_i - \beta_{i-1}) \qquad [65]$$
$$+ F_{a_i+1} \sin(\beta_{i+1} - \beta_i) - F_{p_i} = 0$$

$$F_{f_i} \cos(\alpha_i + \beta_i) + F_{a_i} \cos(\beta_i - \beta_{i-1}) \qquad [66]$$
$$- F_{a_i} \cos(\beta_{i+1} - \beta_i) = 0$$

$$F_{a_i} \sin(\beta_i - \beta_{i-1})\partial/2 \qquad [67]$$
$$- F_{a_i+1} \sin(\beta_{i+1} - \beta_i)\partial/2 = 0$$

Equation [65] describes the sum of the force components perpendicular to the ith element, while equation [66] describes the sum of the force components in the plane of the ith element in the direction of the chain of elements described above. Equation [67] describes the sum of the moments acting on the ith element. The forces acting between chains, in planes other than the one in which the above-mentioned vectors lie, are neglected, which can be done if the muscle fibers lie in planes parallel to the line of pull of the muscle. If we define

$$\Delta F_{a_i} = F_{a_{i-1}} - F_{a_i} \qquad [68]$$

and divide [67] by $\partial/2$, we obtain

$$F_{a_i} \sin(\beta_i - \beta_{i-1}) = F_{a_i} \sin(\beta_{i+1} - \beta_i) + \Delta F_{a_i} \sin(\beta_{i+1} - \beta_i) \quad [69]$$

For very small ∂, approaching $\partial = 0$, the following relations hold:

$$\frac{d\beta^2}{d^2s} \approx \frac{(\beta_{i+1} - \beta_i)/\partial - (\beta_i - \beta_{i-1})/\partial}{\partial} \qquad [70]$$

$$\sin(\beta_{i+1} - \beta_i) \approx (\beta_{i+1} - \beta_i); \qquad \sin(\beta_i - \beta_{i-1}) \approx (\beta_i - \beta_{i-1}) \quad [71]$$
$$\frac{\Delta F_{a_i}}{\partial} \approx \frac{dF_{a_i}}{ds} \qquad [72]$$

in which s is the position parameter along the chain of infinitesimal small elements of the tendinous sheet. Substituting [71] in [70] and the result together with [72] in [69] gives

$$\frac{F_a \, d\beta^2}{d^2s} + \frac{dF_a}{ds} \frac{d\beta}{ds} = 0 \qquad [73]$$

Here the subscript i has been left out because, if the equation applies to the ith element, it applies to all elements of the chain. If the fiber stress is called T, the following relation holds:

$$F_{f_i} = T \, \partial \, \Omega \, \sin (\alpha_i + \beta_i) \qquad [74]$$

The term $\sin(\alpha_i + \beta_i)$ corrects for the angle between the fibers and the ith element of the sheet, because this angle determines the cross-sectional area of muscle fibers that attaches to the element. The component of F_{f_i} in the plane of the ith element is

$$F_{f_{a_i}} = \Delta F_{a_i} = T \, \partial \, \Omega \, \sin (\alpha_i + \beta_i) \cos (\alpha_i + \beta_i) \qquad [75]$$

which is the amount of force added to the chain of elements at the location of the ith element. Dividing this by ∂ and putting it in infinitesimal form yields:

$$\frac{dF_a}{ds} = T \, \Omega \, \sin (\alpha + \beta) \cos (\alpha + \beta) = T \, \Omega \, 1/2 \sin (2\alpha + 2\beta) \qquad [76]$$

If we rewrite [73] we obtain

$$\frac{d\beta^2/d^2s}{d\beta/ds} = -\frac{dF_a/ds}{F_a} \qquad [77]$$

Integrating both sides of [77] in the β domain and substituting [76] in it produces

$$\int \frac{dk}{k} = -\int \frac{T \, \Omega \, 1/2 \sin (2\alpha + 2\beta)}{F_a k} \, d\beta \qquad [78]$$

in which

$$k = \frac{d\beta}{ds} \qquad [79]$$

which is the curvature of the sheet. Since

$$\frac{d(F_a d\beta/ds)}{ds} = \frac{F_a d\beta^2}{d^2s} + \left(\frac{dF_a}{ds}\right)\left(\frac{d\beta}{ds}\right) = 0 \qquad [80]$$

(see formula [73]), we can write

$$F_a k = F_a(0)\, k(0) \qquad [81]$$

in which $F_a(0)$ is the force in the sheet at the edge farthest away from the tendon and $k(0)$ is the curvature there. Since the stress in the tendinous sheet at the edge depends on the fiber stress and the thickness of the sheet at the edge, one may postulate that the thickness of the sheet at the edge is such that (given the strength of tendinous sheet relative to that of muscle fiber) the sheet can carry the force produced by the attaching muscle fibers. If we call the strength of tendinous sheet relative to that of muscle fiber B (that is on the order of 300 if one looks at the cross-sectional area of a tendon and that of the attached muscle fibers) and the thickness of the sheet at the edge $D(0)$, we can write

$$F_a k = F_a(0)\, k(0) = T_a(0)\, D(0)\, k(0)\, \Omega \qquad [82]$$

and since

$$T_a(0) = BT \qquad [83]$$

we can rewrite [78] as

$$\int \frac{dk}{k} = -\frac{1}{2BD(0)\, k(0)} \int \sin(2\alpha + 2\beta)d\beta \qquad [84]$$

which, in turn, leads to

$$\ln k = \frac{\cos(2\alpha + 2\beta)}{4BD(0)\, k(0)} + C \qquad [85]$$

in which C is a constant. Rewriting this formula gives

$$k = A \exp\left[\frac{\cos{(2\alpha + 2\beta)}}{(4BD(0)\ k(0))}\right] \qquad [86]$$

in which A is a constant. This can be solved by substituting the zero conditions and the fact that $\beta(0) = -\alpha(0)$, which means that the fibers attach at the edge of the sheet in a plane tangent to the sheet:

$$k = k(0) \exp\left[\frac{(\cos{(2\alpha + 2\beta)} - 1)}{(4BD(0)\ k(0))}\right] \qquad [87]$$

offering a fairly simple description of the shape of a tendinous sheet with local sheet curvature k, edge curvature $k(0)$, local fiber angle α, local sheet angle β, sheet strength relative to fiber strength B, and edge thickness $D(0)$. The pressure directly under the sheet can be found in the following way: From [65] and [74] we get

$$P\ \Omega\ ds = T\ \Omega\ ds\ \sin^2(2\alpha + 2\beta) + 2Fa\ d\beta$$
$$+ T\ \Omega\ 1/2\sin{(2\alpha + 2\beta)}\ d\beta\ ds \qquad [88]$$

which leads to

$$P = T\sin^2(2\alpha + 2\beta) + \frac{2Fak}{\Omega} \qquad [89]$$

and using [82] and [83]

$$P = T[\sin^2(2\alpha + 2\beta) + 2BD(0)\ k(0)] \qquad [90]$$

Here we have the pressure under a curved tendinous sheet with stress of attaching muscle fibers T, edge curvature $k(0)$, local fiber angle α, local sheet angle β, sheet strength relative to fiber strength B, and edge thickness $D(0)$.

ACKNOWLEDGMENTS

The author would like to thank G.E. Loeb for suggestions regarding the field to cover in this chapter. Mrs. F. Kahabuka is thanked for her cooperation in some experiments. Dr. Boisen Møller was kind enough to point out the early work on muscle architecture by his compatriot, Niels Stensen.

REFERENCES

1. Abrahams, M. Mechanical behaviour of a tendon in vitro. *Med. Biol. Eng.* 5:433–443, 1967.

2. Alexander, R. McN. *Animal Mechanics*. London: Sidgwick and Jackson, 1968, p. 346.
3. Arnold, G. Biomechanische und rheologische Eigenschaften mensliche Sehnen. *Z. Anat. Entwickl. Gesch.* 143:263–300, 1974.
4. Baskin, R.J., and P.J. Paolini. Volume change and pressure development in muscle during contraction. *Am. J. Physiol.* 213:1025–1030, 1967.
5. Benninghoff, A., and H. Rollhäuser. Zur inneren Mechanik des gefiederten Muskels. *Pflügers Arch.* 254:527–548, 1952.
6. Beritoff, J. Über die Kontraktionsfähigkeit des Skelettmuskeln. IV. Mitteilung. Über die physiologische Bedeutung des gefiederten Baues der Muskeln. *Pflügers Arch.* 209:763–778, 1925.
7. Decraemer, W.F., M.A. Maes, and V.J. Vanhuyse. An elastic stress–strain relation for soft biological tissues based on a structural model. *J. Biomechanics* 13:463–468, 1980.
8. Fick, R. Handbuch der anatomie und mechanik der gelenke. In: *Bardelebens Handbuch der Anatomie des Menschen*, Bd. 2, Abt. 1, Teil 2, Jena: Verlag von Gustav Fisher 1910, p. 376.
9. Gans, C., and W.J. Bock. The functional significance of muscle architecture—a theoretical analysis. *Ergebn. Anat. Entw. Gesch.* 38:115–142, 1965.
10. Gans, C. Fiber architecture and muscle function. In R.L. Teijung (ed.). *Exercise and Sport Sciences Reviews*. Philadelphia: Franklin Institute Press, 1982, pp. 160–207.
11. Gaspard, M. Introduction à l'analyse bio-mathématique de l'architecture des muscles. *Extrait Arch. Anat. Hist. Embryol. Norm.* 48:95–146, 1965.
12. Gordon, A.M., F.J. Julian, and A.F. Huxley. The variation in isometric tension with sarcomere length in vertebrate muscle fibers. *J. Physiol.* 184:170–192, 1966.
13. Hatze, H.A. A general myocybernetic control model of skeletal muscle. *Biol. Cybern.* 28:143–157, 1978.
14. Heukelom, B., A. van der Stelt, and P.C. Diegenbach. A simple anatomical model of muscle and the effects of internal pressure. *Bull. Math. Biol.* 41:791–802, 1979.
15. Hill, A.V. The pressure developed in muscle during contraction. *J. Physiol. (Lond.)* 107:518–526, 1948.
16. Huijing, P.A., and R.D. Woittiez. The effect of architecture on skeletal muscle performance: A simple planimetric model. *Neth. J. Zool.* 34:21–32, 1984.
17. Julian, F.J., and R.L. Moss. Sarcomere length–tension relations of frog skinned muscle fibers at lengths above the optimum. *J. Physiol.* 304:529–539, 1980.
18. Loeb, G.E., C.A. Pratt, C.M. Chanaud, and F.J.R. Richmond. Distribution and innervation of short, interdigitated muscle fibers in parallel-fibered muscles of the cat hindlimb. *J. Morphol.* 191:1–17, 1987.
19. Otten, E. Morphometrics and force–length relations of skeletal muscles. In A. Winter et al. (eds.). *International Series on Biomechanics (ISB), Biomechanics*, Vol. IX. Champaign, Ill.: Human Kinetic Publishers, 1985, pp. 27–32.
20. Otten, E. Some numerical reflections upon the simple planimetric muscle model of Huijing and Woittiez. *Neth. J. Zool.* 35:517–520, 1985.
21. Otten, E. Optimal design of vertebrate and insect sarcomeres. *J. Morphol.* 191:49–63, 1987.
22. Otten, E. A myocybernetic model of the jaw system of the rat. *J. Neurosci. Methods.* in press, 1987.
23. Petrofsky, J.S., and D.M. Hendershot. The interrelationship between blood pressure, intramuscular pressure, and isometric endurance in fast and slow twitch skeletal muscle in the cat. *Eur. J. Appl. Physiol.* 53:106–111, 1984.
24. Pfuhl, W. Die gefiederten Muskeln, ihre Form und ihre Wirkungsweise. *Zeitschr. Anat. Entwicklungsgesch.* 106:749–769, 1937.
25. Poliacu Prosé, L. De functionele stabiliteit van de knie van de kat. Thesis, Free University of Amsterdam, 1985, p. 265.
26. Rack, P.M.H., and D.R. Westbury. Elastic properties of the cat soleus tendon and their functional importance. *J. Physiol.* 379:479–495, 1984.

27. Scherz, G. *Pionier der Wissenschaft. Niels Stensen in seinen Schriften.* Copenhagen: Munks-gaard, 1963.
28. Stelt, A. van der. Spiermechanica en myotoombouw bij vissen. Thesis, University of Amsterdam, 1968, p. 9.
29. Stephens, J.A., R.M. Reinking, and D.G. Stuart. The motor units of cat medial gas-trocnemius: Electrical and mechanical properties as a function of muscle length. *J. Morphol.* 146:495–512, 1978.
30. Willemse, J.J. Some characteristics of muscle fibers in a pennate muscle. *Proc. Kon. Ned. Akad. Wet.* Ser. C., 66:162–171, 1963.
31. Woittiez, R.D., P.A. Huijing, H.B.K. Boom, and R.H. Rozendal. A three-dimensional muscle model: A quantified relation between form and function of skeletal muscles. *J. Morphol.* 182:95–113, 1984.

4
Force Sensation in Fresh and Fatigued Human Skeletal Muscle

E. CAFARELLI, Ph.D.

"Force, if unassisted by judgement, collapses through its own mass."
HORACE, circa 45 B.C.

"Thinking is to me the greatest fatigue in the world:"
SIR JOHN VANBRUGH, 1696

INTRODUCTION

The contraction of any skeletal muscle is accompanied by sensations that describe such things as force, velocity and position, as well as the effort needed to accomplish the contraction. The subject of this chapter is the sensation of force that occurs during contraction and the effects that fatigue and, to the extent that data are available, training, have on it. In the course of reviewing these issues, the distinction between sense of force and sense of effort will be clarified. An attempt will be made to place force sensation in its proper functional context within the neuromuscular system and to consider the adaptive value of a sense of force. At the outset, it should be apparent that there would be no precise motor control without feedback. Similarly, it should be apparent that when the acuity of force sensation deteriorates, so does the quality of motor performance. Finally, the force-sensing mechanism is adaptable; the same force produces different sensations when fatigue, training, or disease changes the muscle's capacity to generate force.

To address each of these points, the literature will be discussed in terms of the diagram shown in Figure 1. This particular construction has certain limitations, but it contains those elements that are important for describing force sensations. Three basic areas are shown in the diagram. The first is skeletal muscle itself, which contains metabolic pathways (METAB), the contractile apparatus (CONTR), and peripheral receptors (RECPT). The second area comprises the cardiovascular and respiratory systems that support the energetics of contraction by resupply and removal. The area most difficult to study is contained almost entirely within the central nervous system. Motor output from the motor cortex is shown, along with the force-sensing mechanism (see Terminology). The motor neuron pool represents all the motor neurons available for activity.

139

FIGURE 1

Model of the neuromuscular system, showing the input of feedforward and feedback elements to the force-sensing mechanism. Motor output descends through the motor neuron pool, where it is augmented or reduced by feedback from peripheral receptors (RECPT). The neural drive thus produced operates the contractile elements of muscle (CONTR). Metabolic pathways (METAB) make energy available to fuel the contractile process. Substrate supply and metabolite removal are accomplished as part of the functions of the cardiovascular (CV) and respiratory (RESP) systems. The metabolic rate is coupled to the rate and intensity of activity of the contractile proteins, and both of these influence receptor activity. A copy of the motor output is fed forward directly to the force-sensing mechanism, as well as eliciting an anticipatory response from the cardiovascular and respiratory systems. It is possible that feedforward and feedback are compared either in the force-sensing mechanism or at the segmental level Σ. For simplicity, Renshaw cell activity is included in the comparator Σ.

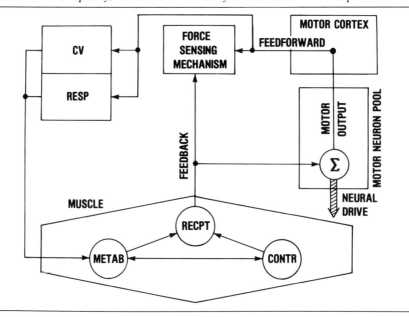

Purposeful motor activity is largely initiated from the motor cortex [22, 61, 65]. This activity descends through the cord and impinges on the motor neuron pool [23]. A copy of the central signal probably irradiates to the cardiovascular and respiratory centers to invoke anticipatory activation of those systems [112, 113]. A wealth of indirect evidence indicates that a copy of the motor outflow is sent to the force-sensing mechanism and produces conscious sensation [26, 44, 45, 96, 97, 100]. Various peripheral receptors detect and transmit information from active muscle to the CNS [84]. Peripheral feedback goes directly to the force-sensing mechanism and also influences central outflow when it arrives at the motor neuron pool [22, 69, 121]. The resulting neural drive to muscle is a version of the central outflow modified by receptor input.

The role of the cardiovascular and respiratory systems, though over-simplified in Figure 1, is to support the energetics of muscle contraction. The pattern of contraction of muscle activated by neural control pro-foundly influences both metabolic and receptor activity [20, 55]. Most of the data in the literature are consistant with this arrangement [65, 66, 67, 69, 104]. It is also the intention of this chapter to suggest the arrangement of the neuromuscular system shown in Figure 1 as a work-ing model of sensory processes in the human neuromuscular system. Future experiments could then be conducted based on hypotheses de-rived from the model and the resulting data used to revise the model.

Terminology

The terms used to describe the mechanisms by which intramuscular force is sensed are as varied as any in physiology. For example, the notion of central feedforward has, at different times, been referred to as the "sense of innervation," "sense of will," "corollary discharge," and "efference copy," to name a few [1, 7, 9, 44, 86, 100, 101, 116, 123, 124, 125]. These terms originally reflected different points of view, but they are currently used almost interchangeably. Since it is beyond the scope of this chapter to consider all of the subtleties of each term, a simplified nomenclature has been adopted. Herewith a glossary of terms and their definitions:

SENSE OF FORCE. The distinct feeling of force generated by an active muscle or a muscle group during contraction. The sense of force, as well as the sensations of position and movement, are thought to constitute the complete muscular or kinesthetic sense [92, 98, 111].

SENSORIUM. The entire sensory apparatus, including the cerebrum, that is the organ of sensation. The force-sensing mechanism shown in Figure 1 is undoubtedly part of the sensorium.

FORCE-SENSING MECHANISM. Hypothetical mechanism within the sensorium that is responsible for sensing force and effort.

FEEDFORWARD. The motor outflow, fed forward from the motor cor-tex to the sensory cortex, that produces conscious force sensation [111]. In some respects, it represents the expectations of the neuromuscular system for a given command [95, 96, 111, 117, 121]. Although anatomical connections exist that could subserve a feedforward signal, no direct measurements of it have ever been made [97]. It must be emphasized that feedforward is a central phenomenon that does not require feedback from peripheral receptors.

FEEDBACK. The afferent inflow from sensory receptors in muscles and joints back to the sensorium. Although Golgi tendon organs are the putative tension receptors, there is some evidence that muscle spindles may also contribute to force sensation [29, 30, 78, 111].

NEURAL DRIVE. The electrical signal that drives the muscle. It arrives via alpha motor neurons, and the best available measure of overall neural drive is the surface electromyogram (EMG) [5, 6, 12, 13, 40, 99]. This means that what leaves the motor cortex is modulated by inhibitory and excitatory influences of segmental reflexes, especially from the gamma system, and depends on high-fidelity transmission of action potentials across the neuromuscular junction [15, 99, 105]. The total electrical energy contained in the EMG is a function of the number of motor units being recruited, the size of the motor units, and their frequency of activation [5, 13, 19].

MAXIMAL VOLUNTARY CONTRACTION (MVC). The most force a muscle or a muscle group can generate in a given position. When used as a reference point for neuromuscular function, force is often expressed relative to MVC when all motor units are maximally activated. As early as 1954, Merton [99] demonstrated that MVC is truly maximal and that no amount of additional stimulation can significantly increase force production. However, recent reports suggest that true maximality may be muscle or muscle group dependent [8, 90].

HISTORY

Several excellent reviews give an account of contemporary thinking about the muscular sense from 1800 to the present. Perhaps the most complete treatment of this area of physiology is provided by McCloskey [96, 97]. Granit's introductory chapter in the *Handbook of Physiology* offers an excellent review and puts the question of the muscle sense in the larger context of motor control [60]. Another thoughtful synthesis of data on the muscular sense is Matthews' review, in which he discusses the role of the muscle spindle in muscle sensation [92]. The reviews of Roland [111], Evarts [44], and, in an earlier volume of this series, Goodwin [57] all discuss, from different perspectives, sensory processes in muscle that may contribute to force sensation. For a more general overview and an introduction to the topic, see the paper by Merton in *Scientific American* [102].

The number of recent reviews makes it unnecessary to reiterate the entire history of force sensation. Instead, this chapter will provide a synopsis of that history, concentrating especially on the question of central feedforward and peripheral feedback elements and how they may contribute to our understanding of muscle sensory processes during fatigue and after training.

In 1826 Sir Charles Bell published a paper in the *Transactions of the Royal Society* in which he discussed neural connections from skeletal muscle to brain and from brain back to muscle [9]. These neural circuits implied that the brain somehow "told" the muscles what to do and the muscles, in turn, informed the brain of the consequences of muscular actions. Later in the nineteenth century, George Henry Lewes warily suggested that outgoing motor impulses might somehow contribute to the "degree of . . . effort . . . a movement demands" [86]. One of the facts upon which he based his speculation was that passive movement (a limb being moved by someone else) was largely devoid of sensation. To Lewes this meant that the motor drive to muscle, absent in passive movement, was part of the sensory process.

The notion that muscle sensation can be generated entirely within the central nervous system without benefit of feedback from peripheral receptors is usually credited to Herman von Helmholtz [123] but according to Steinbach, the idea dates back to the ancient Greeks [116]. Helmholtz's arguments were based on his observations of position sense in the eyes. He noted that when the ocular muscles were paralyzed, an attempt to rotate the eyeballs was sensed as if movement actually occurred, even though nothing at all had happened. Moreover, if the paralysis was incomplete, the rotation was grossly exaggerated. Helmholtz reasoned that this was because the partially paralyzed muscles required a greater amount of conscious effort to drive them. Hence, he said that muscle sensation, at least as far as it is represented by eyeball rotation, is "simply the result of the effort of will" [123].

Von Helmholtz's view of muscle sensation prevailed into the mid-twentieth century [99, 100]. In contrast, C.S. Sherrington, who was well aware of the density and complexity of muscle receptors, argued that not only did these receptors participate in motor reflexes, but they also transmitted information to the sensorium and thus "subserved the muscular sense" [114]. Nevertheless, the idea that muscular sensations were centrally generated held sway, and the formidable array of peripheral receptors known to exist in muscle were consigned to mediating reflexes, an activity that was thought to be insentient [100, 101].

One of the most convincing demonstrations that force sensation is not just a simple analogue of intramuscular tension is the observation that during fatigue any weight feels progressively heavier. It was speculated that the growing sensory intensity was due to the constantly increasing amount of motor output required to maintain any force [86, 100]. Similarly, it was observed that muscles weakened by partial paralysis or stroke responded in the same way [45, 46, 47]. Presumably, the total motor output always stays the same, and only muscle tissue can alter its ability to respond to any given signal.

The literature before 1970 is almost completely devoid of data that would suggest the participation of peripheral muscle receptors in signaling force to the sensorium. In making a case for the preeminence of peripheral feedback, Sherrington and others defended their positions with philosophical arguments rather than empirical data [114]. Thus the idea that force sensation is a centrally generated phenomenon remained firmly in place until about the middle of the twentieth century. In fact, the entire question slipped into obscurity and was replaced by other questions that seemed less metaphysical and could be answered with the techniques available to contemporary investigators.

An exception is the body of work published in Europe that supports the idea that peripheral muscle receptors contribute to conscious sensation of force. VonFrey, Renqvst, and Goldscheider [all cited in 60] each published papers that were essentially in agreement with Sherrington, while at the same time not completely dismissing the Helmholtzian premise that force sensation may have a centrally generated component. The work of these investigators and its relevance in the context of motor control is reviewed by Granit [60].

The question of muscular sentience was revived in the 1950s. First, Sperry's work with fish [115] and then von Holst's with insects [124] indicated that the position of the visual field is determined by contraction of the ocular muscles and that the efferent drive to these muscles is sensed somewhere in the animal's brain. Similar and perhaps more compelling arguments were made by Brindley and Merton with data from experiments on human ocular muscles [21]. They observed that when the eyeballs were rotated passively, there was no sense of which way the eyes were pointing. If the eyeballs were rotated voluntarily, eye position was known even when the movement was made in darkness or when the ocular muscles had been anesthetized [21]. These authors concluded that skeletal muscle was incapable of signaling conscious sensations of force and position. This view was supported by Gelfan and Carter [53], who reported that when the exposed wrist tendons of patients undergoing surgery were pulled, there was no appreciable sensation, but when the subjects moved their fingers voluntarily, it was clearly sensed. However, Matthews and Simmonds were unable to replicate this study [93].

The past two decades have seen a resurgence of interest in this area, much of the research attempting to show that peripheral feedback is indeed important in sensing force [47, 110, 111]. This research has been conducted on humans, and considerable effort has been directed to separating out central and peripheral sources of force sensation. Attempts to uncouple muscle receptor activity from muscle function include such perturbations as local anesthesia, paralysis, and high-frequency vibration. The last excites peripheral receptors far in excess of muscle tension or stretch. These experiments indicate that when the normal peripheral feedback is disrupted, the sensation of force is also disrupted, indicating that force sensation requires an element of peripheral feedback [29, 47, 48, 50, 78, 111].

Current research has reinforced the idea that force sensation probably comprises both feedforward and feedback elements [44, 92, 96, 97]. This has led to the resolution of the question "Is there a difference between the sense of force and the sense of effort?". There seems to be little doubt that these are separate entities and that the sense of force is derived from peripheral feedback and the sense of effort from central feedforward. This explanation goes a long way toward explaining why a given force feels greater as fatigue progresses. Nevertheless, the manner in which feedforward and feedback interact to permit judgments about muscular performance has yet to be elucidated. Although it appears that humans prefer to attend to feedforward at the expense of feedback information [97], it is also likely that both elements are required to sense force at different muscle lengths. Moreover, it is not known how these mechanisms function during progressive fatigue or how they respond to hypertrophy.

Experiments to determine the interaction of feedforward and feedback elements in force sensation often attempt, in a variety of ways, to uncouple muscle tension from neural drive. The most obvious methods are anesthesia or paralysis by injection of various drugs to block afferent feedback or to prevent an otherwise normal muscle from responding to neural drive [35, 45, 47, 51, 58, 91]. Another manipulation is to induce fatigue, which increases neural drive to maintain a desired force [2, 14, 30, 49, 74, 75, 77, 85]. A useful perturbation is to alter the starting length of a muscle before producing a static contraction [27]. Because the maximal force that a muscle can produce is a function of its length, a muscle can be made weaker or stronger by altering the position of its joint.

Other methods of uncoupling muscle tension from neural drive require special attention. The first is vibration, which is a powerful tool for studying neuromuscular function [29, 42, 63, 64, 78, 98]. Vibration experiments, however, have produced conflicting results; therefore, a separate subsection of this chapter will be devoted to vibration experiments and their interpretation. Training is a method not often used, probably because of the amount of time required to induce it, but is one that may be of paramount interest to the readers of this volume. When muscle is exposed to a resistance overload, its normal adaptive mechanism is to hypertrophy and thus to increase its maximal force-generating capacity [55, 56]. The sensory consequence of this adaptation is that any absolute force feels like less than it did before training began. We know this intuitively, but there are almost no experimental data in the literature that support the intuition. The mechanism for this sensory adaptation is not known, and there are only preliminary data available, which suggest that the answer is not as straightforward as it may seem [36].

MEASUREMENT

The study of conscious force sensation in humans limits the number of experimental techniques that are permissible [126]. Therefore, many experiments must combine behavioral observations with physiological data to explain this phenomenon.

When measuring force sensation, it is necessary to use the subject as an instrument of measurement [4]. As with any measurement, the instrument must have a scale and the scale must be calibrated. The measurement of force sensation depends on two basic elements. The first is the instructions given to subjects prior to the experiment. In some cases, they are instructed to judge the degree of effort required to perform a contraction; in others, they are specifically instructed to judge force; and in still others, they are simply told to judge how a contraction feels in some unspecified way. The instructions determine the cast of the data and hence their interpretation [89]. The second element is the method of measurement itself. Force sensation is usually measured by matching sensory intensity to a number or to a contraction in a contralateral limb that feels exactly the same [27, 98]. Some of these techniques are described below.

Category Scales
When force is matched to a number, the method can take several forms. A convenient method is to use a category scale with a short sequence of consecutive numbers and perhaps some descriptive words or phrases such as the scale for rating perceived exertion (RPE) or the scale used by Killian and Campbell to measure dyspnea [81]. Category scales are useful for comparing the absolute level of sensation between subjects and have been used extensively to study sensory processes during dynamic exercise [18]. The major disadvantage of category scales is that they have no ratio properties and thus are inappropriate for studying the gain of the sensory system over a range of stimulus intensities [54, 89]. Another disadvantage of category scales is that they have an obvious upper limit. This means that the subject maps out some strategy for conserving numbers on the scale during the course of the experiment; for example, "20" on the RPE scale must correspond to either maximal oxygen consumption, MVC, the limit of endurance, or the end of the experiment. The effect this has on the true response characteristics of a sensory system is not known.

Direct Scaling Techniques: Magnitude Estimation and Production
An alternative method for measuring sensory processes in man is the method of magnitude estimation. This is a direct scaling technique whereby the subject assigns numbers in proportion to the magnitude of the simulus intensity. A faithful representation of the response characteristics

FIGURE 2

Fictitious data from a magnitude estimation experiment of force sensation during brief static contractions. When the data are plotted in linear coordinates, they form a positively accelerated curve showing that the sensory response of the system is more sensitive to changes in force production at higher forces. The curve can be straightened by plotting the data in logarithmic coordinates as shown. Linear regression analysis of the logarithmically transformed data fits a power function of the form $y = a + x^b$. The function shown here has an exponent, or slope, of 1.7, a standard value for data obtained in this way. The slope describes the gain of the system or how it responds to changes in force production.

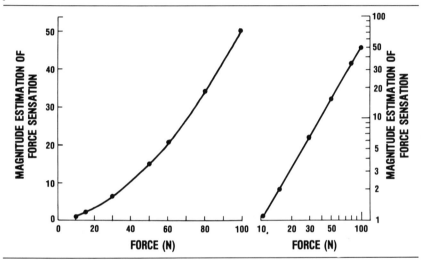

of the system is produced because there are no limits to the number scale [54, 89]. For the same reason, magnitude estimation is not the technique of choice for making absolute interindividual comparisons; it is better suited to determining the rate at which sensation increases per unit increase in stimulus intensity. Another way to express this is to ask if the increase in force sensation is the same for every unit increase in force production over the whole force range. In fact it is not, and this illustrates another disadvantage of magnitude estimation: It generates nonlinear functions that require transformation and curve fitting [120]. It turns out that the sensations generated during various forms of exercise behave in the way other sensory modalities do and conform to the power law [119]. This means that the data that relate how sensory intensity varies as a function of stimulus intensity are best fit with a power function (see Figure 2). Using this method, it has been confirmed that the exponent of the function (the regression coefficient calculated from logarithmically transformed data) that relates force sensation to achieved force is about 1.7, which means that sensory intensity varies as the stimulus intensity raised to the 1.7th power [117, 119]. More importantly, this exponent represents the gain of the system and is invariant among subjects and among a variety of skeletal muscles [117, 119]. The reader who is using this technique for the first time should see the chapter on the magnitude estimation experiment in Marks [89].

Other direct scaling techniques have been used infrequently to study force sensation. A companion to magnitude estimation is magnitude production, in which the subject produces a force to match a given numerical magnitude. The ratio techniques of estimation and production require that forces be generated or judged in proportion to each other. For example, the instruction to "produce a force that is twice as great as the previous one" or the question "if the first force was 20% of your maximum, what percentage is this one?" are typical of these methods. These techniques all share the advantages and disadvantages of magnitude estimation and, in some cases, may depend on the subject's ability to use numbers. Magnitude estimation, because of its simplicity and because it reveals the operating characteristics of the modality, appears to be the method of choice in experiments requiring direct scaling [54, 89].

The Matching Technique
All psychophysical scaling techniques involve matching sensory intensity of one modality to something else, either a number or another sensory modality, such as the loudness of a tone to the force of muscular contraction [89]. There is, however, a technique that involves matching the force of one muscular contraction to the force of another. This works best in bilateral muscle pairs but is also possible in muscles that are vastly different in size and usage, such as adductor pollicis matched to quadriceps femoris [R.J. Cannon, unpublished observations].

The technique was first introduced by McCloskey et al. [98] and has since been used with considerable success in other laboratories [27, 28]. The subject is provided with visual feedback about the force of a contraction in the muscle of interest. Instructions are given to make a contraction of the contralateral, or matching, muscle that feels like the same force. The force of the matching contraction is thus a measure of force sensation in the reference muscle. A more complete description of this technique may be found in reference 26. A disadvantage of the matching technique is that it is technically more elaborate than scaling with numbers, because it requires force-measuring devices for two muscle groups as well as visual feedback for the subject. Moreover, it is suitable only for static contractions of bilateral muscle pairs.

There are several advantages in using the matching technique, pri-

FIGURE 3

Matching forces for several reference forces produced by the triceps. Data are from one subject. When muscle lengths were adjusted so that MVC (symbols with error bars) was about equal in both arms, the slope of the matching function was about 1.0. Adjusting muscle lengths so that there was about a 2 to 1 difference in MVC gave a matching function with slope of about 2.0 (middle function). When the muscle lengths were changed so that the difference between the MVCs was fourfold, the matching function had a slope of about 4.0 (upper function). These data illustrate that the neuromuscular system is capable of adjusting its sensory response to acute changes in force-producing capacity. (From Cafarelli, E., and B. Bigland-Ritchie. Sensation of static force in muscles of different length. Exp. Neurol. *65:511–525, 1979.)*

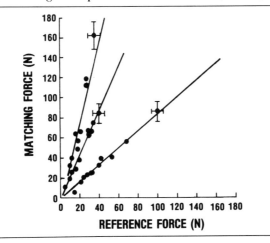

mary among them being the precision of measurement and the sensitivity of the technique to a wide variety of perturbations [27]. The matching technique provides linear functions because the exponent for force sensation in both muscles will be about 1.7 and plotting these two similar but nonlinear functions against each other will give a linear function.

A noteworthy characteristic of the force-sensing mechanism is that it is apparently capable of making relative judgments. For example, when two muscles have quite different MVCs, 50% MVC in one muscle feels like 50% MVC in the other muscle even though the absolute forces are considerably different [27]. An example of this is given by a subject who showed large left-right differences in triceps MVC when the muscle lengths were changed independently (Figure 3). When length was adjusted so that the MVCs in both muscles were about the same, the matching function had a slope of about 1.0. When the lengths were adjusted so that the left MVC was twice as great as the right, the slope of the line was about 2.0 (middle function). When the left muscle was at optimal length and the other was weakened by shortening it, the ratio between the MVCs and the slope of the matching function was about 4.0 [27]. These data illustrate the sensitivity of the matching technique and the ability of the neuromuscular system to adjust immediately for acute changes in force-generating capacity. They also illustrate the importance of the central feedforward element in muscle sensations.

Constant Effort

Some investigators have studied force sensation using a technique called "constant effort" [31, 32, 33, 34, 76, 107]. In this method, the subject is initially instructed to make a contraction, the intensity of which is controlled by visual feedback. Once the desired intensity has been achieved, the visual feedback is removed and the subject then attempts to keep the force or effort constant, depending on the instructions. Invariably, the force sensation or effort is kept constant by reducing the force, and the time course of this function is extremely reproducible (Figure 4). Constant effort functions are best fit with a double exponential function to an asymptote after about 2 minutes, and both rate constants are independent of the initial force [32, 107]. The complex curve fitting involved is of little relevance, except insofar as the constants help describe some physiological process. This technique is highly reproducible and does not rely on the subject's use of the number scale. On the other hand, it does not permit steady-state measurements and the functions generated require extensive curve fitting. However, given that it is one of the few nonnumber matching techniques available for measuring force sensation during dynamic work, its use has been relatively limited [107].

EFFECT OF VIBRATION ON FORCE SENSATION

High-frequency vibration has been used on several occasions to study neuromuscular function [29, 30, 38, 58, 59, 63]. When vibration between 100 and 200 Hz is applied to a muscle tendon, it excites most muscle receptors, especially the spindle primary endings [11, 25, 39]. Golgi tendon organs, pacinian corpuscles, and probably the free nerve endings also respond to vibration, but to a lesser extent than spindles [11]. As a result of spindle activation, a continuous tonic vibration reflex (TVR) is initiated and the muscle shortens [41, 43]. In the unloaded state, this can be demonstrated by flexing the shoulder with the upper arm horizontal and the forearm perpendicular. A vibrator held against the triceps tendon will cause the triceps to contract and the elbow to extend. If the joint is prevented from moving, TVR may produce anywhere from 5 to 30% MVC force [29, 41].

The value of the TVR in studying muscle sensory processes is that force produced by a spinal reflex does not require any central motor

FIGURE 4

Constant effort functions for handgrip contractions at three different starting intensities. Once the initial force was achieved, subjects were instructed to keep force sensation constant. No visual feedback was provided. The data have been fit with a double exponential of the form $y = ae^{-\alpha t} + be^{-\beta t} + c$. Functions on the left are from Pandolf and Cain, 1974 (N = 6), and those on the right are from an earlier study by Cain and Stevens, 1971 (N = 12). Note the similarity between these two sets of data obtained in separate experiments 3 years apart. The facsimilies of actual records (lower panel) are from Stevens and Cain, 1970. They show the repeatability of performance of three individual subjects on five repeated contractions at two different starting intensities. (Modified from Cain, W. S., and J. C. Stevens. Effort in sustained and phasic handgrip contractions. Am. J. Psychol. 84:52–65, 1971. Also modified from Pandolf, K. B., and W. S. Cain. Constant effort during static and dynamic muscular exercise. J. Mot. Behav. 6:101–110, 1974.)

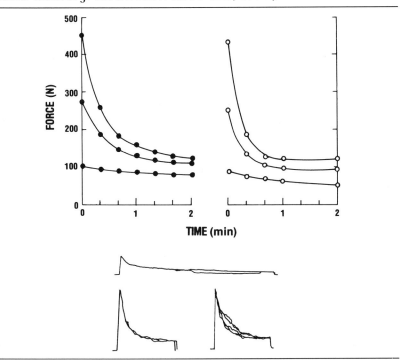

outflow. Thus, any force generated completely or partially by vibration should feel like less force than a normal contraction because central feedforward has been reduced by the augmented spindle afferent activity. The first mention of the effect of vibration on force sensation was by Hagbarth and Eklund, who referred anecdotally to the subject's "feeling . . . relief or lessening of tension" when a contracting muscle was vibrated [63, page 179]. Later, McCloskey and colleagues [98] reported that force sensation declined when the biceps tendon was vibrated. This conclusion was based on their observation that 9 out of 15 of their subjects "consistently" indicated that a given force felt like less force during vibration. That is the extent of the data, and given what we know about the effects of vibration and central feedforward, they are reasonable. These data were used subsequently to argue against muscle spindles and other peripheral receptors as participants in feedback about muscle sensation [96, 97].

In fact, the suggestion of Hagbarth and Eklund [63] and McCloskey et al. [98] that vibration reduces force sensation has not been substantiated. On the contrary, recent studies have shown that vibrating the patellar tendon increases force sensation during quadriceps contraction [29, 30, 78]. There is little doubt that this effect is robust, and it suggests that muscle receptors, primarily spindle Ia fibers, are capable of signaling intramuscular tension (Figure 5). If the instructions to the subjects were to judge force sensation and the matching forces were higher during vibration, it would mean that muscle receptors contribute to force sensation. Since spindle Ia fibers are the most susceptible to vibration, the preliminary conclusion must be that they contribute to force sensation. There are aspects of force sensation in fatigue and following training that could be explained by an active spindle role in this sensory process. This point will be discussed in a later section.

BASIC RESPONSE CHARACTERISTICS OF THE FORCE SENSING MECHANISM

It is apparent that there is a sense of force that is separate from the sense of the effort required to generate force [44, 45, 46, 49, 81, 111]. In a neuromuscular system that is capable of the most precise and sophisticated motor activities, it would be surprising if it were otherwise. As in any regulatory system, the operating characteristics of the sense of force during static contractions show a threshold, a gain, and a maximum. However, it is not known if the sensory maximum is a function of the maximal force-producing capacity of muscle or actually represents a true maximal sensory intensity.

The relationship between force sensation and force production during brief contractions was shown in Figure 2. If these data are transformed

FIGURE 5

Effect of vibration on static force sensation in the quadriceps. Brief static contractions of the reference muscle were made at 10, 25, and 45% MVC and matched with contractions of the opposite quadriceps that felt like the same force. In half of the trials, and without the subject knowing in which trial it would occur, the patellar tendon of the reference muscle was vibrated. There was a significant increase in matching force for all three reference forces. When the matching leg was vibrated, matching force was significantly less at all three references (data not shown). Symbols are the mean and standard error of 35 observations on three subjects. (From Cafarelli, E., and C. E. Kostka. Effect of vibration on static force sensation in man. Exp. Neurol. *74:331–340, 1981.)*

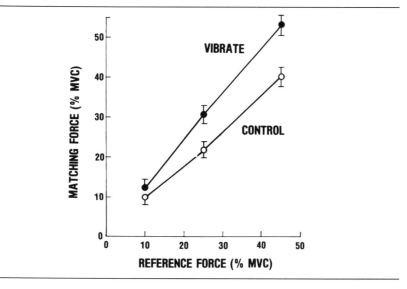

logarithmically, as they have been in the right-hand panel, and a regression line is fit to the transformed data, the regression coefficient, or slope, gives the gain of the system under that specific set of conditions. With data of these kind the slope is usually about 1.7, which means that sensory intensity increases as the 1.7th power of the actual force produced [117, 119]. A similar power relationship between the molar concentration of solutions and the frequency of action potentials in the human chorda tympani has been observed by Borg et al. and by Uttal and Smith [17, 122]. The curvature of the function shows that the gain is lowest with small forces and increases with larger forces. This is consistent with the common observation that a change in force production has a greater effect on sensory intensity while supporting a heavy weight.

The operating characteristics of the force-sensing mechanism shown in Figure 2 can be obtained only with direct ratio scaling techniques. Other techniques, such as category scales and matching procedures, have measurement artifacts associated with them that must be taken into account before the data can be properly interpreted. Two excellent primers on sensory measurement are recommended to the interested reader: first, the work by Gesheider that covers ratio scaling techniques and signal detection theory, and second the treatise by Marks that is an extensive discussion of most psychophysical techniques [54, 89].

The basic question of how force sensation works has not yet been definitely answered, although a considerable amount of research has been conducted. The possibilities are (a) that conscious sensations of muscular activity are derived from afferent information originating in sensory receptors in muscle and connective tissue and around joints [111] and (b) that central motor outflow leaving the motor cortex is copied and sent directly to the sensorium, and hence provides sensations of what the musculature is doing [1, 101, 102]. These are the so-called peripheral feedback and central feedforward mechanisms described in an earlier section on history. It is probably correct that these two mechanisms work together to provide the system with the best possible assessment of neuromuscular activity so that the most precise control may be achieved [26, 44, 96, 97]. On the other hand, the argument has been advanced that force sensations are derived entirely from muscle receptors and that it is the so-called sense of effort or the sense of how hard one must try in order to accomplish a motor task that is subserved by central feedforward [97].

THE EFFECTS OF FATIGUE AND TRAINING

The neuromuscular system constantly adjusts the calibration of the force-sensing mechanism to alterations in the ability of muscle to produce force. As a consequence of any change in capacity, such as fatigue, disease, hypertrophy, or even a deviation of muscle from optimal length, the degree of sensation associated with any force is approximately and inversely proportional to the decrement of MVC [27, 30, 35, 45, 49, 75, 77]. One would predict a similar adaptation to muscular atrophy, but the idea has never been put directly to the test. An intriguing question is whether there is a direct central adaptation in the sensory system itself or if the system is simply sensitive to changes in maximal force-producing capacity. The observation that acute perturbations such as fatigue or altered muscle length produce sensory changes suggests that the sensory apparatus is a slave to changes in maximal efferent capacity and undergoes no adaptation of its own [28].

Fatigue

The precise etiology of fatigue is unknown [see 70]. Several changes occur during the course of fatiguing contractions such as accumulation of metabolites, depletion of substrates, increases in temperature, and shifts in inorganic ions, any one of which is sufficient to hamper contraction [70, 79]. In addition, there are adjustments in the nervous system; for example, the firing frequency of most motor units declines, and there are changes in muscle spindle gain [10, 37, 71, 80, 105]. However, these adjustments do not necessarily contribute to force loss, and it is not known if they have any influence on force sensation. Nevertheless, the general pattern of these changes fits the increase in sensory intensity seen during fatigue [30, 49, 73, 85, 98].

The overall effects of fatigue on force sensation are well known. It is a common experience that the more a muscle is used, the greater the intensity of force sensation for any force. The data shown in Figure 6 were obtained by having subjects support a weight with the elbow flexors on one side and then choosing a weight that felt the same on the contralateral side [98]. If the reference side is rested between trials, the matching force is always about the same. However, when the reference muscle supports the weight continuously, the matching weights increase. The same thing occurs during repeated submaximal and maximal contractions if the rest interval is short enough [28, 30].

There are at least two possible explanations for this phenomenon. The first is that force sensation is adjusted to the reduced maximal force-generating capacity. This would be a cumbersome process because the neuromuscular system would have to compute the relative force of each submaximal contraction. As each becomes a larger proportion of the maximum, a greater sensory intensity would be assigned to it. The second possibility is that the sensory system simply remains attentive to the motor outflow required to make the contraction. As motor units fatigue, additional recruitment is required in order to achieve a submaximal force [87, 99]. Whether the potentiated recruitment is achieved by an increase in motor output or at the level of the motor neuron pool is not known [13].

It can be seen in Figure 1 that the increase in motor output and the peripheral feedback that would potentiate neural drive are both accessible to the force-sensing mechanism. Future experiments will have to block peripheral feedback in order to gain some insight into how force sensation adjusts to muscle fatigue.

Two broad lines of evidence support the notion that feedforward and feedback both contribute to force sensation during progressive fatigue. First, even though subjects are specifically instructed to judge only force and ignore the sense of effort, force sensation still increases during

FIGURE 6

Effect of fatigue on force sensation. The subject was asked to lift a weight with one hand and then to choose a weight that felt the same with the other hand. When the reference arm rested between trials, the matching weight was always about the same (open symbols). When the reference arm supported the weight continuously, the matching weight was ever larger (filled symbols). The matching weights are expressed as a percentage of the reference weight (4.1 kg). After 10 minutes of supporting the reference weight, force sensation for the same force nearly doubled. (Modified from McCloskey, D. I., P. Ebeling, and G. M. Goodwin. Estimation of weights and tensions and apparent involvement of a sense of effort. Exp. Neurol. 42:220–232, 1974.)

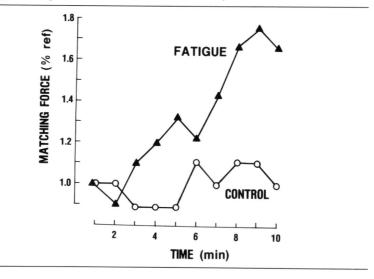

fatigue [28, 77]. Although we may prefer to attend to the centrally generated sense of effort, we are quite capable of entertaining peripheral sensations. Increased force sensation during fatigue suggests that we are either incapable of completely ignoring the central feedforward of motor outflow or that there is something about peripheral feedback that is altered during fatigue.

The second line of evidence is from a recent report on the effect of vibration on fatigued muscle [30]. The usual effect of vibration is to increase the sense of force [29, 30, 78]. However, as a muscle becomes fatigued, the effect of vibration is almost completely attenuated, while force sensation in the vibrated muscle continues to increase, just as it does in the unvibrated muscle [28, 30]. The fact that the vibration effect is attenuated during fatigue, but that force sensation still increases, suggests that the receptors that respond to vibration in fresh muscle (spin-

FIGURE 7

The relationship between force sensation and neural drive is illustrated by this plot of matching force as a function of the EMG from a muscle undergoing progressive fatigue. Data were obtained from quadriceps muscles of nine subjects. Fatigue was induced with repeated MVCs. Matching contractions with the unfatigued leg were made after every 10 MVCs at 50% of the reference leg's unfatigued MVC. The filled symbol is the matching force when the patellar tendon of the reference muscle was vibrated. Since neural drive (EMG) was the same, this excitatory effect of vibration indicates the contribution of the peripheral receptors. No such effect was observed during progressive fatigue. (Modified from Cafarelli, E., and J. Layton-Wood. Effect of vibration on force sensation in fatigued muscle. Med. Sci. Sports Exerc. *18:516–521, 1986.)*

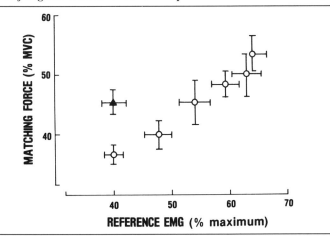

dles, Golgi tendon organs pacinian corpuscles, and free nerve endings), do not play a sensory role during fatigue.

The data in Figure 6 show that force sensation increases with muscle use, but this does not necessarily mean that the increase is caused by fatigue [98]. In fact, most of the studies cited in this section did not measure fatigue. Nevertheless, the rate of fatigue—the continuous loss of MVC force—depends on the intensity of the fatiguing contractions [108]. The rate of increase in force sensation is also a function of contraction intensity [75, 77]. Thus there is some evidence that fatigue and force sensation are linked.

Despite the association between loss of maximal force-producing capacity and force sensation, a reciprocal trade-off between the two does not obtain. When fatigue is induced by repeated MVCs, force sensation increases considerably less than either MVC force or maximal EMG declines (Figure 7) [28, 30]. Compare this result to the much closer association between force sensation and the submaximal EMG from the

FIGURE 8

Time course of fatigue and force sensation during MVCs repeated at a rate of 8.5 · min⁻¹. Fatigue is the decline of maximal force seen in the top panel. Force sensation (bottom panel) is the matching force of the unfatigued leg when the fatigued leg made a contraction at 50% of its unfatigued MVC. Note that the maximal force fell considerably more than force sensation increased. (Modified from Cafarelli, E., and J. Layton-Wood. Effect of vibration on force sensation in fatigued muscle. Med. Sci. Sports Exerc. *18:516–521, 1986.)*

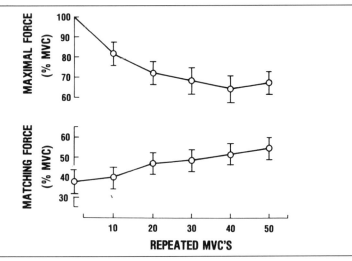

fatigued reference muscle (Figure 8). Combine this observation with the finding that vibration has no effect on submaximal force sensation in fatigued muscle and the implication is that peripheral receptors do not signal elevated force sensation during progressive fatigue [30].

A final important question is the manner in which fatigue and force sensation, both time-dependent processes, interact. Several years ago, Stevens and Cain determined the time course of force sensation at different force levels as a function of contraction duration [118]. According to their data, the intensity of force sensation varies as a function of the product: $F^{1.4} \cdot t^{0.57}$, where F is force in newtons and t is time in seconds (Figure 9). In other words, the initial level of sensation is a function of force raised to the 1.4th power, and thereafter sensation increases as the 0.57th power of time. An interesting aspect of muscle sensory processes illustrated by these data is that the rate of increase in sensory intensity is invariant at any force and for any duration, although absolute intensity is proportional to both [32].

In summary, fatigue is associated with several metabolic, electrical,

FIGURE 9

Magnitude estimations of force sensation as a function of force raised to the 1.4th power and time raised to the 0.57th power. Data from 18 subjects and the function were derived from two separate experiments: one where the duration of handgrip contractions was held constant for 2–4 seconds and force was varied, and another where the force was held constant and the duration was varied. In these experiments the authors report that the exponents for force and time are independent of each other. (Modified from Stevens, J. C., and W. S. Cain. Effort in isometric muscular contractions related to force level and duration. Percept. Psychophysics *8:240–244, 1970.)*

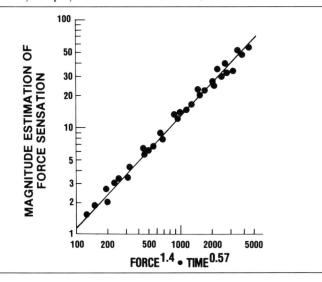

and thermal changes that may hamper contraction. Although the effect of fatigue on force sensation is to increase sensory intensity for any force, the mechanism that makes this adjustment is not clearly understood. The most likely explanation is that the sensorium attends to central feedforward exclusively during fatiguing contractions. The fact that vibration does not intensify force sensation in fatigued muscle, as it does when muscle is fresh, lends considerable support to this possibility.

Training

Muscle hypertrophy occurs when there is increased synthesis and decreased degradation of protein [55, 56]. This leads to an increase in the number of crossbridges and an increase in maximal force-generating capacity. There are no known ultrastructural changes in response to chronic overload in peripheral receptors, particularly in muscle spindles that play no part in load bearing [88, 94, 128]. However, it has been observed that the sensitivity of the stretch reflex has adaptive plasticity

[127]. Nevertheless, because of the increase in total protein, the density of all receptors becomes diluted. According to the feedforward hypothesis, it takes less neural drive to generate the same force after training because fewer motor units are required, and therefore motor output and central feedforward are reduced. The experimental approach that would answer this question would be to train a muscle in the usual way and then compare its sensory responses with those of a muscle trained without using the normal efferent pathways. Recently, Cannon and Cafarelli trained subjects with direct neural stimulation of the adductor pollicis muscles and compared their sensory responses over a range of forces with those of subjects who had trained with voluntary contraction [36]. They found that sensory intensity was about 6–10% less for the same force after training over a range of forces from light to heavy (Figure 10). However, there was also no change in either maximal or submaximal central drive (EMG) following training. These results beg the question of whether force sensation is a function of central feedforward. An extensive search of the literature found no other report of the effects of training on static force sensation. Thus, the answers to this question await the attention of future investigators.

SUMMARY

For more than a century, investigators have pondered the question of muscle sensation. Initially it was suggested that the command for movement was copied somewhere in the brain and gave rise to the sensations of force, movement, and position. The bases for this hypothesis were philosophy and speculation rather than experimental data. In the first half of this century, the central outflow hypothesis was rejected in favor of the hypothesis that peripheral muscle receptors fed back information to the sensorium. However, by the mid-1950s, it was widely accepted that muscle was insentient and that muscle sensation was dependent on central feedforward. Since then, and as more experimental data have become available, it has become apparent that muscle sensations arise from both peripheral feedback and central feedforward, and that both are required for optimal control of the musculature.

A remarkable characteristic of the neuromuscular system is the adaptability of sensory processes to acute and chronic changes in the ability to generate force. Loss of force-generating capacity as a consequence of fatigue or myopathy is immediately apparent to the sensorium, and force sensation is adjusted accordingly. An increase in force-generating capacity through training is similarly accommodated by the force-sensing mechanism, and any absolute force feels like less after training. Although the exact mechanism of this accommodation is not fully appreciated, there is considerable evidence indicating that it is the fluctuating level

FIGURE 10

The effect of training on force sensation in the adductor pollicis. Right hand muscles were trained for 5 weeks with either voluntary contractions or contractions stimulated through the ulnar nerve. Force sensation was measured with the matching technique before and after training. The difference between these two measures is shown in the plot. There was no significant difference after voluntary training because the untrained, matching muscle showed an increase in MVC, which meant that the "calibration" of the measuring instrument (the matching muscle) had changed. This so-called crossover effect has been observed on other occasions. In those subjects who trained with stimulated contractions, there was no increase in MVC force of the matching muscle and there was a 7–10% decrease in force sensation after training. (Modified from Cannon, R. J., and E. Cafarelli. Neuromuscular adaptations to training. J. Appl. Physiol. 63:2396–2402, 1988.)

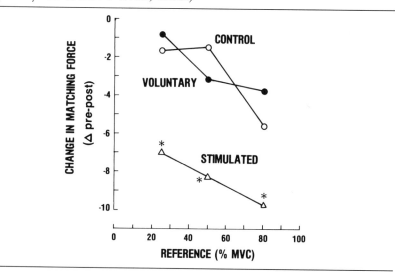

of central drive that is responsible for the adjustment of sensory intensity. Additional evidence also suggests that the peripheral receptors may not be involved in the increase in force sensation during fatigue.

It is not possible to explain precisely how the brain "knows" what the muscles are doing. Even a single aspect of muscle sensory processes, such as force sensation, remains largely unexplained. It has been the purpose of this chapter to review the literature related to the mechanism of force sensation, the effects of fatigue and training, the distinction between the sense of force and the sense of effort, and the role of force sensation in neuromuscular control. Each of these points has been examined and discussed, and the gaps in our understanding of muscle sensory phenomena have become apparent. Probably one of the most compelling aspects of this area of physiology is the meager data base from which to draw conclusions and generate hypotheses about the mechanism(s) of force sensation. This is especially true with respect to the mechanisms by which force sensation is altered by fatigue and training.

FUTURE RESEARCH DIRECTIONS

What are the questions that should now be asked? First of all, they should be directed toward increasing our understanding of the basic mechanism of force sensation and how it adapts to changes in force-producing capacity. Moreover, we need to understand how force sensation contributes to neuromuscular control and how this control can be improved when it is lacking. The model of the neuromuscular system in Figure 1 is suggested as a construct for posing specific experimental questions.

Despite 150 years of research, the role of mechanoreceptors such as muscle spindles and tendon organs in communicating conscious sensations has not been clearly elucidated [96]. Although the tendon organs are putative force receptors [66], it is not clear how they would alter the sensation of an absolute force under conditions of fatigue. Experiments with vibration suggest that muscle spindles somehow contribute to force sensation, yet we know that intramuscular extrafusal tension is not transmitted to spindles because they are arranged in parallel with the extrafusal fibers [52]. It may well be that the gamma motor drive to spindles is the main determinant of sensory intensity.

Future studies may also reveal that central feedforward is not a copy of motor output to the force-sensing mechanism, but instead arises from modulation of central drive by peripheral feedback. The site of this modulation is suggested by the comparator (sigma) shown in Figure 1. Such a mechanism would allow for a constant central drive and would be more in keeping with the "executive" structure that has been suggested for the motor control system [22, 62, 72, 103].

Finally, it is appropriate to point out the correspondence between the study of force sensation in static exercise with the study of perceived exertion during dynamic locomotor exercise. Since the work of Borg [16], in the early 1960s, it has been suggested that the nonspecific sensations that accompany dynamic exercise such as running and cycling may come from "local cues" from working muscles and "central cues" from the heart and lungs [41; see also [18] and [106] for a complete discussion of these ideas]. Over the years, it has become apparent that the so-called local cue, i.e., *force sensation*, from muscle is quite robust but that there are no central cues from the heart and viscera [109]. This is probably because there are no sensory nerves subserving conscious sensation arising from these structures, and thus there is no way to transmit information to the sensorium.

According to Robertson [109], ventilatory activity contributes in some way, but only after exceeding some level of relative maximal oxygen uptake. This agrees with the work of Killian and co-workers [24, 81, 82, 83] and others [3] who have studied respiratory sensations in healthy people, and in patients at rest and during exercise. Their general conclusion is that respiratory sensations arise from contraction of the respiratory muscles and, like all muscle sensations, are composed of force sensation as well as the sense of effort [81]. Thus the study of force sensation and the mechanisms of peripheral feedback and central feedforward are capable of accounting for changes in muscle sensory processes over a vast range of activities from single, brief, static contractions to long-term dynamic exercise.

ACKNOWLEDGMENTS

Some of the work cited was supported by NSERC grant A6633 to E. Cafarelli. The author is grateful to Dr. H. Hutton and Dr. K. Killian for their critical evaluation of the manuscript and to Mrs. V. Baddon for her invaluable word processing skills.

REFERENCES

1. Angel, R.W. Efference copy in the control of movement. *Neurology* 26:1164–1168, 1976.
2. Asmussen, E. Muscle fatigue. *Med. Sci. Sports Exerc.* 11:13–21, 1979.
3. Bakers, J.H.C.M., and S.M. Tenney. The perception of some sensations associated with breathing. *Respir. Physiol.* 10:85–92, 1970.
4. Bartley, S. The homeostatic and comfort perceptual systems. *J. Psychol.* 75:157–162, 1970.
5. Basmajian, J.V. Electromyography comes of age. *Science* 176:603–609, 1972.
6. Basmajian, J.V., and C. DeLuca. *Muscles Alive: Their Functions Revealed by Electromyography*, 5th ed. Baltimore: Williams & Wilkens, 1985.
7. Bastian, C. The "muscular sense": Its nature and cortical localization. *Brain* 10:1–89, 1887.
8. Belanger, A.Y., and A.J. McComas. Extent of motor unit activation during effort. *J. Appl. Physiol.* 51:1131–1135, 1981.
9. Bell, C. On the nervous circle which connects the voluntary muscles with the brain. *Philos. Trans. R. Soc. Lond. (Biol.)* 116:162–167, 1826.
10. Bellemare, F., J.J. Woods, R.S. Johansson, and B. Bigland-Ritchie. Motor-unit discharge rates in maximal voluntary contractions of three human muscles. *J. Neurophysiol.* 50:1380–1392, 1983.
11. Bianconi, R., and J.P. van der Meulen. The response to vibration of the end organs of mammalian muscle spindles. *J. Neurophysiol.* 26:177–190, 1963.
12. Bigland, B., and O.C.J. Lippold. Motor unit activity in the voluntary contraction of humanmuscle. *J. Physiol. (Lond.)* 125:322–335, 1954.
13. Bigland-Ritchie, B. EMG/force relations and fatigue of human voluntary contractions. In D. Miller (ed.). *Exercise and Sport Sciences Review*. Philadelphia: Franklin Institute, 1981, pp. 75–117.

14. Bigland-Ritchie, B., R. Johansson, O.J.C. Lippold, and J.J. Woods. Contractile speed and EMG changes during fatigue of sustained maximal voluntary contractions. *J. Neurophysiol.* 50:313–324, 1983.

15. Bigland-Ritchie, B., C.G. Kukulka, O.C.J. Lippold, and J.J. Woods. The absence of neuromuscular transmission failure in sustained maximal voluntary contractions. *J. Physiol. (Lond.)* 330:265–278, 1982.

16. Borg, G. *Physical Performance and Perceived Exertion.* Lund, Sweden: Gleerup, 1962.

17. Borg, G., H. Diamart, L. Strom, and Y. Zotterman. The relation between neural and perceptual intensity: A comparative study on the neural and psychophysical response to taste stimuli. *J. Physiol. (Lond.)* 192:13–20, 1967.

18. Borg, G., and B. Noble. Perceived Extention. In J. Wilmore (ed.). *Exercise and Sport Sciences Reviews.* New York: Academic Press, 1974, pp. 131–153.

19. Borg, J., L. Brimby, and J. Hannerz. Motor neuron firing range, axonal conducting velocity, and muscle fiber histochemistry in neuromuscular diseases. *Muscle Nerve* 2:423–430, 1979.

20. Boulange, M., J.C. Cnockaert, G. Lensel, E. Pertuzon, and B. Vigreux. Muscular fatigue and rate of tension development. *Eur. J. Appl. Physiol.* 41:17–25, 1979.

21. Brindley, G.S., and P.A. Merton. The absence of position sense in the human eye. *J. Physiol. (Lond.)* 153:130–137, 1960.

22. Brooks, V.B. *The Neural Basis of Motor Control.* New York: Oxford University Press, 1986.

23. Budingen, H.J., and H.J. Freund. The relationship between the rate of rise of isometric tension and motor unit recruitment in a human forearm muscle. *Pflugers Arch.* 362:61–67, 1976.

24. Burdon, J.G.W., K.J. Killian, and E.J.M. Campbell. Effect of ventilatory drive on the perceived magnitude of added loads of breathing. *J. Appl. Physiol.* 53:901–907, 1982.

25. Burke, D., K.-E. Hagbarth, L. Lofstedt, and B.G. Wallin. The responses of human muscle spindle endings to vibration during isometric contraction. *J. Physiol. (Lond.)* 261:695–711, 1976.

26. Cafarelli, E. Peripheral contributions to the perception of effort. *Med. Sci. Sports Exerc.* 14:382–389, 1982.

27. Cafarelli, E., and B. Bigland-Ritchie. Sensation of static force in muscles of different length. *Exp. Neurol.* 65:511–525, 1979.

28. Cafarelli, E., and B. Bigland-Ritchie. Effect of fatigue on force sensation in human skeletal muscle. *Med. Sci. Sports Exerc.* 15:179, 1983. (Abstract)

29. Cafarelli, E., and C.E. Kostka. Effect of vibration on static force sensation in man. *Exp. Neurol.* 74:331–340, 1981.

30. Cafarelli, E., and J. Layton-Wood. Effect of vibration force sensation in fatigued muscle. *Med. Sci. Sports Exerc.* 18:516–521, 1986.

31. Cain, W.S. Nature of perceived effort and fatigue: Roles of strength and blood flow in muscle contractions. *J. Mot. Behav.* 5:33–47, 1973.

32. Cain, W.S., and J.C. Stevens. Effort in sustained and phasic handgrip contractions. *Am. J. Psychol.* 84:52–65, 1971.

33. Cain, W.S., and J.C. Stevens. Constant-effort contractions related to the electromyogram. *Med. Sci. Sports Exerc.* 5:121–127, 1973.

34. Caldwell, L.S., and E.E. Grossman. Constant effort scaling of isometric muscle contractions. *J. Mot. Behav.*, 5:9–16, 1973.

35. Campbell, E.J.M., R.H.T. Edwards, D.K. Hill, D.A. Jones, and M.K. Sykes. Perception of effort during partial curarization. *J. Physiol. (Lond.)*, 263:186P–187P, 1976.

36. Cannon, R.J., and E. Cafarelli. Neuromuscular adaptations to training. *J. Appl. Physiol.* 63:2396–2402, 1987.

37. Christakos, C., and U. Windhorst. Spindle gain increase during muscle unit fatigue. *Brain Res.* 365:388–392, 1986.
38. Craske, B. Perception of impossible limb positions induced by tendon vibration. *Science* 196:71–73, 1977.
39. DeGail, P., J.W. Lance, and P.D. Neilson. Differential effects on tonic and phasic reflex mechanisms produced by vibration of muscles in man. *J. Neurol. Neurosurg. Psychiatry* 29:1–11, 1966.
40. Edwards, R.G., and O.C.J. Lippold. The relation between force and integrated electrical activity in fatigued muscles. *J. Physiol. (Lond.)* 132:677–681, 1956.
41. Ekblom, B., and A.N. Goldbarg. The influence of training and other factors on the subjective rate of perceived exertion. *Acta Physiol. Scand.* 83:399–406, 1971.
42. Eklund, G. Some physical properties of muscle vibrators used to elicit tonic proprioceptive reflexes in man. *Uppsala J. Med. Sci.* 76:271–280, 1971.
43. Eklund, G., and K.-E. Hagbarth. Normal variability of tonic vibration reflexes in man. *Exp. Neurol.* 16:80–92, 1966.
44. Evarts, E.V. Feedback and corollary discharge: A meeting of the concepts. *Neurosci. Res. Prog. Bull.* 9:86–112, 1971.
45. Gandevia, S.C. The perception of motor commands of effort during muscular paralysis. *Brain* 105:151–159, 1982.
46. Gandevia, S.C., and C.K. Mahutte. Theoretical requirements for the interpretation of signals of intramuscular tension. *J. Theor. Biol.* 97:141–153, 1982.
47. Gandevia, S.C., and D.I. McCloskey. Changes in motor commands, as shown by changes in perceived heaviness, during partial curarization and peripheral anaesthesia in man. *J. Physiol. (Lond.)* 272:673–689, 1977.
48. Gandevia, S.C., and D.I. McCloskey. Effects of related sensory inputs on motor performances in man studied through changes in perceived heaviness. *J. Physiol. (Lond.)* 272:653–673, 1977.
49. Gandevia, S.C., and D.I. McCloskey. Sensations of heaviness. *Brain* 100:345–354, 1977.
50. Gandevia, S.C., and D.I. McCloskey. Interpretation of perceived motor commands by reference to afferent signals. *J. Physiol. (Lond.)* 283:493–499, 1978.
51. Gandevia, S.C., D.I. McCloskey, and E.K. Potter. Alterations in perceived heaviness during digital anaesthesia. *J. Physiol. (Lond.)* 306:365–375, 1980.
52. Gardner, E. *Fundamentals of Neurology*, 6th ed. Toronto: W.B. Saunders Co., 1975.
53. Gelfan, S., and S. Carter. Muscle sense in man. *Exp. Neurol.* 18:469–473, 1967.
54. Gescheider, G.A. *Psychophysics: Method and Theory*, Hillsdale, N.J.: Lawrence Earlbaum Associates, 1976.
55. Goldspink, D.F. The influence of activity on muscle size and protein turnover. *J. Physiol. (Lond.)* 264:283–296, 1971.
56. Gollnick, P.D., and W.L. Sembrowich. E.A. Amsterdam, J.H. Wilmore and A.N. DeMaria (eds.). *Adaptations in Human Skeletal Muscle as a Result of Training.* In *Exercise in Cardiovascular Health and Disease.* New York: Yorke Medical Books, 1977, pp. 70–94.
57. Goodwin, G.M. The sense of limb position and movement. In J. Keogh and R.S. Hutton (ed.). *Exercise and Sport Sciences Reviews.* Santa Barbara, CA: Journal Publishing Affiliates, 1976, pp. 87–124.
58. Goodwin, G.M., D.I. McCloskey, and P.B.C. Matthews. The contribution of muscle afferents to kinaesthesia shown by vibration induced illusions of movement and by the effects of paralysing joint afferents. *Brain* 95:705–748, 1972.
59. Goodwin, G.M., D.I. McCloskey, and P.B.C. Matthews. Proprioceptive illusions induced by muscle vibration: Contribution by muscle spindles to perception? *Science* 175:1382–1384, 1972.

60. Granit, R. Comments on the history of motor control. In V. Brooks (ed.). *Handbook of Physiology, Section 1: The Nervous System*. Vol. II, *Motor Control*, Part 1. Bethesda, Md.: American Physiological Society, 1981, pp. 1–16.

61. Gregory, J.E., and U. Proske. Motor unit contractions initiating impulses in a tendon organ in the cat. *J. Physiol. (Lond.)* 313:251–262, 1981.

62. Grodins, F.S. *Control Theory and Biological Systems*. New York: Columbia University Press, 1963.

63. Hagbarth, K.-E. and G. Eklund. Motor effects of vibratory muscle stimuli in man. In R. Granit (ed.). *Muscular Afferents and Motor Control*. Proceedings of the first Nobel Symposium. New York: John Wiley & Sons, 1966, pp. 177–186.

64. Hagbarth, K.-E., and G. Eklund. The muscle vibrator—a useful tool in neurological therapeutic work. *Scand. J. Rehab. Med.* 1:26–34, 1966.

65. Henneman, E. Organization of the motor systems—a preview. In V.B. Mountcastle (ed.). *Medical Physiology*, Vol. II, St. Louis: C.V. Mosby Co., 1974, pp. 1675–1680.

66. Hobbs, S.F. Central command during exercise: Parallel activation of the cardiovascular and motor systems by descending command signals. In O.A. Smith, R.A. Galosy, and S.M. Weiss, (eds). *Circulation, Neurobiology, and Behaviour*, New York: Elsevier Science Publishing Co., 1982, pp. 217–231.

67. Hobbs, S.F., and S.C. Gandevia. Cardiovascular responses and the sense of effort during attempts to contract paralysed muscles: Role of the spinal cord. *Neurosci. Lett.* 57:85–90, 1985.

68. Houk, J., and E. Henneman. Responses of Golgi tendon organs to active contractions of the soleus muscle of the cat. *J. Neurophysiol.* 30:466–481, 1967.

69. Houk, J., and E. Henneman. Feedback control of movement and posture. In V.B. Mountcastle (ed.). *Medical Physiology*, Vol. II. St. Louis: C.V. Mosby Co., 1974, pp. 1681–1696.

70. *Human Muscle Fatigue: Physiological mechanisms*. (CIBA Foundation Symposium 82), London: Pitman Medical, 1981.

71. Hutton, R.S., J.L. Smith, and E. Eldred. Postcontraction sensory discharge from muscle and its source. *J. Neurophysiol.* 36:1090–1103, 1973.

72. Ito, M. Neural systems controlling movement. *Trends Neurosci.* 9:515–518, 1986.

73. Jones, L.A. Role of central and peripheral signals in force sensation during fatigue. *Exp. Neurol.*, 81:497–503, 1983.

74. Jones, L.A., and I.W. Hunter. The relation of muscle force and EMG to perceived force in human finger flexors. *Eur. J. Appl. Physiol.* 50:125–131, 1982.

75. Jones, L.A., and I.W. Hunter. Effect of fatigue on force sensation. *Exp. Neurol.* 81:640–650, 1983.

76. Jones, L.A., and I.W. Hunter. Force and EMG correlates of constant effort contractions. *Eur. J. Appl. Physiol.* 51:75–83, 1983.

77. Jones, L.A., and I.W. Hunter. Perceived force in fatiguing isometric contractions. *Percept. Psychophysics* 33:369–374, 1983.

78. Jones, L.A., and I.W. Hunter. Effect of muscle tendon vibration on the perception of force. *Exp. Neurol.* 87:35–45, 1985.

79. Karlsson, J., B. Diamant, and B. Saltin. Muscle metabolites during submaximal and maximal exercise in man. *Scan. J. Clin. Lab. Invest.* 26:385–394, 1970.

80. Kernell, D., and A.W. Monster. Motoneurone properties and motor fatigue. An intracellular study of gastrocnemius motoneurones of the cat. *Expr. Brain Res.* 46:197–204, 1982.

81. Killian, K.J., and E.J.M. Campbell. Dyspnea and exercise. *Ann. Rev. Physiol.* 45:465–479, 1983.

82. Killian, K.J., C.K. Mahutte, and E.J.M. Campbell. Resistive load detection during passive ventilation. *Clin. Sci.* 59:493–495, 1980.

83. Killian, K.J., E. Summers, M. Basalygo, and E.J.M. Campbell. Effect of frequency on perceived magnitude of added loads to breathing. *J. Appl. Physiol.* 58:1616–1621, 1985.

84. Kniffki, K.-D., S. Mense, and R.F. Schmidt. Responses of group IV afferent units from skeletal muscle to stretch, contraction and chemical stimulation. *Exp. Brain Res.* 31:511–522, 1978.

85. Kostka, C.E., and E. Cafarelli. Effect of pH on sensation and vastus lateralis electromyogram during cycling exercise. *J. Appl. Physiol.* 52:1181–1185, 1982.

86. Lewes, G.H. Motor feelings and the muscular sense. *Brain* 1:14–28, 1879.

87. Lippold, O.C.J. The relation between integrated action potentials in a human muscle and its isometric tension. *J. Physiol. (Lond.)* 117:492–499, 1952.

88. Maier, A., E. Eldred, and V.R. Edgerton. The effects on spindles of muscle atrophy and hypertrophy, *Exp. Neurol.* 37:100–123, 1972.

89. Marks, L.E. *Sensory Processes: The New Psychophysics.* New York: Academic Press, 1974.

90. Marsden, C.D., J.C. Meadows, and P.A. Merton. "Muscular wisdom" that minimizes fatigue during prolonged effort in man: Peak rates of motoneuron discharge and slowing of discharge during fatigue. In J.E. Desmedt, (ed.). *Motor Control Mechanism in Health and Disease.* New York: Raven Press, 1983, pp. 169–211.

91. Marsden, C.D., J.C. Rothwell, and M.M. Traub. Changes in perceived heaviness in man after thumb anaesthesia are associated with corresponding changes in the degree of muscle activation. *J. Physiol. (Lond.)* 280:66P–67P, 1978.

92. Matthews, P.B.C. Where does Sherrinton's "muscular sense" originate? Muscles, joints, corollary discharges? *Ann. Rev. Neurosci.* 5:189–218, 1982.

93. Matthews, P.B.C., and A. Simmonds. Sensations of finger movement elicited by pulling upon flexor tendons in man. *J. Physiol. (Lond.)* 234:27P–28P, 1974.

94. Maynard, J.A., and C.M. Tipton. The effects of exercise training and denervation on the morphology of intrafusal muscle fibers. *Int. Z. Angew. Physiol.* 30:1–9, 1971.

95. McCloskey, D.I. Differences between the senses of movement and position shown by the effects of loading and vibration of muscles in man. *Brain Res.* 63:119–131, 1973.

96. McCloskey, D.I. Kinesthetic sensibility. *Physiol. Rev.* 58:763–792, 1978.

97. McCloskey, D.I. Corollary discharges: motor commands and perception. In V. Brooks (ed.). *Handbook of Physiology,* Section1: *The Nervous System,* Vol. II, *Motor Control,* Part II. Bethesda: *American Physiological Society,* 1981.

98. McCloskey, D.I., P. Ebeling, and G.M. Goodwin. Estimation of weights and tensions and apparent involvement of a sense of effort. *Exp. Neurol.* 42:220–232, 1974.

99. Merton, P.A. Voluntary strength and fatigue. *J. Physiol. (Lond.)* 123:553–564, 1954.

100. Merton, P.A. Human position sense and sense of effort. *Soc. Expl. Biol.* 18:387–400, 1964.

101. Merton, P.A. The sense of effort. In R. Porter (ed.). *Breathing: Hering-Breuer Centenary Symposium.* London: Churchill Livingstone, 1970, pp. 207–211.

102. Merton, P.A. How we control the contraction of our muscles. *Sci. Am.* 226:5, 1972.

103. Miles, F.A., and E.V. Evarts. Concepts of motor organization. *Ann. Rev. Psychol.* 30:327–362, 1979.

104. Miller, R.G., A. Mirka, and M. Maxfield. Rate of tension development in isometric contractions of human hand muscle. *Exp. Neurol.* 73:267–285, 1981.

105. Nelson, D.L., and R.S. Hutton. Dynamic and static stretch responses in muscle spindle receptors in fatigued muscle. *Med. Sci. Sports Exerc.* 17:445–450, 1985.

106. Pandolf, K.B. Advances in the study and application of perceived exertion. In R. Terjung (ed.). *Exercise and Sport Sciences Reviews.* Philadelphia: Franklin Institute Press, 1983, pp. 118–158.

107. Pandolf, K.B., and W.S. Cain. Constant effort during static and dynamic muscular exercise. *J. Mot. Behav.* 6:101–110, 1974.

108. Petrofsky, J.S. Quantification through the surface EMG of muscle fatigue and recovery during successive isometric contractions. *Aviat. Space Environ. Med.* 52:545–550, 1981.

109. Robertson, R.J. Central signals of perceived exertion during dynamic exercise. *Med. Sci. Sports Exerc.* 14:390–396, 1982.

110. Roland, P.E. Do muscular receptors in man evoke sensations of tension and kinaesthesia? *Brain Res.* 99:162–165, 1975.

111. Roland, P.E. Sensory feedback to the cerebral cortex during voluntary movement in man. *Behav. Brain Sci.* 1:129–171, 1978.

112. Rowell, L.R. What signals govern the cardiovascular response to exercise? *Med. Sci. Sports Exerc.* 12:307–315, 1980.

113. Rowell, L.B. Human Circulation: *Regulation during Physical Stress.* New York: *Oxford University Press,* 1986.

114. Sherrington, C.S. The muscular sense. In Schafer, E.A. (ed.). *Textbook of Physiology.* London: Pentland, 1900.

115. Sperry, R.W. Neural basis of the spontaneous optokinetic response produced by visual inversion. *J. Comp. Physiol.* 43:482–489, 1950.

116. Steinbach, M.J. Muscles as sense organs. *Arch. Ophthalmol. (Editorial).* In press.

117. Stevens, J.C. Psychophysical invariances in proprioception. In F.A. Geldard (ed.). *Conference in Vibrotactile Communication.* Austin, Texas: The Psychonomic Society, 1974, pp. 73–77.

118. Stevens, J.C., and W.S. Cain. Effort in isometric muscular contractions related to force level and duration. *Percept. Psychophysics* 8:240–244, 1970.

119. Stevens, J.C., and J.D. Mack. Scales of apparent force. *J. Exp. Psych.* 58:405–413, 1959.

120. Stevens, S.S. On the psychophysical law. *Psych. Rev.* 64:153–181, 1957.

121. Tatton, W.G., and I.C. Bruce. Comment: A schema for the interactions between motor programs and sensory input. *Can. J. Physiol. Pharmacol.* 59:691–699, 1981.

122. Uttal, W.R., and P. Smith. On the psychophysical discriminability of somatosensory nerve action potential patterns with irregular intervals. *Percept. Psychophysics* 2:341–348, 1967.

123. von Helmholtz, H. *Helmholtz's Treatise on Physiological Optics,* 3rd ed. J.P.C. Southall (ed.). Menasha, Wisc.: Optical Society of America, 1925.

124. von Holst, E. Relations between the central nervous system and the peripheral organs. *Br. J. Anim. Behav.* 2:89–94, 1954.

125. Waller, A.D. The sense of effort: An objective study. *Brain* 14:179–249, 1891.

126. Warren, R.M. Measurement of sensory intensity. *Behav. Brain Sci.,* 4:175–223, 1981.

127. Wolpaw, J., D. Braitman, and R. Seegal. Adaptive plasticity in primate spinal stretch reflex: Initial development. *J. Neurophysiol.* 50:1296–1311, 1983.

128. Yellin, H. Intrafusal fiber immutability in the presence of extrafusal fiber plasticity. *Anat. Rec.* 172:468, 1972.

5
Biomechanics of the Human Spine and Trunk*

JAMES A. ASHTON-MILLER, Ph.D.
ALBERT B. SCHULTZ, Ph.D.

INTRODUCTION

In this chapter we review the mechanical properties of the human spine and trunk, its functional capacities, how and why it is loaded in quasistatic and dynamic activities, and the possible role of mechanical factors in producing symptoms and back pain.

FUNCTIONAL ANATOMY

The trunk musculoskeletal system is composed of the spine, rib cage, and pelvis, together with associated fascia and musculature. The spine itself is composed of 24 semirigid presacral vertebrae, each separated by a flexible element, the intervertebral disc (see Figure 1). More than six intervertebral ligaments span adjacent vertebrae, which articulate via the intervertebral disc, and two synovial joints, called the "zygoapophyseal" or "facet joints" which help constrain motions in certain directions. In the thoracic region, 12 pairs of ribs articulate with the spine at the costovertebral joints, the upper 10 articulating anteriorly with the sternum at the costosternal articulations. The pelvis is composed of the sacrum and the right and left ilia (or inominate bones); the latter articulate with the sacrum at the sacroiliac joints and with each other at the pubic symphysis.

SKELETAL COMPONENTS OF THE SPINE AND TRUNK

Apart from the upper cervical vertebrae, C1 and C2, whose structure is unique, each vertebra is composed of the vertebral centrum, the neural arch (consisting of the pedicles and laminae), and structures primarily for muscle attachment, the spinous and transverse processes (see Figure 2a). Each vertebra also has two superior and two inferior articular processes that comprise half of their respective facet joint. The centrum

*This work was supported in part by National Institute of Arthritis and Musculoskeletal Disease Grants AM 33948 and 36047, and National Institutes of Neurological Disease and Stroke Grants NS 20536 and NS 24058.

169

itself consists of trabecular bone surrounded by a thin cortical shell. The centrum must primarily resist compression and shear loading. Its superior and inferior margins are called "vertebral endplates," their central region being covered by a thin layer of hyaline cartilage about 1 mm thick in the young adult. Studies have shown that under a 7500-N compressive load, such as can occur in heavy lifts, the endplate can deflect 0.5 mm, reflecting up to 3% compressive strain in the vertebral trabecular bone [20].

The largest avascular structure in the human body, the intervertebral disc, is composed of an outer annulus and an inner nucleus. It acts as a flexible spacer between adjacent vertebrae, while carrying the significant compressive loads due to gravitational and muscular forces outlined below with relatively little bulge [19, 106]. The annulus consists of 10 or more concentric lamellae, each about 1 mm thick and reinforced with collagen lamellae oriented at alternating angles to the longitudinal axis of the spine (see Figure 2b). Moving from the periphery, type I collagen content decreases, while type II content increases [38]. The inner lamellae become progressively less distinct as they merge with the nucleus pulposus, a gelatinous substance consisting of a strongly hydrophylic proteoglycan gel enmeshed in a random collagen matrix [139]. The young and nondegenerate disc behaves as a short, thick-walled, deformable cylinder containing the fluid nucleus under pressure. Nutrition of the disc is accomplished by diffusion of nutrients into and waste products out of the disc via the central 40% of the cartilaginous endplate and the annulus (see e.g., [138]). With age the nucleus gradually loses its ability to bind water under mechanical pressure and becomes fibrocartilaginous.

Axial compression is by far the most common form of spine loading. The compression force imposed on a healthy disc by the adjacent vertebrae is resisted by both the annulus and the nucleus. The hydration of these components is proportional to the applied compression stress. At a given load, the osmotic swelling pressure developed by the proteoglycans balances the applied compression stress (see Figure 3). However, a disc loaded *in vitro* for 4 hours by 100% body weight will lose 6% of the fluid from the nucleus and 13% of the hydration in the annulus [3]. This effect is also seen *in vivo* as the exponential decrease in overall standing height of about 1 cm that occurs over the course of the day [29, 32].

The facet joints act as kinematic constraints for the intervertebral joint, causing marked coupling between lateral bending and axial torsion motions [146] in the cervical spine, but not elsewhere. The joint surfaces themselves are often complex and nonplanar; one way to measure their geometry and orientation is by using computed tomography (CT) scans [140]. Increasing attention has been focused on the facet joints, partly

FIGURE 1
Frontal (left) and left lateral (right) views of the human spine.

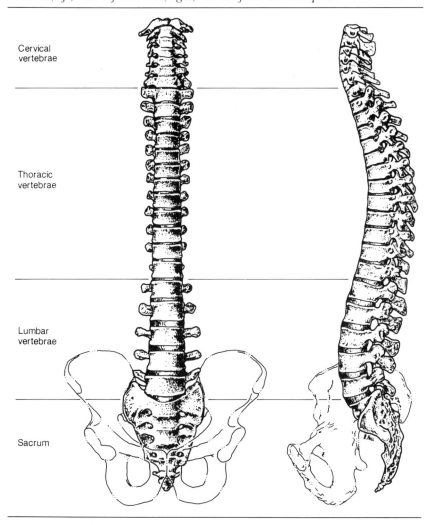

Cervical
vertebrae

Thoracic
vertebrae

Lumbar
vertebrae

Sacrum

because the rich innervation of their facet capsules [52] has raised the possibility that they could be the source of some painful symptoms.

The overall mechanical properties of the lumbar facet joints were studied by Skipor et al. [131]. The goal of these studies was to estimate the loads carried by the facet joints in different situations. One way of estimating the load sharing between the disc and the facets is by mathematical models [77, 129, 148]. Alternatively, the contact pressure between facet joint surfaces can be measured directly by introducing a

FIGURE 2

Lumbar spine motion segment. View of the right half when sectioned in the sagittal plane (left). Ligaments are omitted for clarity. Intervertebral disc sectioned to expose the annular organization (right).

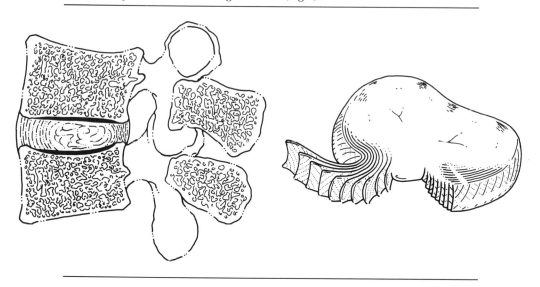

pressure-sensitive film [69] or by utilizing a miniature pressure transducer to record synovial fluid pressure under load [34]. In torsion, for example, the relationship between the applied moment and experimentally measured pressure increased linearly and ranged from 4 to 26 Nm/kPa from one specimen to another. The highest facet pressures were recorded with combined torsion, flexion, and compression.

By categorizing the loads carried by the facets under carefully controlled experimental conditions, studies such as the one cited above will help determine when the facet joints are loaded heavily and whether clinical conditions such as spondylolysis occur because of a fatigue fracture of the pars interarticularis [25], presumably due to increased and more frequent loading of the posterior elements.

As in most joints, the purpose of ligaments is to limit excessive joint rotation. Spinal ligaments run between each vertebra and along the length of the spine [146]. Strains in some ligaments farthest from the axis of rotation can reach nearly 20% when lumbar motion segments are loaded in flexion under a moment of 15 Nm [95]. One way to examine the effect of ligaments on spine segments is to perform repeated tests in one direction, say flexion, while serially sectioning ligaments from posterior to anterior [97]. The facet joint capsules also act as tensile, load-bearing structures between the articular processes [131].

FIGURE 3

Graph of human intervertebral disc hydration versus osmotic swelling pressure. (From Urban, J.P.G., and J.F. McMullin. Swelling pressure of the interverte- bral disc: Influence of proteoglycan and collagen contents. Biorheology 22:145–157, 1986.)

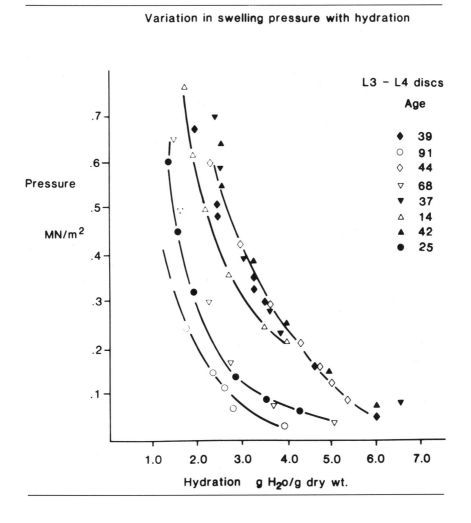

The reader is referred to classic texts for general descriptions of trunk muscle anatomy [133]. Mathematical models of the spine often re- quire detailed descriptions of the origin and insertion points of mus- cles and muscle slips, their anatomic and physiological cross-sectional areas, and even their fiber lengths and fiber types. Many of these data are incomplete. Thus, the detailed anatomy of trunk muscles is continually being updated [15, 16, 66, 83]. The advent of CT and magnetic resonance imaging (MRI) scans has allowed easier and more accurate estimation of muscular lever arms about, say, the cervical or lumbar spine [93].

ANTHROPOMETRY

Anthropometry is the study of human size and form. Mathematical models of the spine require as input data the linear dimensions and shape of the spine and trunk. Often these must be gotten from a variety of sources, depending upon the purpose of the model.

In general, the healthy spine is approximately straight when viewed frontally because each vertebral centrum is approximately symmetric about the midline. A slight lateral deviation or scoliosis is common. For example, Rogala et al. [109] found an incidence of 4.5% for adolescent idiopathic scoliosis curves over 5° (0.09 rad) Cobb angle [25], and 2% for curves over 10° (0.17 rad). If all types of scoliosis are considered, including nonstructural types, the incidence may approach the 10–20% estimate in college men [36].

In a lateral view, the spine has four curves. In the cervical and lumbar spines each curve is convex-forward, a lordosis. In the thoracic and sacral spines each curve is concave-forward, a kyphosis. The thoracic kyphosis normally ranges from 20° (0.35 rad) to 40° (0.70 rad), values outside that range being considered abnormal [107]. Most of the thoracic kyphosis is due to slight wedging of the vertebral bodies; a thoracic disc tends to have endplates that are approximately parallel. Wedging over three or more thoracic vertebrae that exceeds 15° (0.26 rad) is considered abnormal, occurring in conditions such as Scheuermann's kyphosis. Normal lumbar lordosis averages 57° (0.99 rad), ranging from 38° (0.66 rad) to 75° (1.31 rads) [41]. There are no significant differences in the angle of lordosis between males and females [40].

The lumbosacral angle was defined by Ferguson as the angle that the plane of the upper S1 endplate makes with the forward horizontal. In upright stance, this angle averages 41° in the adult male, with 95% lying within the range 26–57° [45].

Among many studies of vertebral morphometry, Lanier [67] focused on the overall geometry of adult macerated vertebrae, while Brandner [18] investigated disc and vertebral dimensions during growth. On a more global scale, marked variations exist between individuals, as can be seen in Figure 4, which shows the variation in sagittal curvatures of a sample of 18 adolescent females with a mean age of 12 years. The equation of a fifth-order polynomial regression ($r^2 = 0.80$) fitted to the coordinate values is

FIGURE 4

Graph showing variation in healthy spine configuration. Mean (denoted by O) and standard deviation (denoted by bars) vertebral center coordinates (in centimeters) are given. Note that the axis is oriented horizontally and the y axis vertically and the difference in scales. The solid line is fifth-order regression whose equation is given in the section on Anthropometry. Data are for 18 adolescents between 10 and 18 years of age. (From Miller, J.A.A., H. Steen, L.B. Skogland, and A. B. Schultz. Sagittal geometry of the spine in females with and without idiopathic scoliosis. Spine *(In press).)*

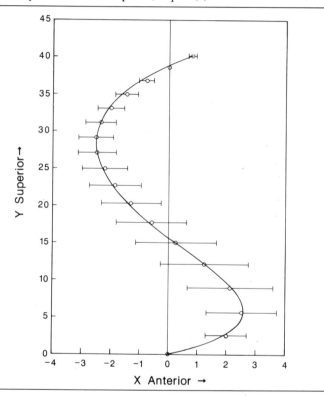

$$X = 1.02030Y - 0.12767Y^2 + 0.00543Y^3$$
$$- 0.10504 \times 10^{-3}Y^4 \qquad (1)$$
$$+ 0.83552 \times 10^{-6}Y^5$$

Table 1 gives the vertebral center coordinates and angle of disc inclination for these spines.

For rigid body models, linear dimensions, as well as cross-sectional dimensions, mass, and inertia data, are required for the trunk. Linear

TABLE 1

Average Segmental Range of Motion at Each Spine Level

Level	Flexion		Extension	Lateral Bending	Torsion†
Occ–C1	13*		13*	8*	0
C1–2	10*		9	0*	47
C2–3	8		3	10*	9
C3–4	7		9	11	11
C4–5	10		8	13	12
C5–6	10		11	15	10
C6–7	13		5	12	9
C7–T1	6		4	14	8
T1–2	5	(F/E)	3	2	9
T2–3		4		3	8
T3–4		5		4	8
T4–5		4		2	8
T5–6		5		2	8
T6–7		5		3	8
T7–8		5		2	8
T8–9		4		2	7
T9–10		3		2	4
T10–11		4		3	2
T11–12		4		3	2
T12–L1		5		3	2
L1–2	8		5	6	1
L2–3	10		3	6	1
L3–4	12		1	6	2
L4–5	13		2	3	2
L5–S1	9		5	1	1

Cervical data are from Kottke and Mundale [65] unless otherwise specified. Thoracic data are from Bakke [9].

Values are total flexion/extension values. Lumber data are from Pearcy et al. [102] and Pearcy and Tibrewal [103].

*Data from White and Panjabi [145].

†Cervical and thoracic data from White and Panjabi [146], lumbar data from Pearcy et al. [102] and Pearcy and Tibrewal [103].

and cross-sectional data can be measured directly from subjects using calipers (see, e.g. [75]). These data can be used to scale cadaver segmental mass and inertia data from sources such as Clauser et al. [14], McConville et al. [73], and Jensen [55].

FUNCTIONAL CAPACITIES

This section will cover *in vivo* measurements of spine ranges of motion in adults. There are many techniques that have been developed to measure spine ranges of motion. Many are noninvasive, using linear or angular measures from surface landmarks [76]. Although convenient, these methods are not as reliable as radiological techniques. For this reason, we shall discuss only radiological data. The data are summarized in Table 1. Due to the difficulty of measuring the range of thoracic

TABLE 2.
Average Stiffness Values (N/mm and Nm/rad) for the Adult Human Spine

Spine Level	Comp.	Shear Ant./Post.	Shear Lat.	Bending Flex./Ext.	Bending Lat.	Axial Torsion
Occ–C1	—	—	—	2.29/1.15	5.16	3.44
C1–2	—	—	—	3.44/2.87	5.16	40.12
C2–7	1317	125/55	33	22.92/40.12	40.12	68.77
T1–12	1250	86/87	101	154.73/189.11	171.92	149.00
L1–L5	667	145/143	132	80.23/166.19	91.69	395.42
L5–S1	1000	78/72	97	120.34/171.92	206.30	263.61

Shear values are given in Newtons per millimeter and bending and axial torsion in Newton metus per rad.
Occ–C1 data from Goel et al. [41].
C2–7 data from Moroney et al. [84].
T1–12 data from Panjabi and White [96].
L1–5 data from Schultz et al. and Berkson et al. [14, 126].
L5–S1 data from McGlashen et al. [74].

torsion to better than 5° (0.09 rad) using traditional planar radiographs [31], these data are only approximate.

IN VITRO MECHANICAL PROPERTIES OF THE SPINE

Knowledge of the load-displacement behavior of the spine and its components is required for mathematical models of the spine. For convenience, most tests of the mechanical properties of the spine have used short lengths of spine consisting of two vertebrae and their intervening soft tissues. This is called a "spine motion segment" or "spine functional unit." In most cases, the load-displacement properties are obtained by gripping the lower vertebra securely, applying known test forces and/or moments to a point on the upper vertebra, and measuring the resulting displacements [96]. In this way the coefficients of the flexibility matrix can be measured directly. Table 2 gives averaged stiffness values for each spine region.

The properties of the occiput–C1–2 complex have recently been studied for the first time by Goel et al. [41]. These workers found that a test moment of 0.3 Nm could give rise to rotations ranging from only 3° (0.05 rad) in lateral bending to 14.5° (0.25 rad) at C1–2 in axial torsion and to 16° at Occ–C1 in extension. Moroney et al. [84] found the lower cervical spine to be an order of magnitude more stiff, being least stiff in flexion and most stiff in axial torsion.

The properties of the adult thoracic spine have been reported by Panjabi et al. [94]. They found average stiffness values ranging from 100 N/mm in lateral shear, to 900 N/mm in anterior or posterior shear, to 1250 N/mm in compression. Rotational stiffness ranges were about 155–172 Nm/rad in flexion, extension, lateral bending and axial torsion.

The overall static load-displacement behavior of lumbar spine motion segments has been well documented over the last 10 years (see e.g., [14, 126]). These tests show that considerable interindividual variations exist. In general, the stiffness of intact spine motion segments is in the range 6–700 N/mm in axial compression; and 1–200 N/mm in anterior, posterior, or lateral shear when test forces of 86 N in shear and 400 N in compression were applied at the vertebral body center. Rotational stiffnesses ranged from 57 to 115 Nm/rad in flexion, extension, and lateral bending to 390 Nm/rad in axial torsion when tested with test moments of 4.7 Nm. To simulate the *in vivo* compression loading of the spine, these results were obtained with a 400-N compressive preload. More recently, the lumbosacral (L5–S1) spine motion segment has been found to have lower (0.5–0.75) shear stiffnesses, larger (1.4–3.3 times) bending stiffnesses, and 1.5 times less stiff torsion behavior than the L1–5 lumbar segments [74].

The influence of the posterior elements has been investigated by first testing the motion segments intact, then removing the posterior elements by excising the pedicles, and finally comparing the behavior of the isolated vertebra-disc-vertebra unit. Not surprisingly, this always leads to a decrease in stiffness. For example, McGlashen et al. [74] found that removal of the posterior elements gave a 1.7-fold increase in shear translations in response to a given test shear force, a 2.1-fold increase in bending rotations in response to a given test moment, and a 2.7 increase in axial rotation in response to a given axial torsion moment.

The ultimate compressive strength of the vertebral centrum varies widely, depending on a number of factors, which include age, sex, and level of activity. Hansson et al. [44] found that the static compressive strength of the lumbar vertebrae averaged about 4000 N. Furthermore, they noted that strength increased in a craniocaudal direction from L1 to L4 by 380 N per level. Most sports require training, which in itself means repetitious loading of the skeleton. Depending on the load levels and the number of repetitions, this can sometimes lead to vertebral fatigue failures that are demonstrable as endplate fractures. The fatigue life of vertebral centra has been found to be surprisingly low [21]. Brinckmann et al. estimated that 2 weeks of athletic training might impose 5000 load cycles on lumbar vertebrae. Using *in vitro* tests, they estimated the probability of fatigue failure at various load levels, expressed as a percentage of maximum static compressive strength. Table 3 shows that the probability of a fatigue failure in 5000 cycles rises from 36% at a 30–40% load level to 92% at a 60–70% load level. Even 10 cycles at the latter load level carried an 8% probability of an endplate fracture.

The mechanical properties of the sacroiliac joints have received little attention compared with the extensive anatomic, histologic, and clinical investigations reviewed by Bellamy et al. [12]. Recently, the load displacement of the adult sacroiliac joint was found to be 100–300 N/mm

TABLE 3.
Probability of Vertebral Fatigue Failure in the Lumbar Spine

Load Level (%)	Cycles to Failure				
	10	100	500	1000	5000
30–40	0	0	21	21	36
40–50	0	38	56	56	67
50–60	0	45	64	82	91
60–70	8	62	76	84	92

Data from Brinckmann et al. [21].

for superior, inferior, anterior, and posterior shear of the sacrum relative to the ilium. Bending stiffness was lowest in axial torsion at 401 Nm/rad, higher in extension at 688 Nm/rad, and highest in flexion and lateral bending at 917 and 1719 Nm/rad, respectively [78]. Thus depending on the test direction, these joints have 0.05 to 7.00 times the stiffness of intact L1–5 lumbar motion segments. No test data are available for the load-displacement behavior of the pubic symphysis. The motions and loads within the human pelvis have recently been simulated using computer models [111].

The load-displacement properties of adult ribs and costovertebral and costosternal articulations have been measured. In general, for the costosternal articulations, a 7-N test force gave rise to displacements of about 5–20 mm in the superior/inferior or anteroposterior (AP) directions at a point 1 cm lateral to the sternal cartilage [121]. Similarly, for the costovertebral articulations, the same test load applied to the rib about 5 cm from the vertebral body resulted in similar displacements of the loading point in the AP and superior/inferior directions, but of only 1 mm in the lateral direction. Human ribs are also flexible. A 7-N test force applied at transverse to the end of a rib whose other end is gripped securely causes displacements of about 30 and 60 mm in upper and lower thoracic ribs, respectively [122].

The bending stiffness of the trunk has been measured in flexion [112], in which the trunk was simply supported at the pelvis and shoulder/neck region and three-point bending applied. Bending stiffness was found to be 0.153×10^8 N/mm^2, or roughly 10 times that of the isolated spine. A second type of measurement is of intact rib cage stiffness when compressed by an indenter, mainly for modeling thorax behavior in automobile crash situations.

EFFECT OF DISC INJURY

One of the most common causes of back and extremity pain is due to compression of the dura and/or nerve root(s) by a disc protrusion. Disc protrusions usually occur on the posterior or posterior-lateral aspect of the disc. It is not known what causes a disc protrusion, but it is believed to be a combination of disc degeneration and either excessive loading [1, 2] or a fatigue failure of the inner posterior annular fibers. Several studies have attempted to address how changes in disc integrity can affect the load-displacement behavior of the disc and intact spine motion segment. Brinckmann [19], for example, found that sectioning the posterior inner annulus fibers to within 1 mm of the periphery results in a small localized bulge of only 0.5 mm in that region under compression loading. This evidence supports the argument that the adult annulus acts as a thick- and not a thin-walled cylinder. On overload, he found that the endplate failed before the injured annulus. In fact, endplate failure is a possible precursor of disc degeneration, because it can disrupt disc nutritional pathways. The link between endplate failure and back pain is not well established, however.

In animals, experimental removal of the nucleus pulposus or enucleation of the disc has been found to cause a significant increase in disc flexibility in shear and bending [134]. Such an increase can lead to increased loading of posterior elements. For example, in humans, derangement of the facet joints does not precede the advent of disc degeneration, but usually follows it. Thus disc enucleation may be one useful animal model for studying the consequences of disc degeneration.

STRENGTH TESTING IN VIVO

Measurements of trunk strength fall into several categories. The simplest, from a biomechanical point of view, are isometric tests of the moments developed about lower lumbar levels in trunk extension, flexion, lateral bending, and axial twisting. Healthy young adult males can develop moments of about 210, 150, 145, and 90 Nm, respectively, in these directions, while females can develop moments with approximately 60% of these values [75].

In recent years, so-called isokinetic strength testing has gained popularity. This form of testing is similar to isometric testing, with the exception that subjects develop maximum force against a force transducer while their trunk is constrained to move at a predetermined angular velocity [68, 72, 136]. Intraindividual correlations between isometric and isokinetic test results are not strong [99].

Other forms of testing include endurance testing, in which subjects are asked either to hold a specified level of trunk moment for as long as possible or, alternatively, to exert a percentage of maximum voluntary strength for given periods, interspersed with rest periods. As an example of the former, Parnianpour et al. [100] found that adults could exert 75% of maximum isometric trunk extensor moment for about 1 minute and a 50% moment for 4–5 minutes.

The simplest form of testing requires no equipment. It consists of repetitions of simple exercises such as sit-ups, curls, and the like. Although simple to conduct, these tests are not necessarily simple to interpret from a biomechanical point of view. This is because they are often performed with widely varying kinematics or body segment accelerations, meaning that the various movements and postures are poorly controlled. Thus, two persons of identical size and shape could subject their muscles to widely varying force-time histories, with very different results. In addition, if the two vary in size and shape as well, the forces required to be developed by the same muscles will be quite dissimilar (see the section on Biomechanical Model Analyses).

Another type of testing involves free weights. Capozzo et al. [22] estimated spine compression during half-squat weight lifting and estimated L3–4 compression range to from 6 to 10 times body weight. Trunk flexion angle was the variable found to affect these loads most significantly.

EFFECT OF AGE AND AGING

Age affects the spine and trunk in two ways. Firstly, in the young, growth increases the linear and cross-sectional dimensions of most structures, consequently increasing body mass and inertia. Not surprisingly, the young spine is more flexible than that of the adult; *in vitro* tests demonstrate that the adolescent spine is 1 to 10 times more flexible than that of the adult, depending on the test direction [87]. Secondly, age can affect both tissue properties and structure. For example, the loss of trunk muscle strength approaches about 1%/year [57], and the decrements in passive tissue strength in cartilage, bone, and tendon/ligament between the third and eighth decades, for example, approach 30, 20, and 18%, respectively [147].

Growth has little effect on the magnitude of thoracic kyphosis; only a few degrees of increase occur from age 5 to age 20. However, lumbar lordosis increases by about 10% between 7 and 17 years of age [141]. During this time, the spine increases in length by about 26% [132].

The range of spine flexion does not increase with age, but lateral bending does [43]. In the elderly, increased thoracic kyphosis and decreased lumbar lordosis occur [82], partially due to a decrease in overall disc height. This loss of disc height is due partly to disc degeneration and partly to an increased curvature of the vertebral endplate [35], perhaps resulting from osteoporotic changes of the vertebral cancellous bone.

Disc degeneration itself starts in the second decade of life and continues steadily thereafter, as Figure 5 shows. Disc degeneration is part of the normal aging process and is itself unrelated to pain or symptoms. Does degeneration affect the mechanical properties of the spine? In one study, Nachemson et al. [92] found no effect of degeneration on the

FIGURE 5

*Percentage of intervertebral discs in each degeneration grade by age. Grade 1
discs are nondegenerate, while grade IV discs are severely degenerate [87].
Data are for 600 discs (Miller et al. [80]).*

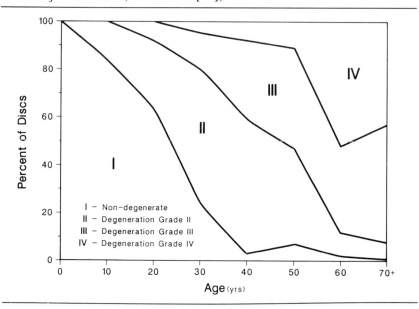

behavior of lumbar vertebrae. Koeller et al. [64] also found little effect
of age on compression stiffness, but did find an increase in creep in
elderly spines.

IN VIVO MEASUREMENTS

Myoelectric Measurements of Trunk Muscle Activity
Direct measurements *in vivo* of the loads imposed upon spine motion
segments and the muscle contraction forces developed in physical task
performances are not practical. However, those loads can be quantified
indirectly by measurements of intradiscal pressures (described subsequently) and measurements of myoelectric activities. The latter arise
because motor nerves engender muscle contractions through the transmission of electrical signals.

Semiquantitative measurements of myoelectric activities have been reported, for example, by Walters and Partridge [142] in the anterior
abdominal muscles; by Carlsoo [23] in an array of trunk muscles; and
by Morris et al. [85], Pauly [101], and Donish and Basmajian [30] in back
muscles.

TABLE 4
Typical Mean Myoelectric Signal Levels in Lumbar Trunk Muscles during Static Exertions in Upright Standing

		Muscles							
		Left Side				Right Side			
Task		ES	RA	OM	OL	ES	RA	OM	OL
Stand Relaxed		3	1	0	0	2	1	1	0
Ext MVS	(204 Nm)	100	7	32	29	100	6	34	17
Flx Res	(43 Nm)	30	1	0	1	27	1	0	1
Flex MVS	(191 Nm)	2	100	100	55	4	100	100	44
Ext Res	(37 Nm)	2	25	39	13	1	27	25	11
RLB MVS	(164 Nm)	7	14	22	10	64	53	91	100
LLB Res	(39 Nm)	2	1	3	1	22	10	22	18
LLB MVS	(180 Nm)	44	43	96	100	6	21	24	9
RLB Res	(39 Nm)	23	12	23	20	3	4	3	1
RTw MVS	(91 Nm)	19	8	87	44	18	13	69	39
LTw Res	(51 Nm)	5	0	15	6	7	1	6	4
LTw MVS	(85 Nm)	24	22	64	59	26	20	66	38
RTw Res	(51 Nm)	6	3	8	10	6	2	10	5

ES = erector spinae, RA = rectus abdominus, OM = medial oblique abdominals, OL = lateral oblique abdominals.
MVS = maximum voluntary strength exertion, Res = resist externally applied force. Flex = flexion, Ext = extension, RLB = right lateral bend, LLB = left lateral bend, RTw = right twist, LTw = left twist. The mean moments developed during these tasks are indicated in parentheses.
Data from Schultz et al. [123]. Readings are normalized to maximum voluntary exertion levels and expressed in percentages.

Quantitative measurements of trunk muscle activities have more recently been reported by Andersson et al. [4], Schultz et al. [125] and Pope et al. [105], for example. Myoelectric signals are noisy, and their absolute values are affected by many variables that cannot easily be controlled. However, when signals are averaged over subject population means and compared on a relative basis from task to task, they can more readily be interpreted quantitatively (Table 4 provides sample data). The papers last cited use these ideas to interpret the activities measured. A chief use of such measurements is for validation of biomechanical model analyses of muscle contraction forces.

Disc Pressures
Nachemson [87] demonstrated that the pressure developed within the nucleus pulposis of a nondegenerated cadaver lumbar intervertebral disc is nearly proportional to the compressive load on the motion segment

TABLE 5
Typical Values of Pressures within the L3–4 Disk

Task	Intradiscal Pressure (kPa)*	Corresponding Spine Compression ((N)†)
Quiet standing	270	380
Resist applied moments in:		
Flexion (41 Nm)	710	990
Extension (28 Nm)	720	1010
Lateral bending (43 Nm)	620	870
Twisting (28 Nm)	480	670
Arms forward, 4 kg in each hand	670	940
Trunk flexed 30° (0.52 rad), arms		
forward, 4 kg in each hand	1620	2270

*Data from Schultz et al. [118]. Means over four subjects are reported.
†Data assume that the L3 cross-sectional area is 17.5 cm² and that nucleus pressure is 1.25 times applied pressure.

containing that disc. Schultz et al. [126] showed that other modes of loading seldom substantially modify this proportionality, and found intradiscal pressure to be approximately 1.3 times the compression load divided by the transverse cross-sectional area of the disc. Thus, measurements of intradiscal pressure provide a means to estimate spine compression loads.

Nachemson and Morris [91] used this idea to determine compression loads on the lumbar spine *in vivo* that result from task performances. Subsequent studies have been reported and/or reviewed by Nachemson and Elfstrom [90], Andersson et al. [5], Nachemson [88], and Schultz et al. [118], for example. Pressures within the nucleus of the L3–4 disc are typically 300 kPa in quiet upright standing configurations, corresponding roughly to a compression on the order of the weight of the body segments superior to L3, but they can easily be five or more times this value in even relatively modest exertions (Table 5). A chief use of intradiscal pressure measurements has been for validation of biomechanical model predictions of spine loads.

Trunk Cavity Pressurization
It was recognized as early as 1923 [58] that trunk cavity pressurization is sometimes used to relieve loads on the spine. Davis [27], Bartelink [10], and Morris et al. [86] contributed some of the earlier reports of abdominal cavity pressure measurements during physical task performances. Typically, in heavy exertion, abdominal cavity pressure peaks are on the order of 13.3 kPa (100 mm Hg), but Eie and Wehn [33] found cavity pressures in a weight lifter as large as 26.7 kPa (200 mm Hg). Morris et al. [86] reported thoracic cavity pressure measurements as well, and analyzed the load-relieving effects of such pressures.

Scaled anatomical cross sections [37] show that the area of the abdominal cavity is on the order of 50% of the product of lumbar trunk width times depth, or approximately 300 cm^2 in an average-sized male adult. A cavity pressure of 13.3 kPa, then, yields a pressure resultant of approximately 400 N. The cavity cross-section centroid lies anterior to the intervertebral disc center at a distance that is approximately 42% of trunk depth, or about 8.4 cm. Thus, large abdominal cavity pressures can produce flexion-relieving moments about a lumbar intervertebral disc center on the order of 37 Nm. This moment is relatively small compared to the approximately 200-Nm extension moment that can be developed in maximum voluntary exertions.

Measurements of abdominal cavity presures during task performances that have been proposed as indicators of spine load. Davis and Mairiaux et al. [27, 71] provide recent expositions of this idea, but some evidence to the contrary has been reported [118, 137]. Moreover, whether abdominal cavity pressurization actually reduces loads on the spine has been questioned (see, e.g., [89]).

Other In Vivo Measurements

In experiments that began to investigate the neuromuscular control of the spine and the trunk posture control system, Jakobs et al. [54] made measurements of spine position sense in which they compared the accuracy with which the spine and trunk may be positioned over the pelvis in the upright and supine positions. They found that positioning was three times better in the upright position, presumably due to the contribution of the vestibular system. Visual feedback was eliminated in these tests. In a follow-up study, Jepsen et al. [56] compared positioning accuracy in the frontal and sagittal planes and found the former to be 27% better than the latter. Such data are valuable baseline data when evaluating patients for possible trunk/spine postural control system dysfunction.

BIOMECHANICAL MODEL ANALYSES

Rigid Body Models to Determine Trunk Loads

The easiest and safest way of determining the loads placed on the trunk structures when a physical task is performed is biomechanical model analysis. Concepts of rigid body equilibrium when tasks are performed slowly, and concepts of rigid body dynamics when they are performed rapidly, underlie these analysis. Morris et al. [86] were among the first to attempt a biomechanical analysis of trunk loads. The relevant ideas will be illustrated through calculations of lumbar trunk internal loads, but similar ideas can be used to calculate internal loads on any musculoskeletal system structures.

FIGURE 6

Free body diagram for a simple weight-holding task. (a). Q is the weight held, W's are the weights of the various body segments, and x's are their distances anterior to the intervertebral disc center. F_z and M_y are the nonzero components of the net reaction. (b). E is the contraction force in the back muscles and C is the compression on the intervertebral disc. E and C together must provide the required F_z and M_y.

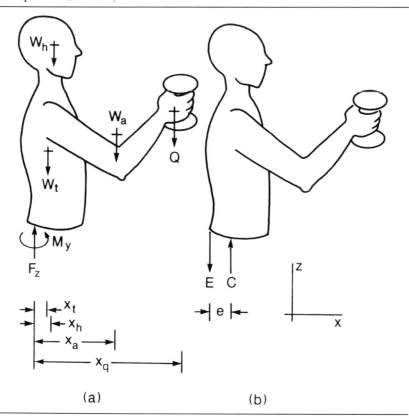

(a) (b)

Calculation of Contraction Forces and Internal Loads Given Net Reactions: A Simple Case

An illustration of a simple internal load calculation is afforded by an analysis of a sagittally symmetric weight-holding task. To gauge the muscle contraction forces needed and the loads that this task imposes on the lumbar trunk structures, consider the free body diagram (Figure 6a) of the body segments above an imaginary transverse cutting plane at the L3 level. The net reaction across the cutting plane required to keep the upper body segments in equilibrium consists of the force F_z and the moment M_y. The values of these follow from the equations expressing longitudinal force and flexion-extension moment equilibrium:

$$F_z = W_a + W_h + W_t + Q \tag{2}$$
$$-M_y = x_a W_a + x_n W_n + x_t W_t + x_q Q$$

where the W's represent the weights of the arms, head, trunk, and the weight held, and the x's their moment arms about the center of the L3 spine motion segment. Appropriate values of those weights might be 60, 40, 250 and 50 N, and 20, 5, 1, and 40 cm. In that case, the nonzero components of the net reaction are F_z = 400 N and M_y = 36.5 Nm.

Once the net reaction is known, a set of internal loads that can provide it can be calculated. Assume, to make the calculation simple, that the required net reaction is developed solely by a spine compression force C and an equivalent back muscle tension E acting over moment arm e (Figure 6b). Balance of forces and moments now requires that

$$F_z = C - E \tag{3}$$
$$-M_y = -eE$$

An appropriate value of e is 5 cm. Then, for the data given above, E = 730 N and C = 1130 N. Note that this spine compression is about three times the superincumbent body weight. Its value is dictated largely by the need to balance the flexion moments.

Calculation of Contraction Forces and Internal Loads from Given Net Reactions: More Complicated Cases
Animals move and exert forces on their surroundings through the use of their muscles. Cross-section muscle models, based on concepts of rigid body equilibrium, enable analyses of the effects that the contraction of muscles produce in more complicated cases. Simple calculations of muscle contraction forces from given net reactions like the one illustrated above are "statically determinate," because the number of unknowns is three or fewer, and up to three equations of moment equilibrium are available to find them. However, such calculations are "statically indeterminate." In these calculations, typically three net reaction equilibrium requirements are given, but more than three muscles contract to produce them. Moreover, other resulting internal load components need to be calculated. Thus, the number of unknowns exceeds the number of equations available to find them.

Figure 7 shows a 10-single-equivalent muscle model through a transverse section of the lumbar trunk at the L3 level (data from [125]). It is convenient to choose this level for analysis, because a cutting plane does

FIGURE 7
Schematic representation of a lumbar trunk cross-sectional model with 10 sin-gle-equivalent muscles. The muscle equivalents represent the rectus abdominis (R), the internal (I) and the external (X) oblique abdominal, the erector spinae (E) and the latissimus dorsi (L) muscles. C, S_a, and S_r are the motion segment compression and shear forces. P is the abdominal cavity pressure resultant.

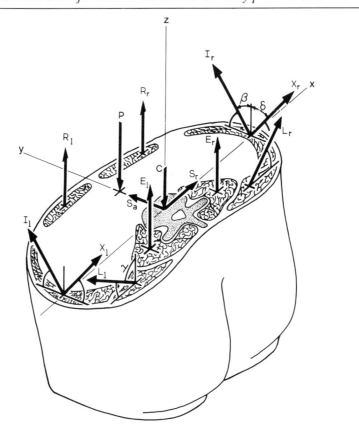

not intersect bony structures other than those of the spine; load trans-mission paths through bony structures may be complex. Table 6 gives the representative values of the areas, and the centroidal locations and lines of action of those muscles. Similar data have been gathered by, for example, Nemeth and Ohlsen [93]. Table 7 presents the equations of statics that govern the calculation of the net force at and moment about the center of the L3 intervertebral disc that these muscles develop. So-lutions of these equations serve to predict how a physical task perfor-mance will load the structures of the trunk. These equations incorporate

TABLE 6
Data Incorporated into the 10-Single-Equivalent Muscle L3 Cross-Sectional Model

Muscle	Symbol	Line of Action	Area Ratio per Side*	Location of Centroid	
				Anteroposterior Offset Ratio†	Lateral Offset Ratio‡
Rectus abdominus	R	Longitudinal	0.0060	0.540	0.121
Oblique abdominals		Inclined 45° (0.79 rad) to longitudinal in sagittal plane			
Internal	I		0.0168	0.189	0.453
External	X		0.0148	0.189	0.453
Erector spinae	E	Longitudinal	0.0390	0.220	0.179
Latissimus dorsi	L	Inclined 45° (0.79 rad) to longitudinal in frontal plane	0.0037	0.276	0.211

The vertebral body center lies in the midsagittal plane at 0.66 times the trunk depth from the anteriormost edge of the cross section.
*In ratio to trunk width times trunk depth.
†From vertebral body center, in ratio to trunk depth.
‡From vertebral body center, in ratio to trunk width.

TABLE 7

The Equations of Equilibrium That Govern the 10-Muscle Cross-Sectional Model of Figure 7

Equations of force equilibrium

$$F_x = S_r + (L_r - L_1) *\sin(\gamma)$$
$$F_y = S_a + (I_1 - L_r) *\sin(\beta) - (X_1 + X_r) *\sin(\delta)$$
$$F_z = (E_1 + E_r) + (R_1 + R_r) + (L_1 + L_r) *\cos(\gamma) + (I_1 + I_r) *\cos(\beta) + (X_1 - X_r) *\cos(\delta) - C$$

Equations of moment equilibrium

$$M_x = (R_1 + R_r) *x_r + ((I_1 + I_r) *\cos(\beta) + (X_1 + X_r) *\cos(\delta)) *x_0 - (E_1 + E_r) *x_e - (L_1 - {}_r) *\cos(\beta) *x_1$$
$$M_y = (R_r - R_1) *y_r + ((I_r - I_1) *\cos(\beta) + (X_r - X_L) *\cos(\delta)) *y_0 - (E_1 + E_r) *y_e - (L_1 + L_r) *\cos(\gamma) *y_1$$
$$M_z = ((I_r - I_1) *\sin(\beta) + (X_1 - X_r) *\sin(\delta)) *x_0 + (L_r - L_1) *\sin(\gamma) *y_1$$

F_x, F_y, F_z are the net reaction force components.
M_x, M_y, M_z are the net reaction moment components.
C, S_a, S_r are the motion segment compression and shear forces.
E_1, L_1, R_1, I_1, X_1 are the forces in the left-side erector spinae, latissimus dorsi, rectus abdominus, and internal and external oblique muscles.
E_r, L_r, R_r, I_r, X_r are the corresponding right-side muscle forces.
β, γ, δ are the angles shown in Figure 7.
x_e, x_1, x_r, x_0 are the (positive) distances from the y axis for the corresponding muscles.
y_e, y_1, y_r, y_0 are the corresponding distances from the x axis.

the assumption that the lumbar motion segment can resist compression and shear forces, but not significant bending moments. The reason for this assumption is that the passive bending resistance developed by a lumbar motion segment in small rotations is only a few Nm per degree, while net moments are often of the order of 100 Nm.

Statically indeterminate calculations of internal loads can be made in a number of ways, but only one technique will be described and that only in brief. In this technique, two quantities are optimized in two successive applications of linear programming. In the first linear program, the maximum muscle contraction intensity (force per unit area) for which solutions exist is first minimized, subject to constraints that moment equilibrium be satisfied (expressed in the last three equations of Table 7) and that no contraction force can be negative. In the second linear program, a set of contraction forces that minimize the value of spine compression is calculated (using the third equation of Table 7), subject to the above two constraints plus the requirement that the maximum contraction intensity used at this stage not exceed the value first calculated. Details of the calculation schemes are given by Bean et al. [11].

To illustrate the results from four sets of calculations of this kind, consider four upright standing tasks in which a pure moment of 40 Nm about the L3 disc center is applied and is to be resisted. Let the applied moment be in flexion, then in extension, then in right lateral bending,

TABLE 8

Net Reaction Moments for 40-Nm Moment-Resist Tasks in Relaxed Standing

	Mx	My	Mz
Flexion	40	0	0
Extension	−40	0	0
Right lateral bend	0	40	0
Right twist	0	0	−40

Body weight moments would be small and are neglected.
Axis directions are as shown in Figure 7.

then in right twisting. The three net reaction moment components for each of these tasks are give in Table 8.

Using the 10-muscle cross-sectional model shown in Figure 7, the geometry data from Table 6, and the calculation scheme just outlined, the internal loads that result are shown in Table 9. The maximum muscle contraction intensities are considerably smaller than those for human muscle reported by Ikai and Fukunaga [51], which were 400–1000 kPa.

In the flexion and extension resist tasks, the calculated muscle contraction forces are sagittally symmetric, as might be expected. The bend and twist resist contraction sets are less easily interpreted. In twisting, the left internal obliques and the left latissimus dorsi contract, but the external obliques contract on the right side. This merely reflects the different line of action of those muscles.

Both erector spinae muscles contract during the twist resist, yet neither contributes a twist moment. Similarly, two left-side muscles contract during the bend-resist task, despite the fact that they produce antagonistic lateral bending moments. The reason for these events is the same in both situations. All three components of the moments must be equilibrated, and Table 9 shows the set of contraction forces that can accomplish this with a minimum of maximum intensity, and within that constraint, a minimum spine compression. The outcome of a statically indeterminate calculation is not always obvious.

Detailed discussions about various trunk muscle models and their use are given by, for example, Andersson et al. [6], Schultz and Andersson [115], Schultz et al. [116, 117, 118], Schultz et al. [125], and Schultz et al. [113, 114, 123].

Extension to Dynamic Performances

In tasks that are performed rapidly, the inertial forces and moments needed to accelerate body segments can become large compared to the forces and moments needed to equilibrate those segments in the same tasks performed slowly. In such dynamic performances, inertial loading needs to be accounted for in the computation of the net reaction. Dy-

TABLE 9
Calculated Muscle Contraction Forces for 40-Nm Resist Tasks, Using 10-Muscle Model of Figure 7 and Geometry Data of Table 6

| Resist Test | Muscle Contraction Forces (N) | | | | | | | | | | Spine Cmp. (N) | Maximum Intensity (kPa) |
| | Left Side | | | | | Right Side | | | | | | |
	ES	RA	IO	XO	LT	ES	RA	IO	XO	LT		
Flexion	419	0	0	0	40	419	0	0	0	40	894	179
Extension	0	80	224	198	0	0	80	224	198	0	757	223
Left lateral bend	0	12	16	0	0	306	47	132	116	0	551	131
Right twist	59	0	212	0	47	143	0	0	187	0	518	211

ES = erector spinae, RA = rectus abdominus, IO = internal oblique abdominals, XO = external oblique abdominals, LT = latissimus dorsi.

FIGURE 8

A single block model for analysis of upper body dynamics. The mass, m, of all body segments superior to the trunk level of interest is assumed to pivot as a single rigid body about the disc center. a_h and a_v are the components of the mass center acceleration. H, V, and M are the nonzero force and moment components of the net reaction.

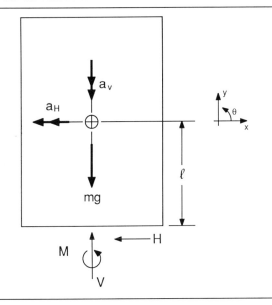

namic performance of a task may also alter the calculation of the internal loads, if for no other reason than that significant cocontractions of antagonistic muscles probably will arise. However, few studies of this latter phenomenon are available to guide biomechanical analyses. Hence, this section will illustrate only how inertial loading effects on net reactions can be calculated.

Consider the simple free-body model of upper body sagittal rotation dynamics shown in Figure 8. The model assumes that all body segments above the L3 level are rotated about L3 as a single rigid body, and the rotation angle is measured by θ. Those segments are represented as a block of mass m whose mass center lies at a distance l superior to L3. The problem is, given values $\dot{\theta}$ and $\ddot{\theta}$ for the angular velocity and acceleration of the block, calculate the net reaction components at L3. These are taken to be a horizontal reaction H, a vertical reaction V, and a trunk moment M. In the course of calculating them, knowledge of the horizontal and vertical components of the mass center acceleration, a_H and a_V, will be needed.

The equations of plane rigid body dynamics become

$$H = ma_H$$
$$V = m(g - a_V) \qquad (4)$$
$$M = I\ddot{\theta}$$

The kinematic equations governing the mass center accelerations are

$$a_H = l\ddot{\theta} \qquad (5)$$
$$a_V = l\dot{\theta}^2$$

To get a feeling for the order of magnitude of the numbers involved, suppose that values for $\dot{\theta}$ and $\ddot{\theta}$ are chosen as the maximum angular velocity and angular acceleration that would occur during a sinusoidal oscillation of double amplitude equal to 0.70 rad (40°). Then the maximum values of $\dot{\theta}$ and $\ddot{\theta}$ would be 2.14 rad/s and 13.8 rad/s². Suppose the block has a mass of 40 kg and a radius of gyration in the sagittal plane about L3 of 0.29 m, so that its moment of inertia is 3.3 kgm². Substituting these numbers into equations (4) and (5), obtain

$$a_H = 3.45 \text{ m/s}^2 \qquad a_V = 1.20 \text{ m/s}^2$$
$$H = 138 \text{ N} \qquad V = 344 \text{ N} \qquad (6)$$
$$M = 45.9 \text{ Nm}$$

Note that the centripetal acceleration causes the vertical reaction to be less than the weight of the upper body segments. The required inertial moment is on the order of one-fourth of the typical maximum voluntary static trunk muscle strength and corresponds roughly to the moment required to support the upper body when the trunk is statically flexed 30° (0.52 rad). Dynamic performances of physical tasks clearly can load musculoskeletal structures heavily, even in the absence of externally applied loads. In fact, it is the strengths of the muscles that determine the largest linear and angular accelerations that can be produced.

Once the net reaction for a dynamic task performance is calculated, sets of muscle contraction and other internal forces that produce it would be calculated, just as for slow performance. What assumptions are appropriate when doing this in dynamic situations, however, is a topic of current research. Moreover, the example just given was quite simple. It considered the dynamics of a single body in plane motion. Biomechanical models that realistically represent a high-speed athletic performance are likely to incorporate many rigid bodies mutually linked. At best, the motions of those bodies might be considered to be plane, but they are more likely to be fully three-dimensional. The computational requirements of realistic body dynamics simulations usually are very substantial.

DEFORMABLE ELEMENT AND FINITE ELEMENT MODELS

The previous section showed how rigid body models can be used to calculate the net reaction imposed by a static or dynamic task performance across an imaginary cutting plane through any section of the body. It also showed how a cross-sectional muscle model can be used to calculate sets of muscle contraction forces capable of balancing that net reaction.

Rigid body models are inappropriate to determine how the human body deforms when loads are applied to it. Models appropriate for this sort of investigation usually consist of a collection of rigid bodies interconnected by a series of deformable elements. Usually each rigid body represents a bone, and the deformable elements are used to represent the passive resistances to relative motions among those bones provided by ligaments, intervertebral discs, and similar soft tissues. Such deformable element models are also useful to determine how structural loads are distributed among multiple soft tissues that interconnect bones, or to determine what relative movements of skeletal structures are produced when various muscles contract with known tensions.

Finite element models are useful to investigate stress and strain distributions within various structures of the musculoskeletal system. In finite element models, the structure of interest is represented by a series of elements, each of which is deformable.

Neither deformable element nor finite element models have so far been used extensively in sports biomechanics research, so they will not be further described here. General description of their use are given, for example, by King [63] and by Schultz and Miller [119].

Descriptions of deformable element models of the trunk are given by, for example, Andriacchi et al. [7], Belytschko et al. [13], and Schultz et al. [120]. Takashima et al. [135] describe the use of such models to examine the actions of each of the major trunk muscles. Models of this kind have been used to investigate the biomechanics underlying the progression and correction of idiopathic scoliosis (e.g., [42, 81, 124]). Shirazi-Adl et al. [127, 128, 130] provide recent examples of the use of finite element models of spine motion segments to analyze stress and pressure distributions within them.

EPIDEMIOLOGY OF BACK PAIN

Between 60 and 80% of the population suffer from back pain at some time in their lives [49, 50, 70]. Impairments of the back and spine are the most frequent cause of chronic limitation of physical activity among persons under 45 years of age and are second only to natural childbirth in accounting for stays in hospitals [104]. In persons aged 45 to 64 years, they rank third after heart disease, and arthritis and rheumatism [59]. Most back pain is idiopathic, meaning that it is of unknown origin. Mechanical factors are clearly implicated in the etiology of some forms of back pain. For example, Kelsey et al. [61] found that workers who lifted weights exceeding 11.3 kg (25 lb) more than 25 times per day while twisting the body were 7.2 times more likely to suffer a prolapsed lumbar disc than those who did not. Similar results were found for the cervical spine [62]. Why the preponderance of disc protrusions occur at the C5–6, C6–7, L4–5, and L5–S1 [60, 62] levels is unknown.

Back pain is uncommon in young children [46]. However, Fairbank et al. [39] studying a group of adolescents aged 13 to 17 years, found that 25.8% (115 of 446) had a history of back pain. These adolescents were found to have increased trunk length when compared with those with no pain. Somewhat paradoxically, back pain was found to be more common in those who avoided sports. However, participation in sports does entail the risk of injury, although this risk varies widely among sports. The most common athletic injuries are to the knee and ankle, accounting for 54 of 72% of male and female injuries, respectively, in 3431 cases at one university over a 7-year period [28]. While strains/sprains dominated, back strain represented only 2–3% of all sprains compared to knee and ankle injuries (63–79%).

Because of the possibility of increasing the intensity and duration of training too rapidly for the musculoskeletal system to adapt, athletic overuse injuries can occur in the spine and trunk, just as they can in the extremities [47]. The example of vertebral endplate fractures occurring within only 2000 cycles of compression has already been noted. As another example of overuse injuries affecting the spine, let us consider the neural arch, which is prone to spondylolysis. This is probably a fatigue fracture of the pars interarticularis [144] and occurs in a number of athletic activities, ranging from gymnastics to American football. Many of these activities require repetitive movements that include large ranges of spine motion, often combined with considerable inertial loads due to rapid accelerations and decelerations. In the pole vault, for example, the thoracic and lumbar spine is first extended 40° (0.70 rad) at pole plant and then flexed through 130° (2.27 rad) in 650 ms [110].

Spondylolysis rarely occurs before the age of 7 or 8 years and is seldom associated with a single traumatic event [46]. Female gymnasts have an incidence of spondylolysis that is four times higher (11%) than that of the general female population [53]. Similarly, male high school and university athletes have an incidence of 20.7% [48], or roughly four to five times the 4–6% found in the general population [108].

Other examples include nontraumatic cervical spine injuries in diving and high jumping [98], presumably related to chronic repeated external forces to the head and neck region. The latter was a subluxation injury of C5 on C6 caused by biweekly training sessions consisting of 12–16 jumps per session, combined with peculiarities in landing technique.

Scheuermann's disease is a condition in which increased kyphosis over 35° (0.61 rad) and wedging of 5° (0.09 rad) of one or more vertebrae is present in the thoracic spine [17]. Although its etiology is unknown, Scheuermann noted that this condition was common among patients subjected to heavy work loads and suspected that mechanical factors may play a role in causing the abnormalities in vertebral endplate and growth cartilages. The incidence in adolescents between 10 and 14 years is about 1% [8]. This condition has been noted among competitive butterfly swimmers [143], with one multiple Olympic champion being a notable example. The total number of spine loading cycles due to the trunk muscle contractions required to perform butterfly or other swimming arm strokes in 4 hours of daily training must exceed several thousand.

SUMMARY

This chapter has reviewed the past 30 years of experimental biomechanical studies of the spine and trunk. In the last 10 years, computers have allowed the development of simulation techniques and models to predict spine and muscle loading in most static and quasi-static activities. Some problems remain, however, particularly with activities involving bending and twisting and those that entail maximal efforts.

Current research is focused on trying to validate models for the analysis of dynamic activities involving simple planar motions. Although the body segment kinematics and external support forces in complex motions can be measured fairly easily with modern motion analysis equipment, models that correctly predict the internal trunk forces have yet to be fully developed and validated. These models will be useful in studying how, why, and where failure of the soft and bony tissues is most likely to occur in a given activity, and whether it is related to work or athletics.

The challenge for the future is to develop models that adequately reflect the anatomical sophistication of the spine and trunk. Thus the stress and strain distributions in any trunk musculoskeletal component, whether the posterior wall of the annulus, a muscle slip of the semispinalis group, or the lumbosacral endplate, will be able to be found. These results can then be combined with models of cumulative trauma response to successfully identify potential failure sites.

REFERENCES

1. Adams, M.A., and W.C. Hutton. Prolapsed intervertebral disc. A hyperflexion study. *Spine* 7:184–191, 1982.

2. Adams, M.A., and W.C. Hutton. Gradual disc prolapse. *Spine* 10:524–531, 1985.

3. Adams, M.A., and W.C. Hutton. The effect of posture on the fluid content of lumbar intervertebral discs. *Spine* 8:665–671, 1983.

4. Andersson, G.B.J., R. Ortengren, and P. Herberts. Quantitative electromyographic studies of back muscle activity related to posture and loading. *Orthop. Clin. North Am.* 8:85–96, 1977.

5. Andersson, G.B.J., R. Ortengren, and A. Nachemson. Intradiscal pressure, intra-abdominal pressure and myoelectric back muscle activity related to posture and loading. *Clin. Orthop. Res.* 129:156–164, 1977.

6. Andersson, G.B.J., R. Ortengren, and A.B. Schultz. Analysis and measurement of the loads on the lumbar spine during work at a table. *J. Biomech.* 13:513–520, 1980.

7. Andriacchi, T., A. Schultz, T. Belytschko, and J. Galante. A model for studies of mechanical interactions between the human spine and rib cage. *J. Biomech.* 7:497–507, 1974.

8. Ascani, E., and A. Montanaro. Scheuermann's disease. In D.S. Bradford and R.N. Hensinger (eds.). *The Pediatric Spine.* New York, Georg Thieme Verlag, 1985, pp. 307–324.

9. Bakke, S.N. Roentgenologische Beobachtungen ueber die bewegungen der wirbel-saule. *Acta Radiol.* 13(suppl.):56–69, 1931.

10. Bartelink, D.L. The role of abdominal pressure in relieving the pressure of the lumbar intervertebral disc. *J. Bone Joint Surg.* 39B:718–725, 1957.

11. Bean, J.C., D.B. Chaffin, and A.B. Schultz. Biomechanical model calculation of muscle contraction forces: A double linear programming method. *J. Biomech.* 21:59–66, 1988.

12. Bellamy, N., W. Park, and P.J. Rooney. What do we know about the sacroiliac joint? *Semin. Arthritis Rheum.* 12:282–313, 1983.

13. Belytschko, T.B., T.P. Andriacchi, A.B. Schultz, and J.O. Galante. Analog studies of forces in the human spine: computational techniques. *J. Biomech.* 6:361–371, 1973.

14. Berkson, M.H., A.L. Nachemson, and A.B. Schultz. Mechanical properties of human lumbar spine motion segments, part II: Responses in compression and shear: Influence of gross morphology. *J. Biomech. Eng.* 101:53–57, 1979.

15. Bogduk, N. A reappraisal of the anatomy of the human lumbar erector spinae. *J. Anat.* 131:525–540, 1980.

16. Bogduk, N., and J.E. Macintosh. The applied anatomy of the thoracolumbar fascia. *Spine* 9:164–170, 1984.

17. Bradford, D.S., J.H. Moe, F.J. Montalvo, and R.B. Winter. Scheuermann's kyphosis and roundback deformity, results of Milwaukee brace treatment in twenty two patients. *J. Bone Joint Surg.* 57A:439–448, 1975.

18. Brandner, M.E. Normal values of the vertebral body and intervertebral disc index during growth. *Am. J. Roentgenol.* 110: 618–627, 1970.

19. Brinckmann, P. Injury of the annulus fibrosus and disc protrusions. An in vivo investigation of human lumbar motion segments. Internal Report No. 22, Munster, Orthopadische Universitatsklinik, 1985.

20. Brinckmann, P., W. Frobin, E. Hierholzer, and M. Horst. Deformation of the vertebral end-plate under axial loading of the spine. *Spine* 8:851–856, 1983.

21. Brinckmann, P., N. Johannleweling, D. Hilweg, and M. Biggemann. Fatigue fracture of human lumbar vertebrae. Internal Report No. 32, Munster: Orthopadische Universitatsklinik, 1986.

22. Capozzo, A., F. Felici, F. Figura, and F. Gazzani. Lumbar spine loading during half squat exercises. *Med. Sci. Sports Exerc.* 17:613–20, 1985.

23. Carlsoo, S. The static muscle load in different work positions: An electromyographic study. *Ergonomics* 4:193–211, 1961.

24. Clauser, C.E., J.T. McConville, and J.W. Young. Weight, volume and center of mass

of segments of the human body. AMRL-TR-69-70. Dayton, Ohio: Aerospace Medical Laboratories, Wright-Patterson Air Force Base, 1969.

25. Cobb, J.R. Outline for the study of scoliosis. Instructional Course Lectures. St. Louis: American Academy of Orthopedic Surgeons, 1984, pp. 261–275.

26. Cyron, B.M., and W.C. Hutton. The fatigue strength of the lumbar neural arch in spondylolysis. *J. Bone Joint Surg.* 60B:234–238, 1978.

27. Davis, P.R. Variations of the human intraabdominal pressure during weight lifting in different postures. *J. Anat. (Lond.)* 90:601, 1956.

28. Dehaven, K.E., and D.M. Lintner. Athletic injuries: Comparison by age, sport and gender. *Am. J. Sports Med.* 14:218–224, 1986.

29. DePuky, P. The physiological oscillations of the length of the body. *Acta Orthop. Scand.* 6:338–347, 1935.

30. Donish, E.W., and J.V. Basmajian. Electromyography of deep back muscle in man. *Am. J. Anat.* 133:25–36, 1972.

31. Drerup, B. Improvements in measuring vertebral rotation from the projections of the pedicles. *J. Biomech.* 18:369–378, 1985.

32. Ecklund, J.A.E., and E.N. Corlett. Shrinkage as a measure of the effect of load on the spine. *Spine* 9:189–194, 1984.

33. Eie, N., and P. Wehn. Measurements of the intra-abdominal pressure in relation to weight bearing of the lumbosacral spine. *J. Oslo City Hosp.* 12:205–217, 1962.

34. El-Bohy, A.A., and A.I. King. Intervertebral disc and facet contact pressure in axial torsion. *Adv. Bioeng.* 2:26–27, 1986.

35. Ericksen, M.F. Aging on the lumbar spine II, L1 and L2. *Am. J. Physiol. Anthropol.* 48:241–246, 1978.

36. Estes, W.L. The causes and occurrence of functional scoliosis in college men. *J.A.M.A.* 75:1411–1414, 1921.

37. Eycleshymer, A.C., and D.M. Schoemaker. *A Cross-Section Anatomy.* New York: Appleton-Century-Crofts, 1911.

38. Eyre, D.R., and H. Muir. Types I and II colagens in intervertebral disc. *Biochem. J.* 157:267–270, 1976.

39. Fairbank, J.C., P.B. Pynsent, J.A. Van-Poortvliet, and H. Phillips. Influence of anthropometric factors and joint laxity in the incidence of adolescent back pain. *Spine* 9:461–464, 1984.

40. Farfan, H.F., R.M. Huberdeau, and H.I. Dubow. Lumbar intervertebral disc degeneration: The influence of geometrical features on the pattern of disc degeneration. *J. Bone Joint Surg.* 54A:492–510, 1972.

41. Goel, V.K., C.R. Clark, K. Galles, and Y.K. Liu. The biokinetics of occipito-atlanto-axial joint. *Adv. Bioeng.* 2:42–43, 1986.

42. Haderspeck, K., and A. Schultz. Progression of idiopathic scoliosis—an analysis of muscle actions and body weight influences. *Spine* 6:447–455, 1981.

43. Haley, S.M., W.L. Tada, and E.M. Carmichael. Spinal mobility in young children. A normative study. *Phys. Ther.* 66:1697–1703, 1986.

44. Hansson, T., B. Roos, and A. Nachemson. The bone mineral content and ultimate compressive strength of lumbar vertebrae. *Spine* 5:46–55, 1980.

45. Hellems, H.K, and T.E. Keats. Measurement of the normal lumbrosacral angle. *Am. J. Roentgenol.* 113:642–645, 1971.

46. Hensinger, R.N. Back pain in children. In D.S. Bradford and R.N. Hensinger (eds.). *The Pediatric Spine.* New York: George Thieme Verlag, 1985, pp. 41–60.

47. Herrin, G.D., M. Jaraiedi, and C.K. Anderson. Prediction of overexertion injuries using biomechanical and psychophysical models. *Am. Ind. Hyg. Assoc. J.* 47:322–330, 1986.

48. Hoshina, H. Spondylolysis in athletes. *Physician Sportsmed.* 3:75–78, 1980.

49. Hult, L. Cervical, dorsal and lumbar spinal syndromes. *Acta Orthop. Scand* 17(suppl.):1–102, 1954.

200 | Ashton-Miller, Schultz

50. Hult, L. The Mukfors investigation. *Acta Orthop. Scand.* 16(suppl.):1–76, 1954.
51. Ikai, M., and J. Fukunaga. Calculation of muscle strength per unit cross-sectional area of human muscle by means of ultrasonic measurement. *Int. Z. Angew. Physiol.* 26:26–32, 1968.
52. Jackson, H.C., R.K. Winkelmann, and W.H. Nickel. Nerve endings in the human lumbar spinal column and related structures. *J. Bone Joint Surg.* 48:1272–1281, 1966.
53. Jackson D.W., L.L. Wiltse, and R.J. Civincione. Spondylolysis in the female gymnast. *Clin. Orthop.* 117:68–73, 1976.
54. Jakobs, T., J.A.A. Miller, and A.B. Schultz. Trunk position sense in the frontal plane. *Exp. Neurol.* 90:129–138, 1985.
55. Jensen, R.K. Body segment mass, radius and radius of gyration proportions of children. *J. Biomech.* 19:359–368, 1986.
56. Jepsen, K.M., J.A.A. Miller, M. Green, and A.B. Schultz. Spine proprioception in the sagittal and frontal planes. *Trans. Orthop. Res. Soc.* 12:373, 1987.
57. Karvonen, M.J., J. Mainzer, W. Rohmert, I. Lowenthal, K. Undentsch, R. Kupper, K.H. Gartner, and J. Rutenfranz. Occupational health studies on air transport workers II. Muscle strength of air transport workers. *Int. Arch. Occup. Environ. Health* 47:233–244, 1980.
58. Keith, A. Man's posture: Its evolution and disorders. *Br. Med. J.* 1:587–590, 1923.
59. Kelsey, J.L. Idiopathic low back pain. Magnitude of the problem. In A.A. White and S.L. Gordon (eds.). *Symposium on Idiopathic Low Back Pain.* St. Louis: C.V. Mosby, 1982, pp. 5–8.
60. Kelsey, J.L., P.B. Githens, T. O'Conner, U. Weil, J.A. Calogero, T.P. Holford, A.A. White, S.D. Walter, A.M. Ostfeld, and W.O. Southwick. Acute prolapsed lumbar intervertebral disc. An epidemiological study with special reference to driving automobiles and cigarette smoking. *Spine* 9:608–613, 1984.
61. Kelsey, J.L., P.B. Githens, T., A.A. White, S.D. Walter, W.O. Southwick, U. Weil, T.R. Holford, A.M. Ostfeld, J.A. Calogero, and T. O'Connor. An epidemiologic study of lifting and twisting on the job and risk for acute prolapsed lumbar intervertebral disc. *J. Orthop. Res.* 2:61–66, 1984.
62. Kelsey, J.L., P.B. Githens, S.D. Walter, W.D. Southwick, U. Weil, T.R. Holford, A.M. Ostfeld, J.A. Calogero, T. O'Connor, and A.A. White. An epidemiological study of acute prolapsed cervical intervertebral disc. *J. Bone Joint Surg.* 66A:907–914, 1984.
63. King, A.I. A review of biomechanical models. *J. Biomech. Eng.* 106:97–104, 1984.
64. Koeller, W., S. Muehlhaus, W. Meier, and F. Hartmann. Biomechanical properties of human intervertebral discs subjected to axial dynamic compression—influence of age and degeneration. *J. Biomech.* 19:807–816, 1986.
65. Kottke, F.S., and M.O. Mundale. Range of mobility of the cervical spine. *Arch. Phys. Med.* 40:379–382, 1959.
66. Langenberg, W. Morphologie, physiologischer Querschnitt und Kraft des M. erector spinae in Lumbalbereich des Menschen. *Z. Anat. Entwickl.-Gesch.* 132:158–190, 1970.
67. Lanier, R.R. The presacral vertebrae of American white and negro males. *Am. J. Phys. Anthropol.* 25:341–420, 1939.
68. Langrana, N.A., and C.K. Lee. Isokinetic evaluation of trunk muscles. *Spine* 9:171–175, 1984.
69. Lorenz, M., A. Patwardhan, and R. Vanderby. Load-bearing characteristics of lumbar facets in normal and surgically-altered spinal segments. *Spine* 8:122–130, 1983.
70. Magora, A. Investigation of the relation between low back pain and occupation. *Indust. Med.* 39:504–510, 1970.
71. Mairiaux, PH., P.R. Davis, D.A., Stubbs, and D. Baty. Relation between intra-abdominal pressure and lumbar moments when lifting weights in the erect posture. *Ergonomics* 27:883–894, 1984.
72. Marras, W.S., A.I. King, and R.L. Joint. Measurement of loads on the lumbar spine under isometric and isokinetic conditions. *Spine* 9:176–187, 1984.

73. McConville, J.T., T.D. Churchill, C.E. Clauser, and J. Cuzzi. Anthropometric relationships of body and body segment moment of inertia. AFAMRL-TR-80-119. Dayton, Ohio: Aerospace Medical Research Laboratories, Wright-Patterson Air Force Base, 1980.

74. McGlashen, K.M., J.A.A. Miller, A.B. Schultz, and G.B.J. Andersson. Load-displacement behavior of the human lumbosacral joint. *J. Orthop. Res.* 5:488–496, 1987.

75. McNeill, T., D. Warwich, G. Andersson, and A. Schultz. Trunk strengths in attempted flexion, extension, and lateral bending in healthy subjects and patients with low-back disorders. *Spine* 6:529–538, 1980.

76. Merritt, J.L., T.J. McLean, R.P. Erickson, and K.P. Offord. Measurement of trunk flexibility in normal subjects: Reproducibility of three clinical methods. *Mayo Clin. Proc.* 61:192–197, 1986.

77. Miller, J.A.A., K.A. Haderspek, and A.B. Schultz. Posterior element loads in lumbar motion segments. *Spine* 8:331–337, 1983.

78. Miller, J.A.A., A.B. Schultz, and G.B.J. Andersson. Loading-displacement behavior of sacroiliac joints. *J. Orthop. Res.* 5:92–100, 1987.

79. Miller, J.A.A., H. Steen, L.B. Skogland, and A.B. Schultz. Sagittal geometry of the spine in females with and without idiopathic scoliosis. *Spine* (In press).

80. Miller, J.A.A., C. Schmatz, and A.B. Schultz. Lumbar disc degeneration: A review of age, sex and level correlations in 600 autopsy specimens. *Spine* (In press).

81. Miller, J.A.A., and L.B. Skogland. Musculoskeletal interactions in the adolescent spine. A study of the effect of some geometric and material property changes in a three-dimensional mathematical model. In: On the importance of growth in idiopathic scoliosis. A biochemical, radiological and biomechanical study. Ph.D. dissertation by L.B. Skogland and J.A.A. Miller, University of Oslo, 1982.

82. Milne, J.S., and I.J. Lauder. Age effects in kyphosis and lordosis in adults. *Ann. Human Biol.* 1:327–337, 1974.

83. Monkhouse, W.S., and A. Khalique. Variations in the composition of the human rectus sheath: A study of the anterior abdominal wall. *J. Anat.* 145:61–66, 1986.

84. Moroney, S.P., A.B. Schultz, J.A.A. Miller, and G.B.J. Andersson. Load-displacement properties of lower cervical spine motion segments. *J. Biomech.* (In press).

85. Morris, J.M., G. Benner, and D.B. Lucas. An electromyographic study of the intrinsic muscle of the back in man. *J. Anat. Lond.* 96:509–520, 1962.

86. Morris, J.M., D.B. Lucas, and B. Bresler. Role of the trunk in stability of the spine. *J. Bone Joint Surg.* 43:327–351, 1961.

87. Nachemson, A. Lumbar interdiscal pressure. Experimental studies of post-mortem material. *Acta Orthop. Scand.* 43(suppl.):10–104, 1960.

88. Nachemson, A.F. Disc pressure measurements. *Spine* 6:94–99, 1981.

89. Nachemson, A.L., G.B.J. Andersson, and A.B. Schultz. Valsalva maneuver biomechanics—effects on lumbar trunk loads of elevated intraabdominal pressures. *Spine* 11:476–479, 1986.

90. Nachemson, A., and G. Elfstrom. Intravital dynamic pressure measurements in lumbar discs. *Scand. J. Rehabil. Med.* 1(suppl):1–40, 1970.

91. Nachemson, A., and J.M. Morris. In vivo measurements of intradiscal pressure. Discometry, a method for the determination of pressure in the lower lumbar discs. *J. Bone Joint Surg.* 46A:1077–1092, 1964.

92. Nachemson, A.L., A.B. Schultz, and M.H. Berkson. Mechanical properties of human lumbar spine motion segments. Influences of age, sex, disc level and degeneration. *Spine* 4:1–8, 1979.

93. Nemeth, G., and H. Ohlsen. Moment arm lengths of trunk muscles to the lumbosacral joint obtained in vivo with computed tomography. *Spine* 11:158–160, 1986.

94. Panjabi, M.M., R.A. Brand, and A.A. White. Mechanical properties of the human thoracic spine. *J. Bone Joint Surg.* 58A:642–652, 1976.

95. Panjabi, M.M., V.K. Goel, and K. Takata. Physiologic strains in the lumbar spinal ligaments: An in vitro biomechanical study. *Spine* 7:192–203, 1982.

96. Panjabi, M.M., and A.A. White. Three-dimensional flexibility and stiffness properties of the human thoracic spine. *J. Biomech.* 9:185–192, 1976.

97. Panjabi, M.M., A.A. White, and R.M. Johnson. Cervical spine mechanics as a function of transection of components. *J. Biomech.* 8:327–336, 1975.

98. Paley, D., and R. Gillespie. Chronic repetitive unrecognized flexion injury of the cervical spine (high jumper's neck). *Am. J. Sports Med.* 14:92–95, 1986.

99. Parnianpour, M., M. Nordin, U. Moritz, and N. Kahanovitz. Correlation between different tests of trunk strength. *Adv. Bioeng.* 2:13, 1986.

100. Parnianpour, M., S. Schecter, U. Moritz, and N. Nordin. Back muscle endurance in repsonse to external load. *Trans. Orthop. Res. Soc.* 12:375, 1987.

101. Pauly, J.E. An electromyographic analysis of certain movements and exercises. *Anat. Rec.* 155:223–234, 1966.

102. Pearcy, M.J., J. Portek, and J. Shepherd. Three-dimensional x-ray analysis of normal measurement in the lumbar spine. *Spine* 9:294–300, 1984.

103. Pearcy, M.J., and S.B. Tibrewal. Axial rotation and lateral bending in the normal lumbar spine measured by three-dimensional radiography. *Spine* 9:582–587, 1984.

104. Pokras, R., and K.K. Kubishke. Diagnosis-related groups using data from the national hospital discharge survey: United States. *NCHS Advance Data 105.* National Center for Health Statistics, Hyattsville, MD, 1985.

105. Pope, M.H., G.B.J. Andersson, II. Broman, M. Svensson, and C. Zetterberg. Electromyographic studies of the lumbar trunk musculature during the development of axial torques. *J. Orthop. Res.* 4:288–297, 1986.

106. Reuber, M., A. Schultz, F. Denis, and D. Spencer. Bulging of lumbar intervertebral discs. *J. Biomech. Eng.* 104:187–192, 1982.

107. Roaf, R. Vertebral growth and its mechanical control. *J. Bone Joint Surg.* 42B:40–59, 1960.

108. Roche, M.B., and G.G. Rowe. The incidence of separate neural arch and coincident bone variations. *J. Bone Joint Surg.* 34A:491–494, 1952.

109. Rogala, E., D.S. Drummond, and J. Gurr. Scoliosis: Incidence and natural history. A prospective epidemiological study. *J. Bone Joint Surg.* 60A:173–176, 1978.

110. Rossi, F. Spondylolysis, spondylolistheses and sports. *J. Sports Med. Phys. Fit.* 18:317–340, 1978.

111. Scholten, P.J., A.B. Schultz, C.W. Luchies, and J.A.A. Miller. Motions and loads within the human pelvis: A biomechanical model study. *J. Orthop Res.* (In press).

112. Scholten, P.J., and A.G. Veldhuizen. The bending stiffness of the trunk. *Spine* 11:463–467, 1986.

113. Schultz, A. Biomechanics of the human spine and trunk. In D.E. Skalak and S. Chien (eds.). *Handbook of Bioengineering.* New York: McGraw-Hill, 1987, pp. 41.1–41.20.

114. Schultz, A. Loads on the lumbar spine. In I.V. Malcolm and M.J. Jayson (eds.). *The Lumbar Spine and Back Pain.* New York: Churchill Livingstone, 1987, pp. 204–214.

115. Schultz, A.B., and G.B.J. Andersson. Analysis of loads on the lumbar spine. *Spine* 6:76–82, 1981.

116. Schultz, A.B., and G.B.J. Andersson, K. Haderspeck, R. Ortegren, M. Nordin, and R. Bjork. Analysis and measurement of lumbar trunk loads in tasks involving bends and twists. *J. Biomech.* 15:669–675, 1982.

117. Schultz, A., and G.B.J. Andersson, R. Ortengren, R. Bjork, and M. Nordin. Analysis and quantitative myoelectric measurements of loads on the lumbar spine when holding weights in standing postures. *Spine* 7:390–397, 1982.

118. Schultz, A., and G. Andersson, R. Ortengren, K. Haderspeck, and A. Nachemson. Loads on the lumbar spine—validation of a biomechanical analysis by measurements of intradiscal pressures and myoelectric signals. *J. Bone Joint Surg.* 64A:713–720, 1982.

119. Schultz, A., and J.A.A. Miller. Biomechanics of the human spine. In V.C. Mow, and W.C. Hayes (eds.). *Basic Orthopaedic Biomechanics.* New York: Raven Press (in press).
120. Schultz, A.B., T.B. Belytschko, and T.P. Andriacchi. Analog studies of forces in the human spine: Mechanical properties and motion segment behavior. *J. Biomech.* 6:373–383, 1973.
121. Schultz, A.B., D.R. Benson, and C. Hirsch. Force-deformation properties of human ribs. *J. Biomech.* 7:303–309, 1973.
122. Schultz, A.B., D.R. Benson, and C. Hirsch. Force-deformation properties of human costo-sternal and costo-vertebral articulations. *J. Biomech.* 7:311–318, 1973.
123. Schultz, A., R. Cromwell, D. Warwick, and G. Andersson. Lumbar trunk muscle use in standing isometric heavy exertions. *J. Orthop. Res.* 5:320–329, 1987.
124. Schultz, A., K. Haderspeck, and S. Takashima. Correction of scoliosis by muscle stimulation—biomechanical analyses. *Spine* 6:468–476, 1981.
125. Schultz, A., K. Haderspeck, D. Warwick, and D. Portillo. Use of lumbar trunk muscles in isometric performance of mechanically complex standing tasks. *J. Orthop. Res.* 1:77–91, 1983.
126. Schultz, A.B, D.N. Warwick, M.H. Berkson, and A.L. Nachemson. Mechanical properties of human lumbar spine motion segments, part 1: Responses in flexion, extension, lateral bending and torsion. *J. Biomech. Eng.* 101:46–52, 1979.
127. Shirazi-Adl, A., A.M. Ahmed, and S.C. Shrivastava. A finite element study of a lumbar motion segment subjected to pure sagittal plane moments. *J. Biomech.* 19:331–350, 1986.
128. Shirazi-Adl, A., A.M. Ahmed, and S.C. Shrivastava. Mechanical response of a lumbar motion segment in axial torque alone and combined with compression. *Spine* 11:914–927, 1986.
129. Shirazi-Adl, A., and G. Dronin. Load-sharing function of lumbar intervertebral disc and facet joints in compression, extension and flexion. *Adv. Bioeng.* 2:18–19, 1986.
130. Shirazi-Adl, A., S.C. Shrivastava, and A.M. Ahmed. Stress analysis of the lumbar disc-body unit in compression—a three-dimensional nonlinear finite element study. *Spine* 9:120–134, 1984.
131. Skipor, A.F., J.A.A. Miller, D.L. Spencer, and A.B. Schultz. Stiffness properties and geometry of lumbar spine posterior elements. J. Biomech. 18:821–830, 1985.
132. Skogland, L.B., and J.A.A. Miller. The length and proportions of the thoracolumbar spine in children with idiopathic scoliosis. *Acta Orthop. Scand.* 51:779–789, 1981.
133. Sobotta, J., and F.H.J. Figge. *Atlas of Human Anatomy,* Vol. 1. New York: Hafner Press, 1974.
134. Spencer, D.L., J.A.A. Miller, and A.B. Schultz. The effects of chemonucleolysis on the mechanical properties of the canine lumbar disc. *Spine* 10:555–561, 1985.
135. Takashima, S.T., S.P. Singh, K.A. Haderspeck, and A.B. Schultz. A model for semi-quantitative studies of muscle actions. *J. Biomech.* 12:929–939, 1979.
136. Thorstensson, A., and J. Nilsson. Trunk muscle strength during constant velocity movements. *Scand. J. Rehabil. Med.* 17:121–127, 1982.
137. Troup, J.D.G., T.P.J. Leskinen, H.R. Stalhammar, and I.A.A. Kuorinka. A comparison of intraabdominal pressure increases, hip torque, and lumbar vertebral compression in different lifting techniques. *Hum. Factors* 25:517–525, 1983.
138. Urban, J.P.G., S. Holm, and A. Moroudas. Diffusion of small solutes into the intervertebral disc: An in vivo study. *Biorheology* 15:203–223, 1978.
139. Urban, J.P.G., and J.F. McMullin. Swelling pressure of the intervertebral disc: Influence of proteoglycan and collagen contents. *Biorheology* 22:145–157, 1986.
140. Van Schaik, J.P.J., H. Verbiest, and F.D.J. Van Schaik. The orientation of laminae and facet joints in the lower lumbar spine. *Spine* 10:59–63, 1985.
141. Voutsinas, S.A., and G.D. MacEwan. Sagittal profiles of the spine. *Clin. Orthop.* 210:235–242, 1986.

142. Walters, C.E., and M.J. Partridge. Electromyographic study of the differential action of the abdominal muscles during exercise. *Am. J. Phys. Med.* 36:259–268, 1957.
143. Wilson, F.D., and R.E. Lindseth. The adolescent "swimmer's back." *Am. J. Sports Med.* 10:174–176, 1982.
144. Wiltse, L.L., E.H. Widell, and D.W. Jackson. Fatigue fracture: The basic lesion in isthmic spondylolisthesis. *J. Bone Joint Surg.* 57A:17–22, 1975.
145. White, A.A., and M.M. Panjabi. The basic kinematics of spine. *Spine* 3:12–20, 1978.
146. White, A.A., and M.M. Panjabi. *Clinical Biomechanics of the Spine.* Philadelphia: J.B. Lippincott Co., 1978, p. 22.
147. Yamada, H. Ratios for age changes in the mechanical properties of human organs and tissues. In F. Gaynor Evans (ed.). *Strength of Biological Materials.* Baltimore: Williams & Wilkins Co., 1970, pp. 255–282.
148. Yang, K.H., and A.I. King. Mechanism of facet load transmission as a hypothesis for low back pain. *Spine* 9:557–565, 1984.

6
Semilunar Cartilage of the Knee: Function and Pathology

CHARLES E. HENNING, M.D.

INTRODUCTION

The menisci contribute to both load transmission and stability in the knee. The meniscus is frequently injured as a result of trauma in the young athlete and gradual degenerative processes in the older athlete. Concepts of treatment of the symptomatic injured meniscus include rest and decreased activity, meniscectomy of varying degrees by varying means, and meniscus repair. These treatments vary in the same order in the degree of difficulty of achieving the desired result. Removal of part or all of the deranged meniscus has been the approach most frequently used until quite recently. Meniscus repair has gained recent interest and is also surgically the most risky and difficult treatment. It is the long-term outcomes of various methods of dealing with the symptomatic meniscus that are the most difficult to evaluate, yet become perhaps the most important when a patient is making a decision about the treatment of a particular problem. Because of the important functions of load bearing and stability of the meniscus, loss of a portion of load bearing and stability of the meniscus, loss of a portion of this structure in the young athlete with associated ligamentous injury results in significant degenerative changes, typically within the first decade. Since more than 80% of the young athletic population has an associated tear of the anterior cruciate ligament, this injury must also be discussed and dealt with.

LOAD TRANSMISSION

Walker and Erkmann [20] demonstrated that the meniscus transmitted 50% of the compression load in the medial compartment and an even higher percentage of the load in the lateral compartment. Seedhom and Hargreaves [19] demonstrated that removal of only 16–34% of the meniscus increased joint surface contact forces by approximately 350%.

The concave shape on the superior border of the meniscus and the flat shape on the inferior border of the meniscus allow this structure to play such an important role in load transmission. The femur can articulate with the superior surface of the meniscus to allow flexion and rotation in a portion of a ball-and-socket joint. On the inferior surface, the flat contour of the meniscus allows gliding motion on the tibia so that rotation of the tibia on the femur can occur. This anatomic arrangement allows for the complex rolling and gliding motions that occur with combinations of flexion-extension and internal-external rotation of the knee. With walking, the flexion-extension range is 70° and the internal-external rotation is approximately 10°. The knee system requires a central pivot consisting of the anterior and posterior cruciate ligaments. The axis of rotation of the knee is a slightly changing point projected vertically down from the instant center of the posterior cruciate attachment of the femur to the plane of the tibia. Since this point is slightly more medial than lateral, more gliding motion takes place in the lateral compartment than in the medial compartment with rotation of the tibia. Loss of an anterior cruciate ligament results in repeated forward subluxation of the tibia on the femur, selectively loading the most posterior part of the menisci.

Dye et al. [6] have shown that the bicondylar knee with the menisci and cruciate ligaments was well developed 320 million years ago. Since the knee retains essentially the same form today, it is reasonable to assume that all the components of the knee are essential for this system to work properly.

STABILITY

The menisci play a significant role in stability of the knee. Markolf et al. [14] demonstrated the stabilizing effect of the medial meniscus, particularly with the knee flexed at 90° of flexion. Levy et al. [12] demonstrated that the posterior horn of the meniscus contributes greatly to anterior stability of the knee.

In an anterior cruciate-deficient knee, the anterior drawer test is positive only 35% of the time when the medial meniscus is intact, compared to 83% of the time following a medial meniscectomy. The Lachman's test is positive 90% of the time with an intact medial meniscus and 95% of the time following a medial meniscectomy [9] (Figure 1).

A less commonly reported medial shift of the femur on the tibia occurs in a knee following medial meniscectomy. The entire femoral condyle complex slides medially, thus increasing the load between the lateral tibial spine and the lateral femoral condyle. These findings are best appreciated by the Rosenberg view [17]. This x-ray is taken with the patient bearing weight and the knee flexed 30–45°.

Thus, the menisci serve an important role in both load transmission

FIGURE 1

Lachman's test. (From Henning, C.E., M.A. Lynch, and K.R. Glick, Jr. Physical examination of the knee. In J.A. Nicholas and E.B. Hershman (eds.). The Lower Extremity and Spine in Sports Medicine. *St. Louis: C.V. Mosby Co., 1986, pp. 765–800.)*

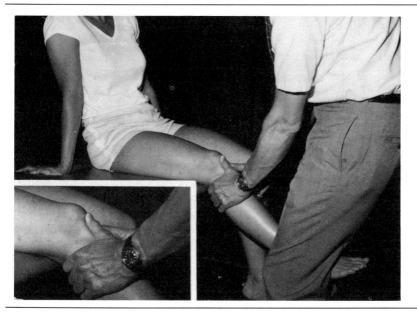

and stability of the knee. Loss of function of the meniscus, either by degenerative changes or surgical removal, will result in a change in the mechanics of the knee. Articular surface contact forces rise 2 to 3.5 times the original value, and degenerative changes ensue.

CLINICAL STUDIES OF MENISCECTOMY

Since the majority of patients with a meniscus tear are in their twenties, studies with less than 10-year follow-up should be considered preliminary unless they already demonstrate bad results. Gudde and Wagenknecht [8] followed up 50 patients after meniscectomy in anterior cruciate-deficient knees and found disastrous results. Johnson et al. [11] reported poor results following meniscectomy in the anterior cruciate-deficient group, with progressive symptoms and degenerative changes. McDaniel and Dameron [15] reported that more than 80% of their anterior cruciate-deficient patients had been treated by meniscectomy. These patients were unable to pursue vigorous lateral-movement sports.

Using long-term follow-up roentgenograms, Fairbank in 1948 [7] described the joint changes observed after total meniscectomy. These changes include narrowing, ridging, and flattening, as well as combinations of the three. Lynch et al. [13] demonstrated one or more Fairbank's changes in more than 88% of patients with a stable anterior cruciate ligament reconstruction and associated meniscectomy. There was no significant difference between the results produced by various methods of meniscectomy, whether total, open partial, or arthroscopic partial. This may be best understood by referring to the previously referenced work by Seedhom and Hargreaves [19]. At least the inner one-third of the meniscus is removed in all partial meniscectomies (regardless of the method), and the loss of this thin, weight-bearing portion of the meniscus is most significant.

Chondromalacia of the articular surfaces at the time of surgery for an anterior cruciate-deficient knee correlates with the status of the meniscus and with preoperative activity. Only 4.8% of the knees with two intact menisci demonstrate degenerative changes, while the incidence of changes with even a left-alone meniscus tear is almost 50%. The appearance of the joint surfaces appears to be related to the length of time of the instability and particularly to the variety of use of the knee following the injury [9]. These findings also raise significant questions about attempts to rehabilitate a cruciate-deficient knee with the intention to participate in sport.

METHOD OF TREATMENT OF MENISCAL TEARS

Meniscus tears may be managed by leaving them alone, meniscectomy by various means, and meniscus repair, again by various means. In general, tears that are 10 mm or less in length and partial thickness tears (involving 50% or less of the vertical height of the meniscus) may be left alone. Although these tears are typically considered asymptomatic, Lynch et al. [13] demonstrated a slightly higher incidence of residual pain in stable anterior cruciate ligament-reconstructed knees compared to a leave-alone medial meniscus or the combination of medial and lateral menisci that were left alone. Functionally, the patients demonstrated a low incidence of Fairbank's changes and did far better than a comparable group in whom partial or total meniscectomy was carried out. Since the meniscus is compressed during load bearing, any cleavage planes are typically compressed together and the meniscus undoubtedly transmits the significant portion of the load.

Casscells [3] reported a high incidence of degenerative meniscus tears in a study of over 300 autopsy specimens, but there was no clear correlation between areas of meniscus degeneration and areas of degenerative change of the articular surface. Only a few knees that had prior surgery showed distinctive degenerative changes.

Black and DeHaven [4] reported on a series of smaller stable meniscus tears that were left alone in both isolated meniscus lesions and in combination with the anterior cruciate ligament. Less than 5% of these ultimately became unstable, and the significant benefit of the presence of the meniscus was a virtual absence of degenerative changes in these joints by x-ray.

Meniscectomy over the last decade has changed from an open procedure to a primarily arthroscopic procedure. The techniques have been developed and advanced by many authors; unfortunately, a description of this development is beyond the scope of this chapter. However, loss of meniscus function by either means, open or arthroscopic, still results in loss of the meniscus substance. The fact that scarring and early postoperative complaints are reduced, and that rehabilitation is somewhat more favorable with arthroscopic meniscectomy, has overshadowed the observation that meniscectomy associated with an anterior cruciate ligament tear results in significant long-term disability beginning after only a few years. This again can best be understood when one realizes that the inner one-third of the meniscus or more is removed in a partial meniscectomy, and the resulting increased contact forces of the joint have been predicted experimentally by Seedhom and Hargreaves [19].

ARTHROSCOPIC MENISCUS REPAIR WITH POSTERIOR INCISION

Meniscus repair is not new. Thomas Annadale [1] in 1885 described what is probably the first meniscus repair. DeHaven [5] in 1981 described early results from an open repair technique. Ikeuchi [10] described an arthroscopically aided procedure in 1975. Scott and Jolly [18] in 1986 described the technique that we are presently using to suture the meniscus. This is a transarticular arthroscopic approach using a posterior incision and a posterior retractor.

The technique reported by Scott and Jolly was used from 1980 to 1983. Vascularity for healing of the repairs was improved with the added use of a rasp to abrade the parameniscal synovium, as suggested by Dil Cannon. The failure rate with this modification decreased from 22% to 9.5%.

Beginning in February 1986, the exogenous blood clot was used to stimulate healing. This has been shown to be effective in a dog model by Arnoczky et al. [2]. From 50 to 80 ml of the patient's blood is allowed to coagulate. This yields 1.5 to 2 ml of thick clot. After parameniscal synovial abrasion, meniscus suturing, and now placement of Surgicel to help stabilize the clot, this thick clot is injected by a means of a blunt needle into the seam of the meniscus tear in the inferior surface of the meniscus.

210 | *Henning*

FIGURE 2
A. Meniscus repair has been carried out with the sutures visible. B. Exogenous blood clot injection.

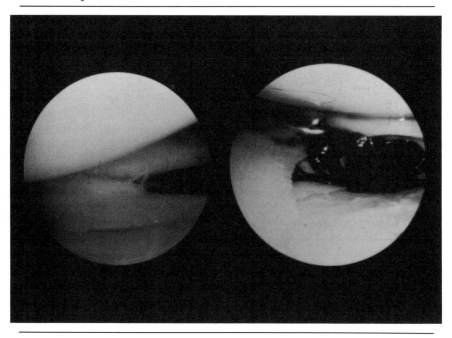

The preliminary results of the use of the rasp and clot combination at first appear worse than those achieved with the rasp alone. The failure rate in tears with a single cleavage plane is nill, while in tears with multiple injuries or in more complex tears it is 40%. Of more significance, however, is the lower incidence of failure in an isolated meniscus repair by the use of the exogenous clot injection. The numbers are still too small to be statistically significant, but the use of the clot to augment healing in the isolated meniscus repair appears to be one of its most promising results. The meniscus repair has been carried out in Figure 2A, with the sutures being just visible. The clot has been injected in Figure 2B. In Figure 3A the superior surface of the meniscus can be inspected and is seen to be healed. Figure 3B demonstrates the significant panus on the inferior surface of the meniscus.We regularly see prolific panus only on the inferior surface. Rim preparation on the inferior surface is extremely important and must be thoroughly carried out. It is of the utmost importance that none of the peripheral white rim is removed so that the cross-sectional area of the meniscus is not altered.

Patients who are healed over 90% or more of the vertical height of the tear are classed as healed, those healed between 50 and 90% of the

FIGURE 3
A. Superior surface of the meniscus can be inspected and seen to be healed.
B. Vascular panus on the inferior surface of the meniscus.

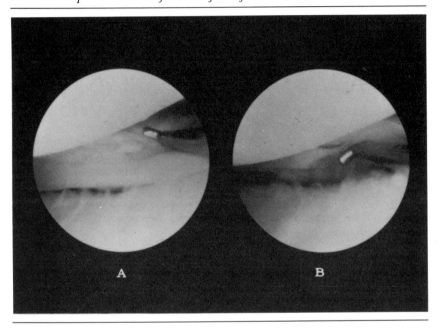

vertical height are considered incompletely healed, and those healed less than 50% of the vertical height are considered failures.

The meniscus is clinically unstable if there is pain or catching symptoms referable to the joint line. This occurred in 8% of the group from 1980 to 1983 and in 2% of the rasp group from 1983 to 1986; so far none of the patients in the blood clot-treated group from February, 1986, through the present have reported symptoms. Follow-up on this last series is too short to allow any conclusions to be made. Fairbank's changes are an early indicator of loss of function of the meniscus in predicting future symptoms.

Lynch et al. [13] reported a 3% incidence of two or more Fairbank's changes and a 4% incidence of pain when both menisci were intact. Those patients with Fairbank's changes had a 66% incidence of pain, however. When a partial or total meniscectomy was done, there was an 88% incidence of two or more Fairbank's changes. The most common changes were ridging and flattening. In patients with two or more changes, the incidence of pain symptoms ranged from one-third with a partial medial meniscectomy only to 90% with total medial meniscectomy and 100% with either partial or total lateral meniscectomy.

CONCLUSIONS

It was the initial premise of this chapter that the menisci and the cruciates are an integral part of the system of load-bearing and stabilizing elements comprising the knee joint. One can anticipate that degenerative changes result from alteration of this system. It is unfortunate that the most difficult operative procedures are the ones that have the best long-term outlook. When repair of the meniscus and precise reconstruction of an intra-articular anterior cruciate ligament are not possible, one must reduce the stress on the system in order to preserve its life.

Thus, there has been a gradual trend toward removal of less of the meniscus and finally to repair of the meniscus without removing any part of it. Significant advances have been made with reconstruction of the anterior cruciate ligament. Numerous reconstructive procedures are now available. Substantial additional work needs to be done to determine which of these procedures are best and to refine them so that good reproducibility is obtained.

Allografting of the meniscus has been done by Milachowski and associates [16], using fresh frozen and freeze-dried preparations. Although the allograft healed, it decreased in size by 2 years, so that it was essentially nonfunctional for weight bearing. To date, there are no synthetic materials that are suitable for the combination of resisting compression load and abrasion by the moving femoral condyle. These observations put even more pressure on the orthopedic community to improve the techniques of meniscus repair.

Perhaps in the near future allografting of the meniscus will become common. It will have the usual problems of difficulty of implantation, determining proper function in terms of the percentage of the total load actually borne by the meniscus, and durability. The allograft probably will need to be done before substantial articular surface changes occur and almost certainly in a stable knee.

To date, all efforts to redesign the knee that has remained essentially unchanged for 320 million years have resulted in a poor outcome. Efforts must continue to reverse engineer the knee in order to determine the exact load-bearing and stabilizing attributes of each component, with special emphasis on the meniscus. Continuing combined efforts by functional anatomists, biomedical engineers, and clinicians will aid in this pursuit. In the meantime, when the system is altered by loss of a stabilizer (the anterior cruciate) or a load bearer (a portion of the meniscus), we must recognize that the knee will not withstand normal use and stop trying to rehabilitate it back to a normal functional level, only to see accelerating degenerative changes as the result.

REFERENCES

1. Annandale, T. An operation for displaced semilunar cartilage. *Br. Med. J.* 1:799, 1885. (Abstract)
2. Arnoczky, S.P., C.A. McDevitt, R.F. Warren, J. Spivak, and A. Allen. Meniscal repair using an exogenous fibrin clot—An experimental study in the dog. *Orthop. Res. Soc.* 2:452, 1986. (Abstract)
3. Casscells, S.W. Torn or degenerated meniscus and its relationship to degeneration in the weight-bearing areas of the femur and tibia. *Clin. Orthop.* 132:196–200, 1978.
4. Black, K.P., and K.E. DeHaven. Meniscus repair. *Orthop. Trans.* 3:561, 1986. (Abstract)
5. DeHaven, K.E. Peripheral meniscus repair. An alternative to meniscectomy. *Orthop. Trans.* 5:399–400, 1981.
6. Dye, S.F., M.W. Via, and C. Andersen. An evolutionary perspective of the knee. *Orthop. Trans.* 10:70, 1986. (Abstract)
7. Fairbank, T.J. Knee joint changes after meniscectomy. *J. Bone Joint Surg.* 30:664–670, 1948.
8. Gudde, P., and R. Wagenknecht. Untersuchungsergebnisse bei 50 Patienten 10–12 Jahre nach der Innenmeniskusoperation bei gleichqeitig vorliegender Ruptue des vordren Kreuzbandes. *Z. Orthop.* 111:369–372, 1973.
9. Henning, C.E., and M.A. Lynch. Current concepts of meniscal function and pathology. Symposium on the knee. *Clin. Sports Med.* 4:259–265, 1985.
10. Ikeuchi, H. Surgery under arthroscopic control. In proceedings of the Societé Internationale d'Arthroscopie. *Rhumatologie* (special issue) 1:57–62, 1975.
11. Johnson, R.J., D.B. Kettelkamp, W. Clar, and P. Leaverton. Factors affecting later results after meniscectomy. *J. Bone Joint Surg.* 56:710–729, 1974.
12. Levy, I.M., P.A. Torzilli, and R.F. Warren. The effect of medial meniscectomy on anterior-posterior motion of the knee. *J. Bone Joint Surg.* 64:883–888, 1982.
13. Lynch, M.A., C.E. Henning, and K.R. Glick. Knee joint surface changes—long-term follow-up meniscus tear treatment in stable anterior cruciate ligament reconstructions. *Clin. Orthop.* 172:148–153, 1983.
14. Markolf, K.L., J.S. Mensch, and H.C. Amstutz. Stiffness and laxity of the knee—the contributions of the supporting structures. A quantitative in vitro study. *J. Bone Joint Surg.* 58:583–593, 1976.
15. McDaniel, W.J., and T.B. Dameron. Untreated ruptures of the anterior cruciate ligament. *J. Bone Joint Surg.* 62A:696–705, 1980.
16. Milachowski, K.A., K. Weismier, C.J. Wirth, and D. Kohn. Meniscus transplantation—experimental study and first clinical report. Presented at the 13th annual meeting of the American Orthopaedic Society for Sports Medicine, Orlando, Florida, June 29–July 2, 1987.
17. Rosenberg, T. Personal communication.
18. Scott G., and B. Jolly. Combined posterior incision and arthroscopic intra-articular repair of the meniscus. *J. Bone Joint Surg.* 68A:847–861, 1986.
19. Seedhom, B. B., and D.J. Hargreaves. Transmission of the load in the knee joint with special reference to the role of the menisci. Part II: Experimental results, discussion and conclusions. *Engineering Med.* 8:220–228, 1979.
20. Walker, P.S., and M.J. Erkmann. The role of the menisci in force transmission across the knee. *Clin. Orthop.* 109:184–192, 1975.

7
Common and Uncommon Dermatologic Diseases Related to Sports Activities

GARY R. KANTOR, M.D.
WILMA F. BERGFELD, M.D.

INTRODUCTION

The dermatologic disorders of athletes may be classified into the broad categories of physical factors, infections and infestations, contact dermatitis, and exacerbation of preexisting skin disease. These diseases are usually minor, with the exception of infections, which may prevent the athlete from participating in an activity, especially a contact sport.

Most skin diseases affecting athletes are common dermatologic problems. This chapter will describe the clinical aspects and treatment of these common skin diseases, as well as newly recognized dermatologic diseases related to sports activities

COMMON DISEASES

Physical Factors

MECHANICAL OR FRICTIONAL. *Blisters.* Friction blisters develop on the feet in running sports such as track, basketball, baseball, and soccer; on the hands in stick and crew sports such as rowing and tennis; and on specific fingers in sports such as fencing and baseball [50]. Shearing forces, primarily horizontal, are responsible and cause an intraepidermal split, with the accumulation of serum and, occasionally, blood. Heat, humidity, and underlying bony abnormalities also contribute to blister development [50]. Clinically, blisters with clear or blood-tinged fluid are present at the affected site. The lesions are only slightly tender but are much more symptomatic when they occur under calluses [50].

Prevention is often difficult, and most padding materials, such as Moleskin or felt, are ineffective. However, properly fitted shoes, wearing two pairs of powdered socks, and using protective hand and foot gear are often helpful [7, 9]. Various padding materials based on organic polymers have also shown promise as preventive measures [61, 62]. Treatment consists of draining a tense blister with a sterile needle and covering the area with a topical antibiotic such as Polysporin. An occlusive dressing such as an adhesive tape may also be used [9]. A commercially available

215

FIGURE 1
Calluses on the pressure-bearing surface of the foot.

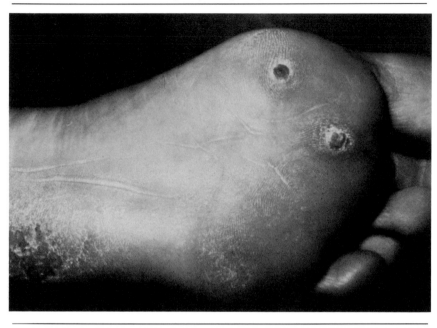

synthetic skin [48] or the use of a small patch of a hydrocolloid dressing such as Duoderm often decreases pain and accelerates healing [68].

Calluses. Calluses often occur over bony prominences as a protective response to chronic, prolonged pressure and friction. Common sites for calluses include the metatarsal region and medial-great toe of the foot and metacarpal and palmodigital aspects of the hand. Calluses are not always undesirable and may be advantageous in sports such as gymnastics, dancing, running, bowling, golfing, and tennis. Clinically, calluses appear as ill-defined, hyperkeratotic plaques (Figure 1). When they occur in response to abnormal pressure or as a consequence of a structurally or functionally defective part, significant pain or tenderness may be present.

Preventive measures help to distribute applied pressure evenly and include properly fitted shoes, shoe inserts, metatarsal bars, arch supports, or the use of a properly designed padding [63]. When needed, treatment consists of paring or sanding of the callus with a scalpel or a pumice stone after hydration. Topical agents such as 5–10% salicylic acid in flexible collodion [63], 40% salicylic acid plaster [47], or 12% lactic acid cream (Lac Hydrin), applied nightly, are helpful to reduce the hyperkeratosis.

Black heel. Black heel is known by many synonyms, including "calcaneal petechiae," "talon noir," "schwarze ferse," "basketball or runner's heel," and "posttraumatic punctate hemorrhage of the skin" [12, 71]. It arises from sudden, forceful halting and twisting movements of the foot, which produce a shearing stress on the delicate papillary dermal capillaries. As a result, extravasated red blood cells move upward throughout the epidermis into an intracorneal location to produce the clinical lesions. The posterior or lateral aspects of the heel are the most common sites; rarely, the palm may be involved [31]. Lesions may be bilateral or multiple [12]. Adolescents or young adults of both sexes are most commonly predisposed to this condition due to their participation in sports such as basketball, tennis, volleyball, jogging, and lacrosse.

Clinically, black heel is marked by the development of painless aggregates of tiny black dots or streaks, often horizontally oriented [3]. Because of their black color, patients will often become alarmed and seek medical advice. Differential diagnosis should appropriately include malignant melanoma, benign melanocytic nevi, and verruca vulgaris. However, the sudden appearance, age of the patient, and characteristic location enable the correct diagnosis to be made. In addition, horizontal paring of black heel with the scalpel blade will reveal the intracorneal location of the lesion. No treatment is needed once it is recognized as a benign, trauma-induced condition. Preventive measures, including the use of two pairs of thick socks, Moleskin or other padding materials, and reinforced heel pieces are often helpful [12, 67].

Striae distensae. Striae distensae or "stretch marks" are commonly seen on the abdomen and thighs with pregnancy, obesity, idiopathic and iatrogenic Cushing's syndrome, or the prolonged use of potent fluorinated topical steroids. However, athletes who utilize weight training such as body builders, gymnasts, or football players may develop striae of the chest, shoulder, upper-outer arm, thighs, and legs. The etiology is not entirely clear, although rapid growth and physical stress are believed to contribute to the loss and fragmentation of elastic fibers [9].

Clinically, striae distensae appear as linear pink or flesh-colored, atrophic patches (Figure 2). Treatment is ineffective, although the use of bland emollients help minimize the symptoms. There is variability in susceptibility to striae development, so preventive measures are unpredictable; however, less strenuous weight training may be successful. Avoidance of anabolic steroids is mandatory.

Abrasions, contusions, and hematomas. Abrasions are common in athletes who participate in sports that utilize turf or mats. These sports include football, baseball, soccer, wrestling, and gymnastics. Abrasions result when superficial layers of the skin are avulsed due to sudden frictional forces exerted on them [63]. Clinically, linear weeping or crusted erosions of the skin are present. Bacterial contamination or foreign bodies

FIGURE 2
Striae of the shoulder region of a weight lifter.

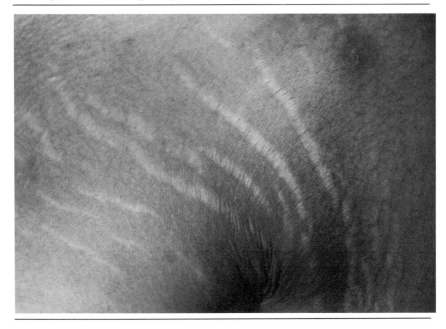

may cause complications [50]. Treatment involves cleansing the area with a mild soap and water or hydrogen proxide and the application of an antibacterial ointment such as Polysporin [22]. Crusts should not be permitted to develop, since moist wounds reepithelialize faster than dry, crusted wounds [15]. Abrasions are easily prevented by the use of sliding pads, long sleeves, protective stockings, knee and elbow pads, and other devices [63].

Contusions occur as a result of blunt trauma and produce more damage to underlying soft tissue than to the skin [60]. If underlying blood vessels are damaged, bruises or a painful hematoma may be produced. Immediate application of an ice pack will decrease pain and edema. After approximately 24–48 hours and when pain has subsided, local heat in the form of a hot water bottle or heating pad may hasten absorption of the hematoma [60]. Aspiration is to be avoided, since it is likely to introduce infection. The use of padding and head gear may prevent most contusions and hematoma formation.

Subungual hemorrhage and tennis toe. Subungual hemorrhage or hematoma results from repeated or sudden blunt trauma to the nail unit and is most common under the hallux or second toenail. When hemorrhage occurs in the nail matrix, it is incorporated into the nail plate,

FIGURE 3
Subungual hematoma of the proximal great toenail.

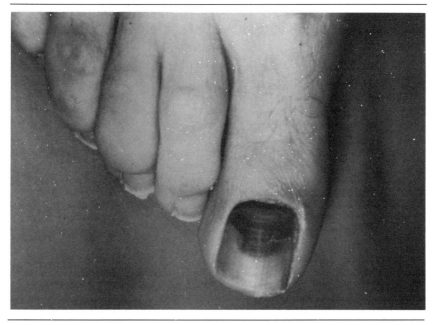

while bleeding distal to the lunula is found in the nail bed [49]. Subungual hemorrhage is particularly common in jogging or racquet sports. Clinically, it appears as a blue-black spot under the nail and must be distinguished from a subungual melanocytic nevus or melanoma (Figure 3). When it is acute or painful, incisional drainage or hot-wire puncture of the nail plate is indicated [9, 24, 47].

A particular form of subungual hemorrhage, which occurs in tennis players, has been referred to as "tennis toe" [25]. It usually occurs on the longer of the first two toes. Tennis toe is believed to result from frequent trauma of the toe into the box toe and tip of the sneaker with the frequent abrupt stops made during tennis play [25]. Hard surfaces and ill-fitting shoes are important aggravating factors [50]. We have found that tennis toe appears more commonly on the dominant foot. This may be because this toe bears a major portion of the body's weight during the thrust of a serve (unpublished observation). Tennis toe clinically appears as painful, vertically oriented lines of hemorrhage similar to splinter hemorrhages. The use of properly fitted shoes and padding of the distal toes may prevent hemorrhage from occurring. Some authors propose tightly lacing the shoes and retying the laces when they become loosened as helpful preventive measures [9, 50].

FIGURE 4
Swelling and inflammation characteristic of an ingrown toenail.

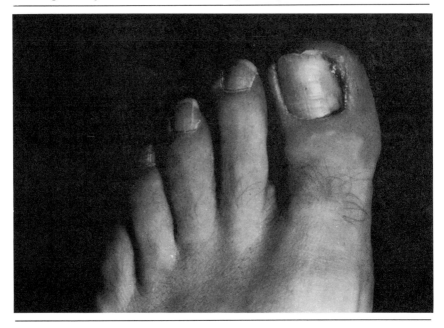

Ingrown toenail. Ingrown toenail most commonly involves the great toe, although any toe may be affected. Multiple factors may contribute to the development of ingrown toenail, including (a) trauma, (b) improper trimming of the toenails, (c) ill-fitting footwear, (d) hyperhidrosis, (e) developmental abnormality of the nail, and (f) overcurvature of the nail plate [49]. Once the nail plate embeds into the surrounding soft tissue, a self-perpetuating process of granulation tissue development and infection results [49].

Clinically, ingrown toenails appear as painful, inflammatory, edematous, soft tissue masses (Figure 4). Conservative treatment should be pursued first, including warm antiseptic soaks in Burow's solution 1:40, analgesics, rest, intralesional corticosteroid use, and elevating the corner of the nail with cotton. If conservative therapy fails, surgical excision including the lateral nail bed is indicated [25]. Cryosurgery [58] or electrodesiccation and curettage to destroy the granulation tissue may also be performed.

Preventive measures are crucial. These include trimming the nails straight across, rather than rounding them off, and allowing the nail to grow over the edge of the toe [55]. Properly fitting and appropriate footwear is also recommended for prevention. If all of these measures fail, permanent removal of the nail with destruction of the nail matrix may be warranted.

COLD-INDUCED. *Pernio.* Pernio or chilblains results from repeated exposure to cold and dampness and commonly affects the acral sites of the body, including the hands, feet, nose, cheeks and ears. It usually occurs in children or people with poor circulation [17, 33]. Pernio is frequently associated with wearing waterproof boots with linings [17]. Cold water accumulates in the inner lining of the boots and is prevented from evaporating, leaving the skin in contact with a cold, moist environment. Vasospasm occurs and produces reddish-blue, edematous plaques that itch and burn. A dermatitis with blisters may develop, and lesions may become chronic [17]. Participants in alpine or cross-country skiing, winter hiking, ice skating, and ice fishing are most susceptible [7].

Treatment consists of rapid rewarming indoors of the affected part and temporary avoidance of further exposure [7, 17]. Prevention by wearing wool socks that are changed as soon as dampness sets in, gentle massage of the affected area, and properly fitted boots are helpful measures. An herbal powder called Warm Feet is available in many ski stores [33]. It is sprinkled in the socks, where its irritant effect on the skin is said to produce increased blood flow to the feet to keep them warmer [33].

Frostnip and frostbite. Frostnip is a very superficial frostbite that affects exposed areas of the face, nose, cheeks, chin, and ears. It is common in skiers due to exposure in subfreezing temperatures with a significant wind-chill factor [7, 17]. Clinically, insensitive white patches of skin are present. Blistering may occur and numbness may last for several days [7, 17]. Rapid rewarming indoors is the recommended treatment. Frostnip may be prevented by avoiding bathing and shaving the face until after the day's outing, thus minimizing removal of the skin's protective oils [17]. We also feel that the application of a petrolatum-based sunscreen cream or other emollient is useful.

Frostbite is severe, deep cold injury affecting skin, subcutaneous tissue, muscle, and even bone [7]. It occurs from prolonged exposure to temperatures of at least $-2°C$ where anoxia and vasoconstriction cause cellular metabolism to halt [17]. Frostbite is unusual in downhill skiers, but may occur in cross-country skiers and winter hikers and climbers who become lost or trapped in a snow storm [17]. Muscles, nerves, and blood vessels are damaged most rapidly. Depending on the time of presentation, a white, cold, and insensitive part, with or without tissue necrosis, is present. The preferred treatment is rapid rewarming in a warm-water bath regulated at 38°C. Analgesics, sedatives, whirlpool baths, and antibiotics are often needed [17]. The proper apparel and proper safety precautions are the best measures to prevent frostbite.

FIGURE 5
Miliaria crystallina resembles rain drops on the skin.

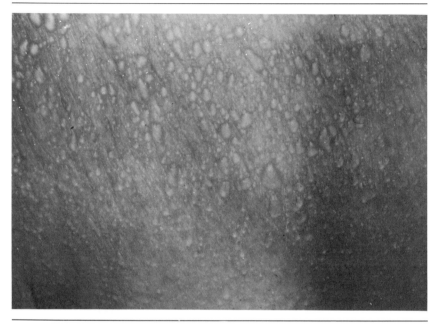

HEAT-INDUCED. *Miliaria.* Miliaria, commonly referred to as "prickly heat," results from occlusion of the sweat duct. It develops on body sites that are covered by clothing and occurs in patients who participate in football, baseball, rugby and skiing [22]. Miliaria may occur in several different forms. The first type, miliaria crystallina, develops when duct occlusion occurs superficially within the epidermis. Asymptomatic, clear, noninflammatory blisters are present, which resolve within hours of cooling the area (Figure 5). Miliaria rubra, the second clinical type, develops when sweat duct occlusion occurs in the lower epidermis [36]. Clinically, discrete reddish papules and blisters that itch are present. Treatment consists of allowing the area to contact cool air and applying a 1% hydrocortisone lotion for itching. Loose clothing that is changed at regular intervals as sweat accumulates may help reduce recurrences of miliaria. Two other types of miliaria, miliaria profunda and miliaria pustulosa, are rare in athletes and result from sweat duct occlusion deeper in the skin, with associated inflammation.

Intertrigo. Intertrigo is inflamed, itchy dermatitis that occurs in body folds, especially in the groin, from friction, maceration, and overheating. It is not a particular problem in lean, muscular athletes but is common in football linemen and weight lifters who have been recruited for their large size and weight [50]. The abdominal, gluteal, axillary, and neck folds may be involved. Intertrigo appears clinically as reddish, macerated patches that may be secondarily colonized by bacteria or yeast.

Treatment includes the application of compresses of Burow's solution 1:40 for 15–20 minutes three times daily followed by the application of diiodohydroxyquin with 1% hydrocortisone cream (Vytone) [63]. Loose-fitting cotton underclothing, weight reduction, and gentle cleansing once daily with warm water and mild soap are helpful preventive measures [63].

SUN-INDUCED. *Acute sunburn.* Everyone, not only athletes, should be concerned about an acute injury from the sun with outdoor activity. Individuals who participate in sports as diverse as swimming, sailing, golfing, fishing, mountain climbing, and skiing are susceptible [7, 30, 32, 42, 44]. Sunburns can be painful and disfiguring and may prevent participation in an athletic event. In addition, recent evidence has incriminated acute sunburns at a young age in the later development of skin cancer and malignant melanoma.

The sun's rays most responsible for acute sunburn are ultraviolet B (UVB) in the range of 290–320 nm. However, longer-wavelength ultraviolet A (UVA), in the range of 320–400 nm, also contributes to skin damage, but to a much lesser degree. An acute sunburn from UVB develops 2–6 hours after exposure, peaks at 20–24 hours and resolves 72–120 hours later [52]. Ultraviolet exposure intensifies as one approaches the equator and at higher elevations. Exposed areas of the body are most affected, but reflection off sand, water, and snow may injure sites such as the area under the chin that are usually not exposed to the sun.

Clinically, acute sunburn appears as a diffuse, warm redness, which may blister and later scale. Systemic symptoms such as fever, chills, nausea, and prostration may be associated. Treatment usually consists of topical steroid sprays or lotions after cool compresses are applied. If the patient presents within 4 hours of the acute sunburn, systemic nonsteroidal anti-inflammatory agents such as ibuprofen (200 mg) or aspirin (650 mg) every 4 hours for 24 hours may abate or reduce the intensity of the reaction [30]. Systemic steroids may be necessary in a severe case [7, 42].

Prevention is the key with sun-related disorders. Sunscreens are widely available, highly effective, and cosmetically acceptable. They are rated according to a sun protection factor (SPF), which ranges from 2 to 15. The greater the SPF, the greater the protection. The proper choice of a sunscreen and SPF will vary according to the patient's skin type and preference. We recommend at least an SPF of 8, and preferably 15, for all of our athletic patients. A list of selective sunscreens is given in Table 1 [34, 52]. These are based on para-aminobenzoic acid or its ester or a

TABLE 1
Sunscreens

Sunscreen	Trade Name
Para-aminobenzoic acid (PABA)	PreSun
PABA ester	Sundown
	Block Out
	Sea and Ski
PABA-ester combination	SuperShade
	Sundown
	Presun
	Total Eclipse
Non-PABA sunscreens	Uval
	Solbar

benzophenone. Most commercially available sunscreens cannot withstand the stress of sweating and water immersion, so it is best to reapply the sunscreen after sweating or swimming [52]. The lips should be protected with a suitable sunscreen stick. Wearing long sleeves and a cap, if feasible, will offer partial protection. If the sports participant takes these proper precautions, a number of uncomfortable days and spoiled vacations can be prevented.

Chronic actinic injury. Chronic sun exposure is associated with the development of wrinkling, aging, elastosis, and premalignant and malignant skin tumors [72]. Light-complexioned, blue-eyed redheads and blonds are most susceptible to the chronic effects of the sun; however, few individuals are absolutely immune to adverse effects of the sun [28, 52]. One study compared the prevalence of skin cancer in professional and amateur female golfers [28]. The professional golfers were considerably younger than the amateurs (average age, 28.4 vs. 54.5 years) but had five times as much sun exposure as the amateurs. Correspondingly, the professional golfers had a high prevalence of skin cancer at a young age.

Clinically, a variety of skin changes occur from sun exposure. These include furrowing, wrinkling, and a yellow discoloration of the skin, comedones around the eyes, red scaly plaques, and frank skin cancer. The most common sun-damaged areas are the ones most exposed to the sun, such as the face, the scalp in bald men, and the neck, arms, and hands.

Unfortunately, our society equates health with the presence of a golden tan. This is even more evident when we consider the popularity of so-called tanning salons. One can still enjoy the sun and outdoor activities by using sunscreens and appropriate clothing. These measures will prevent acute injury and reduce the aging and carcinogenic potential of the sun's rays.

FIGURE 6
Weeping, crusted lesion of impetigo.

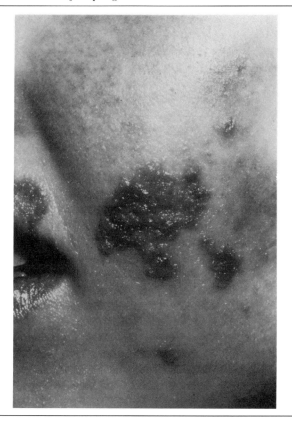

Infections and Infestations

BACTERIAL. *Impetigo.* Impetigo is a common superficial cutaneous infection caused by streptococcal and staphylococcal microorganisms. The infection may be acquired by contact with infected persons or fomites, such as mats, equipment, or towels [4]. Wrestlers, swimmers, and gymnasts are particularly susceptible to impetigo. Clinically, lesions appear as flaccid blisters or erosions with golden-yellow crusting (Figure 6). Bacterial culture will confirm the clinical diagnosis. Because of the potential, though small, for associated glomerulonephritis, a urinalysis to examine for red blood cells and protein should also be obtained if a streptococcal infection is found.

Treatment for impetigo consists of a 7- to 10-day course of systemic antibiotics. Erythromycin or a penicillinase-resistant penicillin in therapeutic doses are effective antimicrobials. Topical cleansing with a mild

FIGURE 7

Inflammatory papules and pustules of acne vulgaris.

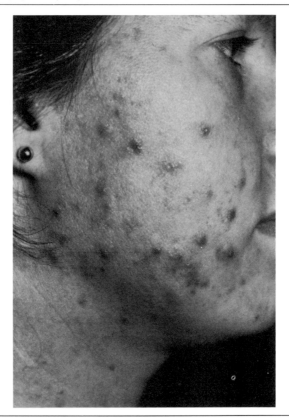

soap and water is helpful for debridement [22]. Since impetigo is highly contagious, the athlete must refrain from contact or water sport activities until the infection has resolved [4, 7, 56]. Towels and equipment must not be shared with other individuals.

Acne and related conditions. Acne vulgaris is a common disease of the hair follicles and sebaceous glands. Causative or exacerbating factors include heredity, increased sebum production, occlusion by topically applied oils or cosmetics, friction from protective equipment, heat, perspiration, hormonal dysfunction, bacterial colonization, anxiety, and certain oral medications. Blackheads and whiteheads are the earliest clinical lesions, which subsequently may become inflammatory papules, pustules, and cysts (Figure 7). The face, chest, shoulders, back, upper arms, and, occasionally, thighs may be involved. Sports activity may aggravate an existing acne problem, especially wrestling, hockey and football [22]. A common site for acne lesions is under the football chin strap [21] or beneath shoulder pads. In addition, the use of anabolic steroids by weight lifters and football players can exacerbate the condition.

Treatment consists of topical cleansing and the use of antibacterial agents such as Dial Soap or pHiSoderm, and/or astringents such as Sea Breeze or 1006, two to three times daily after the sporting activity [21]. In addition, topical antibiotics, topical tretinoin, benzoyl peroxide, and systemic antibiotics such as tetracycline or erythromycin may be needed. Surgical drainage of lesions and intralesional injections of corticosteroids are also helpful adjunctive measures. Isotretinoin (Accutane), a vitamin A analogue, is used in patients with severe cystic acne or treatment-resistant disease. Even though athletes' acne usually improves when their sports activity ceases, they may be treated during the season with good results. Acne is not contagious and does not prevent participation in sports.

Folliculitis. Bacterial folliculitis may develop in the areas of the body occluded by clothing or protective equipment such as the back, chest, arms, and legs. Staphylococcal species are the most common organisms isolated. Clinically, reddish papules and pustules perforated by a central hair are present. These lesions may be itchy or tender [63].

Treatment consists of reducing friction in the affected area. Cotton underwear is often helpful when there is leg involvement [63]. Topical treatment with astringents and drying lotions is usually effective [22]. Systemic antibiotics such as erythromycin or penicillinase-resistant penicillins may also be needed occasionally. Because the risk of spreading infection is low, contact sports activity may be resumed after 2 or 3 days of treatment.

Furunculosis. A furuncle is a cutaneous abscess originating from a hair follicle and is usually caused by *Staphylococcus aureus.* Furuncles may develop from preexisting lesions of folliculitis or may arise *de novo.* The extremities or trunk may be involved. Friction from clothing or equipment, trauma, sweating, oily skin, and poor hygiene are other contributing factors [4,5]. Clinically, warm, tender, inflamed nodules or abscesses are present. Lesions are usually of low infectivity, but since epidemics affecting a whole team can occur with virulent staphylococcal strains [5, 50], precautionary isolation of the patient's equipment and towels is recommended.

Oral penicillinase-resistant penicillin for 10 days is the treatment of choice. Topical application of warm compresses often relieves discomfort. Incision and drainage is often unnecessary if treatment is initiated early [8]. The athlete should refrain from swimming or contact sports until the lesions totally resolve[8]. For recurrent cases, nasopharyngeal cultures of the patient and his or her personal contacts are needed to identify staphylococcal carriers.

FIGURE 8
Erythrasma involving the axilla.

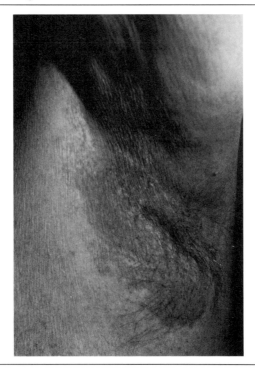

Erythrasma. Erythrasma is a cutaneous bacterial infection that mimics a fungal infection or intertrigo. It is caused by the diphtheroid *Corynebacterium minutissimum.* Intertriginous areas such as the groin, toe webs, axillae, inframammary crease, and intergluteal area provide an ideal warm, moist environment for this infection. Clinically, an asymptomatic, well-demarcated, reddish-brown patch with little scaling is present (Figure 8). Wood's light examination will reveal a coral-red fluorescence that is diagnostic for erythrasma. Local treatment with antibacterial soaps or topical antibiotics is usually effective [63]. Stubborn cases respond rapidly to oral erythromycin [31]. Adequate aeration and loose underclothing are helpful preventive measures.

Pitted keratolysis. Pitted keratolysis is a superficial infection of the skin of the feet believed to be caused by a species of *Corynebacterium.* It is seen primarily in basketball and tennis players and is precipitated by occlusive footwear and hyperhidrosis [31]. The patient presents with the complaint of malodorous feet, and 1- to 3-mm pits with a dirty-brown to black pigmentation are seen, primarily involving the weight-bearing surfaces of the foot. The lesions clear rapidly when the occlusive, mois-ture-contained environment is eliminated. When this fails, topical 5% formalin or 3% erythromycin in 10% benzoyl proxide gel twice daily is effective [6, 31]. Long-term treatment may be necessary [6]. For resistant cases, oral erythromycin in therapeutic doses can be used [31].

VIRAL. *Herpes simplex.* Herpes simplex infections of the skin and mu-cous membranes are common problems in the general population. There are two types of herpes simplex virus. Type I generally infects the lip and areas of the body above the waist; type II causes genital infections and infections below the waist. Participants in contact sports such as wrestling or rugby are particularly susceptible; this infection has been termed "herpes gladiatorum" [69, 70]. Epidemic infections in these ath-letes have been described [18, 53, 69, 70]. Common sites of involvement are the head, neck, and upper extremities, although the trunk may also be affected [7]. The right side of the face and head is more frequently infected because of the common "lock-up" position in wrestling, in which the right cheeks of the opponents are repeatedly pressed together (Fig-ure 9) [31].

Typically, painful, grouped blisters on an inflamed base are present; however, ulceration develops rapidly, with secondary crusting. Because the fragile blisters are frequently traumatized, the characteristic eruption is not always present in the athlete and may be misdiagnosed as bacterial pyoderma or herpes zoster [22, 31]. Microscopic examination of the blister base for multinucleated giant cells and viral culture are helpful diagnostic aids. The infection heals in 10–14 days but often recurs in the same anatomic site. Factors or events such as trauma, sunlight, illness, surgery, stress, or menstruation may trigger a recurrence [63].

Cutaneous herpes infections are highly contagious and precludes in-volvement in contact sports or swimming. Recommendations as to how long participation is prohibited vary. Some authors believe that 4 days is sufficient, since viral shedding ceases after that time [6, 7]. Other recommend at least 120 hours away from contact sports [63]. Still others do not allow the athlete to compete until the lesions have fully healed [31]. We favor the last, most conservative recommendation for our pa-tients. However, some patients shed virus in nasolacrimal secretions even during asymptomatic periods, which complicates the issue [63].

Treatment of herpes gladiatorum is indicated to prevent complications such as herpes keratitis, meningitis, arthritis, or disseminated disease [59]. Topical treatment with drying agents such as Burow's solution 1:40 or benzoyl peroxide gel 5% two to three times daily is helpful. Topical or systemic antibiotics for secondary bacterial colonization may be nec-essary. The use of oral acyclovir (Zovirax), an antiviral drug, is contro-versial. Acyclovir accelerates healing and decreases viral shedding in the treatment of genital herpes infection. However, studies on the treatment

FIGURE 9
Herpes gladiatorum on the face of a wrestler.

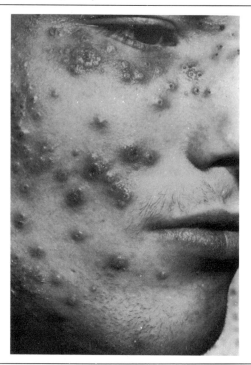

of herpes labialis and recurrent skin infections are inconclusive. Acyclovir has proven to be safe in therapeutic doses for primary or recurrent genital infection. We currently recommend a therapeutic trial of acyclovir, 200–400 mg, five times daily for 5–10 days for acute herpes infections in our athletic patients. For chronic recurrent cutaneous herpes infections in these patients, we have found that prophylactic acyclovir, 200 mg three times daily during the competitive season, reduces the frequency of recurrences.

Verrucae. Verrucae or warts are epidermal tumors caused by the papilloma virus of the papova group. Over 40 different papilloma viruses have been described that produce benign and malignant lesions at different body sites. The plantar wart is the most disabling verrucous lesion affecting athletes, but common warts and flat warts may be cosmetically disfiguring. Because of the effect of perspiration on the skin of the feet, athletes seem to have a greater predilection for plantar warts [6]. Although inoculation may result from exposure to a wart (contaminated floors, equipment, clothing, or other fomites), warts are not highly con-

FIGURE 10
Plantar wart with pinpoint capillary thromboses.

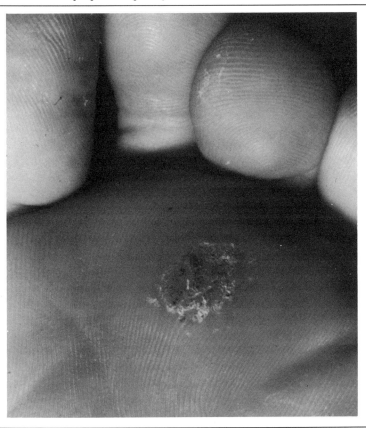

tagious, with an incubation period estimated at greater than 6 months [63]. Calluses are more prone to papilloma virus infections than normal skin, and gymnasts may develop verrucae in their thickly callused hands [7].

When present on a pressure surface such as the foot, the lesions are endophytic and a hyperkeratotic plaque that disrupts the normal skin lines is present (Figure 10). At other sites, brown to tan hyperkeratotic papules or plaques may be seen (Figure 11). A useful diagnostic sign is that when verrucae are pared with a sharp scalpel blade, pinpoint bleeding points are produced.

Multiple destructive modalities are used for treating warts. In the athlete, a more conservative approach is indicated so that sports participation can be continued. Topical agents such as 16% salicylic acid and

FIGURE 11
Common wart on the thumb.

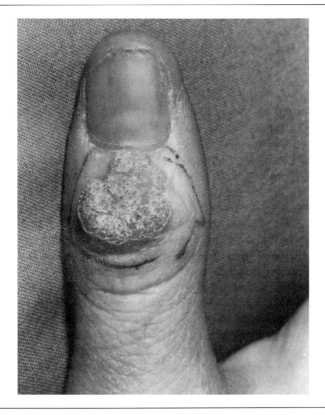

16% lactic acid (Duofilm) applied nightly, 40% salicylic acid plaster applied daily, or Retin-A gel 0.025% applied twice daily produce slow resolution in many patients [7, 8]. In addition, drying powders or solutions should be used routinely by wart-prone athletes. Wearing rubber sandals or other footwear in the locker rooms is also recommended [4]. More aggressive treatment may be used in the off season, such as chemical cautery with 50–75% trichloroacetic acid, liquid nitrogen cryotherapy or electrodesiccation and curettage. For treatment-resistant lesions or verrucae that recur several times, carbon dioxide laser vaporization [43] or intralesional bleomycin have produced favorable results. Cold steel excision and radiotherapy are no longer recommended modalities.

Molluscum contagiosum. Molluscum contagiosum is a viral infection of the skin caused by a pox virus. It is more contagious than verrucae and is acquired by personal contact, contaminated swimming pools, or gymnastic equipment. Minor epidemics have been reported in wrestlers and swimmers [7, 46, 51]. The lesions are found most commonly on the trunk, axillae, face, perineum, and thighs [8]. Clinically, molluscum contagiosum presents as solitary or multiple pearly, umbilicated papules on a noninflammatory base. Occasionally, hyperkeratosis on frictional sites such as the elbows and knees may make the lesions difficult to recognize [22]. These lesions may be spread by direct inoculation through scratching.

Treatment consists of curettage of each lesion, followed by the use of a chemical cauterizing agent [7, 22, 60]. Liquid nitrogen cryotherapy and electrodesiccation are also effective. Topical agents such as Retin-A or skin abrasion after bathing with a Buff-Puff pad, which is disposed after each treatment, have also been used [8].

FUNGAL. *Tinea.* Superficial cutaneous fungal infections have been intimately associated with athletic participation, as evidence by the phrases "athlete's foot" and "jock itch" [7]. Factors that predispose to tinea infections include moisture, as created by constantly perspiring feet in athletic shoes, occlusion, increased carbon dioxide tension, and individual host factors [37]. Overgrowth of resident aerobic bacteria is considered by some to be a significant factor in the production of symptoms [40]. Showers and locker rooms provide a reservoir of dermatophyte infections, and reinfection is common if proper precautions are not followed [37, 55].

Tinea pedis, or athlete's foot, is the most common superficial fungal infection in athletes. It is most often caused by *Trichophyton rubrum* or *T. mentagrophytes* [55]. Infection by the former generally causes an asymptomatic reddish plaque with peripheral scaling and central clearing, whereas infection by the latter may be associated with painful or itchy blisters. Many patients treat themselves, and the clinical picture may be obscured. However, an important clue to the diagnosis is involvement of the fourth toe web, which is nearly always affected in fungal infections [7]. Examination of potassium hydroxide scrapings from affected skin for the presence of fungal hyphae will confirm the diagnosis.

Other dermatoses in the differential diagnosis include dyshidrosis, allergic or irritant contact dermatitis, erythrasma, and psoriasis. Treatment is often helpful if measures are used to reduce dampness of the feet, such as frequent changes of absorbent socks and the use of a drying lotion or powder. Topical antifungals available without a prescription include Micatin and Desenex; prescription topical agents are clotrimazole (Lotrimin) and econazole (Spectazole). For widespread or acute inflammatory lesions, oral griseofulvin, 250–1000 mg daily, may be used [8]. Prophylactic use of tolnaftate powder can reduce the incidence of tinea pedis in high-risk groups [37]. Wearing sandals in public showering facilities is also recommended [55]. However, a patient or athlete may have a localized immune defect for certain fungal strains, making irradication impossible and recurrences common [7].

Tinea cruris is a fungal infection of the groin and upper thighs and is often associated with tinea pedis. The organisms most often responsible for infection are *T. rubrum, T. mentagrophytes,* and *Epidermophyton floccosum* [22]. The infection most likely begins on the feet and spreads to the groin by clothing, towels, or other fomites. The moist, warm microenvironment is ideal for fungal growth. Clinically, lesions appear as reddish plaques with peripheral scaling and central clearing (Figure 12). Itching may be associated with tinea cruris. Examination of the feet and potassium hydroxide scrapings should always be performed. Treatment is similar to that of tinea pedis, with emphasis on loose, clean clothing for proper aeration and good hygiene [31]. Other recommendations are for the athlete to wear socks before putting on underwear and to towel-dry the feet last after a shower to reduce the chance of spreading infection from the feet [4].

Tinea corporis is a superficial fungal infection involving the body. The same organisms responsible for tinea cruris cause this condition. The

FIGURE 12
Tinea cruris of the inguinal region and upper thigh.

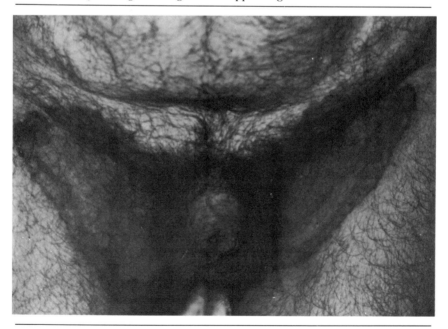

FIGURE 13
Characteristic circular scaling plaques of tinea corporis.

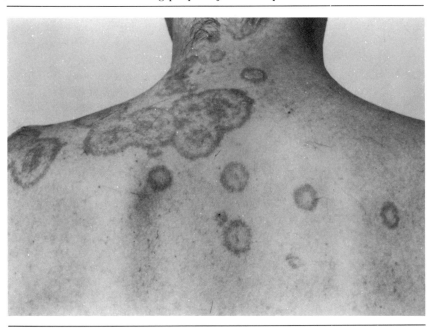

popular term "ringworm" is applied because the lesions appear as annular or circinate plaques with peripheral scaling and central clearing (Figure 13). Although it is not as common in athletes as tinea pedis and tinea cruris, epidemics among wrestlers have been reported [23]. Treatment with topical antifungals or oral griseofulvin is effective.

Tinea versicolor is a superficial fungal infection of the skin caused by *Malassezia furfur*, which is the pathogenic form of a common yeast, *Pityrosporum orbiculare*. Although contagiousness is low and athletes are no more susceptible than the general population, an athlete may be prevented from participating in his or her sport until the skin eruption is diagnosed [22]. The upper back and chest are usually involved first, and lesions spread to the arms, abdomen, thighs, legs, neck, and face. White, pink, or fawn-colored, slightly scaling spots are present clinically. A potassium hydroxide examination of the superficial scale will reveal small hyphae and spores. Treatment consists of the application of selenium sulfide shampoo 2.5% for 15 minutes daily for 3 days from the neck to the ankles [22]. Maintenance/preventive treatment once weekly is also recommended [63]. Ketoconazole, 200 mg/daily for 3 days, may also be used; few side effects have been reported. The patient should be informed that treatment kills the fungus but that the pigment changes in the skin will remain until pigment is naturally restored.

Candidiasis. Although less common than tinea infection, *Candida albicans* may also infect the skin of athletes, particularly those engaged in running sports and swimming [55]. Warm, moist areas of the skin such as the groin, vagina, perineum, and interdigital web spaces are most susceptible. Diabetics have a higher incidence of cutaneous candidiasis than nondiabetics. Infection may be transmitted by shower floors, towels, equipment, or, as reported in one epidemic, by a protective skin lubricant [41]. The clinical appearance is characterized by an inflamed, macerated plaque with satellite papules or pustules. Potassium hydroxide examination of the superficial scale reveals hyphae and numerous spores.

Treatment consists of adequate aeration of the affected area and topical antifungals such as miconazole (Micatin) or clotrimazole (Lotrimin) twice daily. A new product, Lotrisone, is a patented combination of clotrimazole and betamethasone dipropionate. It has proven to be an effective treatment for cutaneous candidiasis because the betamethasone dipropionate, a medium-potency steroid, is useful for its anti-inflammatory effect. However, Lotrisone should be used with caution for no more than 2 weeks in areas such as the groin and genitals, axillae, and face because of the possibility of the steroid component's inducing atrophy of the skin. Absorbent powders are helpful in reducing moisture, but powders containing starch should be avoided, since *C. albicans* can grow readily on it [55]. Zeasorb contains 45% microporous cellulose and can be used as an absorbent powder in these patients.

PARASITIC. *Scabies.* Scabies is a highly contagious infestation caused by *Sarcoptes scabiei*. It may be transmitted by sexual, routine, or frictional contact [22]. A pregnant female mite invades the upper layer of the skin to lay her eggs and produces the characteristic clinical lesion, a burrow. Vesicles or papules may develop but these are rapidly excoriated, since itching is severe. The most common sites for lesions are the finger webs, flexor wrists, elbows, axillae, buttocks, female breasts, and male genitalia [63]. The diagnosis may be confirmed by scraping the burrow's content on a microscopic slide wetted with mineral oil and examining for mites, eggs, or feces (Figure 14).

The treatment of choice for scabies is gamma benzene hexachloride (Kwell). All contacts should be treated, including family members, roommates, team members, friends, coaches, and trainers [63]. The patient is instructed to apply Kwell lotion to all areas from the neck down at night; he or she should shower the following morning and repeat the application in 1 week. This regimen is highly effective, whereas more frequent applications may result in irritant dermatitis [22]. Kwell has a long safety record, and the reports of adverse effects have resulted from inappropriate use or industrial exposure. Clothing and bedding should

FIGURE 14
Sarcoptes scabiei *is the causative agent of scabies.*

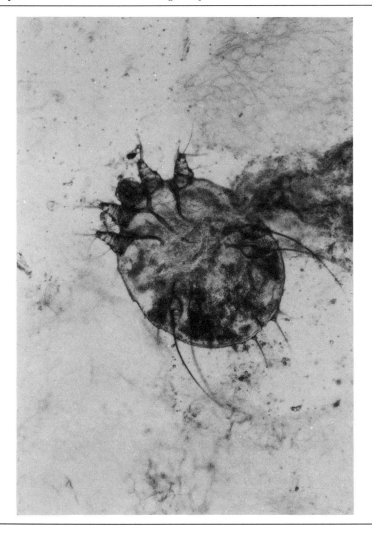

be washed or cleaned and stored for 7–10 days [22]. We recommend that our athletes refrain from contact sports while undergoing treatment. Occasionally, itchy papules will persist for 5–6 weeks after treatment. These lesions should be treated with a medium-potency topical steroid cream twice daily.

A new topical agent for the treatment of scabies is permethrin 5% dermal cream. It is an alternative to Kwell therapy, and one study showed

FIGURE 15
Pediculosis lice, one of which is still grasping a hair.

permethrin to be superior to Kwell for the treatment of scabies in an endemic population [64].

Pediculosis. There are three forms of pediculosis: pediculosis capitis, pediculosis corporis, and pediculosis pubis. The last is more common in the athlete and is better known as "crabs." Pediculosis pubis is caused by the louse, *Phthirus pubis.* It is mainly transmitted by intimate contact. The louse attaches itself to the hair shaft and periodically feeds on the host's blood (Figure 15). Excoriations are the only apparent lesions seen.

The louse or its eggs (nits) may be seen with the aid of a magnifying lens.

Gamma benzene hexachloride (Kwell) is the treatment of choice. It is used as a shampoo, lathered, and allowed to remain in place for 4 minutes. An alternative treatment is the use of pyrethrin with piparonyl butoxide (Rid, A-200). The nits may be removed with a nit comb or tweezers or by trimming the hair.

Contact Dermatitis

Contact dermatitis presents as an acute, subacute, or chronic inflammatory disorder of the skin. There are two types of contact dermatitis. Irritant contact dermatitis is nonallergic and results from exposure to a physical agent or irritating substance that produces dermatitis [8]. Allergic contact dermatitis develops from acquired hypersensitivity to a specific allergen applied to the skin, such as poison ivy.

Irritant contact dermatitis in athletes may be due to mechanical or chemical irritants. Mechanical irritants include head bands or wrist bands (runners), helmets (football players), gloves and fiberglass (hockey players), and adhesive tape (football and basketball players) [9]. Irritant contact dermatitis due to chemicals may occur following application of antiseptics, medicaments, insect repellents, cosmetics, leakage of "cold pack" chemicals, or oily sunscreens [9].

The most common causes of allergic contact dermatitis in the general population include plants (poison ivy, poison oak, ragweed), metals (nickel, chromium, cobalt), organic dyes (paraphenylenediamine), rubber products, chemicals, medicaments, and cosmetics (Figure 16). Athletes are also susceptible to allergic contact dermatitis from these materials, but some specific causes are more common sensitizers in this population.

A report identified tape, especially rubber-backed adhesive tape, as the most common material causing allergic contact dermatitis in athletes [22]. Topical medications are an important cause of allergic contact dermatitis. These include topical antibiotics (neomycin, nitrofurazone, penicillin), antihistamines (diphenhydramine, promethazine), anesthetics (benzocaine, dibucaine), and antiseptics (iodine) (Figure 17) [9]. Allergic contact dermatitis from tincture of benzoin, used to secure tape to the skin, is a common problem [9]. Shoe dermatitis due to sensitivity to rubber, adhesives, dyes, or chemicals used in the tanning of leather may be seen in athletes [7]. This characteristically presents on the dorsal aspects of the toes and feet. The excessive moisture of the athlete's foot makes it more susceptible to shoe dermatitis [37]. In addition, common agents such as poison ivy or ragweed may produce dermatitis that mimics other skin disorders such as atopic eczema or photosensitivity [9].

A thorough and complete history is essential to determine the un-

FIGURE 16
Linear blisters characteristic of poison ivy.

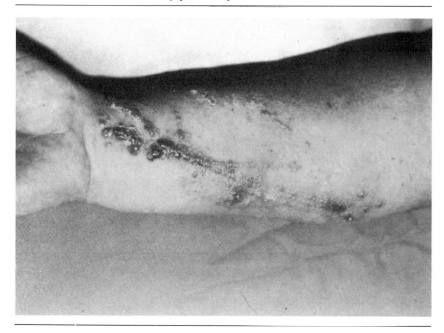

derlying cause of allergic contact dermatitis. Examination of the patient to determine the nature, configuration, and distribution of the eruption is also important. Acute dermatitis is blistering, weeping, and oozing; crusting develops later. Subacute dermatitis is red, edematous, and crusting, whereas chronic dermatitis is dull red and scaling. In contact dermatitis, the clinical lesions are well demarcated and may be linear. Often, the history and physical examination alone will identify the causative agent, but patch testing may be needed to determine the specific incriminating allergen.

Treatment for irritant and allergic contact dermatitis is similar, with elimination or avoidance of the precipitating cause being crucial. Acute dermatitis should be treated with cool compresses (Burow's solution) and a medium-potency topical steroid such as betamethasone valerate (Valisone) in aerosolized or lotion form. A short course of systemic steroids may be required. Subacute and chronic dermatitis may require treatment with medium- or high-potency topical steroid creams or ointments and bland emollients. Oral antihistamines for itching and oral antibiotics for secondary pyoderma may also be needed.

EXACERBATION OF PREEXISTING DERMATOSES. Patients with *atopic dermatitis* often have flares of their disease with sweating, friction, irritation, and the increased bathing associated with strenuous athletics [9]. Atopics are very susceptible to dry skin, especially swimmers [50]. Patients with mild forms of atopy may still qualify for competition if certain protective skin measures are taken [50]. These include frequent use of emollients, avoidance of excessive cold or prolonged exposure, and reduction of bathing to no more than once daily. However, it should be noted that atopic patients are also particularly prone to generalized herpes simplex infections and cutaneous bacterial infections. They should be informed of this risk and discouraged from participation in sports where this exposure is frequent, such as wrestling. Atopic patients with cutaneous viral or bacterial infections are restricted from athletic competition.

Athletes who are susceptible to *dry skin* need to follow measures similar to those of atopic patients. Dry skin is especially prominent during the winter season, when humidity is low. Swimmers, skiers, skaters, and hikers are particularly affected. Bathing with lukewarm water daily or every other day, use of a superfatted soap such as Basis, daily use of emollients, and humidification of the home are often helpful preventive measures.

Dyshidrotic eczema occurs on the hands and feet as recurrent itchy blis-

FIGURE 17
Contact dermatitis due to a topical antibiotic ointment (Polysporin).

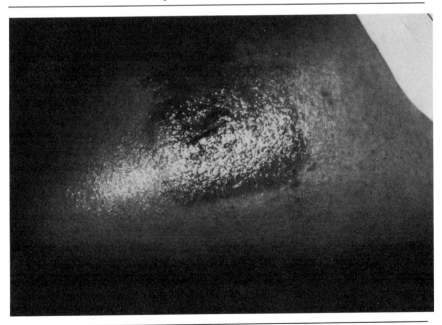

ters accompanied by redness, edema, and crusting. Stress is often associated with flares, although irritants and sweating may exacerbate the disorder. Differentiation of dyshidrotic eczema from contact dermatitis or tinea pedis is difficult. Tiny blisters on the lateral aspects of the toes favor a diagnosis of dyshidrosis, since they are rarely seen in contact dermatitis or tinea infections. In addition, potassium hydroxide examination and patch testing give negative results in dyshidrotic eczema. Treatment includes measures to reduce moisture of the feet, including application of an absorbent powder and frequent changing of white socks and shoes [22]. Compresses with Burow's solution 1:40 and use of topical steroid lotions or creams are also helpful.

Other common skin diseases such as *psoriasis* and *seborrheic dermatitis* are affected by athletic participation. Psoriasis often appears in areas susceptible to trauma such as the elbows, knees, and knuckles. Skin subjected to frictional or abrasional trauma may develop plaques of psoriasis, known as the "Koebner phenomenon." Topical steroids and tar preparations are the mainstay of treatment for psoriasis. Seborrheic dermatitis presents as reddish plaques with greasy yellow scaling. The scalp, ears, eyebrows, and nasal crease are the most common sites, although the axillae, mid-chest, umbilical area, and groin may also be affected. These latter sites are most typically exacerbated in the athlete. Shampoos containing zinc pyrethionine (Head and Shoulders), salicylic acid (Ionil) or tar (T Gel), mild steroid creams containing diiodohydroxyquin (Vytone 1%), topical steroid lotions (Texacort), and topical ketoconazole cream (Nizoral) are effective for treatment.

UNCOMMON DISEASES

Physical Factors

MECHANICAL OR FRICTIONAL. *Dermal and subcutaneous nodules.* Repeated local trauma and hemorrhage at specialized sites may induce fibrotic dermal or subcutaneous masses [50]. Surfer's nodules are an example, consisting of nontender nodular collections caused by kneeling on the surfboard. Common sites include the tibial prominences, mid-dorsa of the feet, and dorsal aspect of one or more metatarsophalangeal joints [19]. Osseous changes may also be associated, and ulceration may develop occasionally [19]. These nodules will resolve if the surfer paddles in a prone position or avoids surfing temporarily [19].

Alopecia. Traction alopecia resulting from wearing a tight-banded, wide-stripped headphone while jogging has been reported [16]. The use of a lighter headpiece halted the hair loss. Patchy alopecia in the occipitoparietal area was described in two male adolescents who practiced break dancing [16]. Gymnasts who repeatedly practice head stands and roll-overs on the balance beam may develop alopecia [20].

Joggers' and bicyclists' nipples. A frictional injury seen in joggers is abrasion of the nipple and areola resulting from frictional contact with the coarse fabric of a shirt during a long run [6]. The condition has been called "joggers' nipples" and manifests as painful, inflamed, fissured, and occasionally bleeding nipples [38]. Wearing a brassiere made of soft fabric is curative in women. In men, the use of a garment made of a semisynthetic fabric or silk, taping the nipples, cutting out the fabric over the breasts, or applying petrolatum before running are helpful measures [13, 37].

Bicyclists' nipples are primarily a thermal injury to the nipples that occurs during a cold-weather ride [54]. Evaporation of sweat and the chill of the wind lower the temperature of the nipples, producing a painful injury that may continue for several days [54]. Use of a cycling jacket, thermal undergarment, or some other protective material will prevent further recurrences.

Dermographism and pressure urticaria. There are three types of physical urticaria: mechanical urticaria, thermal urticaria, and actinic urticaria. Mechanical urticaria consists of two subtypes: dermographism and pressure urticaria. Dermographism is characterized by itchy or asymptomatic, localized or generalized, urticarial plaques following insignificant trauma or pressure (Figure 18). It can be precipitated in athletes by occlusive clothing or sporting gear [45]. The etiologic mechanism of dermographism is unclear, but the disorder has been passively transferred. Dermographism may also be provoked by infection (bacteria or parasites) and drugs (antibiotics) [45]. Pressure urticaria is uncommon but may develop in athletes such as long-distance runners. Erythematous, edematous plaques occur on the feet after continuous running. Both dermographism and pressure urticaria may respond to treatment with protease inhibitors such as epsilon-aminocaproic acid (Amicar) or cyproheptadine (Periactin) [45].

COLD-INDUCED. *Cold urticaria.* Cold urticaria is the most common form of acquired physical urticaria in athletes [45]. The most frequent pathogenic mechanism is nonallergic, with direct histamine liberation from mast cells [45]. Cold agglutinins, cold hemolysins, and cryofibrinogens may be occasionally associated with cold urticaria [45]. Clinically, symptomatic or asymptomatic, localized or generalized, urticarial wheals develop in response to cold exposure. Cold urticaria responds better than most other types of physical urticaria to cyproheptadine (Periactin) and small doses of oral corticosteroids [62], so affected athletes need not abandon training and exercise [62].

Raynaud's disease. Raynaud's disease is an idiopathic cold hypersensitivity and results in vascular spasm with pallor, cyanosis, and, in severe cases, gangrene of the affected digits [17]. Raynaud's phenomenon is secondary to systemic connective tissue diseases such as scleroderma,

FIGURE 18
A dramatic example of dermographism.

lupus erythematosus, and cryoglobulinemia [17]. Patients with Raynaud's disease or phenomenon can find winter sports devastating and must be instructed to protect their hands and feet during these activities [31]. Treatment with topical medications and steroids has been generally unfavorable, although recent evidence shows benefit with use of the calcium antagonist nifedipine [57]. Smoking must be prohibited in these patients. Battery-operated heated gloves and boots may be useful. Severe cases have been treated with surgical sympathectomy, but the benefits are only temporary [17].

HEAT-INDUCED. *Cholinergic urticaria.* Cholinergic urticaria is an acetylcholine-mediated disorder provoked by heat, emotion, and exertion [17, 45]. The etiology is unknown, but autoallergy to sweat and sweat metabolites, as once proposed, is probably not causative [45]. Boxers, runners, swimmers, and weight lifters have been affected [45]. Clinically, 1- to 2-mm urticarial wheals surrounded by an erythematous axonal reflex flare are seen. Systemic symptoms such as generalized sweating, abdominal cramps, dizziness, wheezing, and bradycardia may also be associated.

Treatment is not as effective as in cold urticaria. Antihistamines, such as hydroxyzine (Atarax) and cyproheptadine (Periactin), may relieve the symptoms but do not cure the disorder. Some athletes may have to give up training and participation in their sport for an indefinite period [45].

Exercise-induced urticaria. Exercise-induced urticaria is believed by some authors to be a variant of cholinergic urticaria [35], while others feel that it is a distinct entity [10]. It differs from cholinergic urticaria by its failure to develop after exposure to heat without exercise [39]. Exercise-induced urticaria usually occurs sporadically, although familial cases have recently been reported [27]. Cutaneous manifestations include giant urticaria, lesions indistinguishable from cholinergic urticaria, or angioedema (soft tissue swelling) [39]. The skin changes may be accompanied by systemic manifestations such as wheezing or hypotension, so that some cases may resemble exercise-induced anaphylactic syndrome [35].

Treatment for exercise-induced urticaria has proven difficult. Antihistamines, anticholinergics, beta agonists, or phosphodiesterase inhibitors given prophylactically have not been successful. Cromolyn sodium (Intal) 20 mg three to four times daily, given by inhalation, not orally, has been reported to prevent attacks of exercise-induced urticaria and angioedema [29]. When the condition is accompanied by systemic symptoms, the treatment of choice is subcutaneous epinephrine [10].

SUN-INDUCED. *Solar urticaria.* Solar urticaria is a rare type of physical urticaria and an uncommon cause of urticaria in athletes [45]. It may be associated with porphyria or medications such as sulfonamides [42]. Pathogenically, solar urticaria is believed to result from nonallergic liberation of histamine by a direct effect of ultraviolet rays on mast cells. Clinically, urticarial wheals develop shortly after exposure to the causative wavelength of electromagnetic energy. Antihistamines may be helpful for acute episodes, and antimalarial drugs may be beneficial in some patients for prevention [45].

Photosensitivity dermatitis. Photosensitivity dermatitis is classified into two types: phototoxic and photoallergic. Phototoxic dermatitis is a severe, exaggerated sunburn occurring after exposure to a small dose of ultraviolet light. Photoallergic dermatitis is a sun-induced, eczematous dermatitis characterized by severe itching and blister formation. Outdoor sports activities may expose a susceptible individual to sufficient ultraviolet light to precipitate a photosensitivity dermatitis.

Photosensitivity dermatitis has multiple causes [30, 42], including systemic drugs (tetracycline, demeclocycline, sulfonamides, griseofulvin, hydrochlorothiazide, chlorpropamide, chlorpromazine); topical preparations (coal tar derivatives, antimicrobial soaps, sunscreens); plants and vegetables (fig, parsnip, parsley, dill, wild carrot, lime, celery, anise); and fragrances (colognes, perfumes, after-shave lotions). Often the offending agent may be determined from the history, but photopatch testing may be needed to determine the cause. Treatment is similar to that previously described for acute sunburn and contact dermatitis. Once the

FIGURE 19
Scattered, inflamed papules and pustules on the back of a patient with hot tub folliculitis. (Courtesy of Ronald G. Wheeland, M.D., F.A.C.P., University of California at Davis.)

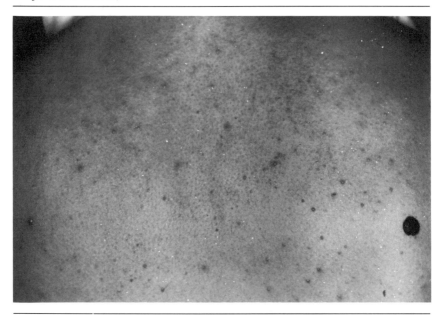

cause is found and eliminated, or an alternative nonphotosensitizing agent is substituted, the athlete may resume normal sports participation.

Infections

BACTERIAL. *"Hot tub" folliculitis.* Outbreaks of a papulopustular skin eruption associated with the use of hot tubs, jaccuzis, whirlpools, and swimming pools have been described [14]. These epidemics have occurred in hotels, motels, and health spas. The causative organism is *Pseudomonas aeruginosa*, which flourishes in the warm, turbulent, heavily used, low-chlorinated water found in public hot tubs and whirlpools. Clinically, reddish papules, pustules, or blisters develop within 2 days of exposure, predominantly on the lateral trunk, axillae, proximal extremities, and buttocks (Figure 19) [14]. The disease appears to be self-limited, lasting from 7–10 days. Topical or systemic therapy does not appear to shorten the duration of the dermatitis. Since the disease was first recognized, measures such as frequent changing of water, automatic chlorination, frequent monitoring of disinfectant levels, and maintenance of water at higher temperatures and at a pH of 7.2–7.8 have reduced the prevalence of pseudomonal folliculitis. Other cutaneous infections may also be transmitted in public bathing facilities, especially herpes and staphylococcal infections.

Otitis externa. Acute otitis externa or "swimmer's ear" occurs uniquely in this specific group of athletes. It develops because prolonged exposure to water causes epidermal maceration and dissolution of cerumen in the ear canal, removing the protective bacteriostatic seal for the skin [43]. Trauma and anatomic anomalies also allow invasion of bacteria, principally pseudomonas species [43, 62]. Pain, swelling, itching, fever, and diminished hearing are the most common symptoms. The most important aspect of therapy is cleaning the external auditory canal by gentle lavage and suctioning, followed by the topical application of antibiotics or astringents [43]. Prevention may be maintained by prophylactic instillation of an acidic solution such as 2% acetic acid in propylene glycol (VoSol) and the use of petrolatum-coated earplugs.

Atypical mycobacteria. Accidental inoculation of *Mycobacterium marinum* may occur in participants of water sports. The most common sites of involvement are the elbows and knees following abrasion received while swimming in a pool, hence the term "swimming pool granuloma" [30]. Clinically, a plaque or nodule is present, which may ulcerate and be associated with lymphadenopathy or lymphangitis. A skin biopsy for bacterial culture of the infected tissue is the most reliable means of diagnosis [31]. The lesions may heal spontaneously, but treatment with cryotherapy, excision, tetracycline, and minocycline has also been used successfully [31].

VIRAL. *Herpes zoster.* Herpes zoster or "shingles" occurs rarely in young athletes [22]. The infection is characterized by painful, grouped blisters on an inflamed base, but, unlike herpes simplex, is arranged in a dermatomal distribution, and recurrences are infrequent. When the orbital division of the trigeminal nerve is involved, infection involving the ipsilateral eye may develop. Herpes zoster is the same virus that causes varicella or chicken pox and is believed to result from either reactivation of a latent viral infection or contact with an infected individual.

Treatment, which is similar to the treatment of herpes simplex, consists of cool soaks and drying agents. Analgesics such as acetaminophen (Tylenol) or codeine may be needed for pain. The benefit of oral acyclovir (Zovirax), an antiviral agent, in herpes zoster infection is inconclusive to date; however, we recommend treatment using acyclovir, 200 mg, five times daily for 10 days. The patient must be prohibited from engaging in contact or water sports, especially when blisters are present, to prevent transmission of varicella to other susceptible athletes not previously infected by the virus [22].

FUNGAL. *Sporotrichosis.* Deep fungal infections are rarely related to sports activities [31]. However, sporotrichosis may be seen in hikers, hunters, gardeners, or fishermen who contact contaminated plants, moss, or soil. Clinically, an ulcerated nodule develops on an extremity, with associated painless nodules along the draining lymphatic chain. The infection rarely disseminates.

Diagnosis is made by demonstrating the causative organism, *Sporotrichum schenckii*, in culture and occasionally on histologic examination. The treatment of choice is an oral supersaturated solution of potassium iodide. Sporotrichosis may be prevented by wearing gloves and other protective materials when contacting possible contaminated plants.

Contact Dermatitis
Common causes of contact dermatitis in athletes were discussed in the first section of this chapter. Some rarer examples of sports-related contact dermatitis will be reviewed here.

Participants in water sports are susceptible to allergic contact dermatitis from a number of unique sources. Swim goggles containing thioureas may produce a periorbital dermatitis [2, 9]. Similarly, contact periorbital leukoderma has been reported from swim goggles due to the neoprene rubber or glue [26]. Scuba divers may develop facial dermatitis from their face masks due to isopropyl aminodiphenylamine, which is used to prevent weathering of rubber [65]. A professional diver was reported to develop a widespread dermatitis from a rubber wet suit containing diethylthiourea [1]. Wind surfers may acquire hand eczema from contact with black rubber components of the wishbone of the sail [66].

Runners are susceptible to contact dermatitis from running shoes. As previously noted, perfuse sweating of the runner's feet makes them more likely to develop shoe dermatitis. The most common incriminating allergens are rubber, adhesives (ethylbutylthiourea), and dyes [9].

Contact dermatitis in bowlers may occur from exposure to the carrying case or its metal parts, the material of the ball itself, or the materials used to aid in the grip of the ball [11]. One patient was reported to have a blotchy facial erythema believed to be secondary to allergy to a resin used in a bowler's grip [11].

EXACERBATION OF PREEXISTING DERMATOSIS. *Vitiligo* is an autoimmune disease characterized by symmetric, depigmented spots and patches of skin (Figure 20). The disorder may be worsened by sports participation in two ways: First, vitiligo may develop in sites of the body subjected to trauma (Koebner phenomenon); second, since depigmented skin may be highly susceptible to acute sunburn and the chronic effects of the sun, the athlete who participates in outdoor activity must be diligent to protect the affected areas from ultraviolet light exposure.

Lichen planus is a common dermatologic problem manifested by itchy, polygonal purple papules on the volar wrist, ankles, genitalia, mucous membranes, and, occasionally, the nails (Figure 21). Since lichen planus commonly develops in abraded skin, the athlete with this disorder must utilize the proper protective gear to prevent it from occurring.

Epidermolysis bullosa is an inherited or acquired blistering disorder of the skin. Patients with a specific superficial form, known by the eponym "Weber-Cockayne," may lead normal lives and participate in sports activities; however, blistering develops in these patients on the hands and feet at trauma sites, particularly in the summer. Drying agents such as aluminum chloride or glutaraldehyde reduce sweating and the development of blisters in these patients. Phenytoin (Dilantin) has also been used in these patients with variable results.

Other photosensitive skin diseases such as *lupus erythematosus* and *polymorphous light eruption* may be exacerbated by outdoor athletic participation. The diligent use of sunscreens may prevent problems in many patients. Topical and systemic corticosteroids are useful for the treat-

FIGURE 20
Depigmented skin around the eyes and mouth characteristic of vitiligo.

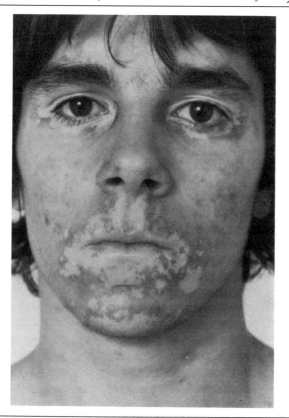

250 | *Kantor, Bergfeld*

FIGURE 21
Lichen planus on the wrists and forearms.

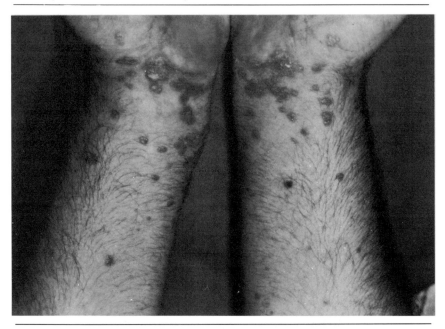

ment of disease exacerbation. Antimalarial medication usually improves sun tolerance in patients with systemic lupus erythematosus.

SUMMARY

The athlete is exposed to a whole spectrum of skin diseases that may or may not be unique to the particular sport or activity. Although the athlete is usually a healthy young adult and sports-related skin diseases are often minor, it is important for these disorders to be recognized by physicians, nurses, coaches, and trainers. Prevention, early diagnosis, and treatment will enable the athlete to resume participation as early as medically possible.

1. Adams, R.M. Contact allergic dermatitis due to diethylthiourea in a wet suit. *Contact Dermatitis* 8:277–278, 1982.
2. Alomar, A., and I. Vilatella. Contact dermatitis to dibutylthiourea in swimming goggles. *Contact Dermatitis* 13:348–349, 1985.
3. Ayres, S., and R. Mihan. Calcaneal petechiae. *Arch. Dermatol.* 106:262, 1972.

4. Bart, B. Skin problems in athletics. *Minnesota Med.* 66:239–241, 1983.
5. Bartlett, P.C., R.J. Martin, and B.R. Cahill. Furunculosis in a high school football team. *Am. J. Sports Med.* 10:371–374, 1982.
6. Basler, R.S.W. Dermatologic aspects of sports participation: *Curr. Concepts Skin Dis.* 15–19, Fall 1985.
7. Basler, R.S. Skin lesions related to sports activity. *Primary Care* 10:479–494, 1983.
8. Bergfeld, W.F. Dermatologic problems in athletes. *Primary Care* 11:151–160, 1984.
9. Bergfeld, W.F., and J.S. Taylor. Trauma, sports, and the skin. *Am. J. Indust. Med.* 8:403–413, 1985.
10. Berman, B.A., and R.N. Ross. Exercise-induced anaphylaxis. *Cutis* 32:216–218, 1983.
11. Blair, C. The dermatologic hazards of bowling. Contact dermatitis to resin in a bowler's grip. *Contact Dermatitis* 8:138–139, 1982.
12. Bodine, K.G. Black heel. *J. Am. Podiatry Assoc.* 70:201, 1980.
13. Brazin, S.A. Dermatologic hazards of long distance running. *J. Am. Mil. Dermatol.* 5:8–9, 1979.
14. Chandrasekar, P.H., K.V.I. Rolston, D.W. Kannangara, J.L. LeFrock and S.A. Binnick. Hot tub-associated dermatitis due to *Pseudomonas aeruginosa. Arch. Dermatol.* 120:1337–1340, 1984.
15. Clark, R.A.F. Cutaneous tissue repair: Basic biologic consideration I. *J. Am. Acad. Dermatol.* 13:701–725, 1985.
16. Copperman, S.M. Two new causes of alopecia. *J.A.M.A.* 25:367, 1984.
17. D'Ambrosia, R.D. Cold injuries encountered in a winter resort. *Cutis* 20:365–368, 1977.
18. Dyke, L.M., U.R. Merikangas, O.C. Bruton, S.G. Trask, and F.M. Hetrick. Skin infection in wrestlers due to herpes simplex virus. *J.A.M.A.* 194:1001–1002, 1965.
19. Erickson, J.G., and G.R. von Gemmingen. Surfer's nodules and other complications of surfboarding. *J.A.M.A.* 201:134–136, 1967.
20. Ely, P.H. Balance beam alopecia. *Arch. Dermatol.* 114:968, 1978.
21. Farber, G.A., J.W. Burks, A.M. Hegre, and G.R. Brown. Football acne—an acneiform eruption. *Cutis* 20:356–360, 1977.
22. Freeman, M.J., and W.F. Bergfeld. Skin diseases of football and wrestling participants. *Cutis* 20:333–341, 1977.
23. Frisk, A., H. Heilborn, and B. Melen. Epidemic occurrence of trichophytosis among wrestlers. *Acta. Dermatol. Venereol.* 46:453–456, 1966.
24. Garfinkel, D., and L.A. Rothenberger. Foot problems in athletes. *J. Fam. Pract.* 19:239–250, 1984.
25. Gibbs, R.C. "Tennis toe." *Arch. Dermatol.* 107:918, 1973.
26. Goette, D.K. Racoon-like periorbital leukoderma from contact with swim goggles. *Contact Dermatitis* 10:129–131, 1984.
27. Grant, J.A., J. Farnam, R.A. Lord, D.O. Thueson, M.A. Lett-Brown, H. Wallfisch, D.P. Fine, and F.C. Schmalstieg. Familial exercise-induced anaphylaxis. *J. Allergy Clin. Immunol.* 54:35–38, 1985.
28. Hanke, C.W., T.W. Zollinger, J.J. O'Brien, and L. Bianco. Skin cancer in professional and amateur female golfers. *Physician Sportsmed.* 13:51–68, 1985.
29. Hatty, S., G.J. Mufti, and T.J. Hamblin. Exercise-induced urticaria and angioedema with relief from cromoglycate insufflation. *Postgrad. Med. J.* 59:586–587, 1983.
30. Hicks, J.H. Swimming and the skin. *Cutis* 19:448–450, 1977.
31. Houston, S.D., and J.M. Knox. Skin problems related to sports and recreational activities. *Cutis* 19:487–491, 1977.
32. Howe, N. Skiing may be hazardous to your skin. *Skiing* 35:91–93, 102, 1983.
33. Jenkins, G. Skin problems related to skating. *Skating Mag.* 61:18–20, 24, 1984.

34. Kaidbey, K. Sunscreens. J. Am. Acad. Dermatol. 5:476, 1981.
35. Kaplan, A.P. Exercise-induced hives. J. Allergy Clin. Immunol. 73:704–707, 1984.
36. Lever, W.F., and G. Schaumberg-Lever. Noninfectious vesicular and bullous diseases. In W.F. Lever and G. Schaumberg-Lever (eds.). Histopathology of the Skin. Philadelphia: J.B. Lippincott Co., 1983, pp. 92–135.
37. Levine, N. Dermatologic aspects of sports medicine. J. Am. Acad. Dermatol. 3:415–424, 1980.
38. Levit, F. Jogger's nipples. N. Engl. J. Med. 297:1127, 1977.
39. Lewis, J., P. Lieberman, G. Treadwell, and J. Erffmeyer. Exercise-induced urticaria, angioedema, and anaphylactoid episodes. J. Allergy Clin. Immunol. 68:432–437, 1981.
40. Leydon, J.J. and A.M. Kligman. Interdigital athlete's foot. Arch. Dermatol. 114:1466–1472, 1978.
41. Malamatinis, J.E., E.D. Mattmiller, and J.N. Westfall. Cutaneous moniliasis affecting varsity athletes. J. Am. Coll. Health Assoc. 16:294–295, 1968.
42. Mattikow, M.S. The ubiquitous golfer. Cutis 19:471–474, 1977.
43. McBurney, E.I., and D.A. Rosen. Carbon dioxide laser treatment of verruca vulgaris. J. Dermatol. Surg. Oncol. 10:45–48, 1984.
44. Mikelionis, J. Mountains, snow, and skin. Cutis 20:346–347, 1977.
45. Mikhailov, P., N. Berova, and V.C. Andreev. Physical urticaria and sport. Cutis 20:381–384, 389–390, 1977.
46. Editorial: Molluscum contagiosum. Br. Med. J. 1:459–460, 1968.
47. Montgomery, R.M. Tennis and its skin problems. Cutis 19:480–482, 1977.
48. Moore, M. Synthetic skin covers blisters, abrasions. Physician Sportsmed 8(12):15, 1980.
49. Mortimer, P.S., and R.P.R. Dawber. Trauma to the nail unit including occupational sports injuries. Dermatol. Clin. 3:415–420, 1985.
50. Muller, S.A. Dermatologic disorders in athletes. J. Ky. Med. Assoc. 74:225–228, 1976.
51. Niizeki, K., O. Kano, and Y. Kondo. An epidemic study of molluscum contagiosum. Dermatologica 169:197–198, 1984.
52. Pathak, M.A. Sunscreens: Topical and systemic approaches for protection of human skin against harmful effects of solar radiation. J. Am. Acad. Dermatol. 7:285–312, 1982.
53. Porter, P.S., and R.D. Baughman. Epidemiology of herpes simplex among wrestlers. J.A.M.A. 194:150–152, 1965.
54. Powell, B. Bicyclist's nipples. J.A.M.A. 249:2457, 1983.
55. Resnik, S.S., L.A. Lewis, and B.H. Cohen. The athlete's foot. Cutis 20:351–353, 355, 1977.
56. Robinson, A.M. Skin problems in athletes. Md. State. Med. J. 18:81–82, 1969.
57. Rodeheffer, R.J., J.A. Rommer, F. Wigley, and C.R. Smith. Controlled double-blind trial of nifedipine in the treatment of Raynaud's phenomenon. N. Engl. J. Med. 308:880–883, 1983.
58. Savastano, A.A. Problems of the foot in athletes. Med. Times 93:1276–1282, 1965.
59. Shelley, W.B. Herpetic arthritis associated with disseminated herpes simplex in a wrestler. Br. J. Dermatol. 103:209–212, 1980.
60. Snook, G.A. How I manage skin problems in wrestling. Physician Sportsmed. 12:97–98, 1984.
61. Spence, W.R., and M.N. Shields. New insole for prevention of athletic blisters. J. Sports Med. Phys. Fitness 8:177–180, 1968.
62. Spence, W.R., and M.N. Shields. Prevention of blisters, callosities, and ulcers by absorption of shear forces. J. Am. Podiatry Assoc. 58:428–434, 1968.
63. Stauffer, L.W. Skin disorders in athletes: Identification and management. Physician Sportsmed. 11:101–121, 1983.

64. Taplin, D., T.L. Meinking, S.L. Porcelain, P.M. Castillero, and J.A. Chen. Permethrin 5% dermal cream: A new treatment for scabies. *J. Am. Acad. Dermatol.* 15:995–1001, 1986.

65. Tennstedt, D., and J.M. Lachapelle. Windsurfer dermatitis from black rubber components. *Contact Dermatitis* 7:160–161, 1981.

66. Tuyp, E., and J.C. Mitchell. Scuba diver facial dermatitis. *Contact Dermatitis* 9:334–335, 1983.

67. Verbov, J. Calcaneal petechiae. *Arch. Dermatol.* 107:918, 1973.

68. Wheeland, R.G. The newer surgical dressings and wound healing. In P.L. Bailin, J.L. Ratz, and R.G. Wheeland (eds.). *Dermatology Clinics: Advanced Dermatologic Surgery.* Philadelphia: W.B. Saunders Co., 1987, pp. 393–407.

69. Wheeler, C.E., and W.H. Cabaniss. Epidemic cutaneous herpes simplex in wrestlers (herpes gladiatorum). *J.A.M.A.* 194:145–149, 1965.

70. White, W.B., and J.M. Grant-Kels. Transmission of herpes simplex virus type I infection in rugby players. *J.A.M.A.* 252:533–535, 1984.

71. Wilkinson, D.S. Black heel—a minor hazard of sport. *Cutis* 20:393–396, 1977.

72. Zaynoun, S., L.A. Ali, J. Shaib, and A. Kurban. The relationship of sun exposure and solar elastosis to basal cell carcinoma. *J. Am. Acad. Dermatol.* 12:522–525, 1985.

8
Endocrinological Responses to Exercise in Stressful Environments

RALPH P. FRANCESCONI, Ph.D.

INTRODUCTION

The metabolic, thermoregulatory, and fluid regulatory adjustments that occur during exercise, even under relatively moderate environmental conditions, may be concomitant with endocrine and neuroendocrine responses involving the hypothalamus, pituitary, adrenal, thyroid, sex glands, and pancreas. Reviews of studies investigating these relationships have been published [22, 66, 87, 153]; the imposition of an environmental stress in the form of heat, cold, or high terrestrial altitude in many cases exacerbates the intensity of these endocrinological responses in humans and higher animals. The responsivity and lability of these hormonal adjustments, the availability and accessibility of the biological medium in humans (plasma, serum, urine) and the recent development of specific quantitative techniques for microassay (high-pressure liquid chromatography, radioimmunoassay) have combined to produce numerous reports on the human endocrine/neuroendocrine response to exercise during heat, cold, or hypoxic stress. The results of many of these studies. will be summarized in this chapter.

Environmental Stress
As early as 1968, Collins and Weiner [22] reviewed the effects of heat exposure on endocrinological responses and concluded that thyroid hormones, corticosteroids, mineralocorticoids, and antidiuretic hormone levels in humans were all affected by sedentary exposure to heat stress. These alterations might be generally associated with a suppression of heat production and a requirement to conserve body fluids and electrolytes during periods of accelerated sweat secretion. Collins [20] later reviewed data indicating that acute exposure to cold stress in humans resulted in elevated norepinephrine excretion. Budd and Warhaft [13] reported that when test subjects were challenged by a cold stress test following nearly 6 months of residence in Antarctica, the prior cold exposure resulted in elevated urinary 17-hydroxycorticosteroids and 17-ketosteroids; however, urinary norepinephrine and epinephrine increments were similar to those recorded in midsummer in Australia. Eastman et al. [36] reported increments in circulating levels of triiodothyronine (T_3)

255

and thyroxine (T_4) upon exposure of four lightly clad test subjects to an ambient temperature of 6°C for 4 days. Thus, hormone responses to cold exposure might be logically related to increased calorigenesis, gluconeogenesis, and lipolysis.

Acute exposure to high-altitude hypobaric hypoxia may elicit a requirement for an increased metabolic rate, and the decreased oxygen availability has often been reported to stimulate the activity of the sympathoadrenocortical axis. Mackinnon et al. [99] reported that within 24 hours of exposure to an altitude of 4300 m, urinary 17-hydroxycorticosteroids were significantly elevated, with an apparent return toward baseline levels by 5 days of exposure. Similar results were reported by Moncloa et al. [109], who also observed a transient (4- to 7-day) elevation in urinary 17-hydroxycorticosteroids upon translocation of sea-level natives to an altitude of 4300 m. During successive sojourns to altitude (3800 m), Timiras et al. [146] had earlier noted not only an attenuating trend of 17-hydroxycorticosteroids after several days at altitude, but also a reduced magnitude of response during consecutive altitude sojourns. Later, Becker and co-workers [5, 6, 30] described elevated epinephrine and hydroxymethoxymandelic acid excretion upon exposure to a simulated altitude of 4000 m. These authors also discussed other factors that might affect endocrine/neuroendocrine responses to environmental stressors: physical activity, confinement, discomfort, and affect state. We later reported [48] that elevated levels of plasma cortisol and urinary 17-hydroxycorticosteroids prior to simulated high-altitude exposure can significantly modulate the response elicited by the environmental stressor. In an attempt to explain the electrolyte and water fluxes that occur upon acute exposure to hypobaric hypoxia, Hogan et al. [73] reported decreased plasma renin activity and urinary aldosterone excretion after exposure of test subjects to 3660 m of simulated altitude. Thus, most early studies that examined the effects of high altitude on human endocrinological responses centered on the sympathicoadrenal axis as the system most responsive to the demands created by the stress of hypobaria and reduced oxygen availability in the inspired air.

ADAPTATION TO EXERCISE AND ENVIRONMENT

One of the themes to be developed in this chapter is the inherent variability of endocrinological responses engendered by the seemingly endless combination of independent variables studied: exercise type, conditioning, intensity of exercise or environment, sampling time, exposure duration, test subject age, physical characteristics, acclimation, and physiological status. As early as 1952, von Euler and Hellner [152] reported that not only is physical exercise accompanied by an increase in the urinary excretion of epinephrine and norepinephrine, but also that the excretion rate may be correlated with the exercise intensity. Gray and Beetham [65] demonstrated that plasma norepinephrine levels were markedly elevated immediately after acute exhaustive exercise and returned to normal levels within 15–30 minutes of exercise completion, while Peronnet et al. [116] reported that both epinephrine and norepinephrine increased significantly after several intensities of exercise. Further, von Euler [151] attributed the increased catecholamine secretion during exercise to the need for fuel mobilization, as well as the homeostatic maintenance of blood pressure by vasoconstriction in nonactive areas to compensate for the hyperemia and vasodilation in actively contracting muscle groups. Thus, the level of catecholamine responses may also be affected by the mass of the actively contracting muscle.

The issue of hormonal responses to exercise prior and subsequent to a training program has been addressed in experimental subjects ranging from rats to humans. Although some of the cited studies did not include the imposition of an environmental paradigm, a brief summation of important observations may be appropriate for this chapter inasmuch as the variability elicited by training levels could be increased by environmental stress. Tharp and Buuck [143] used *in vitro* techniques to demonstrate that the adrenal glands from rats that had been trained for 8 weeks responded to ACTH stimulation with less corticosterone production than glands removed from nontrained control animals. Winder et al. [161] and Ostman and Sjostrand [114] also demonstrated in rats that, following training, stress-induced or exercise-induced increments in urinary norepinephrine, as well as plasma norepinephrine and glucagon, were attenuated in the trained groups. In humans, various investigators have reported that exercise-induced increments in norepinephrine [69], glucagon and catecholamines [162], and plasma renin activity [62] were moderated during exercise subsequent to physical training. Our own work [52, 53] has indicated that heat acclimation can modulate the responses of stress hormones and fluid regulatory hormones to a heat stress test. All of these results are compatible with the observations that following physical training or environmental acclimation metabolic efficiency is increased, thermoregulatory strain is reduced, perceived exertion is attenuated, and blood volume is increased. The control of these physiological and behavioral variables is partially governed by the endocrinological effects noted above. Intuitively, it seems reasonable to conclude—and data are generally confirmatory—that the status of full environmental or exercise adaptation is accompanied by an attenuated response of the effector mechanism.

Karagiorgios et al. [84] observed that both continuous and intermittent exercise elicited significant elevations in plasma growth hormone levels in moderately fit volunteers. Moreover, Johnson et al. [82] investigated the effects of training on hormonal responses, and reported that in racing cyclists elevations of growth hormone and catecholamines were attenuated, while insulin, frequently reported to decrease during muscular activity [19, 79, 89], fell less during exercise in this group in comparison with a less fit control group. The implication here is that the high physical fitness of the trained group dictates less need for the mobilization of oxidizable substrates than in the untrained group. Concurrent with decrements in plasma insulin levels during exercise are apparent elevations in circulating levels of glucagon [9, 40]. Analogously, Sutton [138] reported that unfit subjects were characterized by a greater elevation of growth hormone and cortisol than fit subjects when all subjects exercised at a fixed rate. Cronan and Howley [29] were unable to demonstrate any effects of training on norepinephrine and epinephrine excretion, but Howley [77] later reported a clear correlation between norepinephrine excretion and exercise intensity, with less consistent responses for epinephrine. Daniels and Chosy [32] had earlier imposed a moderate altitude stress (2200 m) on fit athletes during a training program, and observed no changes in epinephrine excretion and a moderate increase in urinary norepinephrine by 2 days of altitude exposure, which persisted throughout 3 weeks at altitude. Later, White et al. [156] reported that the physiological strain of increasingly intense exercise, as manifested by serum corticosteroid levels, can be attenuated by increased physical fitness.

In female test subjects, Boyden et al. [11] reported that increasing the weekly training distance from 21.7 to 48.3 km effected a decrease in circulating T_3, reverse T_3, and a greater thyroid-stimulating hormone response to thyroid-releasing hormone treatment. However, all of these apparent alterations were reversed when weekly training distances increased from 48 to 80 km [10]. Irvine [80] reported that physical training significantly increased the turnover of circulating T_4, and Balsam and Leppo [4] noted differential effects of training on the turnover of T_4 and T_3. As early as 1954, Lashof et al. [95] had reported no effects of moderate or intense exercise on the concentration or clearance of T_4. Later, DeNayer et al. [34] demonstrated a slight but significant decrement in free T_4 30 minutes after strenuous exercise, while Terjung and Tipton [142] concluded that moderate (61% $\dot{V}O_2$max) exercise resulted in an increasing trend of free T_4, which failed to achieve statistical significance. Thus, it appears likely that the intensity of either the exercise or the training regimen may affect the thyroidal response to exercise under normal environmental conditions. Viru [150] also noted the effects of exercise duration, environmental temperature, and interindividual variation in contributing to the range of responses noted for thyroidal activity during exercise.

The effects of exercise, fitness, and training regimens on the response of circulating testicular hormones have also been evaluated. For example,

FIGURE 1

Effects of exercise at sea level and at a simulated altitude of 4550 m on circulating levels of cortisol, growth hormone, and insulin. (From Sutton, J. R. Effect of acute hypoxia on the hormonal response to exercise. J. Appl. Physiol. *42:587–592, 1977.)*

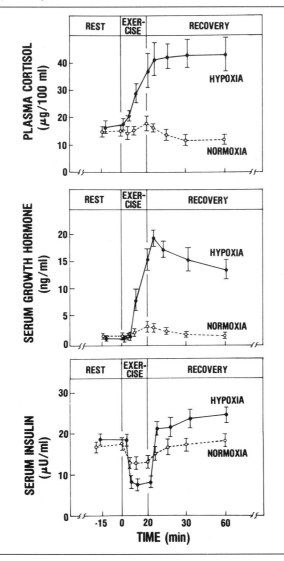

in highly trained swimmers and rowers, Sutton et al. [139] reported increments in serum androgens (predominantly testosterone) during maximal swimming and rowing exercise. Although Galbo et al. [58] observed slightly increased levels of testosterone at the completion of exercise, they demonstrated much larger increments 40 minutes after exercise completion, which declined rapidly consonant with the decrements observed by Dessypris et al. [35] subsequent to a marathon run. Wilkerson et al. [157] exercised men for 20 minutes at five intensities up to 90% $\dot{V}o_2$max; they reported that apparent increments in plasma testosterone concentrations were negated when decreases in plasma volume were considered. The latter results may be compatible with those of Galbo et al. [58], who concluded that minor increments at the conclusion of exercise were the result of a decrease in plasma volume and that more prolonged exercise is required to elicit a true testosterone effect. However, Wilkerson et al. [157] concluded that the effects of exercise duration and intensity, as well as those of physical training, are less than clear. Generally, however, it appears that hormonal responses that are designed to increase substrate availability, increase lipolysis, promote ion conservation, and reduce fluid losses are modulated in the well-trained or environmentally acclimated individual.

ALTITUDE AND EXERCISE

The environmental and endocrinological literature is replete with reports describing the sympathicoadrenal response to real or simulated high-altitude exposure [67, 74, 94, 98, 99, 108, 109, 146]. As early as the 1940s, several investigators [91, 145] had reported the effects of adrenocortical extracts on the ability of small animals to withstand extreme hypoxia. Roosevelt et al. [125] updated these earlier studies and reported that sham-adrenalectomized and sham-hypophysectomized rats survived extreme hypoxia significantly longer than adrenalectomized and hypophysectomized animals. Further, they reported that cortisol administration to adrenalectomized animals attenuated the increases in circulating lactate levels induced by hypoxia. The latter observation could have practical application to exercise endurance during altitude exposure, since it is known that glucocorticoids stimulate the reconversion of pyruvate to glycogen, but subsequent studies have apparently not been performed.

Moreover, the application of exercise or work stress supplemental to exposure to altitude or simulated hypobaric hypoxia has been reported to induce a multiplicity of hormonal responses, many of which are associated with the stimulated activity of the hypothalamic-pituitary-adrenal axis. However, Moncloa et al. [108] examined adrenal function during exercise after acute exposure to high altitude and reported a significant decrement in plasma cortisol levels after exercise. They attributed this observation to increased hepatic blood flow and clearance of cortisol during high-altitude exercise. In their report on the ascent of Mt. Paril, Guilland et al. [67] also reported a significantly increased clearance and catabolism of cortisol with exercise at high altitude. Alternatively, Humpeler et al. [78] reported progressively increasing levels of cortisol after 10 days of exposure to 2850 m when test subjects walked an average of 12.7 km · day^{-1}; however, in this study, the blood was taken before the initiation of exercise, and effects of altitude exposure on hepatic blood flow and cortisol clearance were not evaluated. In a more recent study, Maresh et al. [103] examined the adrenal responses of low-altitude natives (373 m or less) and moderate-altitude natives (1800–2200 m) to maximal bicycle ergometry at a simulated altitude of 4270 m. These investigators reported that serum cortisol levels were increased following exercise in both groups; however, in the latter experiments the exercise test was maximal and of brief duration, unlike the regimen imposed in the earlier studies [67, 78, 108].

Maresh et al. [103] also reported that exercise at either low, moderate, or high altitude induced significant elevations of plasma aldosterone levels, but levels both pre- and postexercise were moderated during high-altitude exposure. Earlier, Maher et al. [102] had reported that increasing intensity of exercise at 4300 m was accompanied by an increase in circulating levels of aldosterone. Further, they observed that aldosterone levels were reduced by acute (14 hours) exposure to high altitude, and that with increasing sojourn (11 days) at high altitude, levels returned toward those recorded at sea level. At a lower altitude (2040 m), Humpeler et al. [78] did not observe this acute decrement in aldosterone levels. Milledge et al. [107] studied subjects who exercised (hill walking) for 6–7 hours each day at 3100 m, and reported that aldosterone levels were significantly elevated immediately after exercise, but this increment was attenuated over the 5 days of altitude exposure. Maher et al. [102] acknowledged the apparent dichotomy of decreased aldosterone levels at a time of apparent contraction of plasma volume upon acute exposure to high altitude; they attributed this response to a possible peripheral venoconstriction, and thus decreased vascular capacity, which could be sensed as an increase in relative blood volume. Hogan et al. [73] had previously speculated that decreased aldosterone secretion at moderate altitudes is a direct result of diminished plasma renin activity.

Generally, investigators have examined the renin-angiotensin-aldosterone systems simultaneously, and have observed close correlative responses between angiotensin I levels and aldosterone [122]. Angiotensin I levels are ordinarily estimated from plasma renin activity following appropriate incubation periods during which angiotensin-converting enzyme is inhibited. Thus, Milledge et al. [107] reported increments in

262 | *Francesconi*

FIGURE 2

Effects of exercise (hill walking) and altitude (3100 m) on plasma levels of aldosterone and renin activity. Blood samples at altitude were taken immediately upon completion of the exercise. (From Milledge, J. S., D. M. Catley, E. S. Williams, W. R. Withey, and B. D. Minty. Effect of prolonged exercise at altitude on the renin-angiotensin system. J. Appl. Physiol. *55:413–418, 1983.)*

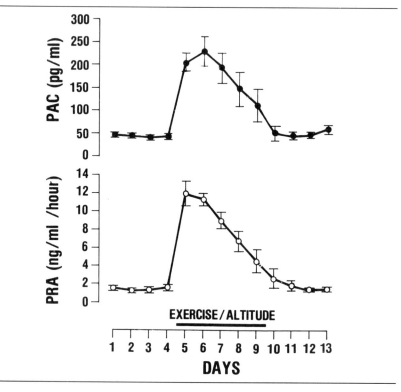

plasma renin activity following exercise at altitude; like aldosterone responses, these increments moderated with increasing time of altitude exposure. The data of Maher et al. [102] were essentially identical to those they had noted for aldosterone: Plasma renin activity was reduced by acute altitude exposure and increased during exercise with chronicity of exposure. Alternatively, Humpeler et al. [78] reported that plasma renin activity was unaffected by exposure to moderate altitude, although the effects of exercise could not be directly assessed because blood was drawn after an overnight fast and 2 hours of supine bed rest. Thus, while aldosterone and plasma renin activity levels may be reduced or not greatly affected by altitude exposure, they are both increased by exercise under either sea level or altitude conditions; further, the chronicity of the altitude exposure and the intensity of the exercise may both affect these responses.

In his report on the scientific and medical aspects of the Australian Andean expedition, Sutton [136] described the effects of exercise and altitude acclimatization on circulating levels of insulin, glucagon, cortisol, thyroxin, and growth hormone. Of these variables, the "most interesting finding" was the response of plasma growth hormone levels to exercise at sea level, during acute exposure to a simulated altitude of 4550 m, and following 3 months of acclimatization in the Andes (4540 m). Significant elevations in plasma growth hormone levels during submaximal exercise were observed during the trial at simulated altitude, but no such increments occurred at sea level or after altitude acclimatization. Later, Sutton and Garmendia [140] reported that maximal physical exercise was necessary to induce a growth hormone response in sea-level dwellers who had been acclimatized to 4500 m for 3 months. These investigators also observed an increased baseline level of growth hormone in high-altitude natives, a finding that was later confirmed by Raynaud et al. [121]. The latter workers compared the effects of exercise at sea level, after a 5-day sojourn at 2850 m, and again at sea level but while test subjects breathed a gas mixture with O_2 equivalent to that at 2850 m. These test subjects were lowland natives and exercised on a bicycle ergometer for 1 hour in each of the three conditions. Again, under all three conditions, plasma growth hormone levels increased significantly during exercise, most rapidly and to the greatest degree under high-altitude conditions. During 1 hour of recovery under each environmental condition, growth hormone levels returned to normalcy. While several studies have indicated an association between the growth hormone response to exercise and high-altitude exposure [136, 137], elevations in growth hormone levels may be more closely correlated with the intensity and duration of exercise [141]. Growth hormone may be effective during exercise in stimulating the release of fatty acids for energy production; the stress of high-altitude hypoxia evidently elevated the response through generally increased hypophyseal activity.

A limited number of studies have focused on the thyroidal response to exercise at altitude. The most detailed of these is probably the report of Stock et al. [132], who examined the effects of moderate exercise (20 minutes) prior to, during, and after a 3-week sojourn at high altitude (3650 m). Generally, the results indicated that the combination of altitude exposure and exercise stimulated thyroidal activity. Other observations were a slightly increased thyroidal response when subjects were fasting and a notable decreasing response after 3 weeks of exposure to high altitude in comparison with 1 week of residence. The next year, Wright [164] also reported increased thyroidal activity, as manifested by plasma

T_4 and reverse T_3 levels, during a high-altitude trek for 13 days between 1000 and 5000 m. Altitude exposure in the absence of exercise has been reported [120] to elicit increases in plasma levels of T_3 and T_4. The combination of exercise and high-altitude exposure apparently causes increased metabolic demands, which may be partially met by elevated thyroidal activity; however, it should probably be noted again that the generally increased activity of the pituitary-adrenal axis during hypoxic stress results partially in similarly increased thyroidal activity.

Increased sympathicoadrenal activity pursuant to exercise under high-altitude conditions has been reported in animals as small as rats [104] and as large as steers [8]. In humans, Guilland et al. [67] have reported that urinary levels of epinephrine, norepinephrine, metanephrine, and vanillylmandelic acid were increased during exercise at high altitude; the increments were maximal above 6000 m and persisted during the descent to sea level. Even earlier, Becker and Kreuzer [5, 6] observed that when high-altitude exposure was combined with a physical work regimen, increased norepinephrine excretion occurred in the absence of significant effects on epinephrine excretion. The same investigators noted that sedentary exposure to simulated high altitude (3000–4000 m) for 90 minutes resulted in no effects on either norepinephrine or epinephrine secretion. Thus, the stimulation of the sympathicoadrenal axis by altitude exposure and exercise may be affected by the elevation, the level of physical activity, and the degree of acclimation to the selected altitude. Mobilization of free fatty acids, stimulation of glycogenolysis, and the perception of the stress of hypobaric hypoxia may all be associated with the catecholamine response to exercise at high altitude.

The effects of exercise and altitude exposure on circulating levels of several additional hormones have been described; some discrepancies persist. For example, Humpeler et al. [78] described a significant elevation in testosterone levels 2 days after arrival at 2040 m and in combination with daily walking over 12.7 km to 2850 m. Interestingly, luteinizing hormone and follicle-stimulating hormone fell under the same conditions. While Vander et al. [149] observed similar results at 4300 m, Guilland et al. [67] described "hypoandrogenicity" during exercise at high altitude, as manifested by urinary testosterone and metabolites of testosterone. The latter workers stated that the "duration, altitude, and the level of physical exertion" were all important variables that probably affected the results. In their report, Sutton and Garmendia [140] observed that high-altitude natives manifested a higher basal concentration of glucagon, and elevations in glucagon were correlated with length of time of altitude exposure. Interestingly, both glucagon [14] and glucocorticoids [125] have been reported to have salutary effects in protecting *in vitro* heart preparations from severe hypoxia.

Thus, it can be concluded that the combination of hypoxia and exercise generally stimulates the secretory activity of the hypothalamic-hypophyseal-sympathicoadrenal axis, as manifested by elevations in circulating levels of the respective hormones (cortisol, corticosteroids, ketosteroids) and neuroendocrines (epinephrine, norepinephrine). Further, the increased metabolic demands, not only of exercise, but also of altitude exposure [63, 85], are compatible with the increments reported in hormones that are associated with an elevated metabolic rate. Several additional points, however, are worth emphasizing. Increased circulating levels of any hormone may indeed be the direct result of heightened secretory activity, but it should be remembered that they may also result from decreased uptake by target organs, decreased catabolism, decreased excretion, or increased release rate in the absence of *de novo* synthesis. While the vast majority of studies have quantitated the circulating or urinary levels of hormones, the other effectors of hormonal concentrations have been far less extensively investigated. The use of radioactive tracers and exercising animal models could provide abundant information on the kinetics and dynamics of endocrinological responses. All of these variables may be affected by the type and intensity of exercise, fitness, duration and level of altitude exposure, origin and acclimatization of test subjects, and real or simulated high-altitude exposure. Further complicating an already overwhelming battery of potential variables are the time of day of sampling, time of sampling with respect to exercise duration or completion, sample handling and storage, particularly in field experiments, and assay technique and variability.

HEAT AND EXERCISE

Exercise in a hot environment can be expected to induce endocrinological alterations designed to reduce urinary fluid loss, increase peripheral vasodilation, promote heat dissipation, maintain blood flow to the exercising muscles, and simultaneously preserve plasma volume and cardiac stability. One of the many physiological responses among humans and higher animals to achieve these sometimes disparate goals is a stimulated secretion of vasopressin (VP) or antidiuretic hormone, which reduces urinary water loss and conserves body fluids and electrolytes [49]. Moreover, in the absence of adequate fluid replenishment, exercise in the heat may lead to progressive dehydration, with significant effects on plasma volume and osmolality [28, 128]. This increased osmolality may be sensed by hypothalamic osmoreceptors and may result in stimulated secretion of pituitary VP [22], with striking results. For example, Strydom et al. [133] reported that during an 18-mile road march in the heat, mean urine volume was reduced to only 134 ml, while sweat losses were greater tham 4 liters. When Shvartz et al. [130] administered orthostatic tilt tests to subjects prior and subsequent to exercise in the heat for 8 days (heat acclimation), they observed a 50-fold elevation of VP during the tilt test before acclimation and a 75% decrement in this response following acclimation. They attributed this decrement to the increased plasma volume ordinarily elicited by heat acclimation.

Convertino et al. [24] attempted to separate the exercise and thermal factors effecting the increase in plasma volume, and concluded that increments in VP levels with exercise contributed significantly to the elevated plasma volume. However, severe (70–75°C) sedentary heat exposure has also been reported to induce significant increments in VP [124], while acclimation, in the absence of further exercise or heat stress, had no effects on plasma VP levels [126]. Studying hidromeiosis (sweat suppression) during prolonged and repeated heat exposures, Candas et al. [15] concluded that changes in sweat rates were not associated with alterations in plasma levels of VP. The results generally indicate that acute exposure to intense heat or exercise in the heat stimulates the synthesis and release of VP to reduce urinary fluid loss; that hyperhydration may reduce the intensity of this response; and that this response may be related to plasma osmolality [61, 105]. However, it should be noted that Wade [153] has argued that the observed increases in vasopressin levels during exercise in the heat may be mediated by a variety of additional factors, including blood pressure and renal and hepatic blood flow. Since the excretion rate of free water may be increased during exercise in the heat [153], it is possible that the physiological significance of elevations in VP may be related to hemodynamic effects.

Widespread reports of elevations in plasma aldosterone levels during single or consecutive exercise trials in a hot environment prompted Braun et al. [12] to examine the effects of exogenous aldosterone administration on the acquisition of heat acclimation. Despite the fact that these investigators found no shortening in the time required for acclimation, they did report some beneficial effects on heart rates and rectal temperatures. Even in the absence of exercise, heat stress alone has been frequently reported to induce significant increments in circulating aldosterone levels [46, 90]. When heat exposure was combined with consumption of a low-sodium diet, increments in circulating aldosterone levels were increased [3, 46]. While exercise in the heat is ordinarily accompanied by rapid increments in plasma aldosterone levels [27], this response is apparently attenuated following acclimation of the test subjects [25, 42, 52]. Further, whereas plasma volume expansion [51], glucose-electrolyte replacement solutions [55], or saline ingestion [33] also moderate the effects of exercise in the heat on plasma aldosterone levels, we have demonstrated that hypohydration [52] and increasing intensity of hypohydration [54] may intensify these responses. Thus, the stimulated secretion of aldosterone during a heat exposure/exercise contingency is clearly adaptive to water and sodium conservation.

Similarly, exercise in the heat is accompanied by a reduction in renal blood flow, some degree of hypohydration, and, if prolonged, decrements in total body sodium content, all of which are conducive to elevated plasma renin activity (PRA). As with aldosterone, sedentary exposure to high ambient temperatures has been reported [3, 90] to elicit significant elevations in PRA. Introduction of an acute exercise regimen to the heat stress generally results in further elevations in PRA [7, 43, 54], and these increments may be affected by the state of heat acclimation [42, 43, 52], hydration status [52, 54], sodium balance [3, 43, 55], physical conditioning [61], and even age [115]. Since plasma levels of angiotensin II may be partially responsible for the control of plasma aldosterone concentrations, it is anticipated that alterations in PRA may be mirrored in plasma aldosterone fluxes during exercise in the heat; however, environmental and exercise conditions, as well as the physiological status of the test volunteers, may preclude such correlations [41].

Collins and Weiner [22] reviewed data indicating that the adrenocorticotrophic response to exercise/heat exposure may be affected by the intensity of the stress, its duration, and the physiological strain induced by this combination. Just a year later, Collins et al. [21] provided evidence that the stimulation of glucocorticoid secretion in humans may be closely related to the achievement of a "critical" rectal temperature during the experimental protocol. Follenius et al. [45] hypothesized that increasing plasma cortisol levels may indeed be a useful measure of heat intolerance. Generally, our own results have indicated that mild exercise in a hot environment can be tolerated with minor effects on glucocorticoid hormones when the subjects are reasonably fit and well hydrated. For example, we have observed [50] that exercise (1.56 m · sec^{-1}) in the heat (49°C db) prevented the normally occurring circadian reductions in plasma cortisol [93] but did not elicit increases in these levels. We later reported that during exercise in the heat, plasma cortisol levels may be increased by hypohydration [53], but if test subjects are well heat acclimated, exercise/heat stress may again only prevent the aforementioned circadian reductions [54].

These effects of heat acclimation are consistent with the report of Davies et al. [33], who also observed attenuated effects on plasma cortisol levels during exercise in the heat following heat acclimation. In a recent review, Viru [150] argued that exercise in the heat may be accompanied by a decrement in adrenocortical activity in humans, but one of the references cited [70] attributed the observed reduction to differences in adrenocortical activity before heat exposure. Earlier, Sulman et al. [134] attributed the catecholamine deficiency in patients during prolonged

FIGURE 3

Effects of hypohydration (5%) and acclimation on responses of circulating cortisol, plasma renin activity, and aldosterone during exercise in a hot-dry environment. (Top figure from Francesconi, R. P., M. N. Sawka, and K. B. Pandolf. Hypohydration and acclimation: Effects on hormone responses to exercise/heat stress. Aviat. Space Environ. Med. *55:365–369, 1984. Middle and bottom figures from Francesconi, R. P., M. N. Sawka, and K. B. Pandolf. Hypohydration and heat acclimation: Plasma renin and aldosterone during exercise.* J. Appl. Physiol. *55:1790–1794, 1983.)*

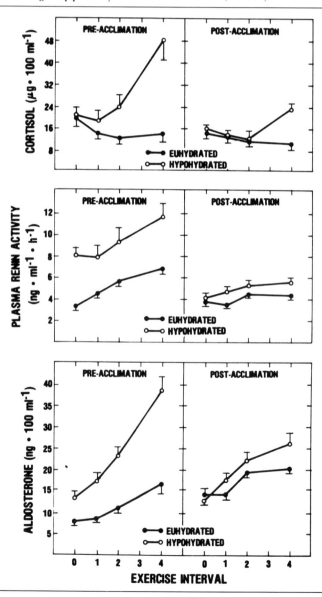

and recurrent exposure to heat stress to an adrenal exhaustion syndrome, but it is unlikely that young, healthy test subjects exposed to acute exercise/heat regimens in a natural or chamber environment would manifest such symptoms.

Using a comprehensive study design, Sedgwick et al. [127] compared the effects of smoking, psychological stressors, heat, exercise, and fat ingestion on the neuroendocrine response profiles of 12 healthy test subjects. They reported that while the norepinephrine excretion rate was increased by exercise (bicycle ergometer, 3- to 18-minute periods, heart rate 130–140 beats per minute), heat exposure (1 hour, 42.5°C db, 28.8°C wb) had no effects on either epinephrine or norepinephrine excretion. Using consecutive daily heat exposures in combination with light exercise, Polozhentsev et al. [117] reported that norepinephrine excretion was increased sharply on the first experimental day in the exercising group, but that this increment disappeared in the ensuing experimental days. Also notable in this experiment was an apparent anticipatory response both upon initiation and upon completion of the 12-day scenario. Powers et al. [118] attempted to separate the thermal and exercise effects on catecholamine levels, and reported that exercise combined with heat elicited an increase in plasma norepinephrine that was greater than the sum of the increments induced by exercise or passive heating alone, with smaller effects on epinephrine responses. Maher et al. [101] reported that heat acclimation reduced urinary norepinephrine levels following exercise in the heat. The variable results indicate that the adrenomedullary and sympathetic response to heat and exercise may be directly correlated with the intensity of either the environmental or the exercise stress.

As noted earlier [134], there have appeared reports of adrenal exhaustion syndrome in individuals exposed to extreme heat for prolonged periods. The authors reported that treatment of such patients with monoamine oxidase inhibitors was effective in reducing the extensive symptomatology of the disorder. Since the manifestations of exercise in the heat (dehydration, increased perceived exertion and core temperature, hypoglycemia) may all affect catecholamine secretion and are generally attenuated by heat acclimation, it is reasonable that the magnitude of the catecholamine response may be affected by the intensity and duration of the exercise, the ambient temperature, the fitness level, and the degree of acclimation of the test subjects.

Considering the role of thyroid hormones in stimulating oxidative metabolism and heat generation, it is probably not surprising that in their early review of endocrinological responses to heat exposure, Collins and Weiner [22] first discussed the rather extensive literature on depressed thyroid activity during heat exposure. More recently, Epstein et al. [38, 39] have reported that light exercise in the heat is accompanied by significant decrements in T_3 levels, while reverse T_3, the noncalorigenic metabolite, actually increases in serum. Gertner et al. [60] examined thyroid gland activity in winter and summer in Israeli laborers and reported lower circulating levels of T_3 during the summer. Since T_4 levels were unaffected, they concluded that extrathyroidal conversion of T_4 to T_3 may be integral to the regulation of energy metabolism. Earlier, Yoshimura et al. [165] had speculated that the seasonal variation of basal metabolic rate in Japanese subjects may be related to reduced thyroid activity during the summer season, and Sulman et al. [135] attributed the symptomatology of heat stress syndrome to hyperthyreosis. The results generally indicate that T_3 levels may be affected before T_4 levels and that exercise under more chronic conditions induced the more physiologically significant changes in human thyroid activity.

Winter [163] used growth hormone-deficient adolescents to demonstrate that during prolonged exercise growth hormone release is necessary for maintenance of free fatty acids as a fuel source. In the absence of a physical work paradigm, Leppaluoto et al. [97] reported an increase in circulating growth hormone levels shortly after exposure to severe heat. When we combined exercise with a hot-dry or hot-wet environment, we observed inconsistent responses of growth hormone that were affected by hydration [53] and, to a much lesser degree, by acclimation [50]. Frewin et al. [56] reported a marked difference in plasma growth hormone responses to exercise when the exercise was carried out at 40°C vs. 10°C. At the hot temperature there occurred a significant increase in growth hormone, while at 10°C no such increment occurred. However, it should be noted that growth hormone responses of humans to exercise/ environmental stress are markedly variable and, in the report of Frewin et al. [56], levels of growth hormone ranged from 3 to 70 ng · ml^{-1} during exercise in the heat. Weeke and Gunderson [154] also observed increments in growth hormone induced by heating, while cool immersion repressed plasma growth hormone levels. In summary, it should be pointed out that in humans growth hormone secretion is episodic in nature [155], and interindividual variability in the sporadic pattern and timing of growth hormone secretion may contribute to the divergence of results reported, as well as the inability to achieve consistent responses during exercise in cool environments.

Thus, there is abundant evidence to demonstrate the many hormonal adaptations that occur in humans during exercise in the heat. The most consistent responses, those of the aldosterone-angiotensin-plasma renin system, are designed to conserve body fluids and electrolytes, and, quite logically, these alterations are exaggerated by hypohydration and electrolyte deprivation and repressed by acclimation and increased plasma volume. It should be noted that in most of the studies cited, test subjects were young, healthy, and moderately fit, all of which could affect test results. For example, in our own studies, mild/moderate exercise in a hot environment usually did not elicit a significant glucocorticoid response when the subjects were well hydrated. It is conceivable, however, that in a group of less fit, older, or heavier subjects, stress perception and reality could be far greater, and adrenocorticotrophic and catecholamine responses could likewise be more prominent. Generally, hormones affecting metabolic activity are either repressed or unaffected by heat exposure and exercise unless either paradigm is sufficiently intense to induce a stress response. An imminent study in our laboratory has been designed to assess the effects of age on some endocrinological responses to exercise in the heat.

COLD AND EXERCISE

In a recent volume in this series, Horvath [75] reviewed the physiological responses of humans to exercise in a cold environment and specifically noted the paucity of information on the endocrinological effects induced by this regimen. Research reports over the last 6 years indicate that the apparent imbalance between investigations concerned with hormonal responses of humans to exercise in hot vs. cold environments has persisted. Literature on the endocrinological responses to work in a cold environment remains limited; in fact, in his review, Horvath [75] reported on the endocrine responses to cold water immersion only. The limited interest in this area of investigation may be surprising considering the enormous metabolic demands elicited by exercise in a cold environment, which are met by hormonal adaptations stimulating oxidative processes and heat production [129].

For example, when Timmons et al. [147] examined fat metabolism in humans during exercise at $-10°C$ and $+22°C$, they reported that oxygen consumption, energy utilization, and fat expenditure were all significantly higher in the cold environment. Analogously, Jacobs et al. [81] compared glycogen depletion in men exercising (50–65 W) on a bicycle ergometer at 21°C and 9°C. While they reported no change in glycogen content at 21°C, the same exercise at 9°C elicited a 23% decrement in glycogen. Hormonal profiles were not reported in these studies.

Fisher [44] observed that even neonatal or premature infants can respond to cold stress with elevations in thyroid-stimulating hormone and T_3, deiodination of T_4 to T_3, and elevations in basal metabolic rate. Considering their thermogenic role [31], it is probably not surprising that thyroid hormones in subjects ranging from rats [96] to humans [63, 113] are elevated pursuant to cold exposure, although the literature is not wholly consistent on this point [154]. In relevant human investigations, Nagata et al. [110] observed that exercise in a cold (4–6°C) environment for 3 hours had no effects on T_4 or T_3, but individuals who exercised in the cold more chronically (i.e., the winter season) did manifest elevated T_3 levels. Alternatively, Wilson [159] had earlier reported that minor changes in protein-bound iodine and cellular/plasma ratios of T_3 during increased physical activity in a cool environment were attributable to decreases in plasma volume. Premachandra et al. [119] investigated the effects of distance swimming and cycle ergometry on thyroid hormones and reported relatively minor effects on T_3 during swimming; Terjung and Tipton [142] had previously reported minor effects of cycle ergometry (30 minutes) on thyroid hormones including thyroid stimulating hormone. During 3.5 hours of bicycle ergometry, O'Connell et al. [111] observed increased concentrations of reverse T_3, which was moderated by dextrose infusion. Thompson et al. [144] administered exogenous thyroid hormones to cold-exposed test subjects, and demonstrated that heat production increased in three of four subjects receiving T_3 and one hypothyroid subject administered T_4. In humans, brief (0.5–3 hours) cold exposure without physical activity had either no [71, 159, 160] or minor [148] effects on thyroid hormone levels. Clearly, the thyroid responses to exercise and cold exposure may be affected by the duration and intensity of the cold stress, as well as the exercise, the absorptive and glycemic status of the subject, and the type of physical exercise.

Studying both hyper- and hypothyroid subjects, Copinschi et al. [26] reported a remarkably close association between plasma levels of thyroid hormones and cortisol, although no reports have addressed the correlative responses of thyroid and glucocorticoid hormones to exercise in a cold environment. In their comprehensive paper, Galbo et al. [57] investigated the effects of water temperature and prolonged swimming in humans on circulating hormones, and reported that cortisol levels fell 15 minutes after a 1-hour swim in 21°C water, while increments occurred after swimming at 27°C and 33°C. We [47] and others [64] had previously reported that cold stress can disrupt the consistent daily periodic oscillations in circulating cortisol levels, but no physiologically significant changes were demonstrated. Hartley et al. [69] used heavy (98% $\dot{V}O_2$max) bicycle exercise to elicit a significant elevation in circulating cortisol, while both mild (42%) and moderate (75%) exercise failed to elicit any effects on this variable; physical conditioning also affects this response [156]. Moreover, cold exposure in the absence of a physical work regimen did elicit significantly elevated cortisol levels [158, 160]. Surprisingly enough, no studies were identified that compared the glucocorticoid responses in humans during increasing intensity or chronicity of exercise under cold ambient conditions.

Mager and Robinson [100] exposed men to 4°C intermittently for 5 weeks and observed significantly increased excretory rates of norepi-

FIGURE 4

Effects of exercise (breast stroke swimming) in three water temperatures (21, 27, 33°C) on serum or plasma hormone levels. (From Galbo, H., M. E. Houston, N. J. Christensen, J. J. Holst, B. Nielsen, E. Nygaard, and J. Suzuki). The effect of water temperature on the hormonal response to prolonged swimming. Acta Physiol. Scand. *105:326–337, 1979.)*

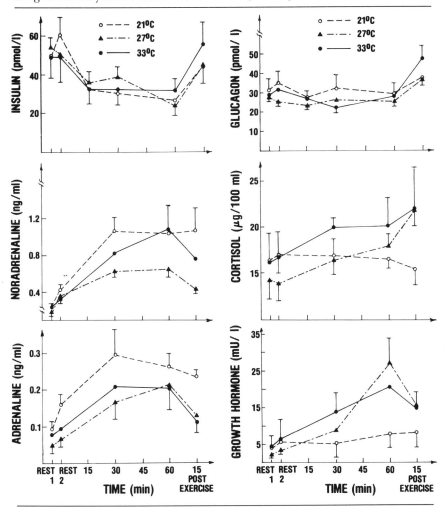

nephrine initially, which returned to control levels after 7 days; in contrast, circulating epinephrine was unaffected during the entire cold exposure. Of course, catecholamine responses to the cold pressor test have been monitored frequently, and generally significant increments in both circulating norepinephrine and epinephrine have been reported [2, 123]. While a considerable number of reports have documented the responsivity of circulating norepinephrine and epinephrine to acute exercise stress [65, 69, 72], whole body exercise in combination with cold stress has not been extensively investigated for these variables in humans. In rats Chin et al. [17] and Harri et al. [68] have demonstrated that exercise training can attenuate the increments in plasma and urinary norepinephrine and epinephrine pursuant to exposure of animals to cold stress. Exogenous administration of norepinephrine to Korean diving women in winter elicited a statistically significant, but physiologically minimal, increase in oxygen consumption of a magnitude insufficient to conclude that nonshivering thermogenesis had developed in these test subjects [83]. Galbo et al. [57] reported that during the first 30 minutes of swimming, there occurred significant elevations in circulating norepinephrine and epinephrine, which appeared to reach steady-state levels between 30 and 60 minutes. It is also relevant to note that the greatest absolute increments in these variables occurred during swimming in the coldest water ($21°C$ vs. $27°C$ or $33°C$), an indication of the necessity for increased thermogenesis during cold water immersion. A similar study at various air temperatures has not been done.

Christensen et al. [18] observed that when men exercised sufficiently to increase their rectal temperature (T_{re}) by $1°C$, small but significant elevations of growth hormone were noted; however, when the same exercise intensity and duration were duplicated in a cold room with no increase in T_{re}, growth hormone release was repressed. Similarly, Galbo et al. [57] reported unchanged levels of growth hormone when their subjects swam in $21°C$ water, while swimming at either $27°C$ or $33°C$ induced elevations in this variable. Generally, the same results have been reported during passive exposure to cold temperatures [64], although Okada et al. [112] did observe significant increments in plasma growth hormone in both male and female test subjects upon rewarming following no changes during 1–2 hours of cold stress.

The repressive effects of the combination of cold exposure and exercise on growth hormone levels may be related to the concurrent insulin/glucose response to exercise in the cold. For example, both cold exposure and exercise have been extensively reported to depress circulating insulin levels to maintain circulating glucose levels in a variety of experimental species [37, 72, 88, 131]. Hypoglycemia is ordinarily stimulatory to growth hormone secretion. Thus, if normo- or hyperglycemia is maintained during exercise in the cold, an important stimulus for growth hormone release may be neutralized.

In 1981 Horvath [75] wrote: "It is hoped that investigations into the area of physiological adjustments to cold will receive the same degree of attention as has been given to hot environment studies." Over the past 6 years, it appears that little progress has been made in addressing this apparent imbalance. Thorough literature searches have revealed a dearth of studies investigating the effects in humans of exercise on hormonal responses in cold air environments. The hormonal adaptations necessary to support the increased metabolic demands of muscular work and heat production during exercise in the cold are clearly identified as an area of environmental physiology requiring further research effort.

ENDOGENOUS OPIOIDS, EXERCISE, AND ENVIRONMENTAL STRESS

The burgeoning research field of endogenous opioid polypeptides and their relationship to stress physiology is relatively new but certainly deserves note in this chapter. According to Akil et al. [1], there are three opioid peptide families—the beta-endorphins, enkephalins, and alpha-endorphins, all of which may be found in appreciable concentrations in the "stress" glands frequently mentioned in this chapter—the hypothalamus, the pituitary, and the adrenal. These endogenous opioids are hypothesized to act as pain moderators and may be intimately involved in the development of stress-induced analgesia.

Colt et al. [23] measured beta-endorphin immunoreactivity in 35 runners after mild and moderate runs and reported significant increments in plasma extracts, which were probably related to the intensity of the run. At approximately the same time, Gambert et al. [59] reported similar results in both men and women exercising at fairly heavy intensities for short durations; they suggested that increments in beta-endorphin immunoreactivity may be associated with the so-called runner's high.

The potential of these endogenous opioids to act as modulators of pain or the affect state has, quite naturally, been adequate stimulus for a flurry of research activity to quantitate and characterize these responses at various exercise intensities [92], at various levels of physical training [16], in women [76], and during altered physiological states [106]. It should be noted that, to date, very few studies have addressed the response of these peptides to exercise during any type of environmentally stressful condition. However, Kelso et al. [86] did examine the effects of cycling (50% $\dot{V}O_2max$) at 24°C and 35°C on plasma beta-endorphin/beta-lipotropin levels and observed slightly increased concentrations at the warmer environmental condition. To the best of my knowledge, no reports have appeared examining the combination of exercise and altitude or cold stress on these responses, but this area of investigation is certainly identified as fertile for additional studies. Responses to such a combination of stressors might be extremely helpful in identifying the role of these compounds in physical training and in mood modulation.

CONCLUSION

Clearly, the physiological or fitness status of an individual may play a pivotal role in the initiation, duration, and intensity of a hormonal response to exercise in a stressful environment. Given the wide variability in the fitness and acclimation levels of a population of potential test subjects, interindividual response differences in such variables as circulating hormones are inevitable. Thus, when evaluating the endocrinological responses to exercise in a stressful environment, it must be noted that the perception and the reality of stress will vary among subjects according to their level of training, hydrational status, acclimation level, nutritional condition, and, importantly, the novelty of the situation. Equally or more divergent is the number of experimental conditions that can be applied to the exercise/environmental scenario. While it is likely and desirable that future research reports maintain this diversity of independent variables, investigators should provide maximal physical and physiological information relative to test subjects, as well as complete information on test scenarios. Such information will be invaluable to the interpretation of results and useful in explaining inconsistencies in results.

While the endocrinological responses to exercise at altitude or in hot/wet, hot/dry environments have been fairly well characterized, much less is known about these responses during exercise in cold-air environments. Further, little has been reported of the hormonal responses to exercise in hyperbaric or gravitational environments. These environments are identified as areas fertile for additional human research to provide a comprehensive understanding of the multiple roles of the endocrine system in meeting the metabolic and physiological demands of exercise in all stressful environments.

ACKNOWLEDGMENTS

The author gratefully acknowledges the skilled technical assistance of Mrs. Susan E.P. Henry and Mrs. Diane Danielski in the preparation and typing of this manuscript.

The views of the author do not purport to reflect the position of the Department of the Army or the Department of Defense.

REFERENCES

1. Akil, H., S.J. Watson, E. Young, M.E. Lewis, H. Khachaturian, and J.M. Walker. Endogenous opioids: Biology and function. *Ann. Rev. Neurosci.* 7:223–255, 1984.
2. Atterhog, J.H., K. Eliasson, and P. Hjemdahl. Sympathoadrenal and cardiovascular responses to mental stress, isometric handgrip, and cold pressor test in asymptomatic young men with primary T-wave abnormalities in the electrocardiogram. *Br. Heart J.* 46:311–319, 1981.
3. Bailey, R.E., D. Bartos, F. Bartos, A. Castro, R.L. Dobson, D.P. Grettie, R. Kramer, D. Macfarlane, and K. Sato. Activation of aldosterone and renin secretion by thermal stress. *Experientia* 28:159–160, 1972.
4. Balsam, A., and L.E. Leppo. Effect of physical training on the metabolism of thyroid hormones in man. *J. Appl. Physiol.* 38:212–215, 1975.
5. Becker, E.J., and F. Kreuzer. Sympathoadrenal response to hypoxia. In J.R. Poortmans (ed.). *Biochemistry of Exercise*, Vol. 3. Baltimore: University Park Press, 1968, pp. 188–191.
6. Becker, E.J., and F. Kreuzer. Sympathoadrenal response to hypoxia. *Pflugers Arch.* 304:1–10, 1968.
7. Berlyne, G.M., J.P.M. Finberg, and C. Yoran. The effect of β-adrenoceptor blockade on body temperature and plasma renin activity in heat-exposed man. *Br. J. Clin. Pharmacol.* 1:307–312, 1974.
8. Blum, J.W., W. Bianca, F. Naf, P. Kunz, J.A. Fischer, and M. DaPrada. Plasma catecholamine and parathyroid hormone responses in cattle during treadmill exercise at simulated high altitude. *Horm. Metab. Res.* 11:246–251, 1979.
9. Böttger, I., E.M. Schlein, G.R. Faloona, and R.H. Unger. The effect of exercise on glucagon secretion. *J. Clin. Endocrinol. Metab.* 35:117–125, 1972.
10. Boyden, T.W., P.W. Pamenter, T.C. Rotkis, P. Stanforth, and J.H. Wilmore. Thyroidal changes associated with endurance training in women. *Med. Sci. Sports Exerc.* 16:243–246, 1984.
11. Boyden, T.W., R.W. Pamenter, P. Stanforth, T. Rotkis, and J.H. Wilmore. Evidence for mild thyroidal impairment in women undergoing endurance training. *J. Clin. Endocrinol. Metab.* 54:53–56, 1982.
12. Braun, W.E., J.T. Maher, and R.F. Byrom. Effect of exogenous *d*-aldosterone on heat acclimatization in man. *J. Appl. Physiol.* 23:341–346, 1967.
13. Budd, G.M., and N. Warhaft. Urinary excretion of adrenal steroids, catecholamines and electrolytes in man, before and after acclimatization to cold in Antarctica. *J. Physiol.* 210:799–806, 1970.
14. Busuttil, R.W., R.J. Paddock, and W.J. George. Protective effect of glucagon on the isolated perfused rat heart following severe hypoxia. *Proc. Soc. Exp. Biol. Med.* 147:527–532, 1974.
15. Candas, V., G. Brandenberger, B. Lutz-Bucher, M. Follenius, and J.P. Libert. Endocrine concomitants of sweating and sweat depression. *Eur. J. Appl. Physiol.* 52:225–229, 1984.
16. Carr, D.B., B.A. Bullen, G.S. Skrinar, M.A. Arnold, M. Rosenblatt, I.Z. Beitins, J.B. Martin, and J.W. McArthur. Physical conditioning facilitates the exercise-induced secretion of beta-endorphin and beta-lipotropin in women. *N. Engl. J. Med.* 305:560–563, 1981.
17. Chin, A.K., R. Seaman, and M. Kapileshwarker. Plasma catecholamine response to exercise and cold adaptation. *J. Appl. Physiol.* 34:409–412, 1973.
18. Christensen, S.E., O.L. Jorgensen, N. Moller, and H. Orskov. Characterization of growth hormone release in response to external heating. Comparison to exercise induced release. *Acta Endocrinol.* 107:295–301, 1984.
19. Cochran, B., E.P. Marbach, R. Poucher, T. Steinberg, and G. Guinup. Effect of acute

muscular exercise on serum immunoreactive insulin concentration. *Diabetes* 15:838–841, 1966.

20. Collins, K.J. The endocrine component of human adaptation to cold and heat. In I. Assenmacher and D.S. Farner (eds.). *Environmental Endocrinology.* New York: Springer-Verlag, 1978, pp. 294–301.

21. Collins, K.J., J.D. Few, T.J. Forward, and L.A. Giec. Stimulation of adrenal glucocorticoid secretion in man by raising the body temperature. *J. Physiol.* 202:645–660, 1969.

22. Collins, K.J., and J.S. Weiner. Endocrinological aspects of exposure to high environmental temperatures. *Physiol. Rev.* 48:785–839, 1968.

23. Colt, E.W.D., S.L. Wardlaw, and A.G. Frantz. The effect of running on plasma β-endorphin. *Life Sci.* 28:1637–1640, 1981.

24. Convertino, V.A., J.E. Greenleaf, and E.M. Bernauer. Role of thermal and exercise factors in the mechanism of hypervolemia. *J. Appl. Physiol.* 48:657–664, 1980.

25. Convertino, V.A., and C.R. Kirby. Plasma aldosterone and renal sodium conservation during exercise following heat acclimation. *Fed. Proc.* 44:1562, 1985. (Abstract)

26. Copinschi, G., R. Leclercq, O.D. Bruno, and A. Cornil. Effects of altered thyroid function upon cortisol secretion in man. *Horm. Metab. Res.* 3:437–442, 1971.

27. Costill, D.L., G. Branam, W. Fink, and R. Nelson. Exercise induced sodium conservation: Changes in plasma renin and aldosterone. *Med. Sci. Sports* 8:209–213, 1976.

28. Costill, D.L., and W.J. Fink. Plasma volume changes following exercise and thermal dehydration. *J. Appl. Physiol.* 37:521–525, 1974.

29. Cronan, T.L., III, and E.T. Howley. The effect of training on epinephrine and norepinephrine excretion. *Med. Sci. Sports* 6:122–125, 1974.

30. Cunningham, W.L., E.J. Becker, and F. Kreuzer. Catecholamines in plasma and urine at high altitude. *J. Appl. Physiol.* 20:607–610, 1965.

31. Danforth, E., Jr., and A. Burger. The role of thyroid hormones in the control of energy expenditure. *J. Clin. Endocrinol. Metab.* 13:581–595, 1984.

32. Daniels, J.T., and J.J. Chosy. Epinephrine and norepinephrine excretion during running training at sea level and altitude. *Med. Sci. Sports* 4:219–224, 1972.

33. Davies, J.A., M.H. Harrison, L.A. Cochrane, R.J. Edwards, and T.M. Gibson. Effect of saline loading during heat acclimatization on adrenocortical hormone levels. *J. Appl. Physiol.* 50:605–612, 1981.

34. DeNayer, P., P. Malvaux, M. Ostyn, H.G. Van den Schrieck, C. Beckers, and M. DeVisscher. Serum free thyroxin and binding proteins after muscular exercise. *J. Clin. Endocrinol. Metab.* 28:714–716, 1968.

35. Dessypris, A., K. Kuoppasalmi, and H. Adlerkreutz. Plasma cortisol, testosterone, androstenedione and luteinizing hormone (LH) in a noncompetitive marathon run. *J. Ster. Biochem.* 7:33–37, 1976.

36. Eastman, C.J., R.P. Ekins, I.M. Leith, and E.S. Williams. Thyroid hormone response to prolonged cold exposure in man. *J. Physiol.* 241:175–181, 1974.

37. Edwards, C.I.W., and R.J. Howland. Adaptive changes in insulin and glucagon secretion during cold acclimation in the rat. *Am. J. Physiol.* 250:E669–E676, 1986.

38. Epstein, Y., G. Keren, and J. Sack. Thyroid functions in heat-intolerant persons. (Letter to the editor.) *Ann. Intern. Med.* 92:1980.

39. Epstein, Y., R. Udassin, and J. Sack. Serum 3,5,3′ triiodothyronine and 3,3′,5′ triiodothyronine concentrations during acute heat load. *J. Clin. Endocrinol. Metab.* 49:677–678, 1979.

40. Felig, P., J. Wahren, R. Hendler, and G. Ahlborg. Plasma glucagon levels in exercising man. *N. Engl. J. Med.* 287:184–185, 1972.

41. Finberg, J.P.M., and G.M. Berlyne. Renin and aldosterone secretion following acute environmental heat exposure. *Israel J. Med. Sci.* 12:844–847, 1976.

42. Finberg, J.P.M., and G.M. Berlyne. Modification of renin and aldosterone response to heat by acclimatization in man. *J. Appl. Physiol.* 42:554–558, 1977.

43. Finberg, J.P.M., M. Katz, H. Gazit, and G.M. Berlyne. Plasma renin activity after acute heat exposure in nonacclimatized and naturally acclimatized man. *J. Appl. Physiol.* 36:519–523, 1974.

44. Fisher, D.A. Thyroid function in the premature infant. *Am. J. Dis. Child.* 131:842–844, 1977.

45. Follenius, M., G. Brandenberger, S. Oyono, and V. Candas. Cortisol as a sensitive index of heat-intolerance. *Physiol. Behav.* 29:509–513, 1982.

46. Follenius, M., G. Brandenberger, M. Simeoni, and B. Reinhardt. Plasma aldosterone, prolactin and ACTH: Relationships in man during heat exposure. *Horm. Metab. Res.* 11:180–181, 1979.

47. Francesconi, R.P., A.E. Boyd III, and M. Mager. Human tryptophan and tyrosine metabolism: Effects of acute exposure to cold stress. *J. Appl. Physiol.* 33:165–169, 1972.

48. Francesconi, R.P., and A. Cymerman. Adrenocortical activity and urinary cyclic AMP levels: Effects of hypobaric hypoxia. *Aviat. Space Environ. Med.* 46:50–54, 1975.

49. Francesconi, R., J. Maher, G. Bynum, and J. Mason. Recurrent heat exposure: Effects on levels of plasma and urinary sodium and potassium in resting and exercising men. *Aviat. Space Environ. Med.* 48:399–404, 1977.

50. Francesconi, R.P., J.T. Maher, J.W. Mason, and G.D. Bynum. Hormonal responses of sedentary and exercising men to recurrent heat exposure. *Aviat. Space Environ. Med.* 49:1102–1106, 1978.

51. Francesconi, R.P., M.N. Sawka, R.W. Hubbard, and M. Mager. Acute albumin-induced plasma volume expansion and exercise in the heat: Effects on hormonal responses in men. *Eur. J. Appl. Physiol.* 51:121–128, 1983.

52. Francesconi, R.P., M.N. Sawka, and K.B. Pandolf. Hypohydration and heat acclimation: Plasma renin and aldosterone during exercise. *J. Appl. Physiol.* 55:1790–1794, 1983.

53. Francesconi, R.P., M.N. Sawka, and K.B. Pandolf. Hypohydration and acclimation: Effects on hormone responses to exercise/heat stress. *Aviat. Space Environ. Med.* 55:365–369, 1984.

54. Francesconi, R.P., M.N. Sawka, K.B. Pandolf, R.W. Hubbard, A.J. Young, and S. Muza. Plasma hormonal responses at graded hypohydration levels during exercise-heat stress. *J. Appl. Physiol.* 59:1855–1860, 1985.

55. Francis, K.T., and R. MacGregor III. Effect of exercise in the heat on plasma renin and aldosterone with either water or a potassium-rich electrolyte solution. *Aviat. Space Environ. Med.* 49:461–465, 1978.

56. Frewin, D.B., A.G. Frantz, and J.A. Downey. The effect of ambient temperature on the growth hormone and prolactin response to exercise. *Aust. J. Exp. Biol. Med. Sci.* 54:97–101, 1976.

57. Galbo, H., M.E. Houston, N.J. Christensen, J.J. Holst, B. Nielsen, E. Nygaard, and J. Suzuki. The effect of water temperature on the hormonal response to prolonged swimming. *Acta Physiol. Scand.* 105:326–337, 1979.

58. Galbo, H., L. Hummer, I.B. Petersen, N.J. Christensen, and N. Bie. Thyroid and testicular hormone responses to graded and prolonged exercise in man. *Eur. J. Appl. Physiol.* 36:101–106, 1977.

59. Gambert, S.R., T.L. Garthwaite, C.H. Pontzer, E.E. Cook, F.E. Tristani, E.H. Duthie, D.R. Martinson, T.C. Hagen, and D.J. McCarty. Running elevates plasma β-endorphin immunoreactivity and ACTH in untrained human subjects. *Proc. Soc. Exp. Biol. Med.* 168:1–4, 1981.

60. Gertner, A., R. Israeli, A. Lev, and Y. Cassuto. Thyroid hormones in chronic heat-exposed men. *Int. J. Biometeorol.* 27:75–82, 1983.

61. Geyssant, A., G. Geelen, C. Denis, A.M. Allevard, M. Vincent, E. Jarsaillon, C.A. Bizollon, J.R. Lacour, and C. Gharib. Plasma vasopressin, renin activity, and aldosterone: Effect of exercise and training. *Eur. J. Appl. Physiol.* 46:21–30, 1981.

62. Gharib, C., M. Vincent, G. Annat, A.M. Allevard, G. Geelen, A. Geyssant, J.P. Eclache, R. Lacour, and C.A. Bizollon. Activite renine et aldosterone plasmatiques au cours d'un exercice submaximal. Effets de l'entrainement. *J. Physiol. (Paris)* 77:911–914, 1981.

63. Gill, M.B., and L.G.C.E. Pugh. Basal metabolism and respiration in men living at 5,800 m (19,000 ft). *J. Appl. Physiol.* 19:949–954, 1964.

64. Golstein-Golaire, J., L. Vanhaelst, O.D. Bruno, R. Leclercq, and G. Copinschi. Acute effects of cold on blood levels of growth hormone, cortisol, and thyrotropin in man. *J. Appl. Physiol.* 29:622–626, 1970.

65. Gray, I., and W.P. Beetham, Jr. Changes in plasma concentration of epinephrine and norepinephrine with muscular work. *Proc. Soc. Exp. Biol. Med.* 96:636–638, 1957.

66. Grossman, A., and J.R. Sutton. Endorphins: What are they? How are they measured? What is their role in exercise? *Med. Sci. Sports Exerc.* 17:74–81, 1985.

67. Guilland, J.C., D. Moreau, M. Malval, R. Morville, and J. Klepping. Evaluation of sympathoadrenal activity, adrenocortical function, and androgenic status of five men during a Himalayan mountaineering expedition. *Eur. J. Appl. Physiol.* 52:156–162, 1984.

68. Harri, M., T. Dannenberg, R. Oksanen-Rossi, E. Hohtola, and U. Sundin. Related and unrelated changes in response to exercise and cold in rats: A reevaluation. *J. Appl. Physiol.* 57:1489–1497, 1984.

69. Hartley, L.H., J.W. Mason, R.P. Hogan, L.G. Jones, T.A. Kotchen, E.H. Mougey, F.E. Wherry, L.L. Pennington, and P.T. Ricketts. Multiple hormonal responses to graded exercise in relation to physical training. *J. Appl. Physiol.* 33:602–606, 1972.

70. Hellman, K., K.J. Collins, C.H. Gray, R.M. Jones, J.B. Lunnon, and J.S. Weiner. The excretion of urinary adrenocortical steroids during heat stress. *J. Endocrinol.* 14:209–216, 1956.

71. Hershman, J.M., D.G. Read, A.L. Bailey, V.D. Norman, and T.B. Gibson. Effect of cold exposure on serum thyrotropin. *J. Clin. Endocrinol.* 30:430–434, 1970.

72. Hickson, R.C., J.M. Hagberg, R.K. Conlee, D.A. Jones, A.A. Ehsani, and W.W. Winder. Effect of training on hormonal responses to exercise in competitive swimmers. *Eur. J. Appl. Physiol.* 41:211–219, 1979.

73. Hogan, R.P., III, T.A. Kotchen, A.E. Boyd III, and L.H. Hartley. Effect of altitude on renin-aldosterone system and metabolism of water and electrolytes. *J. Appl. Physiol.* 35:385–390, 1973.

74. Hoon, R.S., S.C. Sharma, V. Balasubramanian, and K.S. Chadha. Urinary catecholamine excretion on induction to high altitude (3658 m) by air and road. *J. Appl. Physiol.* 42:728–730, 1977.

75. Horvath, S.M. Exercise in a cold environment. In D.I. Miller (ed.). *Exercise and Sport Sciences Reviews*. New York: Macmillan Co., 1981, pp. 221–263.

76. Howlett, T.A., S. Tomlin, L. Ngahfoong, L.H. Rees, B.A. Bullen, G.S. Skrinar, and J.W. McArthur. Release of β-endorphin and met-enkephalin during exercise in normal women: Response to training. *Br. Med. J.* 288:1950–1952, 1984.

77. Howley, E.T. The effect of different intensities of exercise on the excretion of epinephrine and norepinephrine. *Med. Sci. Sports* 8:219–229, 1976.

78. Humpeler, E., F. Skrabal, and G. Bartsch. Influence of exposure to moderate altitude on the plasma concentration of cortisol, aldosterone, renin, testosterone, and gonadotropins. *Eur. J. Appl. Physiol.* 45:167–176, 1980.

79. Hunter, N.M., and M.Y. Sukkar. Changes in plasma insulin levels during muscular exercise. *J. Physiol.* 225:47p–48p, 1968.

80. Irvine, C.H.G. Effect of exercise in thyroxine degradation in athletes and nonathletes. *J. Clin. Endocrinol. Metab.* 28:942–948, 1968.

81. Jacobs, I., T.T. Romet, and D. Kerrigan-Brown. Muscle glycogen depletion during exercise at 9°C and 21°C. *Eur. J. Appl. Physiol.* 54:35–39, 1985.

82. Johnson, R.H., D.M. Park, M.J. Rennie, and W.R. Sulaiman. Hormonal responses to exercise in racing cyclists. *J. Physiol.* 241:23p–25p, 1974.

83. Kang, B.S., D.S. Han, K.S. Paik, Y.S. Park, J.K. Kim, C.S. Kim, D.W. Rennie, and S.K. Hong. Calorigenic action of norepinephrine in the Korean women divers. *J. Appl. Physiol.* 29:6–9, 1970.

84. Karagiorgios, A., J.F. Garcia, and G.A. Brooks. Growth hormone response to continuous and intermittent exercise. *Med. Sci. Sports* 11:302–307, 1979.

85. Kellogg, R.H., N. Pace, E.R. Archibald, and B.E. Vaughn. Respiratory response to inspired CO_2 during acclimatization to an altitude of 12,470 feet. *J. Appl. Physiol.* 11:67–71, 1957.

86. Kelso, T.B., W.G. Herbert, F.C. Gwazdauskas, F.L. Goss, and J.L. Hess. Exercise-thermoregulatory stress and increased plasma β-endorphin/β-lipotropin in humans. *J. Appl. Physiol.* 57:444–449, 1984.

87. Koeslag, J.H. Post-exercise ketosis and the hormone response to exercise. *Med. Sci. Sports Exerc.* 14:327–334, 1982.

88. Koivisto, V.A., S-L. Karonen, and E.A. Nikkila. Carbohydrate ingestion before exercise: Comparison of glucose, fructose, and sweet placebo. *J. Appl. Physiol.* 51:783–787, 1981.

89. Koivisto, V., V. Soman, E. Nadel, W.V. Tamborlane, and P. Felig. Exercise and insulin: Insulin binding, insulin mobilization, and counterregulatory hormone secretion. *Fed. Proc.* 39:1481–1486, 1980.

90. Kosunen, K.J., A.J. Pakarinen, K. Kuoppasalmi, and H. Adlerkreutz. Plasma renin activity, angiotensin II, and aldosterone during intense heat stress. *J. Appl. Physiol.* 41:323–327, 1976.

91. Kottke, F.J., C.B. Taylor, W.G. Kubicek, D.M. Erickson, and G.T. Evans. Adrenal cortex and altitude tolerance. *Am. J. Physiol.* 153:16–20, 1948.

92. Kraemer, W.J., B. Noble, B. Culver, and R.V. Lewis. Changes in plasma proenkephalin peptide F and catecholamine levels during graded exercise in men. *Proc. Natl. Acad. Sci. U.S.A.* 82:6349–6351, 1985.

93. Krieger, D.T., W. Allen, F. Rizzo, and H.P. Krieger. Characterization of the normal temporal pattern of plasma corticosteroid levels. *J. Clin. Endocrinol. Metab.* 32:266–284, 1971.

94. Langley, L.L., and R.W. Clarke. The reaction of the adrenal cortex to low atmospheric pressure. *Yale J. Biol. Med.* 14:529–546, 1942.

95. Lashof, J.C., P.K. Bondy, K. Sterling, and E.B. Man. Effect of muscular exercise on circulating thyroid hormone. *Proc. Soc. Exp. Biol. Med.* 86:233–235, 1954.

96. LeBlanc, J., A. Labrie, D. Lupien, and D. Richard. Catecholamines and triiodothyronine variations and the calorigenic response to norepinephrine in cold-adapted and exercise-trained rats. *Can. J. Physiol. Pharmacol.* 60:783–787, 1982.

97. Leppaluoto, J., T. Ranta, U. Laisi, J. Partanen, P. Virkkunen, and H. Lybeck. Strong heat exposure and adenohypophyseal hormone secretion in man. *Horm. Metab. Res.* 7:439–440, 1975.

98. Levin, C. The effects of several varieties of stress on the cholesterol content of the adrenal glands and of the serum of rats. *Endocrinology* 37:34–43, 1945.

99. MacKinnon, P.C.B., M.E. Monk-Jones, and K. Fotherby. A study of various indices of adrenocortical activity during 23 days at high altitude. *J. Endocrinol.* 26:555–566, 1963.

100. Mager, M., and S.M. Robinson. Substrate mobilization and utilization in fasting men during cold exposure. *Bull. N.J. Acad. Sci. Symp. Issue* 26–30, 1969.

101. Maher, J.T., D.E. Bass, D.D. Heistad, E.T. Angelakos, and L.H. Hartley. Effect of posture on heat acclimatization in man. *J. Appl. Physiol.* 33:8–13, 1972.
102. Maher, J.T., L.G. Jones, L.H. Hartley, G.H. Williams, and L.I. Rose. Aldosterone dynamics during graded exercise at sea level and high altitude. *J. Appl. Physiol.* 39:18–22, 1975.
103. Maresh, C.M., B.J. Noble, K.L. Robertson, and R.L. Seip. Adrenocortical responses to maximal exercise in moderate altitude natives at 447 torr. *J. Appl. Physiol.* 56:482–488, 1984.
104. Meerson, F.Z., M.G. Pshennikova, and E.S. Matlina. Effect of preliminary adaptation to altitude hypoxia on the content of catecholamines in the hypothalamus, adrenal glands, and heart during intense physical activity. *Vopr. Med. Khim.* 23:172–175, 1977.
105. Melin, B., J.P. Eclache, G. Geelen, G. Annat, A.M. Allevard, E. Jarsaillon, A. Zebidi, J.J. Legros, and C. Gharib. Plasma AVP, neurophysin, renin activity, and aldosterone during submaximal exercise performed until exhaustion in trained and untrained men. *Eur. J. Appl. Physiol.* 44:141–151, 1980.
106. Mikines, K.J., M. Kjaer, C. Hagen, B. Sonne, E.A. Richter, and H. Galbo. The effect of training on responses of β-endorphin and other pituitary hormones to insulin-induced hypoglycemia. *Eur. J. Appl. Physiol.* 54:476–479, 1985.
107. Milledge, J.S., D.M. Catley, E.S. Williams, W.R. Withey, and B.D. Minty. Effect of prolonged exercise at altitude on the renin-aldosterone system. *J. Appl. Physiol.* 55:413–418, 1983.
108. Moncloa, F., A. Carcelen, and L. Beteta. Physical exercise, acid-base balance, and adrenal function in newcomers to high altitude. *J. Appl. Physiol.* 28:151–155, 1970.
109. Moncloa, F., J. Donayre, L.A. Sobrevilla, and R. Guerra-Garcia. Endocrine studies at high altitude. II. Adrenal cortical function in sea level natives exposed to high altitudes (4300 meters) for two weeks. *J. Clin. Endocrinol. Metab.* 25:1640–1642, 1965.
110. Nagata, H., T. Izumiyama, K. Kamata, S. Kono, Y. Yukimura, M. Tawata, T. Aizawa, and T. Yamada. An increase of plasma triiodothyronine concentration in man in a cold environment. *J. Clin. Endocrinol. Metab.* 43:1153–1156, 1976.
111. O'Connell, M., D.C. Robbins, E.S. Horton, E.A.H. Sims, and E. Danforth, Jr. Changes in serum concentration of 3,3',5'-triiodothyronine and 3,5,3'-triiodothyronine during prolonged moderate exercise. *J. Clin. Endocrinol. Metab.* 49:242–246, 1979.
112. Okada, Y., K. Miyai, H. Iwatsubo, and Y. Kumahara. Human growth hormone secretion in normal adult subjects during and after exposure to cold. *J. Clin. Endocrinol.* 30:393–395, 1970.
113. O'Malley, B.P., N. Cook, A. Richardson, D.B. Barnett, and F.D. Rosenthal. Circulating catecholamine, thyrotrophin, thyroid hormone, and prolactin responses of normal subjects to acute cold exposure. *Clin. Endocrinol.* 21:285–291, 1984.
114. Ostman, I., and N.O. Sjostrand. Reduced urinary noradrenaline excretion during rest, exercise and cold stress in trained rats: A comparison between physically trained rats, cold acclimated rats and warm acclimated rats. *Acta Physiol. Scand.* 95:209–218, 1975.
115. Paolone, A.M., A.O. Ajiduah, J.T. Troup, C.W. Stevens, and Z.V. Kendrick. The effects of age and heat stress on plasma renin activity and plasma volume during exercise. *Med. Sci. Sports Exerc.* 15:97–98, 1983.
116. Peronnet, F., J. Cleroux, H. Perrault, G. Thibault, D. Cousineau, J. de Champlain, J-C. Guilland, and J. Klepping. Plasma norepinephrine, epinephrine, and dopamine β-hydroxylase activity during exercise in man. *Med. Sci. Sports Exerc.* 17:683–688, 1985.
117. Polozhentsev, S.D., G.N. Novozhilov, K.V. Mazurov, and V.N. Denisov. Activity of the sympathico-adrenal system as an indicator of heat adaptation. *Hum. Physiol.* 4:688–690, 1978.
118. Powers, S.K., E.T. Howley, and R. Cox. A differential catecholamine response during prolonged exercise and passive heating. *Med. Sci. Sports Exerc.* 14:435–439, 1982.

119. Premachandra, B.N., W.W. Winder, R. Hickson, S. Lang, and J.O. Holloszy. Circulating reverse triiodothyronine in humans during exercise. *Eur. J. Appl. Physiol.* 47:281–288, 1981.

120. Rastogi, G.K., M.S. Malhotra, M.C. Srivastava, R.C. Sawhneg, G.L. Dua, K. Sridharan, R.S. Hoon, and I. Singh. Study of the pituitary-thyroid functions at high altitude in man. *J. Clin. Endocrinol. Metab.* 44:447–452, 1977.

121. Raynaud, J., L. Drouet, J.P. Martineaud, J. Bordachar, J. Coudert, and J. Durand. Time course of plasma growth hormone during exercise in humans at altitude. *J. Appl. Physiol.* 50:229–233, 1981.

122. Reid, I.A., B.J. Morris, and W.F. Ganong. The renin-angiotensin system. *Ann. Rev. Physiol.* 40:377–410, 1978.

123. Robertson, D., G.A. Johnson, R.M. Robertson, A.S. Nies, D.G. Shard, and J.A. Oates. Comparative assessment of stimuli that release neuronal and adrenomedullary catecholamines in man. *Circulation* 59:637–643, 1979.

124. Rocker, L., K. Kirsch, and B. Agrawal. Long-term observations on plasma antidiuretic hormone levels during and after heat stress. *Eur. J. Appl. Physiol.* 49:59–62, 1982.

125. Roosevelt, T.S., A. Ruhmann-Wennhold, and D.H. Nelson. A protective effect of glucocorticoids in hypoxic stress. *Am. J. Physiol.* 223:30–33, 1972.

126. Sciaraffa, D., E. Shvartz, L.C. Keil, P.J. Brock, and J.E. Greenleaf. Heat acclimation and resting blood pressure of normotensive men. *Med. Sci. Sports* 9:51, 1977. (Abstract)

127. Sedgwick, A.W., A.H. Davidson, R.E. Taplin, and D.W. Thomas. A pilot study of some associations between behavioral stressors and physiological processes in healthy men. *Eur. J. Appl. Physiol.* 46:409–421, 1981.

128. Senay, L.C., Jr., and M.L. Christensen. Changes in blood volume during progressive dehydration. *J. Appl. Physiol.* 20:1136–1140, 1965.

129. Shephard, R.J. Adaptation to exercise in the cold. *Sports Med.* 2:59–71, 1985.

130. Shvartz, E., V.A. Convertino, L.C. Keil, and R.F. Haines. Orthostatic, fluid-electrolyte and endocrine responses in fainters and nonfainters. *J. Appl. Physiol.* 51:1404–1410, 1981.

131. Smith, O.L.K. Insulin response in rats acutely exposed to cold. *Can. J. Physiol. Pharmacol.* 62:924–927, 1984.

132. Stock, M.J., C. Chapman, J.L. Stirling, and I.T. Campbell. Effects of exercise, altitude, and food on blood hormone and metabolite levels. *J. Appl. Physiol.* 45:350–354, 1978.

133. Strydom, N.B., C.H. Wyndham, C.H. VanGraan, L.D. Holdsworth, and J.F. Morrison. The influence of water restriction on the performance of men during a prolonged road march. *S. Afr. Med. J.* 40:539–544, 1966.

134. Sulman, F.G., Y. Pfeifer, and E. Superstine. The adrenal exhaustion syndrome: An adrenal deficiency. *Ann. N.Y. Acad. Sci.* 301:918–930, 1977.

135. Sulman, F.G., E. Tal, Y. Pfeifer, and E. Superstine. Intermittent hyperthyreosis—a heat stress syndrome. *Horm. Metab. Res.* 7:424–428, 1975.

136. Sutton, J. Scientific and medical aspects of the Australian Andean expedition. *Med. J. Aust.* 2:355–361, 1971.

137. Sutton, J.R. Effect of acute hypoxia on the hormonal response to exercise. *J. Appl. Physiol.* 42:587–592, 1977.

138. Sutton, J.R. Hormonal and metabolic responses to exercise in subjects of high and low work capacities. *Med. Sci. Sports* 10:1–6, 1978.

139. Sutton, J.R., M.J. Coleman, J. Casey, and L. Lazarus. Androgen responses during physical exercise. *Br. Med. J.* 1:520–522, 1973.

140. Sutton, J., and F. Garmendia. Variaciones hormonales durante el esfuerzo ficico en la altura. *Arch. Biol. Andina* 7:83–93, 1977.

141. Sutton, J.R., N.L. Jones, and C.J. Toeus. Growth hormone secretion in acid-base alterations at rest and during exercise. *Clin. Sci. Molec. Med.* 50:241–247, 1976.

142. Terjung, R.L., and C.M. Tipton. Plasma thyroxine and thyroid stimulating hormone levels during submaximal exercise in humans. *Am. J. Physiol.* 220:1840–1845, 1971.

143. Tharp, G.D., and R.J. Buuck. Adrenal adaptation to chronic exercise. *J. Appl. Physiol.* 37:720–722, 1974.

144. Thompson, R.H., E.R. Buskirk, and G.D. Whedon. Temperature regulation against cold: Effect of induced hyperthyroidism in men and women. *J. Appl. Physiol.* 31:740–745, 1971.

145. Thorn, G.W., M. Clinton, Jr., B.M. Davis, and R.A. Lewis. Effect of adrenal cortical hormone therapy on altitude tolerance. *Endocrinology* 36:381–390, 1945.

146. Timiras, P.S., N. Pace, and C.A. Hwang. Plasma and urine 17-hydroxycorticosteroid and urine 17-ketosteroid levels in man during acclimatization to high altitude. *Fed. Proc.* 16:340, 1957. (Abstract)

147. Timmons, B.A., J. Araujo, and T.R. Thomas. Fat utilization enhanced by exercise and a cold environment. *Med. Sci. Sports Exerc.* 17:673–678, 1985.

148. Tuomisto, J., P. Mannisto, B-A. Lamberg, and M. Linnoila. Effect of cold exposure on serum thyrotrophin levels in man. *Acta Endocrinol.* 83:522–527, 1976.

149. Vander, A.J., L.G. Moore, G. Brewer, K. Menon, and B. England. Effects of high altitude on plasma concentrations of testosterone and pituitary gonadotropins in man. *Aviat. Space Environ. Med.* 49:356–357, 1978.

150. Viru, A. *Hormones in Muscular Activity*, Vol. I. Boca Raton: Fla.: CRC Press, 1985, p. 56.

151. von Euler, U.S. Sympatho-adrenal activity in physical exercise. *Med. Sci. Sports* 6:165–173, 1974.

152. von Euler, U.S., and S. Hellner. Excretion of noradrenaline and adrenaline in muscular work. *Acta Physiol. Scand.* 16:183–191, 1952.

153. Wade, C.E. Response, regulation, and action of vasopressin during exercise: A review. *Med. Sci. Sports Exerc.* 16:506–511, 1984.

154. Weeke, J., and H.J.G. Gundersen. The effect of heating and central cooling on serum TSH, GH, and norepinephrine in resting normal man. *Acta Physiol. Scand.* 117:33–39, 1983.

155. Weitzman, E.D., C. Nogeire, M. Perlow, D. Fukushima, J. Sassin, P. McGregor, T.F. Gallagher, and L. Hellman. Effects of a prolonged 3-hour sleep-wake cycle on sleep stages, plasma cortisol, growth hormone and body temperature in man. *J. Clin. Endocrinol. Metab.* 38:1018–1030, 1974.

156. White, J.A., A.A. Ismail, and G.D. Bottoms. Effect of physical fitness on the adrenocortical response to exercise stress. *Med. Sci. Sports* 8:113–118, 1976.

157. Wilkerson, J.E., S.M. Horvath, and B. Gutin. Plasma testosterone during treadmill exercise. *J. Appl. Physiol.* 49:249–253, 1980.

158. Wilkerson, J.E., P.B. Raven, N.W. Bolduan, and S.M. Horvath. Adaptations in man's adrenal function in response to acute cold stress. *J. Appl. Physiol.* 36:183–189, 1974.

159. Wilson, O. Field study of the effect of cold exposure and increased muscular activity upon metabolic rate and thyroid function in man. *Fed. Proc.* 25:1357–1362, 1966.

160. Wilson, O., P. Hedner, S. Laurell, B. Nosslin, C. Rerup, and E. Rosengren. Thyroid and adrenal response to acute cold exposure in man. *J. Appl. Physiol.* 28:543–548, 1970.

161. Winder, W.W., M.A. Beattie, and R.T. Holman. Endurance training attenuates stress hormone responses to exercise in fasted rats. *Am. J. Physiol.* 243:R179–R184, 1982.

162. Winder, W.W., R.C. Hickson, J.M. Hagberg, A.A. Ehsani, and J.A. McLane. Training induced changes in hormonal and metabolic responses to submaximal exercise. *J. Appl. Physiol.* 46:766–771, 1979.

163. Winter, J.S.D. The metabolic response to exercise and exhaustion in normal and growth-hormone-deficient children. *Can. J. Physiol. Pharmacol.* 52:575–582, 1974.

164. Wright, A.D. Birmingham Medical Research Expeditionary Society 1977 Expedition: Thyroid function and acute mountain sickness. *Postgrad. Med. J.* 55:483–486, 1979.

165. Yoshimura, M., S. Hori, and H. Yoshimura. Effect of high-fat diet on thermal acclimation with special reference to thyroid activity. *Jpn. J. Physiol.* 22:517–531, 1972.

9
Exercise and Type I Diabetes Mellitus

ANGELICA VITUG, M.D.
STEPHEN H. SCHNEIDER, M.D.
NEIL B. RUDERMAN, M.D.

INTRODUCTION

The concept that physical activity is beneficial for patients with diabetes mellitus is centuries old [80]. Throughout the years, however, there has been considerable controversy as to its value. For instance, early in this century, exercise was felt to be contraindicated, since in some patients clinical deterioration was observed following heavy physical activity [67]. After the discovery of insulin, exercise was repopularized for the treatment of diabetes by Joslin [38] and Katsch [39], who portrayed it as one of the three basic modalities of therapy, along with diet and insulin. In recent years, there has been a resurgence of interest in the interactions of exercise, physical training, and the diabetic state. It has become apparent that the effects of exercise differ among different subgroups of patients with diabetes, and that the risks and benefits of exercise are dependent on the specific type of the diabetic syndrome, as well as the state of metabolic control.

The syndrome of diabetes mellitus consists of a heterogeneous group of disorders with varying pathophysiologies. The two largest subgroups of patients with diabetes have been labeled "type I" and "type II." Type II, or non-insulin-dependent diabetes millitus, formerly called "maturity-onset diabetes," tends to occur in older individuals. Early in the course of this disorder it is associated, in most patients, with significant resistance to insulin's actions, an abnormal but relatively well-maintained insulin secretion, and normal to elevated plasma insulin levels. Type I, or insulin-dependent diabetes, formerly called "juvenile-onset diabetes," generally occurs in younger individuals and is associated with an absolute deficiency of insulin and often of other pancreatic hormones secondary to the destruction of the pancreatic islets by what appears to be an immunologically mediated inflammatory reaction. These patients generally have a more severe abnormality of glucose homeostasis, the effects of exercise on the metabolic state are more pronounced, and management of exercise-related problems is more difficult. In this chapter, we

285

will address the problems and potential benefits of exercise in patients with type I diabetes mellitus. We will review briefly the physiology of exercise, the metabolic abnormalities commonly seen in patients with type I diabetes during and after exercise, and an approach to understanding and treating some of the difficulties caused by exercise in these patients.

FUEL METABOLISM AND ITS REGULATION DURING EXERCISE

Physical activity is the most profound challenge to fuel homeostasis in normal humans. Total body O_2 consumption and glucose turnover may increase more than 10-fold, and O_2 consumption and glucose uptake by exercising muscles may increase even more. Remarkably, in the face of these large changes in glucose turnover, plasma glucose levels remain stable for hours [22, 84]. To accomplish this, glucose delivery from digested food in the gut or from hepatic glycogenolysis and gluconeogenesis are precisely regulated to match peripheral gluocse utilization.

The mechanisms responsible for the increased glucose uptake that occurs in exercising skeletal muscle are incompletely understood. As plasma insulin levels generally decrease during exercise of moderate to severe intensity [85], insulin is not likely to be a major mediator of this effect. Increases in both the affinity and number of insulin receptors occur following physical training [43, 58]. However, there is little evidence that such changes occur during exercise itself [11, 44]. An increase in receptor number has been reported following periods of physical training, but it appears to be secondary to improved insulin sensitivity rather than a primary event.

Increased glucose delivery could hypothetically result in enhanced glucose uptake due to the large increase in capillary surface area and blood flow that occurs in skeletal muscle during exercise [8]. On the other hand, increased glucose uptake has been demonstrated in experimental conditions in which glucose delivery is not a factor [29, 64]. Based on these findings, it is likely that exercise exerts its major effects on skeletal muscle glucose uptake by postreceptor mechanisms that regulate glucose transport and/or intracellular glucose metabolism [90]. One possibility, presently under study, is that it increases the availability of glucose transporters at the cell surface, as has recently been demonstrated in trained rats [82].

The signal that initiates the increases in glucose uptake and utilization by skeletal muscle during and after exercise is also not well understood. Glycogen depletion is temporally related to enhanced

FIGURE 1

Various glycemic responses to exercise based on the degree of insulinization.

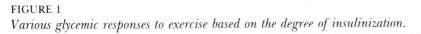

INSULIN AND THE METABOLIC RESPONSE TO EXERCISE

glucose uptake; however, following exercise, enhanced insulin-stimulated glucose uptake can be demonstrated after glycogen stores have been repleted [61, 64]. Conversely, in perfused rat muscle, the increase in glucose transport that follows electrically induced contractions ceases even if glycogen stores have not been fully repleted [7, 51, 59]. Thus, while glycogen depletion may play a role in initiating glucose uptake, other as yet unidentified factors are also likely to be important.

Despite the absence of an increase in plasma insulin levels during exercise, a permissive role for basal levels of insulin in exercise-enhanced glucose uptake has been proposed. Studies by Berger et al. [6] clearly show that the ability of muscle contraction to increase glucose uptake and utilization is severely decreased in rats with diabetic ketoacidosis, consistent with the idea that some insulin is required for the effects of exercise to become manifest. On the other hand, recent studies by Richter et al. [64] and Wallberg-Henriksson and Holloszy [89] have challenged this view. It is possible that the influence of diabetic ketoacidosis on glucose uptake during exercise is not mediated through insulin deficiency alone. For the present, the relative importance of insulin and glycogen depletion in regulating exercise-mediated glucose uptake remains unclear.

GLUCOSE HOMEOSTASIS AND THE HORMONAL RESPONSE TO EXERCISE

Glucose homeostasis is maintained during exercise by a precise coordination of hormonal and metabolic events. With the onset of exercise, plasma insulin levels decline as a result of increased alpha-adrenergic input to the beta cell [25]. This should enhance hepatic glucose output both directly and by sensitizing the liver to the effects of basal levels of glucagon and epinephrine [36, 76]. With more prolonged exercise, even of moderate intensity, blood glucose levels begin to fall, and plasma levels of glucagon, growth hormone, cortisol, and epinephrine increase [24, 26, 83]. Thus far, only glucagon and epinephrine have a well-established role in acutely maintaining glucose homeostasis [23, 26, 37, 63, 91]. Their precise role during exercise is unresolved, however, Bjorkman et al. [9] and Hoelzer et al. [33] have shown that inhibition of glucagon release by somatostatin has little effect on glucose homeostasis in humans during exercise, whereas beta-adrenergic blockade results in a mild tendency toward hypoglycemia [28, 41, 81]. The combination, however, of somatostatin and beta-adrenergic blockade results in significant impairment of glucose homeostasis [33, 77]. This suggests a hierarchy of counterregulatory hormones that differs from that observed during insulin-induced hypoglycemia in that epinephrine and possibly norepinephrine appear to play the major role initially in maintaining plasma glucose levels during exercise, while glucagon is important when beta-adrenergic activity becomes deficient. In keeping with this notion, hepatic glucose output is increased during the first few minutes of exercise when no changes in glucagon levels are evident, and of the potential mediators measured, only norepinephrine appears to be increased [27] (see Table 1).

FUEL METABOLISM DURING EXERCISE IN PATIENTS WITH TYPE I DIABETES MELLITUS

Changes in glucose homeostasis in patients with type I diabetes are quite complex and depend upon a number of factors, including the degree of insulinization, prior metabolic control, the presence or absence of autonomic neuropathy, and recent food intake. Patients who are in a state of chronic insulin deficiency of moderate degree have decreased glycogen stores in liver and, to a lesser extent, in skeletal muscle [65, 66]. This results in impaired aerobic exercise endurance and a more

TABLE 1
Glucose Metabolism During Exercise

Factors that may influence increased hepatic glucose production during exercise
  Decreased insulin levels
  Increased norepinephrine (local)
  Increased epinephrine levels
  Increased glucagon levels
Factors that may influence increased glucose utilization by exercising muscle
(?) Permissive concentrations of insulin
  Increased glucose delivery
  Glycogen depletion
  Increased number of glucose transporters at the cell surface
  Increased numbers of insulin receptors (with physical training)

rapid switch of fuels during prolonged exercise to the utilization of free fatty acids. Thus, after 40 minutes of exercise, such individuals may have a metabolic profile similar to that of nondiabetic subjects who have exercised for as long as 4 hours—the so-called accelerated adaptation to exercise [86]. Treatment with insulin but not with oral hypoglycemic agents returns glycogen stores, metabolic profiles, and aerobic exercise capacity in such individuals to normal [5, 30, 95].

An important metabolic complication of exercise in the poorly controlled patient with severe insulin deficiency may be a worsening of the metabolic state. These patients generally have a fasting glucose level in excess of 300 mg/dl and are often mildly dehydrated. Berger et al. [5] and Hagenfeldt [31] have shown a rise in plasma glucose levels, as well as mild to moderate ketosis, following exercise in such individuals. Presumably a deficiency of insulin and an excess of counterregulatory hormones cause excessive hepatic glucose and ketone body production, as well as a modest impairment in peripheral glucose and possibly ketone body utilization. Because of this, patients with type I diabetes mellitus who are poorly controlled should avoid exercise until adequate insulinization has been achieved.

HYPOGLYCEMIA AND EXERCISE IN TYPE I DIABETES

The most common disturbance of glucose homeostasis during exercise in type I diabetes is hypoglycemia. This is a particularly severe problem in patients whose diabetes is "brittle" or in those who are undergoing intensive insulin therapy in an attempt to normalize plasma glucose levels throughout the day. Most commonly, hypoglycemia occurs during a relatively prolonged session of moderately intense exercise when hepatic glucose production cannot keep pace with the increased use of glucose by exercising muscle. In addition to stimulation of glucose uptake acutely, glucose uptake and insulin sensitivity are

TABLE 2
Factors that Contribute to Hypoglycemia During Exercise in Type I Diabetes

Accelerated absorption of insulin
Nonsuppressible plasma insulin levels
Increased sensitivity to insulin
? Impaired counterregulatory hormonal response
Drugs

enhanced for many hours after activity has ceased [1, 49, 64, 87]. In the rat, this increased glucose uptake is at least partially independent of insulin-mediated glucose transport [29, 64]. It is not surprising, therefore, that in addition to occurring during exercise, hypoglycemic episodes are not uncommon 4–6 hours following an exercise bout. In many cases, the etiology of hypoglycemia during or following exercise in type I diabetes is not clear. However, a number of factors have been identified that may contribute (Table 2).

a. Inappropriately high levels of insulin in the circulation. When insulin levels are inappropriately high during and after exercise, hepatic glucose production may be depressed and hypoglycemia could result. One possible cause of such hyperinsulinemia is accelerated absorption of insulin from its injection site. Repetitive contraction of skeletal muscle immediately under the injection site of an insulin depot can alter its absorption [42, 96]. This generally occurs when short-acting insulin is administered, and it appears to be important only when exercise takes place within an hour or less of the insulin injection. Accelerated absorption of insulin during exercise may result in hypoglycemia at the time of exercise or shortly thereafter. Also, by decreasing the amount of insulin remaining, this may result in hyperglycemia later in the day and overall deterioration of glucose control. Changing the site of insulin injection to an area away from the exercising muscle, or delaying exercise for some hours after the injection of short-acting insulin, can correct these problems. While in some individuals accelerated absorption of depot insulin is the cause of hyperinsulinemia leading to hypoglycemia, in most patients hyperinsulinemia is simply the result of a previous insulin injection and changing the injection site is of little benefit [40, 97]. Parenthetically, the absence of the physiologic fall in plasma insulin, at least in normal humans, does not readily cause hypoglycemia [13], and a number of studies suggest that insulin infusion during exercise in diabetics has only minor effects on hepatic glucose output [18, 55, 71, 97]. Thus, while a lack of physiologic insulin suppression may be an important contributor to hypoglycemia, additional factors are likely to be involved.

b. Impaired counterregulatory response. In some instances, defects in the response of counterregulatory hormones during exercise may contribute to the hypoglycemic response in type I diabetes. This is particularly likely in patients with established autonomic neuropathy who are unable to increase their plasma catecholamine levels appropriately [32]. It might also occur, however, in patients with no clinical evidence of autonomic dysfunction. Recent studies indicate that many individuals with relatively long-standing type I diabetes mellitus lose their ability to secrete glucagon and epinephrine in the face of insulin-induced hypoglycemia, even in the absence of clinically evident autonomic neuropathy. Loss of these counterregulatory hormones results in an increased tendency to develop hypoglycemia. While Sotsky et al. [78] could not demonstrate a defective hormonal response to exercise of short duration in a group of type I diabetics, we have found a decreased response of epinephrine to exercise of greater than 30 minutes' duration [74] in a subgroup of patients who had had type I diabetes for 10 or more years. Whether such a defective counterregulatory hormone response is important in determining which patients develop exercise-related hypoglycemia remains to be determined.

c. Increased insulin sensitivity. It should be reemphasized that clinically important episodes of hypoglycemia often occur many hours after an exercise bout. In clinical practice, such episodes are often the most troublesome, as they tend to be unanticipated, and if exercise is performed in the evening, they may occur when the patient is asleep. As previously mentioned, an increased sensitivity of muscle to insulin persists for many hours after exercise [1, 64] and, along with inappropriately high levels of insulin, is probably responsible for some of these late hypoglycemic reactions. Nevertheless, the etiology of many of these hypoglycemic episodes is even less well understood than that of episodes that occur during exericse.

d. Drugs. Various commonly prescribed medications may play a role in exercise-induced hypoglycemia in some patients with type I diabetes. Beta-adrenergic blocking agents may aggravate insulin-induced hypoglycemia, especially in the subgroup of patients who may have an impaired glucagon response [10]. Ethanol can inhibit gluconeogenesis and, in the absence of adequate hepatic glycogen stores or food in the gut, may predispose individuals to exercise-related hypoglycemia. In patients with type I diabetes for whom exercise-related hypoglycemia is a problem, avoidance of these agents is probably well advised.

APPROACH TO AVOIDING HYPOGLYCEMIA DURING EXERCISE

The following guidelines may be useful for the well-controlled insulin-dependent diabetic who wishes to participate in strenuous exercise without the risk of hypoglycemia.

TABLE 3
Guidelines for Avoiding Hypoglycemia During and After Exercise

1. Consume carbohydrates (15–30 gm) for every 30 minutes of moderately intense exercise.
2. Consume a snack of slowly absorbed carbohydrate following prolonged exercise sessions.
3. Decrease the insulin dose
   a. Intermediate-acting insulin—decrease by 30–35% on the day of exercise.
   b. Intermediate- and short-acting insulin—omit dose of short-acting insulin that precedes exercise.
   c. Multiple doses of short-acting insulin—reduce the dose prior to exercise by 30–35% and supplement carbohydrates.
   d. Continuous subcutaneous infusion—eliminate mealtime bolus or increment that precedes or immediately follows exercise.
4. Avoid exercising muscle underlying injections of short-acting insulin for 1 hour.
5. Avoid late evening exercise.

a. During prolonged exercise, such a patient can take an additional 15–30 g of readily absorbable carbohydrates every 30 minutes. At the end of a prolonged exercise session, more slowly absorbed carbohydrates such as milk may be useful in preventing delayed hypoglycemic episodes. Studies have shown that well-insulinized patients have a normal capacity to oxidize (up to 90% of) an ingested glucose load during exercise [47].

b. Hypoglycemia can be prevented by decreasing of the dose of insulin on the day of exercise. The necessary reduction varies considerably, depending on individual sensitivity and the duration and type of exercise and time of day. In general, for patients taking intermediate-acting insulin, a reduction of 30–40% in the morning dose is typical. Individuals taking combinations of intermediate- and short-acting insulin can generally omit the dose of regular insulin prior to exercise.

c. Patients treated with continuous subcutaneous insulin infusion, with normalization of plasma glucose throughout the day, may be at particularly high risk for hypoglycemia. When exercise follows a meal, maintaining the insulin infusion at the basal rate while eliminating the mealtime bolus or increment generally prevents a severe hypoglycemic response [60].

Although these guidelines are helpful, the response of an individual diabetic to exercise may be unpredictable because of the heterogeneity of the diabetic population. Patient strategies need to be individualized. Home blood glucose monitoring is very useful in this respect. Nevertheless, in some patients in whom metabolic control is difficult to achieve, it may not be possible to institute an exercise program without worsening metabolic control and/or causing frequent hypoglycemic episodes (Table 3).

SPECIAL PROBLEMS RELATED TO EXERCISE IN PATIENTS WITH VASCULAR AND NEUROLOGICAL COMPLICATIONS

VASCULAR. Exercise of moderate to severe intensity results in major hemodynamic changes, including a widening of pulse pressure and a large increase in systolic but not diastolic blood pressure. The increase in systolic blood pressure that occurs during exercise varies greatly on an individual basis, but exercise of even moderate intensity is not uncommonly associated with a sustained increment in systolic blood pressure of well over 200 mm of mercury. The possibility that these hemodynamic changes could worsen large- or small-vessel disease in patients with diabetes needs to be considered.

At present, there is no evidence that programs of intensive physical training accelerate the progression of diabetic retinopathy. It is clear that exercise that results in large increments in systolic pressure, i.e., high-intensity aerobic exercise, or exercise that involves Valsalva-type maneuvers, such as bending, excessive stretching, or heavy lifting, can cause retinal hemorrhage in the presence of preexistent proliferative diabetic retinopathy and should be avoided.

Transient exercise-induced proteinuria is a common finding in patients with long-standing type I diabetes mellitus, and the degree of proteinuria is related to the level of elevation in systolic blood pressure [57]. It is not known whether the hemodynamic changes associated with exercise that are believed to result in proteinuria have any ill effects on the kidney, although sustained hypertension is a major factor in the progession of diabetic nephropathy. Because of its potentially adverse effects, it is prudent at present for patients with established microvascular disease of the eye or kidney to avoid exercise that results in systolic hypertension greater than 180–200 mm Hg for a sustained period of time.

A serious concern in type I diabetes of long duration, above age 35 and even at younger ages if renal disease is present, is silent myocardial ischemia due to coronary artery disease. For this reason, such patients should have a careful cardiovascular examination, including a stress electrocardiogram, prior to embarking on an exercise program

NEUROLOGICAL. Patients with significant autonomic neuropathy generally have impaired aerobic exercise performance associated with a decrease in maximal heart rate and an increase in resting heart rate. These patients are more likely to encounter problems during exercise. In addition to silent ischemia, these patients have an increased risk of developing hypotensive episodes following strenuous exercise, particularly in the untrained state. A predisposition to dehydration in the heat and a poor tolerance for exercise in the cold are commonly seen. Finally, patients with loss of sensory function and distortion of the normal anatomy of the foot due to diabetic peripheral neuropathy are predisposed

TABLE 4
Risks Associated with Exercise In Type I Diabetes

Metabolic
    Hyperglycemia and ketosis
    Hypoglycemia
Vascular
    Ischemic coronary events
    Retinal hemorrhage
    Proteinuria
Neurologic
    Silent myocardial ischemia
    Orthostatic hypotension
    Dehydration
    Predisposition to foot trauma

to traumatic injury and foot ulceration. Use of proper footwear, foot inspection following every exercise session, and avoidance of exercise that results in repeated foot trauma such as jogging on hard surfaces should be advised. Instead, activities such as swimming and cycling should be encouraged.

BENEFITS OF REGULAR EXERCISE FOR THE PATIENT WITH TYPE I DIABETES MELLITUS

The role of regular exercise and physical training in improving glycemic control in patients with type I diabetes remains controversial. Repetitive exercise bouts result in alterations in the body referred to as the "trained state." These include improved efficiency of the cardiovascular system and increased capillary and mitochondrial density in the active skeletal muscle. Patients with type I diabetes are able to increase their $\dot{V}O_2$max and the activities of mitochondrial enzymes normally in response to physical training [16, 87], but in patients with long-standing disease new capillary formation may be decreased [70, 88].

In normal humans, an increase in insulin receptor number and improved insulin sensitivity during physical training have been well demonstrated. In addition, DeFronzo et al. [19] have shown that the increase in insulin sensitivity following physical training in patients with type I diabetes is similar to that demonstrated in normal humans. Utilizing the glucose clamp technique, exercise appears to have a synergistic rather than an additive effect on isulin's ability to enhance glucose uptake [19, 87]. While much of this is due to improved glucose disposal in skeletal muscle, recent work in individuals who do not have type I diabetes has raised the possibility that changes in hepatic insulin sensitivity may be at least as important [20].

Despite the clear association between physical training and improved insulin sensitivity, the clinical utility of physical training in improving glucose control in type I diabetes has not been demonstrated. Improved metabolic control of children during periods of increased activity, such as at summer camp, are well documented but difficult to interpret due to the large number of confounding variables [2, 53]. Caron et al. [12] have demonstrated that a single moderate bout of exercise in type I diabetes can result in decreased postmeal glycemic excursions for many hours. Recent studies suggest, however, that improved overall glycemic control in patients with type I diabetes is difficult to demonstrate during physical training despite sustained improvements in insulin sensitivity [34, 48, 49, 87, 88, 98]. In patients with type I diabetes, in whom absolute insulin deficiency is the rule, the major clinical problem is hypoglycemia. Common strategies include a decrease in insulin dosage, alteration of the timing of insulin administration, and an increase in carbohydrate intake. These actions, while preventing hypoglycemia, may partially negate the improved glycemic control that might be anticipated to result from exercise-induced enhancement of insulin sensitivity. Although most patients with type I diabetes do not demonstrate a major improvement in glycemic control with regular exercise, some are more likely to benefit than others. In our experience, these include patients who are less prone to hypoglycemia and are willing and able to carefully regulate their timing and amount of exercise each day. Even when regular exercise fails to achieve better glycemic control, it often results in decreased insulin requirements and psychological benefits. In addition, it may afford some protection against premature atherosclerosis. In many patients with very difficult-to-control type I diabetes mellitus, it is, for all practical purposes, impossible to devise an exercise regimen that does not result in unacceptable swings of plasma glucose. Thus, based on our current understanding, a general recommendation for using exercise therapy to improve glycemic control in type I diabetes mellitus is not justified at this time.

Other Potential Benefits of Exercise in Patients with Type I Diabetes Mellitus
Exercise therapy may be of value to patients with type I diabetes as a means of protecting them from premature atherosclerosis. Accelerated atherosclerosis is becoming an increasingly important problem in type I diabetes mellitus [46, 69]. Epidemiologic studies have demonstrated that cerebrovascular, coronary, and peripheral arterial diseases are more common in type I diabetes than in the general population and that they occur at an earlier age. Significant atherosclerotic vascular disease may occur in patients with type I diabetes mellitus prior to the age of 30, especially if they have renal disease.

Few studies have examined the effects of exercise on cardiovascular risk factors in patients with type I diabetes mellitus. Studies of the effect of exercise on risk factors in normal populations and patients with type II diabetes, however, suggest a potential utility for this approach. Major risk factors for atherosclerosis known to be influenced by exercise include hyperlipidemia, abnormal coagulation profiles, and hyperinsulinemia.

Significant hyperlipidemia is not a common problem in patients with type I diabetes mellitus under good metabolic control, and in well-controlled patients with type I diabetes, high-density lipoprotein (HDL)-cholesterol levels are generally normal or elevated [35]. Little is known about the effects of exercise on plasma lipids and lipoproteins in these patients. In patients with type II diabetes mellitus and normal individuals, however, regular exercise does result in a significant decrease in plasma very-low-density lipoprotein (VLDL) levels [50] and, if exercise is of sufficient intensity and duration, an increment in plasma HDL-cholesterol levels [94]. Although VLDL cholesterol is generally not considered to be a major risk factor for atherosclerosis, the VLDL particles in some patients with diabetes may be abnormal and may have an increased atherogenic potential [75]. In insulin-deficient rats, exercise results in a significant improvement in triglyceride metabolism [17]. More investigation needs to be done on the potential value of exercise for type I diabetics in this respect.

The association of abnormalities of the coagulation system frequently noted in patients with type I diabetes and the risk of developing myocardial infarction have been confirmed in a number of studies [45, 93]. Elevated levels of fibrinogen and factor VIII complex activity, enhanced platelet aggregability, increased thromboxane, decreased prostacyclin synthesis, and a decreased fibrinolytic response to a variety of stimuli have been observed in patients with type I diabetes mellitus [15]. In many instances, it is unclear whether these changes precede or result from vascular injury. The effects of exercise on the coagulation system of patients with type I diabetes mellitus are not known. Studies in both normal individuals and patients with type II diabetes mellitus suggest that exercise may result in a significant improvement in fibrinolytic capacity and other coagulation parameters [72, 73, and review in 14].

Hyperinsulinemia has been associated with cerebral, coronary, and peripheral arterial disease in normal individuals and type II diabetics with insulin resistance [21, 62, 92]. In addition, insulin resistance has been associated prospectively with a predilection to macrovascular disease in patients with type I diabetes [54]. Insulin has been shown to alter metabolic pathways in vascular cells and to stimulate the growth of vascular smooth muscle [79]. Most patients with type I diabetes mellitus treated with intensive or conventional insulin therapy in an attempt to normalize plasma glucose have elevated plasma insulin levels [4]. In addition, a secondary increase in IGF-1, a growth factor that may affect atherogenesis, has been demonstrated in patients with type I diabetes mellitus receiving continuous subcutaneous insulin infusions [3]. While most studies demonstrate that physical training decreases insulin requirements in patients with type I diabetes, little information is available about the effects of physical training on 24-hour plasma insulin or growth factor levels.

In summary, little is known about the effects of exercise and physical training on known cardiovascular risk factors in type I diabetes mellitus. Based on studies of normal individuals and patients with type II diabetes, it would seem reasonable to conclude that regular exercise might have some beneficial effect. This represents an interesting area for future work.

EXERCISE RECOMMENDATIONS FOR PATIENTS WITH TYPE I DIABETES MELLITUS

Children, adolescents, and young adults with uncomplicated diabetes in general need not restrict their physical activity, except insofar as it causes hypoglycemia or worsening of diabetes control. On the other hand, older patients and those with suspected complications who wish to engage in significant physical activity require a thorough evaluation. A history and physical examination in these individuals should be directed specifically at findings suggestive of (a) occult coronary artery disease; (b) significant microvascular disease, particularly proliferative retinopathy, in which case major limitations on exercise intensity may be required; (c) autonomic neuropathy, which may increase the risk of exercise-related hypotension and impaired aerobic exericse capacity; (d) sensory neuropathy, which increases the risk of musculoskeletal injury and damage to the feet; and (e) overall metabolic control, which will be a major determinant of the metabolic response. If metabolic control is inadequate, improved insulinization should be achieved prior to initiating the exercise program. As already noted, children and young adults without complications of diabetes can successfully engage in a wide variety of recreational sports and should be encouraged to do so with minimal regimentation or prior testing. However, in this case, education of patients, parents, coaches, and other supervisory personnel is of primary importance. We believe that all sedentary diabetic patients over the age of 40 or those who have had type I diabetes mellitus for 10 or more years require formal exercise testing. Such testing not only identifies patients with occult cardiovascular disease but may also serve as a basis for formulating exercise recommendations.

Specific Recommendations

TYPE. Aerobic exercise which involves repetitive submaximal contraction of major muscle groups, such as swimming, cycling and brisk

TABLE 5
Exercise Recommendations in Patients with Long-Standing Type I Diabetes

Type	Aerobic
Duration	20–40 minutes
Frequency	4–7 days/week
Intensity	50–60% $\dot{V}O_{2max}$
	BP < 200 mm Hg
Time of day	morning

walking, is usually recommended for patients with diabetes mellitus (Table 5). Recently it has been demonstrated that high-resistance anaerobic exercise also results in improved glucose disposal, at least in normal humans [56]. Nevertheless, since high-intensity training results in large increases in systolic blood pressure and may cause detrimental hemodynamic changes, it is not recommended for older patients and those with established vascular disease. In addition, strenuous calisthenics, and excessive bending, stretching, and squatting, which result in Valsalva-type maneuvers, should be discouraged in this group of patients. Highly competitive sports, such as racketball, basketball, and singles tennis should be avoided, and for patients with significant retinopathy, proper eye protection is essential if there is any risk of trauma, such as occurs in most racket sports.

WARM-UP AND WARM-DOWN. Exercise sessions should always begin with a warm-up period of 5–10 minutes, with mild stretching not involving Valsalva-type activities to decrease the chance of musculoskeletal injury. This should be followed by a 5- to 10-minute warm-down to decrease the risk of postexercise arrhythmias and speed recovery from fatigue.

DURATION. There are no studies regarding the optimal duration of exercise in patients with type I diabetes mellitus. However, studies on normal individuals suggest that exercise sessions of less than 20–30 minutes are of little utility. On the other hand, exercise of more than 30–40 minutes' duration is most commonly associated with hypoglycemia in patients with type I diabetes. It seems reasonable that an exercise session of about 30 minutes is ideal for most such individuals.

FREQUENCY. The optimal frequency of exercise regimens for patients with type I diabetes is not known. In relatively brittle type I diabetes, consistency in the timing and nature of exercise is extremely important so that an insulin regimen can be established. Such patients often do best when they exercise at the same approximate time every day of the week.

INTENSITY. Maehlum and Pruett have demonstrated in type I diabetics that there is little effect of exercise on glucose disposal when the relative exercise intensity is much below 30–50% of maximal [52]. At higher intensities, effects of exercise on subsequent glucose disposal are roughly proportional to the total work performed (i.e., time × intensity). The increment in systolic blood pressure is roughly proportional to the relative exercise intensity [57], and it therefore seems reasonable to recommend for older patients and those with established vascular disease that exercise should be performed at around 50–60% of the $\dot{V}o_2$max. Tables of maximal heart rate used to estimate relative exercise intensity in normal people need to be used with caution in patients with long-standing type I diabetes mellitus, as autonomic neuropathy will result in a significant decrease in both $\dot{V}o_2$max and maximal heart rate.

The blood pressure response to exercise in diabetic patients with vascular disease has not been adequately studied. It is probably prudent to limit exercise intensity to prevent systolic pressure from exceeding 180–200 mm Hg for prolonged periods in patients with established vascular disease. The relative exercise intensity that results in such a rise in systolic pressure will vary considerably from individual to individual. The blood pressure response in such patients needs to be determined during initial exercise testing and probably should be confirmed during a typical exercise session. Proof that limiting the rise in systolic pressure during regular bouts of exercise will result in fewer vascular complications is not yet available.

TIME OF DAY. Because of the relatively transient effects of exercise on glucose disposal, it is likely that exercise done in the early morning prior to breakfast will have the greatest impact on glycemic excursions throughout the day. Patients with a tendency to develop hypoglycemia following exercise often do better when exercise is performed in the morning, at which time postexercise hypoglycemic effects appear to be less prominent [68]. Exercise in the evening is generally a poor strategy for such patients, as this is when hypoglycemic effects are most pronounced and delayed hypoglycemia may occur during periods of sleep.

CONCLUSION

The use of exercise therapy in improving overall glycemic control remains controversial. While a subgroup of patients with type I diabetes mellitus can probably achieve improved control with lower insulin requirements, in many cases exercise therapy will result in either no improvement or a deterioration of metabolic control. In addition, exercise therapy is associated with significant risks, including hypoglycemia and, possibly, worsening of vascular complications. In all cases, education and proper supervision are essential for safe and effective exercise regimens. Often the physician's primary role is helping the patient to enjoy a reasonable amount of recreational work activity with minimal side effects. More effective use of exercise to improve glycemic control will depend upon a better understanding of the control of glucose homeostasis and the etiology of vascular disease in type I diabetes. Nevertheless, most patients with type I diabetes mellitus who do not have major vascular complications can perform mild to moderate recreational and work-related physical activity with proper education and precautions. This may result in improved self-image, in a better overall quality of life, and possibly in a decreased risk for some forms of vascular disease.

REFERENCES

1. Ahlborg, G., and P. Felig. Lactate and glucose exchange across the forearm, legs and splanchnic bed during and after prolonged leg exercise. *J. Clin. Invest.* 69:45–54, 1982.
2. Akerblom, H.K., T. Koivukanges, and J. Ilkka. Experience from a winter camp for teenage diabetics. *Acta Paediatr. Scand.* 283(suppl):50–52, 1979.
3. Ameil, S.A., R.S. Sherwin, R.L. Hintz, J.M. Gertner, C.M. Press, and W.V. Tamborlane. Effect of diabetes and its control on insulin like growth factors in young subjects with type I diabetes. *Diabetes* 33:1175–1179, 1984.
4. Bergenstal, R.M., J. Dupre, P.M. Lawson, R.A. Rizza, and A.H. Rubenstein. Observations on C-peptide and free insulin in the blood during continuous subcutaneous insulin infusion and conventional insulin therapy. *Diabetes* 34(suppl 3):31–36, 1985.
5. Berger, M., P. Berchtold, H.J. Cupper, H. Drost, H.K. Kley, W.A. Muller, W. Wiegelmann, H. Zimmerman-Telschow, F.A. Gries, H.L. Kruskemper, and H. Zimmerman. Metabolic and hormonal effects of muscular exercise on juvenile type diabetes. *Diabetologia* 13:355–365, 1977.
6. Berger, M., S. Hagg, and N.B. Ruderman. Glucose metabolism in perfused skeletal muscle. Interaction of exercise on glucose uptake. *Biochem. J.* 146:231–238, 1975.
7. Bergstrom, J., and E. Hultman. Muscle glycogen synthesis after exercise: An enhancing factor localized to the muscle cells. *Nature* 210:309–310, 1966.
8. Berregard, B.S., and J.T. Shepherd. Regulation of the circulation during exercise in man. *Physiol. Rev.* 47:178–213, 1967.
9. Bjorkman, O., P. Felig, L. Hagenfeldt, and J. Wahren. Influence of hypoglucagonemia on splanchnic glucose output during leg exercise in man. *Clin. Physiol.* 1:43–57, 1981.
10. Bolli, G., P. DeFeo, P. Compagnucci, M.G. Cartechini, G. Angeletti, F. Santeusano, and P. Brunetti. Important role of adrenergic mechanism in acute glucose counterregulation following insulin-induced hypoglycemia in type I diabetes. *Diabetes* 31:641–647, 1982.
11. Bonen, A., N.J. Tal, P. Glune, and R.L. Kirby. Effects of exercise on insulin binding to human muscle. *Am. J. Physiol.* 248:E403–E408, 1985.
12. Caron, D., P. Poussier, E.B. Marliss, and B. Ziman. Effects of postprandial exercise on meal related glucose intolerance in insulin dependent diabetic individuals. *Diab. Care* 5:364–369, 1982.
13. Chisholm, D.J., A.B. Jenkins, D.E. James, and E.W. Kraegen. Effect of hyperinsulinemia on glucose homeostasis during moderate exercise in man. *Diabetes* 31:603–608, 1982.
14. Colwell, J.A. Effects of exercise on platelet function, coagulation, and fibrinolysis. *Diab./Metab. Rev.* 1:501–512, 1986.
15. Colwell, J.A. and P.J. Halushka. Platelet function in diabetes mellitus. *J. Haematol.* 44:521–526, 1980.
16. Costill, D.L., P. Cleary, W.J. Fink, C. Foster, J.L. Ivy, and F. Witzmann. Training adaptations in skeletal muscle of juvenile diabetes. *Diabetes* 28:818–822, 1979.
17. Dall'aglio, E., F. Chang, H. Chang, J. Stern, and G. Reaven. Effect of exercise and diet on triglyceride metabolism in rats with moderate insulin deficiency. *Diabetes* 32:46–50, 1983.

18. DeFeo, P., G. Bolli, G. Perriello, S. deCosmo, P. Compagnucci, G. Angeletti, F. Santeusanio, J. Gerich, M. Motolese, and P. Brunetti. The adrenergic contribution to glucose counterregulation in type I diabetes mellitus. Dependency on A-cell function and mediation through beta-adrenergic receptors. *Diabetes* 32:887–893, 1983.

19. DeFronzo, R.A., E. Ferrannini, Y. Sato, P. Felig, and J. Wahren. Synergistic interaction between exercise and insulin on peripheral glucose uptake. *J. Clin. Invest.* 68:1468–1474, 1981.

20. Devlin, J.T., M. Hirshman, E.D. Horton, and E.S. Horton. Enhanced peripheral and splanchnic insulin sensitivity in NIDDM men after a single bout of exercise. *Diabetes* 36:434–439, 1987.

21. Ducimetiere, P., L. Eschwege, J.L. Papoz, J.L. Richard, J.R. Claude, and G. Rosselin. Relationship of plasma insulin levels to the incidence of myocardial infarction and coronary heart disease mortality in a middle-aged population. *Diabetologia* 19:205–210, 1980.

22. Felig, P., A. Cherif, A. Minagawa, and J. Wahren. Hypoglycemia during prolonged exercise on normal man. *N. Engl. J. Med.* 306:895–900, 1982.

23. Felig, P., and J. Wahren. Influence of endogenous insulin secretion on splanchnic glucose and amino acid metabolism in man. *J. Clin. Invest.* 50:1702–1711, 1971.

24. Felig, P., J. Wahren, R. Hendler, and G. Ahlberg. Plasma glucagon levels in exercising man. *N. Engl. J. Med.* 287:184–185, 1972.

25. Galbo, H., N.J. Christensen, and J.J. Holst. Catecholamines and pancreatic hormones during autonomic blockade in exercising man. *Acta Physiol. Scand.* 101:428–437, 1977.

26. Galbo, H., N.J. Christensen, and J.J. Holst. Glucose-induced decrease in glucagon and epinephrine responses to exercise in man. *J. Appl. Physiol.* 42:525–530, 1977.

27. Galbo, H., J.J. Holst, and N.J. Christensen. Glucagon and plasma catecholamine responses to graded and prolonged exercise in man. *J. Appl. Physiol.* 38:70–76, 1975.

28. Galbo, H., J.J. Holst, N.J. Christensen, and J. Hilsted. Glucagon and plasma catecholamines during β-receptor blockade in exercising man. *J. Appl. Physiol.* 40:855–863, 1976.

29. Garetto, L.P., E.A. Richter, M.N. Goodman, and N.B. Ruderman. Enhanced muscle glucose metabolism after exercise in the rat. The two phases. *Am. J. Physiol.* 246:E471–E475, 1984.

30. Hagan, R.D., J.F. Marks, and P.A. Warren. Physiologic responses of juvenile onset diabetic boys to muscular work. *Diabetes* 28:1114–1119, 1979.

31. Hagenfeldt, L. Metabolism of free fatty acids and ketone bodies during exercise in normal and diabetic man. *Diabetes* 28(suppl 1):66–70, 1979.

32. Hilsted, J., H. Galbo, and N.J. Christensen. Impaired response of catecholamines, growth hormone, and cortisol to graded exercise in diabetic autonomic neuropathy. *Diabetes* 29:257–262, 1980.

33. Hoelzer, D.R., G.P. Dalsky, W.E. Clutter, S.D. Shah, J.O. Holloszy, and P.E. Cryer. Glucoregulation during exercise. *J. Clin Invest.* 77:212–221, 1986.

34. Holm, G., and G. Stromblad. Type I diabetes and physical exercise. *Acta Med. Scand.* 671(suppl):95–96, 1983.

35. Howard, B. Lipoprotein metabolism in diabetes mellitus. *J. Lipid Res.* 28:619–622, 1987.

36. Issekutz, B. The role of hypoinsulinemia in exercise metabolism. *Diabetes* 29:629–635, 1980.

37. Issekutz, B., and M. Vranic. Role of glucagon in regulation of glucose produced in exercising dogs. *Am. J. Physiol.* 238:E13–E20, 1980.

38. Joslin, E.P. The treatment of diabetes mellitus. In E.P. Joslin, H.F. Root, P. Shite, and A. Marble (eds.). *Treatment of Diabetes Mellitus*. Philadelphia: Lea & Febiger, 1959, pp. 243–300.

39. Katsch, G. Die arbeitstherapie und zuckerkranken. *Erg. Physikal Diet Ther.* 1:1–36, 1939.

40. Kemmer, F.W., P. Berchtold, M. Berger, A. Starke, H.J. Cuppers, F.A. Gries, and H. Zimmerman. Exercise induced fall of blood glucose in insulin-treated diabetes unrelated to alterations of insulin mobilization. *Diabetes* 28:1131–1137, 1979.
41. Koch, G., I.W. Franz, A. Gubba, and F.W. Lohman. β-adrenoceptor blockade and physical activity—cardiovascular and metabolic aspects. *Acta Med. Scand.* 214 (suppl 672):55–62, 1983.
42. Koivisto, V.A., and P. Felig. Effect of leg exercise on insulin absorption in diabetic patients. *N. Engl. J. Med.* 298:79–83, 1978.
43. Koivisto, V.A., V.R. Soman, and P. Felig. Effects of acute exercise on insulin binding to monocytes in obesity. *Metab. Clin. Exp.* 29:168–172, 1980.
44. Koivisto, V.A., and H. Yki-Jarvinen. Influence of prolonged exercise on insulin binding and glucose transport in adipocytes. *Diabetes* 34 (suppl I):26A, 1985.
45. Kostis, J., J. Baughman, and P. Kuo. Association of recurrent myocardial infarction with hemostatic factors. A prospective study. *Chest* 81:571–574, 1982.
46. Krolewski, A.S., E.J. Kosinski, J.H. Warren, O.S. Leland, E.J. Busick, A.C. Asmal, L.I. Rand, A.R. Christlieb, R.F. Bradley, and C.R. Kahn. Magnitude and determinants of coronary artery disease in insulin-dependent diabetes. *Am. J. Cardiol.* 59:750–755, 1987.
47. Krzentowski, G., F. Pirnay, N. Pallikarakis, A.S. Luycky, M. Lacroix, F. Mosora, and P.J. Lefebvre. Glucose utilization during exercise in normal and diabetic subjects. *Diabetes* 30:983–989, 1981.
48. Landt, K.W., B.N. Campaign, F.W. James, and M.A. Sperling. Effects of exercise training on insulin sensitivity in adolescents with type I diabetes. *Diabetes Care* 8:461–465, 1985.
49. LeBlanc, J., A. Nadeau, D. Richard, and A. Tremblay. Studies on the sparing effect of exercise on insulin requirements in human subjects. *Metabolism* 30:1119–1124, 1981.
50. Lopez, S., R. Ural, L. Balant, A. Lopez, R. Vial, and L. Balart. Effect of exercise and physical fitness on serum lipids. *Atherosclerosis* 20:1–9, 1974.
51. MacDougall, J.D., G.R. Ward, D.G. Sale, and J.R. Sutton. Muscle glycogen repletion after high-intensity intermittent exercise. *J. Appl. Physiol.* 42:129–132, 1977.
52. Maehlum S., and E.D.R. Pruett. Muscular exercise and metabolism in male juvenile diabetics. Glucose tolerance after exercise. *Scand. J. Clin. Lab. Invest.* 32:149–153, 1973.
53. Marble, A. Insulin in the treatment of diabetes. In A. Marble, P. White, R. Bradley, L. Krall (eds.). *Joslin's Diabetes Mellitus*. Philadelphia: Lea & Febiger, 1971, p. 291.
54. Martin, F.I.R., and J.L. Hopper. Relationship of acute insulin sensitivity to the progression of vascular disease in long term type I (insulin-dependent) diabetes mellitus. *Diabetologia* 30:149–153, 1987.
55. Martin, M.J., D.C. Robbins, R. Bergenstal, B. LaGrange, A.H. Rubenstein. Absence of exercise-induced hypoglycemia in type I diabetic patients during maintenance of normoglycemia by short-term-open loop infusion. *Diabetologia* 23:337–342, 1982.
56. Miller, W.J., W.M. Sherman, and J.L. Ivy. Effect of strength training on glucose tolerance and post-glucose insulin response. *Med. Sci. Sports Exerc.* 16:539–543, 1984.
57. Mogensen, C.E., C.K. Christensen, and E. Vittinghus. The stages in diabetic renal disease. *Diabetes* 32(suppl 2):64–78, 1983.
58. Pedersen, O., H. Beck-Nielsen, and L. Heding. Increased insulin receptors after exercise in patients with insulin-dependent diabetes mellitus. *N. Engl. J. Med.* 302:886–892, 1980.
59. Ploug, T., H. Galbo, J. Vinten, M. Jorgensen, and E.A. Richter. Kinetics of glucose transport in rat muscle: Effects of insulin and contraction. *Am. J. Physiol.* 16:E12–E20, 1987.
60. Poussier, P., B. Ziman, E.B. Marliss, A.M. Albisser, K. Perlman, and D. Caron. Open-loop intravenous insulin waveforms for postprandial exercise in type I diabetes. *Diabetes Care* 6:129–134, 1983.

61. Pruett, E.D., and S. Oseid. Effect of exercise on the glucose and insulin response to glucose infusion. *Scand. J. Clin. Lab. Invest.* 26:277–285, 1970.
62. Pyorala, K. Relationship of glucose tolerance and plasma insulin to the incidence of coronary heart disease, results from two population studies in Finland. *Diabetes Care* 2:131–141, 1979.
63. Richter, E.A., H. Galbo, J.J. Holst, and B. Sonne. Significance of glucagon for insulin secretion and hepatic glycogenolysis during exercise in rats. *Horm. Metab. Res.* 13:323–326, 1981.
64. Richter, E.A., L.P. Garetto, M.N. Goodman, and N.B. Ruderman. Enhanced muscle glucose metabolism after exercise: Modulation by local factors. *Am. J. Physiol.* 246:E476–E482, 1984.
65. Roch-Norlund, A.E. Muscle glycogen synthetase in patients with diabetes mellitus. Basal values effects of glycogen depletion by exercise, and effect of treatment. *Scand. J. Clin. Lab. Invest.* 29:237–242, 1972.
66. Roch-Norlund, A.E., J. Berstrom, H. Castenfors, and E. Haltman. Muscle glycogen in patients with diabetes mellitus. Glycogen content before and after treatment and the effects of insulin. *Acta Med. Scand.* 187:445–453, 1970.
67. Rollo, J. *Cases of Diabetes Mellitus with the Results of the Trials of Certain Acids and Other Substances in the Cure of the Lues Venerea*, 2nd ed. London: 1798.
68. Ruegener, J.J., R.W. Squires, H.M. Marsh, and J.M. Miles. Diurnal differences in the glycemic response to exercise in insulin-dependent patients on intensive insulin therapy. *Diabetes* 36(suppl 1):4A, 1987.
69. Rytter, L., S. Troelsen, and B.N. Henning. Prevalence and mortality of acute myocardial infarction in patients with diabetes. *Diabetes Care* 8:230–234, 1985.
70. Saltin, B., M. Houston, E. Nygaard, T. Graham, and J. Wahren. Muscle fiber characteristics in healthy man and patients with juvenile diabetes. *Diabetes* 28(suppl 1):93–99, 1979.
71. Schiffrin A., S. Parikh, E.B. Marliss, and M.A. Desrosiers. Metabolic responses to fasting exercise in adolescent insulin-dependent diabetic subjects treated with continuous subcutaneous insulin infusion and intensive conventional therapy. *Diabetes Care* 7:255–260, 1984.
72. Schneider, S.H., H. Kim, N.B. Ruderman, A.K. Khachadurian, L.F. Amorosa, and P. Saidi. Effects of exercise and physical training on certain coagulation parameters in diabetes. *Clin. Res.* 30:403A, 1982.
73. Schneider, S.H., H.C. Kim, N.B. Ruderman, and A.K. Khachadurian. Impaired fibrinolytic responses to exercise in type 2 diabetes: Effects of exercise and physical training. *Metabolism* (submitted).
74. Schneider, S.H., A. Vitug, M.A.L. Mertz, R. Ananthakrishnan, A. Apelian, and A.K. Khachadurian. Abnormal hormonal response to prolonged exercise in type I diabetes. *Diabetes* 36(suppl I):16A, 1987. (Abstract)
75. Schwandt, P. Very low density lipoproteins in type II diabetes mellitus and risk of atherosclerosis. *Horm. Metab. Res.* 15(suppl):80–83, 1985.
76. Shamoon, H., R. Hendler, and R.S. Sherwin. Altered response to cortisone, epinephrine and glucagon in insulin infused juvenile onset diabetes. *Diabetes* 29:284–291, 1980.
77. Simonson, D.C., V. Koivisto, R.S. Sherwin, E. Ferranini, R. Hendler, A. Juhlin-Dannfelt, and R.A. DeFronzo. Adrenergic blockade alters glucose kinetics during exercise in insulin-dependent diabetes. *J. Clin. Invest.* 73:1648–1658, 1984.
78. Sotsky, M., S. Shilo, and H. Shamoon. Regulation of epinephrine and glucagon responses to exercise and hypoglycemia in non-diabetic and type I diabetic subjects. *Diabetes* 36(suppl I):11A, 1980. (Abstract)
79. Stout, R.W. Overview of the association between insulin and atherosclerosis. *Metabolism* 34(suppl 1):7–12, 1985.
80. Sushruta, S.C.S. *Vaidya Jadavaji Trikamji Acharia.* Bombay: Nirnyar Sagar Press, 1938, pp. 11–13.

81. Uusitupa, M., O. Siitohen, M. Harkonen, A. Gordin, A. Aro, K. Hersio, G. Johansson, T. Koronen, and R. Rauramaa. Metabolic and hormonal response to physical exercise during β₁ selective and non-selective β-blockade. *Horm. Metab. Res.* 14:583–589, 1982.

82. Vinten, J., P.L. Norgaard, B. Sonne, and H. Galbo. Effect of physical training on glucose transporters in fat cell fractions. *Biochem. Biophys. Acta* 841:223–227, 1985.

83. Vranic, M., C. Gauthier, D. Bilinski, D. Wasserman, K. El Tayeb, G. Hetenyi, and H.L.A. Lickley. Catecholamine responses and their interaction with other glucoregulatory hormones. *Am. J. Physiol.* 247:E145–E156, 1984.

84. Wahren, J. Glucose turnover during exercise in healthy man and in patients with diabetes mellitus. *Diabetes* 28(suppl 1):82–88, 1979.

85. Wahren J., P. Felig, G. Ahlborg, and L. Jorfeldt. Glucose metabolism during leg exercise in man. *J. Clin. Invest.* 50:2715–2725, 1971.

86. Wahren, J., Y. Sato, J. Ostman, L. Hagenfeldt, and P. Felig. Turnover and splanchnic metabolism of free fatty acids and ketones in insulin dependent diabetes at rest and in response to exercise. *J. Clin. Invest.* 73:1367–1376, 1984.

87. Wallberg-Henriksson, H., R. Gunnarsson, J. Henriksson, R. deFronzo, P. Felig, J. Ostman, and J. Wahren. Increased peripheral insulin sensitivity and muscle mitochondrial enzymes but unchanged blood glucose control in type I diabetics after physical training. *Diabetes* 31:1044–1050, 1982.

88. Wallberg-Henriksson, H., R. Gunnarsson, J. Henriksson, J. Ostman, and J. Wahren. Influence of physical training on formation of muscle capillaries in type I diabetes. *Diabetes* 33:851–857, 1984.

89. Wallberg-Henriksson, H., and J.O. Holloszy. Contractive activity increases glucose uptake by muscle in severely diabetic rats. *J. Appl. Physiol.* 57:1045–1049, 1984.

90. Wardzala, L.J., E.D. Horton, M. Crettaz, B. Jeanrenaud, and E.S. Horton. Physical training of lean and genetically obese Zuker rats. Am. J. Physiol. 243:E418–E426, 1982.

91. Wasserman, D.H., H. Lavin, A. Lickley, and M. Vranic. Interactions between glucagon and other counterregulatory hormones during normoglycemic and hypoglycemic exercise in dogs. *J. Clin. Invest.* 74:1404–1413, 1984.

92. Welborn, T.A., and K. Wearne. Coronary heart disease incidence and cardiovascular mortality in Busselton with reference to glucose and insulin concentrations. *Diabetes Care* 2:154–160, 1979.

93. Wilhelmsen, L., K. Suardsudd, K. Korsan-Bengtsen, B. Lawson, L. Welin, and G. Tibblin. Fibrinogen as a risk factor for stroke and myocardial infarction. *N. Engl. J. Med.* 311:501–505, 1984.

94. Wood, F., and W. Haskell. The effect of exercise on plasma high density lipoproteins. *Lipids* 14:417–427, 1979.

95. Yki-Jarvinen, H., and V.A. Koivisto. Effects of body composition on insulin sensitivity. *Diabetes* 32:965–969, 1983.

96. Zinman, B., F.T. Murray, M. Vranic, A.M. Albisser, B.S. Liebel, P.A. McClean, and E.P. Marliss. Glucoregulation during moderate exeircse in insulin treated diabetics. *J. Clin. Endocrinol. Metab.* 45:641–652, 1977.

97. Zinman, B., M. Vranic, A.M. Albisser, B.S. Leibel, and E.B. Marliss. The role of insulin in the metabolic response to exercise in diabetic man. *Diabetes* 28(suppl 1):76–81, 1979.

98. Zinman, B., S. Zunica-Guajarno, and D. Kelly. Comparison of the acute and long-term effects of exercise on glucose control in type I long-term effects of exercise on glucose control in type I diabetes. *Diabetes Care* 7:515–519, 1984.

10
Exercise in End-Stage Renal Disease

PATRICIA L. PAINTER, Ph.D.

INTRODUCTION

The success of rehabilitative programs employing exercise as a therapeutic intervention in cardiac disease has led to increasing interest in exercise training in other patient populations. Many patients with end-stage renal disease (ESRD) suffer from muscle weakness, fatigue, bone disease, cardiovascular disease, and multiple psychosocial problems. Advances in medical technology such as dialysis and transplantation have been effective in maintaining life. Despite this, attention has only recently been directed at the functional status and rehabilitation of this patient group.

This chapter is a review of the role of exercise in ESRD. A discussion of the basic pathophysiology and treatment of the disease is included to orient exercise professionals to the multitude and complexity of the problems associated with renal failure. The goal of this chapter is to stimulate interest in developing research and appropriate rehabilitation programs for these patients in order to enhance their functional ability and possibly their quality of life.

CHRONIC RENAL FAILURE

Chronic renal failure (CRF) results from structural renal damage and progressively diminished renal function. Once initiated, the disease generally progresses to ESRD, requiring some form of renal replacement therapy such as dialysis or transplantation. The incidence of ESRD in the United States is approximately 1 in 10,000 per year. The average age of dialysis patients is 48 years, with 46% of patients over the age of 55 [110]. The initial damage to the kidney may be the result of hypertension, diabetes mellitus, autoimmune processes, chronic infection, congenital abnormalities, or unknown causes. The rate of progression varies; however, the biochemical, endocrine, and metabolic disorders associated with decreased renal function are similar regardless of the initial cause of dysfunction. [6].

A damaged kidney initially responds with higher filtration and excretion rates per nephron, thereby masking symptoms until only 10–15%

TABLE 1

*Some of the Compounds Implicated in the Toxicity of Uremia**

Organic Metabolites
Urea
Creatinine
Guanidine compounds
Aliphatic amines
Phenols and aromatic amines
Uric acid
Oxalic acid
Myoinositol
2,3-Butylene glycol
Peptides and protein degradation products
Middle molecules
Amino acids
β_2-Microglobulin
Enzymes
Renin
Ribonuclease
Lysozyme
Hormones
Parathyroid hormone
Glucagon
Growth hormone
Calcitonin
"Natriuretic hormone"

*From Blachley J.D., and J.P. Knochel. The biochemistry of uremia. In B.M. Brenner and J.H. Stein (eds). *Contemporary Issues in Nephrology: Chronic Renal Failure.* New York: Churchill Livingstone, 1981. Reprinted by permission.

of renal function remains [61]. Progressive renal failure results in the inability to excrete substances, resulting in uremic syndrome, which is characterized by fatigue, nausea, malaise, anorexia, and subtle neurologic symptoms. Uremia also secondarily impairs the function of other metabolic and organ systems [101]. The multisystemic nature and the psychosocial implications of the disease and treatment affect the functional status of the patients, as well as the rehabilitation potential.

BIOCHEMICAL AND REGULATORY ABNORMALITIES IN UREMIA

The pathophysiology of ESRD results from the loss of both excretory and regulatory function of the kidney. The accumulation in the blood of substances normally excreted by the kidney is responsible for many complications associated with renal failure. Blood urea nitrogen (BUN) and creatinine are two of these substances, and are the primary clinical markers for assessing the level of kidney function and the adequacy of treatment. Many other substances have been implicated in the toxicity of uremia. A list of these compounds is presented in Table 1. Theories on the mechanisms of these "toxins" include (a) modulation of enzyme activities that affect the rate of glycoloysis and respiration, resulting ultimately in impaired energy production, and (b) inhibition of the Na/K-ATPase system, which may result in altered active transport across cell membranes and altered membrane potentials [6, 101].

Loss of the regulatory function of the kidney results in the inability to regulate extracellular volume and electrolyte concentration, which adversely affects cellular function [6, 28]. Other regulatory malfunctions include (a) impaired generation of ammonia and hydrogen ion excretion, resulting in metabolic acidosis, and (b) decreased erythropoietin production, which is the primary cause of anemia in ESRD patients [2, 6, 35].

Various normal substances may be excessively produced or inappropriately regulated in response to the chemical derangements of renal failure. Parathyroid hormone (PTH) may be the most important of these [6]. PTH is produced in excess secondary to hyperphosphatemia, reduced conversion of vitamin D to its most active forms, and malabsorption and impaired release of calcium ions from bone. The attempt to maintain an adequate circulating calcium ion concentration in the face of hypocalcemia results in hyperparathyroidism and renal osteodystrophy [6, 105].

Endocrine Abnormalities

Numerous endocrine metabolic disorders are associated with uremia. Many of these abnormalities are the result of delayed degradation and accumulation of peptide hormones that affect feedback control mechanisms, abnormal receptor function and/or number, and ultimately end-organ responses [28]. This chapter will review only endocrine disorders that may be associated with exercise responses and/or substrate utilization in uremic patients. For further information, readers are referred to other comprehensive reviews on the endocrine status of uremia [28].

Carbohydrate Metabolism

Over 50% of nondiabetic uremic patients exhibit glucose intolerance, characterized by normal fasting blood sugar levels with hyperinsulinemia and a blunted decline in the plasma glucose concentration after an oral or infused glucose challenge. Possible mechanisms that contribute to the glucose intolerance include (a) insulin resistance, (b) impaired insulin secretion, (c) enhanced gluconeogenesis, (d) reduced degradation of insulin, and (e) reduced degradation of glucagon [21, 23].

Reduced insulin sensitivity in uremic patients is suggested by the observations of elevated fasting insulin levels in the presence of normal fasting glucose values and a normal early insulin response to a glucose challenge, with a significant increase in the late insulin response. Decreased insulin sensitivity is the primary factor in the glucose intolerance of uremia, however; some patients exhibit impaired secretion of insulin from the beta cell [22].

Beta cell secretion of insulin should increase secondary to tissue resistance to insulin and the resultant increased glucose levels, which would contribute to hyperinsulinemia. In some patients, however, uremia may directly inhibit insulin secretion from the beta cell, which further impairs glucose tolerance [23]. Decreased insulin sensitivity and the resulting hyperglycemia may have significant clinical implications in uremic patients, including hypertriglyceridemia and impaired amino acid and protein metabolism. Hyperinsulinemia is known to increase hepatic triglyceride synthesis. Insulin is a primary regulator of lipoprotein lipase. If the resistance to insulin affects the activity of the lipase enzyme, very-low-density lipoprotein (VLDL) triglyceride removal will be affected [22, 23].

Insulin is known to promote net muscle uptake of branched chain amino acids. If insulin resistance affects amino acid transport, an intracellular amino acid deficiency could result. This may account for the muscle wasting that is common in uremic patients [23].

Renal failure results in a significant decrease in glucagon degradation and hyperglucagonemia [60]. There is enhanced hepatic sensitivity to glucagon in uremia, which results in augmented gluconeogenesis from alanine. This could also contribute to the muscle wasting and negative nitrogen balance observed in uremia, due to increased flow of protein nitrogen from the peripheral tissues to the liver [60].

Decreased activity of several key glycolytic enzymes has been reported and may also contribute to abnormal carbohydrate metabolism. Pyruvate kinase, glucose-6-phosphate dehydrogenase, phosphofructokinase, phosphorylase, and lactate dehydrogenase activities have been shown to be reduced in uremic subjects [80, 84].

Lipid Metabolism
Sixty percent of uremic patients have hyperlipidemia, which is characterized by hypertriglyceridemia and normal (or low) cholesterol concentrations. Of the transport lipoproteins, VLDL is elevated, with low high-density lipoprotein (HDL) concentrations and normal low-density lipoprotein (LDL), which can be classified as a type IV hyperlipidemic phenotype [9, 16]. This pattern is equally prevalent in dialysis patients (peritoneal or hemodialysis), as well as in predialysis patients. Following successful renal transplantation, the lipid profile becomes hypercholesterolemic, characterized as lipoprotein phenotypes IIa and IIb, with elevated levels of LDL particles [16]. The hypertriglyceridemia is primarily due to decreased removal of VLDL particles. Defective VLDL removal has been shown in triglyceride turnover studies regardless of lipid levels or the type of dialysis [14].

Abnormalities in the apoprotein composition of lipoproteins have been reported in uremic patients with type IV hyperlipidemia—specifically, a reduction in apoprotein CII and an increase in the apoprotein E content of VLDL and HDL [25, 98]. The impaired lipolytic activity of uremic plasma and the accumulation of VLDL particles may be a result of decreased concentration of the CII activation of peripheral lipoprotein lipase [98]. Others have reported decreased activities of peripheral and hepatic triglyceride lipase [83]. Adipose tissue lipase is also depressed in uremic patients with type IV hyperlipoproteinemia [40]. The decrease in lipase activity may be due to accumulation of circulating inhibitors [25].

Several iatrogenic interventions may also contribute to the hypertriglyceridemia. These include (a) androgens administered for the treatment of anemia, (b) β-blockers for hypertension, (c) depletion of carnitine by the hemodialysis procedure, (d) exposure to high carbohydrate loads in the dialysate used for peritoneal dialysis, and (e) the use of acetate dialysate. Intermittent heparin injections necessary for anticoagulation in the dialysis treatment may contribute to the "exhaustion" of tissue lipoprotein lipases, thus affecting the removal of the VLDL, and may aggravate the hyperlipidemic tendency [28].

Following transplantation, the LDL fraction increases and the VLDL concentration decreases (type II) [16]. Studies in renal transplant recipients are difficult to interpret due to the variations in corticosteroid dosage, which is widely accepted as the main pathogenic factor responsible for the lipid abnormalities observed [28]. Little information exists on lipase activity following transplantation.

TREATMENT

Treatment of CRF consists of medical management until creatinine clearance is <5 ml/min, at which time more aggressive therapy is required. Conservative management is directed at minimizing the consequences of accumulated nitrogenous waste products normally excreted by the kidneys. Dietary measures play a primary role in the initial management of CRF, with protein restriction to decrease the symptoms of uremia, as well as possibly delaying the progression of the disease.

Dietary sodium intake is regulated carefully in patients with renal damage. These patients excrete sodium at a relatively fixed rate and are unable to regulate excretion over a wide range of intake [82]. Thus, severe restriction can lead to volume depletion, and excess sodium may result in edema and/or heart failure. Water restriction is indicated with hyponatremia and when there is an excess of total body sodium.

Dietary protein is restricted in pre–end-stage patients in order to decrease (a) hydrogen ion production, (b) potassium intake, (c) phosphorus intake, and (d) the nitrogen load on the kidney and to (e) decrease the source of preformed creatine, which is converted to creatinine. Limitation of the nitrogenous wastes typically reduces the symptoms of uremia [39].

Net catabolism exists in CRF, as indicated by significant loss of amino acids from the muscles. Levels of albumin, transferrin, and certain complement factors are used to assess the catabolic status of the patient. Amino acid supplements are given, which may improve the levels of these proteins and the nutritional status of the patient [39, 82]. Keto acids that are transaminated to their respective amino acids are also given to decrease the nitrogen load, and are often effective in maintaining the nitrogen balance [82].

Control of renal osteodystrophy is achieved by (a) dietary phosphate restriction and (b) administration of phosphate binders that prevent gastrointestinal absorption. Calcium intake is increased primarily by supplementation and by administration of vitamin D_3 analogues [82]. Control of hypertension is essential in the earlier phases of renal disease in order to delay the progression of the disease [113].

Progressive deterioration of renal function will ultimately require the initiation of some form of renal replacement therapy for maintenance of life. Treatment options include in-center hemodialysis, home hemodialysis, peritoneal dialysis, and transplantation. The decision as to when to initiate dialysis is determined by many factors, including cardiovascular status, neuropathy, electrolyte elevation (especially of potassium) that cannot be controlled with conservative measures, chronic fluid overload, severe and irreversible oliguria or anuria, significant uremic symptoms, and excessively abnormal laboratory values (usually creatinine >8–12 mg/dl, BUN >100–120 mg/dl) and creatinine clearance (<5 ml/min). Factors such as age and economic status have not been considered in the initiation of dialysis treatment in the United States since the passage of the ESRD act in 1972, which requires Medicare funding for all eligible patients with diagnosed ESRD [73]. Table 2 shows some of the signs and symptoms of uremia and the effect of dialysis on those problems [101].

Hemodialysis

Hemodialysis (HD) is the most common form of therapy, with approximately 79% of all patients treated in a center or at home. HD is a process of ultrafiltration (fluid removal) and clearance of excess toxic solutes from the blood. It necessitates vascular access by way of an arteriovenous fistula constructed by a prosthetic conduit or by utilizing native vessels [12, 73].

Two needles are placed in the fistula—one for removal and one for return of blood. The blood is drawn from the body to the dialyzer by

TABLE 2
Signs and Symptoms of Uremia

System	Corrected by Dialysis	Not Corrected by Dialysis
Musculoskeletal		Renal osteodystrophy Metastatic calcifications Decreased growth Muscle weakness
Neurological	Encephalopathy Peripheral neuropathy (early)	Peripheral neuropathy (late)
Cardiopulmonary	Volume-dependent hypertension Pericarditis Pleuritis Pulmonary edema Congestive failure Heart murmurs	Hyperreninemic hypertension Accelerated atherogenesis Calcifications
Hematologic	Platelet and white cell dysfunction	Anemia
Electrolytes	Hyperkalemia Hyponatremia	Hyperphosphatemia Hypocalcemia Hyperuricemia Metabolic acidosis
Endocrine/metabolic	Carbohydrate intolerance Malnutrition Sexual dysfunction Amenorrhea	Hyperlipidemia Thyroid dysfunction Infertility (females) Hyperparathyroidism Vitamin D deficiency

the action of a blood pump at an average rate of 200–300 ml·min^{-1}. Blood returns from the dialyzer through a venous blood line. No more than 400 ml of blood is removed from the body at any time. Pressures are monitored in both the arterial and venous lines to set ultrafiltration rates and to detect clotting or obstruction in the blood lines or dialyzer. Sensors and filters are incorporated throughout the system to prevent air from entering the body [73].

The dialyzer is a chamber with a semipermeable membrane that separates blood and dialysate. Removal of substances from the blood to the dialysate is dependent upon a number of factors, including the characteristics of the membrane, the surface area of the membrane, transmembrane pressures, osmotic gradient, concentration gradients, blood flow, dialysate flow, and convection. Manipulation of the blood flow rate, dialysate flow rate, and number of hours of treatment can be used to remove more or less smaller molecular weight substances. New membranes are being developed that are designed to accommodate a greater blood flow rate and are biocompatible, which ultimately will provide more efficient and safer dialysis [73].

The dialysate is a solution composed of appropriate concentrations of sodium, potassium, chloride, magnesium, calcium, and buffer to develop ideal plasma constituents. The concentrates of some solutes in the dialysate may vary among patients according to their needs (e.g., decreased sodium is used to control total body sodium and hypertension). The potassium concentration is selected depending on the patient's dietary potassium intake and, to some extent, on residual renal function. The buffer capacity of the dialysate is provided by acetate or bicarbonate [73]. The use of bicarbonate dialysate may decrease some of the complications of the dialysis treatment, such as decreased arterial oxygen tension, cramping, and hypotension [24].

The prescription of dialysis depends on the quantity of fluid to be removed or gained and the required clearance of toxins. The duration of hemodialysis, type and size of the dialyzer, and blood flow are the most commonly altered parameters and are based on the degree of residual renal function, body size, dietary intake, and clinical status. A typical dialysis schedule is 3–4 hours thrice weekly [17]. The adequacy of dialysis is evaluated by monitoring at (a) biochemical parameters of azotemia, acidosis, and anemia and (b) clinical parameters such as energy levels, cardiac status, feeling of well-being, and appetite. Other approaches include urea kinetics and modeling.

Prior to each dialysis, the patient is evaluated for volume status by weighing, blood pressure measurement, and physical examination. Blood pressure is monitored and evaluated throughout the dialysis procedure to assess the progress of fluid removal [18]. Complications resulting from the dialysis procedure typically include hypotension, cramping due to electrolyte and fluid shifts, and anticoagulation problems. Fatigue following dialysis typically lasts for up to 12 hours [74].

Additional therapeutic measures include (a) anticoagulant therapy, which involves systemic heparinization to prevent clotting in the dialyzer during the treatment, [103] and (b) replacement therapy of blood, hormones, and other substances that may be removed by the dialysis process (specifically various water-soluble vitamins of particular molecular size, such as B-complex, vitamins, ascorbic acid, and folic acid) [32].

HD is relatively ineffective in lowering serum phosporus due to significant tissue binding of phosphate. Administration of aluminum hydroxide with food binds the dietary phosphate and decreases absorption.

Aluminum bone disease may result from long-term administration of these aluminum-containing phosphate binders. Hemodialysis may also not improve hypocalcemia, which requires the administration of calcium supplements and vitamin D preparations to prevent osteomalacia and secondary hyperparathyroidism [32, 105].

Anemia is a continuing problem in dialysis patients and is probably the primary cause of symptoms of fatigue and lethargy [2, 35]. Many patients receive regular transfusions. Oral and/or parenteral androgen therapy have been shown to increase erythropoeisis and are used in many patients [112]. Development of erythropoeitin through genetic engineering is a promising treatment for the problem of anemia and is currently being tested [29].

Peritoneal Dialysis

Approximately 14% of patients are treated with peritoneal dialysis. The peritoneal membranes are effective for ultrafiltration of fluids and clearance of toxic substances in the blood of uremic individuals. Peritoneal dialysis is accomplished by introducing a dialysis fluid into the peritoneal cavity via a permanent catheter placed in the abdominal wall. The fluid may be introduced either by a machine, which cycles fluid continuously over a 12-hour period, or manually by 2-liter bags, which are attached to tubing and emptied by gravity into the peritoneum. The latter process is called "continuous ambulatory peritoneal dialysis (CAPD)" and allows the patient to dialyze while ambulating. These patients exchange fluid every 4 hours, using sterile technique [86].

In peritoneal dialysis, ultrafiltration is primarily via an osmotic gradient. Maximal ultrafiltration is thus less efficient than HD, and there are fewer large pores in the peritoneal membranes; however, the increased time during which the blood is exposed to the dialysis fluid compensates for this inefficiency. Peritoneal dialysis allows continuous steady-state dialysis and avoids the rapid and often dramatic shifts in body fluids experienced in HD, which makes it the preferred treatment for patients with an unstable cardiovascular status [86].

Typically, the hematocrit is maintained at a higher level without androgen therapy in patients on CAPD. Calcium absorption from the dialysis fluid maintains calcium levels within normal limits without supplementation. Phosphate and PTH appear to be better controlled, as is blood glucose in diabetics (insulin is often infused into the dialysis fluid and absorbed through the membranes). Blood pressures are typically normalized without antihypertensive agents, and patients may often exhibit orthostatic hypotension [86].

Hypertriglyceridemia is a problem in patients on CAPD due to the exposure and absorption of glucose in the dialysate [16]. Peritonitis is the primary complication of this form of therapy. Hernias also develop with increased intra-abdominal pressures. Patients often develop obesity and lower back pain with long-term CAPD treatment [86].

Renal Transplantation

Transplantation of kidneys has become the treatment of choice for younger patients with ESRD. Approximately 7–10% of all patients receive transplants. Kidneys are obtained from either a living related source (family member) or a cadaver. Patients considered for renal transplantation are generally healthier than the general dialysis population; patients with severe cardiac, cerebrovascular, or pulmonary disease and neoplasia are not considered candidates. Extensive immunological studies are performed on the recipient to minimize the immunological response to the transplanted kidney. This includes tissue typing, crossmatching, and pretransplant blood transfusions. When an appropriate matched kidney is found, it is placed in a extrailiac position [109].

Patients are placed on immunosuppressive medication, which includes combinations of the following agents: (a) azothioprine, (b) corticosteroids, (c) antilymphocyte globulin, and (d) cyclosporin A. Patients may experience early acute rejection, or chronic rejection may occur later [109]. Current statistics indicate that mortality at the end of the first year is <5%. Survival of the transplanted kidney varies and is improving with advances in immunosuppression therapy. One-year graft survival is 75–90% in living related transplants and 45–70% in cadaver transplants. Most metabolic, endocrine, and biochemical derangements of uremia are corrected following transplantation [114].

Complications from kidney transplantation are primarily related to immunosuppressive therapy, infection being the most common. Atherosclerotic cardiovascular disease is prevalent in these patients due to hypertension, hypertriglyceridemia, low HDL fraction of cholesterol, and arterial calcification. Hypertension may result from steroid therapy and excessive release of renin from the native kidneys. Uremic osteomalacia may resolve following transplantation, with improved vitamin D metabolism and correction of metabolic acidosis. Long-term steroid therapy can result in osteonecrosis, particularly affecting the hip, knee, and shoulder joints. Obesity is common after transplantation, with a redistribution of body fat due to corticosteroid therapy [109].

CARDIOVASCULAR CONSEQUENCES OF ESRD

Cardiovascular disease is the leading cause of death in chronic dialysis patients and the second most common cause in renal transplant recipients [75]. Death from atherosclerosis in chronic dialysis patients 25–45 years of age is four times greater than in the general population [72]. Multiple factors contribute to the cardiovascular complications encountered in uremia, and include hypertension, left ventricular dysfunction, and hyperlipidemia [34, 63].

The mechanisms of hypertension in renal failure include (a) volume overload, resulting in increased cardiac output (many hypertensive patients normalize blood pressure after initiating dialysis), (b) hyperreninemia, (c) elevated total peripheral resistance, and (d) autonomic dysfunction [34]. As stated by Guyton [50], numerous blood pressure control systems in the body are designed to balance sodium intake and output by the kidneys. The decreased ability to excrete sodium in renal disease

FIGURE 1

Factors causing myocardial dysfunction in patients with chronic renal disease. (From Forst, D. H., and R. A. O'Rourke. Cardiovascular complications of chronic renal failure. In B. M. Brenner and J. H. Stein (eds.). Contemporary Issues in Nephrology: Chronic Renal Failure. *New York: Churchill Livingstone, 1981. Reprinted by permission.)*

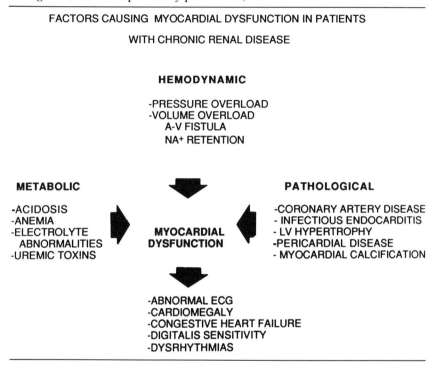

at a given blood pressure activates these controls to increase blood pressure until sodium output equals sodium intake, with the final result being hypertension.

Myocardial Dysfunction

Myocardial dysfunction commonly occurs in patients with ESRD. Multiple factors contribute to this problem, including metabolic, pathologic, and hemodynamic conditions (Figure 1). Ventricular volume and pressure overload are common. Volume overload is due to sodium retention, anemia, and the resulting increased total blood volume and increased venous return through the atrioventricular (A-V) shunt established for dialysis therapy. Pressure overload is a result of chronic hypertension, and the ensuing hypertrophy increases wall stress [3, 34]. The physiological response to this overload condition is increased stroke volume and cardiac output via the Starling mechanism. This mechanism facilitates cardiac output up to a certain point, beyond which further increases in volume result in pulmonary congestion and peripheral edema. Thus, congestive heart failure can occur in these patients without decreased left ventricular performance. Treatment may be initiated to effectively maintain appropriate volume and correct the loading condition in order to prevent progressive deterioration of left ventricular function [3].

The balance between myocardial oxygen supply and demand in ESRD is often compromised by the volume and pressure overloading conditions. Left ventricular hypertrophy may also lead to a mismatch between myocardial tissue and coronary blood flow. Anemia further compromises the oxygen supply [3, 34].

Uremia directly affects myocardial function in several ways. Metabolic abnormalities such as hyper- or hypokalemia, hypocalcemia, hypomagnesiumemia, and metabolic acidosis all alter the electrical and contractile properties of the myocardium. Increased calcium/phosphorus product over time can lead to calcification and eventual mitral valve dysfunction, aortic valve stenosis, and/or myocardial conduction blocks [3, 34].

Atherosclerosis
Virtually all the conditions known to promote the atherosclerotic process are prevalent in dialysis patients [3, 44]. Factors such as advanced age, genetic abnormalities, uremia, sedentary life-style, sex steroid use, and stress promote hypertriglyceridemia; low HDL-cholesterol, diabetes mellitus, hyperinsulinemia, glucose intolerance, cigarette smoking, and hypertension all contribute to atherogenesis [44, 53]. In the presence of ischemic heart disease, problems associated with dialysis such as anemia, stress, infection, fluid overload, electrolyte imbalance, and thrombosis increase the likelihood of myocardial infarction [44]. Reports of accelerated atherosclerosis caused by hemodialysis exist [47, 75]; however, risk factors [53], and not hemodialysis per se, are most likely responsible for the higher incidence of this disease in these patients [76].

NEUROMUSCULAR FUNCTION

Neuromuscular dysfunction is present in a significant number of uremic patients [99]. Evidence of autonomic dysfunction comes from reports of abnormal eccrine sweat gland function, reduced Valsalva ratio, attenuated blood pressure and heart rate responses to handgrip, and decreased baroreflex activity [31, 71, 97, 99]. Blood pressure and heart rate responses to handgrip, Valsalva, and orthostatic challenge improve within 2 months of successful renal transplantation and are normalized within 1 year [56, 115].

Plasma catecholamines are reported to be variable; however, methodological complications using radiochemical assays make the results problematic due to an inhibition of methylation reactions in uremic serum [64]. The use of internal standardization methods or high-pressure liquid chromatography results in norepinephrine levels elevated 75% above normal [65]. End-organ resistance to norepinephrine is suggested, via either down-regulation of receptors or decreased affinity of the receptors. Uremic rats demonstrate a 28% decreased affinity to beta-receptor–specific radioligands [79].

Somatic neuropathy is manifested by symptoms of pain, burning, and tingling in the distal extremities. Legs are affected more often than arms, with progressive weakness and atrophy of muscles [85, 99]. Nielson [85] and Thomas [111] reported that 93% of patients demonstrate decreased deep tendon reflexes, with 50% exhibiting clinical or electrical evidence of neuropathy. Only 18% had clinical problems associated with the neuropathy.

A condition termed "restless legs syndrome" is common. It is characterized by electromyographic (EMG) findings of fibrillation, increased amounts of polyphasic units, and increased duration of the motor units [85]. Motor and sensory nerve conduction is slow, which is not directly related to the blood chemistries [85]. Dialysis improves conduction velocity by approximately 16% [26], and the neuropathy is corrected with renal transplantation [7].

Neuropathological findings indicate decreased numbers of large myelinated fibers. In the remaining fibers the sheath is swollen and fragmented, with degeneration of the axon cylinders. The myelin sheath is damaged only where there is a degenerated axon. This leads researchers to believe that uremia causes a metabolic defect that leads to a decrease in the size of the axon, causing a rearrangement of myelin that results in destruction of the nerve fiber [26, 85].

Uremic myopathy that primarily affects proximal muscles is also described. Wasting of the quadriceps is common, with intact sensation and preservation of muscle reflexes. Hip flexors, hip extensors, and shoulder abductors are most often affected [70]. Muscle biopsy reveals type II fiber atrophy, variably-sized fibers, and rounding of fibers with few internal nuclei. A study of muscle biopsy specimens [33] in uremic patients showed abnormal results in 69%. Overlap of the myopathy and neuropathy was found in 29% of the patients, with pure myopathy in 11% and pure neuropathy in 29% [1, 33]. Arterial calcification has been noted mainly in the medial and external lamina of the vessels within the muscles, which may result in ischemic myopathy. The severity of this condition relates to the calcium-phosphorus product and is improved following parathyroidectomy [99].

Altered energy metabolism within the muscle has been reported [8]. Evidence for this comes from animal studies that indicate enhanced glycogen breakdown secondary to increased activities of regulatory enzymes of glycogenolysis. Cyclic AMP–dependent protein kinase and phosphorylase activity are significantly increased in uremic rats, as are the levels of the active I form of glycogen synthetase [60]. Reduction in phosphofructokinase and other key glycolytic enzymes in uremic patients has been reported by Nakao et al. [84] and Metcoff et al. [80]. Animal studies also indicate a reduction in the contractile force of skeletal muscles in uremic rats and a reduction in all measures of cellular calcium transport via the sarcoplasmic reticulum of uremic rabbits, indicating abnormal excitation-contraction coupling [59].

Factors implicated in the abnormal muscle energy metabolism in uremia include abnormalities in vitamin D metabolism, excess PTH, various uremic toxins, malnutrition and reduced energy intake, abnormalities in cellular energetics, impaired protein synthesis and amino acid metabolism, hypophosphatemia and reduction in intracellular phosphorus stores, and impaired biochemical integrity of cell membranes [8].

REHABILITATION STATUS

In 1981, in an editorial in the *New England Journal of Medicine* entitled "Renal Rehabilitation—Where Are the Data?" [100], Dr. Drummond Rennie brought attention to the discrepancy between the expected and observed rates of rehabilitation and the insufficient availability of information concerning the functional and rehabilitation status of the patients treated through the ESRD program.

Gutman et al. [48] reported that in a sample of 2481 patients treated with dialysis, only 60% of nondiabetic and 23% of diabetic patients were capable of physical activity beyond caring for themselves. Another attempt to assess the quality of life in ESRD patients has been made by Batelle Institute [30]. This study revealed that employment and objective and subjective measures of quality of life depend on the treatment, with renal transplant patients faring better in all cases than dialysis patients. Those patients on home HD, however, were most closely associated with the transplant patients, with in-center hemodialysis and CAPD patients being similar on most measures [30].

This study showed that over 80% of all patients were limited in vigorous activities such as running or participating in strenuous sports. More than half reported difficulty in walking several blocks or climbing a few flights of stairs, lifting or carrying weights of up to 25 lb, and bending, stooping, and lifting. The most prevalent symptoms were fatigue, weakness, and difficulty in sleeping, and were common with all treatment modalities [5].

Subjective measures of the quality of life such as well-being index, psychological affect, and life satisfaction showed that the patients perceived their quality of life to be adequate. However, objective measures

TABLE 3
Reported Studies of Exercise Tolerance in Patients with ESRD

Reference	N	Treatment (N)	Age (Years)	Sex (M/F)	Test Type	Exercise Capacity
Ulmer et al.	40	Pre-HD	13	NR	PWC 170	22nd percentile
		HD	23			
		RTX	14			
Roseler et al.	13	NR	47	7/6	PWC	73.2 Watts
Barnea et al.	22	HD	37	17/5	PWC	51% of normal
Lundin et al.	10	HD	32.7	9/1	$\dot{V}O_2$max	28.6 ml · kg^{-1} · min^{-1}
Zabetakis et al.	12	HD	45	NR	$\dot{V}O_2$max	17.4 ml · kg^{-1} · min^{-1}
Goldberg et al.	14	HD	38.5	8/6	$\dot{V}O_2$max	21.0 ml · kg^{-1} · min^{-1}
Painter et al.	50	HD (18)	45	11/7	$\dot{V}O_2$max	19.1 ml · kg^{-1} · min^{-1}
		CAPD (12)	34	6/6		21.1 ml · kg^{-1} · min^{-1}
		RTX (20)	36	13/7		31.7 ml · kg^{-1} · min^{-1}
Shalom et al.	14	HD (11)	45.5	7/7	$\dot{V}O_2$max	15.4 ml · kg^{-1} · min^{-1}
		CAPD (3)				
Painter et al.	171	HD	48	103/68	Estimated max (BE)	3.5 METS

N = number of patients, M = male, F = female, HD = hemodialysis, CAPD = continuous ambulatory peritoneal dialysis, RTX = renal transplant, TM = treadmill, BE = bicycle ergometer, PWC = physical working capacity; $\dot{V}O_2$max = maximal oxygen consumption.

of the quality of life showed that the dialysis patients were below the functioning levels of the general population [30].

The discrepancy between subjective and objective measures of rehabilitation and quality of life must be pursued. More intensive studies focusing on assessment and on improving rehabilitation outcomes in this population have been recommended by the Task Force on Rehabilitation established by the Health Care Financing Administration [49].

RESPONSES TO ACUTE EXERCISE

Patients with ESRD treated with dialysis have markedly impaired exercise tolerance. Barnea et al. [4] reported that physical work capacity (PWC) in 22 adult HD patients averaged only 51% of that of normal persons. PWC was not significantly different when the tests were done before or within 12 hours after dialysis. Direct measurement of $\dot{V}O_2$max has been reported in several studies [43, 91, 104, 118], and most values fall between 15.3 and 21.0 ml · kg^{-1} · min^{-1} (Table 3). Lundin et al. [77] reported somewhat higher values in 10 patients, averaging 28.6 ml · kg^{-1} · min^{-1}. Patients treated with CAPD do not differ significantly in their $\dot{V}O_2$max from HD patients [89, 91], with average $\dot{V}O_2$max values of 21.1 ml · kg^{-1} · min^{-1} in a group of 12 patients. Successful renal transplant recipients have normalized levels of $\dot{V}O_2$max [91]. This was shown in a cross-sectional group of patients who had average $\dot{V}O_2$max values of 31.7 ml · kg^{-1} · min^{-1} [91], as well as in a longitudinal study of 20 patients pre- and posttransplant who showed changes in $\dot{V}O_2$max values from 23.5 to 29.3 ml · kg^{-1} · min^{-1} within 7.5 weeks of transplantation [95]. This dramatic improvement could not be attributed to physical conditioning during the time posttransplant. Squires et al. [108] estimated maximal exercise capacity from treadmill tests performed 3 weeks posttransplant to be 5.7 METS.

No complications associated with maximal exercise testing have been reported. All reported studies have involved patients with no documented heart disease or other major complications such as diabetes. Exercise capacity in a large group of patients who are more representative of the general population of HD patients has only recently been reported [93]. Symptom-limited cycle ergometer testing was performed on 171 HD patients for preexercise screening. The average estimated peak exercise capacity was 3.5 METS. Eighty-nine percent of the tests were terminated due to leg and/or general fatigue.

Patients treated with CAPD may exhibit abnormal blood pressure responses to graded exercise [89]. In the only study of exercise responses in patients treated with CAPD, 10 of 11 patients who completed maximal graded exercise testing on a treadmill showed abnormal blood pressure responses. Tests were performed with 2 liters of dialysis fluid present in the abdomen. Blood pressures fell significantly at approximately 84% of the $\dot{V}O_2$max. The average fall in systolic pressure was 34 mm Hg, and all patients except one were asymptomatic with this blood pressure drop. Four patients were then tested without the dialysis fluid present, which resulted in appropriate blood pressure responses, with no change in maximal exercise capacity [89]. The abnormal blood pressure responses in the "full" condition may be associated with a decrease in venous return with altered peripheral vascular resistance, which may not fully compensate for the decrease in peripheral resistance accompanying exercise.

Limiting Factors to Exercise in ESRD

The factor(s) that limit exercise capacity in uremic subjects are unknown; however, any or all of the abnormal endocrine, biochemical, cardiovascular, and neuromuscular functions associated with uremia may contribute to abnormal integration and control of exercise responses. The normalization of $\dot{V}O_2$max following transplantation [95] suggests that removal of the uremic state may cause improved functioning of one or more of the systems involved in oxygen transport and utilization that determine exercise capacity. Figure 2 shows the physiologic systems and controls involved in the oxygen transport chain and how these controls may be affected by uremia.

Anemia has been implicated in the low exercise capacity; however, variable relationships between hematocrit and exercise capacity have been reported. Uremic patients compensate for their anemia with in-

FIGURE 2

Physiologic systems and controls involved in the transport of oxygen from the atmosphere to the working muscles in healthy subjects (left) and factors that may affect oxygen transport in patients with chronic renal disease (right). (From Painter, P., and P. Hanson. A model for clinical exercise prescription: application to hemodialysis patients. J. Cardiopul. Rehabil. *7:177, 1987.)*

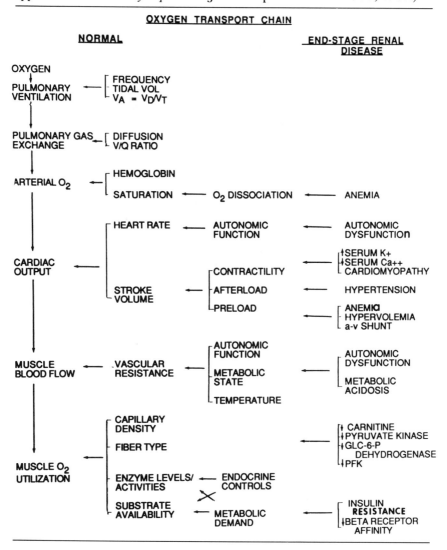

creased levels of 2,3-diphosphoglycerate (2,3-DPG), modification of the hemoglobin molecule, and metabolic acidosis, all which facilitate oxygen release at the periphery [81].

A strong correlation between hematocrit and PWC was shown in pediatric patients by Ulmer et al. [117]. Zabetakis et al. [118] reported a strong correlation between hemoglobin levels and $\dot{V}O_2$max levels in a combined group of HD patients and normal subjects. When data for HD, CAPD, and transplant patients were grouped together, there was a positive correlation between hematocrit and $\dot{V}O_2$max [91]; however, when the dialysis patient data were analyzed independently, the correlation was insignificant. Sill et al. [106] reported that PWC increased in only 6 of 10 patients when the hematocrit was increased from 20.6 to 37.6 by packed red cell transfusion. The increased $\dot{V}O_2$max following renal transplantation [95] was not correlated with the increased hematocrit ($r = 0.04$). Exercise training studies have also shown an increased $\dot{V}O_2$max without parallel increases in hematocrit or hemoglobin [92, 104, 118].

The lack of a significant correlation between the degree of anemia and PWC led Barnea et al. [4] to suggest cardiovascular limitations to exercise. Lundin et al. [77] reported that patients with histories of hypertension and abnormal echocardiograms had lower $\dot{V}O_2$max levels than patients with no such histories. Shalom et al. [104], however, showed that left ventricular ejection fractions measured by multigated radionuclide angiography increased an average of 8% above resting levels during upright graded bicycle exercise in HD patients. A study performed at the University of Wisconsin showed that maximal cardiac output significantly increased following renal transplantation due to increased maximal heart rates,with no change in maximal stroke volume [90].

Many conditions exist that may affect the left ventricular response to exercise (Figure 1). Increased left ventricular preload and afterload (from hypertension, anemia, shunting through the A-V fistula, left ventricular hypertrophy) and negative inotropic states such as hyperkalemia, hypocalcemia, hypermagnesemia, acidosis, and cardiomyopathy all may decrease left ventricular response and stroke volume during exercise.

Bullock et al. [10] investigated the interactions between abnormal exercise tolerance and cardiac abnormalities in 54 HD and transplant patients. They categorized the patients into those with normal exercise tests (results that fell within one standard deviation of the normal control group mean) and abnormal tests (those that fell below two standard deviations of the control mean). M-mode echocardiography and radionuclide angiography were performed to identify cardiac abnormalities. The investigators found that with decreasing exercise tolerance, there was an increased incidence of cardiac abnormalities. The proportion of patients who lost their jobs within the first year of treatment increased with decreasing exercise tolerance.

Abnormal heart rate responses to exercise are well documented in dialysis patients. These patients exhibit low maximal heart rates compared to age-predicted normal values and compared to those of renal transplant recipients [91]. Ketner et al. [68] showed that HD patients have subnormal heart rate responses to submaximal work of various intensities, averaging 20% lower than those of normal subjects at any given relative $\dot{V}O_2$max.

Other evidence of an impaired chronotropic response to exercise in uremic patients comes from the reports of heart rate changes following renal transplantation [90, 95]. Maximal heart rates increased from 155 to 178 b · min^{-1} in a group of young renal transplant patients (average age, 28 years). In addition, the heart rate at 70% of $\dot{V}O_2$max in the anemic, pretransplant condition was significantly lower than the heart rate posttransplantation [95]. Normal individuals with induced anemia have heart rates similar to those in the control, nonanemic state at the same relative $\dot{V}O_2$max [116]. Exercise heart rates at the same absolute submaximal exercise intensity were also lower pretransplant, again different from the responses seen in normal persons with induced anemia [67, 116].

In addition, induced anemia in normal persons has been shown to decrease the maximal heart rates by 6 [116] to 11 [67] b · min^{-1}. The magnitudes of these heart rate reductions are much less than those seen in the uremic patients pretransplant, which were 23 b · min^{-1} lower than posttransplant, nonanemic values [95].

The control of the peripheral circulation in uremic subjects has not been studied; however, both autonomic dysfunction and metabolic acidosis could affect the redistribution of blood flow to the working muscles. Following transplantation, it is also unknown whether the denervated kidney responds to exercise by decreasing flow and contributing to the redistribution of cardiac output to the working muscles.

Peripheral metabolic factors in uremia may play a major role in limiting exercise capacity. Termination of most exercise tests is due to localized leg fatigue. Parrish et al. [96] reported elevated lactic acid levels at submaximal exercise on a treadmill in HD patients. These patients had lactate levels 65% higher than those of the normal controls; however, the absolute exercise level was the same for both groups (1.0 mph/0% grade), and no indication of the relative percentages of $\dot{V}O_2$max was given. Indirect evidence of early onset of anaerobic metabolism comes from Zabetakis et al. [118], who reported low ventilatory thresholds (40% of $\dot{V}O_2$max). Direct lactate measurements by Barnea et al. [4] and Kettner et al. [68] have shown lactate levels to be similar to those of normals during submaximal exercise intensities, at the same relative percentage of maximal capacity and at near-maximal levels.

Plasma glucose levels are similar to those of normals during submaximal exercise, suggesting normal substrate mobilization, at least at exercise levels of 50% of $\dot{V}O_2$max [68]. Reports of altered levels of carnitine and activities of key glycolytic and lipolytic enzymes may be of importance and warrant further study in this patient group. The abnormal hormonal regulation affecting carbohydrate and lipid metabolism in these patients may also be important in determining exercise capacity. Further study of muscle oxidative capacity and control of substrate utilization at various exercise intensities must be encouraged in order to determine the role of peripheral metabolism as a limitation to exercise tolerance in this patient group.

General physical deconditioning is also a possible contributory factor in the low exercise tolerance observed. Reports of physical activity levels [48] indicate that less than 60% of nondiabetic patients on HD were capable of physical activity beyond that of caring for themselves. A 1-week physical activity recall in 30 in-center HD patients revealed that only 20% ever participated in activities that required an energy expenditure of more than 3 METS (Painter, unpublished data). Eight percent of all patients stated that they participated in a regular exercise program at home, which involved activities other than necessary daily tasks [93].

EXERCISE TESTING IN ESRD

The use of exercise testing as a diagnostic tool in dialysis patients is questionable. Baseline electrocardiograms (ECGs) may be abnormal due to electrolyte changes such as hyper- or hypokalemia and hyper- or hypocalcemia. There is a high prevalence of left ventricular hypertrophy, often with strain patterns on the ECG, and many patients are on digitalis preparations [107]. These conditions may render the exercise ECG uninterpretable for ischemic changes.

The very low exercise tolerance of these patients and the subnormal heart rate responses may limit the information obtained from standard exercise testing [102]. The average maximal heart rates attained in a group of 171 patients was 70% of the age-predicted maximum [93]. The inability to achieve appropriate maximal heart rates (at least 85% of age-predicted levels) may result in a high frequency of false-negative tests [27]. In this large group of patients given symptom-limited tests (peak METS = 3.5), only 7% had to discontinue the tests due to cardiovascular conditions such as arrhythmia or angina. Only one showed significant ST-segment depression with angina. In all other patients, tests were discontinued due to leg or general fatigue [93].

Orie et al. [88] used exercise ECGs, thallium exercise tests, and catheterization in 20 uremic patients (ESRD secondary to type I diabetes mellitus; mean age, 33 years) who were asymptomatic for coronary disease to study the incidence of coronary artery disease. All patients were scheduled for living related renal transplant and were studied prior to surgery. Eleven patients had significant coronary artery disease (six with multiple-vessel and five with single-vessel involvement), and only two had positive exercise ECG evidence of ischemia. Eighteen had nondiagnostic exercise tests due to a low peak heart rate. Thallium results increased the sensitivity of the tests to 73% but did not discriminate the extent of coronary artery disease in any of these patients. The authors concluded that exercise ECGs and a history alone are unreliable as diagnostic criteria for coronary artery disease, primarily due to the low functional capacity and low peak heart rates achieved. The patients in this study were diabetic, and their probability of coronary disease is high. Similar studies must be performed on nondiabetic uremic patients to document the sensitivity of standard exercise testing as a diagnostic tool.

Increasing potassium concentrations with exercise have been a theoretical concern in exercise testing of dialysis patients. Hagberg [51] suggests that potassium values should be measured prior to exercise testing in these patients, and the test not be performed with any value greater than 5.0 meq $\cdot$ l^{-1}. Potassium levels were not evaluated prior to exercise testing in a group of 171 patients who were tested immediately prior to their HD treatment [93], when blood chemistry values are most abnormal and fluid accumulation may be present. No cardiovascular events were reported in this group of patients.

Huber and Marguard [62] studied changes in potassium and blood gases with maximal exercise in a group of 17 normal subjects and 17 dialysis patients. The dialysis patients had higher resting levels of potassium, which increased approximately 1.4 meq $\cdot$ l^{-1} at maximal exercise. The normal subjects increased their potassium approximately 0.9 meq $\cdot$ l^{-1} above resting levels. The potassium dropped to resting levels within 5 minutes of recovery from exercise in both groups. The dialysis patients had a greater drop in pH at maximal exercise (to approximately 7.15) compared to the normal subjects, and regulatory mechanisms to correct the metabolic acidosis postexercise were ineffective within the 30 minutes of recovery observed. The authors indicated that the rise in plasma potassium with exercise (to 8.42 meq $\cdot$ l^{-1} in one patient) was tolerated well by the dialysis patients; however, this may be a reason for the muscle fatigue and weakness associated with vigorous exertion. Similar results were reported by Lundin et al. [78].

Latos et al. [69] studied four patients with maximal treadmill exercise and a 30-minute bout of submaximal exercise to evaluate electrolyte responses prior to dialysis and on nondialysis days. They showed no significant differences in exercise responses in the two conditions. Serum potassium, CO_2, $PaCO_2$, and pH at maximal exercise were all similar. During prolonged submaximal exercise, potassium rose less than 1.0 $meq \cdot l^{-1}$ and CO_2 dropped 22–25% on both days. The recovery in pH was faster on the nondialysis day, with normalization of pH and CO_2 within 1 hour, compared to 4 hours on the dialysis day.

Timing of the exercise test in HD patients may also be important, considering the changes in physiological status resulting from the HD treatment. Hagberg [51] suggests that since blood chemistry values are at their optimum postdialysis, testing may be appropriate at that time. Although Barnea et al. [4] have reported no difference in PWC before or after dialysis, the postdialysis tests were performed within 12 hours of the treatment and not immediately afterwards. Exercise testing immediately after HD may result in significant postexercise hypotension due to the complex hemodynamic regulation of arterial pressure associated with dialysis, including reflex control of peripheral resistance in response to a decrease in cardiac output [15]. In our experience of 12 symptom-limited tests performed within 2 hours after HD, 6 were discontinued due to a decrease or an inappropriate rise in blood pressure, and 4 others revealed symptomatic postexercise hypotension (Painter, unpublished data). Exercise testing immediately postdialysis may limit the information obtained from the test and may result in significant hypotension.

EXERCISE TRAINING IN ESRD

One of the first published reports on the benefits of regular exercise training in HD was by Jette et al. [66], who reported the results of a comprehensive fitness program on one 21-year-old patient over a 15-month period. The benefits were significant, with increases in estimated $\dot{V}O_2$max (from 15.0 to 28.3 $ml \cdot kg^{-1} \cdot min^{-1}$) and improvements in strength measurements and several blood chemistry values. An editorial written in 1977 by Dr. Terry Oberley [87], an HD patient, suggested the importance of regular exercise training for HD patients. In 1979, the results of two exercise training studies were reported [41, 42, 46]. A summary of the results of reported training studies is provided in Table 4.

Green et al. [46] exercise six patients for 25–45 minutes of a walk/jog program on 3 days/week (off-dialysis days) for 10 weeks. Patients exhibited no changes in serum glucose, bicarbonate, potassium, or albumin levels following the exercise conditioning program. BUN was unchanged; however, serum creatinine rose significantly and serum calcium and phosphorus were lowered. No changes were seen in serum lipids in this study. A later report [118] of changes in functional capacity in this group of patients indicated a 21% increase in $\dot{V}O_2$max and significant

TABLE 4
Summary of Reported Effects of Exercise Training in Dialysis Patients

Study	Goldberg et al.	Zabetakis et al.	Shalom et al.	Painter et al.
n (ex, control)	13, 12	6, 6	7, 7*	14, 7
Treatment	HD	HD	HD, CAPD	HD
Study duration	12 ± 4 months	10 weeks	12 weeks	6 months
Time of ex	Off dialysis	Off dialysis	Off dialysis	On dialysis
Type of ex	Cycle, walk, walk-jog	Walk-jog	Cycle, walk, walk-jog	Cycle
$\dot{V}O_2$max	↑ (21%)	↑ (21%)	↑ (42%)	↑ (26%)
Test duration	↑	↑	↑	↑
Resting BP	↓	—	—	↓
Triglycerides	↓	—	—	—
Total cholesterol	—	—	NR	—
VLDL-cholesterol	↓	—	NR	—
LDL-cholesterol	—	—	NR	—
HDL-cholesterol	↑	—	NR	—
Hematocrit	↑ (27%)	—	—	—
BUN	NR	—	NR	—
Creatinine	NR	↑	NR	—
Calcium	NR	↓	NR	NR
Phosphorus	NR	↓	NR	NR
Fasting glucose	↓	—	NR	NR
Plasma insulin	↓	NR	NR	NR
Psychosocial function	Improved	NR	—†	Improved
Other	↑ glc tolerance	↑ AT	Poor compliance	Good compliance

*Seven exercisers attended > 50% of sessions, controls < 50% of sessions.
†See text; — = no change.
ex = exercise, cont = control, HD = hemodialysis, AT = anaerobic threshold,
CAPD = continuous ambulatory peritoneal dialysis, NR = not reported, glc = glucose.

increases in test duration and ventilatory threshold. No changes were seen in hematocrit, hemoglobin, or 2,3-DPG.

A major study of the effects of exercise training in HD was completed at the Washington University School of Medicine and the Chromalloy American Kidney Center, and has resulted in numerous reports [13, 36, 43, 45, 52, 54]. This study randomly assigned 25 HD patients ($\bar{x}$ age, 37.9 years) into an exercise training group ($N = 13$) and a group of sedentary controls ($N = 12$) following maximal exercise testing and measurement of $\dot{V}O_2$max. The exercise training program consisted of walking, cycling, and walk/jogging of progressive intensity from 50–60% to 70–80% of $\dot{V}O_2$max for up to 20–45 minutes per session. Exercise was held on nondialysis days.

After 12 (±4) months, there was a 19% increase in the duraton of the graded treadmill exercise test and a 21% increase in $\dot{V}O_2$max in the exercise group [43, 54]. Also associated with the exercise training were improvements in blood pressure, with a significant reduction in systolic pressures of hypertensive patients (N = 6) from 155 ($\pm$ 10) to 124 ($\pm$ 7) mm Hg with a reduction in dosage and/or number of antihypertensive medications [52]. Plasma triglycerides were significantly lower following exercise training, as were VLDL triglyceride concentrations. Total cholesterol did not change; however, the VLDL-cholesterol concentration decreased and the HDL fraction increased significantly [43]. Changes in apoprotein A-I paralleled the rise in HDL-cholesterol level, while plasma apoproteins A-II and B did not change. The HDL_2-cholesterol fraction rose from 9 ($\pm$ 2) mg $\cdot$ dl^{-1} to near normal at 15 ($\pm$ 2) mg $\cdot$ dl^{-1}. Significant increases in postheparin plasma lipoprotein lipase activity and decreased hepatic lipase activity occurred in the exercisers [45, 54]. Control subjects showed no changes in any of these parameters.

Metabolic changes observed following training in this study included a decrease in fasting plasma insulin, with no change in the fasting glucose concentration. There was also a 42% increase in the glucose disappearance rate in the trained group. Insulin receptor binding to mononuclear cells improved by 70% after training, indicating improved insulin sensitivity [36, 43, 54]. Exercise training resulted in a 27% increase in hematocrit, which was associated with a 27% increase in red cell mass, with no changes in plasma volumes. These changes were related to a twofold increase in reticulocyte count and a significant rise in red blood cell survival [36, 43].

Psychological testing showed a reduction of depression in the exercise group. This group also maintained levels of hostility, anxiety, and reported frequency of pleasant events, all of which worsened over time in the control group [13].

Shalom et al. [104] reported that of 50 maintenance dialysis patients eligible to participate in an exercise training study, only 14 completed all testing and initiated the 12-week exercise training program. The exercise involved stationary cycling and walking at a level of 75–80% of the attained maximal heart rate, three times per week, off dialysis. Only seven of these patients attended 50% or more of the scheduled exercise sessions. This group significantly increased their peak treadmill duration by 2.4 METS, as well as their peak $\dot{V}O_2$max. The group that did not adhere to the exercise did not show any changes. No changes were noted in left ventricular ejection fraction, hematocrit, resting blood pressure, body weight, or antihypertensive medication in either group. The two groups of patients did not differ in demographics or initial hemodynamic data; however, the noncompliant group showed greater impairment on several psychological tests. A stepwise multiple regression that determined the best set of predictors of compliance to exercise revealed that anxiety and hostility, as measured by the SCL-90, accounted for more than 55% of the variance in attendance. Shalom et al. stated that the patients in the noncompliant group may be representative of the larger population on maintenance dialysis in terms of psychological profiles and indicated that exercise training programs may be applicable only to those dialysis patients who are psychologically better adjusted. Because of this, the authors suggested that the overall impact of this type of program may be limited by low participation rates.

Squires et al. [108] reported positive results with exercise training early after renal transplantation. Patients exercised in the cardiac rehabilitation center 16 times over a 5.8-week period following surgery. Exercise session duration was 25–40 minutes at an intensity of 40–60% of maximal capacity. The estimated METS increased from 5.7 to 9.2, with peak heart rates increasing from 127 to 153 b · min^{-1}. The subjects tolerated the exercise testing and training without complications. The results indicate an increase in exercise capacity, which may be due to improved renal function and recovery from surgery, as well as to the exercise training. Further study of the long-term effects of exercise training following renal transplantation is warranted. No exercise training studies in patients treated with CAPD have been reported.

Animal Studies
Davis et al. [20] studied the effects of exercise training on muscle protein catabolism in uremic female rats. Nephrectomized rats were compared to controls under the conditions of swimming training or no exercise. The release of amino acids from *in vitro* muscle was measured. It was found that uremia caused increased release of phenylalanine, tyrosine (33%), and alanine (50%), as well as decreased citrate synthase activity. Exercise training corrected these changes in the uremic rats.

Muscle sensitivity to insulin was decreased in uremia and was improved by 75% with exercise training, which also reduced amino acid release from the muscle by 50%. Conclusions drawn in this study suggest that exercise training reduces muscle protein catabolism in uremia by increasing insulin sensitivity.

The finding of hematuria, proteinuria, and red cell casts following strenuous activity in normal persons has raised the question of whether exercise may actually exacerbate renal injury and should be contraindicated in pre-ESRD patients. No studies have been performed to address this question, and conflicting evidence from two animal studies exists.

Heifets et al. [55] showed that partially nephrectomized rats subjected to swimming exercise had significantly higher inulin clearances, higher filtration fractions, lower serum creatinine, and lower 24-hour urine output than sedentary rats with the same degree of uremia. It was concluded that chronic exercise improves renal function in partially nephrectomized rats, and it was suggested that exercise training has the potential to reduce the progression of renal disease in moderate renal insufficiency. Another study has shown adverse effects of exercise on glomerulonephritis [19]. Glomerulonephritis was induced in rabbits by injection of bovine serum albumin, which caused significant albuminuria and increased serum BUN. The abnormal albuminuria was more frequent, and tended to persist at a higher level in the exercise group and during the course of the experiment, while BUN continued to rise only in the exercise group. The exercised animals showed a greater frequency of abnormal findings in the biopsy indices of glomerular injury, although only one index (blood in the tubules) achieved statistical significance. The authors concluded that exercise superimposed on active immune complex–mediated glomerulonephritis may cause worsening of the abnormal glomerular function.

The mechanism postulated to explain these findings is the increased capillary hydrostatic pressure that results with decreased renal blood flow and increased efferent capillary pressure during exercise. This response may increase the bulk flow and movement of plasma protein across the glomerular capillary walls and cause trapping of cellular immune complexes or increase formation of the complexes in the capillary walls. The applicability of these findings to patients with pre-ESRD remains to be studied.

Exercise Training During Hemodialysis
Stationary cycling during the HD treatment is an alternative approach to exercise training in this patient group that may enhance compliance with a regular exercise training program. The acute effects of exercise during dialysis have been studied by Germain et al. [37] and Burke et al. [11]. They had six patients pedal a stationary cycle at approximately 56% of $\dot{V}O_2$max (measured off dialysis) for 15 minutes. A drop in PaO_2 at rest on HD from 102 to 92 mm Hg was observed, associated with a decreased alveolar ventilation rate from 5.15 to 4.0 $l \cdot min^{-1}$. $\dot{V}CO_2$ also fell from 204 to 175 ml $\cdot min^{-1}$. With exercise the arterial PO_2 increased to 102, probably as a result of the increase in V_A and the increase in $\dot{V}CO_2$ to 440 ml $\cdot min^{-1}$. Hemodynamic changes showed increased heart rates with exercise from 84 to 120 b $\cdot min^{-1}$, which returned to normal within 15 minutes. Systolic and diastolic pressures also increased with exercise (150 to 181, and 84 to 97 mm Hg, respectively). In those patients on acetate dialysis, there is a clear advantage for exercise to maintain arterial oxygen tension.

Germain et al. [38] also compared maximal exercise during and off HD in four patients. Although these patients were able to perform more work off dialysis, $\dot{V}O_2$max values were not significantly different. Systolic blood pressure and the rate-pressure product were higher at maximal

FIGURE 3

Bicycle setup for exercise training during hemodialysis.

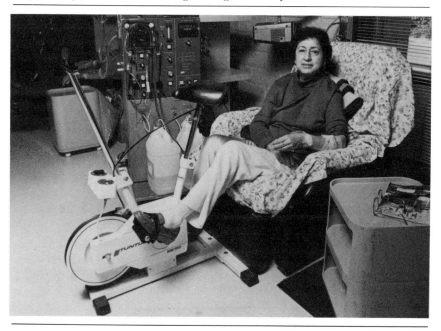

work off dialysis. Potassium levels were higher off dialysis; however, the differences were not significant. The authors suggested that maximal exercise testing may be safer when done during dialysis because of the lower potassium levels. However, if the purpose of the exercise test is to detect ischemia, the rate-pressure product is higher off dialysis and there is a greater chance of eliciting ischemic changes when the test is performed at this time. It is also unclear how maximal efforts during dialysis would affect the average dialysis patient's treatment.

Exercise training at submaximal levels during the dialysis treatment (Figure 3) results in benefits similar to those described in training on off-dialysis days. A study to evaluate these benefits was conducted by Painter et al. [92]. Thirteen patients volunteered to exercise during the dialysis treatment following treadmill testing for determination of $\dot{V}O_2$max values. The program started with 5 minutes of exercise and gradually progressed according to individual tolerance to 30 minutes of cycling during every treatment. The intensity of exercise was prescribed according to the rating of perceived exertion, approximating 70–85% of peak capacity. $\dot{V}O_2$max increased significantly (26%) over the 6 months of exercise training. Improved blood pressure control was observed in six of eight hypertensive patients, with decreased antihypertensive med-

TABLE 5

Hemodynamic Responses to a Standard Exercise Intensity at Different Times During the Dialysis Treatment (N = 8)

Time of Exercise	Heart Rate	SBP	RPE	HR > Rest	SBP > Rest
Predialysis	115 (13)	145 (20)	13	27 (15)	19 (11)
Hour 1	121 (13)	144 (21)	13	35 (19)*	27 (12)
Hour 2	128 (17)*	140 (23)	15*	46 (17)*	24 (13)
Hour 3	139 (18)*	132 (17)	16*	55 (17)*	23 (18)

Mean (SD).
*$P < .05$ compared to predialysis values.

ication requirements. Several patients were able to discontinue antihypertensive medications. No changes were observed in plasma lipid concentrations or hematocrit, although there was a trend toward increased hematocrit by the end of the 6 months of training. Subjective responses to the exercise training were very positive, and compliance with the exercise program was high (91% in the first 3 months and 75% in the second 3 months). Exercise training during the treatment was recommended for improving compliance with regular exercise training and providing a supervised setting for exercise for this high-risk group of patients.

Participation rates in a program of exercise training during dialysis have been reported [93]. Of a total of 358 patients in five clinics, 171 were tested for admission to the program. A total of 187 patients were not tested, primarily for medical reasons. Of those patients tested, 58 (34%) did not start the exercise program due to lack of interest, cardiovascular conditions, orthopedic problems, and other medical reasons. Of the 113 who started the program, 52 (46%) dropped out, due primarily to medical reasons (transplantation [13], home exercise [9], lack of interest [7], death [7], and other medical conditions [14]). Participation rates in those who continued the program (61 patients) were surprisingly good, with 78% of all participants exercising during >50% of all possible sessions. Forty-four percent of these participating patients (8% of the total patient population) exercised every dialysis treatment. No medical complications related to the exercise training were reported in this study.

The timing of exercise during dialysis may be important in prescribing an exercise regimen. A study to evaluate the heart rate and blood pressure responses to standard submaximal exercise (approximating 85% of the off-dialysis maximal capacity) was conducted in eight patients [94]. A standard exercise intensity was performed for 15 minutes immediately prior to HD and during the last 15 minutes of each hour of the treatment. Heart rates, blood pressure, and perceived exertion ratings were similar to those at rest only during the first hour of treatment (Table 5). Exercise later in the treatment resulted in higher heart rates and higher perceived exertion ratings and lower blood pressure responses to the same standard exercise intensity. Due to the changing hemodynamics resulting from the HD procedure, heart rate testing may be an inappropriate method for prescribing exercise intensity. This increases the importance of using ratings of perceived exertion for this purpose.

Research Considerations

Preliminary results indicate potential benefits to ESRD patients from exercise training; however, the need for further study is substantial. The multisystemic nature of renal disease and the complexity of the treatment will require compromise with the ideal scientific design of exercise studies. Researchers must respect the treatment mode as an absolute priority, and study design must respect the time and psychosocial demands placed on these patients.

The changing physiological status of these patients must also be considered. Fluid and dietary intake, as well as the adequacy of their dialysis treatments, must be taken into account. The potential for rapid changes in clinical status further complicates systematic, long-term studies. It is possible for patients to go into congestive heart failure with pulmonary edema as a result of fluid indiscretion and inadequate dialysis. Arrhythmias may surface due to electrolyte changes. Patients are frequently hospitalized due to infection, access-site problems, or other complications. Patients who require frequent transfusions may often experience chronic fatigue and may be unwilling to participate in exertion. The treatment modes are not permanent, and patients may choose an alternative form of dialysis at any time. Failure of a transplant obviously requires reinitiation of dialysis, and often dialysis patients will be called on very short notice when a kidney for transplantation becomes available. Psychosocial factors should always be considered when working with this patient group, and adjustments in study design may be required to accommodate patient schedules. ESRD is an end-stage disease, and loss of study subjects due to death should be expected. Many factors associated with the treatment of this disease may affect the results of exercise studies, including (a) the timing of dialysis in relation to the exercise test and/or the training; (b) weight changes between dialysis treatments; (c) dietary compliance; (d) timing of medications (many patients on HD do not take medications on dialysis days); (e) timing of transfusions in relation to the testing; and (f) intermittent treatment regimens (i.e., decadurobulin administration for anemia). For optimal cooperation by patients, and to ensure that study procedures will not adversely affect the clinical status of the patient, it is recommended that dialysis staff be appropriately informed and possibly included as a part of the research team.

Reimbursement is a major issue in developing exercise rehabilitation programs for ESRD patients. Medicare funding of the treatment does not cover such rehabilitation efforts at this time. In addition, many patients qualify for disability status, which may limit their ability to pay for rehabilitation and may reduce the incentive to participate in rehabilitation programs.

ACKNOWLEDGMENTS

The author wishes to thank Dr. Toby Gottheiner for his thorough review and comments on the pathophysiology and treatment section of this chapter.

REFERENCES

1. Ahonen, R.E. Light microscopic study of striated muscle in uremia. *Acta Neuropathol.* *(Berl.)* 49:51–55, 1980.
2. Anagnostou, A., and N.A. Kurtzman. The anemia of chronic renal failure. *Semin. Nephrol.* 5:115–127, 1985.
3. Ayus, J., P. Frommer, and J.B. Young. Cardiac and circulatory abnormalities in chronic renal failure. *Semin. Nephrol.* 1:112–123, 1981.
4. Barnea, N., Y. Drory, A. Iaina, C. Lapidot, E. Reisin, H. Eliahou, and J.J. Kellermann. Exercise tolerance in patients on chronic hemodialysis. *Isr. J. Med. Sci.* 16:17–21, 1980.
5. Battelle Human Affairs Research Centers. National kidney dialysis and kidney transplantation study: A summary of results. *Contemp. Dial. Nephrol.* 6:41–47, 1985.
6. Blachley, J.D., and J.P. Knochel. The biochemistry of uremia. In B.M. Brenner and J.H. Stein (eds.). *Contemporary Issues in Nephrology: Chronic Renal Failure.* New York: Churchill Livingstone, 1981, pp. 28–45.
7. Bolton, C. Effects of renal transplantation on uremic neuropathy. *N. Engl. J. Med.* 284:1170–1175, 1971.
8. Brautbar, N. Skeletal myopathy in uremia: Abnormal energy metabolism. *Kidney Int.* 24(suppl. 16):S81–S86, 1983.
9. Brunzell, J.D., J.J. Albers, L.B. Haas, A.P. Goldberg, L. Agadoa, and D.J. Sherrard. Prevalence of serum lipid abnormalities in chronic hemodialysis. *Metabolism* 8:903–910, 1977.
10. Bullock, R.E., H.A. Amer, I. Simpson, M.K. Ward, and R.J. Chall. Cardiac abnormalities and exercise tolerance in patients receiving renal replacement therapy. *Br. Med. J.* 289:1479–1484, 1984.
11. Burke, E.J., M.J. Germain, G.L. Graden, and J.P. Fitzgibbons. Mild steady-state exercise during hemodialysis treatment. *Physician Sportsmed.* 12:153–157, 1984.
12. Butt, K.M.H. Vascular access for chronic hemodialysis. In A.R. Nissenson and R.N. Fine (eds.). *Dialysis Therapy.* St. Louis: C.V. Mosby Co., 1986, pp. 5–9.
13. Carney, R.M., P.M. McKevitt, A.P. Goldberg, J.M. Hagberg, J.A. Delmez, and H.R. Harter. Psychological effects of exercise training in hemodialysis patients. *Nephron* 33:179–181, 1983.
14. Cattran, D.C., S.S.A. Fenton, D.R. Wilson, and G. Steiner. Defective triglyceride removal in lipemia associated with peritoneal dialysis and haemodialysis. *Ann. Int. Med.* 85:29–33, 1976.
15. Chaignon, M., W.T. Chen, R.C. Tarazi, S. Nakamoto, and E.L. Bravo. Blood pressure response to hemodialysis. *Hypertension* 3:333–339, 1981.
16. Chan, M.K., A. Barghese, and J.F. Moorhead. Lipid abnormalities in uremia, dialysis and transplantation. *Kidney Int.* 19:625–627, 1981.

17. Corea, A.L. Hemodialysis orders. In A.R. Nissenson and R.N. Fine (eds.). *Dialysis Therapy*. St. Louis: C.V. Mosby Co., 1986, pp. 73–74.
18. Corea, A.L. Pre- and post-hemodialysis assessment. In A.R. Nissenson and R.N. Fine (eds.). *Dialysis Therapy*. St. Louis: C.V. Mosby Co., 1986, pp. 75–77.
19. Cornacoff, J.B., L. A. Hebert, H.M. Sharma, W.H. Bay, and D.C. Young. Adverse effect of exercise on immune complex-mediated glomerulonephritis. *Nephron* 40:292–296, 1985.
20. Davis, T.A., I.E. Karl, A.P. Goldberg, and H.R. Harter. Effects of exercise training on muscle protein catabolism in uremia. *Kidney Int.* 24(suppl. 16):S52–S57, 1983.
21. DeFronzo, R.A., R. Andres, P. Edgar, and W.G. Walker. Carbohydrate metabolism in uremia: A review. *Nephron* 52:469–481, 1973.
22. DeFronzo, R.A. Pathogenesis of glucose intolerance in uremia. *Metabolism* 27:1866–1880, 1978.
23. DeFronzo, R.A., and J.D. Smith. Is glucose intolerance harmful for the uremic patient? *Kidney Int.* 28(suppl. 17):S88–S97, 1985.
24. Diamond, S.M., and W.L. Henrich. Acetate dialysate versus bicarbonate dialysate: A continuing controversy. *Am. J. Kidney Dis.* 9:3–11, 1987.
25. Drueke, T., B. Lacour, J.B. Roullet, and J.L. Funck-Brentano. Recent advances in factors that alter lipid metabolism in chronic renal failure. *Kidney Int.* 24(suppl. 16):S134–S138, 1983.
26. Dyck, P.J. Comparison of symptoms, chemistry and nerve function to assess adequacy of hemodialysis. *Neurology* 29:1361–1368, 1979.
27. Ellestadt, M.H. *Stress Testing: Principles and Practice*, 2nd ed. Philadelphia: F.A. Davis Co., 1980, p. 157.
28. Emmanouel, D.S., M.D. Lindheimer, and A.I. Katz. Metabolic and endocrine abnormalities in chronic renal failure. In B.M. Brenner and J.H. Stein (eds.). *Contemporary Issues in Nephrology: Chronic Renal Failure*. New York: Churchill Livingstone, 1981, pp. 46–84.
29. Eschbach, W.W., J.C. Egrie, M.R. Downing, J.K. Browne, and J.W. Adamson. Correction of the anemia of end-stage renal disease with recombinant human erythropoietin: results of a combined phase I and II clinical trial. *N. Engl. J. Med.* 316:73–78, 1987.
30. Evans, R.W., D.L. Manninen, L.P. Garrison, L.G. Hart, C.R. Blagg, R.A. Gutman, A.R. Hull, and E.G. Lowrie. The quality of life of patients with end-stage renal disease. *N. Engl. J. Med.* 312:553–559, 1985.
31. Ewing, D.J., and R. Winney. Autonomic function of patients with chronic renal failure on intermittent hemodialysis. *Nephron* 15:424–429, 1975.
32. Feinstein, E.I. Nutritional therapy in maintenance hemodialysis patients. In A.R. Nissenson and R.N. Fine (eds.). *Dialysis Therapy*. St. Louis: C.V. Mosby Co., 1986, pp. 142–145.
33. Floyd, M., D.R. Ayyar, D.D. Barwick, P. Hudgson, and D. Weightman. Myopathy in chronic renal failure. *Q. J. Med.* 172:509–524, 1974.
34. Forst, D.H., and R.A. O'Rourke. Cardiovascular complications of chronic renal failure. In B.M. Brenner and J.H. Stein (eds.). *Contemporary Issues in Nephrology: Chronic Renal Failure*. New York: Churchill Livingstone, 1981, pp. 85–116.
35. Fried, W. Hematological abnormalities in chronic renal failure. *Semin. Nephrol.* 1:176–185, 1981.
36. Gavin, J.R., A.P. Goldberg, J.M. Hagberg, J.A. Delmez, E. Geltman, and H.R. Harter. Endurance exercise improves insulin sensitivity in uremia. *Clin. Res.* 40:393–397, 1982.
37. Germain, M.J., E.J. Burke, G.L. Braden, and J.P. Fitzgibbons. Amelioration of hemodialysis-induced fall in PaO$_2$ with exercise. *Am. J. Nephrol.* 5:351–354, 1985.
38. Germain, M.J., E. Burke, J. Fitzgibbons, and G. Braden. Maximal exercise during hemodialysis: Physiologic effects. *Kidney Int.* 29:63A, 1985. (Abstract)

39. Giordano, C. Early dietary protein restriction protects the failing kidney. *Kidney Int.* 28(suppl. 17):S66–S70, 1985.
40. Goldberg, A.P., D.J. Sherrard, and J.D. Brunzell. Adipose tissue lipoprotein lipase in chronic hemodialysis: A role for plasma trigyceride metabolism. *J. Clin. Endocrinol. Metab.* 47:1173–1182, 1978.
41. Goldberg, A.P., J.M. Hagberg, J.A. Delmez, G.W. Heath, and H.R. Harter. Exercise training improves abnormal lipid and carbohydrate metabolism in hemodialysis patients. *Trans. Am. Soc. Artif. Int. Organs* 25:431–436, 1979.
42. Goldberg, A.P., J.M. Hagberg, J.A. Delmez, R.W. Florman, and H.R. Harter. Effects of exercise training on coronary risk factors in hemodialysis patients. *Proc. Dialysis Transplant Forum.* 9:39–42, 1979.
43. Goldberg, A.P., E.M. Geltman, J.M. Hagberg, J.R. Gavin, J.A. Delmez, R.M. Carney, A. Naumowicz, M.H. Oldfield, and H.R. Harter. The therapeutic effects of exercise training for hemodialysis patients. *Kidney Int.* 24(suppl. 16):S303–S309, 1983.
44. Goldberg, A.P. Lipid abnormalities in hemodialysis patients: Prevalence, implications and treatment. *Perspect. Lipid Dis.* 2:17–24, 1984.
45. Goldberg, A.P., E.M. Geltman, J.R. Gavin, R.M. Carney, J.M. Hagberg, J.A. Delmez, A. Naumovich, M.H. Oldfield, and H.R. Harter. Exercise training reduces coronary risk and effectively rehabilitates hemodialysis patients. *Nephron* 42:311–316, 1986.
46. Greene, M.C., P.M. Zabetakis, G.W. Gleim, F.L. Pasternak, A.J. Saraniti, M.F. Michelis, and J.A. Nicholas. Effects of exercise on lipid metabolism and dietary intake in hemodialysis patients. *Proc. Dialysis Transplant Forum* 9:80–85, 1979.
47. Greene, D., N.J. Stone, and F.A. Krumlovsky. Putative atherogenic factors in patients with chronic renal failure. *Progr. Cardiovas. Dis.* 26:133–144, 1983.
48. Gutman, R.A., W.W. Stead, and R.R. Robinson. Physical activity and employment status of patients on maintenance dialysis. *N. Engl. J. Med.* 304:309–313, 1981.
49. Gutman, R.A. Rehabilitation of chronic renal disease patients: Are we meeting our objectives? In N.G. Kutner, D.D. Cardenas, and J.D. Bower (eds.). *Rehabilitation and the Chronic Renal Disease Patient.* New York: Spectrum Publications, 1985, pp. 3–15.
50. Guyton, A.R. Personal views on mechanisms of hypertension. In J. Genest, W. Koiw, and O. Kuchel (eds.). *Hypertension: Physiopathology and Treatment.* New York: McGraw-Hill Book Co., 1977, pp. 149–166.
51. Hagberg, J. Exercise testing and prescription for the end-stage renal disease patient. In B. Franklin, S. Gordon, and G. Timmis (eds.). *Exercise in Modern Medicine: Testing and Prescription in Health and Disease.* In press.
52. Hagberg, J.M., A.P. Goldberg, A.A. Eshani, G.W. Heath, J.A. Delmez, and H.R. Harter. Exercise training improves hypertension in hemodialysis patients. *Am. J. Nephrol.* 3:209–212, 1983.
53. Haire, H.M., D.J. Sherrard, and D. Scardapane. Smoking, hypertension, and mortality in a maintenance dialysis population. *Cardiovasc. Med.* 3:1163–1168, 1978.
54. Harter, H.R., and A.P. Goldberg. Endurance exercise training: An effective therapeutic modality for hemodialysis patients. *Med. Clin. North Am.* 69:159–175, 1978.
55. Heifets, M., T.A. Davis, and S. Klahr. Exercise training improves renal function in rats with a remnant kidney. *Kidney Int.* 31:386, 1986. (Abstract)
56. Hennemann, R.H., A. Sternagel-Haase, and A. Heidland. Uraemic sympathetic neuropathy after haemodialysis and transplantation. *Eur. J. Clin. Invest.* 9:23–27, 1979.
57. Henry, D. Phosphate binders. In A.R. Nissenson and R.N. Fine (eds.). *Dialysis Therapy.* St. Louis: C.V. Mosby Co., 1986, pp. 187–188.
58. Heuk, C., and E. Ritz. Hyperlipoproteinemia in renal insufficiency. *Nephron* 25:1–7, 1980.
59. Horl, W.H., J. Sperling, and A. Heidland. Enhanced glycogen turnover in skeletal

muscles of uremic rats: Cause of uncontrolled actomyosin ATPase. *Am. J. Clin. Nutr.* 31:1861–1864, 1978.

60. Horl, W.H., and A. Heidland. Glycogen metabolism in uremia. *Am. J. Clin. Nutr.* 33:1461–1467, 1980.

61. Hostetter, T.H., and B.M. Brenner. Glomerular adaptations to renal injury. In B.M. Brenner and J.H. Stein (eds.). *Contemporary Issues in Nephrology: Chronic Renal Failure.* New York: Churchill Livingston, 1981, pp. 1–27.

62. Huber, W., and E. Marguard. Plasma potassium and blood pH following physical exercise in dialysis patients. *Nephron* 40:383–384, 1985.

63. Ibels, L.S., J.H. Stewart, J.F. Mahony, F.C. Neale, and A.G.R. Sheil. Occlusive arterial disease in uraemic and haemodialysis patients and renal transplant recipients. *Q. J. Med.* 66:197–214, 1977.

64. Izzo, J.L., M.S. Izzo, R.H. Sterns, and R.B. Freeman. Sympathetic nervous system hyperactivity in maintenance hemodialysis patients. *Trans. Am. Soc. Artif. Organs* 28:604–606, 1982.

65. Izzo, J.L., and R.H. Sterns. Abnormal norepinephrine release in uremia. *Kidney Int.* 24(suppl. 16):S1–S3, 1983.

66. Jette, M., G. Posen, and C. Cardarelli. Effects of an exercise programme in a patient undergoing hemodialysis treatment. *J. Sports Med.* 17:181–184, 1977.

67. Kanstrup, I., and B. Ekblom. Blood volume and hemoglobin concentration as determinants of maximal aerobic power. *Med. Sci. Sports Exuc.* 16:256–262, 1984.

68. Ketner, A., A.P. Goldberg, J.M. Hagberg, J.A. Delmez, and H.R. Harter. Cardiovascular and metabolic responses to submaximal exercise in hemodialysis patients. *Kidney Int.* 26:66–71, 1984.

69. Latos, D., D. Strimel, M. Drews, and T. Allison. Acid-base and electrolyte changes following acute exercise. *Am. J. Kidney Dis.* (in press).

70. Lazaro, R.P., and H.S. Kirshner. Proximal muscle weakness in uremia. *Arch. Neurol.* 37:555–558, 1980.

71. Lazarus, J.M., C.L. Hampers, E.G. Lowrie, and J.P. Merrill. Baroreceptor activity in normotensive and hypertensive uremic patients. *Circulation* 47:1015–1021, 1973.

72. Lazarus, J.M., E.G. Lowrie, C.L. Hampers, and J.P. Merrill. Cardiovascular disease in uremic patients on hemodialysis. *Kidney Int.* 2 (suppl.):S167–S175, 1975.

73. Lazarus, J.M. Hemodialysis in chronic renal failure. In B.M. Brenner and J.H. Stein (eds.). *Contemporary Issues in Nephrology: Chronic Renal Failure.* New York: Churchill Livingstone, 1981, pp. 153–193.

74. Levin, N.W., and F. Dumler. Common clinical problems during hemodialysis. In A.R. Nissenson and R.N. Fine (eds.). *Dialysis Therapy.* St. Louis: C.V. Mosby Co., 1986, pp. 85–88.

75. Lindner, A., B. Charra, D.J. Sherrard, and B.H. Scribner. Accelerated atherosclerosis in prolonged maintenance hemodialysis. *N. Engl. J. Med.* 260:697–699, 1974.

76. Lundin, A.P., and E.A. Friedman. Vascular consequences of maintenance hemodialysis—an unproven case. *Nephron* 21:177–180, 1978.

77. Lundin, A.P., R.A. Stein, F. Frank, P. LaBelle, G.M. Berlyne, N. Krasnow, and E.A. Friedman. Cardiovascular status in long-term hemodialysis patients: An exercise and echocardiographic study. *Nephron* 28:234–238, 1981.

78. Lundin, A.P., R.A. Stein, C.D. Brown, P. LaBelle, F.S. Kalman, B.G. Delano, W.F. Heneghan, N.A. Lazarus, N. Krasnow, and E.A. Friedman. Fatigue, acid-base and electrolyte changes with exhaustive treadmill exercise in hemodialysis patients. *Nephron* 46:57–62, 1987.

79. Meggs, L.G., and A.I. Goodman. Adrenergic dysfunction in uremia. *Kidney Int.* 29:215, 1985. (Abstract)

80. Metcoff, J., R. Lindemann, and D. Baxter. Cell metabolism in uremia. *Am. J. Clin. Nutr.* 38:1627–1637, 1978.
81. Miller, M.E. Oxygen transport in uremia. *Semin. Nephrol.* 5:140–141, 1985.
82. Mitch, W.E. Conservative management of chronic renal failure. In B.M. Brenner and J.H. Stein (eds.). *Contemporary Issues in Nephrology: Chronic Renal Failure.* New York: Churchill Livingstone, 1981, pp. 117–153.
83. Mordasini, R., F. Frey, W. Flury, G. Klose, and H. Greten. Selective deficiency of hepatic triglyceride lipase in uremic patients. *N. Engl. J. Med.* 297:1362–1366, 1977.
84. Nakao, T., S. Fujiwara, K. Isoda, and T. Miyahara. Impaired lactate production by skeletal muscle with anaerobic exercise in patients with chronic renal failure. *Nephron* 31:111–115, 1982.
85. Nielson, V. The peripheral nerve function in chronic renal failure. *Acta Med. Scand.* (suppl. 573):1–32, 1974.
86. Nolph, K.D., and M.I. Sorkin. Continuous ambulatory peritoneal dialysis. In B.M. Brenner and J.H. Stein (eds.). *Contemporary Issues in Nephrology: Chronic Renal Disease.* New York: Churchill Livingstone, 1981, pp. 193–218.
87. Oberley, T. Success in self-dialysis. *Dialysis Transp.* 6:47–48, 1977.
88. Orie, J.E., H. Jabi, N. Glass, M. Besozzi, G.G. Rowe, W.P. Miller, H. Solllinger, and F. Belzer. Thallium 201 myocardial perfusion imaging and coronary arteriography in asymptomatic patients with end-stage renal disease secondary to juvenile onset diabetes mellitus. *Transplant Proc.* 27:1709–1710, 1986.
89. Painter, P.L., D. Messer, C. Weidener, and S.W. Zimmerman. Response to graded exercise testing in patients treated with CAPD. *Peritoneal Dial. Bull.* (suppl.)4:S94–S97, 1984.
90. Painter, P., P. Hanson, D. Messer-Rehak, M. Besozzi, and N.R. Glass. Ventricular function during exercise following renal transplantation. *Clin. Res.* 32:773A, 1984. (Abstract)
91. Painter, P.L., D. Messer-Rehak, P. Hanson, S.W. Zimmerman, and N.R. Glass. Exercise capacity in hemodialysis, CAPD, and renal transplant patients. *Nephron* 42:47–51, 1986.
92. Painter, P., J.N. Nelson-Worel, M.M. Hill, D.R. Thornbery, W.R. Shelp, A.R. Harrington, and A.B. Weinstein. Effects of exercise training during hemodialysis. *Nephron* 43:87–92, 1986.
93. Painter, P. Participation in exercise training during hemodialysis: A multicenter trial program. *Med. Sci. Sports Exerc.* 19:S19, 1987. (Abstract)
94. Painter, P., and M. Paris. Heart rate and blood pressure responses to exercise during hemodialysis. Washington, D.C.: National Kidney Foundation, 1987. (Abstract)
95. Painter, P.L., P. Hanson, D. Messer-Rehak, S.W. Zimmer, and N.R. Glass. Exercise tolerance changes following renal transplantation. *Am. J. Kidney Dis.* 10:452–456, 1987.
96. Parrish, A.E., M. Zikria, and R.A. Kenney. Oxygen uptake in exercising subjects with minimal renal disease. *Nephron* 40:455–457, 1985.
97. Pickering, T.G., B. Gribbin, and D.O. Oliver. Baroreflex sensitivity in patients on long-term hemodialysis. *Clin. Sci.* 43:645–657, 1972.
98. Rapoport, J., M. Aviram, C. Chaimovitz, and J.G. Brook. Defective high-density lipoprotein composition in patients on chronic hemodialysis. *N. Engl. J. Med.* 299:1326–1329, 1978.
99. Reese, G.N., and S.H. Appel. Neurologic complications of renal failure. *Semin. Nephrol.* 1:137–150, 1981.
100. Rennie, D. Renal rehabilitation—where are the data? *N. Engl. J. Med.* 304:351–352, 1981. (Editorial).
101. Rose, B.D. (ed.). Pathophysiology of uremia. In *Pathophysiology of Renal Disease.* New York: McGraw-Hill Book Co., 1981, pp. 419–474.
102. Rostrand, S.G. Management of ischemic heart disease, heart failure, and pericarditis

inpatients on hemodialysis. In A.R. Nissenson and R.N. Fine (eds.). *Dialysis Therapy.* St. Louis: C.V. Mosby Co., 1986, pp. 166–169.

103. Sanders, P.W., and J.J. Curtis. Management of anticoagulation for hemodialysis. In A.R. Nissenson and R.N. Fine (eds.). *Dialysis Therapy.* St. Louis: C.V. Mosby Co., 1986, pp. 39–40.

104. Shalom, R., J.A. Blumenthal, R.S. Williams, R.G. McMurray, and V.W. Dennis. Feasibility and benefits of exercise training in patients on maintenance dialysis. *Kidney Int.* 25:958–963, 1984.

105. Sherrard, D. Renal Osteodystrophy. *Semin. Nephrol.* 6:56–67, 1986.

106. Sill, V.V., K.G. Lanser, and W. Bauditz. Ein Flub der Anaie und der arteriovenosen fistel auf die Korperliche Leistungsfahigkeit der Dauerdialysepatenten. *Z. Kardiol.* 62:164–175, 1972.

107. Silverstein, D.K., and J.S. Karliner. Ischemic heart disease. In R.A. O'Rourke, B.M. Brenner, and J.H. Stein (eds.). *Contemporary Issues in Nephrology: The Heart and Renal Disease.* New York: Churchill Livingstone, 1984, pp. 209–240.

108. Squires, R.W., J.D. Brekke, G.T. Gau, A. Muri, and P.P. Frohnert. Early exercise testing and training after renal transplantation. *Med. Sci. Sports Exerc.* 17:184, 1985. (Abstract)

109. Strom, T.B., and N.L. Tilnery. Clinical management of the renal transplantation recipient. In B.M. Brenner and J.H. Stein (eds.). *Contemporary Issues in Nephrology: Chronic Renal Failure.* New York: Churchill Livingstone, 1981, pp. 255–287.

110. U.S. ESRD Program: Selected 1984 statistics. *Contemp. Dialysis Nephrol.* 6:18, 1985.

111. Thomas, P.K. Screening for peripheral neuropathy in patients treated by chronic hemodialysis. *Muscle Nerve* 1:396–399, 1978.

112. Vasiri, N.D. Anemia in ESRD patients. In A.R. Nissenson and R.N. Fine (eds.). *Dialysis Therapy.* St. Louis: C.V. Mosby Co., 1986, pp. 158–162.

113. Vincenti, F., W.J. Amend, J. Abele, N.J. Feduska, and O. Salvatierra. The role of hypertension in hemodialysis-associated atherosclerosis. *Am. J. Med.* 68:363–367, 1980.

114. Vollmer, W.M., P.W. Wahl, and C.R Blagg. Survival with dialysis and transplantation in patients with end stage renal disease. *N. Engl. J. Med.* 308:1553–1558, 1983.

115. Wilson, J.A., T.M. Yahya, G.R. Giles, and A.M. Davison. The effect of haemodialysis and transplantation on autonomic neuropathy. *Proc. EDTA* 16:261–265, 1979.

116. Woodson, R.D., R.E. Willis, and C. Lenfant. Effects of acute and established anemia on oxygen transport at rest, submaximal and maximal work. *J. Appl. Physiol.* 44:36–43, 1978.

117. Ulmer, H.E., H. Greiner, H.W. Schuler, and K. Scharer. Cardiovascular impairment and physical working capacity in children with chronic renal failure. *Acta Paediatr. Scand.* 67:43–48, 1978.

118. Zabetakis, P.M., G.W. Gleim, F.L. Pasternak, A. Saraniti, J.A. Nicholas, and M.F. Michelis. Long-duration submaximal exercise conditioning in hemodialysis patients. *Clin. Nephrol.* 18:17–22, 1982.

11
Exercise and the Elderly

BRYANT A. STAMFORD, Ph.D.

INTRODUCTION

The decline of physical work capacity in the elderly has been known since the earliest times, and the burgeoning geriatric population has increased interest in why this occurs. Is the decline inevitable, arising from the natural anatomical and physiological consequences of aging? Or do factors such as reduced daily physical activities and underlying disease processes play a significant role? Can the decline be arrested or, better yet, reversed? These and other questions have preoccupied exercise gerontologists in recent years. Unfortunately, research on the elderly is difficult at best, and there are a number of obstacles that are not encountered when research is conducted on younger individuals.

The extent to which a given subset of individuals represents the elderly population in general is a major obstacle. This problem is inherent in all research on humans, but may be amplified in the elderly because of increased anatomical and/or physiological diversity among elderly individuals. The situation is complicated further by the extremes of activity patterns among those comprising the elderly population and the likelihood that those who volunteer for testing are the most active. These and other methodological problems may be responsible for the gross lack of agreement between cross-sectional and longitudinal data in some areas. The rate of decline in maximal oxygen uptake with age is one example.

A longitudinal approach does not necessarily avoid problems caused by diversity. Within elderly individuals there is increased diversity in functional capacity among organ systems, and a decline in one area may affect a seemingly unrelated area. Orthopedic limitations imposed on cardiovascular function is one example. Studying younger and middle-aged subjects through time creates a different set of problems, as changes observed in the elderly may not be due to a gradual transition over many years and extrapolations could lead to erroneous conclusions. For example, strength loss late in life would not be reflected in aging trends assessed in the earlier years.

Finally, much of the available literature does not provide evidence that permits isolation of the effects of aging per se from other confounding

341

factors. Rather, much of the reported research is a description of those individuals who have lived for a minimal number of years and must be interpreted carefully. Animal studies may provide the controls necessary for isolation of causal effects, but limits on the external validity are obvious.

Despite the broad array of inherent limitations, the body of knowledge concerning physical performance and the elderly is expanding rapidly in scope and sophistication. This chapter presents a selective review of literature pertinent to the anatomical and physiological status of the elderly and their effects on the capacity of the elderly to perform physical work and exercise. In addition, the ability of the elderly to undergo training to improve physical performance capacity will be discussed.

MAXIMAL OXYGEN UPTAKE ($\dot{V}O_2$max)

The best single indicator of physical working capacity is the maximal oxygen uptake ($\dot{V}O_2$max). Documentation that $\dot{V}O_2$max has been achieved is often difficult in young, healthy subjects. A true indication is no further increase in oxygen consumption, the plateau, despite an increase in external work. In the elderly, a plateau may be extremely difficult to achieve, especially in those unfamillar with vigorous exercise owing to fear, muscular weakness, and shortness of breath [17, 97, 121, 149, 264]. Electrocardiographic abnormalities are also more likely to occur in the elderly during maximal exertion [23].

Other criteria have been used to document $\dot{V}O_2$max, such as a blood lactate level in excess of 8 mM plasma, a respiratory exchange ratio in excess of 1.15, and/or reaching the estimated maximal heart rate [18, 210]. These methods are not as reliable, but there seems to be no other alternative. Repeat testing may result in a greater number of subjects attaining the plateau, but this is impractical when testing a large number of subjects.

In view of these methodological complications, a variety of prediction tests have been employed. Prediction tests are based upon the facts that a given amount of external work requires a given amount of oxygen consumption and that there is a linear relationship between heart rate and oxygen consumption. This relationship is similar for young and elderly persons [14, 15, 92, 188, 242, 253], although a slight increase in the oxygen cost of a given submaximal work load has been reported in older individuals [266]. Notwithstanding the fact that there may be a large error factor when attempting to predict the $\dot{V}O_2$max of individuals, the random nature of the error does not preclude the use of such tests for grossly describing large populations. The research literature is a mixture of studies in which $\dot{V}O_2$max has been measured directly, and predictive tests.

Cross-sectional studies indicate that with age $\dot{V}O_2$max declines progressively in both males and females [15, 21, 30, 66, 110, 190, 197, 214]. From these cross-sectional data, the rate of decline in $\dot{V}O_2$max for sedentary men was found to be approximately 0.40–0.45 ml $\cdot$ kg^{-1} $\cdot$ min^{-1} per year, and the rate of decline for active men was 0.44 ml $\cdot$ kg^{-1} $\cdot$ min^{-1} per year. This represents a decrement of slightly less than 1% per year, beginning at an approximate age of 25 years [229], or approximately 9% per decade [108]. In sedentary women, the rate of decline was less, 0.30 ml $\cdot$ kg^{-1} $\cdot$ min^{-1} per year [110]. Similar results for women were found in longitudinal studies [185].

Longitudinal studies offer several advantages over cross-sectional studies with regard to assessment of changes in $\dot{V}O_2$max with age. The same individuals are observed through time, which allows each subject to serve as his/her own control; confounding hidden factors such as heredity can be controlled as well [43]. Longitudinal studies [39, 59, 112] indicate that the rate of decline in $\dot{V}O_2$max in sedentary men is greater than that reported in cross-sectional studies (Figure 1A). This may be due to the fact that cross-sectional studies include highly fit individuals in the study population [192]. There is some question, however, as to whether the accelerated rate of decline demonstrated in longitudinal studies, approximately 1.0 ml $\cdot$ kg^{-1} $\cdot$ min^{-1} per year, is more indicative of certain segments of the life span rather than the full life span. Shephard and Sidney point out in their review [216] that a loss of 1.0 ml $\cdot$ kg^{-1} $\cdot$ min^{-1} per year over a span of 40 years, from ages 25 to 65 years, would result in a $\dot{V}O_2$max of less than 10 ml $\cdot$ kg^{-1} $\cdot$ min^{-1}. This level is, of course, much lower than expected for 65-year-olds.

There is a tendency to gain weight consistently from the age of 20 to the mid-forties. This is due, at least in part, to the fact that the early adult years tend to be busy years, which precludes the level of physical activity enjoyed earlier in life. Weight gain and reduced physical activity would suggest an accelerated decline in $\dot{V}O_2$max during these years. However, the 32-year longitudinal study by Robinson et al. [198] revealed a decrement of approximately 0.42 ml $\cdot$ kg^{-1} $\cdot$ min^{-1} per year from early life (approximately 20 years of age). There is the possibility that within this 32-year span, there were segments (e.g., ages 20–30) that were accelerated. Other segments of accelerated decline could also exist, such as beyond age 60.

The suggestion that sedentary and active men decline in $\dot{V}O_2$max at the same rate was challenged by Dehn and Bruce [59], who found that the rate of decline was much greater in sedentary men (Figure 1B). Subsequent studies support the fact that chronic vigorous physical activity can reduce the decline in $\dot{V}O_2$max with age [108, 116, 186]. Others [66, 185] have reported similar findings in women.

Kasch and Wallace [126] followed a group of active men for 10 years,

FIGURE 1

A. *Longitudinal versus cross-sectional changes in* $\dot{V}O_2max$: *(a) Cross-sectional data from 17 studies* ($-0.40\ ml \cdot kg^{-1} \cdot min^{-1}$ *per year); Dehn and Bruce, J. Appl. Physiol. 33:805–807, 1972; (b) data* ($-1.04\ ml \cdot kg^{-1} \cdot min^{-1}$ *per year) from Dill et al., J. Sports Med. 7:4–32, 1967; (c) data* (-0.93 $ml \cdot kg^{-1} \cdot min^{-1}$ *per year) from Hollmann, 1965; cited in Dehn and Bruce, J. Appl. Physiol. 33:805–807, 1972; (d) data* ($-0.94\ ml \cdot kg^{-1} \cdot min^{-1}$ *per year) from Dehn and Bruce, J. Appl. Physiol. 33:805–807, 1972. B. Longitudinal changes in* $\dot{V}O_2max$ *in active versus inactive men: (b) data from Dill et al., J. Sports Med. 7:4–32, 1967; (c) data from Hollmann, 1965; cited in Dehn and Bruce, J. Appl. Physiol. 33:805–807, 1972; (d) data from Dehn and Bruce, J. Appl. Physiol. 33:805–807, 1972. (Figures A and B redrawn from Dehn, M.M., and R.A. Bruce. Longitudinal variations in maximal oxygen intake with age and activity. J. Appl. Physiol 33:805–807, 1972.*

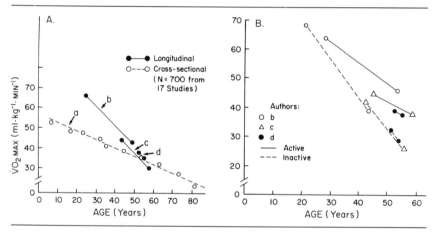

from ages 45 to 55, and found no loss in $\dot{V}O_2max$ as a result of vigorous training. The men in this study exercised by running or swimming three times per week for approximately 1 hour per session at 86% of maximal capacity. It must be noted that exercise of this intensity, frequency, and duration would be expected to increase $\dot{V}O_2max$, but it did not. The men needed to work very hard in order to sustain their $\dot{V}O_2max$ at a modest 44 ml $\cdot$ kg^{-1} $\cdot$ min^{-1} over the 10-year span. This suggests progressive physiological deterioration despite exercise training.

Changes in body composition confound assessment of the changes in $\dot{V}O_2max$ with age. For example, the longitudinal study by Irving et al. [116] demonstrated that chronic exercise reduced the rate of decline in $\dot{V}O_2max$. However, a significant weight gain in the sedentary comparison group could essentially account for the difference in the rates of decline between the two groups. Similarly, in a follow-up study by Kasch et al. [127] after an additional 8 years (18 years total), there was a loss in $\dot{V}O_2$max when expressed in liters per minute. However, a loss of body weight offset this decline, and there was no change when $\dot{V}O_2$max was expressed in milliliters per kilogram per minute.

The loss of muscle mass in the elderly may be masked by an increase in connective tissue [64], which could influence interpretation of $\dot{V}O_2$max differences in the old and young. For example, since muscle mass is decreased and body fat is increased in the elderly, comparisons with the young for $\dot{V}O_2$max normalized for total body mass are misleading. Even when attempting to correct this situation by expressing $\dot{V}O_2$max per kilogram of lean tissue as determined from measurement of body density, the compensation of connective tissue for muscle tissue would still provide misleading results. It has been demonstrated that when employing 24-hour creatinine excretion as an index of lean (muscle) tissue, the $\dot{V}O_2$max per kilogram of lean tissue was not decreased in the elderly [80]. Moreover, it must be considered that in the elderly who initiate training late in life, a key effect of physical training to increase $\dot{V}O_2$max could be modulated through an increased muscle mass, with a resultant increase in a-$\overline{v}O_2$ difference [210].

Some elderly individuals in their late sixties and beyond have demonstrated a high $\dot{V}O_2$max [46, 123, 188, 270]. However, when the $\dot{V}O_2$max is high early in life, as is the case with former endurance athletes, intensive training will not sustain it at the same level in later years [64, 108]. Is the loss of muscle mass primarily responsible? It has been reported that physical training continued throughout life and into the later years may contribute to a body composition in the elderly comparable to that of younger endurance athletes [108]. However, data derived from fat-fold caliper measurements, hydrostatic weighing, and other traditional approaches to the measurement of body composition do not preclude the possibility that the lean body mass of the elderly contains a greater proportion of connective tissue.

The wide range of values reported in cross-sectional and longitudinal studies for the rate of decline in $\dot{V}O_2$max with age, and confounding factors such as heredity, changes in body weight and body composition, and physically active versus sedentary life-style, suggest that a single rate may not adequately describe this phenomenon. Dr. E. R. Buskirk [44] offers a possible explanation that encourages a broader perspective on the issues: "changes in $\dot{V}O_2$max over the entire age range may be curvilinear, with active individuals declining slowly as long as they maintain a regular exercise program, and sedentary individuals declining at a rapid rate during their 20's and 30's followed by a slower rate of decline of their $\dot{V}O_2$max as they age further."

DETERMINANTS OF $\dot{V}O_2$max

$\dot{V}O_2$max is the product of maximal cardiac output ($\dot{Q}$max) and maximal extraction of oxygen from the blood by working tissues (a-$\bar{v}O_2$ difference). This is expressed as $\dot{V}O_2$max = $\dot{Q}$max × a-$\bar{v}O_2$ diff max. Maximal cardiac output is the product of maximal heart rate (HR) and maximal stroke volume (SV). This is expressed as $\dot{Q}$max = HRmax × SVmax. a-$\bar{v}O_2$ difference is influenced by a variety of factors including muscle mass, the capacity of arterial blood to transport and relinguish oxygen, and the capacity of the tissues to take up and utilize oxygen. Each of these factors will be considered as affecting $\dot{V}O_2$max in the elderly.

Cardiac Output: Heart Rate
The decline in $\dot{V}O_2$max with age may be due, at least in part, to a decline in maximal heart rate [3, 40, 114, 121, 201, 212, 241, 263]. Recent evidence suggests that a reduced maximal heart rate may be the primary factor. Hagberg et al. [102] reported that the decline in maximal heart rate was solely responsible for differences in $\dot{V}O_2$max between older and younger endurance athletes, as maximal stroke volume and maximal a-$\bar{v}O_2$ difference were similar (Table 1).

The decline in maximal heart rate is substantial according to several early reports [15, 197]. However, it should be noted that a host of factors such as muscle weakness, shortness of breath, and fear of excessive exertion can cause premature termination of a maximal test and underestimation of the maximal heart rate. The exercise mode will also influence the maximal heart rate, especially in the untrained individual; for example, the maximal heart rate achieved on the treadmill is likely to be higher than that achieved on a cycle ergometer. On the other hand, the decline in maximal heart rate is evident in older endurance athletes who have sustained a high level of training over the years [102, 108].

Some investigations have demonstrated higher maximal heart rates in the elderly than expected from earlier reports [149, 152]. For example, in the study by Seals et al. [210], the mean age of subjects was 63 years, and the mean maximal heart rate achieved during graded treadmill exercise was 174 b · min^{-1}. The often used estimate of 220 minus the age would predict a maximal heart rate of 157 b · min^{-1} in these subjects. The rate of decline in maximal heart rate with age appears to be less in women than in men [114].

The age-related reduction in maximal heart rate could be associated with decreased sympathetic drive [53], although the preponderance of evidence argues to the contrary. For example, several studies have demonstrated the need for increased levels of infused catecholamines to reach a given heart rate in elderly versus younger subjects [28, 153, 260]. These studies support a decreased responsiveness to sympathetic stimulation in the elderly.

TABLE 1

Hemodynamic Comparison of Young and Older Endurance Athletes*

	Master Athletes ($N = 8$)	Young Runners		Sedentary Age-Matched Subjects ($N = 15$)
		Matched ($N = 8$)	Competitive ($N = 8$)	
Age, years	56 (5)	25 (3)	26 (3)	58 (5)
$\dot{V}O_2$max, $l \cdot min^{-1}$	3.69 (0.46)	4.24† (0.34)	4.56† (0.36)	2.44† (0.44)
$\dot{V}O_2$max, $ml \cdot kg^{-1} \cdot min^{-1}$	56.6 (5.2)	62.2† (5.9)	70.3†§ (2.5)	29.7†§ (5.4)
$\dot{V}O_2$max, $ml \cdot kg$ $LBW^{-1} \cdot min^{-1}$	63.9 (6.7)	71.1† (5.7)	77.8†§ (2.6)	35.9† (5.3)
Heart rate, $b \cdot min^{-1}$	172 (15)	195† (11)	195† (6)	176 (10)
O_2 pulse, $ml \cdot kg^{-1}$ $min^{-1} \cdot b^{-1}$	0.33 (0.01)	0.32 (0.04)	0.36†# (0.02)	0.17† (0.03)
O_2 pulse, $ml \cdot kg$ $LBW^{-1} \cdot min^{-1} \cdot b^{-1}$	0.37 (0.02)	0.37 (0.04)	0.40‡# (0.03)	0.21† (0.03)
$\dot{V}E_{max}$, $l \cdot min^{-1}$	117 (24)	126 (8)	131‡ (11)	85† (18)
Maximum stroke volume, ml ‖	133 (9)	131 (12)	139 (9)	109† (19)
Maximal cardiac output, $l \cdot min^{-1}$¶	22.9 (2.2)	25.5† (2.2)	27.1† (1.8)	19.2† (3.5)
Maximal a-$\bar{v}O_2$ difference, $ml \cdot 100$ ml^{-1}	16.2 (2.5)	16.7 (1.7)	16.9 (1.5)	13.0† (2.6)

*From Hagberg, J.M., et al. A hemodynamic comparison of young and old endurance athletes during exercise. *J. Appl. Physiol.* 58:2041–2046, 1985.
Values are means (SD) and LBW, lean body weight.
†Significantly different from master athletes; $P < 0.01$.
‡Significantly different from master athletes; $P < 0.05$.
§Significantly different from matched young runners; $P < 0.05$.
#Significantly different from matched young runners; $P < 0.01$.
‖ Average stroke volume measured at the three submaximal exercise work rates.
¶Estimated by multiplying maximum stroke volume by maximum heart rate.

Several studies indicate a decreased end-organ sensitivity to the effects of catecholamines in the elderly [89, 122, 204, 273, 277]. In addition, a blunted responsiveness has been inferred from observations of increased plasma norepinephrine levels in the elderly when exposed to various stressors [28, 177, 276, 277]. However, this could be due to a higher relative stress experienced by older individuals compared to their younger counterparts.

Further evidence supporting reduced "responsiveness" rather than "drive" is presented by Fleg et al. [81], who reported substantially lower heart rates and greater plasma catecholamine levels in older subjects compared with younger subjects over a series of aerobic work loads adjusted for relative stress. Some may argue that work at 60–70% $\dot{V}O_2$max represents a different level of stress for a young versus an old man due to differences in submaximal indices such as the anaerobic threshold.

348 | *Stamford*

FIGURE 2

Norepinephrine (A) and epinephrine (B) responses in subjects varying in age from 29 to 72 years at rest, during maximal exercise, and following exercise. Subjects were participants of the Baltimore Longitudinal Study on Aging. Each subject was judged to be free from occult coronary artery disease from results obtained on a variety of screening tests. (From Fleg, J. L., et al. Age-related augmentation of plasma catecholamines during dynamic exercise in healthy males. J. Appl. Physiol. *59:1033–1039, 1985. Redrawn by E. G. Lakatta and republished in Lakatta, E. G. Cardiovascular system. In B. Kent and R. N. Butler [eds.]* Human Aging Research: Concepts and Techniques. *New York: Raven Press. In press).*

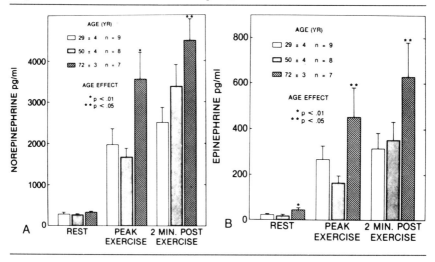

However, the fact that the plasma catecholamine levels were approximately twice as high in old subjects (age 72) as in young ones (age 29) at maximal effort is persuasive [81, see Figure 2]. The authors [81] acknowledge the fact that plasma catecholamine levels provide a reflection of catecholamine production, release, and degradation, and this could influence their results if there was a decreased clearance of norepinephrine in elderly subjects. Conflicting results have been reported on this issue [77, 276].

Decreased responsiveness to sympathetic stimulation could be due to changes in the aged beta-adrenergic receptors [1, 65, 79, 82], although no change was noted in beta-adrenergic receptor number or affinity [99]. Other possibilities exist as well. A postsynaptic breakdown in the coupling of receptor and effector is possible, as catecholamines influence biochemical reactions, which in turn affect contractile responses [141].

Cardiac Output: Stroke Volume
Several studies have reported a lower cardiac output in older versus younger subjects at given levels of oxygen consumption and similar heart rates due to a decreased stroke volume [92, 98, 121, 241]. Others have reported an increased stroke volume and cardiac output in the elderly during submaximal exercise [26, 105].

The introduction of radionuclide measurement techniques provides a noninvasive means by which ventricular performance can be investigated in the elderly. Port et al. [189] reported that with aging there is a reduced exercise ejection fraction. In some individuals, this could be associated with occult coronary disease. A lack of adequate blood supply can result in weakened contractions in the affected areas and regional wall motion abnormalities that can influence the interpretation of results obtained [138].

Rodeheffer et al. [201] reported that older subjects, vigorously screened in an effort to detect underlying coronary disease, did not experience a decline in ejection fraction. Rather, there was an increased stroke volume attributable to an increase in end-diastolic volume and use of the Frank-Starling mechanism (Figure 3). Thus, cardiac output was maintained despite a lower maximal heart rate. In the studies by Port et al. [189] and Rodeheffer et al. [201], exercise was performed in the upright position.

Higginbotham et al. [109] examined men aged 20 to 50 years during upright exercise and found a 25% age-related reduction in $\dot{V}O_2$max. They found no relationship between age and exercise stroke volume index, end-diastolic or end-systolic volume index, ejection fraction, or a-$\bar{v}O_2$ difference. They concluded that the lower $\dot{V}O_2$max in older men was due to a decrease in maximal heart rate, which resulted in a concomitant decrease in maximal cardiac output. In contrast to the findings of Rodeheffer et al. [201], there was no increase in end-diastolic volume and stroke volume, and thus a drop in maximal heart rate was translated directly into a drop in cardiac output. Similar findings for men were reported by Hossack and Bruce [114]. These results also support the findings of Hagberg et al. [102] for older endurance athletes.

Results reported by Mann et al. [157] indicate that stroke volume during supine exercise is maintained by the Frank-Starling mechanism mediated by an increased end-diastolic volume, as suggested by Rodeheffer et al. [201]. Van Tosh et al. [259] reported similar findings from echocardiographic studies during semisupine exercise.

Greater dependence upon the Frank-Starling mechanism would seem to compensate for a reduced responsiveness to catecholamines [88]. However, structural changes in the aging myocardium and arteries can

FIGURE 3

Heart rate (A), end-diastolic volume (B), end-systolic volume (C), and stroke volume (D) as related to cardiac output during progressively increasing up-right work loads. The relationship between stroke volume and end-diastolic volume is depicted in (E). Subjects were participants of the Baltimore Longitudinal Study on Aging and represented three age groups ranging from 25 to 80 years. Each subject was judged to be free from occult coronary artery disease from results obtained on a variety of screening tests. (From Rodeheffer, R. J., et al. Exercise cardiac output is maintained with advancing age in healthy human subjects: Cardiac dilatation and increased stroke volume compensate for diminished heart rate. Circulation *69:203–213, 1984. Redrawn by E. G. Lakatta and republished in Lakatta, E. G. Cardiovascular system. In B. Kent and R. N. Butler [eds.],* Human Aging Research: Concepts and Techniques. *New York: Raven Press. In press.)*

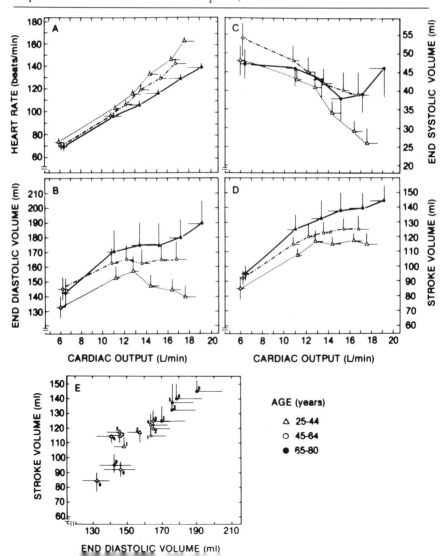

result in an increased preload (resistance to filling of the heart) and an increased afterload (systemic and pulmonary vascular resistance) [16, 87, 92, 121, 173, 177, 241, 243, 249]. The presence or absence of underlying disease conditions could influence the impact of these factors, and thus vigorous screening of subjects for occult coronary disease could significantly affect the findings. For example, the results of an investigation by Hakki et al. [103] suggest that older individuals with demonstrable (angiographic) coronary heart disease do not rely upon the Frank-Starling mechanism during exercise.

Separating age-related causes from mere disuse and deconditioning (of the heart) permeates the geriatric literature and cannot be ignored [14, 87, 124]. For example, in the elderly, there is an increased contraction time due to a longer time to peak tension and a longer half-relaxation time [106, 136, 140]. In part, these effects may be due to reduced myosin ATPase activity and/or impairment of the rate of calcium sequestration by the sarcoplasmic reticulum [50, 139]. Are these factors due to aging or reduced physical activity? On the one hand, exercise training has been shown to reverse these effects in animals [199, 238]. On the other hand, a study by Schocken et al. [208] indicated that exercise training did not improve ventricular function in elderly subjects.

The use of different (dye dilution, rebreathing, direct Fick, echocardiographic, radionuclide) measurement techniques, upright versus supine exercise, relative versus absolute work loads, physical training history and status, and other factors such as a small sample size may contribute to the different interpretations regarding the potential decline in stroke volume as a product of aging. Actual measurement of stroke volume during maximal exercise versus extrapolation from submaximal values is another possible confounding factor.

A major complication, and perhaps the most important, could be the high prevalence of asymptomatic ischemic heart disease in the elderly [248, 265, 268]. This is supported by autopsy studies that demonstrate a high incidence of significant coronary disease not only in those dying from coronary heart disease but also in those dying from cancer, accidents, and other causes [75]. Thus, differences in results among recent studies could be attributable, in part, to vigorous screening for underlying pathological complications [137].

The use of sophisticated screening measures presents the provocative dilemma of whether to use as research subjects only those elderly individuals who are proven to be free of underlying pathological complications, even though such individuals may not be representative of the elderly population at large. This has obvious clinical and academic implications, but may be necessary in order to isolate the impact of aging per se on cardiac performance in elderly humans.

Arteriovenous Oxygen (a-$\bar{v}O_2$) *Difference*

In simplistic terms, a-$\bar{v}O_2$ difference represents a peripheral adjustment to exercise stress, whereas heart rate and stroke volume represent adjustments that are centralized. Although relatively little is known about the maximum a-$\bar{v}O_2$ difference in the elderly, there is some evidence that it is decreased [87, 98, 121]. There is also evidence to the contrary [109]. A comparison of young and old athletes revealed a similar a-$\bar{v}O_2$ difference despite a difference in $\dot{V}O_2$max [102]. Repeated maximal tests on one individual (D. B. Dill) from age 35 to 92 revealed that the a-$\bar{v}O_2$ difference was maintained through the years, despite a drop in heart rate and possibly stroke volume [113].

Several factors could operate to reduce the maximal a-$\bar{v}O_2$ difference in the elderly. There appears to be no change in the metabolic potential of muscle per unit mass, as indicated by enzymatic activity [7, 94, 176]. Thus, the loss of muscle mass, which can be rather substantial in the elderly despite little or no change in body mass [33], would directly affect the utilization of oxygen in the periphery. In addition, during maximal exercise, 80–85% of the cardiac output is redistributed to the working skeletal muscles [18]. This effect may be diminished in the elderly, owing to a reduced heat tolerance and a greater blood flow to the skin [148, 151, 195]. This, combined with a lower capillary/fiber ratio in exercising muscles [178], would result in a reduced extraction of oxygen from the blood.

The ability to transport oxygen in the arterial blood (i.e., circulating red blood cells and hemgloblin concentration) does not appear to be affected negatively to a significant degree by age [57, 76, 113, 215, 217, 218]. However, a shift in the oxygen dissociation curve to the left, possibly due to a drop in 2,3-diphosphoglyceric acid (2,3-DPG) content, could affect the delivery of oxygen to working muscles [63, 128, 191]. Tweeddale et al. [256], on the other hand, did not find a relationship between age and oxygen-binding capacity, and they reported no change in 2,3-DPG.

Pulmonary Function

Maximal ventilation during exercise is reduced in the elderly [196]. However, this is not likely to be a limitation on $\dot{V}O_2$max. With training and an increase in $\dot{V}O_2$max in the elderly, the maximal exercise ventilation increases, and this represents a larger proportion of the maximal ventilatory capacity that remains unchanged with training [272, see Table 2].

Some characteristics of pulmonary function decline in the elderly, but the extent to which this influences physical working capacity in healthy individuals is not certain [155]. The vital capacity declines with age, with no apparent change in the total lung capacity, and the residual volume is increased, which results in an increased ratio of residual volume to total lung capacity [52, 160, 174, 175, 180, 209]. Compliance of the lung may increase with age, while compliance of the thoracic wall may decrease [161, 194, 255, 261], and thus more energy is required to sustain any given level of ventilation [62]. There are obvious implications for ventilatory capacity as well [128].

Ventilation may be higher for a given amount of submaximal work in the elderly [62, 96, 179, 196]. The ventilatory equivalent for oxygen may be higher in the elderly as well [62, 96]. One explanation could be the greater ventilatory response to CO_2 production in the elderly [35], which may be the means by which the elderly compensate for lower gas exchange efficiency [57, 69]. On the other hand, the ability to regulate ventilation may decline in the elderly, and several reports indicate a reduced sensitivity to hypercapnia and hypoxia with age [6, 133, 181, 205), which is apparently unchanged by physical training [272, see Table 2].

It is certainly possible that a higher ventilation and ventilatory equivalent may be due to the fact that older men "are simply exercising at a higher percentage of their $\dot{V}O_2$max" [164]. The data of Yerg et al. [272] support this possibility. They found that the ventilatory response and the ventilatory equivalent for oxygen were reduced at the same absolute work rate following training, which resulted in a 25% increase in $\dot{V}O_2$max (Table 2).

Another important consideration when assessing responses to submaximal exercise is the anaerobic threshold or ventilation threshold [179]. When expressed as an absolute work load, the ventilation threshold has been shown to be much lower in the elderly [54, 193]. At work loads above the ventilation threshold, the respiratory exchange ratio (R) and blood lactate concentration indicate a greater dependence upon carbohydrate for fuel. There is a shift toward greater oxidation of fat at a given submaximal work level after training in the elderly, as evidenced by a reduction in R and blood lactate [211]. Ventilation was reduced as well [211].

PHYSICAL TRAINING

Cardiorespiratory Fitness

The ability of the elderly to increase their cardiorespiratory fitness has received considerable attention in the past two decades. Earlier, it was widely accepted that older individuals who did not engage in physical training early in life could not respond to exercise training initiated in their later years [111]. Others suggested that some response was possible, but the degree of response was less than expected for younger individuals [131, 203, 269].

TABLE 2
Effect of Training on Ventilatory Function*

	Ventilatory Capacity and Maximal Exercise Response		
	Before Training	After Training	*P*
BSA, m^2	1.87 (0.12)	1.85 (0.10)	NS
MVV, l · min^{-1}	130.4 (33.3)	130.0 (32.5)	NS
$\dot{V}O_2$max, l · min^{-1}	1.91 (0.43)	2.39 (0.55)	<0.005
$\dot{V}O_2$max, ml · kg^{-1} · min^{-1}	25.7 (4.9)	32.9 (7.6)	<0.005
$\dot{V}E$max, l · min^{-1}	66.7 (18.6)	86.1 (17.4)	<0.005
$\dot{V}E$max · MVV^{-1} × 100%	53 (15)	69 (14)	<0.005
	Responses to Submaximal Exercise and to Hypercapnia		
$\dot{V}E/\dot{V}O_2$	27.7 (2.6)	25.1 (2.8)	<0.005
$\dot{V}E/\dot{V}CO_2$	28.5 (3.4)	27.4 (4.3)	NS
Heart rate, b · min^{-1}	141 (18)	125 (13)	<0.025
Blood lactate, mmol · l^{-1}	3.00 (1.09)	1.67 (0.77)	<0.005
S, l · min^{-1} mmHg^{-1}	1.53 (0.53)	1.67 (0.72)	NS
S · m^{-2} BSA	0.82 (0.27)	0.85 (0.36)	NS

*From Yerg, J.E., et al. Effect of endurance exercise training on ventilatory function in older individuals. *J. Appl. Physiol.* 58:791–794, 1985.
Values are means (SD) for 11 subjects (7 men and 4 women, ages 63 (±2) years).
BSA = body surface area; S = slope of hypercapnic ventilatory response.
$\dot{V}E/\dot{V}O_2$, heart rate, and blood lactate were determined at $\dot{V}O_2$ of 1.53 ± 0.37 and 1.51 ± 0.35 l · min^{-1}, *P* = NS, respectively; $\dot{V}E/\dot{V}CO_2$ was calculated at $\dot{V}CO_2$ of 1.49 ± 0.35 and 1.49 ± 0.36. l · min^{-1}, *P* = NS, respectively.

Stamford [240] investigated the effects of physical training on institutionalized geriatric patients who had been confined since early childhood. It was ascertained that these individuals had not engaged in vigorous physical labor or exercise during their lives, and for at least the latter two decades, the sum total of their daily exercise had consisted of slow walking to destinations such as the cafeteria or bathrooms located within the same building and on the same floor. These individuals demonstrated a significant cardiorespiratory training effect, and their response to physical training was at least comparable to that observed among a group of recently admitted patients with a history of considerably greater physical activity. These findings suggest that the capacity to respond to physical training is independent of the physical activity history.

Whether older individuals respond to physical training to the same degree as their younger counterparts is not certain. Such factors as the initial fitness level complicate matters. For example, the lower the fitness level initially, the greater the expected improvement. Also, when the initial level of fitness is low, the degree of change expressed as a percentage is likely to be exaggerated. A lack of motivation and/or fear on the pretest could provide artificially low initial values, which would create the illusion of a huge change. These factors favor a large increase for the elderly, and in fact, an increase in $\dot{V}O_2$max of 38% has been reported [23]. On the other hand, the elderly may not be capable of engaging in vigorous exercise early in training due to orthopedic limitations and unfamiliarity with excessive exertion. Regardless, several studies suggest that older subjects can respond to physical training over an 8- to 20-week period in a manner expected of younger subjects, with a range of increases in $\dot{V}O_2$max extending from approximately 5% to 20% [2, 20, 41, 72, 187, 224, 258].

It is well established that the greater the intensity of training, the greater the training effects. A minimal intensity of training of 60% of the heart rate range has been suggested for young, healthy males [125]. For the elderly, however, lower intensities can be effective in the early stages of training, probably due to the low initial level of fitness. deVries [60] reported a significant change in the cardiorespiratory fitness in old subjects resulting from training at only 40% of the heart rate range. As fitness improved, however, the degree of change was reduced. Badenhop et al. [20] reported a similar improvement in $\dot{V}O_2$max whether training was conducted at a low intensity of 30–45% of the heart rate range or at 60–75% of the heart rate range. In contrast, Seals et al. [210] and Sidney and Shephard [224] reported that high-intensity exercise was more effective in increasing $\dot{V}O_2$max than low-intensity exercise.

Stamford [240] reported that the initial level of fitness in old subjects dictated whether or not they were likely to respond to low-intensity training. In accordance with the established principle of overload, following an initial change, greater intensity of training is required for continued improvement. This was demonstrated very well by Sidney and Shephard [224], who reported that fitness gains after 7 weeks of training in elderly subjects accounted for most of the total fitness gains over 1 year.

Changes in cardiorespiratory fitness in the elderly are not related to sex. This has been documented in younger [42, 90, 203] and older subjects [171, 220, 222, 224, 225, 246]. Similarly, changes in cardiorespiratory fitness in the elderly can be achieved with a variety of training modes, including cycling, walking, and jogging/running [27, 41, 129, 131, 206, 224, 258, 269].

Cardiorespiratory Training Effects
Relatively few studies have measured directly the changes in maximal oxygen uptake resulting from training in the elderly [20, 23, 27, 171, 172, 210]. In many cases, assumptions concerning mechanisms associated with the cardiorespiratory training effect have been made on the basis of submaximal responses and responses of the middle-aged to training.

At present, the mechanisms responsible for increases in $\dot{V}O_2$max in the elderly are unclear [70].

In younger individuals, increased maximal oxygen uptake is due to increased cardiac output and a-$\bar{v}O_2$ difference, each contributing to about the same degree [18, 73, 74, 130]. There appears to be no conclusive evidence to support an increased maximal cardiac output arising from an increased maximal stroke volume in the elderly. Moreover, in middle-aged and elderly men, it has been reported that there is little, if any, change in maximal a-$\bar{v}O_2$ difference [31, 107, 130, 172, 206, 213, 216]. These factors combined (no change in cardiac output and no change in a-$\bar{v}O_2$ difference) would indicate that no change in $\dot{V}O_2$max is likely to occur as a result of physical training. There is sufficient evidence to the contrary [20, 101, 210, 245, 250].

Conflicting findings are always difficult to explain, but methodological problems could play a part. Measurement of cardiac output during maximal exercise is difficult at best, and noninvasive procedures may not yield adequate data. There is also the possibility that the initial test administered prior to training in the elderly is not maximal due to limiting factors discussed earlier. After several weeks of physical training, a true maximal test may be achieved, and thus submaximal initial values could unwittingly be compared with true maximal posttraining values.

Seals et al. [210] reported an increased a-$\bar{v}O_2$ difference in the elderly as a result of high-intensity training, but there was no effect as a result of low-intensity training (Table 3). In addition, the data of Heath et al. [108] suggest the possibility that stroke volume and/or a-$\bar{v}O_2$ difference could have contributed to the high maximal oxygen pulse demonstrated by master athletes that was comparable to that of younger athletes. There is obviously a need for more definitive studies in this area before accurate conclusions can be formulated.

Other physiological changes typically associated with training in younger subjects have also been reported in the elderly. These include increased blood volume, increased hemoglobin, increased muscle glycogen, and an increase in mitochondria and aerobic enzyme activity [27, 129, 245, 246]. An increased myoglobin level has not been found in elderly humans [117, 162], but exercise training in animals has produced such an increase [29].

Changes in physiological responses during submaximal exercise of a fixed absolute work rate before and after training are similar for younger and older individuals. Common findings in the elderly include a reduced heart rate [2, 23, 27, 61, 172, 210, 224, 239, 240], reduced blood lactate concentration [23, 211, 245], and increased oxygen pulse [2, 23, 61, 240]. Reductions in systolic blood pressure have also been reported [23, 239, 240].

TABLE 3

*Maximal Exercise Responses Before and After Low- and High-Intensity Training**

	Before Training	After Low-Intensity Training	After High-Intensity Training
$\dot{V}O_2$max, ml · kg^{-1} · min^{-1}	25.4 (4.6)	28.2 (5.2)†	32.9 (7.6)‡δ
$\dot{V}O_2$max, l · min^{-1}	1.91 (0.4)	2.10 (0.4)†	2.39 (0.6)‡δ
Heart rate, b · min^{-1}	174 (10)	168 (7)	174 (7)
Estimated stroke volume, ml	101 (18)	107 (17)†	108 (16)†
Estimated cardiac output, l · min^{-1}	17.6 (3.2)	18.1 (2.8)	18.7 (2.9)
Estimated arteriovenous O_2 difference, ml O_2 · 100 ml	11.0 (3.0)	11.7 (2.1)	12.8 (2.5)‡δ
Estimated left ventribular stroke work, g · m	160 (35)	169 (36)	172 (32)
Mean blood pressure, mm Hg	116 (12)	116 (14)	117 (12)
Estimated systemic vascular resistance, dyn · s · cm^5	543 (112)	520 (97)	512 (96)
Ventilation, l · min^{-1}	67.2 (16.4)	74.2 (20.0)†	86.5 (17.4)‡δ
Respiratory exchange ratio, U	1.21 (0.07)	1.17 (0.05)	1.20 (0.08)
Blood lactate, mM	8.1 (1.9)	7.9 (2.1)	8.8 (2.7)

*From Seals, D.R., et al. Endurance training in older men and women. I. Cardiovascular responses to exercise. *J. Appl. Physiol.* 57:1024–1029, 1984.
Values are means (SD) for 11 subjects (8 men and 3 women, ages 63 (±2) years).
†$P < 0.05$.
‡$P < 0.01$ vs. before training.
δ$P < 0.01$ vs. after low-intensity training.

Submaximal oxygen uptake at standardized work loads remains unchanged as a result of training [23, 27, 240]. This indicates that the above-mentioned changes were not due to improved mechanical efficiency during exercise. Respiratory minute volume and ventilatory equivalent for oxygen during submaximal exercise were not changed as a result of short-term physical training [2, 23, 27, 240]. However, with long-term training (12 months), Yerg et al. [272] reported a lower ventilatory equivalent for oxygen during submaximal exercise. This suggests that the higher ventilatory equivalent for oxygen observed in the elderly [96, 164, 179] can be reversed with endurance training.

STRENGTH

Strength seems to peak in the third decade, followed by a plateau through approximately the age of 50 years, followed in turn by a loss of strength amounting to 20% by age 65 and progressing further as age increases [13, 146, 166]. Within these general guidelines, actual performance varies somewhat and the results may be dependent upon a number of methodological factors. The type of test employed (isometric vs. dynamic) may influence the results, although it has been demonstrated that the age-related pattern for strength was similar for isometric and dynamic strength [146], and a loss of both isometric and dynamic strength occurs with advanced age [12, 144, 169, 274, 275]. The muscles employed in testing may also influence the results, as the age-related loss of strength in leg muscles may be greater than the loss in arm muscles [95].

The hand grip dynamometer provides an easy and convenient method for measuring isometric strength, and many studies have employed it. Generalizations based upon hand grip strength must be applied carefully to the body as a whole, however, because leg strength, for example, declines more rapidly than hand grip strength [226]. The loss of hand grip strength in males by age 65 compared with that of 20-year-olds has been shown to be about 20%, and the loss in females over the same 45 years may range from 2 to 20% [32, 134, 215]. A lesser decline in females could be attributable to a lower peak in the younger years due to less occupational use of the hands [213]. This interpretation is supported by the findings of Petrofsky and Lind [183], who reported no appreciable loss in grip strength among men 22–62 years of age who performed similar occupational duties. This suggests the potential confounding impact of loss of occupational duties when assessing age-related changes in strength.

Data obtained from individuals beyond age 65 suggest that the loss of isometric strength is accelerated [9, 11, 37, 45]. The overall degree of age-related loss reported varies from 24 to 45% [146, 169]. The age range and/or the age of groups of subjects compared may influence the results. For example, a particularly large age-related loss of strength (40–45%) involved the comparison of young (20–35 years) and very old (70–86 years) individuals [169].

Peak power and total work performed in a brief period of time (30 seconds) have been studied as a function of age. The decline in peak power and total work performed in 30 seconds was 6% per decade and paralleled the decline in $\dot{V}O_2$max with age [156]. This degree of loss also approximates the degree of strength loss expected over four decades. Isometric endurance, as measured by the ability to sustain an isometric contraction at a given percentage of maximal contraction strength, may not decline with age [144]. Petrofsky et al. [182] demonstrated no loss in males and an increase in isometric endurance in females. Johnson [119] reported that endurance in older females did not change despite a significant loss of strength.

TABLE 4
*Fiber Type Distribution and Fiber Areas in Different Age Groups**

Age Group (Years)	N	Mean Age (Years)	Fiber Type Distribution %, Type II	Fiber Areas (μm^2) Type I	Type II
20–29	11	26.1 (0.8)	59.5 (3.9)	2944 (249)	3663 (224)
30–39	10	35.3 (1.0)	63.2 (1.5)	2854 (178)	3509 (282)
40–49	8	42.6 (0.8)	51.8 (5.1)	3133 (230)	3361 (296)
50–59	12	54.5 (0.6)	48.3 (3.0)	2877 (160)	2802 (125)
60–65	10	61.6 (0.6)	45.0 (4.5)	2264 (245)	2120 (174)

*From Larsson, L., et al. Muscle strength and speed of movement in relation to age and muscle morphology. *J. Appl. Physiol.* 46:451–456, 1979.
Values are means (SE).
Biopsy specimens taken from the vastus lateralis muscle.

Factors Underlying Strength Loss

Muscle mass decreases with age and is reflected in reduced creatinine excretion [257]. The loss of muscle mass would seem to be an obvious explanation for the loss of strength. Young et al. [274] demonstrated a 33% reduction in the cross-sectional area of the quadriceps muscle (measured with ultrasound scanning) in elderly women and a loss of quadriceps strength amounting to 35%. Others question whether the loss in muscle mass can account fully for the loss in strength [154]. When Young et al. [275] studied elderly males, they found a 39% loss in quadriceps strength and only a 25% loss in the cross-sectional area of the muscle. Aniansson et al. [7] reported a 6% loss of muscle mass and a loss in quadriceps strength in 10–22% over a 7-year period in elderly men.

The loss of muscle volume may be due to a reduced fiber size, particularly in fast-twitch (type II) fibers [7, 11, 94, 95, 254]. A reduced fiber size in fast-twitch fibers would result in an increased slow-twitch (type I) area proportional to the fast-twitch area [146; see Table 4]. There may also be a reduction in the total number of muscle fibers [150]. This conclusion is supported by electromyographic studies that indicate a loss of functioning motor neurons in elderly individuals [37, 45, 47]. The loss of motor neurons could be responsible for the loss of muscle fibers, as denervation would lead to atrophy and eventual replacement by connective tissue. Damage and loss of function in the peripheral nerve is possible, as is damage to the muscle fiber itself [150].

The relative proportion (number) of fast-twitch to slow-twitch fibers may be altered by aging, with an increase in the proportion of slow-twitch fibers [143, 145, 227]. This is not a consistent finding, however, and some controversy exists [7, 8, 11]. Lexell et al. [150] reported a tendency toward the selective atrophy of fast-twitch fibers in the elderly, but this was not statistically significant. Electromyographic studies indicate the loss of fast-twitch neurons [45], and fast-twitch fibers may be more susceptible to damage arising from local ischemia due to atherosclerotic lesions in the peripheral circulation [227, 228].

The selective loss of fast-twitch fibers would help to explain the discrepancy between muscle volume loss and the loss of strength in the elderly, as well as the lack of loss of isometric endurance in the face of a significant loss of strength. On the other hand, a selective loss of fast-twitch fibers would influence maximal velocity [251], but the shape of the force–velocity curve is similar in the young and the old [12]. More than one interpretation is possible when reviewing this area, and further research is required.

Maximum speed of movement does not appear to decrease to the same degree as strength [146], and the loss of muscle fibers with aging may not influence the speed of muscle contraction until the loss is severe in the elderly [247]. Loss of muscle fibers and speed of movement may not be uniform throughout the body. The difference observed between arm and leg strength in the elderly could be due to selective changes in the muscles and nerves. It has been suggested that the muscles of the legs are affected to a greater degree by atrophy than those of the arms [254]. There may also be a tendency for increased neurological dysfunction in the legs compared with the arms [94, 118].

Effects of Strength Training

Resistance training can result in increased strength in old persons, but the adaptation mode may differ from that observed in younger individuals. Moritani and deVries [167] reported that strength gains for young men were accompanied by hypertrophy of the trained muscle mass, while in older men, the increased ability to recruit motor units was the primary mechanism for improved strength. In contrast, Larsson [147] reported, as a result of biopsy studies, that hypertrophy of slow-twitch and fast-twitch muscle fibers was possible in older men. Aniansson and Gustafsson [10] also demonstrated hypertrophy in fast-twitch fibers as a result of training in 70-year-old subjects.

Several additional studies have reported increased strength in old subjects as a result of resistance training [49, 58, 202]. Other studies, which emphasized cardiorespiratory exercise training, reported either no gains in strength or only modest gains, as would be expected from this type of training [24, 61, 221].

There is a loss of muscular strength with age that may be due, in part, to a loss of muscle mass. The loss of fast-twitch fibers, whether selectively higher than the loss of slow-twitch fibers or not, would reduce the power potential of older persons [56]. Studies of humans and animals suggest that the rate of adaptation of skeletal muscle to the stimulus applied by vigorous chronic exercise is retarded in the elderly [230]. The balance between protein synthesis and protein degradation essentially controls muscle growth, and there is evidence supporting a reduced rate of protein synthesis in the elderly [158]. Changes at the neuromuscular junction are likely to occur as well [85], and the combination of these factors supports a reduced ability to respond to training.

Despite the possibility that the rate of adaptation of skeletal muscle to training may change with age, there is also the possibility that overall adaptation, regardless of the time course, may be greater than assumed at present. There are some data to support this belief [36, 100, 47]. There is also the possibility that exercise training can reverse the trend toward a reduced rate of protein synthesis and other negative changes. More research concerning the mechanisms of change through training is required.

BODY COMPOSITION

Two obvious changes occur in body composition with age. There is accumulation of fat and a substantial loss of muscle mass in the elderly. Loss of muscle mass could be as high as 10–12% and can occur even with no appreciable loss in body mass [33]. The loss of lean tissue may be responsible, at least in part, for the decline in basal metabolic rate with age [219].

Increased body weight with age is a common phenomenon, so common, in fact, that not gaining weight with age is highly unusual. Weight gain generally continues unchecked from age 25 to approximately age 50 [252]. In sedentary populations, weight gain with age is assumed to be in the form of fat [215, 267], but in the latter years the amount of fat gained can be masked by losses in bone and muscle tissues [218]. Thus, although there may be no gain in absolute body fat, there can be an increase in relative body fat due to a loss of body density [84, 170].

According to the data of Brozek [38], a gain in body fat of approximately 12.24 kg is likely from age 20 to age 55. This is combined with a concomitant loss of approximately 3 kg of lean tissue. Tzankoff and Norris [257] reported that men in their eighth decade of life demonstrated a reduction in muscle mass of approximately 9 kg coupled with an increased body fatness of 3.4 kg when comparisons were made with men in their fifth decade.

Chronic exercise can reduce fat accumulation with age, and old persons can demonstrate a level of body fatness similar to that of younger persons if they have a consistent physical activity history throughout life. This has been demonstrated in lumberjacks in Norway [231] over an age range of 20 to 70 years. Body fatness was held in check in this population, averaging only 13% over five decades. In addition, a com-

TABLE 5
Body Composition of Older and Younger Endurance Athletes*

	N	Age (Years)	Height (cm)	Weight (kg)	Fat (%)	LBW (kg)
Young athletes	16	22† (2)	175.8 (7.2)	65.2 (5.7)	9.3 (1.8)	59.2 (4.4)
Masters athletes	16	59 (6)	173.0 (5.3)	63.3 (7.1)	9.8 (1.2)	57.1 (6.4)
Untrained	9	50† (6)	175.3 (8.1)	85.0† (10.7)	20.4† (2.6)	67.7† (6.2)
Lean untrained	9	52† (10)	174.8 (6.3)	69.1‡ (6.7)	14.2†‡ (2.2)	59.3‡ (5.3)

*From Heath, G.W., et al., A physiological comparison of young and older endurance athletes. *J. Appl. Physiol.* 51:634–640, 1981.
Values are means (SD).
LBW = lean body weight.
†Significantly different from masters athletes; $P < 0.01$.
‡Significantly lower than in untrained persons; $P < 0.05$.

parison of master athletes ranging in age from 50 to 72 years with young athletes revealed a similar level of body fatness [108, see Table 5].

Exercise initiated late in life can bring about a modest change in body composition. Sidney and Shephard [223] reported that skinfold thickness was significantly reduced following 52 weeks of aerobic exercise. There was no change in body weight, which indicates an increase in lean tissue. deVries [61] also reported a reduction in body fatness following an exercise program.

Hydrostatic weighing is the preferred method for determining body composition, but this technique has several shortcomings when applied to the elderly. Residual volume may be variable in the elderly and difficult to predict; thus, direct measurement is necessary [213]. In addition, the density of lean tissue may be different from that of younger individuals, and there may also be fear of the need to submerge completely and exhale air from the lungs. Skinfold (fatfold) measurements and the potassium whole body counter are convenient, but there are shortcomings associated with these techniques as well. For example, skinfold measurements assume a set relationship between subcutaneous and deep body fat, and the potassium counter assumes a set relationship between potassium and lean body mass. These relationships have been questioned in the elderly [68, 83, 184].

BONES AND JOINTS

Bones change with age, and there may be changes in the composition of bone, and/or a loss in the amount of bone [78]. For example, the inorganic/organic component ratio is essentially equal in children, whereas in the elderly it may reach 7:1 [18].

Bone loss in females has received increased attention in recent years. Compared with males, who lose bone at a rate of approximately 0.4%

per year beginning at age 50, females begin earlier and the rate of bone loss is higher [235]. A loss of cortical thickness beginning at approximately age 35 and progressing to a 30% loss by old age in females as compared to 20% in males has been reported [86]. The rate of bone loss immediately following menopause may be accelerated by a magnitude of two- to threefold and may be sustained for 5 years [235]. Extreme bone loss contributes to the high rate of bone fractures in older compared with younger women [25, 48], and these alarming trends underscore the importance of investigating approaches that can arrest or even reverse this process.

The loss of hormones may be an important factor, as bone loss is greater in estrogen-deficient females, and osteoblast activity increases when estrogen is administered [252]. Amenorrheic females demonstrate lower vertebral bone density when compared with normal cycling females [67].

For males and females, inactivity resulting in the loss of mechanical forces applied to bones is thought to be a key factor in bone changes and bone loss. A sedentary existence can result in a loss of thickness and bone density [19, 71, 142, 200, 207, 236, 244]. The loss of compressional stress on long bones is also thought to be an important factor in bone loss [67, 93]. Inactivity and loss of compressional stress associated with the weightlessness of space flight have resulted in significant demineralization of bone [262].

The extent to which bone loss can be arrested or reversed by physical activity has been investigated. Montoye et al. [163] reported that the volume and circumference of bone in the dominant hand and forearm of tennis players who participated in the sport for over four decades were greater than those in the unused arm. Similar results were reported by Huddleston et al. [115]. These athletes were engaged in vigorous and demanding physical activity. Similar results have been reported for runners [55, 120].

Montoye [165] reported, in a cross-sectional study, that moderate physical activity did not appear to prevent bone loss. In contrast, several longitudinal studies support the use of moderate physical activity in the prevention of bone loss, especially in postmenopausal females [132, 225]. Moreover, there is evidence from longitudinal studies (Table 6) that moderate physical activity may increase bone mineral content in the elderly [34, 232, 233, 234].

A number of changes occur in the joint components (cartilage, tendons, ligaments, synovial fluid) with age, but many of these changes may not create symptoms [4]. Common changes include degenerative changes in the spine [237], loss of stability due to reduced thickness and other alterations in collagen structure in synovial joints [91, 104], and calcification of cartilage [51]. Changes in the elastin component of connective

TABLE 6
*Bone Mineral Increases in Older Women Following Exercise Training**

Study Group	N	Age Years Mean (SD)	Weight (kg) Mean (SD)
Control			
Before study	18	81.9 (7.4)	59.3 (14.4)
After 36 months	18	84.9 (7.4)	58.4 (14.7)
Physical activity			
Before study	12	82.9 (6.1)	58.4 (11.1)
After 36 months	12	85.9 (6.1)	58.6 (9.4)

Age and Weight of Subjects Before and After a 36-Month Study of Older Women

Bone Mineral Content (BMC) and Bone Content Mineral/Width (BMC/W) Changes of the Radius Over 36 Months

	Control	Physical Activity	*t*-Ratio
BMC	−3.28†	+2.29	<0.005
BMC/W	−2.59	+1.71	<0.01

*From Smith, E.L., et al. Physical activity and calcium modalities for bone mineral increase in aged women. *Med. Sci. Sports Exerc.* 13:60–64, 1981.
†The percentage change and comparison of the groups was done by regression analysis, using indicator variables.

tissue, as well as complications such as arthritis and osteoporosis [135, 271], can lead to loss of mobility and stability in the joints of the elderly [5].

Exercise can improve these conditions to a large extent [49, 168]. Therefore, it is uncertain whether aging or disuse is the primary cause. In addition, since restrictions on joint mobility can arise from muscle shortening or stiffness, as well as neuromuscular factors, the joint may be restricted by factors not inherent to the joint per se [22].

SUMMARY

Data from cross-sectional studies suggest that VO_2max declines in adulthood at a rate of 0.40–0.45 ml $\cdot$ kg^{-1} $\cdot$ min^{-1} per year in males and 0.30 ml $\cdot$ kg^{-1} $\cdot$ min^{-1} per year in females. Longitudinal studies suggest that the loss is much greater for males, approximating 1.0 ml $\cdot$ kg^{-1} $\cdot$ min^{-1} per year or more. The rate of loss may be greater in sedentary compared to active individuals.

The decline in $\dot{V}O_2$max with age appears to be inevitable, and a major contributing factor may be the decline in maximal cardiac output. A reduced maximal heart rate is a consistent finding, and this may be due to decreased end-organ sensitivity to catecholamines. Maximal stroke volume may or may not decrease, and physical training status may be a determining factor. The most recent evidence suggests increased dependence upon the Frank-Starling mechanism, resulting in an increased stroke volume to offset the decline in maximal heart rate. Cardiac output is thought to be maintained in this manner. Use of this mechanism may depend upon the absence of underlying disease. Therefore, investigators who vigorously screen potential subjects for occult coronary disease may report findings different from those who do not.

Maximal a-$\bar{v}O_2$ difference may or may not decline in the elderly. The research is divided, and there is support for both beliefs. Several factors typical of the elderly, including a decline in muscle mass, increased blood distribution to the skin during exercise, and a potentially lower capillary/fiber ratio, would contribute to a lower a-$\bar{v}O_2$ difference. On the other hand, in those subjects with reduced cardiac output, there may be greater dependence upon a-$\bar{v}O_2$ difference during maximal exercise.

Pulmonary function does not appear to limit $\dot{V}O_2$max, although the elderly may be less efficient while breathing during exercise. However, the higher ventilation and higher ventilatory equivalent for oxygen observed during submaximal exercise could be due to higher relative stress in the elderly.

Elderly males and females are capable of demonstrating a training effect in response to endurance training regardless of previous physical activity patterns and current training status. The degree of change with training, expressed in relative terms, appears to be comparable to that demonstrated by younger subjects. Physiological factors contributing to an increased $\dot{V}O_2$max as a result of training appear to be similar in elderly and younger subjects, with the possible exception of no change in maximal a-$\bar{v}O_2$ difference in the elderly. This point is somewhat controversial. When responses to an absolute amount of submaximal work are used to assess pre- and posttraining changes, the responses of older and younger subjects are similar, with the possible exception of a reduced systolic blood pressure in the elderly.

Strength peaks in the third decade and appears to be sustained until late in life, with a loss of strength amounting to approximately 20% by age 65 and progressing further as age increases. The loss of muscle mass may not account fully for the loss in strength. There may be a decreased fiber size, particularly in fast-twitch fibers, and there may be a reduction in the number of fibers as well. Controversy exists as to whether there is a selective loss of fast-twitch fibers, resulting in an increased proportion of slow-twitch fibers. Strength can be increased in the elderly through training, but the adaptation mode may differ from that observed in younger subjects. Hypertrophy of the trained muscle mass is a common finding in the young. In older men, although hypertrophy has been observed, the increased ability to recruit motor units may be the primary mechanism for improved strength.

There are two obvious changes in the body composition of the elderly. There is a substantial loss of muscle mass and an accumulation of body fat. The loss of muscle mass may be responsible for the decline in basal metabolic rate. There is also speculation that the decline in $\dot{V}O_2$max is closely associated with the loss of muscle mass. Loss of muscle mass may be disguised by its replacement with connective tissue. Therefore, standard densiometric methods for assessing body composition may provide misleading results, especially when addressing the issue of $\dot{V}O_2$max per unit of lean tissue.

Bones change with age, and the inorganic/organic component ratio can be substantially greater in the elderly. Bone loss is also tied to aging. Hormonal factors (in females), inactivity, and the loss of mechanical and compressional forces applied to the bones are thought to be key factors. Exercise training appears to prevent bone loss and may even increase bone mineral content in the elderly. Exercise may also improve joint function, which has a tendency to dissipate with advanced age.

REFERENCES

1. Abrass, I.B., and P.J. Scarpace. Catalytic unit of adenylate cyclase: Reduced activity in aged-human lymphocytes. *J. Clin. Endocrinol. Metab.* 55:1026–1028, 1982.
2. Adams, G.M., and H.A. deVries. Physiological effects of an exercise training regimen upon women aged 52 to 79. *J. Gerontol.* 28:50–55, 1973.
3. Adams, W.C., M.M. McHenry, and E.M. Bernauer. Multistage treadmill walking performance and associated cardiorespiratory responses of middle-aged men. *Clin. Sci.* 42:355–370, 1972.
4. Adrian, M.J. Flexibility in the aging adult. In E.L. Smith and R.C. Serfass (eds.). *Exercise and Aging: The Scientific Basis.* Hillside, N.J.: Enslow Publishers, 1981, pp. 45–57.
5. Allman, F.L. Conditioning for sports. In A.J. Ryan and F.L. Allman (eds.). *Sports Medicine.* New York: Academic Press, 1974, pp. 161–179.
6. Altose, M.D., W.C. McCauley, and S.G. Kelson. Effects of hypercapnia and inspiratory flow-resistive loading on respiratory activity in chronic airways obstruction. *J. Clin. Invest.* 59:500–507, 1977.
7. Aniansson, A., M. Hedberg, G.B. Henning, and G. Grimby. Muscle morphology, enzymatic activity, and muscle strength in elderly men: A follow-up study. *Muscle Nerve* 9:585–591, 1986.
8 Aniansson, A., G. Grimby, E. Nygaard, and B. Saltin. Muscle fiber composition and fiber area in various age groups. *Muscle Nerve* 2:271–277, 1980.
9. Aniansson, A., G. Grimby, and A. Rundgren. Isometric and isokinetic quadriceps muscle strength in 70-year-old men and women. *Scand. J. Rehab. Med.* 12:161–168, 1980.
10. Aniansson, A., and E. Gustafsson. Physical training in elderly men with special reference to quadriceps muscle strength and morphology. *Clin. Physiol.* 1:87–98, 1981.
11. Aniansson, A., G. Grimby, M. Hedberg, and M. Krotkiewski. Muscle morphology,

enzyme activity and muscle strength in elderly men and women. *Clin. Physiol.* 1:73–86, 1981.

12. Aniansson, A., G. Grimby, M. Hedberg, A. Rungren, and L. Sperling. Muscle function in old age. *Scand. J. Rehab. Med.* 6(suppl.):43–49, 1978.

13. Asmussen, E. Growth in muscular strength and power. In G.L. Rarick (ed.). *Physical Activity Human Growth and Development.* New York: Academic Press, 1973, p. 60.

14. Asmussen, E., and P. Mathiasen. Some physiological functions in physical education students reinvestigated after twenty-five years. *J. Am. Geriatr. Soc.* 20:379–387, 1962.

15. Astrand, I. Aerobic work capacity in men and women with special reference to age. *Acta Physiol. Scand.* 49(suppl. 169):1–92, 1960.

16. Astrand, I. Exercise electrocardiograms recorded twice with an 8-year interval in a group of 204 women and men 48–63 years old. *Acta Med. Scand.* 178:27–39, 1965.

17. Astrand, I., P.O. Astrand, and K. Rodahl. Maximal heart rate during work in older men. *J. Appl. Physiol.* 14:562–566, 1959.

18. Astrand, P.O., and K. Rodahl. *Textbook of Work Physiology.* New York: McGraw Hill Book Co., 1986.

19. Atkinson, P.J., J.A. Weatherell, and S.M. Weidmann. Changes in density of human femoral cortex with age. *J. Bone Joint Surg.* 44B:496–502, 1962.

20. Badenhop, D.J., P.A. Cleary, S.F. Schal, E.L. Fox, and R.L. Bartels. Physiological adjustments to higher or lower intensity exercise in elders. *Med. Sci. Sports Exerc.* 15:496–502, 1983.

21. Baily, D.A., R.J. Shephard, R.L. Mirwald, and G.A. McBride. A current view of cardiorespiratory fitness levels of Canadians. *Can. Med. Assoc. J.* 111:25–30, 1974.

22. Barry, H.C. Exercise prescriptions for the elderly. *Am. Fam. Physicians* 34:155–162, 1986.

23. Barry, A.J., J.W. Daly, E.D.R. Pruett, J.R. Steinmetz, H.F. Page, N.C. Birkhead, and K. Rodhal. The effects of physical conditioning on older individuals. I. Work capacity, circulatory-respiratory function, and electrocardiogram. *J. Gerontol.* 21:182–191, 1966.

24. Barry, A.J., J.R. Steinmetz, H.F. Page, and K. Rodahl. The effects of physical conditioning on older individuals. II. Motor performance and cognitive function. *J. Gerontol.* 21:192–199, 1966.

25. Bauer, G. Epidemiology of fracture in aged persons. *Clin. Orthop.* 27:219–225, 1960.

26. Becklake, M.R., H. Frank, G.R. Dagenais, G.L. Ostiguy, and G.A. Guzman. Influence of age and sex on exercise cardiac output. *J. Appl. Physiol.* 20:938–947, 1965.

27. Benestad, A.M. Trainability of old men. *Acta Med. Scand.* 178:321–327, 1965.

28. Bertel, O., F.R. Buhler, W. Klowski, and B.E. Lutold. Decreased beta-adrenoreceptor responsiveness as related to age, blood pressure, and plasma catecholamines in patients with essential hypertension. *Hypertension* 2:130–138, 1980.

29. Beyer, R.E., and J.E. Fattore. The influence of age and endurance exercise on the myoglobin concentration of skeletal muscle of the rat. *J. Gerontol.* 39:525–530, 1984.

30. Binkhorst, R.A., J. Pool, P. VanLeeuwen, and A. Bouhuys. Maximum oxygen uptake in healthy non-athletic males. *Int. Z. Angew. Physiol. Einschl. Arbeitsphysiol.* 22:10–18, 1966.

31. Blomqvist, C.G., and B. Saltin. Cardiovascular adaptations to physical training. *Ann. Rev. Physiol.* 45:169–189, 1983.

32. Bookwalter, K.W. Grip strength norms for males. *Res. Q.* 21:249–273, 1950.

33. Borkan, G.A., D.E. Hults, A.F. Gerzof, A.H. Robbins, and C.K. Silbert. Age changes in body composition revealed by computer tomography. *J. Gerontol.* 38:673–677, 1983.

34. Brewer, V., B.M. Meyer, M.S. Keele, S.J. Upton, and R.D. Hagan. Role of exercise in prevention of involutional bone loss. *Med. Sci. Sports Exerc.* 15:445–449, 1983.

35. Brischetto, M.J., R.P. Millman, D.D. Peterson, D.A. Silage, and A.I. Pack. Effect of aging on ventilatory response to exercise and CO_2. *J. Appl. Physiol.* 56:1143–1150, 1984.

36. Brown, M. Long-term endurance exercise effects on skeletal muscle in aging rats. *Med. Sci. Sports Exerc.* 17:245, 1985. (Abstract)

37. Brown, W.F. A method for estimating the number of motor units in thenar muscles and the change in motor unit count with ageing. *J. Neurol. Neurosurg. Psychiatry* 35:845–852, 1972.

38. Brozek, J. Changes of body composition in man during maturity and their nutritional implications. *Fed. Proc.* 11:784–793, 1952.

39. Bruce, R.A. Exercise, functional aerobic capacity, and aging-another viewpoint. *Med. Sci. Sports Exerc.* 16:8–13, 1984.

40. Bruce, R.A., L.D. Fisher, M.N. Cooper, and G.O. Gey. Separation of effects of cardiovascular disease and age on ventricular function with maximal exercise. *Am. J. Cardiol.* 34:757–763, 1974.

41. Buccola, V.A., and W.J. Stone. Effects of jogging and cycling programs on physiological and personality variables in aged men. *Res. Q.* 46:134–139, 1975.

42. Burke, E.J. Physiological effects of similar training programs in males and females. *Res. Q.* 48:510–517, 1977.

43. Buskirk, E.R. Health maintenance and longevity: Exercise. In C.E. Finch and E.L. Schneider (eds.). *Handbook of the Biology of Aging*, 2nd ed. New York: Van Nostrand Reinhold Co., 1985, pp. 894–931.

44. Buskirk, E.R., and J.L. Hodgson. Age and aerobic power: The rate of change in men and women. *Fed. Proc.* 46:1824–1829, 1987.

45. Campbell, M.J., A.J. McComas, and F. Petito. Physiological changes in ageing muscles. *J. Neurol. Neurosurg. Psychiatry* 36:174–182, 1973.

46. Cantwell, J.D., and E.O. Watt. Extreme cardiopulmonary fitness in old age. *Chest* 65:357–359, 1974.

47. Carlsson, K.E., W. Alston, and D.J. Feldman. Electromyographic study of aging in skeletal muscle. *Am. J. Phys. Med.* 43:141–145, 1964.

48. Chalmers, J., and K.C. Ho. Geographical variations in senile osteoporosis. The association with physical activity. *J. Bone Joint Surg.* 52:667–675, 1970.

49. Chapman, E.A., H.A. deVries, and R. Swezey. Joint stiffness: Effects of exercise on young and old men. *J. Gerontol.* 27:218–221, 1972.

50. Chesky, J.A., and M. Rockstein. Reduced myocardial actomyosin adenosine triphosphatase activity in the aging male Fischer rat. *Cardiovasc. Res.* 11:242–246, 1977.

51. Chung, E.B. Ageing in human joints. II. Joint capsule. *J. Natl. Med. Assoc.* 58:254–260, 1966.

52. Comroe, J.H., R.E. Forster, A.B. Dubois, W.A. Briscoe, and E. Carlsen. *The Lung.* Chicago: Year Book Medical Publishers, 1962.

53. Conway, J., R. Wheeler, and R. Sannerstedt. Sympathetic nervous activity during exercise in relation to age. *Cardiovasc. Res.* 5:577–581, 1971.

54. Cunningham, D.A., E.A. Nancekievill, D.H. Paterson, A.P. Donner, and P.A. Rechnitzer. Ventilation threshold and aging. *J. Gerontol.* 40:703–707, 1985.

55. Dalen, N., and K.E. Olsson. Bone mineral content and physical activity. *Acta Orthop. Scand.* 45:170–174, 1974.

56. Davies, C.T.M., J. White, and K. Young. Electrically evoked and voluntary maximal isometric tension in relation to dynamic muscle performance in elderly male subjects, aged 69 years. *Eur. J. Appl. Physiol.* 51:37–43, 1983.

57. Davies, C.T.M. The oxygen transporting system in relation to age. *Clin. Sci.* 42:1–13, 1972.

58. Daykin, H.P. The application of isometrics in geriatric treatment. *Am. Corr. Ther. J.* 21:203–205, 1967.
59. Dehn, M.M., and R.A. Bruce. Longitudinal variations in maximal oxygen intake with age and activity. *J. Appl. Physiol.* 33:805–807, 1972.
60. deVries, H.A. Exercise intensity threshold for improvement of cardiovascular-respiratory function in older men. *Geriatrics* 26:94–101, 1971.
61. deVries, H.A. Physiological effects of an exercise training regimen upon men aged 52–88. *J. Gerontol.* 25:325–336, 1970.
62. deVries, H.A., and G.M. Adams. Comparison of exercise responses in old and young men: II. Ventilatory mechanics. *J. Gerontol.* 27:349–352, 1972.
63. Dill, D.B., A. Graybill, A. Hurtado, and A.C. Taguini. Gaseous exchange in the lungs in old age. *J. Am. Geriatr. Soc.* 11:1063–1076, 1963.
64. Dill, D.B., S. Robinson, and J.C. Ross. A longitudinal study of 16 champion runners. *J. Sports Med.* 7:4–32, 1967.
65. Dillon, N., S. Chung, J. Kelly, and K. O'Malley. Age and beta-adrenoceptor–mediated function. *Clin. Pharmacol. Ther.* 27:769–772, 1980.
66. Drinkwater, B.L., S.M. Horvath, and C.L. Wells. Aerobic power of females, ages 10 to 68. *J. Gerontol.* 30:385–394, 1975.
67. Drinkwater, B.D., K.L. Nilson, and C.S. Chestnut III. Bone mineral content of amenorrheic and eumenorrheic athletes. *N. Engl. J. Med.* 311:277–281, 1984.
68. Durnin, J.V.G.A., and J. Womersley. Body fat assessed from total body density and its estimation from skinfold thickness: Measurements on 481 men and women aged from 16–72 years. *Br. J. Nutr.* 32:77–97, 1974.
69. Edelman, N.H., C. Mittman, A.H. Norris, and N.W. Shock. Effects of respiratory pattern on age differences in ventilation uniformity. *J. Appl. Physiol.* 24:49–53, 1968.
70. Ehsani, A.A. Cardiovascular adaptations to exercise training in the elderly. *Fed. Proc.* 46:1840–1843, 1987.
71. Eisenberg, E., and G.S. Gordan. Skeletal dynamics in man measured by nonradioactive strontium. *J. Clin. Invest.* 40:1809–1825, 1961.
72. Eisenman, P.A., and L.A. Golding. Comparison of effects of training on $\dot{V}o_2$max in girls and young women. *Med. Sci. Sports* 2:136–138, 1975.
73. Ekblom, B. Effect of physical training on oxygen transport system in man. *Acta Physiol. Scand.* 328(suppl.):1–76, 1969.
74. Ekblom, B., P.O. Astrand, B. Saltin, J. Stenberg, and B. Wallstrom. Effect of training on circulatory response to exercise. *J. Appl. Physiol.* 24:518–528, 1968.
75. Elveback, L., and J.T. Lie. Combined high incidence of coronary artery disease at autopsy in Olmstead County, Minnesota. *Circulation* 70:345–349, 1984.
76. Ericsson, P. Total hemoglobin and physical work capacity in elderly people. *Acta Med. Scand.* 188:15–23, 1970.
77. Esler, M., H. Skews, P. Leonard, G. Jackman, A. Bobik, and P. Korner. Age-dependence of noradrenaline kinetics in normal subjects. *Clin. Sci.* 60:217–219, 1981.
78. Exton-Smith, A.N. Mineral metabolism. In C.E. Finch and E.L. Schneider (eds.). *Handbook of the Biology of Aging*, 2nd ed. New York: Van Nostrand, 1985, pp. 511–539.
79. Feldman, R.D., L.E. Limbird, J. Nadeau, D. Robertson, and A.J.J. Wood. Alterations in leucocyte β-receptor affinity with aging. A potential explanation for altered β-adrenergic sensitivity in the elderly. *N. Engl. J. Med.* 310:815–819, 1984.
80. Fleg, J.L., and E.G. Lakatta. Loss of muscle mass is a major determinant of the age-related decline in maximal aerobic capacity. *Circulation* 72:Part II,III-464, 1985.
81. Fleg, J.L., S.P. Tzankoff, and E.G. Lakatta. Age-related augmentation of plasma catecholamines during dynamic exercise in healthy males. *J. Appl. Physiol.* 59:1033–1039, 1985.

82. Fleish, J.H. Age-related decrease in beta-adrenoceptor activity of the cardiovascular system. *Trends Pharmacol. Sci.* 2:337–339, 1981.

83. Forbes, G.B., and J.C. Reina. Adult lean body mass declines with age: Some longitudinal observations. *Metabolism* 653–663, 1970.

84. Friis-Hansen, B. Hydrometry of growth and aging. In J. Brozek (ed.). *Human Body Composition.* Oxford: Pergamon Press, 1963, pp. 191–209.

85. Frolkis, V.V., O.A. Martynenko, and V.P. Zamostyan. Ageing of the neuromuscular apparatus. *Gerontology* 22:244–279, 1976.

86. Garn, S.M. Bone loss and aging. In R. Goldman and M. Rockstein (ed.). *The Physiology and Pathology of Aging.* New York: Academic Press, 1975, pp. 281–299.

87. Gerstenblith, G., E.G. Lakatta, and M.L. Weisfeldt. Age change in myocardial function and exercise response. *Prog. Cardiovasc. Dis.* 19:1–21, 1976.

88. Gerstenblith, G., D.G. Renlund, and E.G. Lakatta. Cardiovascular responses to exercise in younger and older men. *Fed. Proc.* 46:1834–1839, 1987.

89. Gerstenblith, G., H.A. Spurgeon, J.J.P. Froelich, M.L. Weisfeldt, and E.G. Lakatta. Diminished ionotropic responsiveness to ouabain in aged rat myocardium. *Circ. Res.* 44:517–523, 1979.

90. Getchell, L.H., and J.C. Moore. Physical training: Comparative responses of middle-aged adults. *Arch. Phys. Med. Rehab.* 56:250–254, 1975.

91. Grahame, R. Diseases of the joints. In J.C. Brocklehurst (ed.). *Textbook of Geriatric Medicine and Gerontology.* Edinburgh: Churchill-Livingstone, 1973, pp. 367–381.

92. Granath, A., B. Jonsson, and T. Strandell. Circulation in healthy old men studied by right-heart catheterization at rest and during exercise in supine and sitting position. In D. Brunner and E. Jokl (eds.). *Medicine and Sport: Physical Activity and Aging.* Baltimore: University Park Press. 1970, pp. 48–79.

93. Greenleaf, J.E. Physiological responses to prolonged bed rest and fluid immersion in humans. *J. Appl. Physiol.* 57:619–633, 1984.

94. Grimby, G., B. Danneskiold-Samsoe, K. Hvid, and B. Saltin. Morphology and enzymatic capacity in arm and leg muscles in 78–81 year old men and women. *Acta Physiol. Scand.* 115:125–134, 1982.

95. Grimby, G., and B. Saltin. The ageing muscle. *Clin. Physiol.* 3:209–218, 1983.

96. Grimby, G., and B. Saltin. Physiological analysis of physically well-trained middle-aged and old athletes. *Acta Med. Scand.* 179:513–523, 1968.

97. Grimby, G., J. Bjure, M. Aurell, B. Ekstrom-Jodal, G. Tibblin, and L. Wilhelmsen. Work capacity and physiologic responses to work. Men born in 1913. *Am. J. Cardiol.* 30:37–42, 1972.

98. Grimby, G., N.J. Nilsson, and B. Saltin. Cardiac output during submaximal and maximal exercise in active middle-aged athletes. *J. Appl. Physiol.* 21:1150–1156, 1966.

99. Guarnieri, T., C.R. Filburn, G. Zitnik, G.S. Roth, and E.G. Lakatta. Contractile and biochemical correlates of β-adrenergic stimulation of the aged heart. *Am. J. Physiol.* 239:H501–H508, 1980.

100. Gutmann, E., and V. Hanzlikova. Basic mechanisms of ageing in the neuromuscular system. *Mech. Ageing Dev.* 1:327–349, 1972.

101. Hagberg, J.M. Effect of training on the decline of VO_2max with aging. *Fed. Proc.* 46:1830–1833, 1987.

102. Hagberg, J.M., W.K. Allen, D.R. Seals, B.F. Hurley, A.A. Ehsani, and J.O. Holloszy. A hemodynamic comparison of young and older endurance athletes during exercise. *J. Appl. Physiol.* 58:2041–2046, 1985.

103. Hakki, A.H., N.L. DePace, and A.S. Iskandrian. Effect of age on left ventricular function during exercise in patients with coronary artery disease. *J. Am. Col. Cardiol.* 2:645–651, 1983.

104. Hall, D.A. *The Aging of Connective Tissue.* London: Academic Press, 1976.

105. Hanson, J.S., B.S. Tabakin, and A.M. Levy. Comparative exercise cardiorespiratory performance of normal men in the third, fourth and fifth decades of life. *Circulation* 37:345–360, 1968.

106. Harrison, T.R., K. Dixon, R.O. Russell, Jr., P.S. Bidai, and H.N. Coleman. The relation of age to the duration of contraction, ejection, and relaxation of the normal heart. *Am. Heart J.* 67:189–199, 1964.

107. Hartley, L.H., G. Grimby, A. Kilbom, N.J. Nilsson, I. Astrand, J. Bjure, B. Ekblom, and B. Saltin. Physical training in sedentary middle aged and older men: III. Cardiac output and gas exchange at submaximal and maximal exercise. *Scand. J. Clin. Lab. Invest.* 24:335–344, 1969.

108. Heath, G.W., J.M. Hagberg, A.A. Ehsani, and J.O. Holloszy. A physiological comparison of young and older endurance athletes. *J. Appl. Physiol.* 51:634–640, 1981.

109. Higginbotham, M.S., K.G. Morris, R.S. Williams, R.E. Coleman, and F.R. Labb. Physiologic basis for the age-related decline in aerobic work capacity. *Am. J. Cardiol.* 57:1374–1379, 1986.

110. Hodgson, J.L., and E.R. Buskirk. Physical fitness and age, with emphasis on cardiovascular function in the elderly. *J. Am. Geriatr. Soc.* 25:385–392, 1977.

111. Hollmann, W. Changes in the capacity for maximal and continuous effort in relation to age. In E. Jokl and E. Simon (eds.). *International Research in Sport and Physical Education.* Springfield, Ill.: C.C. Thomas, 1964, pp. 369–372.

112. Hollman, W. Diminution of cardiopulmonary capacity in the course of life and its prevention by participation in sports. In K. Kato (ed.). *Proceedings of the International Congress of Sports Sciences.* Tokyo: Japanese Union of Sports Sciences, 1966, pp. 91–93.

113. Horvath, S.M., and J.F. Borgia. Cardiopulmonary gas transport and aging. *Am. Rev. Respir. Dis.* 129(suppl.):568–571, 1984.

114. Hossack, K.F., and R.A. Bruce. Maximal cardiac function in sedentary normal men and women: Comparison of age-related changes. *J. Appl. Physiol.* 53:799–804, 1982.

115. Huddleston, A.L., D. Rockwell, D.N. Kulund, and R.B. Harrison. Bone mass in lifetime tennis athletes. *J.A.M.A.* 244:1107–1109, 1980.

116. Irving, J.B., F. Kusumi, and R.A. Bruce. Longitudinal variations in maximal oxygen consumption in healthy men. *Clin. Cardiol.* 3:134–136, 1980.

117. Jansson, E., C. Sylven, and E. Nordevang. Myoglobin in the quadriceps femoris muscle of competitive cyclists and untrained men. *Acta Physiol. Scand.* 114:627–629, 1982.

118. Jennekens, F.G.I., B.E. Tomlinson, and J.N. Walton. Histochemical aspects of five limb muscles in old age. An autopsy study. *J. Neurol. Sci.* 14:259–276, 1971.

119. Johnson, T. Age-related differences in isometric and dynamic strength and endurance. *Phys. Ther.* 62:985–989, 1982.

120. Jones, H.H., J.D. Priest, W.C. Hayes, C.C. Tichenor, and D.A. Nagel. Humeral hypertrophy in response to exercise. *J. Bone Joint Surg.* 59:204–208, 1977.

121. Julius, S., A. Amery, L.S. Whitlock, and J. Conway. Influence of age on the hemodynamic response to exercise. *Circulation* 36:222–230, 1967.

122. Kaijser, L., and C. Sachs. Autonomic cardiovascular responses in old age. *Clin. Physiol.* 5:347–357, 1985.

123. Kaman, R.L., P.B. Raven, C. Carlisle, and J. Ayres. Age related changes in cardiac enzymes as a result of jogging exercise in man. *Med. Sci. Sports* 10:46–47, 1978.

124. Kanstrup, I.L., and B. Ekblom. Influence of age and physical activity on central hemodynamics and lung function in active adults. *J. Appl. Physiol.* 45:709–717, 1978.

125. Karvonen, M.J., E. Kentala, and O. Mustala. The effects of training on heart rate. A longitudinal study. *Ann. Med. Exp. Biol. Fenn.* 35:307–315, 1957.

126. Kasch, F.W., and J.P. Wallace. Physiological variables during 10 years of endurance exercise. *Med. Sci. Sports* 8:5–8, 1976.

127. Kasch, F.W., J.P. Wallace, and S.P. Van Camp. Effects of 18 years of endurance exercise on the physical work capacity of older men. *J. Cardiac Rehabil.* 5:308–312, 1985.

128. Kenney, R.A. Physiology of aging. *Clin. Geriatr. Med.* 1:37–59, 1985.

129. Kiessling, K.H., L. Pilstrom, A.C. Bylund, B. Saltin, and K. Piehl. Enzyme activities and morphometry in skeletal muscle of middle-aged men after training. *Scand. J. Clin. Lab. Invest.* 33:63–69, 1974.

130. Kilbom, A., and I. Astrand. Physical training with submaximal intensities in women. II. Effect on cardiac output. *Scand. J. Clin. Lab. Invest.* 28:163–175, 1971.

131. Kilbom, A. Physical training in women. *Scand. J. Clin. Lab. Invest.* 119(suppl. 28):1–34, 1971.

132. Krolner, B., E. Tondevold, B. Toft, B. Berthelsen, and S. Ports Nielsen. Bone mass of the axial and the appendicular skeleton in women with Colles' fracture: Its relation to physical activity. *Clin. Physiol.* 2:147–157, 1982.

133. Kronenberg, R.S., and C.W. Drage. Attenuation of the ventilatory and heart rate responses to hypoxia and hypercapnia with aging in normal men. *J. Clin. Invest.* 52:1812–1819, 1973.

134. Kutal, I., J. Parizkova, and J. Dycka. Muscle strength and lean body mass in old men of different physical activity. *J. Appl. Physiol.* 29:168–171, 1970.

135. LaBella, F.S., and G. Paul. Structure of collagen from human tendons as influenced by age and sex. *J. Gerontol.* 20:54–59, 1963.

136. Lakatta, E.G. Alterations in the cardiovascular system that occur in advanced age. *Fed. Proc.* 38:163–167, 1979.

137. Lakatta, E.G. Heart and circulation. In C.E. Finch and E.L. Schneider (eds.). *Handbook of the Biology of Aging*, 2nd ed. New York: Van Nostrand, 1985, pp. 377–413.

138. Lakatta, E.G. Cardiovascular system. In B. Kent and R.N. Butler (eds.). *Human Aging Research: Concepts and Techniques.* New York: Raven Press (in press).

139. Lakatta, E.G., and F.C.P. Yin. Myocardial aging: Functional alterations and related cellular mechanisms. *Am. J. Physiol.* 242:H927–H941, 1982.

140. Lakatta, E.G., G. Gerstenblith, C.S. Angell, N.W. Shock, and M.L. Weisfeldt. Prolonged contraction duration in aged myocardium. *J. Clin. Invest.* 55:61–68, 1975.

141. Lakatta, E.G. Age-related alterations in the cardiovascular response to adrenergic mediated stress. *Fed. Proc.* 39:3173–3177, 1980.

142. Lanyon, L.E., and J.A. O'Connor. Adapation of bone artificially loaded at high and low physiological strain rates. *J. Physiol.* 303:36P, 1980. (Abstract)

143. Larsson, L., B. Sjodin, and J. Karlsson. Histochemical and biochemical changes in human skeletal muscle with age in sedentary males, age 22–65 years. *Acta Physiol. Scand.* 103:31–39, 1978.

144. Larsson, L., and J. Karlsson. Isometric and dynamic endurance as a function of age and skeletal muscle characteristics. *Acta Physiol. Scand.* 104:129–136, 1978.

145. Larsson, L. Histochemical characteristics of human skeletal muscle during ageing. *Acta Physiol. Scand.* 117:469–471, 1983.

146. Larsson, L., G. Grimby, and J. Karlsson. Muscle strength and speed of movement in relation to age and muscle morphology. *J. Appl. Physiol.* 46:451–456, 1979.

147. Larsson, L. Physical training effects on muscle morphology in sedentary males at different ages. *Med. Sci. Sports Exerc.* 14:203–206, 1982.

148. Leithead, C.S., and A.R. Lind. *Heat Stress and Heat Disorders.* London: Cassell & Company, 1964.

149. Lester, M., L.T. Sheffield, P. Trammell, and T.J. Reeves. The effect of age and athletic training on maximal heart rate during muscular exercise. *Am. Heart J.* 76:370–376, 1968.

150. Lexell, J., K. Henriksson-Larsson, B. Wimblad, and M. Sjostrom. Distribution of different fiber types in human skeletal muscle. 3. Effects of aging in m. vastus lateralis studies in whole muscle cross-sections. *Muscle Nerve* 6:588–595, 1983.

151. Lind, A.R., P.W. Hunphreys, K.J. Collins, K. Foster, and K.F. Sweetland. Influence of age and daily duration of exposure on responses of men to work in heat. *J. Appl. Physiol.* 28:50–56, 1970.

152. Londeree, B.R., and M.L. Moeschberger. Effect of age and other factors on maximal heart rate. *Res. Q. Exer. Sports* 53:297–304, 1982.

153. London, G.M., M.E. Safar, Y.A. Weiss, and P.L. Milliez. Isoproterenol sensitivity and total body clearance of propranolol in hypertensive patients. *J. Clin. Pharmacol.* 16:174–183, 1976.

154. MacLennan, W.J., M.R.P. Hall, J.I. Timothy, and M. Robinson. Is weakness in old age due to muscle wasting? *Age Ageing* 9:188–192, 1980.

155. Mahler, D.A., D.P.E. Cunningham, and G.D. Curfman. Aging and exercise performance. *Clin. Geriatr. Med.* 2:433–452, 1986.

156. Makrides, L., G.J. Heigenhauser, N. McCartney, and N.L. Jones. Maximal short term exercise capacity in healthy subjects aged 15–70 years. *Clin. Sci.* 69:197–205, 1985.

157. Mann, D.C., B.S. Deneberg, A.K. Gash, P.T. Makler, and A.A. Boue. Effects of age on ventricular performance during graded supine exercise. *Am. Heart J.* 111:108–115, 1986.

158. Markrides, S.C. Protein synthesis and degradation during ageing and senescence. *Biol. Rev.* 58:343–422, 1983.

159. Mazess, R.B. Measurement of skeletal status by noninvasive methods. *Calcif. Tissue Int.* 28:89–92, 1979.

160. Milne, J.S., and J. Williamson. Respiratory function tests in older people. *Clin. Sci.* 42:371–381, 1972.

161. Mittman, C., N.H. Edelman, A.H. Norris, and N.W. Shock. Relationship between chest wall and pulmonary compliance and age. *J. Appl. Physiol.* 20:1211–1216, 1965.

162. Moller, P., and R. Brandt. The effect of physical training in elderly subjects with special reference to energy-rich phosphagens and myoglobin in leg skeletal muscle. *Clin. Physiol.* 2:307–314, 1982.

163. Montoye, H.J., E.L. Smith, D.F. Fardon, and E.T. Howley. Bone mineral in senior tennis players. *Scand. J. Sports Sci.* 2:26–32, 1980.

164. Montoye, H.J. Age and oxygen utilization during submaximal treadmill exercise in males. *J. Gerontol.* 37:396–402, 1982.

165. Montoye, H.J. *Physical Activity and Health: An Epidemiologic Study of an Entire Community.* Englewood Cliffs, N.J.: Prentice-Hall, 1975.

166. Montoye, H.J., and D.E. Lamphiear. Grip and arm strength in males and females, age 10 to 69. *Res. Q.* 48:109–120, 1977.

167. Moritani, T., and H.A. deVries. Neural factors versus hypertrophy in the time course of muscle strength gain in young and old men. *J. Gerontol.* 36:294–297, 1981.

168. Munns, K. Effects of exercise on the range of joint motion in elderly subjects. In E.L. Smith and R.C. Serfass (eds.). *Exercise and Aging: The Scientific Basis.* Hillside, N.J.: Enslow Publishers, 1981, pp. 167–178.

169. Murray, M.P., G.M. Gardner, L.A. Mollinger, and S.B. Sepic. Strength of isometric and isokinetic contractions. *Phys. Ther.* 60:412–419, 1980.

170. Myhre, L.B., and W. Kessler. Body density and potassium 40 measurements of body composition as related to age. *J. Appl. Physiol.* 21:1251–1255, 1966.

171. Niinimaa, V., and R.J. Shephard. Training and oxygen conductance in the elderly. I. The respiratory system. *J. Gerontol.* 33:354–361, 1978.

172. Niinimaa, V., and R.J. Shephard. Training and oxygen conductance in the elderly. II. The cardiovascular system. *J. Gerontol.* 33:362–367, 1978.

173. Nixon, J.V., H. Hallmark, K. Page, P.B. Raven, and J.H. Mitchell. Ventricular performance in human hearts aged 61–73 years. *Am. J. Cardiol.* 56:932–937, 1985.

174. Norris, A.H., N.W. Shock, M. Landowne, and J.A. Falzone. Pulmonary function studies: Age differences in lung volume and bellows function. *J. Gerontol.* 11:379–387, 1956.

175. Norris, A.H., N.W. Shock, and J.A. Falzone. Relation of lung volumes and maximal breathing capacity to age and socio-economic status. In H.T. Blumenthal (ed.). *Medical and Clinical Aspect of Aging.* New York: Columbia University Press, 1962, pp. 163–171.

176. Orlander, J., K.H. Kiessling, L. Larsson, J. Larsson, and A. Aniansson. Skeletal muscle metabolism and ultrastructure in relation to age in sedentary men. *Acta Physiol. Scand.* 104:249–261, 1978.

177. Palmer, G.J., M.G. Ziegler, and C.R. Lake. Response of norepinephrine and blood pressure to stress increases with age. *J. Gerontol.* 33:482–487, 1978.

178. Pariskova, J., E. Eiselt, S. Sprynarova, and M. Wachtlova. Body composition, aerobic capacity and density of muscle capillaries in young and old men. *J. Appl. Physiol.* 31:323–325, 1971.

179. Patrick, J.M., E.J. Bassey, and P.II. Fentem. The rising ventilatory cost of bicycle exercise in the seventh decade: A longitudinal study of nine healthy men. *Clin. Sci.* 65:521–526, 1983.

180. Pemberton, J., and E.G. Flanagan. Vital capacity and timed vital capacity in normal men over forty. *J. Appl. Physiol.* 9:291–296, 1956.

181. Peterson, D.D., A.I. Pack, D.A. Silage, and A.P. Fishman. Effects of ageing on respiratory responses to hypoxia and hypercapnia. *Am. Rev. Respir. Dis.* 124:387–391, 1981.

182. Petrofsky, J.S., R.L. Burse, and A.R. Lind. Comparison of physiological responses of women and men to isometric exercise. *J. Appl. Physiol.* 38:863–868, 1975.

183. Petrofsky, J.S., and A.R. Lind. Aging, isometric strength and endurance and cardiovascular responses to static effort. *J. Appl. Physiol.* 38:91–95, 1975.

184. Pierson, R.N., D.H.Y. Lin, and R.A. Phillips. Total body potassium in health: Effects of age, sex, height and fat. *Am. J. Physiol.* 226:206–212, 1974.

185. Plowman, S.A., B.L. Drinkwater, and S.M. Horvath. Age and aerobic power in women: A longitudinal study. *J. Gerontol.* 34:512–520, 1979.

186. Pollock, M.L., C. Foster, D. Knapp, J.L. Rod, and D.H. Schmidt. Effect of age, training, and competition on aerobic capacity and body composition of masters athletes. *J. Appl. Physiol.* (In press).

187. Pollock, M.L., G.A. Dawson, H.S. Miller, A. Ward, D. Cooper, W. Headley, A.C. Linnerud, and M.M. Nomeit. Physiologic responses of men 49 to 65 years of age to endurance training. *J. Am. Geriatr. Soc.* 24:97–104, 1976.

188. Pollock, M.L., H.S. Miller, and J. Wilmore. Physiological characteristics of champion American track athletes 40 to 75 years of age. *J. Gerontol.* 29:645–650, 1974.

189. Port, S., F.R. Cobb, R.E. Coleman, and R.H. Jones. Effect of age on the response of the left ventricular ejection fraction to exercise. *N. Engl. J. Med.* 303:1133–1137, 1980.

190. Profant, G.R., R.G. Early, K.L. Nilson, F. Kusumi, V. Hofer, and R.A. Bruce. Responses to maximal exercise in healthy middle-aged women. *J. Appl. Physiol.* 33:595–599, 1972.

191. Purcell, Y., and B. Brozovic. Red cell 2,3-diphosphoglycerate concentration in man decreases with age. *Nature* 251:511–512, 1974.

192. Raven, P.B., and J. Mitchell. The effect of aging on the cardiovascular response to dynamic and static exercise. In M.L. Weisfeldt (ed.). *The Aging Heart.* New York: Raven Press, 1980, pp. 269–296.

193. Reinhard, U., P.H. Mueller, and R.M. Schmuelling. Determination of anaerobic

threshold by the ventilation equivalent in normal individuals. *Respiration.* 38:36–42, 1979.

194. Rizzato, G., and L. Marazzini. Thoracoabdominal mechanics in elderly men. *J. Appl. Physiol.* 28:457–460, 1970.

195. Robinson, S. Circulatory adjustments of men in hot environments. In J.D. Hardy (ed.). *Temperature: Its Measurement and Control in Science and Industry,* Vol. 3, Part 3, New York: Reinhold Book Corporation, 1963, p. 287.

196. Robinson, S., D.B. Dill, J.C. Ross, R.D. Robinson, J.A. Wagner, and S.P. Tzankoff. Training and physiological aging in man. *Fed. Proc.* 32:1628–1634, 1973.

197. Robinson, S. Experimental studies of physical fitness in relation to age. *Arbeitsphysiologie* 20:251–323, 1938.

198. Robinson, S., D.B. Dill, S.P. Tzankoff, J.A. Wagner, and R.D. Robinson. Longitudinal studies of aging in 37 men. *J. Appl. Physiol.* 38:263–267, 1975.

199. Rockstein, M., J.A. Chesky, and T. Lopez. Effects of exercise on the biochemical aging of mammalian myocardium. I. Actomyosin ATPase. *J. Gerontol.* 36:294–297, 1981.

200. Rodahl, K., N.C. Birkhead, J. Blizzard, B. Issekutz, and E.D.R. Pruett. Physiological changes during prolonged bed rest. In G. Blix (ed.). *Nutrition and Physical Activity.* Stockholm: Almqvist and Wiksell, 1967, p. 107.

201. Rodeheffer, R.J., G. Gerstenblith, L.C. Becker, J.L. Fleg, M.L. Weisfeldt, and E.G. Lakatta. Exercise cardiac output is maintained with advancing age in healthy human subjects: Cardiac dilatation and increased stroke volume compensate for a diminished heart rate. *Circulation* 69:203–213, 1984.

202. Rodriguez, M.J., J.J. DePalma, and H.P. Daykin. Isometric exercise in general practice. *J. Assoc. Phys. Ment. Rehab.* 19:197–200, 1965.

203. Roskamm, H. Optimum patterns of exercise for healthy adults. In Proceedings of International Symposium on Physical Activity and Health. *Can. Med. Assoc. J.* 96:895–899, 1967.

204. Rubin, C.P., P.J. Scott, K. McLean, and J.C. Reid. Noradrenaline release and clearance in relation to age and blood pressure in man. *Eur. J. Clin. Invest.* 12:121–125, 1982.

205. Rubin, S., M. Tack, and N.S. Cherniack. Effect of aging on respiratory responses to CO_2 and inspiratory resistive loads. *J. Gerontol.* 37:306–310, 1982.

206. Saltin, B., L.H. Hartley, A. Kilborm, and I. Astrand. Physical training in sedentary middle-aged and older men. II. Oxygen uptake, heart rate, and blood lactate concentration at submaximal and maximal exercise. *Scand. J. Clin. Lab. Invest.* 24:323–334, 1969.

207. Sawin, C.S., J.A. Rummel, and E.L. Michel. Instrumental personal exercise during long duration space flights. *Aviat. Space Environ. Med.* 46:394–400, 1975.

208. Schocken, D.D., J.A. Blumenthal, S. Port, P. Hindle, and R.E. Coleman. Physical conditioning and left ventricular performance in the elderly. *Am. J. Cardiol.* 52:359–364, 1983.

209. Schmidt, C.D., M.L. Dickman, R.M. Gardner, and F.K. Brough. Spirometric standards for healthy elderly men and women. *Am. Rev. Respir. Dis.* 108:933–939, 1973.

210. Seals, D.R., J.M. Hagberg, B.F. Hurley, A.A. Ehsani, and J.O. Holloszy. Endurance training in older men and women. I. Cardiovascular responses to exercise. *J. Appl. Physiol.* 57:1024–1029, 1984.

211. Seals, D.R., B.F. Hurley, J. Schultz, and J.H. Hagberg. Endurance training in older men and women. II. Blood lactate response to submaximal exercise. *J. Appl. Physiol.* 57:1030–1033, 1984.

212. Sheffield, L.T., J.A. Maloof, J.A. Sawyer, and D. Roitman. Maximal heart rate and

treadmill performance of healthy women in relation to age. *Circulation* 57:79–84, 1978.

213. Shephard, R.J. *Physical Activity and Aging.* Chicago: Year Book Medical Publishers, 1978.

214. Shephard, R.J. World standards of cardiorespiratory performance. *Arch. Environ. Health* 13:664–670, 1966.

215. Shephard, R.J. *Endurance Fitness,* 2nd ed. Toronto: University of Toronto Press, 1977.

216. Shephard, R.J., and K.H. Sidney. Exercise and aging. In R.S. Hutton (ed.). *Exercise and Sport Sciences Reviews,* Vol. 6. Philadelphia: Franklin Institute Press, 1978, pp. 1–57.

217. Shock, N.W. Aging of homeostatic mechanisms. In A. Lansing (ed.). *Problems of Ageing.* Baltimore: Williams & Wilkins Co., 1952, pp. 415–446.

218. Shock, N.W. Physiological aspects of aging in man. *Ann. Rev. Physiol.* 23:97–122, 1961.

219. Shock, N.W., D.M. Watkin, M.J. Yiengst, A.H. Norris, G.W. Gatney, R.I. Gregerman, and J.A. Falzone. Age differences in the water content of the body as related to basal oxygen consumption in males. *J. Gerontol.* 18:1–8, 1963.

220. Sidney, K.H., and R.J. Shephard. Attitudes towards health and physical training in the elderly. Effects of a physical training program. *Med. Sci. Sports* 8:246–252, 1976.

221. Sidney, K.H., and R.J. Shephard. Activity patterns of elderly men and women. *J. Gerontol.* 32:25–32, 1977.

222. Sidney, K.H., and R.J. Shephard. Training and electrocardiographic abnormalities in the elderly. *Br. Heart J.* 39:1114–1120, 1977.

223. Sidney, K.H., and R.J. Shephard. Maximum and submaximum exercise tests in men and women in the seventh, eighth and ninth decades of life. *J. Appl. Physiol.* 43:280–287, 1977.

224. Sidney, K.H., and R.J. Shephard. Frequency and intensity of exercise training for elderly subjects. *Med. Sci. Sports* 10:125–131, 1978.

225. Sidney, K.H., R.J. Shephard, and J.E. Harrison. Endurance training and body composition of the elderly. *Am. J. Clin. Nutr.* 30:326–333, 1977.

226. Simonson, E. Physical fitness and work capacity of older men. *Geriatrics* 2:110–119, 1947.

227. Sjostrom, M., K.A. Angquist, and O. Rais. Intermittent claudication and muscle fiber fine structure: Correlation between clinical and morphological data. *Ultrastruct. Pathol.* 1:309–326, 1980.

228. Sjostrom, M., P. Neglen, J. Friden, and B. Eklof. Human skeletal muscle metabolism and morphology after temporary incomplete ischaemia. *Eur. J. Clin. Invest.* 12:69–79, 1982.

229. Skinner, J.S. Age and performance. In J. Kuel (ed.). *Limiting Factors of Physical Performance.* Stuttgart: Thiene, 1973, pp. 271–282.

230. Skinner, J.S., C.M. Tipton, and A.C. Vailas. Exercise, physical training and the ageing process. In A. Viidik (ed.). *Lectures on Gerontology,* Vol. 1., Part B. London: Academic Press, 1982, pp. 407–439.

231. Skrobak-Kaczynski, J., and K.L. Andersen. The effect of a high level of habitual physical activity in the regulation of fatness during aging. *Int. Arch. Occup. Environ. Health* 36:41–46, 1975.

232. Smith, E.L., W. Reddan, and P.E. Smith. Physical activity and calcium modalities for bone mineral increase in aged women. *Med. Sci. Sports Exerc.* 13:60–64, 1981.

233. Smith, E.L., P.E. Smith, C.J. Ensign, and M.M. Shea. Bone involution decrease in exercising middle-aged women. *Calcif. Tissue Int.* 36(suppl. 1):S129–S138, 1984.

234. Smith, E.L., and W. Reddan. Physical activity—a modality for bone accretion in the aged. *Am. J. Roentgenol.* 126:1297, 1977. (Abstract)
235. Smith, E.L. Exercise for prevention of osteoporosis: A review. *Physician Sportsmed.* 10:72–83, 1982.
236. Smith, E.L., and C. Gilligan. Physical activity for the older adult. *Physician Sportsmed.* 11:91–101, 1983.
237. Spira, E. Orthopedic observations with physically active elderly subjects. In D. Brunner and E. Jokl (eds.). *Physical Activity and Aging.* Baltimore: University Park Press, 1970, pp. 307–308.
238. Spurgeon, H.A., M.F. Steinbach, and E.G. Lakatta. Chronic exercise prevents characteristic age-related changes in rat cardiac contraction. *Am. J. Physiol.* 244:H513–H518, 1983.
239. Stamford, B.A. Physiological effects of training upon institutionalized geriatric men. *J. Gerontol.* 27:451–455, 1972.
240. Stamford, B.A. Effects of chronic institutionalization on the physical working capacity and trainability of geriatric men. *J. Gerontol.* 28:441–446, 1973.
241. Strandell, T. Circulatory studies on healthy old men. *Acta Med. Scand.* 414(suppl.):1–43, 1964.
242. Strandell, T. Heart rate, arterial lactate concentration and oxygen uptake during exercise in old men compared to young men. *Acta Physiol. Scand.* 60:197–201, 1964.
243. Strandell, T. Cardiac output in old age. In F.T. Carid, J.L.C. Doll, and R.D. Kennedy (eds.). *Cardiology in Old Age.* New York: Plenum Press, 1967, p. 160.
244. Suominen, H., E. Heikkinen, P. Vainio, and T. Lahtinen. Mineral density of calcaneus in men at different ages: A population study with special reference to life-style factors. *Age Ageing* 13:273–281, 1984.
245. Suominen, H., E. Heikkinen, H. Liesen, D. Michel, and W. Hollmann. Effects of 8 weeks' endurance training on skeletal muscle metabolism in 56–70 year old sedentary men. *Eur. J. Appl. Physiol.* 37:173–180, 1977.
246. Suominen, H., E. Heikkinen, and I. Parkatti. Effects of eight weeks' physical training on muscle and connective tissue of the m. vastus lateralis in 69 year old men and women. *J. Gerontol.* 32:33–37, 1977.
247. Syrovy, I., and E. Gutmann. Changes in speed of contraction and ATPase activity in striated muscle during old age. *Exp. Gerontol.* 5:31–35, 1970.
248. Tejada, C., J.P. Strong, M.R. Montenegro, C. Restrepo, and L.A. Solberg. Distribution of coronary and aortic atherosclerosis by geographic location, race, and sex. *Lab. Invest.* 18:509–526, 1968.
249. Templeton, G.H., M.R. Platt, J.T. Willerson, and M.L. Weisfeldt. Influence of aging on left ventricular hemodynamics and stiffness in beagles. *Circ. Res.* 44:189–194, 1979.
250. Thomas, S.G., D.A. Cunningham, P.A. Rechnitzer, A.P. Donner, and J.H. Howard. Determinants of the training response in elderly men. *Med. Sci. Sports Exerc.* 17:667–672, 1985.
251. Thorstensson, A., G. Grimby, and J. Karlsson. Force–velocity relations and fiber composition in human knee extensor muscles. *J. Appl. Physiol.* 40:12–16, 1976.
252. Timiras, P.S. *Developmental Physiology and Aging.* New York: Macmillan Co., 1972.
253. Tlusty, L. Physical fitness in old age. I. Aerobic capacity and the other parameters of physical fitness followed by means of graded exercise in ergometric examination of elderly individuals. *Respiration* 26:161–181, 1969.

254. Tomonaga, M. Histochemical and ultrastructural changes in senile human skeletal muscle. *J. Am. Geriatr. Soc.* 25:125–131, 1977.
255. Turner, J.M., J. Mead, and M.E. Wohl. Elasticity of human lungs in relation to age. *J. Appl. Physiol.* 25:664–671, 1968.
256. Tweeddale, P.M., R.J.E. Leggett, and D.C. Finley. Effect of age on oxygen-binding in normal human subjects. *Clin. Sci. Mol. Med.* 51:185–188, 1976.
257. Tzankoff, S.P., and A.H. Norris. Effect of muscle mass decrease on age-related BMR changes. *J. Appl. Physiol.* 43:1001–1006, 1977.
258. Tzankoff, S.P., S. Robinson, F.S. Pyke, and C.A. Brawn. Physiological adjustments to work in older men as affected by physical training. *J. Appl. Physiol.* 33:346–350, 1972.
259. Van Tosh, A., E.G. Lakatta, J.L. Fleg, J. Weiss, C. Kallman, M. Weisfeldt, and G. Gerstenbith. Ventricular dimension changes during submaximal exercise: Effect of aging in normal man. *Circulation* 62(suppl. 3):129, 1980. (Abstract)
260. Vestal, R.E., A.J. Wood, and D.G. Shand. Reduced β-adrenoceptor sensitivity in the elderly. *Clin. Pharmacol. Ther.* 26:181–186, 1979.
261. Viljanen, A. (ed.). Reference values for spirometric, pulmonary diffusing capacity and body plethysmographic studies. *Scand. J. Clin. Lab. Invest.* 42(suppl. 159):5–50, 1982.
262. Vogel, J.M., and M.W. Whittle. Bone mineral changes: The second manned Skylab mission. *Aviat. Space Environ. Med.* 47:396–400, 1976.
263. Voigt, A.E., R.A. Bruce, F. Kusumi, G. Pettet, K. Neilson, B. Whitkanack, and J. Tapia. Longitudinal variations in maximal exercise performance of healthy sedentary middle aged women. *Sports Med.* 15:323–327, 1975.
264. von Dobelin, W., I. Astrand, and A. Bergstrom. Analysis of age and other factors related to maximal oxygen uptake. *J. Appl. Physiol.* 22:934–938, 1967.
265. Weisfeldt, M.L. Aging of the cardiovascular system. *N. Engl. J. Med.* 303:1172–1173, 1980.
266. Wessel, J.A., D.A. Small, W.D. Van Huss, D.J. Anderson, and D.C. Cederquist. Age and physiological response to exercise in women 20–69 years of age. *J. Gerontol.* 23:269–279, 1968.
267. Wessel, J.A., A. Ufer, W.D. Van Huss, and D. Cederquist. Age trends of various components of body composition and functional characteristics in women aged 20–69 years. *Ann. N.Y. Acad. Sci.* 110:608–622, 1963.
268. White, N.K., J.E. Edwards, and T.J. Dry. The relationship of the degree of coronary atherosclerosis with age, in men. *Circulation* 1:645–654, 1950.
269. Wilmore, J.H., J. Royce, R.N. Girandola, F.I. Katch, and V.I. Katch. Physiological alterations resulting from a ten week program of jogging. *Med. Sci. Sports* 2:7–14, 1970.
270. Wollein, W., N. Bachl, and L. Prokop. Endurance capacity of trained older aged athletes. *Eur. Heart J.* 5(suppl.):21–25, 1984.
271. Wright, V., and R.J. Johns. Physical factors concerned with the stiffness of normal and diseased joints. *Bull. Johns Hopkins Hosp.* 106:215–231, 1960.
272. Yerg, J.E., D.R. Seals, J.M. Hagberg, and J.O. Holloszy. Effect of endurance exercise training on ventilatory function in older individuals. *J. Appl. Physiol.* 58:791–794, 1985.
273. Yin, F.C.P., H.A. Spurgeon, H.L. Greene, E.G. Lakatta, and M.L. Weisfeldt. Age-associated decrease in heart rate response to isoproterenol in dogs. *Mech. Ageing Dev.* 10:17–25, 1979.
274. Young, A., M. Stokes, and M. Crowe. The size and strength of the quadriceps muscles of old and young women. *Eur. J. Clin. Invest.* 14:282–287, 1984.

275. Young, A., M. Stokes, and M. Crowe. The size and strength of the quadriceps muscles of old and young men. *Clin. Physiol.* 5:145–154, 1985.
276. Young, J.B., J.W. Rowe, J.A. Pallotta, D. Sparrow, and L. Landsberg. Enhanced plasma norepinephrine response to upright posture and oral glucose administration in elderly human subjects. *Metabolism* 29:532–539, 1980.
277. Ziegler, M.G., C.R. Lake, and I.J. Kopin. Plasma Noradrenaline increases with age. *Nature* 261:333–335, 1976.

12
Biofeedback Applications in Exercise and Athletic Performance

LEONARD D. ZAICHKOWSKY, Ph.D.
C. ZVI FUCHS, Ed.D.

INTRODUCTION

Biofeedback, as a term and as an area of inquiry and application in psychophysiology and behavioral medicine/health psychology, is a rather recent development, first appearing in the literature in the 1960s. Since that time, psychologists, physicians, and other health professionals have conducted extensive research on the topic. Research on and application of biofeedback (BFK) technology in the exercise and sport sciences is predictably of a more recent vintage, with the first paper appearing only 12 years ago [92]. The purpose of this chapter is to discuss briefly the concept of BFK, and then to review critically the studies that investigated the efficacy of using BFK in order to control performance anxiety, fine tune performance, reduce pain, increase strength and flexibility, and increase exercise tolerance.

Genesis of the Concept of Biofeedback
At the core of BFK is the principle of feedback, a concept that psychologists, motor behavior researchers, and practitioners have researched and applied for decades (see Magill [58] and Newell et al. [68] for excellent reviews of feedback). The biological sciences, however, were also no strangers to the concept of feedback, especially since Sherrington's [81] findings on the proprioceptive system. Indeed, BFK can be thought of as a specialized application of feedback, where the system feeding back information (or what some motor skill researchers would term "augmented information" and/or "knowledge of results") is a biological signal. Biofeedback, thus, is nothing more than the use of instrumentation to detect and amplify internal physiological processes in order to make this ordinarily unavailable information available to the individual in a form that is *meaningful, rapid, precise*, and *consistent*. The feedback, along with practice, theoretically allows an individual to learn to self-regulate biological functions normally not under voluntary control, or functions that were previously under self-control but for which self-regulation has broken down because of trauma or disease.

Figure 1 illustrates, in summary form, the control system that serves as BFK. The process of BFK involves three methodological elements. First, information about the biological function is obtained by having sensing electrodes pick up appropriate signals. Second, these signals are transduced and amplified by the biofeedback instrument (usually electronic). Third, the individual uses this biological feedback (hence the term "biofeedback"), as well as instructions from a trainer or therapist, to try to increase or decrease the biological function. Such efforts usually take the form of some combination of verbal instructions in the use of cognitive strategies that facilitate voluntary control, verbal instructions to make the feedback display change in the desired direction, or the presentation or removal of reinforcers contingent upon changes in the feedback display.

The whole feedback process as illustrated moves clockwise, is continuous, and ideally is precise, immediate, and meaningful. For example, the individual attempts to control (feedforward) heart rate (HR). HR changes in some manner; information about the actual HR change is provided by a light, meter, digital display, or other meaningful presentation. The individual evaluates the outcome, makes appropriate changes, and so on. In general, the individual compares the instructions received with the actual responses produced and seeks to reduce any discrepancy between the two [2].

The term "feedforward," as used above, is a term that, like "feedback," has been borrowed from the field of cybernetics. Although it is traditionally used to indicate the takeover of a subordinate system by a superordinate system [2], such is not the case here. Rather, it merely indicates an important controlling relationship. What is interesting is that the feedback in BFK is not really the important focus, but rather the feedforward. But in order to obtain accurate feedforward, the individual needs to have accurate feedback.

The commonly used modalities of BFK training include muscle or electromyographic (EMG) BFK, cardiovascular BFK that includes HR and thermal feedback, electrodermal (EDR) BFK, and electroencephalographic (EEG) BFK.

The evolution of BFK, from a historical perspective, is interesting in that it apparently grew out of a simultaneous inquiry taking place in the EMG [7] and EEG [13] fields, as well as work in operant conditioning [66]. For a more thorough historical treatment, the reader is referred to Brown [14] and Zaichkowsky [96]. Since the initial inquiry into BFK some 25 years ago, studies on theoretical and applied aspects of BFK have appeared in major journals representing the fields of psychology [12], physiology [25, 31], education [5], medicine [63, 65], and others. Two professional societies, the Biofeedback Society of America and the American Association of Biofeedback Clinicians, have been formed. They publish their own journals: *Biofeedback and Self-Regulation* and the *American Journal of Clinical*

FIGURE 1
Biofeedback as a general control system.

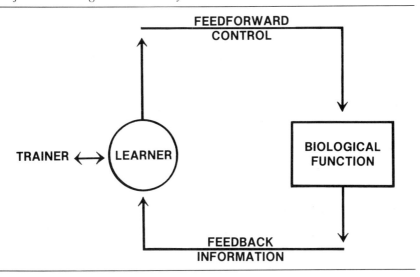

Biofeedback, recently changed to *Clinical Biofeedback and Health,* respectively. Several textbooks have also been published. Among them is the classical textbook edited by Basmajian [8], *Biofeedback: Principles and Practice for Clinicians,* which recently appeared in its second edition.

BFK in Sport and Motor Behavior
Investigations of BFK with athletes or with movement phenomena have occurred only within the last 15 years. In 1978, a Task Force of the Biofeedback Society of America attempted to determine whether BFK had any application to the field of athletics [76]. They reported that a handful of clinical researchers were using BFK in three different ways: as a technique for teaching athletes to deal with general and specific anxiety; as a means of restoring function after muscle injury; and as a means for providing biomechanical and muscle feedback to athletes so that they could perfect highly skilled movements and enhance performance. The Task Force reported that their findings were primarily based on anecdotal reports and not on empirical studies. A 1980 update of this report [77] showed that very little had been added to the literature in 2 years.

Several sport scientists have attempted to establish a theoretical basis for the use of BFK in sports, as well as to review the research literature that has accumulated in the field. The theoretical papers include early speculations on the possible role of BFK in sport psychology [4, 11, 92], motor skill acquisition [87, 90], and rehabilitation of sport injuries [90]. The review papers can be divided into sport psychology–oriented reviews [40, 94, 95], recent psychophysiologically oriented reviews [48, 98], and an edited book *Biofeedback and Sports Science* [78] that includes a mixture of theoretical as well as practical review papers.

The remainder of this chapter will review studies that examined the efficacy of using BFK in sport and exercise training and performance. More specifically, we will review papers that have investigated the effects of different BFK modalities applied to healthy subjects during exercise and/or as a preparation for enhanced performance. We will first examine studies that used EMG feedback as the principal modality, followed by studies using HR feedback, and finally, studies that employed temperature and EDR feedback.

BFK IN EXERCISE, SPORT AND MOTOR PERFORMANCE

EMG BFK is unquestionably the most widely studied modality of BFK for relaxation training and rehabilitation of muscle. Generally in EMG BFK, surface electrodes are attached to the prepared skin, and the electrical activity of the target muscle(s) is presented to the subject, either visually or auditorally or both. In special cases, such as single motor unit (SMU) training, fine wire electrodes are inserted into the muscle itself. For general relaxation training, most researchers and clinicians use the frontalis or trapezius muscles, whereas for rehabilitation, the target muscle is generally used. Once the feedback signal is presented, the subject tries to modify it in the appropriate direction, namely, to decrease EMG output for relaxation of spastic or tense muscles and to increase EMG output for activation of paretic muscles [91]. In the following section, we will review the appropriate studies that used EMG training as the sole or primary mode of intervention in nonathletes performing either gross or fine motor laboratory tasks.

BFK and Motor Performance Anxiety

The first of the laboratory studies was conducted by Teague [85]. This researcher used both systematic desensitization and EMG BFK in an attempt to reduce state anxiety and improve balancing performance on a stabilometer. After providing college students with a total of 4 hours of treatment, Teague found that his subjects were able to reduce state anxiety (although the result was statistically insignificant) and to improve balancing performance.

French [32] likewise used a stabilometer for his measure of motor performance. He hypothesized that EMG feedback training would reduce general performance-debilitating muscle tension and improve balancing performance. Results of the study showed a significant decline in tension between pretesting and posttesting on the stabilometer. Associated with the lower EMG reading was a significant improvement in performance by the experimental group. French's contention was supported by his obtained coefficient of correlation for time-on-balance and concurrently scored EMG values ($r = -0.60$).

In a recent study, Blais and Vallerand [12] trained ten 10- to 13-year-old boys, who scored high on the Sport Competition Anxiety Test (SCAT), with EMG BFK for six sessions. The results showed that in comparison to their placebo controls, BFK-trained subjects showed reduced frontalis EMG, reduced HR, and better performance in a highly competitive balance task (stabilometer). The respiration rate, however, was not significantly different between the experimental and control groups.

In addition to the above studies, which measured the effect of EMG BFK training on anxiety and performance on the gross skill of balancing, several studies examined BFK training on fine motor skill performance. For example, Sabourin and Rioux [75] used a sample of 18 females to compare different regimens of EMG training on pursuit rotor performance and reaction times. The subjects were divided equally into three groups: passive BFK training to decrease EMG levels, active BFK training to achieve given criteria in a bidirectional training paradigm (learning to increase/decrease EMG levels at will), and a control group. The results showed that for pursuit rotor tracking skill, both biofeedback groups showed improved performance over controls. On reaction time, only the active BFK group demonstrated significant improvement. The last finding should not be surprising since it seems that the subjects in the passive BFK group were too relaxed to perform efficiently, as would be predicted by the inverted-U theory [60]. Similar results were also found by Pinel and Schultz [74] on a choice-response time test. These response measures were not significant for the EMG BFK low-muscle-tension condition. Hand steadiness and grip strength tests were, however, better for the EMG BFK low-tension condition compared to the high-tension condition. It is interesting to note that the EMG-trained right forearm (flexor muscle group) was also the one used in testing subjects on the motor performance tests.

More recently, French [33] reported the effects of EMG BFK on the learning and performance of a pursuit-rotor task. As in the Sabourin and Rioux [75] study, subjects reduced tension and significantly improved their performance on the task.

EMG BFK and Sport Performance Anxiety
Another group of studies examined the effects of BFK training on athletes representing a variety of skill levels, as well as different sports. Bennett and Hall [10], in an unpublished paper, reported the findings of a study on archers. The researchers assigned high-competitive and low-competitive novice archers to one of three groups: BFK-cognitive training, BFK single exposure, and no BFK. EMG frontalis muscle training for group 1 con-

sisted of four 10-minute sessions; group 2 received a single 10-minute session. The results indicated that muscle tension levels could be significantly reduced with BFK training. However, Bennett and Hall concluded that reduced EMG tension levels were not accompanied by increases in archery performance. The major weakness of this study was that the training periods were too brief and training was not conducted to a criterion. Thus, it is not feasible to make conclusions about the efficacy of "treatment."

Wenz and Strong [87] also reported on some exploratory work with elite athletes (mainly track and synchronized swimmers) using both EMG and thermal BFK in a clinical rather than a research context. These psychologists reported teaching athletes anxiety management, using biofeedback as well as Jacobsonian relaxation training, autogenic phrases, and imagery. Although their work to date has precluded hypothesis testing, the researchers reported that athletes developed greater "self-regulation" when they became more self-confident and consequently improved their performances.

DeWitt [27] reported on two studies that attempted to determine whether a cognitive BFK training program would help athletes reduce competitive stress reactions and improve performance. In the first study, six football players attended 12 biweekly training sessions, each 1 hour in duration. The training sessions included EMG BFK on either the frontalis, masseter, or trapezius muscle, as well as general relaxation training, training in visual imagery, and cognitive training. The results showed that four of the six athletes improved in game performance, based upon coaches' ratings, accompanied by significant declines in EMG levels across sessions. In the second study reported by DeWitt, 12 university male basketball players were randomly assigned to treatment and contact-control groups. In addition to EMG BFK, training in visual imagery, and cognitive strategies, subjects received HR feedback. The results showed that the athletes were able to reduce EMG and HR levels significantly over 11 sessions. Furthermore, two team managers, who were not aware of which athletes were in the BFK training programs, rated the performance of the treatment group significantly higher than that of the control group. Additionally, the treatment subjects reported feeling more relaxed, had greater control over tension, felt "looser" during games, and reported a decrease in the number of minor injuries during program participation.

Griffiths et al. [37] examined the efficacy of different treatments designed to reduce the level of anxiety in beginning scuba divers. Their treatments included taped relaxation training and meditation, and a combined training program of taped muscle relaxation and EMG BFK. The researchers employed an underwater assembly task (called the U.S. Navy's "Sp^2 task") under stressed conditions in order to test the effects of the various treatments on underwater anxiety. Their results indicated that in comparison to the control group, both the meditation and BFK relaxation groups reduced their state anxiety, but no significant differences were found between the meditation and BFK relaxation groups. A shortcoming of this study is that it is not clear whether highly anxious subjects were used in the study. If the subjects were not in fact highly anxious, it is reasonable to conclude that intervention would be of little value.

Two studies examined the effect of EMG BFK training on gymnastic performance. The first study, reported by Zaichkowsky et al. [97], tested the hypothesis that EMG frontalis biofeedback in combination with systematic desensitization would be effective in reducing state anxiety and improving the performance of college gymnasts. It was found that BFK reduced frontal EMG activity as much as 42% from baseline levels. However, A-state anxiety, although lower than baseline anxiety under two different conditions of competitive stress, was not significantly reduced after training. Even though performance was improved for the treatment group on four out of six events under conditions of moderate and high stress, design limitations prevented unequivocal statements regarding treatment efficacy. This occurred because the gymnasts were not required to compete in all events; thus, sample sizes for particular events became rather small. It was of interest to note that experimental subjects reported BFK to be helpful in managing their anxiety and perceived it to enhance their performance.

Tsukomoto [86] likewise studied the effects of EMG-assisted BFK relaxation on gymnasts. The researcher found no differences on anxiety between groups that learned to relax with BFK and groups that did not. One limitation of this study was the use of subjective judgment for performance evaluation. If the treatment was in fact effective, it may have been masked by the method used to judge performance.

Since all of the papers reviewed so far included EMG frontalis BFK as the primary training modality to teach relaxation and ostensibly to improve motor and exercise performance in athletes, it is appropriate to examine the relationships among frontalis tension control and performance. Kirkcaldy and Christen [47] were interested in determining the effects of EMG frontalis BFK on the rate of recovery after exercise. In order to do so, they studied four experimental groups of physically conditioned subjects. The first group received five sessions of EMG frontalis training at rest. The second group received the same EMG training immediately following submaximal graded exercise intensities (30–150 W) on a bicycle ergometer. The third group was a placebo group, and the fourth used Jacobson's relaxation technique. All groups were tested during exercise stress. The results showed that both BFK groups exhibited a marked reduction in EMG frontalis tension after exercise. This reduction was highly specific to the frontalis muscle and was not manifested in corresponding heart rate reductions.

Kirkcaldy and Christen's main finding indicates that EMG BFK can be given under stressful situations (e.g., right at the end of an exercise bout and before another one) and still be effective. This finding was addressed by Balog [5], who examined the effect of exercise on EMG frontalis BFK relaxation learning. She, however, found no advantage for the exercise group (riding a bicycle ergometer at 33–200 W) over the BFK only trained group in their relaxation (EMG) response after exercise. Similar results were reported by Harrison [38] for highly trained athletes in the control of SMUs. Harrison stated that highly trained athletes might be poorer learners of SMU control than less skilled subjects. The above findings may indicate that athletes or subjects involved in exercise/motor activity may not have an inherent advantage over noexercisers in EMG BFK learning. This, however, is contrary to the early findings of Jacobson [42].

Several researchers have questioned the validity of using frontal muscle activity as an indicator of general muscle tension in patients and healthy subjects [1, 64]. Also, the Graham et al. study [36] showed convincing evidence that frontalis EMG activity is responsive only to changes in head and neck muscles, but does not correlate with changes in exercise-induced muscular tension in the rest of the body. Therefore, as in most of the studies reviewed, subjects may have successfully reduced their frontalis EMG, but their performing muscles may still have remained tense.

On the other hand, if we accept that frontalis EMG activity is a true indicator of general arousal and muscle tension, as most of the reviewed studies did, these studies still failed to demonstrate conclusively that their subjects suffered from performance and/or precompetition anxiety, either by using psychological tests or by demonstrating abnormal EMG frontalis activity. It might be that BFK relaxation treatment actually "tranquilized" subjects who were relaxed already or who needed some arousal in order to perform adequately.

In conclusion, the above-mentioned design faults, combined with too brief a BFK training time in most of the studies, contribute to the confusing results whereby some studies show EMG reduction, on the one hand, but no improvement in performance, on the other hand. The majority of the studies, however, showed reduction in EMG followed by improved performance. Table 1 summarizes the above studies; however, it is important to point out that they must be evaluated with the methodological limitations noted previously.

EMG BFK and Healthy Muscle Strength Training
Improvement in muscle strength and function with EMG BFK in necrologic and paretic patients is a well-documented phenomenon [8]. Voluntary control of SMU activity in healthy persons [7] and athletes [38] also has an established history. The remarkable results of EMG BFK in

TABLE 1
EMG BFK Relaxation

Study	Subjects (Total, Experimental, and Control Groups)	Biofeedback Treatment (Modality, Site, and Adjunctive Treatment)	Length of Biofeedback Treatment (Sessions × Time)	Motor Performance	Results
Teague [85]	$N = 20$ college students (20–40 years) $E = 10$ BFK + relaxation $C = 10$ pseudotherapy	EMG frontalis + systematic desensitization relaxation	4×60 minutes	Balance	State anxiety = NS; balance performance ↑
French [32]	$N = 30$ male college student $E = 20$ BFK $C = 10$	EMG frontalis	9×20 minutes	Balance	EMG ↓; tension ↓; balance performance ↑
Blais and Vallerand [12]	$N = 20$ high-anxiety boys $\overline{X} = 11.7$ years $\overline{X} = 10$ BFK $C = 10$	EMG frontalis	6×30 minutes	Balance	EMG ↓; HR ↓ (trend); RR = NS; balance performance ↑
Sabourin and Rioux [75]	$N = 18$ females $E_1 = 6$ active BFK $E_2 = 6$ passive BFK $C = 6$	EMG frontalis?	5×30 minutes	Pursuit rotor; RT	Pursuit rotor tracking skill ↑ for both BFK groups; RT ↓ for active BFK group only
Pinel and Schultz [74]	$N = 12$ male college students (subjects used as their own control)	EMG forearm flexors	3×30 minutes	Hand steadiness; grip strength; choice response time	Hand steadiness ↑ when EMG is ↓; grip strength ↑ when EMG is ↓; choice reaction time = NS

TABLE 1
(*continued*)

Study	Subjects (Total, Experimental, and Control Groups)	Biofeedback Treatment (Modality, Site, and Adjunctive Treatment)	Length of Biofeedback Treatment (Sessions × Time)	Motor Performance	Results
French [33]	$N = 30$ male college students (18–23 years) $E_1 = 10$ BFK training $E_2 = 10$ BFK training + BFK on posttest $C = 10$	EMG frontalis	9×20 minutes	Pursuit rotor	EMG ↓ for both BFK groups; pursuit tracking skill ↑ for both BFK groups
Bennett and Hall [10]	$N = 30$ undergraduate novice archers, high and low competitors $E_1 = 10$ BFK + cognitive relaxation $E_2 = 10$ BFK only $C = 10$	EMG frontalis	$E_1 = 4 \times 10$ minutes $E_2 = 1 \times 10$ min	Archery	EMG ↓ for both BFK groups; archery performance = NS
DeWitt Study I [27]	$N = 6$ university football players	EMG frontalis, masseter, and/or trapezius + relaxation, cognitive + imagery training	12×30 minutes	Football	EMG ↓; performance ratings
DeWitt Study II [27]	$N = 12$ university basketball players $E = 6$ EMG + HR BFK $C = 6$	As in study I + HR BFK	11×60 minutes	Basketball	EMG ↓; HR ↓; performance ratings ↑; self-report ↑
Griffith et al. [37]	$N = 50$ college students beginning SCUBA class	EMG frontalis + taped relaxation instructions	6×20 minutes	Underwater assembly test (Sp^2)	State anxiety ↓; underwater performance = NS

(*continued*)

Study	Subjects (Total, Experimental, and Control Groups)	Biofeedback Treatment (Modality, Site, and Adjunctive Treatment)	Length of Biofeedback Treatment (Sessions × Time)	Motor Performance	Results
	E_1 = 19 BFK + relaxation E_2 = 14 Meditation + relaxation C = 17				
Zaichkowsky et al. [97]	N = 25 male college gymnasts E_1 = 10 BFK + desensitization E_2 = 8 relaxation + desensitization C = 7	EMG frontalis + desensitization training	6 × 15–20 minutes	Gymnastics	EMG ↓; state anxiety = NS; gymnastic performance = NS
Tsukomoto [86]	N = 24 female gymnasts, provincial level (10–15 years) E_1 = 8 BFK + relaxation E_2 = 8 relaxation C = 8	EMG frontalis + relaxation	7 × ? minutes	Gymnastics	EMG ↓ only for BFK + relaxation group; anxiety level = NS; gymnastic performance = NS
Kirkcaldy and Christen [47]	N = 26 male P.E. students (19–26 years) E_1 = BFK at rest E_2 = BFK right after exercise E_3 = placebo BFK E_4 = Jacobson relaxation	EMG frontalis	5 × 10 minutes	Bicycle ergometer at 30, 70, 100 115 W; 2-minute intervals	EMG ↓ after exercise for BFK groups (E_1 and E_2) only
Balog [5]	N = 20 (10 male and 10 female) college students E_1 = 10 BFK + exercise E_2 = 10 BFK alone	EMG frontalis	8 × 32 minutes	Bicycle ergometer: female = 200–600 kpm, male = 300–1200 kpm; 4-minute intervals at 90–150 b · min^{-1}	EMG for both BFK groups (no better performance for exercised subjects)

N = total number of subjects, E = experimental group, C = control group, NS = no significant differences, RT = reaction time, BFK = biofeedback, ↑ = performance improvement, ↓ = BFK control.

motor rehabilitation and motor control has led some researchers to use EMG BFK training with healthy subjects as an experimental model for future patient neuromuscular rehabilitation in regular and sports-related injuries. In addition, EMG BFK has been offered to enhance athletes' and healthy persons' exercise programs [90].

Simard and Ladd [82] were the first to use wire-inserted electrodes in order to train healthy subjects to control individually the three segments (superior, inferior, and middle) of the trapezius. The success of the subjects (70–90%) in learning the task in a relatively short time (3 hours) demonstrated to the researchers the possibility of preorthotic training for upper-limb amputees. The implications for athletic performance, especially skill learning, are still unexplored.

In a relatively similar research design, LeVeau and Rogers [51] trained two segments of the quadriceps muscle group [vastus lateralis (VL) and vastus medialis (VM)] to contract independently. Since VL and ML have separate neural innervations, surface EMG electrodes were used in order to discriminate the contraction/relaxation patterns of the two segments. The results showed that healthy subjects can lower VL activity and increase VM activity separately, and thus increase significantly the difference in EMG output between them. It seems that strengthening of the VM independently of the VL may be important in the conservative treatment of hypermobile patella and chondromalacia patella in athletes, especially since regular resistance exercise tends to increase strength in both segments, thereby maintaining muscle imbalance. Practical application of EMG BFK for the treatment of sports-related injuries was demonstrated only recently with patellofemoral pain syndrome [89], and voluntary posterior instability of the shoulder [9]. It should be noted that in both studies, the rehabilitation program included EMG BFK as an adjunct to conventional therapeutic exercise.

The practical application of EMG biofeedback for healthy subjects was also demonstrated by Middaugh et al. [65]. In an attempt to understand the learning mechanisms involved in BFK neuromuscular rehabilitation, these researchers used the left abductor hallucis muscle as the model. Since this muscle is poorly used even in healthy persons, the use of normal subjects rather than patients seemed to be justified. The results showed that active abduction of the abductor hallucis was enhanced by EMG BFK from surface electrodes that were placed over the muscle. The significantly greater EMG activity that was exhibited by the subjects during the feedback trials reflected an increase in motor unit recruitment and probably an increase in muscle strength.

The issue of changes in muscle strength due to EMG BFK training was addressed by Lucca and Recchiuti [57]. The subjects in their study were 30 healthy young females who were divided equally into three groups. The experimental group performed isometric contractions of the knee extensors while receiving EMG BFK from surface electrodes that were placed over the belly of the rectus femoris muscle. The second group performed isometric contractions of the same muscle group, but without feedback. The third group did not exercise and was used as a control. After a 19-day program, the experimental group showed significantly greater gains in average peak torque when compared to the group receiving only exercise. It is interesting to note that the BFK training group also demonstrated significant gains in the untrained leg, thus providing evidence for the phenomenon of bilateral transfer.

The quadriceps muscle was also used by Croce [21] to investigate the effectiveness of EMG BFK training with isokinetic exercise. Three groups were used in the experimental design. The experimental group received instantaneous visual and auditory integrated electromyographic (IEMG) feedback of their strength performance during training of the dominant leg on the Cybex machine, at 110–120° of hip joint flexion, while performing at $30° \cdot sec^{-1}$. The placebo group received nonactive ultrasound treatment 30 seconds before training, and a control group performed isokinetic training only. Although all three groups received accurate knowledge of the results regarding their peak torque output and peak EMG levels after each training session, as well as standard verbal encouragement during training, only the BFK group exhibited significantly greater peak torque values on the posttest. However, IEMG values on the posttest were significantly greater not only for the BFK group but also for the placebo group. Overall, the results supported the researcher's hypothesis that a training program of combined isokinetics and EMG BFK produced significant gains in maximal force and IEMG activity of leg extensor muscles.

In another recent study, James [43] examined the effects of different modes of BFK on maximal voluntary contraction (MVC) of the right abductor of the fifth digit. Forty healthy young females were divided into four groups: visual BFK, auditory BFK, MVC without feedback, and no training. All trained groups showed improvement, but both BFK groups demonstrated significantly higher values in isometric strength. It is worth noting that even though no significant differences between BFK modes was found, the visual group showed quicker increases than the audio group in the initial training stages. Table 2 summarizes the six studies that investigated the efficacy of using EMG BFK to facilitate strength development.

It appears that an exercise regimen combined with EMG BFK from the trained muscle may bring about greater gains in strength than exercise alone, especially in isometric exercise, where feedback is usually absent. The implications of these findings for highly trained athletes are

TABLE 2
EMG BFK Strength

Study	Subjects	Modality and Site of Biofeedback Treatment	Length of Biofeedback Treatment (Sessions × Trials × Time)	Motor Performance	Results
Simard and Ladd [82]	$N = 13$ young, healthy subjects (14–18 years) $E_1 = 11$ EMG BKF $E_2 = 1$ EMG BFK $E_3 = 1$ EMG BFK	EMG insert of wire electrodes in three trapezius segments	$E_1 = 1 \times 3$ hours $E_2 = 2 \times 3$ hours $E_3 = 4 \times 2.5$ hours	Motor unit isolation	Individual control over trapezius segments (70–91% success)
LeVeau and Rogers [51]	$N = 10$ (5 male and 5 female) healthy subjects	EMG quadriceps	15×30 minutes	Muscle EMG isolation	Individual control over vastus lateralis vs. vastus medialis (difference between means, 6.5%)
Middaugh et al. [65]	$N = 10$ university students receiving alternated BFK and no BFK trials $E = 6$ trials $C = 6$ trials	EMG left abductor hallucis	$2 \times 6 \times 30$ seconds	Motor unit recruitment	EMG ↑ in BFK trials; recruitment ↑ in BFK trials

TABLE 2
(*continued*)

Study	Subjects/Groups	EMG site	Protocol	Assessment	Results
Lucca and Recchuiti [57]	N = 30 female graduate students E_1 = 10 BFK + isometric exercise E_2 = 10 isometric exercise	EMG quadriceps femoris	19 × 3 × 6 seconds	Peak torque, 50% of MVC	Peak torque ↑; transfer of gains to nontrained leg
James [43]	N = 40 college females E_1 = 10 EMG auditory + MVC E_2 = 10 EMG visual + MVC E_3 = 10 MVC, no BFK C = 10 no training	EMG right abductor digiti quinti	4 × 10 × 10 seconds	MVC against strain gauge apparatus	MVC ↑ for EMG BFK groups (auditory and visual)
Croce [21]	N = 21 male students (18–32 years) E_1 = 7 BFK + isokinetic exercise E_2 = 7 placebo + isokinetic exercise E_3 = 7 isokinetic exercise only	EMG quadriceps of dominant leg	15 × 25 × 15 minutes	Cybex machine; peak torque 1 RM MVC 30° · sec^{-1}; IEMG	peak torque ↑; IEMG ↑ (in comparison to exercise no BFK group only)

↑ = EMG and/or performance increases.

not yet known, but the implications for beginners are obvious. The mechanism underlying the increases in strength can be explained psychologically by greater awareness and knowledge of results inherent in the BFK procedure, and neurophysiologically by the increase in the firing rates of active motor units and/or recruitment of new inactive motor units. Readers interested in the theoretical and possible practical implications of EMG BFK in exercise programs, skill learning, and motor performance are referred to Wolf's [90] paper on the subject.

EMG BFK and Exercise-Induced Muscle Fatigue and Pain
In an early and not well-known study, Lloyd [53] examined the effects of EMG BFK during exercise on muscle endurance and perceived pain. Lloyd, who used young, well-conditioned soldiers, applied auditory EMG BFK during a sustained contraction of 50% of maximum isometric elbow flexion. He found that auditory EMG BFK did not significantly increase endurance time or decrease the degree of perceived pain. It did, however, significantly reduce the amount of muscle activity (EMG) required to sustain the contraction. This last finding is contrary to the findings of Edwards and Lippold [28], who demonstrated that EMG output needs to be increased in order to sustain a given level of tension. This may indicate more efficiency in muscular contraction during the fatigue regimen [65]. More data are needed to confirm the finding that EMG patterns before and/or during the fatigue phase may be altered by BFK training, and if so, to determine the practical implications of these findings.

EMG BFK has also been used to determine its effects on delayed muscle soreness (DMS), which is usually felt in the untrained muscles after initial eccentric exercise exposure. McGlynn et al. [62] trained 20 subjects in the eccentric leg press (60% MVC) until they had to stop exercising because of unbearable pain. The subjects were divided into a control group and a BFK training group, which received EMG BFK from their quadriceps 6, 25, 30, 49, and 54 hours after they stopped their workout and 24, 48, and 72 hours postexercise; at the same times, EMG measurements (without feedback) of the quadriceps muscle were taken for both groups. Results showed that only the BFK group recorded significant reductions in the perceived mean pain level on all measurements. EMG mean levels were not different for both groups, except for 48 hours after exercise, where the BFK group showed a reduction of 50% in comparison to the control group. This reduction, however, was not statistically significant.

Since athletes' perceived level of pain is probably one of the most limiting factors in training and competition, the self-reported reductions in pain levels by the BFK group are quite impressive. On the other hand, even though not statistically significant, the recorded EMG reduction

TABLE 3
EMG BFK/Exercise-Induced Fatigue and Pain

Study	Subjects	Modality and Site of Biofeedback Treatment	Length of Biofeedback Treatment (Sessions × Time)	Fatigue and/or Pain Measure	Results
Lloyd [53]	N = 30 young soldiers E = 15 BFK during exercise C = 15 No BFK	EMG, long head of right biceps brachii	1 × subjects' endurance time	Pain and endurance during 50% MVC	Pain rating = NS; endurance time = NS; EMG ↓
McGlynn et al. [62]	N = 20 healthy (9 females, 18 males) subjects (18–26 years) E = 10 exercise + EMG BFK C = 10 exercise only	EMG rectus femoris	5 × 15 minutes	DMS and EMG levels 6, 25, 30, 49, and 54 hours after sustained 60% MVC	EMG = NS; pain rating ↓
McGlynn et al. [63]	N = 36 healthy males (18–26 years) E_1 = 12 exercise + EMG BFK E_2 = 12 exercise + static stretching C = 12 no treatment	EMG biceps brachii	5 × 15 minutes	DMS and EMG levels 6, 25, 30, 49, and 54 hours after sustained 80% MVC	EMG ↓ (for both experimental groups); pain rating = NS

DMS = delayed muscle soreness.

for the BFK group at 48 hours after exercise is practically important, since pain after eccentric exercise seems to reach its peak 48 hours later [26, 84]. This latter finding may also indicate a relationship between EMG measurements and subjective pain reports by athletes. Nevertheless, the finding that specific EMG feedback significantly reduces muscle pain but not EMG muscle tension is in direct opposition to previous findings by McGlynn et al. [63], who found that BFK training of the biceps muscle significantly reduced mean EMG levels but not muscle pain. Table 3 summarizes the studies done on BFK, fatigue, and pain.

While it is natural to have conflicting and confusing findings during the initial stages of any scientific investigation, the inconclusive findings concerning EMG BFK and exercise-induced muscle pain are puzzling, especially when we take into consideration the successful outcomes of BFK intervention in other forms of acute and chronic pain [8]. More research is clearly needed in this area.

EMG BFK and Flexibility Training
Another physiological parameter that has been investigated is the use of EMG BFK in order to improve flexibility of gymnasts and track athletes. In a two-stage study, Wilson and Bird [88] divided 10 gymnasts into two groups. The control group practiced self-relaxation, while the BFK training group received EMG feedback from their hip extensors. At the end of nine sessions both groups had significantly improved their hip flexion, but the BFK group had improved more quickly across trials. In the second stage of the study, 15 female gymnasts were divided into three groups: control (no treatment), modified progressive relaxation, and EMG hip extensors feedback plus relaxation. Results showed that all groups improved their hip flexion, with no one group superior to the others in any of the parameters studied.

In a similar study with 30 athletes, Cummings et al. [23] studied the effects of specific EMG feedback from the hip extensors in comparison to modified progressive relaxation and an active regimen of flexibility exercises. All three methods improved the athletes' hip flexibility after eight sessions. However, when the athletes were instructed to stop all hip flexibility training for 2 weeks, only the relaxation and EMG BFK groups maintained their near-maximal flexibility level.

These two studies may reveal an alternative procedure for flexibility training. Unfortunately, we are not yet at a stage that enables us to make any conclusions. It seems, however, that EMG training of specific muscles is comparable to active flexibility exercises as far as the end results are concerned, but the process itself may be enhanced by EMG BFK. Table 4 summarizes the studies conducted on EMG BFK and flexibility training.

TABLE 4
EMG BFK Flexibility

Study	Subjects	Modality and Site of Biofeedback Treatment	Length of Biofeedback Treatment (Sessions × Time)	Motor Performance	Results
Wilson and Bird, Study I [88]	N = 10 male gymnasts (19–26 years) E = BFK C = self-relaxation	EMG from hip extensors	$9 \times 5 \times 30$ seconds	Flexibility	Flexibility ↑ in a ↑ rate across trials
Wilson and Bird, Study II [88]	N = 15 female gymnasts E_1 = BFK + relaxation E_2 = progressive relaxation C = no treatment	EMG from hip extensors	8×10 minutes	Flexibility	Flexibility = NS (for all three groups)
Cummings et al. [23]	N = 30 track athletes: 15 males (15–21 years), 15 females (13–19 years) E_1 = BFK E_2 = relaxation C = no treatment	EMG biceps femoris	8×10 minutes	Flexibility; hurdlers' stretch; sprint performance	Male hip extension ↑; Hurdlers' stretch = NS; sprint performance = NS

HEART RATE AND RESPIRATORY CONTROL WITH BFK

Control of the cardiovascular system via BFK training has been successfully demonstrated in patients with cardiac arrhythmias, hypertension, and vasoconstrictive disorders [29]. These encouraging results have led other researchers to believe that BFK training can be used to control the cardiovascular and respiratory systems in healthy active adults in order to improve their exercise performance, as well as for the rehabilitation of cardiac patients in order to increase their exercise tolerance. To train subjects in cardiovascular/respiratory BFK during exercise, a variety of HR, blood flow, and respiration parameters can be used as feedback to the subjects. The most common ones are HR and interbeat interval (IBI), where the subject learns to increase the time span between the R waves, product feedback (IBI × pulse transit time = RPI), and its more conventional equivalent, the rate–pressure product (RPP) of HR and systolic blood pressure [55]. With BFK, subjects may learn to regulate cardiac functions, blood pressure, and respiration in both the same and opposite directions, suggesting the involvement of multiphysiological systems in the self-regulation process [8]. The following section will examine studies that investigated the possibility of decreasing the cardiovascular and respiratory effects of exercise by BFK training before and during the exercise regimen.

HR Control During Static Exercise
The ability to control HR while executing static exercise was first explored by Magnusson [59]. She instructed her subjects to increase HR, while simultaneously using 20% MVC of the right forearm in order to induce HR changes. Subjects were divided into three groups. The first group used a hand-held dynamometer and an HR BFK display in order to accelerate HR during the first two sessions. In the third and last session, subjects used only HR BFK to achieve HR increases. The second group used only a hand-held dynamometer to increase HR for the first two sessions and HR BFK only for the third session. The third group received only HR BFK during all three sessions. The results showed that the first group was superior to the muscle tension group and to the BFK-only group in HR performance during the first two sessions. In the third session (all groups given HR BFK only), the first group deteriorated and performed at the same level as the other two. This study was the first to demonstrate clearly that HR can be controlled during the performance of submaximal static exercise and that this control may be regulated independently of somatic mediation.

Carroll and Rhys-Davies [17] also examined isometric contractions of the forearm flexors on HR acceleration learning. They found that during two-thirds of maximal voluntary contraction, HR BFK produced greater voluntary heart rate increases than instructions alone. It should be noted that RR changes were not influenced by the HR BFK procedure, and neither were the forearm EMG changes. These last two findings suggests, as in Magnusson's [59] study, the existence of two separate control mechanisms.

Since voluntary HR acceleration is an easier skill to master than HR deceleration [61]—especially during exercise, because an exercise intensity on the cardiovascular system automatically accelerates HR—it was of interest to examine the possibility of voluntary HR decreases during static muscular effort. Indeed, convincing evidence of this hypothesis was presented by Clemens and Shattock [18]. They found that bidirectional learning (increase/decrease) of HR control was possible during performance of static exercise with a hand-held dynamometer, while using 0, 10, 30, and 50% of MVC. Here too, no significant relationships were found between chin EMG levels and the control of HR, suggesting independence of somatic and autonomic control mechanisms. The static exercise and HR BFK studies are summarized in Table 5.

Even though the studies reviewed have used static exercise only in order to confirm the possibility of HR control under stress-induced situations, the outcome of these studies may have important implications in the investigation of exercise physiology.

HR and Respiratory Control During Dynamic Exercise

In this section, we will review two pioneering and very-little-known unpublished papers in the field of HR control during exercise stress [50, 67]. The first study to show the significant control of HR prior to and during low-intensity exercise on a bicycle ergometer was by Mize [67]. These reductions, however, were not significant at higher intensities. In another study, LeFevers [50], showed that BFK training to lower HR during rest can be transferred to the exercise situation on a treadmill, even during high-intensity stress levels (160–180 b · min^{-1}).

The first published study, by Goldstein et al. [34], was a breakthrough in establishing exercise HR BFK training procedures and experimental design. The researchers trained 18 young, healthy adults to perform on a treadmill (1.12 m · s^{-1}, 6% grade). Eight of the participants received beat-to-beat HR BFK during the exercise regimen. They were instructed to try to lower their HR without reducing the exercise intensity. The other 10 participants were given instructions to lower their HR but did not receive any feedback. Comparison of the two groups after 25 sessions showed significant lower mean HR (-12 b · min^{-1}), blood pressure (-17 mm Hg), and RPP (-28%) for the BFK group. These results were maintained for 5 weeks after the cessation of training. In contrast, the control group did not show any significant changes during the experiment and failed to change even when they received BFK training later.

TABLE 5
HR Control During Static Exercise

Study	Subjects	Modality of Biofeedback Treatment	Length of Biofeedback Treatment (Sessions × Trial × Time)	Performance Measure	Results
Magnusson [59]	N = 30 females (20–27 years) E_1 = BFK + 20% MVC E_2 = 20% MVC + BFK C = BFK only	HR (beat to beat)	E_1 = 3 × 10 × 1 minute E_2 = 1 × 10 × 1 minute E_3 = 1 × 10 × 1 minute	20% MVC of forearm muscles	E_1 = HR ↑ (indicating control)
Carroll and Rhys-Davies [17]	N = 24 (11 females and 13 males; 19–26 years)	HR (beat to beat)	1 × 20 × 1 minute	Two-thirds MVC of forearm muscles	HR ↑ (indicating control)
Clemens and Shattock [18]	N = 3 undergraduate students (20–30 years)	HR (beat to beat)	4 × 16 × 1 minute	0, 10, 30, and 50% of MVC of forearm muscles	HR ↑ ↓ (indicating bidirectional control)

Replication of the former study by Perski and Engel [72] on a bicycle ergometer also showed a substantial reduction in HR (-20%) compared to the control group, but no significant change in systolic blood pressure. In contrast to the former study, substantial reductions in HR for the control group were noticed when they received BFK training.

Recently, Lo and Johnston published two consecutive studies examining the effects of IBI, pulse transit time, and their product (RPI) on healthy volunteers who performed the same intensity of exercise on a bicycle ergometer. In the first study, Lo and Johnston [55] found that both BFK conditions were superior to verbal instructions in decreasing sympathetic arousal during mild intensity cycling (4 kg, 29–31 rpm). These reductions, however, were limited to the practice sessions and were not transferred to a non-BFK condition. In the second study, Lo and Johnston [54] found that RPI BFK was more effective in decreasing the cardiovascular and respiratory effects of the previous aerobic regimen than relaxation training or cycling alone.

In another recent study, Perski et al. [73] investigated HR control during moderate steady-state exercise on a bicycle ergometer (60–70% of maximum HR). The HR BFK subjects showed 22% less increase in HR than the controls. When controls were given BFK, they reduced their HR by 9%. HR decreases were accompanied by significant decreases in oxygen consumption, pulmonary ventilation, and RPP, but not in systolic blood pressure.

In the studies that have been reviewed so far, respiratory efficiency was achieved indirectly via direct cardiovascular HR BFK. In a unique study, Davies et al. [25] used respiratory BFK to assess the effect of respiratory alkalosis on blood lactate levels during submaximal exercise intervals of 2 minutes at 25-W increments up to 175 W. The results showed that respiratory alkalosis during exercise can be achieved when subjects receive hyperventilation feedback. This method of BFK allowed ventilation and pH to be adjusted voluntarily, independent of metabolic rate. This form of BFK deserves increased study because of the important role that respiration plays in the regulation of other physiological processes.

In conclusion, cardiac and pulmonary functions have been shown to be under volitional control during various exercise regimens of different submaximal intensities. It now remains to pursue this line of research with top athletes who are performing at near-maximal capacity. It would be interesting to determine whether BFK training can help these athletes improve their performance or whether a ceiling effect precludes significant improvement. It should be remembered, however, that an athlete operating at a lower HR and reduced oxygen consumption can, in the long run, be expected to exercise more efficiently. Table 6 summarizes the studies done on HR and respiratory BFK.

TABLE 6
HR/Respiratory Control During Exercise

Study	Subjects	Modality of Biofeedback Treatment	Length of Biofeedback Treatment (Sessions × Trial × Time)	Performance Measure	Results
Mize [67]	N = 30 college females E = 15 BFK C = 15	Visual and verbal HR BFK to criterion at rest	12 × 4 × ?	Bicycle ergometer, SWC 150	HR ↓ with low-intensity exercise; HR = NS with high-intensity exercise
LeFevers [50]	N = 35 college females E_1 = 15 BFK + instrumental conditioning C = 11 no treatment	Visual HR BFK to criterion (10% resting HR) at rest	10 × 4 × ?	Treadmill exercise at four levels of HR: 100–120, 120–140, 140–160, 160–180 b · min^{-1}	E_1 = HR ↓ during all four intensities; E_2 = HR ↓ except at 100–120 b · min^{-1} indicating successful transfer from rest training to exercise stress performance
Goldstein et al. [34]	N = 18 (18–39 years) E = 8 exercise + BFK C = 10 exercise + instruction (During the experiment, both groups switched roles—E = C, C = E; therefore, subjects were used as their own controls)	HR—option of beat-to-beat RR interval; trends in HR	5 × 5 × 10 minutes	Treadmill 2.5 m · s^{-1}, 6% grade	HR ↓; SBP ↓; RPP ↓ (indicating → myocardial O_2 consumption)

TABLE 6
(continued)

Perski and Engel [72]	N = 10 (5 males and 5 females) (experimental design as in Goldstein et al. [34])	HR—option of R wave of ECG, b · min⁻¹, beat-to-beat, threshold criterion	5 × 45 minutes	Bicycle ergometer, fixed intensity of 50% of predicted maximum HR	HR ↓; SBP = NS; RPP ↓
Lo and Johnston [55]	N = 36 university students (18 males and 18 females); 18–30 years) E_1 = IBI + exercise E_2 = product FBK + exercise E_3 = verbal instructions + exercise	IBI, RPI, (IBI × RPI = product FBK)	4 × 5 × 6 minutes	Upright bicycle ergometer fixed at 4 kg force, 29–31 rpm	IBI ↑; product FBK ↑ (indicating smaller decreases in the time between the R wave and peripheral pulse-sympathetic arousal ↓ RPP ↓)
Lo and Johnston [54]	N = 36 university students (18–34 years) E_1 = FBK + exercise E_2 = Benson's relaxation + exercise C = exercise only	Product FBK	(see Lo and Johnston [55])	(see Lo and Johnston [55])	Product FBK ↑ (indicating more exercise tolerance for the FB group); ICI ↑
Perski et al. [73]	N = 10 males 19–24 yr E = FBK + exercise C = exercise only (experimental design as in Goldstein et al. [34])	HR—option of R wave of ECG, b · min⁻¹, threshold criterion	4 × 5 × 2 minutes	Bicycle ergometer, steady work level, 60–70% of maximum HR	HR ↓; VO₂ consumption ↓; pulmonary ventilation ↓; RPP ↓; SBP = NS

TABLE 6
(*continued*)

Study	Subjects	Modality of Biofeedback Treatment	Length of Biofeedback Treatment (Sessions × Trial × Time)	Performance Measure	Results
Davies, et al. [25]	$N = 8$ healthy subjects (7 males and 1 female) $\overline{X} = 26.4$ years $\overline{X}_1 = $ BFK + exercise $E_2 = $ hyperventilation following acetazolamide $(5 \times 250$ mg) $E_3 = $ acetazolamide + spontaneous ventilation $C = $ exercise only (all subjects were tested in all three experimental conditions; therefore, subjects were used as their own controls)	Hyperventilation BFK = maintain end tidal Pa_{CO_2} at 25 torr and increase pH by 0.08–0.10 at each exercise intensity	Not specified (BFK was given during testing routine)	Upright bicycle ergometer: graded work loads of 5, 100, 125, 150, 175 W, 2-minute intervals	Confirm that ventilation and pH can be manipulated by BFK independent of metabolic rate

Cardiac Patients and HR Control During Exercise

Encouraged by the success of healthy subjects to control HR, blood pressure, and respiration during exercise, Johnston and Lo [44] applied a similar procedure to angina pectoris patients. Seven patients with established angina who took medication for anginal pain were trained with HR and EMG relaxation BFK at rest and while cranking at a constant rate on a bicycle ergometer. During HR BFK the patients received either feedback on the product of the pulse transit time, from the R wave on the ECG to the radial pulse (RPI) or the IBI. The patient's task was to increase the product, i.e., decrease the HR and blood pressure. Since the BFK procedure, length of BFK sessions, and exercise intensity of the patients were individualized for each patient, it is very difficult to evaluate the outcome of this study. The results, however, showed that six out of the seven patients decreased the frequency of anginal attacks, decreased the usage of medication to control anginal pain, and increased their exercise tolerance.

In another study, which employed a more rigorous research design, Fredrikson and Engel [31] tested whether borderline hypertension patients ($<160/95$; $>140/90$ mm Hg) could learn to reduce their HR while exercising on a bicycle ergometer at a mild-submaximal fixed intensity (33 W, 50 rpm). The BFK group received beat-to-beat HR BFK and were asked to slow down their HR while exercising. The results, after 5 days and 25 training trials, showed that in comparison to the control group, the HR BFK group had significantly reduced their HR, RPP, and VO_2 consumption. No significant differences in systolic blood pressure were found between the two groups. Table 7 summarizes the BFK studies done on cardiac patients.

It seems that different forms of HR BFK during exercise can benefit cardiovascular patients by making the system more efficient. Since the threshold for anginal pain is closely related to the product of heart rate and systolic blood pressure, RPP or its equivalent, product BFK (IBI × RPI), can be used as a noninvasive measure of myocardial oxygen consumption [55] during HR BFK training in an effort to increase exercise tolerance. In spite of the encouraging results, more research is needed before recommending HR BFK as an adjunctive procedure in cardiac rehabilitation programs.

ELECTRODERMAL AND TEMPERATURE CONTROL WITH BFK

"Electrodermal biofeedback (EDR)" is a term that refers to feedback obtained from electrical activity at various skin sites. Presently, there is a proliferation of terms and a general lack of consensus regarding the measurement of electrodermal activity [20]. The numerous specific mea-

TABLE 7
HR Control in Cardiac Patients During Exercise

Study	Subjects and Condition	Modality of Biofeedback Treatment	Length of Biofeedback Treatment (Sessions × Trials × Time)	Performance Measure	Results
Johnston and Lo [44]	$N = 7$ (6 males and 1 female): angina pectoris patients (52–63 years) S_1 = relaxation S_2 = EMG BFK S_3 = product FB (series of case studies)	S_1 = relaxation S_2 = EMG frontalis S_3 = product FB	Individually adjusted for patients. Range from 3 to 12 BFK sessions (treated as case studies)	Bicycle ergometer, constant rate, low intensity	In six out of seven patients; product BF ↑ (at rest but not during cycling); pain frequency ↓; medication use ↓; exercise tolerance ↑
Fredrickson and Engle [31]	$N = 12$ borderline hypertension $\overline{X}$ = 40 years $\overline{X}$ = exercise + BFK C = exercise only	HR options: beat-to-beat, b·$\min^{-1}$, threshold criterion, trends in HR	$5 \times 5 \times 3$ minutes	Bicycle ergometer fixed load, 33 W, 50 rpm	HR ↓; RPP ↓; $\dot{V}O_2$ consumption ↓; SBP = NS

KEY
HR = heart rate; SBP = systolic blood pressure; IBI = interbeat interval; RPI = pulse transit time; IBI × RPI = product FB (feedback); RPP = rate–pressure product (= HR × SBP or IBI × RPI); ICI = respiratory intercycle time.

sures include galvanic skin response (GSR), skin conductance response (SCR), skin resistance response (SRR), skin conductance level (SCL), skin resistance level (SRL), and skin potential response (SPR). EDR has been used to teach relaxation and as an adjunct in therapy, e.g., systematic desensitization.

Electrodermal BFK and Precompetition Anxiety
Costa et al. [22] used electrodermal GSR BFK with 10 series B handball players in order to reduce precompetition anxiety. They reported that BFK training was useful in decreasing habitual as well as precompetitive anxiety. The success in anxiety management was, however, determined by the athletes' performance on psychological questionnaires (Spielberger's State/Trait Anxiety Inventory) and did not measure actual athletic performance on the court. In addition, this study lacked adequate research design and clarity of procedure.

Hashimoto et al. [39] also used GSR as the sole source of BFK in order to reduce precompetition anxiety in college athletes. Measurements taken 20 minutes before competition confirmed the efficacy of brief (eight sessions) GSR training in reducing somatic anxiety and increasing self-confidence before competition. Even though the researchers used a large sample ($N = 164$) and followed strict and adequate research procedures, they also had not measured athletic outcome as a result of their successful intervention, leaving unsolved the dilemma of external validity.

Temperature BFK and Autonomic Control
Peripheral temperature BFK uses the skin of the fingers and toes as an indirect measure of sympathetic arousal. Since peripheral temperature is determined primarily by blood flow through the small arterioles of the skin, decreases in the diameter of the arterioles, accompanied by high levels of adrenalin in the bloodstream, are responsible for vasoconstriction and therefore lower skin temperature.

The range of peripheral skin temperature is quite variable, with values ranging from 18 to 21°C (high sympathetic arousal) to 32 to 35°C (low sympathetic arousal). Subjects trained in temperature control have been able to change their peripheral skin temperature at rates as high as $4°F \cdot min^{-1}$. In a clinical setting, skin temperature feedback is used for migraine headaches, Raynaud's disease, and the treatment of other vascular disorders that are of psychosomatic origin. In sports and athletics, the use of skin temperature BFK was suggested by Kappes and Chapman [45] as a measure to prevent frostbite in winter sports, but this has not yet been tested with athletes. Kappes et al. [46] measured, by infrared hand temperature, 51 cross-country skiers; indoor, outdoor, mid-race, and finish. They found, contrary to expected results, that warmer hands were associated with slower racing times.

The use of skin temperature BFK to induce relaxation in sports where mental relaxation and concentration are crucial (e.g., gymnastics) has been studied, but since peripheral temperature BFK control is obtained at a relatively slower rate than most of the other BFK modalities, and since temperature control may indicate long-lasting effects on the autonomic nervous system, temperature BFK is usually used in conjunction with EDR BFK and/or other modalities. Indeed, all studies that used peripheral temperature BFK as a treatment for athletic anxiety incorporate EDR training as a mode to learn state anxiety control. It seems that a complete training of the autonomic nervous system, via BFK, for anxiety reduction should include EDR BFK for situational anxiety and peripheral temperature BFK for reducing chronic "trait" anxiety.

Temperature EDR BFK and Competition Anxiety
In her dissertation at Boston University, Goodspeed [35] tested the efficacy of using EDR and temperature BFK as part of a comprehensive mental training program with gymnasts. Study 1 used nine female gymnasts at a division I university as subjects. The gymnasts were able to demonstrate temperature self-regulation and significantly improved their performance over that of the previous year. Although it was not possible to attribute causality to the BFK "treatment," the gymnasts perceived the treatment program as being significant in reducing anxiety and improving their performance. Study 2, which used 16 young gymnasts of various abilities, failed to find any significant differences between the control and treatment groups (which received the same treatment as the subjects in study 1).

In a remarkably similar study, Peper and Schmid [71] studied the effects of autonomic self-regulatory techniques and mental training strategies on members of the U.S. Rhythmic Gymnastics team. The 2-year program included home practice and training camp instruction in progressive relaxation, autogenic training, imagery rehearsal, arousal and energy awareness, skin temperature, EDR, HR, and EMG BFK training. Most of the team members demonstrated voluntary control over peripheral temperature, EMG activity, HR, and skin conductance. Additionally, athletes reported the program to be highly beneficial in enhancing their gymnastic performance, integrating the mental skills into their workouts, using relaxation to reenergize, and controlling their arousal states.

More recently, Peper and Malik [70] reported a case study of an ultramarathoner who was treated with a number of psychophysiological self-regulation techniques, including skin temperature and EMG BFK. Even though it is impossible to distinguish the role of BFK, it should be noted that the ultramarathoner won two races and had to drop out of the third race due to a previous injury. Table 8 summarizes the studies that used temperature BFK.

In conclusion, it seems that EDR and skin temperature BFK may be used together and in conjunction with other relaxation techniques to institute a relaxation response that might be used to combat precompetition anxiety. However, the difficulty of distinguishing BFK treatment from other interventions and the difficulty of measuring the direct effect of BFK treatment in anxiety reduction on actual athletic performance leave us usually with no more than self-reports. These self-reports were all favorable in the studies reviewed.

SUMMARY AND DISCUSSION

This chapter has reviewed 42 data-based publications that examined the effects of BFK training on sports and athletic performance. Thirty-three (79%) were published papers and nine (21%) were unpublished papers (theses, dissertations, presentations, etc.). Out of the total number of studies reviewed, 35 (83%) report some improvement due to BFK intervention. In terms of BFK modalities, 24 of these studies (57%) examined the effect of EMG BFK and 19 (80%) reported positive outcomes. Fourteen (30%) examined HR/respiratory BFK training and 12 (92%) reported successful results. Two (5%) used EDR intervention and both (100%) reported that subjects achieved their training goals. Three studies (7%) evaluated the effect of temperature and EDR BFK intervention. Two of the studies (67%) reported positive outcomes, and in one study the findings were equivocal [35].

It seems that the majority of studies (83%) found BFK procedures to be highly successful in facilitating sport and athletic performance and beneficial for the athletes' well-being. These findings are especially impressive in terms of HR/respiratory BFK control during stress induced by submaximal exercise regimens. However, one must interpret these published positive outcomes with caution, since it is possible that a similar number of studies produced equivocal or no significant differences between subjects trained using BFK and their controls; these studies (because of editorial policy) were not published in refereed journals. It should be noted, however, that in spite of the positive outcomes in the majority of the studies reviewed here, we cannot ignore the fact that a substantial number of studies reviewed in this chapter shared one or more of the research faults that Shellenberger and Green [80] accurately claim to be prevalent in the general BFK literature. Among these faults we find:

a. An insufficient number of training sessions. To paraphrase Shellenberger and Green, this is like attempting to train an athlete to run a 4-minute mile in four sessions and then concluding that humans are not

TABLE 8
Temperature/EDR BFK

Study	Subjects	Biofeedback Treatment (Modality, Site, Adjunct Treatment)	Length of Biofeedback Treatment (Sessions × Trial × Time)	Performance Measure	Results
Goodspeed Study 1 [35]	N = 9 female high-level gymnasts (18–21 years)	Temp + GSR + relaxation + mental imagery + cognitive strategies	8 × 2 × 30 minutes + individual homework 4 × 2 × ? minutes	Gymnastics	Temp ↑; state anxiety = NS; athletic performance ↑
Goodspeed Study 2 [35]	N = 16 female gymnasts (10–15 years) E = 8 BFK + relaxation C = 8 relaxation	(See Goodspeed Study 1)	8 × 2 × 30 minutes	Gymnastics	State anxiety = NS; athletic performance = NS
Peper and Schmid [71]	U.S. Rhythmic Gymnastic Team	Temp + EMG + HR + SCL + relaxation + mental training	2 years of multi-intervention	Rhythmic gymnastics	Self-report of performance ↑; emotional state controlled; Temp. ↑; EMG ↓; SCL ↓

TABLE 8
(continued)

Study	Subjects	Method	Duration	Task	Results
Peper and Malik [70]	1 ultramarathoner (38 years old) (case study)	Temp + EMG + relaxation + behavioral techniques	6 months of multi-intervention	Ultramarathon	2 wins, 1 loss
Costa et al. [22]	$N = 10$ handball team (19–26 years) E = 5 BFK C = 5 no treatment	GSR (?) index and third finger of left hand	7 × 15 minutes	Precompetition anxiety	Precompetition anxiety ↓; state anxiety ↓
Hashimoto et al. [39]	$N = 164$ college athletes (106 males and 58 females) E = BFK C = no treatment	GSR hand-palm	8 × 9 minutes	Precompetition anxiety	Self-confidence ↑; somatic anxiety 20 mintues before the game ↓

KEY
Temp = temperature; SCL = skin conductance level.

able to run the 4-minute mile and, further, that the stop watch is not useful. The Bennett and Hall [10] study exemplifies this methodological shortcoming.

b. Closely related to problem (a) is failure on the part of researchers to train subjects to criterion. In this chapter, we found few studies that trained subjects in self-regulation to a clearly determined criterion. In order to determine if self-regulation is efficacious, one must first demonstrate that self-regulation has in fact been mastered. Evidence for the importance of training to mastery is provided in an excellent study by Libo and Arnold [52].

c. Insufficient length of each training session. As indicated in the previous tables, numerous studies had training sessions that were either brief or not reported. In their review, Shellenberger and Green point out that, in general, researchers run sessions of 16, 10, or 3 minutes in length, which is inconsistent with mastery learning.

d. Failure to give subjects homework exercises, as well as adequate instructions/coaching. Few of the studies reviewed in this chapter reported giving experimental subjects exercises whereby they could practice self-regulation at home. The erroneous assumption is that BFK has specific drug-like effects.

e. Failure to establish reliability measures and confidence bands, seemingly on the assumption that psychophysiological variables are invariant. Few of the studies reviewed in this chapter discussed the concept of reliability. On the contrary, a number of studies discussed the success of BFK training on the basis of statistically significant changes in physiological measures without first demonstrating that the change did not occur beyond the range of normal variation. As such, these studies are statistically significant but not functionally or practically significant.

f. Failure to use appropriate research designs. Numerous studies utilized classical between-subject designs. In some cases, these designs were appropriate because the objective of the study was to determine the efficacy of a specific BFK treatment relative to a no-treatment control group. Other studies, such as the Zaichkowsky et al. [97] study, employed a between-subjects design to determine EMG treatment effects with anxious gymnasts. Although conceptually sound, the design was inappropriate because the researchers had to add borderline anxious gymnasts to the study in order to obtain statistical power. Unfortunately, these subjects did not benefit from the treatment and canceled out the positive effects achieved by truly anxious subjects. A more appropriate paradigm would have been a single-case experimental design [93].

Attention to these shortcomings (where appropriate) would, in our opinion, result in effect sizes that would be greater than those reported to date in the literature.

Based upon our psychophysiological research and review of the work of other sport scientists, it is our belief that the exercise and sport science fields (i.e., sport psychology, motor control, exercise physiology, biomechanics) can benefit a great deal from additional research in psychophysiology and the applied subarea of BFK. To date there has been only a limited utilization of psychophysiological models in the study of motor behavior. Besides our reviewed studies in BFK, researchers have examined perceived exertion [69], anxiety [30], reaction time [79], and centralist vs. peripheralist views of motor control [83]. More recently, Landers and his colleagues have been engaged in exciting psychophysiological research that has examined both physiological correlates of effective motor performance and the use of biological feedback to enhance performance [41, 49].

Although the above citations are only examples of studies employing physiological measures to make inferences about psychological and emotional states, the truth is that the total number of psychophysiological studies in the broad field of exercise science is extremely limited. In a recent paper, Hatfield and Landers [40] reviewed these psychophysiological studies and suggested, much as we do, that motor behavior researchers should engage in more of this type of work. Certainly physiological measures can be utilized to help us learn more about psychophysiological phenomena such as stress/arousal/tension/anxiety, reaction time, and motor control, as well as how these phenomena and other factors, such as motivation, individual differences, etc., relate to optimal human performance.

Studies using the more traditional BFK model are clearly few in number and are deserving of replication; however, the methodologies should be carefully looked at and, where necessary, should incorporate improvements suggested earlier in this chapter. We need to know more about the conditions under which BFK-assisted self-regulation is most effective for enhancing performance or facilitating rehabilitation. For instance, we need to experiment with practice schedules, generalization of practice, retention of acquired self-regulation, and modes of feedback. Mode of feedback is particularly lacking in research. It is our experience that BFK is most effective when the feedback is "exciting" to the learner. This is particularly true when the feedback of a visual display or auditory sounds becomes boring after repeated exposure. Consideration must be given to providing exciting, creative feedback whenever possible. This means using simple feedback devices such as mirrors and goniometers, as well as sohisticated telemetry and computer-aided devices. Additionally, we need to know more about the aptitudes for self-regulation, that is, whether certain individuals learn self-regulation more easily than others. Much remains to be learned about the question of specificity vs.

generalizability of learned self-control within a particular system, such as the muscular system, and across systems (e.g., can transfer occur from the somatic to the autonomic system?).

There is one mode of feedback in the general BFK literature that has not been discussed in this chapter—EEG BFK. This mode has been demonstrated to be successful in the treatment of epilepsy, hyperactivity, and learning disorders [56]. Except for one preliminary study by Browning [16], which showed promising results with alpha EEG BFK in the process of learning a specific tap dance skill, no other studies have been conducted with EEG BFK in sport. However, psychophysiological studies have considered EEG in order to describe brain wave activity during motor activity. These have included studies on marksmen [41] and runners and bikers [24]. Clearly, the EEG field is ripe for further studies by sports scientists. A final comment regarding BFK applications in the field of exercise science deserves mention at this time. Augmented feedback of force, position, range of motion, and other movement parameters have been used successfully as a mode of BFK for many years and are aptly described by Newell et al. [68], Brown et al. [15], Ariel [3], and Clarkson et al. [19]. We, however, have concentrated on the more traditional modes of BFK, namely, those concerned with covert function of the human body and not overt output.

In conclusion, we feel that the evidence to date regarding the application of BFK training, or closely related terms such as "augmented feedback training," "psychophysiological feedback training," "biofeedback therapy," and "self-regulation training in exercise and sport science," clearly supports the need for continued research and application. Psychophysiological self-regulation will perhaps be easier in the future as we continue to develop state-of-the-art instrumentation. Not only will we be able to improve upon the feedback from traditional modalities, but it is likely that we will develop techniques for feeding back information from systems heretofore not attempted or developed such as ocular function, blood sugar, kidney function, and other physiological activities that are essential for optimal health and human performance.

REFERENCES

1. Alexander, A.B. An experimental test of assumptions relating to the use of electromyographic biofeedback as a general relaxation training technique. *Psychophysiology,* 12:656–662, 1975.
2. Anliker, J. Biofeedback from the perspectives of cybernetics and systems science. In J. Beatty and H. Legewie (eds.). *Biofeedback and Behavior.* New York: Plenum Press, 1977, pp. 21–45.
3. Ariel, G.B. Biofeedback and biomechanics in athletic training. In J.H. Sandweiss and

S.L. Wolf (eds.). *Biofeedback and Sports Sciences.* New York: Plenum Press, 1985, pp. 107–145.

4. Ash, M.J., and R.D. Zellner. Speculations on the use of biofeedback training in sport psychology. In D.M. Landers and R.W. Christina (eds.). *Psychology of Motor Behavior and Sport.* Champaign, Ill.: Human Kinetics, 1977, pp. 321–330.
5. Balog, L.F. The effects of exercise on muscle tension and subsequent muscle relaxation training. *Res. Q.* 54:119–125, 1983.
6. Basmajian, J.V. Anatomical and physiological basis for biofeedback and autonomic regulation. In J.V. Basmajian (ed.). *Biofeedback: Principles and Practice for Clinicians,* 2nd ed. Baltimore: Williams & Wilkins Co., 1983, pp. 23–35.
7. Basmajian, J.V. Control and training of individual motor units. *Science* 141:440–441, 1963.
8. Basmajian, J.V. *Biofeedback: Principles and Practice for Clinicians,* 2nd ed. Baltimore: Williams & Wilkins Co., 1983.
9. Beall, M.S., G. Diefenbach, and A. Allen. Electromyographic biofeedback in the treatment of voluntary posterior instability of the shoulder. *Am. J Sports Med.* 15:175–178, 1987.
10. Bennett, B., and C.R. Hall. Biofeedback training and archery performance. Paper presented to the International Congress in Physical Education. Trois Rivieres, Quebec, 1979.
11. Blais, M., and T. Orlick. Electromyographic feedback as a means of competitive anxiety control: problems and potential. In B. Kerr (ed.). *Human Performance and Behavior.* Banff, Alberta, Canada: Scapps, 1977, pp. 13–18.
12. Blais, M.R., and R.J. Vallerand. Multimodal effects of electromyographic biofeedback: Looking at children's ability to control pre-competitive anxiety. *J. Sport Psychol.* 8:283–303, 1986.
13. Brown, B. Recognition of aspects of consciousness through association with EEG alpha activity represented by a light signal. *Psychophysiology* 6:442–452, 1970.
14. Brown, B. *Stress and the Art of Biofeedback.* New York: Harper & Row, 1977.
15. Brown, B.S., M. Daniel, and D.R. Gorman. Visual feedback and strength improvement. *Natl. Strength Condit. Assoc. J.* 6:22–24, 1984.
16. Browning, G.S. The influence of alpha rhythm during mental practice. Unpublished master's thesis, Texas Woman's University, Denton, Texas, 1972.
17. Carroll, D., and L. Rhys-Davies. Heart rate changes with exercise and voluntary heart rate acceleration. *Biol. Psychol.* 8:241–252, 1979.
18. Clemens, W.J., and R.J. Shattock. Voluntary heart rate control during static muscular effort. *Psychophysiology* 16:327–332, 1979.
19. Clarkson, P.M., R. James, A. Watkins, and P. Foley. The effect of augmented feedback on foot pronation during barre exercise in dance. *Res. Q. Exerc. Sport* 57:33–40, 1986.
20. Cohen, A. Basic biofeedback electronics for the clinician. In J.V. Basmajian (ed.). *Biofeedback: Principles and Practice for Clinicians,* 2nd ed. Baltimore: Williams & Wilkins Co., 1983, pp. 336–338.
21. Croce, R.V. The effects of EMG biofeedback on strength acquisition. *Biofeedback Self-Regul.* 11:299–310, 1986.
22. Costa, A., M. Bonaccorsi, and T. Scrimali. Biofeedback and control of anxiety preceding athletic competition. *Int. J. Sport Psychol.* 15:98–109, 1984.
23. Cummings, M.S., V.E. Wilson, and E.I. Bird. Flexibility development in sprinters using EMG biofeedback and relaxation training. *Biofeedback Self-Regul.* 9:395–405, 1984.
24. Daniels, F.S., B. Fernhall, and D.M. Landers. The effect of maximal and submaximal aerobic exercise on temporal EEG alpha activity in runners and bikers. *Psychophysiology* 21:574, 1984. (Abstract)

25. Davies, S.F., C. Iber, S.A. Keene, C.D. McArthur, and M.J. Path. Effect of respiratory alkalosis during exercise on blood lactate. *J. Appl. Physiol.* 61:948–952, 1986.

26. DeVries, H.A. Quantitative electromyographic investigation of the spasm theory of muscular pain. *Am. J. Phys. Med.* 45:119–134, 1966.

27. DeWitt, D.J. Cognitive and biofeedback training for stress reduction with university students. *J. Sport Psychol.* 2:288–294, 1980.

28. Edwards, R.G., and O.C.J. Lippold. The relation between force and integrated electrical activity in fatigued muscle. *J. Physiol.* 132:677, 1956.

29. Engle, B.T., and W.F. Bailey. Behavioral applications in the treatment of patients with cardiovascular disorders. In J.V. Basmajian (ed.). *Principles and Practice for Clinicians,* 2nd ed. Baltimore: Williams & Wilkins Co., 1983, pp. 228–238.

30. Fenz, W., and S. Epstein. Gradients of physiological arousal of experienced and novice parachutists as a function of an approaching jump. *Psychosomatic Med.* 29:33–51, 1967.

31. Fredrikson, M., and B.T. Engel. Learned control of heart rate during exercise in patients with borderline hypertension. *Eur. J. Appl. Physiol.* 54:315–320, 1985.

32. French, S.N. Electromyographic biofeedback for tension control during gross motor skill acquisition. *Percept. Mot. Skills* 47:883–889, 1978.

33. French, S.N. Electromyographic biofeedback for tension control during fine motor skill acquisition. *Biofeedback Self-Regul.* 5:221–228, 1980.

34. Goldstein, D.S., R.S. Ross, and J.V. Brady. Biofeedback heart rate during exercise. *Biofeedback Self-Regul.* 2:107–125, 1977.

35. Goodspeed, G.A. The effects of comprehensive self-regulation training on state anxiety and performance of female gymnasts. Unpublished Ed.D. dissertation, Boston University, 1983.

36. Graham, C., M.R. Cook, H.D. Cohen, M.M. Gerkovich, J.W. Phelps, and S.S. Fotopoulos. Effects of variation in physical effort on frontalis EMG activity. *Biofeedback Self-Regul.* 11:135–141, 1986.

37. Griffiths, J.J., D.H. Steel, P. Vaccaro, and M.B. Karpman. The effects of relaxation techniques on anxiety and underwater performance. *Int. J. Sport Psychol.* 12:176–182, 1981.

38. Harrison, V.F. Voluntary control of low threshold motor unit potentials in the neuromuscularly skilled individual. *Anat. Rec.* 145:237, 1963.

39. Hashimoto, K., M. Tokunaga, H. Tatano, and R. Kanezaki. A study on reducing competitive anxiety in sport: The change in pre-competitive state anxiety and the effect of biofeedback training on anxiety. *J. Electron.* 1:77–86, 1984.

40. Hatfield, B.D., and D.M. Landers. Psychophysiology: A new direction for sport psychology. *J. Sport Psychol.* 5:243–259, 1983.

41. Hatfield, B.D., D.M. Landers, and W.J. Ray. Cognitive processes during self-paced motor performance: An electroencephalographic profile of skilled marksmen. *J. Sport Psychol.* 6:55–70, 1984.

42. Jacobson, E. The course of relaxation in muscles of athletes. *Am. J. Psychol.* 48:98–108, 1936.

43. James, R.J. Comparative effects of different modes of augmented feedback on striate muscle strength scores. Boston: *Proceedings of the 18th Annual Meeting of the Biofeedback Society of America,* 1987, pp. 57.

44. Johnston, D.W., and C.R. Lo. The effects of cardiovascular feedback and relaxation on angina pectoris. *Behav. Psychother.* 11:257–264, 1983.

45. Kappes, B.M., and S.J. Chapman. The effect of indoor versus outdoor thermal biofeedbacktraining in cold weather sports. *J. Sport Psychol.* 6:305–311, 1984.

46. Kappes, B.M., N.A. Latze, and B. Travis. Infrared hand temperature measurements during the 1986 330K IDITASKI cross-country ski race. Boston: *Proceedings of the 18th Annual Meeting of the Biofeedback Society of America,* 1987, pp. 98–101.

47. Kirkcaldy, B.D., and J. Christen. An investigation into the effect of EMG frontalis biofeedback on physiological correlates of exercise. *Int. J. Sport Psychol.* 12:235–252, 1981.
48. Landers, D.M. Psychophysiological assessment and biofeedback. In J.H. Sandweiss and S.L. Wolf (eds.). *Biofeedback and Sports Science.* New York: Plenum Press, 1985, pp. 63–105.
49. Landers, D.M., R.W. Christina, B.D. Hatfield, F.S. Daniels, and L.A. Doyle. Moving competitive shooting into the scientist's lab. *Am. Rifleman* 128:36–37, 76–77, 1980.
50. LeFevers, V.A. Volitional control of heart rate during exercise stress. Unpublished Ph.D. dissertation, Texas Woman's University, Denton, Texas, 1971.
51. LeVeau, B.F., and C. Rogers. Selective training of the vastus medialis muscle using EMG biofeedback. *Phys. Ther.* 60:1410–1415, 1980.
52. Libo, L., and G. Arnold. Does training to criterion influence improvement? A follow-up study of EMG and thermal biofeedback. *J. Behav. Med.* 6:397–404, 1983.
53. Lloyd, A.J. Auditory EMG feedback during sustained submaximum isometric contraction. *Res. Q.* 43:39–46, 1972.
54. Lo, C.R., and D.W. Johnston. The self-control of cardiovascular response to exercise using feedback of the product of interbeat interval and pulse transit time. *Psychosom. Med.* 46:115–125, 1984.
55. Lo, C.R., and D.W. Johnston. Cardiovascular feedback during dynamic exercise. *Psychophysiology* 21:199–206, 1984.
56. Lubar, J.F. Electroencephalographic biofeedback and neurological applications. In J.V. Basmajian (ed.). *Biofeedback: Principles and Practice for Clinicians,* 2nd ed. Baltimore: Williams & Wilkins Co., 1983, pp. 37–61.
57. Lucca, J.A., and S.J. Recchuiti. Effect of electromyographic biofeedback on an isometric strengthening program. *Phys. Ther.* 63:200–203, 1983.
58. Magill, R.A. Knowledge of results and skill acquisition. In L.D. Zaichkowsky and C.Z. Fuchs (eds.). *The Psychology of Motor Behavior: Development, Control, Learning and Performance.* Ithaca, N.Y.: Mouvement Publications, 1986, pp. 51–63.
59. Magnusson, E. The effects of controlled muscle tension on performance and learning of heart rate control. *Biol. Psychol.* 4:81–92, 1976.
60. Martens, R., and D.M. Landers. Motor performance under stress: A test of the inverted-U hypothesis. *J. Personal. Soc. Psychol.* 16:29–37, 1970.
61. McCanne, T.R., and K.M. Hathaway. Individual differences in motor skills ability affect the self-regulation of heart rate. *Biofeedback Self-Regul.* 9:241–452, 1984.
62. McGlynn, G.H., N.T. Laughlin, and S.P. Filios. The effect of electromyographic feedback on EMG activity and pain in the quadriceps muscle group. *J. Sports Med. Physical Fitness* 19:237–244, 1979.
63. McGlynn, G.H., N.T. Laughlin, and V. Rowe. Effects of electromyographic feedback and static stretching on artificially induced muscle soreness. *Am. J. Physical Med.* 58:139–148, 1979.
64. McGowan, W.T., W.N. Haynes, and C.C. Wilson. Frontal electromyographic feedback: Stress attenuation and generalization. *Biofeedback Self-Regul.* 4:323–336, 1979.
65. Middaugh, S.J., M.C. Miller, G. Foster, and M.B. Ferdon. Electromyographic feedback: Effects of voluntary muscle contractions in normal subjects. *Arch. Phys. Med. Rehabil.* 63:254–260, 1982.
66. Miller, N.E. Learning of visceral land glandular responses. *Science* 163:434–445, 1969.
67. Mize, N.J. Conditioning of heart rate under exercise stress. Unpublished master's thesis, Texas Woman's University, Denton, Texas, 1970.
68. Newell, K.M., L.R. Morris, and D.M. Scully. Augmented information and the acqui-

sition of skill in physical activity. In R.L. Terjung (ed.). *Exercise and Sport Science Reviews.* New York: Macmillan Co., 1985, pp. 235–261.

69. Pandolf, K. Differentiated ratings of perceived exertion during physical exercise. *Med. Sci. Sports Exerc.* 14:397–405, 1982.

70. Peper, E., and K. Malik. Biofeedback modulated peak performance program for ultramarathoner. *Proceedings of the 16th Annual Meeting of the Biofeedback Society of America,* 1985, pp.

71. Peper, E., and A. Schmid. The use of electrodermal biofeedback for peak performance training. *Somatics* 4:16–18, 1983.

72. Perski, A., and B.T. Engel. The role of behavioral conditioning in the cardiovascular adjustment to exercise. *Biofeedback Self-Regul.* 5:91–104, 1980.

73. Perski, A., S.P. Tzankoff, and B.T. Engel. Central control of cardiovascular adjustments to exercise. *J. Appl. Physiol.* 58:431–435, 1985.

74. Pinel, J.P., and T.D. Schultz. Effect of antecedent muscle tension levels on motor behavior. *Med. Sci. Sports Exerc.* 10:177–182, 1978.

75. Sabourin, M., and S. Rioux. Effects of active and passive EMG biofeedback training on performance of motor and cognitive tasks. *Percept. Mot. Skills* 49:831–835, 1979.

76. Sandweiss, J. Athletic applications of biofeedback (Task Force Report). Denver, Colo.: Biofeedback Society of America, 1978.

77. Sandweiss, J., and W.A. Greene. Athletic applications of biofeedback (Task Force Report). Denver, Colo.: Biofeedback Society of America, 1980.

78. Sandweiss, J., and S.L. Wolf (eds.). *Biofeedback and Sports Science.* New York: Plenum Press, 1985.

79. Schmidt, R.A., and G.A. Stull. Premotor and motor reaction time as a function of preliminary muscle tension. *J. Mot. Behav.* 2:96–110, 1970.

80. Shellenberger, R., and J.A. Green. *From the Ghost in the Box to Successful Biofeedback Training.* Greeley, Colo.: Health Psychology Publications, 1986.

81. Sherrington, C.S. On the proprioceptive system, especially in its reflex aspect. *Brain* 29:467–482, 1906.

82. Simard, T.G., and W.H. Ladd. Pre-orthotic training: An electromyographic study in normal adults. *Am. J. Phys. Med.* 48:301–312, 1969.

83. Stilson, D.W., I. Matus, and G. Ball. Relaxation and subjective estimates of muscle tension: Implications for a central efferent theory of muscle control. *Biofeedback Self-Regul.* 5:19–36, 1980.

84. Talag, T. Residual muscular soreness as influenced by concentric, eccentric, and static contractions. *Res. Q.* 44:458–469, 1973.

85. Teague, M. A combined systematic desensitization and electromyograph biofeedback technique for controlling state anxiety and improving gross motor skill performance. Unpublished anxiety and improving gross motor skill performance. Unpublished Ph.D. dissertation, University of Northern Colorado, Greeley, Colorado, 1976.

86. Tsukomoto, S. The effects of EMG biofeedback assisted relaxation on sport competition anxiety. Unpublished master's thesis, University of Western Ontario, London, Ontario, 1979.

87. Wenz, B.J., and D.J. Strong. An application of biofeedback and self-regulation procedures with superior athletes. In R.W. Suinn (ed.). *Psychology in Sports: Methods and Applications.* Minneapolis: Burgess, 1980, pp. 328–333.

88. Wilson, V.E., and E.I. Bird. Effects of relaxation and/or biofeedback training upon hip flexion in gymnasts. *Biofeedback Self-Regul.* 6:25–34, 1981.

89. Wise, H.H., I.M. Fiebert, and J.L. Kates. EMG biofeedback as treatment for patellofemoral pain syndrome. *J. Orthop. Sports Phys. Ther.* 6:95–103, 1987.

90. Wolf, S.L. Electromyographic biofeedback in exercise programs. *Physician Sportsmed.* 8:61–69, 1980.
91. Wolf, S.L. Neurophysiological factors in electromyographic feedback for neuromotor disorders. In J.V. Basmajian (ed.). *Biofeedback: Principles and Practice for Clinicians.* Baltimore: Williams & Wilkins Co., 1983, pp. 5–22.
92. Zaichkowsky, L.D. Combating stress: What about relaxation training and biofeedback? *Mouvement* 1:309–312, 1975.
93. Zaichkowsky, L.D. Single case experimental designs: Application to motor behavior research. In G. Roberts and W. Halliwell (eds.). *Psychology of Motor Behavior.* Champaign, Ill.: Human Kinetics, 1980, pp. 171–179.
94. Zaichkowsky, L.D. Biofeedback and the management of competitive stress. In Y. Hanin (ed.). *Stress and Anxiety in Sport.* Moscow: Soviet Press, 1981, pp. 250–261.
95. Zaichkowsky, L.D. Biofeedback and self-regulation of competitive stress. In L.D. Zaichkowsky and W.E. Sime (eds.). *Stress Management for Sport.* Reston, Va.: American Alliance for Health, Physical Education, Recreation and Dance, 1982, pp. 55–64.
96. Zaichkowsky, L.D. The use of biofeedback for self-regulation of performance states. In L.E. Unestahl (ed.). *The Mental Aspects of Gymnastics.* Orebro, Sweden: Veje, 1983, pp. 95–105.
97. Zaichkowsky, L.D., J.A. Dorsey, and T.B. Mulholland. The effects of biofeedback assisted systematic desensitization in the control of anxiety and performance. In M. Vanek (ed.). *IV Svetovy Kongress, ISSP.* Prague: Olympia, 1979, pp. 809–812.
98. Zaichkowsky, L.D., and C.Z. Fuchs. Biofeedback: The psychophysiology of motor control and human performance. In L.D. Zaichkowsky and C.Z. Fuchs (eds.). *The Psychology of Motor Behavior: Development, Control, Learning and Performance.* Ithaca, N.Y.: Mouvement Publications, 1986, pp. 159–173.

13
Self-Confidence and Sports Performance
DEBORAH L. FELTZ, Ph.D.

INTRODUCTION

The cognitive approach to the study of achievement motivation assumes that strivings for achievement are mediated through several cognitive mechanisms. A growing body of evidence suggests that one's perception of ability or self-confidence is the central mediating construct of those achievement strivings [1, 13, 45, 72]. In sport, self-confidence is one of the most frequently cited psychological factors thought to affect athletic achievements. "Self-confidence," as the term is used here, is the belief that one can successfully execute a specific activity rather than a global trait that accounts for overall performance optimism. For example, one may have a high degree of self-confidence in one's driving ability in golf but a low degree of self-confidence in putting.

Although self-confidence is thought to affect athletic performance, its relationship with performance has not been clear in much of the sport science research. Self-confidence has been shown to be significantly correlated with skillful sport performance, but whether there is a causal relationship, and what the direction of that relationship is, cannot be determined from the correlational designs of the studies [33, 41, 50, 66].

This chapter focuses on the nature of the relationship between self-confidence and sport performance. First, definitions of self-confidence and related concepts are given. Second, the major theoretical approaches to studying this relationship are briefly described, research evidence from sport is provided, and general criticisms are reviewed. Third, a summary and comparison of the approaches are provided and the status of the relationship of confidence to sport performance is summarized. Finally, a conclusion is presented with suggestions for future research.

Definitions of Self-Confidence and Related Concepts
Various terms such as "self-confidence," "self-efficacy," "perceived ability," and "perceived competence" have been used to describe one's perceived capability to accomplish a certain level of performance. Bandura [1] uses the term "self-efficacy" to describe the conviction one has to execute successfully the behavior (e.g., a sports performance) required to produce a certain outcome (e.g., a trophy or self-satisfaction) and, thus, can be considered as a situationally specific self-confidence. In

addition, as Bandura [5] notes, self-efficacy is not concerned with the skills an individual has but with the judgments of what an individual can do with the skills he or she possesses. He also distinguishes between perceived self-efficacy and self-confidence. Self-confidence, for him, refers to the strength of the belief or conviction but does not specify the level of perceived competence. Bandura prefers to use the term "self-efficacy" to specify the level of perceived competence and the strength of that belief.

"Perceived competence" and "perceived ability" are terms that have been limited in use to the achievement and mastery motivation literature, and indicate the sense that one has the ability to master a task resulting from cumulative interactions with the environment [45, 72]. In the specific area of sport and movement, Griffin and Keogh [42] use the term "movement confidence" to describe an individual's feeling of adequacy in a movement situation, whereas Vealey [87, p. 222] defines "sport confidence" as "the belief or degree of certainty individuals possess about their ability to be successful in sport."

Some terms are related to self-confidence but should not be confused with the construct. "Self-concept" represents a composite view of oneself that is developed through evaluative experiences and social interactions. As Bandura [5–7] has noted, however, a global self-concept will not predict the intra-individual variability in performance as well as self-confidence perceptions that vary across activities and circumstances.

"Self-esteem" is another concept related to self-confidence and pertains to one's personal judgment of worthiness. Although self-confidence and self-esteem may be related, certain individuals do not have high self-confidence for a given activity, but nevertheless still "like themselves"; by contrast, there are those who may regard themselves as highly competent at a given activity but do not have corresponding feelings of self-worth.

The concept of performance "expectancies" has been used to try to operationalize self-confidence in sport by asking subjects how well they expect to perform or whether they expect to beat their opponent [18, 19, 21, 71, 78, 79]. Most of the expectancy research in sport, however, is actually concerned with competitive efficacy expectations rather than outcome expectations. Bandura [1, 5] distinguishes judgments of personal efficacy from response-outcome expectations. Self-efficacy is a judgment of one's ability to perform at a certain level, whereas outcome expectancy pertains to one's judgment of the likely consequences of such a performance. For example, the belief that one can run a marathon in less than 2 hours is an efficacy judgment; the anticipated social recognition, money, and the self-satisfaction created by such a performance are the outcome expectancies. What Bandura refers to as the "outcome" should not be confused with the typical use of the term "sport outcome" in the sport psychology literature. "Sport outcome" refers to the performance accomplishment itself, not what follows from that accomplishment.

In this chapter, I will address the areas of the literature that conceptualize self-confidence as self-efficacy, perceived competence or ability, sport confidence, and movement confidence. Except when discussing a particular theoretical construct, I will use the term "self-confidence" to represent the perceived ability to accomplish a certain level of performance. The related areas of self-concept, self-esteem, and outcome expectancies are beyond the scope of this chapter and will not be considered. Readers interested in self-concept and self-esteem in sport are referred to recent reviews by Sonstroem [81] and by Weiss [93].

THEORETICAL APPROACHES TO STUDYING SELF-CONFIDENCE IN SPORT

Self-Efficacy

Bandura's [1] theory of self-efficacy has been the most extensively used theory for investigating self-confidence in sport and motor performance. Bandura originally proposed the theory to account for the different results achieved by the diverse methods used in clinical psychology for treating anxiety. It has since been expanded [3] and applied to other domains of psychological functioning, including motivation [8], achievement behavior [9, 80], career choice and development [11, 44], and health behavior [73], in addition to sport behavior.

This theory, developed within the framework of a social cognitive theory [5], poses self-efficacy as a common cognitive mechanism for mediating people's motivation and behavior. People's judgment of their capability to perform at given levels affect their behavior (i.e., choice of activities, effort expenditure, persistence), their thought patterns, and their emotional reactions in demanding or anxiety-provoking situations. Self-efficacy is a major determinant of behavior, however, only when proper incentives and the necessary skills are present.

SOURCE OF INFORMATION. According to Bandura's theory, expectations of personal efficacy are derived from four principal sources of information: performance accomplishments, vicarious experiences, verbal persuasion, and physiological arousal. These four categories of efficacy information are not mutually exclusive in terms of the information they provide, though some are more influential than others. For instance, performance accomplishments provide the most dependable source of efficacy information because they are based on personal mastery experiences. Bandura [1, p. 194] emphasized that the relationship between efficacy expectations and performance is reciprocal: "Mastery expectations influence performance and are, in turn, altered by the cumulative

FIGURE 1

Relationship between major sources of efficacy information, efficacy expectations, and performance as predicted by Bandura's theory.

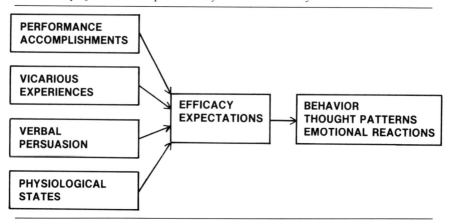

effects of one's efforts." This relationship between the major sources of efficacy information, efficacy expectations, and performance, as predicted by Bandura's theory is presented in Figure 1.

Performance accomplishments. As stated previously, performance accomplishments provide the most dependable source of information upon which to base self-efficacy judgments because they are based on one's mastery experiences. These experiences affect self-efficacy judgments through cognitive processing of such information. If these experiences have been repeatedly perceived as successes, they will raise efficacy expectations; if they have been perceived as failures, they will lower expectations. The influence that performance experiences have on perceived efficacy also depends on the perceived difficulty of the task, the effort expended, the amount of physical guidance received, and the temporal patterns of success and failure [3]. Performance accomplishments on difficult tasks, tasks independently attempted, and tasks accomplished early in learning with only occasional failures carry greater efficacy value than easy tasks, tasks accomplished with external aids, or tasks in which repeated failures are experienced early in the learning process.

Vicarious experiences. Efficacy information can also be obtained through observing or imagining others engaging in a task that observers themselves have never performed. Although vicarious sources of efficacy information are generally weaker than performance accomplishments, their influence on self-efficacy can be enhanced by a number of factors. The less experience one has had with a task or situation, the more one will rely on others to judge one's own capabilities. Similarities to the model in terms of performance or personal characteristics have been shown to enhance the effectiveness of modeling procedures on subjects' self-efficacy and performance [40].

Persuasion. Persuasive techniques are widely used by teachers, coaches, and peers in attempting to influence the learner's behavior. These techniques can include verbal persuasion and/or bogus performance feedback. Efficacy expectations based on this type of information are also likely to be weaker than those based on one's own accomplishments. In addition, persuasive techniques are effective only if heightened appraisal is within realistic bounds. The extent of persuasive influence on self-efficacy also depends on the credibility, prestige, trustworthiness, and expertise of the persuader.

Physiological states. The level and quality of physiological arousal also provide an indication of self-efficacy. Although other theorists [14, 28, 98] postulate that reduction in physiological arousal directly changes behavior through reinforcement, Bandura [1] states that arousal affects behavior through the cognitive appraisal (efficacy expectations) of the information conveyed by arousal. For example, some individuals may interpret increases in their physiological arousal as a fear that they cannot perform the skill successfully, whereas others may interpret this state as being psyched up and ready for performance. Bandura [5] also notes that physiological sources of self-efficacy are not limited to autonomic arousal. People use their levels of fatigue, fitness, and pain in strength and endurance activities as indicants of physical inefficacy [34, 82].

Anxiety or autonomic arousal is viewed not only as a source of efficacy information by Bandura [1] but also as a co-effect of behavior. This suggests another reciprocal relationship in self-efficacy theory: one between self-efficacy and physiological arousal.

Efficacy/behavior relationship. As mentioned previously, Bandura [1] states that self-efficacy is a major determinant of behavior only when people have sufficient incentives to act on their self-percepts of efficacy and when they possess the requisite subskills. He predicts that efficacy expectations will exceed actual performance when there is little incentive to perform the activity or when physical or social constraints are imposed on performance. An individual may have the necessary skill and high self-efficacy but no incentive to perform. Discrepancies will also occur when tasks or circumstances are ambiguous or when one has little information on which to base efficacy expectations.

How individuals cognitively process efficacy information will also influence the relationship between self-efficacy and behavior [1]. For instance, successes and failures may be perceived or distorted in importance. People who overweigh their failures will have lower levels of self-efficacy than those with the same performance levels who do not.

MEASUREMENT OF SELF-EFFICACY. Bandura [1] advocates a microan-alytic approach for testing propositions about the origins and functions of perceived self-efficacy. This requires a detailed assessment of the level, strength, and generality of perceived self-efficacy. "Level of self-efficacy" refers to people's expected performance attainments. "Strength" refers to the strength of people's beliefs that they can attain different levels of performance. "Generality" indicates the number of domains of func-tioning in which people judge themselves to be efficacious. Self-efficacy instruments are typically constructed by listing a series of tasks, usually varying in difficulty, complexity, or stressfulness. People are asked to designate the tasks they believe they can perform (efficacy level). For each task designated, they rate their degree of certainty (efficacy strength) that they can execute it on a 100-point probability scale ranging from high uncertainty to complete certainty.

According to Bandura [5], this method permits a microanalysis of the degree of congruence between self-efficacy and action at the level of individual tasks. However, this method also requires that one conduct a conceptual analysis of the subskills needed to perform a task and a contextual analysis of the level of situational demands. Bandura [5] uses the example of driving self-efficacy to show how the strength of per-ceived self-efficacy may vary for navigating through residential areas, arterial roads, congested city traffic, onrushing freeway traffic, and twist-ing mountain roads. In gymnastics, the subskills needed to perform competitively could be categorized by event (vault, beam, bars, floor exercise) and by the context of stunts within each event that vary in degree of difficulty.

In the sport literature, self-efficacy researchers have typically corre-lated aggregate self-efficacy scores with aggregate performance scores rather than examining the congruence between self-efficacy and per-formance at the level of individual tasks [102]. Perhaps this is due to the nature of the tasks used in sport. In most sports studies, subjects' efficacy expectations and performance have not been assessed in terms of the approach/avoidance to a series of tasks that increase in difficulty. Rather, subjects are asked about their confidence beliefs concerning a single task in terms of how long or at what height they can perform and then are asked to attempt that task in two or more trials.

Ryckman and his colleagues [77] developed the Physical Self-Efficacy Scale to provide an omnibus measure of perceived physical self-efficacy. The scale has two factors: a perceived physical ability factor and a phys-ical self-presentation confidence factor that reflects confidence in the display of physical skills. The authors found significant correlations be-tween total physical self-efficacy scores, perceived physical ability scores, and performance on a reaction-time task and a motor coordination task. Gayton and his colleagues [37] also found predictive validity for the scale with competitive marathon running performance. However, McAuley and Gill [70] found a task-specific measure of self-efficacy that measured expectations in the areas of vault, beam, bars, and floor exercise to be a much better predictor of gymnastics performance than the global measure of physical self-efficacy. This supports a growing body of evidence that particularized measures of self-efficacy have greater explanatory and predictive power than global measures [see 5, 6].

RESEARCH IN SPORT AND PHYSICAL ACTIVITY. Much of the self-efficacy research in sport and motor performance has focused on examining (a) the effects of various methods used to create athletic competence in self-efficacy and performance and (b) the relationship between self-efficacy and performance. The various treatment techniques examined in these studies were based on one or more of the four major sources of efficacy information outlined by Bandura [1].

Sport and exercise research has examined the influence of techniques based on performance accomplishment and has shown them to be effective in enhancing both self-efficacy and performance [27, 33, 51, 54, 68, 89, 90, 91]. Studies have also supported the superiority of performance-based information over other sources of efficacy information [23, 33, 35, 68, 91]. For instance, participant modeling, which involves a model's demonstration plus guided participation of the learner, has been shown to produce superior diving performance and stronger expectations of personal efficacy than either live modeling or videotaped modeling techniques [33].

Information gained through vicarious experiences has been shown to increase perceived efficacy in muscular endurance tasks [34, 40], gymnastic performance [68], exercise activity [20], and competitive persistence [89]. These techniques have included modeling [20, 40], imagery [34], and information acquired about a competitor's competence [89]. Weinberg and his colleagues [89] manipulated subjects' efficacy expectations about competing on a muscular endurance task by having them observe their competitor (a confederate), who either performed poorly on a related strength task and was said to have a knee injury (high self-efficacy) or who performed well and was said to be a varsity track athlete (low self-efficacy). Results indicated that the higher the induced self-efficacy, the greater the muscular endurance. Subjects who competed against an injured competitor endured longer than those who competed against a varsity athlete.

The few studies that have investigated persuasive techniques such as positive self-talk [88, 97] and reinterpreting arousal [103] as a source of efficacy information report mixed results. Wilkes and Summers [97] were the only ones who found self-efficacy techniques (positive self-talk) to influence performance. However, efficacy-related cognitions did not seem to mediate the effect.

Few sport studies have investigated the influence of physiological or emotional states on self-efficacy [29, 35, 55]. In my work on diving [29, 35], I found that although actual physiological arousal did not predict self-efficacy expectancies, perceived autonomic arousal was a significant predictor, but not as strong a predictor as previous performance accomplishments. Kavanagh and Hausfeld [55], however, found that induced moods (happiness/sadness), as measured by self-report, did not alter efficacy expectations in any consistent manner using strength tasks.

In these studies that have examined non-performance-based sources of efficacy information, lack of effects may have been due to confounding with actual performance where multiple performance trials were used. Because personal experiences are so powerful, subjects' perceptions of their performance experience may overshadow any influence that the treatment variable may have on self-efficacy.

A number of studies have examined the relationship between self-efficacy and athletic and exercise performance [10, 29, 31, 33–35, 37, 40, 54, 55, 65, 68, 70, 77, 89, 91, 92, 99]. As Wurtele [102] noted, the results of these studies show a significant relationship between self-efficacy and performance across a number of sport tasks and physical activities. These correlational results, which are summarized in Table 1, do not necessarily demonstrate a causal relationship between self-efficacy and performance.

A few studies in the sport and motor performance area have been conducted to investigate the causal relationships in Bandura's theory [29, 31, 35, 68]. Using path analysis techniques, these studies found that although self-efficacy was indeed a major determinant of performance, direct effects of treatment on performance [68] and direct effects of past performance on future performance [29, 31, 35] were also present. These results indicate that performance-based treatments affect behavior through other mechanisms as well as perceived self-efficacy.

I conducted a study [29] that compared the influence of self-efficacy as a common cognitive mechanism with an alternative anxiety-based model [28] in the approach/avoidance behavior of college females attempting a modified back dive. The self-efficacy model in this study predicted that self-efficacy was the major predictor of performance and that a reciprocal relationship existed between self-efficacy and back-diving performance. The anxiety-based model included related performance experience, self-reported anxiety, and physiological arousal as causal influences on back-diving performance. Self-efficacy was hypothesized as merely an effect.

The results provided little support for the complete network of relationships in either model. Self-efficacy was neither just an effect nor the only significant predictor of performance, although it was the major predictor of performance on the first of four diving attempts. Physio-

TABLE 1

Correlations Between Self-Efficacy and Performance

Study	N	Performance Task	Self-Efficacy Measure	r (All Significant)
Barling and Abel [10]	40	Subjective rating of Tennis performance	Strength	0.53
Ewart et al. [25]	40	Arm strength	Strength	0.73
		Aerobic endurance	Strength	0.54
Ewart et al. [26]	40	Treadmill test performance	Strength	0.66
Feltz [29]	80	Back dive attempts	Strength	0.63 (Trial 1)
Feltz [30]	40	Back dive attempts—females	Strength	0.46 (Trial 1)
	40	Back dive attempts—males	Strength	0.28 (Trial 1)
Feltz et al. [33]	60	Back dive performance	Strength	0.29 (Trial 1)
Feltz et al. [34]	63	Leg endurance	Level	0.39 (Trial 1)
Feltz and Mugno [35]	80	Back dive attempts	Strength	0.59 (Trial 1)
Gayton et al. [37]	33	Marathon running	Ryckman et al. [77] PPA	0.55
Gould and Weiss [40]	150	Leg extension endurance	Level	0.31
			Strength	0.26
Kaplan et al. [54]	60	Walking compliance COPD patients	Strength	0.63
Kavanagh and Hausfeld [55]	16	Hand grip strength (study I)	Strength	0.61, 0.64, 0.70
	12	Hand grip strength (study II)	Strength	0.47, 0.48, 0.50
Lee [65]	14	Gymnastics competition performance	Performance estimate	0.55
McAuley [68]	39	Gymastics balance beam test	Strength	0.71
McAuley and Gill [70]	52	Gymnastics—vault	Strength	0.28
		Beam		0.58
		Bars		0.72
		Floor exercise		0.43
Ryckman et al. [77]	22	Reaction time		0.40
		Motor coordination task	PPA	0.40
Weinberg et al. [89]	60	Leg extension endurance	Strength	0.68
Weinberg et al. [91]	32	Gymnastic task—front mill circle	Level	0.64
Weingberg et al. [92]	112	Leg extension endurance	Strength	0.19
Woolfolk et al. [99]	66	Golf putt accuracy	Level	0.26

logical arousal and past related accomplishments also predicted approach/avoidance behavior on the first trial. After trial 1, however, performance on a previous trial was the major predictor of performance on the next trial. In other words, regardless of what subjects thought they were capable of performing after the first diving attempt, once they stepped to the end of the diving board, their next attempt or avoidance of the dive was determined more by what they did on the previous trial. In accord with Bandura's theory, I found a reciprocal relationship between self-efficacy and performance, although they were not equally reciprocal. As subjects progressed over trials, performance became a stronger influence on self-efficacy than self-efficacy became on performance.

Because I found little support for the complete network of relationships in either the self-efficacy or the anxiety-based model, I proposed a revised model that included both self-efficacy and previous performance as direct predictors of back-diving performance. This revised model was later tested with two different sample populations and found to be supported in terms of its major predictions [31, 35].

McAuley [68] also examined the self-efficacy and anxiety-based models of the relationship of anxiety, self-efficacy, and performance on a gymnastics task and found similar results. Neither model fit the data, though the self-efficacy model provided a better fit than the anxiety-based model. Although these findings, together with mine, suggest that self-efficacy, as a common cognitive mechanism, cannot account for all behavioral change in motor performance, self-efficacy has been found consistently to be an important and necessary cognitive mechanism in explaining motor performance, especially in an initial performance attempt. Furthermore, as Bandura [5–7] notes, commonality of mechanism does not imply exclusivity of mechanism; other mechanisms may also influence behavior. He would conclude, therefore, that McAuley's and my results are not at odds with self-efficacy theory.

Perhaps self-efficacy may have more of an effect on performance under more variable conditions than those used in the preceding studies. Predicting repetitive performance under the invariant conditions of these studies may not be the most informative paradigm for testing the relative contributions of self-efficacy, anxiety, and performance. In most real-life sport situations, people perform with some variation in circumstances (e.g., different meets, different settings) and temporal intervals. Under such conditions, there may be greater leeway for efficacy judgments to exert an effect on subsequent trial attempts. However, there are also occasions in sport where short-term trials under relatively invariant conditions do exist (e.g., archery) and are important to examine in relation to self-efficacy.

Weinberg's research [89, 90, 92] has also attempted to demonstrate the causal influence of self-efficacy on motor performance through experimental manipulation of self-efficacy. However, Biglan [12] has criticized this approach as leading to an arbitrary interpretation of self-efficacy's relationship to performance. He points out that when environmental variables are manipulated in order to manipulate self-efficacy ratings, performance behavior or other factors are also affected. Environmental manipulations may influence some other variable (e.g., anxiety) that influences self-efficacy and performance without any causal role for self-efficacy. "Third variable" causes must be considered. Regression and path analysis have been used to control for the contribution of other possible factors, including anxiety [29, 68].

Recovery and adherence efficacy. More recently, researchers have begun to study the significance of self-efficacy in explaining success of recovery from myocardial infarction and adherence to exercise regimens [23, 25, 27, 54, 82]. In the area of cardiac rehabilitation, Ewart and his colleagues [27] showed that perceived physical efficacy in patients with coronary artery disease was strengthened by having them master increasing exercise intensities on the treadmill and using persuasive medical counseling. Self-efficacy was found to be a good predictor of patients' activity levels after they returned to their home environment. In a subsequent study [25], perceived physical efficacy was used to identify successfully, in advance, coronary artery disease patients who overexerted by exercising at intensities above the prescribed heart rate range, thereby putting themselves at risk. In addition, Taylor and his colleagues [82] demonstrated the importance of raising the spouse's efficacy level regarding the patient's capabilities. Spouses who believed that their partners had a robust heart were more likely to encourage them to resume an active life than those who believed that their partner's cardiac capability was severely reduced.

Researchers have also begun to investigate the influence of self-efficacy in predicting adherence to exercise regimens. Kaplan and his colleagues [54] found that perceived self-efficacy mediated exercise compliance in patients with chronic obstructive pulmonary disease. Desharnais and his colleagues [23] examined the ability of self-efficacy and outcome expectancy (potential benefits from regular exercise) to predict adherence to exercise in an 11-week physical fitness program. Although both efficacy and outcome expectations were significant predictors of exercise adherence, self-efficacy best distinguished adherers from dropouts. Potential dropouts displayed less certainty than adherers about their capacity to attend the program regularly at the outset and expected more benefits from their participation. Efficacy research in this area is just beginning, but it appears to show consistent results in self-efficacy as a predictor of cardiac recovery and adherence to exercise.

CRITICISMS OF SELF-EFFICACY THEORY. Self-efficacy theory has been criticized for being so heavily based on self-report measures because of the demand and suggestion problems that may occur [14, 56]. However, Bandura [5] has presented evidence that in situations where individuals have no reason to distort their reports, self-reports can be quite representative of cognitions. Thus, efficacy judgments are best made when recorded privately. Weinberg et al. [92] compared public with private efficacy-expectation groups and found no differences between the two in terms of expectations or performance. Critics have suggested, however, that just making an efficacy statement, even privately, creates a demand or goal to match the performance with the efficacy judgment [12, 14]. Contrary to this presumption, Telch et al. [83] have shown that variation in social demand has little or no effect on congruence between self-efficacy and performance. If anything, social demand may encourage conservation and thus reduce the congruence between self-efficacy and performance.

Kazdin [56] has also criticized Bandura's measure of self-efficacy for being so closely related to the actual performance task that it ensured high correlations. But one can also be assured of finding low correlations if there is little similarity between the efficacy measure and what people are asked to perform [2]. Moreover, Kazdin was concerned about the possible reactivity occurring when the self-efficacy measure and the behavior test are administered so closely in time. Again, Bandura [2] points out that if the interval between efficacy judgments and performance is too great, efficacy expectations may be changed in the interim.

Self-efficacy, as a construct, has even been questioned as to its necessity in explaining behavior by those with strong behavioristic views [12, 14, 28, 98]. These theorists have argued that environmental events such as anxiety response "habit" were the direct cause of both self-efficacy expectations and behavioral change. Eysenck [28] considered efficacy expectations, as well as any other cognitive determinant of behavior, as merely a by-product of conditioned responses. In describing the role of self-efficacy in athletic performance, therefore, Bandura would argue that successful performance and reduced competitive anxiety are determined primarily by an athlete's self-efficacy expectations; by contrast, Eysenck and others would argue that an athlete's high degree of self-efficacy is merely an effect of reduced anxiety and that this reduced anxiety is the major determinant of successful performance and self-efficacy. However, path analysis studies have indicated that self-efficacy is not merely a by-product of conditioned anxiety [29, 68]. Indeed, evidence also shows that perceived self-efficacy accounts for a substantial amount of variance in behavior when anticipatory anxiety is controlled, whereas the relationship between anticipatory anxiety and behavior essentially disappears when perceived self-efficacy is partialled out [6].

Furthermore, a large body of evidence exists on the failure of conditioned anxiety responses to predict avoidance behavior [see 5].

On a related concern, Kirsch [60] has criticized the concept of "self-efficacy" as being merely old wine with a new label. He contends that self-efficacy is no different from Rotter's [76] concept of "expectancy for success." However, as Bandura [6] has countered, the label "expectancy for success" indicates an outcome expectancy. "Because self-percepts of efficacy are formed through acts of self-appraisal based on multidimensional information, perceived self-efficacy is more closely allied to the field of human judgment than to the subject of expectancy, which refers to an anticipation that something is likely to happen" [6, p. 362].

In summary, while some criticisms have focused on the methods by which self-efficacy ratings are made [12, 56, 59, 61], research on self-efficacy in numerous sport and physical activity settings has shown a consistent significant relationship between self-efficacy and performance. The studies that have been conducted to investigate the causal relationships in Bandura's theory of athletic activities [29, 31, 35, 68] have been consistent in showing that performance factors and perceived self-efficacy are both needed to explain performance.

Perceived Competence
"Perceived competence" and "perceived ability" are terms that have been limited in use to the achievement and mastery motivation literature and indicate the sense that one has the ability to master a task resulting from cumulative interactions with the environment [45, 72]. Harter [45] and Nicholls [72] have developed theories of achievement motivation incorporating the construct of perceived competence (or ability). Although both theoretical models are very similar in their predictions of perceived competence in achievement contexts, Nicholls uses attribution theory (a theory of causal judgment) to explain the cognitions involved in developing a sense of competence, whereas Harter bases her model on socialization and affective processes within a drive theory to explain the development of a child's sense of competence and subsequent behavior. These theories are not as well tested within the sport and physical activity areas as is self-efficacy theory, and where they have been employed, they have been used to explain participation motivation rather than specific task performance. Because Roberts [74] has described Nicholls' model in detail and has reviewed that literature in an earlier volume, I will provide only a brief overview of the model in this section. In addition, cognitive evaluation theory [22] includes perceived competence as a mediator of intrinsic motivation. However, this area was reviewed in the preceding volume of this series [85] and will not be reviewed here.

The concept of competence, as a psychological construct mediating achievement behavior, was first introduced by White [96]. White proposed "effectance" motivation (a global motive) to explain why an individual feels impelled to engage in mastery attempts. Individuals engage in mastery behaviors in order to have an effect on their environment. Being effective (or competent) results in a feeling of efficacy and intrinsic pleasure. White's model did not lend itself readily to empirical investigation, however, because of its global nature and lack of operational definitions. Harter [45], therefore, refined and extended White's model and also developed measurement procedures to test its components empirically.

Harter did not view perceived competence as a global trait or a unitary construct, but rather as a multidimensional motive, having specific domains in the areas of physical, social, and cognitive concerns. Cognitive competence emphasizes school or academic performance; social competence is defined in terms of popularity with one's peers; and physical competence reflects perceived ability at sports and outdoor games. This view of perceived confidence is more specific than the one overall trait view, but is still more global than Bandura's [1] microanalytic conception and is drive oriented rather than self-perception oriented. Harter also focused on the implications of failure as well as success; reconceptualized success as including a condition of "optimal degree of challenge"; considered the role of socializing agents in maintaining, enhancing, or attenuating competence motivation through reinforcement and modeling patterns; considered the effects of reinforcement history on the development of a self-reward system and the internalization of mastery goals; and addressed the relative influence of intrinsic and extrinsic motivation orientations. Harter's model is presented in Figure 2.

According to Harter's [45] model, children's mastery attempts in specific domains result in successes or failures and are evaluated by significant others. If the successes are optimally challenging, this leads to perceived competence and intrinsic pleasure. Approval by significant others also leads to perceived competence, but the need for this approval diminishes with age. Perceived competence and intrinsic pleasure lead to increased motivation to be competent. A history of failure results in perceived lack of competence and anxiety in mastery situations, and decreases children's motivation to continue mastery attempts. In addition, the need for external approval persists developmentally, rather than diminishing.

Harter [45] suggested that perception of control, as well as significant others' approval or disapproval of mastery attempts, influences a child's perceived competence. Children who feel responsible for the outcome of their mastery attempts have a positive sense of competence. When children either do not know who is in control or view powerful others

FIGURE 2

Harter's version of White's competence motivation theory. (From Weiss, M.R. Self-esteem and achievement in children's sport and physical activity. In Gould, D., and M. Weiss [eds.]. Advances in Pediatric Sport Sciences, *Vol. 2:* Behavioral Issues. *Champaign, Ill.: Human Kinetics, Press, 1987, pp. 87–119.)*

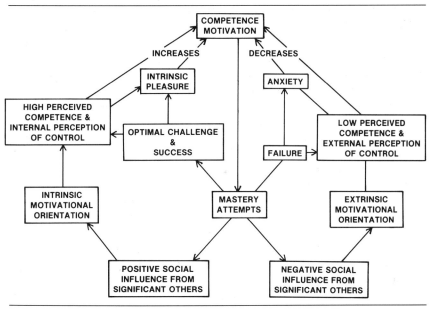

as responsible for their performance, they have a negative or lower sense of competence.

Harter's model is intuitively appealing to the study of motivation in youth sports. From this model, one would predict that young athletes who perceive themselves to be highly competent in a sport, who are oriented toward mastery. in sport, and who identify themselves as primarily responsible for their performance persist longer at the sport and maintain interest in mastering the skills. In contrast, those who perceive themselves to have low competence in sport, who are oriented toward extrinsic mastery, and who believe that others are responsible for their performance do not maintain task performance and interest.

Competence motivation theory differs from self-efficacy theory on the origins of perceived efficacy or competence [5]. In Harter's framework, children's competence motives develop gradually through prolonged transactions with their surroundings and evaluative reinforcement of others. In Bandura's social cognitive framework, perceived efficacy is derived from diverse sources of information conveyed vicariously, as well as through social evaluation and direct experience. In addition, Harter has operationalized perceived competence based on a developmental approach; therefore, the measurement of perceived competence is valid only for children. Although Bandura [5] has provided an explanation of the developmental differences in perceived efficacy, its measurement has not been based on a developmental approach.

Nicholls' [72] theoretical model also relates perceived competence (ability) to effectance motivation. Like Bandura [1] and Harter [45], Nicholls believes that perceived competence is the critical mediator of performance and persistence. In addition, the basic assumption of Nicholls' theory is that people are motivated by a desire to demonstrate and/or develop high ability and avoid demonstrating low ability. Nicholls also conceptualizes two types of ability: ego-involved ability and task ability. Individuals may view competence relative to their peers or relative to their past performances or gains in knowledge. As Duda [24] explained, Harter's theory focuses on how much competence individuals perceive themselves to possess and the corresponding relationship to behavior, whereas Nicholls' theory considers the meaning of ability or how it is construed in relation to performance and persistence in achievement settings.

In sport, an athlete's goal would be to maximize the subjective probability of attributing high ability to the self and minimize the subjective probability of attributing low ability to the self. As long as the athlete is able to make high ability attributions to the self in a sport situation, participation will continue. In contrast, the athlete who makes low ability attributions will discontinue participation in that sport to avoid the unpleasant affect associated with feelings of failure.

Both Harter's [45] and Nicholls' [72] models provide the same explanation for children's discontinuation of an activity such as a sport. Nicholls proposes that athletes who realize that they do not possess enough ability to be successful will drop out. Harter also proposes that when athletes have a low perceived physical competence they will withdraw because this perception produces feelings of failure, anxiety, and sadness.

MEASUREMENT OF PERCEIVED COMPETENCE AND PERCEIVED ABILITY. Harter [45] developed the Perceived Competence Scale for Children to measure perceived competence in children from grades 3 through 9. Harter and Pike [49] later extended this scale to pictorial versions appropriate for preschool-kindergarten and first-second grades. The original scale consists of 28 items, 7 in each of the three specific domains (cognitive, social, physical) and 7 that assess a child's general sense of self-worth. The structured alternative questionnaire format involves first asking the child to choose between one of two statements that was most descriptive of him or her as compared to other children of the same age. For instance, the child must choose between "Some kids do very well at all kinds of sports, BUT others don't feel that they are very good when it comes to sports." After choosing one of the two statements, the child is asked whether the statement is "sort of" or "really" true for him or her. This questionnaire format was designed to reduce social desirability effects. Both responses are worded so that they are perceived as socially legitimate. Each item is scored on a four-point scale, with 4 indicating the highest degree of perceived competence and 1 indicating the lowest. The scores are typically summed and then averaged for each subscale. Harter [46] found that girls consistently rated themselves as less competent than boys in the sports domain. However, if subjects are instructed to use same-sex children as their comparison peer group, these differences are eliminated [95].

Harter [48] has recently developed the Self Perception Profile for Children, which is a revision of the Perceived Competence Scale for Children. The revised scale contains two additional subscales: physical appearance and behavioral conduct. These new subscales assess self-adequacy rather than perceived competence in the form of actual skills. Several items from the original subscales also underwent revision.

In the sport literature, the physical subscale of Harter's Perceived Competence Scale for Children has been predominantly employed [32, 36, 52, 75, 95], and a few studies have employed sport-specific modifications [15, 32, 53, 84, 95]. In one study [32], I modified Harter's perceived physical competence subscale to apply to soccer in order to compare players' more specific perceived soccer competence with their perceived physical competence in predicting players' actual soccer ability. The results indicated that the perceived soccer competence subscale had higher internal consistency and was slightly more predictive of soccer ability than perceived physical competence. However, these sport-specific assessments are more representative of perceived general capacity in a particular sport than of self-efficacy as assessed by the microanalytic approach advocated by Bandura [1].

Harter has also developed scales to measure the construct of perceived control [Multidimensional Measure of Children's Perceptions of Control, 17] and the construct of intrinsic versus extrinsic motivational orientations [Intrinsic Versus Extrinsic Orientation in the Classroom, 47]. Harter's motivational orientations scale pertains only to classroom motivation; a modified version has been adapted for sports [94].

Nicholls [72] has not addressed the issue of how to measure perceived ability. Researchers have typically used a one-item Likert-type scale in which subjects are asked to rate their own ability for a particular task [16]. This type of assessment appears to be more situationally specific than Harter's assessment tool.

RESEARCH IN SPORT AND PHYSICAL ACTIVITY. Despite the intuitive appeal of competence motivation theory to youth sports, relatively little research has been conducted to test Harter's model in sport and physical activity settings. The studies that have been conducted have examined (a) the relationship between perceived physical competence and participation in organized sports, (b) the sources of competence information and significant others' feedback, and (c) the relationship of perceived competence to actual competence, in addition to scale construction efforts [32, 84, 94].

Based on Harter's model, individuals who perceive themselves to be competent in sports should be more likely to participate, while those low in perceived physical competence should be more likely not to participate or to discontinue participation. A few studies in the area of youth sports have examined this hypothesis in terms of participant status [36, 63, 64, 75, 84]. These investigators found that older youth sport participants (9- to 11-year olds) were higher in perceived physical competence than same-age nonparticipants [75] but not higher than younger participants [5- to 9-year-olds] [84]. Interscholastic sport participants [36] and youth wrestlers [16] were found to be higher in perceived physical competence than dropouts, but elite young gymnasts did not differ in perceived physical competence compared to former gymnasts in the same program [63]. The fact that the former elite gymnasts had all experienced some degree of success may explain these contradictory findings. If former and current elite gymnasts are comparing perceptions of their own competence to those of other same-aged children in general, the scale is probably not sensitive enough to discern any differences.

As Klint and Weiss [64] have noted, the investigations just reported were based on the assumption that children participate in sports to demonstrate physical competence. However, children who have low perceptions of their physical competence may still participate in sports for affiliative reasons or to demonstrate social competence [84]. Klint and Weiss examined the relationship between perceptions of competence and particular motives for sport participation and found support for this assumption. Children high in perceived physical competence were more motivated to participate for skill development reasons, whereas those high in perceived social competence were more motivated to participate for the affiliative reasons. These results suggest that researchers should not assume that participation in an activity is due to a certain type of competence motivation or achievement goal.

Harter's model also suggests that the more experience a child has with a sport, the more opportunity that child has to develop a sense of perceived physical competence. Of course, mere participation in sports does not guarantee that a child will have a high sense of physical competence. The degree to which a child has been successful over the sport experience will have a greater influence on his or her perceived competence than will length of involvement. However, the longer a child has been involved in a sport, the more likely he or she has had more successful mastery experiences. Continual failures usually lead to discouragement.

Sport research has not supported this contention, however [32, 36, 75]. Only low [32, 36] or nonsignificant [75] relationships were found between years of playing experience and perceived physical competence. Roberts and his colleagues [75] suggested that the experience of sport participation may not influence children's perceptions of competence; rather, children with a higher perception of competence may select a sport as an activity to demonstrate their abilities. An alternative explanation for the low relationship found may lie in the questionnaire format used to measure perceived competence. Harter's questionnaire is constructed to measure perceived competence relative to one's peers rather than relative to one's own past performances. As children become older and gain more playing experience, their comparison peers change. Thus, they may not view themselves as becoming more competent in comparison to their peers as they gain playing experience, or more competent in absolute terms, because their peers are gaining competence, too. In fact, Ulrich [84] found that as children's age increased, perceived physical competence decreased while actual motor competence increased.

Harter [45] has not specified the sources of information available to children for making judgments about their competence to the same extent as Bandura [1]. Positive reinforcement or approval for independent mastery attempts from adults and optimal challenge plus success are the only two sources specified in the model. Horn and Hasbrook [53] examined what sources of competence information that children use in sport. They found younger children (8–11 years) tended to rate evaluative feedback from parents and game outcome (winning/losing) as more important sources of information about their competence than did older children (12–14 years), who rated social comparison sources as more important. However, adult feedback, especially from coaches, has been shown to be still influential in adolescent athletes' perceived physical competence [52].

Actual sports competence or sports achievement should likewise be a source of competence information, and studies have found significant relationships between perceived physical (or sport-specific) competence and actual skill [32, 52, 84, 95]. Weiss and her colleagues [95] predicted, however, that perceived competence was causally predominant over sports achievement and tested this assumption using causal modeling techniques. They also examined the interrelationships among Harter's contructs of perceived competence, perceived control, and motivational orientation. The results showed that perceptions of competence in sport causally influenced sports achievement and motivational orientation. Perceived control also influenced achievement and motivational orientation, as predicted.

These results do not mean that other competing models may not also fit the data equally well. Whether sports achievement causally influences perceived competence or whether there is a reciprocal relationship, as Bandura [1] would contend, must await additional research. This study was an important step, however, in determining the causal relationships among the constructs of perceived competence, perceived controls, motivational orientation, and actual achievement in the sport domain.

CRITICISMS OF COMPETENCE MOTIVATION. As with self-efficacy assessments, perceived competence is based on self-report and thus could suffer from demand and suggestion problems. Harter's [45] structured alternative format has reduced the likelihood of social desirability effects, however, and is regarded as a great advance in the measurement of children's self-confidence [62]. Nevertheless, as previously stated, the trait nature of the measurement reduces its predictive accuracy in relation to performance [5–7]. Sport researchers have used sport-specific measures to try to increase the predictive power of their tests [15, 53, 95], but some have still found this type of modification not to be specific enough [15].

The measurement of perceived competence has also been criticized for not taking the contextual factors of performance situations into account [5, 24]. For instance, children's perceived competence in a sport may change depending on the environmental pressure to compete, the competitiveness of the sport organization, or the peers with which children are comparing themselves [63]. Duda [24], therefore, has advocated more examination of children's perceived competence in actual sport and physical activity situations. The measurement of self-efficacy, on the other hand, involves a relational judgment between perceived capabilities and different task demands (e.g., can one jump 3 ft, 6 ft, 9 ft?) and thus builds contextual factors into the measurement format.

Bandura [5] has also criticized competence motivation conceptually as being difficult to verify because the motive is inferred from the mastery behavior it supposedly causes. One cannot tell, as Bandura points out, whether individuals engage in mastery behavior because of a competence motive to do so or for any number of other reasons without an independent measure of motive strength.

In summary, Harter's theory is developmentally oriented and thus well suited for studying children's competence motivation in sport. It is also trait oriented in its conception, even though the perceived competence construct is viewed as a multidimensional motive rather than as a global trait or unitary construct. Unfortunately, because perceived competence has been measured as a trait, the contextual factors of performance situations have not been considered and the research on perceived competence in youth sports has not been as consistent as the research on self-efficacy.

Sport Confidence

Vealey [87] was dissatisfied with the way self-efficacy and self-confidence had been operationalized in countless ways for every sport situation studied and noted that Harter's model of perceived competence was limited to children. Therefore, she developed a model and instrumentation for sport confidence (the belief in one's ability to be successful in sport) in an attempt to provide a parsimonious operationalization of self-confidence in sport situations. According to Vealey, this model and instrumentation allow for more consistent predictions of behaviors across different sport situations. Borrowing heavily from Nicholls' and Bandura's theories, she developed an interactional, sport-specific model of self-confidence in which sport confidence is conceptualized into trait (SC-trait) and state (SC-state) components, and also includes a competitive orientation construct to account for individual differences in defining success in sport. This model is presented in Figure 3.

SC-trait represents the perceptions that individuals usually possess about their ability to be successful in sport; SC-state represents the perceptions individuals have at a particular moment about their ability to be successful in sport. However, based on Nicholls' belief that success means different things to different individuals, Vealey recognized a need to include in her model a construct, competitive orientation, as a way to operationalize success. Competitive orientation is a dispositional construct that indicates one's tendency to strive toward achieving a certain type of goal in sport that will demonstrate competence and success. Vealey selected (a) performing well and (b) winning as the goals upon which competitive orientations are based. Performing well is similar in conceptualization to Nicholls' task ability orientation, and winning is similar to his ego-involved ability concept. Even though athletes may pursue both of these goals, through successive sport experiences they may become performance oriented or outcome oriented [87].

Although competitive orientation is not considered a primary construct in the model, both SC-trait and competitive orientation are predicted to influence how athletes perceive factors within an objective sport situation and how they respond with certain SC-state levels. Specifically, SC-state is hypothesized to be positively related to SC-trait and performance orientation and negatively related to outcome orientation. SC-state, in turn, is predicted to be the most important mediator of behavior.

FIGURE 3

Conceptual model of sport confidence. (From Vealey, R. Conceptualization of sport-confidence and competitive orientation: Preliminary investigation and instrument development. J. Sport Psychol. *8:211–246, 1986.)*

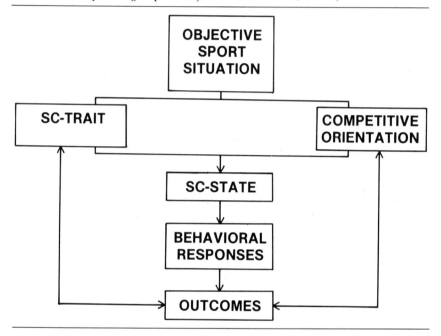

SC-trait and competitive orientation are predicted to influence and be influenced by subjective outcomes. Vealey [87] has used causal attributions for performance, perceived past success, perceived performance rating, and performance satisfaction as measures of subjective outcomes. Performance satisfaction would be what Bandura [5] considers an outcome expectation. SC-trait and performance orientation are hypothesized to be positively related to internal attributions for performance, performance rating, performance satisfaction, and perceived success.

MEASUREMENT OF SPORT CONFIDENCE. Vealey [87] developed three instruments to test the relationships represented in her conceptual model: (a) the Trait Sport-Confidence Inventory (TSCI), (b) the State Sport-Confidence Inventory (SSCI), and (c) the Competitive Orientation Inventory (COI). Both the TSCI and SSCI use a five-point Likert scale for respondents to compare their own self-confidence with the most self-confident athlete they know. Similarly to Bandura [5], Vealey considered the conceptual areas of competence deemed important to sport performance in developing the TSCI and SSCI instruments. Besides physical ability, she noted [86] that abilities such as performing under pressure and being able to make critical decisions were also necessary competencies for success in sport. However, unlike Bandura's measurement of self-efficacy, Vealey considered the competency areas of sport in general in measuring sport confidence rather than conducting a conceptual analysis of each sport under investigation.

One might argue that because one of the dimensions of self-efficacy is generality, some measure of sport, athletic, or exercise self-confidence is warranted to assess how efficacy cognitions can be predictive of action across similar athletic activities. Bandura [6] points out, however, that the use of domain-linked efficacy scales does not mean that one cannot assess generality of perceived capability. He states that "one can derive the degree of generality from multidomain scales, but one cannot extract the patterning of perceived self-efficacy from conglomerate omnibus tests" [6, p. 372].

Researchers interested in sport confidence have also used the Competitive State Anxiety Inventory-2 (CSAI-2) [67] to measure self-confidence in sport situations. In the CSAI-2, self-confidence is viewed as a separate subcomponent of anxiety in addition to cognitive and perceived somatic anxiety. Specifically, self-confidence is thought of as the conceptual opposite of cognitive anxiety. This is in opposition to Bandura's [4] view of self-efficacy, which does not include anxiety in either the definition or the measuring devices. Just because three factors were found in a factor analysis does not mean that confidence is a subcomponent of anxiety or that anxiety is a subcomponent of confidence.

No consistent pattern of results has emerged from using the CSAI-2 measure of self-confidence to predict performance [39, 67, 69]. Gould and his colleagues [38] used an intraindividual analysis in an attempt to correct for the previous inconsistent findings and still did not find the predicted positive relationship between self-confidence and performance. These findings are in accord with a growing body of evidence that the convenience gained by trait approaches is at the cost of explanatory and predictive power [5, 6].

RESEARCH ON THE SPORT CONFIDENCE MODEL. The only published research on the sport confidence model has been Vealey's own preliminary investigation and instrument development [87]. Her validation procedures included five phases of data collection involving 666 high school, college, and adult athletes. The TSCI, SSCI, and COI instruments demonstrated adequate item discrimination, internal consistency, test-retest reliability, content validity, and concurrent validity.

Vealey tested the construct validity of her model using 48 elite gymnasts who were participating in a national meet. The only results that supported her model were that SC-trait and competitive orientation were significant predictors of SC-state as well as of several subjective outcomes. Contrary to her model, precompetition SC-state did not predict performance, nor did a significant correlation emerge between performance and SC-trait. However, performance did predict postcompetition SC-state.

The explanations Vealey provided for SC-state's inability to predict performance were the elite nature of the sample, the importance of this particular competition, and the structure of the competition, which lasted for 2 days. The elite sample, as one might suspect, was very homogeneous and high in reported self-confidence. Vealey proposed that these athletes would not admit to feelings of diffidence. However, using a small and homogeneous sample, whether high or low in ability, makes it difficult to find any predictive relationships. A more heterogeneous group would have provided a better sample with which to test the hypothesized relationships within the model of sport confidence. The facts that the competition lasted for 2 days, and that sport confidence could not be assessed immediately prior to and throughout the competition, also made it difficult to get accurate assessments of SC-state.

Vealey [86] also suggested that perhaps sport performance is too complex to be predicted by SC-state. This is a very important point that sport psychology researchers sometimes fail to recognize in their attempts to explain sport performance solely by psychological variables[30]. In addition, as mentioned earlier, Bandura [1] contends that self-efficacy or confidence affects the choice of activities, effort expenditure, persistence in a given activity, and vulnerability to stress and depression. Competitive sport performance, however, includes more than approach/avoidance behavior, effort expenditure, and persistence; it also includes skills. Those researchers in sport and exercise who have measured self-confidence in terms of how it has influenced the performance behaviors outlined by Bandura have found significant relationships [23, 25–27, 29, 34, 65, 89, 90].

CRITICISMS OF SPORT CONFIDENCE. Vealey's measurement of sport confidence represents an improvement over the physical self-efficacy scale [77] and Harter's physical subscale in that it assesses the generative capabilities necessary for successful performance in most sport situations. However, it does not consider specific sport contexts or assessments of those contexts in the microanalytic approach that will produce the most predictive power. For instance, in ice hockey, an important area of self-confidence is one's perceived ability in making power plays (scoring when the opponents are short-handed). Power play behavior can be assessed directly, which provides a measure that is especially relevant to the behavior being analyzed. As stated previously, measures that are tailored to the domain of functioning being studied have greater predictive power than general trait measures.

Also, in regard to the measurement of sport confidence, Vealey does not provide a rationale for instructing respondents to compare their self-confidence to that of the most self-confident athlete they know. Since people differ in terms of the athletes they know, such a rating procedure can create considerable unsystematic variance. Subjects could appear high or low in confidence, depending on whom they happen to select for comparison. Should the comparison athlete be one the respondent knows personally or a professional that the respondent reads about in the newspaper? Perhaps less variable results would occur if respondents were instructed to make comparisons to an age- and gender-appropriate athlete in terms of sport confidence.

The necessity for including SC-trait in the sport confidence model could be questioned, since the only variable it predicts is SC-state and is therefore redundant. Determining the important sources of SC-state may be more fruitful than assessing athletes' dispositional self-confidence.

In addition, inclusion of the concept of competitive orientation could be called into question. Vealey included the construct of competitive orientation in the model as a way to operationalize individual perceptions of success. However, how one perceives success in one situation may be different from how one perceives it in another. The definition of success may be situationally specific. In using the self-efficacy measurement approach, the questions can be structured to assess comparative confidence (how confident are you that you can beat your opponent?) and/or individual performance-oriented confidence (how confident are you that you can improve your last performance?). A dispositional competitive orientation is not needed.

To test fully the network of relationships hypothesized in the sport confidence model, a path analysis or causal modeling should have been conducted; however, this would have necessitated a larger sample. This type of analysis would better test the necessity for including SC-trait and competitive orientation in the model. In addition, even without a path analysis, a larger sample size is needed for any multivariate analysis.

Movement Confidence
Another model specific to sport and motor performance, one concerning movement confidence, was developed by Griffin and Keogh [42] to describe the feeling of adequacy in a movement situation as both a personal consequence and a mediator in that situation. This model is similar to the models previously reviewed. Griffin and Keogh claim, however, that their model expands these models to include evaluations that an individual makes of sensory experiences directly related to moving. Move-

FIGURE 4

Movement confidence model (From Griffin, N.S., and J.F. Keogh. A model for movement confidence. In Kelso, J.A.S., and J. Clark [eds.]. The Development of Movement Control and Coordination. *New York: Wiley, 1982, pp. 213–236.)*

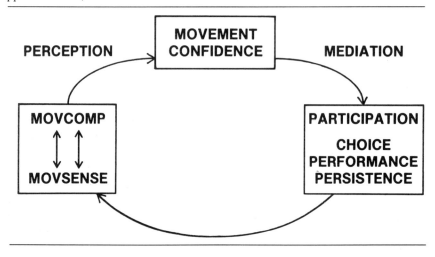

ment confidence is viewed as a consequence of this evaluation process, which then, in turn, mediates participation in a movement situation. This model is presented in Figure 4.

Movement confidence, as a consequence, involves the evaluation of a two-factor personal assessment: movement competence (MOVCOMP) and movement sense (MOVSENSE). MOVCOMP is an individual's perception of personal skill in relation to task demands, and MOVSENSE is an individual's personal expectations of sensory experiences related to moving. These sensory experiences can include muscle aches, breathing hard, sensing of speed, pain of injury, etc. Griffin and Keogh categorize these sensory experiences into two components: personal enjoyment of expected moving sensations and perceived potential for physical harm. Perceived movement competence and perceived movement sense thus interact to produce a sense or state of movement confidence.

Movement confidence as a mediator functions to influence participation choice, participation performance, and participation persistence in a fashion similar to that proposed by Bandura [1]. Participation, in turn, provides information that is added to an individual's experiences for future use in the personal evaluation process.

MEASUREMENT OF MOVEMENT CONFIDENCE. Griffin and Keogh recognized that the difficulty of measuring movement confidence would be in measuring perceived movement competence, personal enjoyment of expected moving sensations, and perceived potential for physical harm as entities separate from each other and separate from movement confidence. They developed a Movement Confidence Inventory [43] in an attempt to identify these components as separate entities and as varying in their contribution to perceived levels of movement confidence. The inventory requires three different ratings to be made for any movement task: level of experience, level of confidence in performing the task, and extent to which each of 22 paired descriptor words (e.g., "safe/dangerous") contributes to one's perceived level of movement confidence. The descriptor words were organized into the three confidence components of competence, enjoyment, and physical harm. Unfortunately, factor analysis of the descriptor words did not reveal three factors organized around the three confidence components, rather, there were simply items loading on one factor, with the partner or opposite word loading on the second factor (e.g., "difficult/easy") [43].

The Movement Confidence Inventory does not provide an external criterion of movement confidence, which Griffin and Keogh [42] indicate is a difficult matter to resolve. One possibility they suggested is to identify observable behavioral manifestations of movement confidence. However, using behavior to measure self-beliefs would entangle one in hopeless circularity. Still, Keogh et al. [58] attempted to develop such an observational measure and appeared to end up measuring behavioral manifestations of fear rather than confidence. For instance, they identified behaviors such as shuffling feet, hesitation, reaching for support, and looking excessively at the instructor. Behavioral indicators of positive levels of movement confidence were much more difficult to observe. Bandura [1] would conceptualize these behavioral manifestations as anxiety or fear co-effects of avoidance behavior resulting from perceived inefficacy. Thus, there would be no fixed relationship between anxiety and actions. In fact, Keogh and his colleagues [58] found that some of the subjects who displayed these anxious behaviors were still able to perform adequately.

CRITICISMS OF MOVEMENT CONFIDENCE. The only research conducted on movement confidence has been in instrumentation development. No research support for the model has been provided. The one study that tried to identify movement competence, personal enjoyment of expected moving sensations, and perceived potential for physical harm as separate entities failed to do so [43].

On conceptual grounds, I see no need for this model in studying self-confidence in movement situations that could not be studied within Bandura's [1] theoretical framework of self-efficacy. Griffin and Keogh [42] believe that movement sense is the unique component that differentiates their model from other conceptions of self-confidence. However, in Bandura's model, expected sensory experiences are implied as a source of confidence information via physiological states. The personal enjoyment of such sensations appears to have more to do with having the incentive to perform the task than it does with having confidence. An increase in enjoyment may increase approach behavior and persistence, but not confidence in one's ability to perform the task more proficiently. In addition, perceived potential for physical harm may be viewed as part of the perceived task demands or task difficulty within Bandura's framework.

Summary and Comparison of Approaches
Self-efficacy theory [1], competence motivation theory [45], and the models of sport confidence [87] and movement confidence [42] have been reviewed in this chapter. All of these models view self-confidence as a critical mediator of motivation and behavior but differ on the origins of self-confidence and how it is measured.

Bandura [1] views self-confidence as specific to particular domains of functioning and as being derived from the cognitive appraisal of diverse sources of information, including enactive and vicarious experiences, social influences, and physiological information. A microanalytic procedure requiring a conceptual analysis of the required generative competencies for a given performance task is used and offers the most predictive power in explaining behavior. On the other hand, in Harter's [45] developmental framework, which is confined to children, self-confidence develops gradually through prolonged transactions with one's surroundings and evaluation reinforcement of others, and is considered to have a multidimensional trait orientation. Harter's measurement of the construct is psychometrically sound and derived from developmental theory, but it does not consider contextual factors within specific performance situations. Her measure also forces the child to assess self-confidence in relation to peers when, according to Nicholls [72] and evidence from sport research [53], the process by which children judge their capabilities changes with age.

Given Bandura's situationally specific model and Harter's developmental model, the models of sport confidence [87] and movement confidence [42] seem unwarranted for studying self-confidence in sport. Vealey's [87] constructs of trait sport confidence and competitive orientation, from which situational sport confidence is derived, do not add any new conceptual dimensions. Furthermore, the comparison "to the most confident athlete you know," used in the measurement of sport confidence, creates considerable unsystematic variance and thus does not provide the parsimonious operationalization of self-confidence that was intended. Regardless of the countless ways that self-confidence (or self-efficacy) has been operationalized for every sport situation studied, the results have been very consistent in finding situationally specific self-confidence to be significantly related to performance.

The research from the sport literature provides clear evidence that a significant relationship exists between self-confidence and performance. This evidence spans different tasks, measures of self-confidence, and major theoretical paradigms [1, 45]. In terms of causal interactions between self-confidence and performance, evidence from sport shows that self-confidence is both an effect and a cause in relation to performance [29, 31, 35, 68]. However, in the athletic domain, other factors, such as prior performance and behavior [29, 32, 35, 68], are also instrumental in influencing performance. Self-confidence, if considered as a common mechanism mediating behavior, should not be expected to fully explain human behavior [4], particularly the complex behavior of sport performance [86].

CONCLUSION

This chapter has compared the major theoretical frameworks used to examine self-confidence in sport and physical activity settings. Both Bandura's model and Harter's model (for studying motivational behavior in youth sports) appear to be viable theoretical frameworks in which to study self-confidence in sport, even though modifications will be required to explain the complex nature of sport performance. Variables such as previous performance, affective self-evaluation, goal setting, and physiological states (e.g., mood or fitness) may exert a direct influence on sport performance. In studying competence motivation in children, situational variables may need to be given greater consideration. The inclusion of these additional determinants should increase the amount of variance in athletic performance that can be explained as, was the case in my model on diving performance [29, 31, 35].

Much of the sport research has examined self-confidence in relation to actual sport performance in terms of skill rather than in terms of the motivational behavior actually specified by the theories, such as persistence or mastery attempts, choice of activities or skills, and effort expended. These behaviors are certainly contributors to skillful performance and should be given more attention in the study of self-confidence in sport.

Other areas that deserve attention in Bandura's model are the generalizability of self-confidence in terms of the number of domains of functioning within a sport (e.g., types of shots in golf) or within exercise, the nonmovement domains of confidence required in exercise and sport (e.g., psychological skills), how people process multidimensional confidence information, the study of self-confidence across a number of situations (e.g., over the course of a season), and the study of team confidence in relation to self-confidence. In terms of the generality of self-confidence, examination of the relative contributions of generality, level, and strength to overall performance would help determine where to focus intervention studies. In the nonmovement aspects of self-confidence, belief in control over one's intrusive thoughts, for instance, may be an important confidence component in the area of exercise behavior and sport performance. Bandura [5] proposes that self-confidence influences thought patterns, as well as behavior, and research has demonstrated its applicability in anxiety-provoking situations [57].

Scant research has been conducted on how people process multidimensional confidence information [5]. The importance of different types of information may vary across different types of activities and situations. In some sport and exercise situations, physiological information may be a more pertinent source of confidence information than previous performance. In processing multidimensional information, people may misjudge or ignore relevant information in trying to integrate it [5]. Results from this research may also have implications for the type and amount of confidence information provided to sport performers and exercise patients.

As mentioned earlier in this chapter, in many real-life sport situations, people perform with some variation in circumstances (e.g., different competitions) and temporal intervals. Studying confidence judgments across a number of competitions or situations may be the most informative paradigm for testing the relative contribution of self-confidence, performance, and other possible mediating variables.

All of the studies cited in this chapter have examined self-confidence in relation to individual athletic or exercise performance. In team sports, however, many of the challenges and difficulties athletes face reflect team problems requiring sustained team efforts to produce successful performance. Drawing from Bandura's [5] concept of collective efficacy, perceived team confidence should influence what athletes choose to do as a team, how much effort they put into it, and their staying power when team efforts fail to produce results. Confidence in one's team to be able to produce the required performance may be just as important as confidence in oneself. Similarly, coaches' perceived efficacy may have an important impact on team performance. Evidence that managerial self-efficacy affects organizational performance is especially relevant to this issue [100, 101].

Finally, in Harter's model, attention should be directed to examining children's self-confidence in actual sport and physical activity situations [24]. Bandura's concept of situationally specific self-confidence could be examined in relation to children's perceived physical competence. This interactional strategy may provide more power in explaining children's sport competence motivation.

REFERENCES

1. Bandura, A. Self-efficacy: Toward a unifying theory of behavioral change. *Psychol. Rev.* 84:191–215, 1977.
2. Bandura, A. Reflections on self-efficacy. In S. Rachman, (ed.). *Advances in Behavior Research and Therapy*, Vol. 1. Oxford: Pergamon Press, 1978, pp. 237–269.
3. Bandura, A. Self-efficacy in human agency. *Am. Psychol.* 37:122–147, 1982.
4. Bandura, A. Recycling misconceptions of perceived self-efficacy. *Cog. Ther. Res.* 8:231–255, 1984.
5. Bandura, A. *Social Foundation of Thought and Action: A Social Cognitive Theory.* Englewood Cliffs, N.J.: Prentice-Hall, 1986.
6. Bandura, A. The explanatory and predictive scope of self-efficacy theory. J. Soc. Clin. Psychol. 4:359–373, 1986.
7. Bandura, A. Self-efficacy mechanisms in physiological activation and health-promoting behavior. In J. Madden IV, S. Matthysse, and J. Barchas (eds.). *Adaptation, Learning and Affect.* New York: Raven Press, 1986.
8. Bandura, A., and D. Cervone. Self-evaluative and self-efficacy mechanisms governing the motivational effects of goal systems. *J. Pers. Soc. Psychol.* 45:1017–1028, 1983.
9. Bandura, A., and D.H. Schunk. Cultivating competence, self-efficacy, and intrinsic interest through proximal self-motivation. *J. Pers. Soc. Psychol.* 41:586–598, 1981.
10. Barling, J., and M. Abel. Self-efficacy beliefs and tennis performance. *Cog. Ther. Res.* 7:265–272, 1983.
11. Betz, N.E., and G. Hackett. The relationship of career-related self-efficacy expectations to perceived career options in college women and men. *J. Counsel. Psychol.* 28:399–410, 1981.
12. Biglan, A. A behavior-analytic critique of Bandura's self-efficacy theory. *Behavior Analyst* 10:1–15, 1987.
13. Bird, A.M., and J.N. Brame. Self versus team attributions: A test of the "I'm ok, but the team's so-so" phenomenon. *Res. Q.* 49:260–268, 1978.
14. Borkovec, T.D. Self-efficacy: Cause or reflection of behavioral change. In S. Rachman (ed.). *Advances in Behavior Research and Therapy.* Oxford: Pergamon Press, 1978, pp. 163–170.
15. Brustad, R., and M.R. Weiss. Competence perceptions and sources of worry in high, medium, and low competitive trait-anxious young athletes. *J. Sport Psychol.* 9:97–105, 1987.
16. Burton, D., and R. Martens. Pinned by their own goals: An exploratory investigation into why kids drop out of wrestling. *J. Sport Psychol.* 8:183–197, 1986.
17. Connell, J.P. *A Multidimensional Measure of Children's Perceptions of Control.* Denver: University of Denver Press, 1980.
18. Corbin, C.B. Sex of subject, sex of opponent, and opponent ability as factors affecting self-confidence in a competitive situation. *J. Sport Psychol.* 3:265–270, 1981.
19. Corbin, C.B., D.M. Landers, D.L. Feltz, and K. Senior. Sex differences in performance estimates: Female's lack of confidence vs. male boastfulness. *Res. Q. Exerc. Sport* 54:407–410, 1983.
20. Corbin, C.B., D.R. Laurie, C. Gruger, and B. Smiley. Vicarious success experience as a factor influencing self-confidence, attitudes and physical activity of adult women. *J. Teach. Phys. Ed.* 4:17–23, 1984.

21. Corbin, C.B., and C. Nix. Sex-typing of physical activities and success predictions of children before and after cross-sex competition. *J. Sport Psychol.* 1:43–52, 1979.

22. Deci, E.L., and R.M. Ryan. *Intrinsic Motivation and Self-Determination in Human Behavior.* New York: Plenum Press, 1985.

23. Desharnais, R., J. Bouillon, and G. Godin. Self-efficacy and outcome expectations as determinants of exercise adherence. *Psychol. Rep.* 59:1155–1159, 1986.

24. Duda, J.L. Toward a developmental theory of children's motivation in sport. *J. Sport Psychol.* 9:130–145, 1987.

25. Ewart, C.K., K.J. Stewart, R.E. Gillilan, and M.H. Kelemen. Self-efficacy mediates strength gains during circuit weight training in men with coronary artery disease. *Med. Sci. Sports Exerc.* 18:531–540, 1986.

26. Ewart, C.K., K.J. Stewart, R.E. Gillilan, M.H. Kelemen, S.A. Valenti, J.D. Manley, and M.D. Kelemen. Usefulness of self-efficacy in predicting overexertion during programmed exercise in coronary artery disease. *Am. J. Cardiol.* 57:557–561, 1986.

27. Ewart, C.K., C.B. Taylor, L.B. Reese, and R.F. DeBusk. Effects of early postmyocardial infarction exercise testing on self-perception and subsequent physical activity. *Am. J. Cardiol.* 51:1076–1080, 1983.

28. Eysenck, H.J. Expectations as causal elements in behavioral change. In S. Rachman (ed.). *Advances in Behavior Research and Therapy.* Oxford: Pergamon Press, 1978, pp. 171–175.

29. Feltz, D.L. Path analysis of the causal elements in Bandura's theory of self-efficacy and an anxiety-based model of avoidance behavior. *J. Pers. Soc. Psychol.* 42:764–781, 1982.

30. Feltz, D.L. Future directions in theoretical research in sport psychology: From applied psychology toward sport science. In J. Skinner (ed.). *Future Directions in Exercise/Sport Research.* Champaign, Ill.: Human Kinetics Press, in press.

31. Feltz, D.L. Gender differences in the causal elements of self-efficacy on a high avoidance motor task. *J. Sport Psychol.* in press.

32. Feltz, D.L., and E.W. Brown. Perceived competence in soccer skills among young soccer players. *J. Sport Psychol.* 6:385–394, 1984.

33. Feltz, D.L., D.M. Landers, and U. Raeder. Enhancing self-efficacy in high avoidance motor tasks: A comparison of modeling techniques. *J. Sport Psychol.* 1:112–122, 1979.

34. Feltz, D.L., S. Marcotullio, and C. Fitzgerald. The effects of different forms of in vivo emotive imagery on self-efficacy and competitive endurance performance. Paper presented at the North American Society for the Psychology of Sport and Physical Activity, Gulfport, Miss., 1985.

35. Feltz, D.L., and D.A. Mugno. A replication of the path analysis of the causal elements in Bandura's theory of self-efficacy and the influence of autonomic perception. *J. Sport Psychol.* 5:263–277, 1983.

36. Feltz, D.L., and L. Petlichkoff. Perceived competence among interscholastic sport participants and dropouts. *Can. J. Appl. Sport Sci.* 8:231–235, 1983.

37. Gayton, W.F., G.R. Matthews, and G.N. Burchstead. An investigation of the validity of the physical self-efficacy scale in predicting marathon performance. *Percept. Mot. Skills* 63:752–754, 1986.

38. Gould, D., L. Petlichkoff, J. Simons, and M. Vevera. Relationship between Competitive State Anxiety Inventory-2 subscale scores and pistol shooting performance. *J. Sport Psychol.* 9:33–42, 1987.

39. Gould, D., L. Petlichkoff, and R.S. Weinberg. Antecedents of temporal changes in, and relationships between, CSAI-2 subcomponents. *J. Sport Psychol.* 6:289–304, 1984.

40. Gould, D., and M. Weiss. Effect of model similarity and model self-talk on self-efficacy in muscular endurance. *J. Sport Psychol.* 3:17–29, 1981.

41. Gould, D., M.R. Weiss, and R. Weinberg. Psychological characteristics of successful and nonsuccessful Big-Ten Wrestlers. *J. Sport Psychol.* 3:69–81, 1981.
42. Griffin, N.S., and J.F. Keogh. A model for movement confidence. In J.A.S. Kelso and J. Clark (eds.). *The Development of Movement Control and Coordination.* New York: Wiley, 1982, pp. 213–236.
43. Griffin, N.S., J.F. Keogh, and R. Maybee. Performer perceptions of movement confidence. *J. Sport Psychol.* 6:395–407, 1984.
44. Hackett, G., and N.E. Betz. A self-efficacy approach to the career development of women. *J. Vocat. Behav.* 18:326–339, 1981.
45. Harter, S. Effectance motivation reconsidered: Toward a developmental model. *Hum. Dev.* 21:34–64, 1978.
46. Harter, S. The development of competence motivation in the mastery of cognitive and physical skills: Is there still a place for joy? In G.C. Roberts and D.M. Landers (eds.). *Psychology of Motor Behavior and Sport—1980.* Champaign, Ill.: Human Kinetics Press, 1981, pp. 3–29.
47. Harter, S. A new self-report scale of intrinsic versus extrinsic orientation in the classroom: Motivational and informational components. *Dev. Psychol.* 17:300–312, 1981.
48. Harter, S. *Manual for the Self-Perception Profile for Children.* Denver: University of Denver Press, 1985.
49. Harter, S., and R. Pike. *The Pictorial Scale of Perceived Competence and Social Acceptance for Young Children.* Denver: University of Denver Press, 1983.
50. Highlen, P.S., and B.B. Bennett. Psychological characteristics of successful and nonsuccessful elite wrestlers: An exploratory study. *J. Sport Psychol.* 1:123–137, 1979.
51. Hogan, P.I., and J.P. Santomier. Effect of mastering swim skills on older adults' self-efficacy. *Res. Q. Exerc. Sport* 55:294–296, 1984.
52. Horn, T.S. Coaches' feedback and changes in children's perceptions of their physical competence. *J. Educ. Psychol.* 77:174–186, 1985.
53. Horn, T., and C. Hasbrook. Informational components influencing children's perceptions of their physical competence. In M. Weiss and D. Gould (eds.). *Sport for Children and Youth.* Champaign, Ill.: Human Kinetics Press, 1986, pp. 81–88.
54. Kaplan, R.M., C.J. Atkins, and S. Reinsch. Specific efficacy expectations mediate exercise compliance in patients with COPD. *Health Psychol.* 3:223–242, 1984.
55. Kavanagh, D., and S. Hausfeld. Physical performance and self-efficacy under happy and sad moods. *J. Sport Psychol.* 8:112–123, 1986.
56. Kazdin, A.E. Conceptual and assessment issues raised by self-efficacy theory. In S. Rachman (ed.). *Advances in Behavior Research and Therapy,* Vol. 1. Oxford: Pergamon Press, 1978, pp. 177–185.
57. Kent, G., and R. Gibbons. Self-efficacy and the control of anxious cognitions. *J. Behav. Ther. Exp. Psychiatry* 18:33–40, 1987.
58. Keogh, J.F., N.S. Griffin, and R. Spector. Observer perceptions of movement confidence. *Res. Q. Exerc. Sport* 52:465–473, 1981.
59. Kirsch, I. "Microanalytic" analyses of efficacy expectations as predictors of performance. *Cog. Ther. Res.* 4:259–262, 1980.
60. Kirsch, I. Self-efficacy and expectancy: Old wine with new labels. *J. Pers. Soc. Psychol.* 49:824–830, 1985.
61. Kirsch, I., and C.V. Wickless. Concordance rates between self-efficacy and approach behavior are redundant. *Cog. Ther. Res.* 7:179–188, 1983.
62. Kleiber, D.A. Of joy, competence, and significant others in children's sports. In G.C. Roberts and D.M. Landers (eds.). *Psychology of Motor Behavior and Sport—1980.* Champaign, Ill.: Human Kinetics Press, 1981, pp. 30–36.
63. Klint, K.A. Participation motives and self-perceptions of current and former athletes

in youth gymnastics. Unpublished master's thesis, University of Oregon, Eugene, 1985.

64. Klint, K.A., and M.R. Weiss. Perceived competence and motives for participating in youth sports: A test of Harter's competence motivation theory. *J. Sport Psychol.* 9:55–65, 1987.

65. Lee, C. Self-efficacy as a predictor of performance in competitive gymnastics. *J. Sport Psychol.* 4:405–409, 1982.

66. Mahoney, M.J., and M. Avener. Psychology of the elite athlete: An exploratory study. *Cog. Ther. Res.* 1:135–141, 1977.

67. Martens, R., D. Burton, R.S. Vealey, L.A. Bump, and D. Smith. Cognitive and somatic dimensions of competitive anxiety. Paper presented at the North American Society for the Psychology of Sport and Physical Activity meeting, University of Maryland, College Park, Md., 1982.

68. McAuley, E. Modeling and self-efficacy: A test of Bandura's model. *J. Sport Psychol.* 7:283–295, 1985.

69. McAuley, E. State anxiety: Antecedent or result of sport performance? *J. Sport Behav.* 8:71–77, 1985.

70. McAuley, E., and D. Gill. Reliability and validity of the physical self-efficacy scale in a competitive sport setting. *J. Sport Psychol.* 5:410–418, 1983.

71. Nelson, L., and M. Furst. An objective study of the effects of expectation on competitive sport setting. *J. Psychol.* 81:69–72, 1972.

72. Nicholls, J.G. Achievement motivation: Conceptions of ability, subjective experience, task choice and performance. *Psychol. Rev.* 91:328–346, 1984.

73. O'Leary, A. Self-efficacy and health. *Behav. Res. Ther.* 23:437–451, 1985.

74. Roberts, G.C. Achievement motivation in sport. In R.L. Terjung (ed.). *Exercise and Sport Sciences Reviews.* Philadelphia: Franklin Institute Press, 1982, pp. 236–269.

75. Roberts, G.C., D.A. Kleiber, and J.L. Duda. An analysis of motivation in children's sports: The role of perceived competence in participation. *J. Sport Psychol.* 3:206–216, 1981.

76. Rotter, J.B. *Social Learning and Clinical Psychology.* Englewood Cliffs, N.J.: Prentice-Hall, 1954.

77. Ryckman, R.M., M.A. Robbins, B. Thornton, and P. Cantrell. Development and validation of a physical self-efficacy scale. *J. Pers. Soc. Psychol.* 42:891–900, 1982.

78. Scanlan, T.K., and M.W. Passer. Determinants of competitive performance expectancies of young male athletes. *J. Pers.* 49:60–74, 1981.

79. Scanlan, T.K., and M.W. Passer. Factors influencing the competitive performance expectancies of young female athletes. *J. Sport Psychol.* 1:212–220, 1979.

80. Schunk, D.H. Self-efficacy perspective on achievement behavior. *Educ. Psychol.* 19:48–58, 1984.

81. Sonstroem, R.J. Exercise and self-esteem. In R.L. Terjung (ed.). *Exercise and Sport Sciences Reviews.* Lexington, Mass.: Collamore Press, 1984, pp. 123–155.

82. Taylor, C.B., A. Bandura, C.K. Ewart, N.H. Miller, and R.F. Debusk. Raising spouse's and patient's perceptions of his cardiac capabilities following a myocardial infarction. *Am. J. Cardiol.* 55:635–638, 1985.

83. Telch, M.J., A Bandura, P. Vinciguerra, S. Agras, and A.L. Stout. Social demand and congruence between self-efficacy and performance. *Behav. Ther.* 13:694–701, 1983.

84. Ulrich, B.D. Perceptions of physical competence, motor competence, and participation in organized sport: Their interrelationships in young children. *Res. Q. Exerc. Sport* 58:57–67, 1987.

85. Vallerand, R.J., E.L. Deci, and R.M. Ryan. Intrinsic motivation in sport. In K.B. Pandolf (ed.). *Exercise and Sport Sciences Review,* Vol. 15. New York: Macmillan Co., 1987, pp. 389–425.

86. Vealey, R.S. The conceptualization and measurement of sport confidence. Unpublished Ph.D. dissertation, University of Illinois, 1984.

87. Vealey, R. Conceptualization of sport-confidence and competitive orientation: Preliminary investigation and instrument development. *J. Sport Psychol.* 8:221–246, 1986.

88. Weinberg, R. Relationship between self-efficacy and cognitive strategies in enhancing endurance performance. *Int. J. Sport Psychol.* 17:280–293, 1986.

89. Weinberg, R., D. Gould, and A. Jackson. Expectations and performance: An empirical test of Bandura's self-efficacy theory. *J. Sport Psychol.* 1:320–331, 1979.

90. Weinberg, R.S., D. Gould, D. Yukelson, and A. Jackson. The effect of preexisting and manipulated self-efficacy on a competitive muscular endurance task. *J. Sport Psychol.* 3:345–354, 1981.

91. Weinberg, R.S., M. Sinardi, and A. Jackson. Effect of bar height and modeling on anxiety, self-confidence and gymnastic performance. *Int. Gymnast.* 2:11–13, 1982.

92. Weinberg, R.S., D. Yukelson, and A. Jackson. Effect of public and private efficacy expectations on competitive performance. *J. Sport Psychol.* 2:340–349, 1980.

93. Weiss, M.R. Self-esteem and achievement in children's sport and physical activity. In D. Gould and M. Weiss (eds.). *Advances in Pediatric Sport Sciences*, Vol. 2: *Behavioral Issues*. Champaign, Ill.: Human Kinetics Press, 1987, pp. 87–119.

94. Weiss, M.R., B.J. Bredemeier, and R.M. Shewchuk. An intrinsic/extrinsic motivation scale for the youth sport setting: A confirmatory factor analysis. *J. Sport Psychol.* 7:75–91, 1985.

95. Weiss, M.R., B.J. Bredemeier, and R. Shewchuk. The dynamics of perceived competence, perceived control, and motivational orientation in youth sport. In M. Weiss and D. Gould (eds.). *Sport for Children and Youths*. Champaign, Ill.: Human Kinetics Press, 1986, pp. 89–102.

96. White, R. Motivation reconsidered: The concept of competence. *Psychol. Rev.* 66:297–323, 1959.

97. Wilkes, R.L., and J.J. Summers. Cognitions, mediating variables, and strength performance. *J. Sport Psychol.* 6:351–359, 1984.

98. Wolpe, J. Self-efficacy theory and psychotherapeutic change: A square peg for a round role. In S. Rachman (ed.). *Advances in Behavioral Research and Therapy*. Oxford: Pergamon Press, 1978, pp. 231–236.

99. Woolfolk, R.L., S.M. Murphy, D. Gottesfeld, and D. Aitken. Effects of mental rehearsal of task motor activity and mental depiction of task outcome on motor skill performance. *J. Sport Psychol.* 7:191–197, 1985.

100. Wood, R.E., and A. Bandura. Impact of conceptions of ability on complex organizational decision-making. Unpublished manuscript, Stanford University, Stanford, Calif.

101. Wood, R.E., A. Bandura, and T. Bailey. Mechanisms governing organizational productivity in complex decision-making environments. Unpublished manuscript, Stanford University, Stanford, Calif.

102. Wurtele, S.K. Self-efficacy and athletic performance; A review. *J. Soc. Clin. Psychol.* 4:290–301, 1986.

103. Yan Lan, L., and D.L. Gill. The relationships among self-efficacy, stress responses, and a cognitive feedback manipulation. *J. Sport Psychol.* 6:227–238, 1984.

14
Discourses on the Gender/Sport Relationship: From Women in Sport to Gender Relations

SUSAN J. BIRRELL, Ph.D.

INTRODUCTION

Women's place in the world of sport has always provided grounds for fascinating and enlightening study, whether the proper focus was conceived of as "women in sport" or, more recently, "gender relations and sport." As participants, women have historically been less involved than men and involved in different ways than men. However, it was not until the past 20 years that a few scholars—mostly women—began to question the disparity between men's and women's rates of participation, to investigate the pattern and sources of the differences between men's and women's styles of involvement, and to theorize about the cultural meaning of women's relative absence from sport.

Since 1965, the development of physical education as an academic discipline and the growth of the sociology of sport as an academic specialty have provided legitimacy to the study of sport as a significant social phenomenon, yet little of that scholarly attention has been diverted to the analysis of women in sport. For example, a survey of the contents of six prominent journals and three important conferences in sociology of sport from 1966 to 1982 found that only 6% of the studies focused on women athletes, while an additional 5% made "purposive comparisons" of male and female athletes [24]. As a result of this lack of attention, we know less about the relationship between women and sport than we should.

One factor contributing to the lack of research is the relative scarcity of women scholars. Currently, only 36% of the membership of the North American Society for the Sociology of Sport is female, and this proportion is apparently not high enough to counterbalance the general lack of attention to women's issues by male scholars.

The purpose of this chapter is to trace the development of our understanding of the relationship between women and sport and to evaluate the current status of our knowledge of that relationship. In part, this chapter provides an intellectual history of the development of the field referred to as "women in sport."

This chapter is based on the premise that academic understandings

459

of women athletes and societal treatment of them are dialectically related. Research might dispel myths about women's participation, thus changing societal attitudes. But researchers themselves are often subject to unconscious assumptions that, if unexamined, affect our work in profound ways. For example, the orienting questions we ask already contain within them theories of women, sport, and society and assumptions about the proper relationships among them. Faced with the reality of women's lower rates of participation in sport, we may ask "Why aren't women more involved in sport?" or "Why aren't women more interested in sport?" These questions elicit a far different research program than one that sees the same patterns and asks "Why are women excluded from sport?" A still different approach is evident in the questions "What is the nature of the relationship between women and sport?" or "Why is the relationship between women and sport problematic?" or "Why do women persist in an activity that has tried to exclude them?" A central thesis of this chapter is that the development of the field is tied to such orienting questions; since questions suggest theory, our ability to ask provoking questions can either enlighten or limit our knowledge.

This chapter has certain historical, geographical, and disciplinary boundaries. Historically, it focuses on the past 25 years, when physical educators formally began to question women's exclusion from sport. Scholarly attention to women in sport developed in three stages that roughly parallel the decades: a slow, tentative start from 1960 to 1971, a period of groping for identity and direction from 1971 to 1980, and the current trend, evident since 1980, toward greater theoretical sophistication and diversity. This chapter is organized to highlight these stages of development.

Geographically, the focus is on the experience of women in sport in North America, with some reference to the work of British scholars writing in the cultural studies tradition. Of course, we will not approach a comprehensive analysis of women in sport until we understand the varieties of cultural experiences surrounding sport for women throughout the world. Such a comprehensive analysis awaits our attention.

In terms of disciplinary boundaries, the focus is on the analysis of women's place in sport as a social phenomenon. Particularly in North America, that analysis has been generated by professionals and scholars within the field of physical education. The first to attend to the issue were professional women physical educators who were concerned about women's limited opportunities in sport. They were joined in the 1970s by the newly trained scholars. Most of the research reviewed here is by sport sociologists; however, earlier work had a decidedly psychological flavor to it, and some recent work blurs the boundaries between sociology and history, with excellent results. Indeed, one might argue that the growth of our knowledge about the meanings of women's sport experiences has increased in theoretical sophistication as we have turned from psychological to cultural models.

Finally, this chapter is limited by the tendency of the field to focus on the experiences of young, white, middle-class women. Until we have expanded our scope to include the experiences of all women, regardless of age, race, class, body size, or sexual preference, we cannot approach a comprehensive analysis of the meaning of women's relationship to sport. This bias is the single greatest flaw in an otherwise progressive field.

A HERITAGE OF EXCLUSION: SPORT FOR WOMEN THROUGH 1960

The proper place of women in sport has always been circumscribed by societal attitudes toward women, filtered through such elements as health, beauty, femininity, women's distinctive nature, physical capabilities, and prevailing ideologies of female behavior. At the turn of the century, as sport became increasingly popular for men, woman's proper place was on the sidelines, cheering her man on to victory. If she herself actively participated, she was expected to do so within the bounds of middle-class taste, and there was to be nothing strenuous, competitive, or, indeed, particularly active about it.

Research has documented the successful exclusion of middle-class women from sport: The ideals of femininity protected her from the strain of physical exertion in sport, thus saving her beauty, her health, her reputation as a lady, and the reproductive machinery of the nation. The physical exertion demanded by housework and by labor outside the home was somehow perfectly acceptable, particularly for working-class women, women of color, or farm women who "escaped" the strictures of the middle-class cult of true womanhood [24, 220], yet we know far less about the leisure pursuits of women of color or working-class women. Works like Peiss' *Cheap Amusements* [168] are beginning to fill the gaps.

Some women persisted in their love for sport, refusing to be limited by polite social arrangements. The few stars who emerged were in the more genteel sports of tennis (Helen Wills Moody) and golf (Glenna Collett). Not until the 1920s was the American public ready to accept active women heroines such as Amelia Earhart, but their acceptance was given only so long as these women could be clearly seen as exceptions [199], and the image had to be just right. For example, despite her exceptional athletic talent, Babe Didrickson Zaharias was never fully accepted by the public because of her unladylike demeanor.

Women's involvement was kept in check primarily by public reaction, but the public good was aided to some extent by an interesting group of allies—professional women physical educators. They were convinced that it was in women's best interests to modify their sporting activities to minimize physical overexertion, to preserve a feminine appearance and manner, and to avoid the abuses of the male sport system. Because their field remained closely aligned with medicine, they were particularly influenced by medical opinion about women's inability to endure strenuous physical activity. And they were dismayed by the increasing elitism, commercialism, and violence in men's sport. Their single-minded determination to control the conditions of sport for women and their unflagging pride in the alternative they provided are evident in their writings [97, 139, 140, 159, 185, 187, 202–204, 228].

As the century progressed and as public interest in Olympic sport grew, the Amateur Athletic Union and the National Amateur Athletic Federation became increasingly interested in developing female talent, particularly in track and field. The women physical educators were staunchly opposed to this highly competitive venture. By 1923, a jurisdictional battle was brewing over women's sport. At Lou Henry Hoover's famous 1923 Conference on Athletics and Physical Recreation for Girls and Women, women physical educators formed the Women's Division of the National Amateur Athletic Federation and adopted the platform that set the agenda for women's high school and college sport for almost 50 years [228]. The platform called for a program of mass participation that eliminated such evils as selfishness, extrinsic rewards, sensational publicity, gate receipts, travel, and exploitation of athletes for the sake of the fans [228]. In the words that were to become the motto for the playday era, they advocated "a game for every girl and every girl in a game." From 1923 through the 1960s, that ideology remained securely in place.

Thus, prior to 1960, our understanding of women athletes was really a misunderstanding based on two sources: notions about what was "good" for women, proscribed by the male medical establishment on the basis of erroneous and often self-serving "evidence" [63, 141], and an ideology of femininity that enforced societal prescriptions about proper behavior for women. Together these interdependent forces produced an image of women as weak, fragile, timid, and unsuited for sport, and they celebrated her beauty and passive femininity. This feminine ideal and its incongruence with male-defined sporting practices was reinforced by physical educators throughout the 1960s.

DISCOVERING WOMEN IN SPORT

Some rumblings of discontent were lurking below the surface during the 1950s, for in the 1960s a growing awareness of the restrictions of past practices began to surface in the writing of prominent women such as Elizabeth Halsey [97] and Margaret Coffey [48]. Their articles are best described as musings on the state of women's sport programs; while they clearly saw past practices as a constraint on the present, they did not speak in outraged tones, nor did they call for reform.

As physical education began to evolve into an academic field, leading professionals like Celeste Ulrich [216] and Madge Phillips [170, 171] recognized the potential for analyzing the social aspects of women's sport experiences. Their articles were understandably tentative. They knew there was something there, but they did not yet have the analytical tools to explore it.

The classic statement of the period was Eleanor Metheny's *Connotations of Movement in Sport and Dance* [160], a work that critically appraised the ideology that worked to keep women from full, meaningful participation in sport. Metheny interpreted Olympic events "as symbolic formulations of man's conception of himself as a consequential force within the universe" [160, p. 43], and in her chapter on "The Feminine Image in Sports," she argued that such "symbolic formulations" and "mythic images of the female role" actually create notions of appropriate female activity that work as powerful social sanctions. Based on the activities deemed acceptable for girls by Olympic standards, Metheny was able to show precisely what physical skills were categorically unacceptable; generally unacceptable or acceptable for a minority of athletes; or generally acceptable. Her focus on these larger social issues, and her reliance on her own ability to read the meanings in social practices, make her work more contemporaneous with the work of the 1980s than of the 1960s. Even today, after dramatic increases in the number of high school girls and college women involved in sport programs, Metheny's framework provides an insightful analysis into the cultural pressures on women athletes.

COMING OF AGE IN THE 1970s

The decade of the 1970s is marked by unevenness in focus and quality as the field struggled first for identity and then for legitimacy. Developments must be seen against a backdrop of other significant social forces, including the women's movement, which had both a political and an intellectual effect on the field of women in sport, and legislative and institutional changes such as the formation of the Association for Intercollegiate Athletics for Women in 1971, the passage of Title IX in 1972, the creation of the Women's Sport Foundation in 1974, and the founding of *WomenSport* magazine in 1974. These forces helped to bring about a dramatic increase in the opportunities for girls and women. Participation rates for girls and women in sport exploded [166, 229], and the field struggled to understand and explain the massive changes that were occurring.

At the 1973 American Association for Health, Physical Education and Recreation (AAHPER) convention at Minneapolis, for example, the implications of these changes were so uncertain that "Even though the official convention theme was 'Unity through Diversity,' every session . . . somehow commented on women's role in society and her desire to participate in athletics. . . . For many in attendance, 'Women's Athletics' seemed to be the theme" [120, unnumbered]. As a result, the Division of Girls and Women in Sport (DGWS) published a monograph composed of papers from the convention, entitled *Women's Athletics: Coping with Controversy* [120]. The topics included historical accounts [198, 205] and calls for reform [58, 66, 117, 186].

In addition to these changes in sport for women, physical education was transforming itself from primarily a profession to an academic discipline. Sport studies and its constituent subdisciplines—sociology of sport, history of sport, psychology of sport, and anthropology of play—were seeking their own intellectual definition and searching for appropriate methodologies and theories from their parent disciplines. As those concerned with focusing on women's experiences in sport sought models, they turned to these new fields, and they were particularly attracted to psychological models.

Psychological Models
The work of the early 1970s was dominated by psychological rather than sociological analyses of women's place in sport. Typical studies focused on attitudes toward female athletes [19, 85, 87, 102, 156], personality traits of female athletes [128, 153, 154, 164, 169, 224], and motivation for involvement [20, 56, 231, 233, 234]. None of these traditions offered a particularly profound conception of the complexity of this issue. Attitude studies are basically descriptive and offer little insight into the production or effects of such images. Research on personality traits, and to a lesser extent motivation, is weakened by conceptual and methodological flaws.* As a whole, the research is undependable: While one study may find "significant differences" between athletes and nonathletes, these results are likely to be inconsistent with the findings of other studies of a similar population. Thus, no clear personality or motivational pattern can be found for female athletes, for team or individual athletes, or for athletes in specific sports [22].

The conceptual problems are equally troubling. Trait research isolates the individual from any social context by assuming that internal, stable traits control behavior. Even the more recent interactional models of personality and motivation, which take account of the individual and

---

* Methodologically, the research suffers from problems of poor operationalization, inadequate sampling, use of inappropriate instruments, poor statistical analysis, generalizing beyond the data, and inferring causal relationships from weak correlational patterns (see [26]).

the social context, trivialize that complex relationship by reducing it to mathematical formulae. By focusing on traits and motives as "stable and internal" dimensions, the research perpetuates a simplistic model of the relationship between women and sport, locating women's "problem" within women themselves, blaming them for their lack of motivation or lack of appropriate personality traits rather than exploring the cultural constraints on behavior.

For a short while, the theory of fear of success was explored as a promising explanation for women's absence from sport [20, 56]. That theory proposes that women avoid achievement situations such as sport because they have been given conflicting messages about their own achievement. However, research on fear of success also contains serious methodological flaws. The inventories probably measure reactions to inappropriate sex role behavior rather than a stable motive; there is no proof that a fear of success actually exists or that it pertains mainly to women; and the approach falsely implies that women's lower rates of participation are their own fault [22].

The most influential topics of this early period focused on notions of sex roles. These traditions had an impact on our understanding of the relationship between women and sport that is still felt today. Particularly prominent was the research on role conflict, a theory proposed by Dorothy Harris. Harris argued that few women were involved in sport because they experienced debilitating conflict over their roles as athletes and females [103, 105, 106].

Harris [103] and Tyler [215] discovered that women saw these roles as distinct from one another; however, researchers have never been able to document the adverse or debilitating effect that such conflict was assumed to have on women athletes. Indeed, several studies by Snyder and his colleagues [193–195] show just the opposite—that the female athlete's self-esteem is enhanced by sport involvement. Nevertheless, numerous accounts assumed that the woman in sport was an "anomaly" [65], a "contradiction" [167], playing "incompatible roles" [109], "in a double bind " [103], "Dr. Jekyll-Mr. [sic] Hyde" [103], and, most often, the possessor of "role conflicts which are both personally and socially difficult to resolve" [85, p. 96].

In historical terms, role conflict represents the first attempt to find a "theory" that would explain why women are less involved in sport than men. Although role conflict has been severely critiqued on methodological, theoretical, and political grounds [22, 92, 94, 207, 210, 211], the tradition continues to have its advocates [11, 16, 184].

Related to role conflict theory was research on the apologetic. Several researchers [68, 230], most notably Pat Del Ray [54, 55], reasoned that one important way for women athletes to resolve their conflict and "reduce cognitive dissonance" [55, p. 107] was to apologize for their involvement by overemphasizing their feminine side, for example, by wearing makeup, jewelry, and pastel colors; by discussing their boyfriends at every opportunity; and by giving every indication that sport was not important to them. While the apologetic may be practiced by a few women, it is far more likely to be exhibited by the press, thus reminding us that the need for the apologetic is a cultural and not an individual creation.

Research that attempted to measure differences between female athletes and nonathletes in terms of their psychological masculinity and femininity [137] is also related to assumptions of role conflict. This tradition suffers from serious conceptual and methodological flaws, and it has serious political consequences. "Male" and "female" are terms that denote real biological differences, whereas "masculinity" and "femininity" are terms that connote culturally constructed stereotypes of "appropriate" male and female behavior. Thus, studies that attempt to measure the masculinity or femininity of an individual not only reify conventional cultural prescriptions but also reproduce the relations they purport only to describe or measure.

The psychological inventories mistakenly conceptualize masculinity and femininity as traits—or a constellation of traits—and thus as stable and enduring personality characteristics. Yet the inventories are notoriously culture bound because masculinity and femininity are not naturally occurring facts of the universe but historically specific, culturally constructed agendas for behavior. Moreover, by conceiving of masculinity and femininity as bipolar, the inventories and the resultant research construct a false model of gender differences, since bipolarity assumes that if men are high in a particular trait, such as independence, women are the direct opposite, i.e., dependent. As the work of Spence and Helmreich [200] has shown, gender differences in behavior are usually relative rather than oppositional [22].

The introduction of a new dimension labeled "psychological androgyny" appeared to correct some of the problems in the sex role research. "Androgyny" refers to the combination in one individual of both feminine and masculine behavioral characteristics. But androgyny remains grounded in sex role stereotypes at both the theoretical and the methodological levels, for it is conceived of as the combination of masculine and feminine traits, not the transcendence of such prescriptions. Moreover, while the theory purports to value equally traditional male and female behavior patterns, in practice androgyny subverts female qualities to male qualities [22]. Despite these criticisms, research on androgyny among female athletes began in the late 1970s [51, 54, 165, 200] and continues in psychology of sport today. Several feminists [60, 68, 167] argue for a reconstruction of sport as an androgynous activity.

These early traditions—attitudes, traits, motives, sex roles, role conflict—shared several characteristics. They grew out of early attempts to come to terms with the patterns of women's sport involvement; they offered psychological rather than social explanations for those patterns; they relied on methodologically primitive attempts to measure complex psychosocial constructs; they conceived of women as not fitting into sport; and, by subtly assuming that the problem behind women's low involvement lay within, they tended to blame women for their own lack of participation. The social context in which sport and women have been defined was dealt with in only the vaguest manner; the real focus was on the responses of the individual to a social world whose power was taken for granted. These approaches are attempts to answer the simplest questions: Why aren't women interested in sport? Why aren't more women involved in sport? They do not question the structure of sport, nor do they see sport as an institution that is produced through human agency and thus subject to social change.

Sociological Beginnings
Several works of the early 1970s represent appreciable advances in the sociological conceptualization of women's sport, particularly the work of Marie Hart and Jan Felshin. Theirs were the first feminist informed critiques of discriminatory attitudes and practices against women in sport. Without the benefit of a theoretically based feminist framework, Hart and Felshin managed to be both sociological and feminist.

Hart's work [109–111] focuses on how pressures to conform to cultural stereotypes hurt those who work against type: female athletes and male dancers. Her focus is clearly cultural. She sees sport as "male cultural territory," and she argues that "a social situation, heavy in prestige for some and laden with stigma for others, has been created and is perpetuated by the archaic male and female role expectations" [111, p. 176].

Felshin's writing on women in sport [65–69] also focuses on social context. In "The Social Anomaly of Women in Sports" [65], she gives examples of the trivialization and devaluation of women's sporting accomplishments, showing how the "Preservation of the masculinized connotations of sport has meant the development of various alternatives for demeaning women's participation in it" [65, p. 122]. Agreeing with Hart that sport is "a preserve of masculinity," she clearly understands sport as a significant symbolic force in women's subordination to men. Moreover, Felshin is not content to argue that women must be accommodated within sport as men have created it. Hers is the earliest voice urging women to create their own definitions of sport:

How can women fight for equality in a domain where the prevailing ethic seems not only masculinized but corrupt and brutalized as well? . . . The task for women in sport may be a difficult one. Male domination and pervading discrimination must be challenged, and so must the ethic of sport as men have defined it [65, p. 124].

In "The Triple Option . . . for Women in Sport" [68], she reflects on the massive changes occurring in women's sport as the result of the AIAW and Title IX. With critical perception, she spells out the assumptions and consequences of the apologetic, the forensic and the futuristic. The apologetic is a conservative stance whose proponents insist that women athletes are feminine and who seek diminutive, "feminine" sport forms to prove it. The forensic is a liberal approach whose advocates assume that women are equal to men and who fight for the rights of women to enter male sport. The dialectic is a loosely defined radical stance that argues that men and women may be different, that sport as presently constituted does not satisfy all humans, and that women can help to redefine sport as a more human practice. Felshin's framework prefigured Jagger and Rothenberg's [126] feminist frameworks, which serve as a point of departure for much of the theoretical work of the early 1980s.

Felshin's section in *The American Women in Sport* [67] made several important contributions, including the conceptualization of women's relationship to sport as a dialectic. While such language is more common in our field today, in the mid-1970s it represented a significant advance over the simplistic, unidirectional "hypodermic" approaches featured by trait, motivation, sex role, and role conflict literature. Instead, Felshin argued, the relationship between women and sport is dynamic and interactive.

The work of Hart and Felshin was grounded in a feminist sensibility, yet little theoretical work was available to help them frame their arguments. Nevertheless, they were clearly forerunners of the feminist perspective of the 1980s. They conceived of sport as a male preserve, understood sport and woman as social constructs and understood the dialectical relationship between the two, tackled sensitive subjects such as homophobia, and clearly saw a connection between sport and other feminist issues.

By 1974, the study of women in sport had reached its first plateau of development. In addition to the work of Hart and Felshin, the first two books on women in sport had just appeared. In *The Femininity Game*, Boslooper and Hayes noted that "Men have gone to a lot of trouble to keep women out of competitive sport" [31, p. 101], and they went on to detail the cultural constraints to women's participation. Consistent with the state of the field, they covered a great deal of territory, with chapters on physiology, psychology, sociology, anthropology, and history. *The American Women in Sport* also took a multidisciplinary approach, offering four separate perspectives to understanding women's sport: a historical chronicle by Ellen Gerber, the sociological context by Felshin, a psychological perspective by Pearl Berlin, and a biophysical perspective by Waneen Wyrick.

In Canada during the same period, significant changes concerning women's sport were occurring as well. Canadians held their first National Conference on Women in Sport in Toronto in 1974 [208], and Abigail Hoffman's *About Face: Towards a Positive Image of Women in Sport* [121] was published in 1976 as part of a series of monographs sponsored by the Ontario government in an attempt to improve the status of women in Canada. The monograph, written for a general audience, includes an indictment of sexist practices in sport, dispels myths about the female athlete, and offers specific recommendations for making changes in one's own community. *About Face* was followed the next year by *Women in Canadian Life: Sports* [47], another monograph aimed at a general audience that documented, with a critical eye, the history of women in Canadian sport.

Evidence of Growing Academic Interest
Academic interest in the field was growing, as evidenced by several important conferences, the first mention of sport in women's studies journals, the appearance of the first journal issue devoted entirely to women and sport, and the development of several new research traditions.

The first national research conference on women in sport, organized by Dorothy Harris, was held at Pennsylvania State University in 1972. The proceedings of the Penn State conference [104] demonstrate the dominance of psychological models, for the "sociological" topics included achievement motivation [233], self-concept [232] and birth order [172], a confusion typical of the early years in the field. However, the Proceedings also included Sherif's "Females in the Competitive Process" [190], an unusually dynamic approach to women's sport, and a typically thorough review of socialization literature by Ingham et al. that bears the enticing title "Socialization, Dialectics and Sport" [125]. That paper presents one of the first critiques of role conflict theory, criticizing the unidirectional model of influence assumed by role conflict and arguing instead for a focus on the dialectical relationship between culture and individual behavior.

A second important conference was organized at Temple University in July 1976 by Carole Oglesby. The program included a mix of psychology and sociology, and a mix of theory and practice. The presentations form the nucleus of Oglesby's edited book *Women and Sport: From Myth to Reality* [167]. Temple also held workshops on Black Women in Sport in 1976 and 1977. The University of Iowa began its yearly series of Women as Leaders in Physical Education workshops in 1978. That same year, the First International Conference on Women and Sport was held in London.

Although feminists outside of sport have often viewed sport as an insignificant feminist issue [65, 110, 210], some feminist journals began to find space for articles on sport. In 1976, *Signs* published its first—and so far only—sport-related article, Kennard's "History of Physical Education" [131]. In 1978, the *Women's Studies International Quarterly* included Prendergast's "Stoolball: The Pursuit of Vertigo?" [173], an interesting analysis of the economic grounding for female bonding in an English village that focused on the game of stoolball, despite male resistance to the practice. In 1979 *Canadian Woman Studies* featured Hall's "Women and the Lawrentian Wrestle" [91], in which she used the naked wrestling scene between two men in D.H. Lawrence's *Women in Love* as an image of the sort of primordial physical competition from which women are so effectively excluded.

In 1977, the feminist journal *Frontiers* published several articles on sport [54, 230]; *Arena Review* [99] became the first journal to focus an entire issue on women in sport; and the third volume of *NAGWS Research Reports: Women in Sport* [7], contained perhaps the first stock taking of the emerging field. In a review of sources relevant to the "sociological perspective" of women in sport, Hall briefly reviewed the state of the field, citing the work of Felshin and Willis as "the only pure sociological analyses of women in sport" [88, p. 40].

In the late 1970s, sociologists began to explore several new areas of women's sport. Some researchers focused on sex differences in the professionalization of attitudes toward play [146, 218] and found that females had a more playful, fairness-oriented attitude toward sport, while males were more oriented toward winning. Following an early tradition in the sociology of sport, other researchers studied the effects of high school athletic participation on female athletes. The studies showed that, like their male counterparts, female athletes got higher grades and had higher educational aspirations than nonathletes [21, 98, 138, 196]. Other studies discovered that female athletes of the 1970s gained social status in high school through their involvement in sport [21, 40, 41, 70]. This finding is in stark contrast to Coleman's observations in *The Adolescent Society* [50] of the 1950s, in which girls were cheerleaders whose status was ascribed by good looks, nice clothes, and family social status, while boys were athletes who could achieve their way into the leading crowd.

The most dominant topic, however, was socialization, and when Susan Greendorfer published her first study on the socialization of female athletes in 1977 [77], the topic had its strongest advocate. Her thesis, that women's involvement in sport is attributable to socialization experiences in youth, dominated the field for several years, as researchers [77–80, 83, 84, 115, 195, 197, 201] tested one population after another in an effort to determine which significant others had the most impact on female participation. Yet, while socialization research on boys has shown a clear pattern of male role models, the sex of the role model for girls has not been firmly established.

While the tradition has provided some general information about the socialization process, it has not advanced significantly since its early years, perhaps because it has limited itself unnecessarily. Although it has adopted a model [132] that proposes interacting influences of personal attributes, significant others, and socializing situations, only one element of the model, the influence of significant others, has ever been tested in sport. Moreover, the research tradition has serious methodological and theoretical shortcomings, particularly its conception of socialization as a uni-directional process [114, 174], its overdeterministic model and its con-ceptualization of the individual as "compliant and conforming" [206, p. 30], and its assumption that sport can be isolated from other social practices [210]. Recently, the primary proponents of this line of research have expressed some doubts as well [71, 81].

In a different approach, Janet Lever [142, 143] used observational techniques to document the play patterns of young girls and boys. Her observations showed that boys play more complex games characterized by larger numbers of players, greater role differentiation, more com-plicated rules, more explicit goals, greater player interdependence, and team formation. Lever suggested that the different play patterns have an effect on adult behaviors. Boys may learn "organizationally relevant skills" that help them solve disputes by learning to "depersonalize the attack" [142, p. 485]. Since girls' play is more intimate and private, they may learn "delicate socioemotional skills" [142, p. 484].

Feminist Developments

The year 1978 seems to be a turning point in our understanding of women's sporting practices for it marks the appearance of Carole Og-lesby's edited book *Women in Sport: From Myth to Reality* [167] and Ann Hall's monograph *Sport and Gender: A Feminist Perspective on the Sociology of Sport* [89].

Oglesby's book was transitional. It can be seen as a catalogue of re-search traditions to date, including socialization [78], achievement-re-lated motives [20], attribution theory [157], historical myths [199], body image and sex stereotyping [155], androgyny [60], and the apologetic [55]. Yet it also featured Wilma Scott Heide [116], former President of the National Organization for Women (NOW), issuing a radical call for reform of sport along feminist lines, and Oglesby made clear in her preface the vision of the text as a whole:

This book is a tale, never told before. Its premise is that a group of women, competent in various fields, can theorize about sport in a unique and insightful way. Its premise is that such a group can effectively describe woman's experiencing of present-day sport and propose alternatives which promise a better sporting future for women and men. [167, p. vii]

Oglesby situated the role conflict dilemma in social context.

Sports feminism, then, is what the book is about. From a pre-feminist vantage point, the label sport feminism is a contradiction: Feminism—a philosophy of the equality of women; Sport—a human endeavor wherein males historically have excelled. In this book, the apparent contradiction is treated as an artifact of our society. [167, p. vii]

Both Oglesby's and Hall's books were clearly feminist, but only Hall sustained a clear feminist focus throughout. Her monograph was the first work to attempt a definition of feminism, the first to understand the feminist critique of social science, and the first to bring feminist paradigms to bear on sport. Hall presented an excellent summary of the existing research on women in sport, but, more important, she outlined a clearly feminist agenda for future research. Her monograph was an indication that a theoretically based feminist perspective would inform the work of the next decade.

Summary
The decade of the 1970s was a period of excitement and diversity in the production of knowledge about women and sport. Increasing public awareness of the need for greater sporting opportunities for girls and women resulted in important changes, and Title IX ushered in an era of participation unequaled in women's sporting history. Interest in understanding women's sport increased as well, as the public and academics both wondered why women's involvement rates had been so low and what sorts of women had persevered in their involvement despite lack of opportunities, subtle discouragement, and outright hostility.

  The earliest attempts to come to terms with the woman/sport relationship focused on attitudes toward women athletes, their personality traits, their motivational patterns, their fear of success, the demands of sex roles, psychological femininity, androgyny, role conflict, the apologetic, and socialization. Most of the topics were psychological in focus; even those that work on the boundaries between culture and the individual, such as sex roles and socialization, were conceived of primarily in psychological terms. Despite calls for the analysis of the dialectical relationships between sport and women and between culture and the individual, researchers tended to factor out confusing and unmeasurable cultural forces or dynamic relationships. The subtle assumption of this research as a whole was that the true barriers to women's full partici- pation in sport are psychological, not cultural.

In sum, during the 1970s, researchers using psychological methods and inventories did generate some information about female athletes, but the quality of the research was often poor and the generalizability of the results was typically limited. Sociologists, on the other hand, de- livered social commentaries on sexist practices in sport but engaged in little formal inquiry. Clearly, the field lacked a theory capable of con- ceptualizing the complex dialectical relationships between women, sport, and culture. As a result, a sociology of women in sport did not truly exist until the 1980s.

TRENDS OF THE 1980s

Research on the Backlash of the 1980s

The early 1980s might be seen as another period of ambivalence about the proper place of women in sport. Public and academic interest in sport for women continued to grow, but that interest was not matched by institutional support. After the dramatic gains for women in sport in the 1970s, a backlash was beginning to be evident. Title IX, challenged by the National Collegiate Athletic Association (NCAA) from the start, was upheld in several court cases [188], but in the Grove City case in 1984, the Supreme Court ruled that athletic programs were exempt from Title IX because they do not receive direct federal funding. The decision severely weakened Title IX. In addition, the relentless pressure of the NCAA to wrest control of women's collegiate athletics from the Asso- ciation for Intercollegiate Athletics for Women (AIAW) was intensifying: In January 1981, against the pleas of the women running women's ath- letic programs, the NCAA voted to begin championships for women in Division I programs. Within a year, the AIAW was out of business.

Although the growth of women's programs created greater oppor- tunities to coach women athletes, the number of women in those positions began a precipitous decline. A similar trend was occurring in adminis- trative positions: As men's and women's athletic programs merged, men were invariably named to head the programs.

In Canada, even without Title IX, the pattern was the same. Men's and women's programs merged in 1978, with the result that men dis- placed women as heads of women's programs. Ontario was the only province in which women managed to retain their coaching and admin- istrative positions, because Ontario alone maintained separate provincial organizations to oversee men's and women's programs [217].

A number of researchers turned their attention to the new develop- ments in women's sport. Acosta and Carpenter [3–6] and Holmen and

Parkhouse [122] have been monitoring since 1974 the loss for women of coaching and administrative positions. Their data show an alarming trend: Between 1974 and 1986, the percentage of women's sports coached by women has declined from 81 to 51% [6, 122]. At the administrative level, the changes are even more dramatic: As men's and women's programs have merged, the percentage of women's programs headed by women has fallen from 79% in 1973–1974 to 15% in 1985–1986 [6]. While the expansion of women's athletic programs created many new opportunities for coaching women's sports, far more men than women found jobs within these programs [1, 122].

In their study of changes in the athletic labor market between 1977–1978 and 1978–1979, Abbott and Smith found that "the women's athletic system is less effectively dominated by women than is the men's system by men" [1, p. 47]. Over the 2-year period studied, they found that different "vacancy-creating events" brought about different results in terms of hiring. When a female coach departed, there was a 48% chance that her replacement would be a female and a 19% chance that it would be male; in contrast, 69% of the replacements for male coaches were male and only 4% were female.* However, if the vacancy-creating event was the creation of a new job, a man got the job 68% of the time and a woman got it only 28% of the time. This finding takes on greater significance when we realize that during this period of time there were 1037 new jobs in women's athletics and a loss of 211 jobs in men's athletics [1]. Abbott and Smith conclude that while Title IX and Equal Employment Opportunity Commission regulations "should pull probabilities of male and female replacement closer together . . . in fact they increase the disparity" [1, p. 46]. Their findings are consistent with other research, which reveals that "males tend to dominate the higher echelons of 'female' occupations" [1, p. 46].

Why women's athletics is being transformed from an employment setting dominated by women to one dominated by men is a topic of great concern. Holmen and Parkhouse [122] suggested three possibilities: (a) better salaries are drawing men into women's athletics; (b) men have greater access to the hiring system, particularly since the trend toward male administrators in women's programs means that men rather than women are now in positions to hire; and (c) men are perceived as being better qualified.

Hart et al. [108] reviewed several other explanations including role conflict, incomplete occupational socialization, and discrimination through perceived limits to opportunities. Their own study tested a career contingency model [174] that considered the link between reasons for entering

---

* The percentages do not total 100 because some jobs were removed from the market and others had not yet been filled.

coaching and reasons for leaving coaching. They discovered that former coaches and present coaches gave different reasons for entering coaching, and they concluded that a shift in value orientations of the coaches coupled with the increasingly competitive nature of girls' and women's sport accounts in part for the reduction in the number of women coaches.

Acosta and Carpenter [4, 6] found that male and female administrators attributed the pattern to different causes. Men thought the decline was the result of women's inadequacies: lack of qualifications, unwillingness to recruit or travel, failure to apply for job openings, and time constraints due to family commitments. Women attributed the decline mostly to structural barriers: success of the old boys' network, weakness of the old girls' network, unconscious discrimination in the selection process, and women's lack of qualifications. Knoppers [135] suggested applying Kanter's [130] model of women in organizations to explain the "male domination of the profession" in terms of limited opportunity, denial of access, and burdens of tokenism.

Finally, Liu [144] explored the career patterns of male and female coaches of women's Division I basketball teams. Women followed the pattern of sponsored mobility that Loy and Sage [150] found for male coaches of men's teams, that is, the best predictor of holding a coaching position at a prestigious program was past association with other prestigious programs. The careers of male coaches of women's teams followed a different pattern. For them, the best predictor of holding a prestigious position was the win/loss record at their previous job. Since the records of male and female coaches were not significantly different, Liu's data raise the possibility that male and female candidates for positions may be judged on different criteria.

The conflict between the AIAW and the NCAA for control of women's college sport has been the subject of several recent studies, many of which focus on the political and ideological dimensions of the confrontation and the differences in policy, procedure, and values between the two organizations [44, 74, 76, 127, 145, 191]. As Slatton [191] showed, the AIAW's practices differed considerably from the NCAA's in terms of representation of student athletes within the governance structure, commitment to fiscal responsibility, and an educational model of sport. The NCAA takeover of women's collegiate athletics can be seen as an example of the need to destroy competing ideologies through the destruction of alternate structures.

Burns [42] focused her attention on the different style of leadership that emerged from this alternative sporting structure. On the basis of her interviews with the presidents of the AIAW, she uncovered a model of leadership that contradicts textbook notions of leadership derived from studies of male leaders. These women, she found, were uncomfortable with the idea of power, preferring to see it as a resource to be shared with others. Moreover, their leadership styles were characterized by four qualities not generally discussed in the leadership literature: a commitment to fairness, even at the expense of self-interest; an extraordinary sense of responsibility and mission to the organization; an openness or trusting style; and a sense of shared leadership. Because of their distinctive commitments and styles, and because the model of women's sport they were fighting to preserve was under constant pressure to conform to the dominant model, Burns found that these women spent an inordinate amount of their time legitimating the organization, the values it held, and themselves as leaders. Such legitimacy work is probably a central feature of all cultural forms that attempt to provide viable alternative ideological choices.

Rosenbrock [179] offered another example of the power of dominant male ideology within women's sport. Rosenbrock's study of women administrators who have been in the field throughout the Title IX years shows they have an enormous amount of ambivalence and have developed elaborate coping strategies as they struggle to maintain old values and commitments in an era of massive change.

Taken as a whole, these studies have a romantic quality, a sadness over the loss of an organization that, within the bounds of institutional constraints, attempted to provide a counterideology for sport. While some maintain hope that change is possible at that level, others argue that the best hope for woman-centered sport is through less formal, recreational sport forms [23, 28]. As Birrell [23] warns, however, this will work only so long as the separate structures have separate and distinct ideologies as well. That theme is developed by other scholars and is discussed more fully below.

Residual and Emergent Traditions
During the 1980s, academic attention to women in sport became more diversified. In Williams' [225] terms, the decade can be seen as a time when residual and emergent traditions struggled for dominance. Thus research traditions rooted in the 1970s persist today, but they do so alongside an increasing number of theoretically based, feminist analyses of sport.

Some traditions such as traits and motives, sex roles, and psychological femininity now reside in psychology. Other residual traditions such as role conflict, androgyny, and socialization remain prominent, and researchers have balanced their interest in socialization with a focus on retirement and desocialization [38, 82].

Attention to the academic performance of women athletes continues, and research has extended to the college setting, where several studies [134, 175, 176] have investigated whether female athletes are better prepared for college and receive better grades than other female students. Continuing studies with the Webb scale have shown that as women become more involved in competitive sport, their attitudes become more professionalized [129, 136, 183, 214]. Blinde [30] discovered a similar shift in values among women who have entered athletics since Title IX. Pre-Title IX athletes were more likely to report that sport was fun and to say that they had adequate time to devote to academics; the post-Title IX group placed more emphasis on athletic-related factors such as team reputation, coach, and facilities. Moreover, the latter group was more likely to feel relieved when their athletic career was over and less likely to say that they would have competed without a scholarship.

Feminist analysis at this time was growing due to the emergence of a small but critical mass of women scholars trained in academic disciplines and excited by the potential of feminist theory.* In the language of Mullins [162] and Loy et al. [149], the field had moved during the 1970s from the "normal" stage of isolated scholars to the "network" stage necessary to generate new ideas.† At the end of the 1970s these women

---

* One can trace the intellectual bloodlines and colleague relationships among this group. When Eleanor Metheny passed away in 1983, she left as her legacy a classic analysis of women in sport [171] and at least two young women whose careers she had affected at the University of Southern California: Marie Hart and Ellen Gerber. Both of these women made significant contributions to the field in the early 1970s, yet both have been burned out by the struggle. Hart now works in film production, while Gerber is a civil rights lawyer. Their colleague, Jan Felshin, who teaches at East Stroudsburg University, made her mark on the field early but does not write in the area presently. Dorothy Harris' work is confined to the psychology of sport. One early feminist who has endured through the generational change is Carole Oglesby, who earned her degree at Purdue in the mid-1960s. These women constitute a diffuse first generation.

A second generation of women began publishing in the late 1970s. They include Susan Greendorfer (Illinois), who studied at Wisconsin; Mary Duquin (Pittsburgh), who studied at Stanford; Ann Hall (Alberta), who studied at Birmingham and Alberta; Janet Lever, who studied at Yale; Nancy Theberge (Waterloo) and Susan Birrell (Iowa), who studied at Massachusetts; Janet Harris (North Carolina at Greensboro), who studied at UCLA; and Brenda Bredemeier (Berkeley), who studied at Temple. Only two of these women were fortunate enough to study with earlier feminists: Birrell worked with Gerber and Oglesby at Massachusetts, and Bredemeier worked with Oglesby at Temple. Strong collegial ties remain among these women, though they rarely publish together. There is a greater tendency for intergenerational co-authorship.

A third generation of students, some trained by these women, is about to make its mark on the 1980s: Cathy Bray and Janice Butcher (Manitoba), who worked with Hall; Cindy Hasbrook (Wisconsin, Milwaukee) and Elaine Blinde (Southern Illinois), who worked with Greendorfer; and Cheryl Cole, who worked with Birrell.

† It is interesting to note that the stages in the development of the field of women in sport occur later than those indicated by Loy et al. [149] for the field of sociology of sport in general. They located the normal stage, 1951–1964; the network stage, 1965–1972; the cluster stage, 1973–1977; and the specialty stage just beginning in the late 1970s. In their scheme, women in sport, or, more precisely, feminist analysis, would be considered a specialty field. But with women in sport as the field, the normal stage appears to be 1965–1980 and the network stage from 1980 to the present. Perhaps a combined cluster/specialty stage is developing in the United States, with students wishing to focus on traditional research on women in sport going to Illinois to study with Greendorfer and those interested in feminist analysis being drawn to Iowa to study with Birrell or to Temple to study with Oglesby.

began to present and publish their work, and in the early 1980s a number of them turned to feminism as the theoretical framework most capable of providing epistemological grounding and theoretical sophistication to the research enterprise.

The feminist agenda for the 1980s began with the increasing realization that there was something wrong with the discipline itself. Safrit [181] wondered why fewer women than men were getting published in the journals, and Hall [90] went even further to describe an atmosphere of intellectual sexism within the field. The contrast between the two approaches is evidence of the differing perspectives of the time. Safrit's seemingly objective analysis leaves the reader with the feeling that women were not pulling their intellectual weight, while Hall offered the more critical evaluation that the context in which intellectual activity takes place is subtly designed to value men's ideas and male notions of appropriate methodology.*

Drawing upon the growing feminist critiques of the social sciences [112, 161, 192], Birrell [24] questioned the superficial practice of adding gender to sport research as a variable and called for a deeper commitment to academic feminism. Finally, Hall [95] exposed the cultural constraints on what counts as knowledge and explored in depth the epistemological foundations of the feminist standpoint as the grounding for feminist methodology and theory.

These articles criticized the methodological, theoretical, and political limitations of the traditions that had dominated the field in the 1970s, and they called for methodological approaches grounded in new epistemological assumptions. Simultaneous with the general critiques of sexist methodology came critiques of specific research traditions and past practices in the field. These ground-clearing critiques focused on psychological traits and motives [22], sex roles [22, 92, 94], role conflict [22, 33, 92, 94, 207, 210, 211], and socialization [24, 206, 210].

It is within this context that the meetings of the North American Society for the Sociology of Sport (NASSS) in Denver in October of 1980 can be considered a symbolic moment in the development of a feminist analysis of the woman/sport relationship. First, the meetings provided the opportunity for women scholars to meet, form networks, and caucus informally over dinner and between sessions. Second, several papers were presented that were of particular importance for developing the identity of the field.

Theberge's "Convergences between the Feminist and Radical Critiques of Sport," later published as "A Critique of Critiques" [207], was the first paper clearly to explore the connections between Marxist critical theories

---

* Safrit's recent update of her article [182], while acknowledging that male bias might exist in the field, nevertheless continues to assess women's productivity as if all other factors were equal.

and feminist critiques of sport. Hall's paper, "Sport, Sex Roles and Sex Identity" [92], was an excellent critique of the narrow-minded models dominating the field at the time, specifically role conflict, psychological femininity, and androgyny. It is a classic example of the ground-clearing work of the time. Duquin [61] argued that the different realities of men's and women's lives must be recognized and taken into consideration in sport; and Harris [107] called for broader acceptance of hermeneutical research, an approach consistent with feminist calls for more qualitative and reflexive methodologies.

But perhaps the most significant paper was Mary Boutilier and Lucinda SanGiovanni's "Women, Sport, and Public Policy" [32], in which they introduced and explained the feminist frameworks of Jagger and Rothenberg [126] and applied them to current issues in women's athletics. The frameworks introduced a sense of form and order to feminist theory and women's studies, illuminating the commonalities and delineating the distinctions among feminist thinkers. For many in women's studies as well as sport sociology, the work of Jagger and Rothenberg provided a much needed theoretical orientation from which to move forward and a way to get a firmer grasp on the diversity of voices in feminist writings.

Boutilier and SanGiovanni's contribution to the field did not end there. Three years later their book, *The Sporting Woman* [33], provided not only the first textbook on women in sport but also a first-rate feminist and sociological analysis of the relations between women, sport, and other social institutions. In critical tradition, they acknowledged the assumptions that produced their own particular analysis of sport, and their statements form an agenda for further analysis that underlies much of the work of the 1980s: "sport is a patriarchal institution," "sexist ideology pervades sport," "if women change, men and sport don't have to," "there is a liberal bias in the study of women and sport," "sport sociology is dominated by sexist research," and "women are not men" (pp. 17–19). Their work has had an enormous impact on the field.

While the NASSS conference marks a turning point in terms of a formal feminist consciousness about sport, it did not occur without precedents. Rather, it seems to mark a theoretical maturation that began with the feminist consciousness about sport evident in the earlier writing of Hart, Felshin, and Oglesby. While often atheoretical, those early writings set an agenda for the comprehension of sport as a feminist issue.

The Critical Agenda

Thus, in a relatively short period of time, feminist work in the field grew from the writings of those politically conscious women, to the liberal feminist approach of adding women to established research traditions and applying the methodologies and theories designed to study and explain male behavior, and finally to the endorsement of methods and theories developed to expand our means of conceptualizing women's lives. By the mid-1980s, as these scholars grew quickly in their understanding of the elaborations and diversity of feminist theory, some of them began to move to the more critical edge of the field where they joined other scholars, such as Ingham, Gruneau, Beamish, and Hardy, who were developing perspectives informed by Marx, Weber, and other materialist theorists.

The most noticeable trend in the sociology of sport at this time was its increasing theoretical self-consciousness. A new critical agenda was emerging, informed by the critical theories of feminism, Marxism, and cultural studies, and a search for more comprehensive theories and models has resulted in a good deal of orienting work. Ann Hall has been particularly active in this regard. Over the years she has called for increased attention to feminist theory [89, 93, 94], has developed an excellent analysis of the need for new feminist epistemologies [95], and, most recently, has explicitly called for the development of appropriate methods for analyzing sport in a capitalist patriarchy [96]. Beamish [14] has suggested comprehending gender relations within a materialist perspective; Theberge [209] has demonstrated the connections between feminist and Marxist theories; Bray [34, 35] has argued for a socialist feminist approach; and Whitson [223], Critcher [52], and McKay [158] have all written about including gender within critical models of sport. Most recently, following the developing regard within sociology of sport for British cultural studies models, Cheryl Cole and Susan Birrell [49] have called for the development of a feminist cultural studies approach to sport that would blend the insights of socialist feminism with those of British cultural studies.

Cultural studies is a critical, Marxist-informed, interdisciplinary approach to the study of culture that developed in Britain in the 1950s as a response to the limitations of orthodox Marxism and American positivist sociology. In Willis' words, cultural studies replaces the "pragmatic linear determinism" which dominated the field with "analytical cultural criticism" and "critical qualitative analysis" [227, p. 120]. One of the chief analytical projects of cultural studies is to clarify the relationship between culture, or, more precisely, the processes of cultural production, and ideology, or the system of representations that actively shape consciousness and reproduce relations of dominance and subordination. Thus cultural studies is based on a recognition of the underlying tension of dominant and subordinate groups over issues of material distribution and ideological ascendency [49].

A feminist cultural studies, as advocated by Cole and Birrell [49], would extend that perspective to an analysis of the processes of domination and subordination as they apply to gender relations in sport and would provide a more powerful and inclusive analysis of the place of sport in cultural production. Feminism and cultural studies are compatible in many ways: They share intellectual roots, including a critique of positivism as ahistorical, decontextualized, and static; both are critical theories; both are historical and material; and they share a focus on the struggle between dominant and subordinate groups. Yet each has something to offer the other. Cultural studies has more developed conceptual tools for comprehending the processes of cultural production and the struggle between dominant and subordinate groups; socialist feminism broadens the agenda of cultural studies by insisting on the necessity of maintaining the articulation between class, race, and gender antagonisms. Without the socialist feminist perspective, cultural studies is essentially gender blind. Left undeveloped by both theories at this point is any sophisticated analysis of race as a significant category of human experience and focus of cultural struggle [49].

EARLY BRITISH CONTRIBUTIONS. The work at this critical edge actually began in the early 1970s with two British articles that were apparently so far advanced for American audiences that they lay almost unnoticed for about 10 years. Kenneth Sheard and Eric Dunning's 1973 article, "The Rugby Football Club as a Type of Male Preserve" [189], gained respect as a subcultural study [147], but because it focused so clearly on males, it was not fully recognized for its importance to feminist scholarship until gender relations was recognized as the proper focus of the field. Sheard and Dunning argued that sport is a significant location for the production of rabidly antifemale sentiments. By focusing on certain rituals of rugby football designed to show contempt for women, particularly the crude lyrics of drinking songs and the practices that surround their performance, Sheard and Dunning revealed some specific forms of cultural practices that exclude and degrade women. They further argued that the players feel a necessity for such spaces for male displays in order to preserve, or reproduce, notions of male dominance and female subordination.

Sheard and Dunning developed several significant themes. They recognized sport as a male preserve—a site for the willful exclusion and degradation of women, and thus an arena for the production of an ideology of dominance and subordination between the sexes; and they provided an explanation for why that action seems necessary to men.

Paul Willis' [226, 227]* 1974 paper on "Performance and Meaning" in women's sport developed more fully the importance of ideology, he-

---

* "Performance and meaning" [226] was distributed by the Centre For Contemporary Cultural Studies in Birmingham, but it reached such a small audience that Willis published a slight revision under the title "Women in Sport in Ideology" [227] in Hargreaves *Sport, Culture and Ideology*, edited by J. Hargreaves, in 1982. Since the 1982 work is easier to find, the pages cited in this chapter are from that source.

gemony, and common sense as they apply to gender relations in sport, and anticipated the arguments current in the field almost 15 years later. It is a most concise and significant statement on the meaning of women's exclusion from sport.

Willis began his analysis by observing that the apparent performance differentials between the sexes are less interesting than

> the manner in which this gap is understood and taken up in the popular consciousness. . . .After all, there are many factual differences facing us in the social world. . . .The analytical sociocultural task is not to measure these differences precisely and explain them physically, but to ask *why* some differences, and not others, are taken as so important, become so exaggerated, are used to buttress social attitudes and prejudice. [227, p. 120]

Willis observed that society makes a great fuss about the gender gaps in athletic performances, and he grounded in Marxist theory his analysis of the meaning of the importance of this performance gap.

Sport is a particularly significant arena of gender relations, he argued, because it appears to be outside of real life. Thus the central lesson of sport, that differences between the sexes are "natural" and men are "naturally dominant," presents itself as common sense. But in reality, sport is an essential ideological tool for producing and reproducing the domination of men over women, thus preserving the gendered division of labor upon which the stability of the social order is imagined to depend.

Willis' two provocative articles were early analyses in the critical tradition that is becoming increasingly prominent within the field. The critical traditions promise to provide new insights into gender relations, including the gendering of sport through the invention of often diminutive, "feminine" forms of physical activity; the reproduction through sport of gender as a relation of domination and subordination; and the tension between differentially privileged groups as they struggle to produce meanings of sport resonant with their own lived experiences [49].

RECENT CRITICAL ADVANCES. The shift in the field is so recent and the insights so exciting that it is difficult to capture all the trends in recent research. Accordingly, analysis is restricted to four themes central to the critical feminist project: (a) the production of an ideology of masculinity and of male power through sport; (b) the media practices through which dominant notions of women are reproduced; (c) the centrality of issues surrounding physicality, sexuality, and the body for defining gender relations; and (d) the resistance of women to dominant sport practices as they create women-centered sporting practices or seek to transform sport into a more humane activity.

It is important to note that the studies reviewed in connection with these themes are not all in the critical tradition. They are grouped together because the insights they produce can be built on by critical theorists to advance the critical project.

SPORTS AND THE IDEOLOGY OF MASCULINITY. The clearest theme emerging from the new critical agenda is the production through sport of an ideology of male dominance. To understand the topic, we begin with several papers that are not in the critical tradition but that furnish a backdrop against which a critical analysis was developed.

Some of the clearest statements of personal attachment to sport as a male activity can be found in Sabo and Runfola's edited book *Jock: Sports and Male Identity* [180], in which reflections by several authors attest to the power of sport to create feelings of personal power in men. Sabo and Runfola critique this obsession in an update of earlier commentaries [119, 186]. On the other hand, Carroll's more recent article, "Sport: Virtue and Grace" [43], is so proud of naked masculine prowess that it is hard to take his anachronistic message seriously. Feminists must thank Carroll for taking the time to commit to print the sexist polemic that underlies patriarchal attempts to exclude women from sport. Not since Weiss [219] has a male academic been bold enough to spell out what he really thinks about women on male turf. With some of the pieces from *Jock,* Carroll's article forms a reminder of dominant notions that sport is a masculine activity that must be zealously guarded against female intrusion. Carroll's article captures the terror of those who fear that not only will sport masculinize women but—far worse—that women will feminize sport.

It is upon precisely that fear that Sheard and Dunning's rugby players act when they attempt to disgust, offend, shock, and otherwise discourage any female intruders who might happen into their male bastion. In a recent revision of that paper, Dunning [59] argues the almost biological necessity for the preservation of such spaces, particularly during times of encroachment by women into traditional male worlds and privileges. Thus the changing relations between the sexes and the ensuing civilizing of society lead men to stake out clearly demarcated male turf.

Birrell [25], Hargreaves [100], Lenskyj [141], Peiss [168], and Willis [227] all provide further evidence of the imagined need for a male preserve at precisely those times and places when male egos feel most battered by the social changes demanded by equality. For example, Susan Birrell [25] argues that American sport developed in the late nineteenth century in a social context dominated by tension surrounding changing gender relations. Birrell argues that the particular conditions of male life—the increasingly vocal and active role of women in society, the mechanization of labor, the ascendance of sedentary middle-class occupations, the fear of feminization of culture and education, the loss of male spaces such as saloons, pool halls, amusement parks and, most symbolically, the loss of the American frontier as a space in which to create heroic male myths—all created a crisis in masculinity that was played out by the claiming of sport as a male territory in which to produce myths of male dominance and restore masculine hegemony. The result of that struggle was the production of an understanding of sport as male territory that held such hegemonic power that it has dominated all other conceptions of sport for almost 100 years.

In a response to Dunning [59] that builds on the work of Dyer and Foucault, Jennifer Hargreaves [101] argues that the ideology of masculinity is rooted in images of male muscularity: "Muscularity is thus a 'sign' of male power" (p. 112). She considers the connection between sport and "the focus on the anatomy of the male body as the embodiment of power" (p. 113). She notes the irony of muscularity as an image of man's "natural" superiority, since muscles "are produced by much 'pumping of iron' and ingesting of drugs" in order to meet the increasing standards of our particular historical time.

In a related vein, Bryson echoes Willis' earlier observation when she concludes her study of sport in Australia by noting that

> certain sports provide ritual support for male dominance, through a process of mobilization of bias which takes place in two key ways. First, they link maleness with highly valued and visible skills; and second, they link maleness with the positively sanctioned use of aggression/force/violence. [39, p. 421]

The result is an ideology of domination based on the "inferiorisation of women's activities" (p. 424). The social consequence is the reproduction of an ideology that represents males as naturally superior to females.

THE PRODUCTION OF IMAGES OF WOMEN IN SPORT. A second topic of concern to critical scholars is the role of the media as producers of dominant images of reality, which they package as commonsense presentations. Communication Studies departments are currently leading the shift toward cultural studies that is visible in some sport studies programs as well, and the obvious fit between the two should lead to a productive partnership in the development of theoretical insights on the sport/media complex.

Research is beginning to move beyond the descriptive confines of content analysis that documented quantitatively the wholesale neglect and trivialization of women athletes by the media [33, 178]. More recent studies have attempted to expand that narrow descriptive model by noting its theoretical flaws [178], conducting qualitative analyses of women's treatment by the media [37, 118], describing the work routines that produce the sport news [213], and focusing on media construction of a particular event [27].

Hilliard [118] and Bresnahan [37] have both documented qualitative differences in the media's treatment of male and female athletes. Hilliard found a "debunking motif" in magazine articles about male and female professional tennis players that focused on their "imperfections and character flaws." These perceived flaws followed predictable gender stereotypes. The males were seen as one-dimensional, unfriendly, or ill-tempered, while the women were portrayed as unable to fulfill their athletic potential, overly dependent on others, particularly men, prone to anxiety and depression, and having doubts about their sexual identity. However, the articles tended to forgive the men their flaws because they also had positive attributes: their superb athleticism, determination to succeed, aggressiveness, toughness, and honesty. In contrast, the women's flaws were not balanced in the articles by redeeming positive attributes.

Bresnahan [37] has uncovered similar patterns in her analysis of the media coverage of women marathoners. She found that even when women runners were being featured on the television screen, commentators were as likely to talk about the unseen male runners as about the women supposedly featured. Moreover, both television and the press emphasized a female runner's physical characteristics and family life; and questions about her training were invariably directed to her male coach. In such ways, the media tempered her image as a powerful athlete with socially preferred images of femininity, domesticity, heterosexuality, and male authority.

Some critics argue that women athletes receive less attention than male athletes because there are too few women sports writers [33]. In "Sharing the Beat," Angell [10] details the crude comments and inhumane behavior encountered by women who enter the locker room in an attempt to do their jobs as sports writers. But Theberge and Cronk [213] argue that "sexism in the sports media is not primarily a function of the prejudices of individual journalists" but rather is a result of apparently rational working practices.

Focusing on the way a newspaper covers women's sport, Theberge and Cronk show how media practices construct the parameters of our understanding of sport and then fill in the spaces with predictable sports content that effectively "reads women out of the sports news." These practices include reliance on the wire services, the structure and spatial limits of the sports section, and the beat, a commitment to cover specific sports such as men's college basketball. Newspapers rely on the beat to produce sport news stories regularly, a practice that results in the routine coverage of sports deemed important and the routine neglect of others, such as women's college basketball, which are considered marginal and thus are reproduced as marginal through this very practice.

Finally, in their study of Renee Richards, Birrell and Cole [27] show how the media constructed a framework of debate around Richards' entrance into women's tennis that privileged Richard's rights over those of the women on the tour and reduced complex issues of the social construction of gender to a discussion of male prerogative and technological wizardry. Also mixed up in this fascinating case are the ways in which Richards' intrusion into women's tennis became an occasion for the trivialization of women's physical accomplishments. The media seemed to delight in reporting the male tennis players' sneering reactions to the women's protests at having to complete against a man, raised in a world of male privilege, who happened to be inhabiting a female-seeming body.

WOMEN, PHYSICALITY, AND POWER. Other recent feminist work has explored the theoretical connection between sport as a physical activity and physicality as the key to women's oppression [26, 101, 141, 151, 152, 212]. This approach is nicely rooted in historical circumstances, for fears that a woman's involvement in sport could compromise her health, her beauty, her reproductive capacity, and her femininity were the earliest rationales for women's exclusion from sport. Advising women to avoid the stress of sport was "for her own good" [63, 141].

In her excellent book, *Out of Bounds: Women, Sport and Sexuality*, Helen Lenskyj [141] shows how the impact of the medical profession and cultural standards of femininity worked together to dampen the enthusiasm and thwart the ambitions of most North American women for sport. Hargreaves [100] and Atkinson [12] document the trend in Britain as well. Myths about women's frailty and disinterest appear to have lost some of their power, but Lenskyj and other show how the same arguments resurface in modern dress, for example, in terms of fears for women about amenorrhea.

In "Toward a Feminish Alternative to Sport as a Male Preserve" [211], Nancy Theberge notes that most analyses "misrepresent the nature and understate the impact" of sport in the reproduction of gender. Following both Dunning [59] and Willis [227], she argues that sport reproduces gender inequality by subtle extension of its model of male physical superiority to a model of male social superiority. Since the key to that bit of common sense is physicality, Theberge argues that "sport as a male preserve has contributed to the oppression of women through the objectification and domination of their physicality and sexuality" [211, p. 193].

Birrell and Cole [26] present a complementary argument based on recent feminist theories as they discuss the many ways in which men control women through control of women's bodies. Such control is accomplished through an ensemble of cultural practices including rape, domestic violence, sexual harassment, pornography, male-defined standards of female beauty, unattainable media images, compulsory heterosexuality, and, of course, sport. They argue that taking back control of one's body, if done with a consciousness of that act as political, can be a significant step toward understanding and practicing resistance to physical and ideological domination.

Theberge expands the thesis in two other papers. In "Sport and Feminism in North America" [210]", she shows the relevance of sport to the women's movement by arguing that women's performances in sport "are a particularly effective means to refute myths of female frailty" (p. 50). As a result, feminists might make "strategic use of women's sporting accomplishment to advance their cause in other domains [such as] restrictions upon women's employment in physically demanding and hazardous occupations" (p. 50).

In "Sport and Women's Empowerment" [212], Theberge elaborates further by exploring the connections among sport, power and sexuality. Beginning with Hartsock's [113] critique of male concepts of power as privilege, strength, and domination, and accepting Hartsock's redefinition of power as energy, potential, and creativity—a redefinition supported by Burns' [42] research on women leaders—Theberge advances her own argument that by taking control of their own physicality in sport, women may actively resist their own subordination. Theberge's argument thus builds on Dunning's [59] and Hargreaves' [101] arguments that "power is not simply about strength or superiority but about domination and more specifically, about the domination of women by men" [212, p. 20]. For Theberge, "The liberatory possibility of sport lies in the opportunity for women to experience the creativity and energy of their bodily power and develop this power in the community of women" [212, p. 20].

One phenomenon in which the connection between power and sexuality is evident is the fitness boom, but Theberge warns that "the feminization of the fitness movement" results in a repossession of women's bodies by emphasizing not bodily strength but enhanced sexuality [212]. The dangers of incorporation and the power of masculine hegemony are thus apparent when activities with liberatory potential are reappropriated into dominant images of femininity [26, 212]. Even body building, an activity that could challenge dominant images of females by producing the muscles that have been a mark of masculine superiority [101], is understood by many of its female practitioners as "a means of enhancing their feminine qualities. To be muscular, fit, strong and healthy is to add to their attractiveness as women and to their sex appeal to men" [57, p. 380].

Birrell and Cole [27] pursue the connection between women's physicality and sport in another direction, through an analysis of the controversy surrounding the entrance of Renee Richards, a male-to-female transsexual, into women's professional tennis. Cole and Birrell examine the controversy over Richards' "true" sexual identity and the experts to whom the United States Tennis Association and eventually the courts turned to determine who is and who is not a woman. Not surprisingly, the experts turned out to be the male-dominated medical establishment that had pioneered the technology that created Renee Richards in the first place. Completely obscured in the debate were the enormously signficant part that culture plays in the production of mutually exclusive gender categories, the strength of cultural prescriptions for gender-appropriate behavior that would make transsexualism appear to be a practical solution to gender dysphoria, and the material and ideological interests of the women athletes who play on the tour.

A final topic focused on sport and women's physicality, but one that receives scant attention is homophobia. While most of the studies reviewed below are not critical in the theoretical sense of that word, taken together their insights suggest important directions for future critical analysis.

One early article is fascinating because its oblique approach provides insight into the felt danger surrounding the topic. In "The Physical Educator: Miss or Mrs.?" [9], Alexander discusses the marital status of women physical educators wholly in terms of their personality. Not until Beck's [15] angry condemnation of physical education as sexist, racist, and homophobic did the issue of sexual preference surface in any meaningful way. Two years later, in 1982, Coblan [46] documented the closeting of lesbians in physical education departments in an attempt to expose the dynamics behind their fears. Going public, Coblan argued, results in the confirmation of an "ancient male fantasy": All women in sport are lesbians.

The power of that equation is startling, for it works in a number of ways. By discrediting all women in sport as lesbians, men can rest assured that their territory is not being invaded by "real" women after all; by mobilizing societal prejudices against homosexuality, they may be able to keep the number of women involved in sport to a safe minimum; by creating an atmosphere of danger, they can, through innuendo, effectively prevent individual women from wanting to be involved in sport; and by keeping women from sport, they keep women from discovering the joy and power of their own physicality and they remove a potential arena for the development of female solidarity [18, 26, 33, 46, 133]. Thus the norms of compulsory heterosexuality accomplish hegemonic closure. As Bennett astutely observes, "Calling one a lesbian is not primarily a way to control lesbians. It is a way to control women" [18, p. 41].

Although all women suffer from the threat of being labeled a lesbian, there is little organized resistance to compulsory heterosexuality, particularly in physical education [46, 133]. Lenskyj [141] notes that lesbianism was not an issue in the field until the theories of Freud became popular in the 1920s and 1930s, but she suggests that our obsession with psychological masculinity and femininity may be a circuitous way to deal with the issue. Whatever its source, it is clear that sexual labeling is a potent weapon in the social control of women in sport.

RESISTANCE AND TRANSFORMATION THROUGH SPORT. If sport accomplishes the reproduction of patriarchal relations through its appeal to a logic of male physical superiority, and if women can produce their own physical strength and a sense of personal power through sport, then sport may serve not only as a site for female oppression but as a site for female liberation as well. Indeed, this is a central tenet of cultural analysis: the conceptualization of culture as contested terrain where dominant and subordinate groups enact the primary cultural struggle [49]. Several writers have developed this theme by focusing not on the ways that the ideology of masculinity works to exclude women from sport but on the ways that women actively resist dominant images of femininity and sport, creating woman-centered alternative sport forms and transforming sport for their own enjoyment. Thus they focus on the struggle over meaning present in all cultural processes, regardless of the power of hegemonic forces.

Because dominant ideological practices have never totally excluded women from sport, Cole and Birrell argue that "the very presence of women in sport is evidence of leaky hegemony" [49, p. 24], and they note that "The gendering of sport and the persistent presence of women in sport can be understood as the result of tension between attempts of a dominant group to establish and maintain sport as a male preserve and the active resistance of a subordinate group to their own subordination" [49, p. 24].

Several researchers not working in the critical tradition have noted that women's values and styles in sport are different from men's. The Webb scale studies [136, 146, 183, 214, 218] report gender differences in orientation toward sport (see also [30]), and Bredemeier [36] notes gender differences in moral reasoning in sport situations. Other research, such as accounts of the differences between the AIAW and the NCAA [42, 74, 191], focus on the distinctive ways men and women organize and practice sport. Grant [74] has documented a "gender gap" in women's field hockey. She shows how the values underlying competition shifted quickly from fair play and friendly competition to antagonism and a selfish concern for the outcome when external pressures to conform to male values and to determine champions for funding purposes prevailed. Grant's example is particularly noteworthy, for her focus is on elite international athletes; most often opportunities for trans-formation occur in less public, lower-profile recreational venues.

Other writers have focused on the creation and maintenance of woman-centered sport forms [23, 33, 45, 61, 116, 212, 221], and some have described the material practices that constitute such a transformation. Thus Wheatley [222] has explored women's rugby as an activity in which women consciously rebel against cultural definitions of appropriate sporting practices for women. As early as 1977, Bishop [29] noted the boldness of women ruggers as they challenged male domination and control of the sport, but Wheatley's descriptions place the women's rugby subculture in juxtaposition to the male preserve documented by Sheard and Dunning [189]. The message of her somewhat outrageous ruggers is clear: Women can penetrate even the malest of male preserves.

Boutilier and SanGiovanni [33] and Grabiner [73] have both discussed feminist attempts to reform softball into a woman-centered activity, but the most complete analysis is Birrell and Richter's "Is a Diamond Forever? Feminist Transformations of Sport" [28]. Birrell and Richter show how feminists reappropriated a previously alienating sport form and, through conscious intervention, transformed it into an experience that had meaning within their own lives. These feminists enacted a sport form that was suffused with the following counterhegemonic practices: an emphasis on the process of play that rejects sport as a rational practice; an inclusiveness that insists on providing opportunities for women of all sizes, ages, classes, and races, and a safe space for those who have not had an opportunity to develop their skills; collective coaching practices that deconstruct the hierarchical relationship between player and coach; and a refusal to see the opponent as other.

The power of a feminist intervention in sport is not limited to trans-forming sport; dominant images of gender are challenged as well [26, 49, 211, 212]. Too few feminists, both in and out of sport, are aware of the ideological power of sport. Sport should be seen as a site not only for producing strong women athletes but for producing strong, confident, politically aware women. That is the true power of sport in the feminist revolution.

THE CONTINUING RACIST BIAS

The greatest flaw in the new scholarship on gender relations and sport is the almost total absence of women of color in our studies and in our theories [49]. Moreover, rather than progressing, our record of neglect has gotten worse.

In the late 1970s, several conferences and workshops on minority women athletes were held in the United States in an effort to overcome the lack of information about women of color. Temple University held two workshops on Black Women in Sport in 1976 and 1977; Howard

University held a National Conference on Minority Women in Sport in 1980; and the University of Iowa held a workshop on Black Women in Sport in 1980. Since then, there has been general silence on the topic at predominantly white institutions.

We take little account of black women in our research, sometimes adding race or ethnic identity as a variable, just as we reduce gender to a variable. Research focusing on black women is scarce [2, 75, 123, 177] and usually unpublished [8, 13, 163]. Some researchers have provided descriptive data on the involvement of black women in college athletics in the United States showing that less than 6% of all women intercollegiate athletes are black [8, 13, 163], and these are concentrated in basketball and track and field [13]. The only book published on the black experience in sport is *Black Woman in Sport* [75], a collection of readings produced in 1981 by several women associated with Temple University. Unfortunately, the book is now out of print.

Sport sociology's attention to black male athletes has been slightly better: Research on race and centrality in sport [148] is the classic example. Moreover, Harry Edwards has almost singlehandedly kept the cause of black male athletes before the eyes of the public and the academy. But even Edwards is guilty of massive neglect of black women: His *Revolt of the Black Athlete* [62] mentions black women only once, spending less than a page on them.

Thus, as a field, we have yet to deal with issues of race in any profound theoretical manner. The experiences of women of color differ from those of white women in significant ways; yet, while our models for analysis provide space for dealing with race as a relation of domination and subordination [49], we have not made the commitment necessary to begin to explore that dynamic. While what we know about black women athletes is small, what we know about the athletic experiences of other women of color—Chicanas, Asian women, Native American women—is virtually nonexistent [8].

As those in feminist theory are aware [53, 124, 126], merely adding women of color to our theories, even those informed by feminism or cultural studies, is an inadequate response. Just as women's different way of being in the world and different epistemologies radically transform male-centered theories of social reality [95, 192], so the ontological and epistemological differences of people of color can be expected to expand our theories in radical and unforeseen ways. Surely the path of the future must lead to a greater commitment to understanding the sport experiences of all women of color.

SUMMARY

In any developing field such as the one that began as "women in sport," key developments can be traced through the evolution of the language we use and the concepts we develop to express our new understandings. Thus the discourse has moved from considerations of sex differences and sex roles, to gender differences and gender roles, to the sex/gender system, and finally to patriarchy and gender relations, and we have progressed from seeing gender as a variable or as a distributive category to conceiving of it as a set of relations created through human agency and sustained or reproduced through cultural practices including, but not limited to, sport. At the same time, our understanding of sport has grown from seeing it as a static social institution, defined in terms of its separation from the real world, to the comprehension of sport as a social practice produced through human agency and reproduced through ideological work [86]. Finally, our view of gender relations has moved from a focus on sex differences, conceived as relatively innate, to an outraged response to sexism, to a deeper understanding of just how complex and culturally situated are the relations of domination and subordination that characterize gender relations in partriarchal cultures.

As our consciousness has grown, our questions have changed from "why aren't more women involved in sport?" to "why are women excluded from sport?" to "what specific social practices accomplish the physical and ideological exclusion of women from sport?", "how and why have women managed to resist the practices that seek to incorporate them?", and "how do women work to transform sport to an activity that reflects their own needs as women?"

The study of gender relations and sport has come a long way in a short time. In less that 20 years, the field has transformed itself from often angry, always well-intentioned, but generally atheoretical investigations of the patterns of women's involvement and the psychological factors that kept women from full participation, to a theoretically informed, critical analysis of the cultural forces that work to produce the ideological practices that influence the relations of sport and gender. Clearly, the direction for the future lies in the development and application of more critical analyses capable of capturing the complexity of the gender/sport relation.

ACKNOWLEDGMENTS

I would like to thank my colleagues at the University of Iowa for their help in the preparation of this Chapter: Kathy Bresnahan for research assistance; Bonnie Slatton for reacting to an earlier draft; and Cheryl Cole for research assistance and critical reading of several drafts.

REFERENCES

1. Abbott, A., and D.R. Smith. Governmental constraints and labor market mobility: Turnover among college athletic personnel. *Sociol. Work Occup.* 11:29–53, 1984.

2. Acosta, R.V. Minorities in sport: Educational opportunities affect representation. *J. Health Phys. Educ.* 57:52–55, 1986.
3. Acosta, R.V., and L.J. Carpenter. Women in athletics—A status report. *J. Health Phys. Educ. Recreat. Dance* 56:30–34, 1985.
4. Acosta, R.V., and L.J. Carpenter. Status of women in athletics: Changes and causes. *J. Health Phys. Educ. Recreat. Dance* 56:35–37, 1985.
5. Acosta, R.V., and L.J. Carpenter. Women in sport. In D. Chu, J.O. Seagrave, and B.J. Becker (eds.). *Sport and Higher Education.* Champaign, Ill.: Human Kinetics Press, 1985.
6. Acosta, R.V., and L.J. Carpenter. Women in intercollegiate sport: A longitudinal study—Nine year update. Unpublished paper, 1986.
7. Adrian, M., and J. Brame (eds.). *NAGWS Research Reports: Women in Sport,* Vol. 3. Washington, D.C.: American Alliance for Health, Physical Education, and Recreation, 1977.
8. Alexander, A. Status of Minority Women in the Association of Intercollegiate Athletics for Women. Master's thesis, University of Iowa, Iowa City, 1978.
9. Alexander, C. The physical educator: Miss or Mrs.? In D. Harris (ed.). *Division for Girls and Women's Sports Research Reports: Women in Sports,* Vol 2. Washington, D.C., American Association for Health, Physical Education, and Recreation, 1973.
10. Angell, R. Sharing the beat. In *Late Innings: A Baseball Companion.* New York: Ballentine Books, 1982, pp. 126–135.
11. Anthrop, J., and M.T. Allison. Role conflict and the high school female athlete. *Res. Q.* 54:104–111, 1983.
12. Atkinson, P. Strong minds and weak bodies: Sports, gymnastics and the medicalization of women's education. *Br. J. Sports Hist.* 2:62–71, 1985.
13. Barclay, V.M. Status of black women in sports among selected institutions of higher education. Master's thesis, University of Iowa, Iowa City, 1979.
14. Beamish, R. Materialism and the comprehension of gender-related issues in sport. In N. Theberge and P. Donnelly (eds.). *Sport and the Sociological Imagination.* Fort Worth: Texas Christian University Press, 1984.
15. Beck, B. No more masks! A feminist perspective on issues and directions in professional preparation. In *NAPEHE Annual Conference Proceedings,* Vol 2. Champaign, Ill.: Human Kinetics Press, 1981, pp. 126–135.
16. Bell, M. Role conflict of women as athletes in the United States. In R. Lapchick (ed.). *Fractured Focus: Sport as a Reflection of Society.* Lexington, Mass.: Lexington Books, 1986, pp. 139–149.
17. Bem, S. The measurement of psychological androgyny. *J. Consult. Clinical Psych.* 45:155–162, 1974.
18. Bennett, R.S. Sexual labelling as social control: Some potential effects of being female in the gym. In *Perspectives: Western Society for Physical Education of College Women* 4:40–50, 1982.
19. Bird, A.M., and J. McCullough. Femininity within social roles as perceived by athletes and nonathletes. In M. Adrian and J. Brame (eds.). *NAGWS Research Reports,* Vol. 3. Washington, D.C.: American Alliance for Health, Physical Education, and Recreation, 1977, pp. 57–63.
20. Birrell, S. Achievement related motives and the woman athlete. In C.A. Oglesby (ed.). *Women and Sport: From Myth to Reality.* Philadelphia: Lea & Febiger, 1978, pp. 143–171.
21. Birrell, S. The neglected half of the adolescent society: Shifts in status conferral in the high school for girls. Paper presented at the American Sociological Association Annual Meetings, New York, August 1980.
22. Birrell, S. The psychological dimensions of female athletic participation. In M. Boutilier and L. SanGiovanni (eds.). *The Sporting Woman.* Champaign, Ill.: Human Kinetics Press, 1983, pp. 49–91.

23. Birrell, S. Separatism as an issue in women's sport, *Arena Rev.* 8:49–61, 1984.
24. Birrell, S. Studying gender in sport: A feminist perspective. In N. Theberge and P. Donnelly (eds.). *Sport and the Sociological Imagination.* Fort Worth: Texas Christian University Press, 1984, pp. 125–135.
25. Birrell, S. Women and the myth of sport. Paper presented at the North American Society for the Sociology of Sport Annual Meetings, Edmonton, Alberta, Canada, November 1987.
26. Birrell, S., and C.L. Cole. The body as political territory. Paper presented at the Women as Leaders conference, University of Iowa, July 1986.
27. Birrell, S., and C.L. Cole. The challenge of Rene Richards: A feminist analysis. Paper presented at the North American Society for the Sociology of Sport Annual Meetings, Boston, November 1986.
28. Birrell, S., and D.M. Richter. Is a diamond forever? Feminist transformations of sport. *Women's Studies Int. Forum* 10:395–409, 1987.
29. Bishop, L. Women and rugby. *Arena Newsletter* 1:1–4, 1977.
30. Blinde, E. Contrasting orientations toward sport: Pre- and post-Title IX athletes. *J. Sport Social Issues* 10:6–14, 1986.
31. Boslooper, T., and M. Hayes. *The Femininity Game.* New York: Stein & Day, 1973.
32. Boutilier, M., and L. SanGiovanni. Women, sport and public policy. In S. Greendorfer and A. Yiannakis (eds.). *Sociology of Sport: Diverse Perspectives.* West Point, N.Y.: Leisure Press, 1981, pp. 181–191.
33. Boutilier, M., and L. SanGiovanni. *The Sporting Woman.* Champaign, Ill.: Human Kinetics Press, 1983.
34. Bray, C. Sport, capitalism and patriarchy. *Can. Woman Studies* 4:11–13, 1983.
35. Bray, C. Gender and the political economy of Canadian sport. In N. Theberge and P. Donnelly (eds.). *Sport and the Sociological Imagination,* Fort Worth: Texas Christian University Press, 1984, pp. 104–124.
36. Bredemeier, B. Not rough and tough: How girls can learn to develop assertiveness in sports without aggression. Presentation at the New Agenda II national conference, Indianapolis, IN, June 1987.
37. Bresnahan, K. Women in the long run: Media portrayals of elite women marathoners. Unpublished paper, University of Iowa, Iowa City, 1987.
38. Brown, B. Factors influencing the process of withdrawal by female adolescents from the role of competitive age group swimmer. *Sociol. Sport J.* 2:111–129, 1985.
39. Bryson, L. Sport and the oppression of women. *Aust. N.Z. J. Sport* 19:413–426, 1983.
40. Buhrmann, H.G., and R.D. Bratton. Athletic participation and status of Alberta high school girls. *Int. Rev. Sport Sociol.* 12:57–67, 1977.
41. Buhrmann, H.C., and M.S. Jarvis. Athletics and status. CAHPER J. 37:14–17, 1971.
42. Burns, K. Reconstructing leadership experiences: Toward a feminist theory of leadership. Ph.D. dissertation, University of Iowa, 1987.
43. Carroll, J. Sport: Virtue and grace. *Theory, Culture and Society* 3:91–98, 1986.
44. Chandler, J. The Association for Intercollegiate Athletics for Women: The end of amateurism in U.S. intercollegiate sport. *West Georgia College Studies Social Sci.* 24:5–17, 1985.
45. Coakley, J. Females in sport: Liberation or equality with males? In *Sport in Society: Issues and Controversies,* 2nd ed. St. Louis: C.V. Mosby, 1982, pp. 213–238.
46. Coblan, L. Lesbians in physical education and sport. In M. Cruikshank (ed.). *Lesbian Studies: Present and Future.* Old Westbury, N.Y.: Feminist Press, 1982, pp. 179–186.
47. Cochrane, J., A. Hoffman, and P. Kincaid. *Women in Canadian Life: Sports.* Toronto: Fitzhenry and Whiteside, 1977.
48. Coffey, M. The sportwoman then and now. *J. Health Phys. Educ.* 36:38–41, 50, 1965.

49. Cole, C.L., and S. Birrell. Resisting the canon: Feminist cultural studies. Paper presented at the NASSS Annual Meetings, Las Vegas, October 1986.
50. Coleman, J.S. *The Adolescent Society.* New York: Free Press, 1961.
51. Colker, R., and C. Widom. Correlates of female athletic participation. *Sex Roles* 6:47–58, 1980.
52. Critcher, C. Radical theories of play. *Sociol. Sport J.* 3:333–343, 1986.
53. Davis, A. *Women, Race and Class.* New York: Vintage Books, 1983.
54. Del Rey, P. Apologetics and androgyny: The past and the future. *Frontiers* 3:8–10, 1977.
55. Del Rey, P. The apologetic and women in sport. In C.A. Oglesby (ed.). *Women and Sport: From Myth to Reality.* Philadelphia: Lea & Febiger, 1978, pp. 107–111.
56. Donnelly, P., and S. Birrell. *Motivation and Sport Involvement.* CAHPER Sociology of Sport Monograph Series. Ottawa: Canadian Association for Health, Physical Education, and Recreation, 1978.
57. Duff, R.W., and L.K. Hong. Women bodybuilders: The new femininity? *Social. Sport J.* 1:374–380, 1984.
58. Dunkle, M. Equal opportunity for women in sport. In B. Hoepner (ed.). *Women's Athletics: Coping with Controversy.* Washington, D.C.: American Association for Health, Physical Education, and Recreation, 1974.
59. Dunning, E. Sport as a male preserve: Notes on the social sources of masculine identity and its transformations. *Theory, Culture and Society* 3:79–90, 1986.
60. Duquin, M.E. The androgynous advantage. In C.A. Oglesby (ed.). *Women and Sport: From Myth to Reality.* Philadelphia: Lea & Febiger, 1978, pp. 89–106.
61. Duquin, M.E. Creating social reality: The case of women and sport. In S. Greendorfer and A. Yiannakis (eds.). *Sociology of Sport: Diverse Perspectives.* West Point, N.Y.: Leisure Press, 1981, pp. 77–82.
62. Edwards, H. *The Revolt of the Black Athlete.* New York: Free Press, 1969.
63. Ehrenreich, B., and D. English. *For Her Own Good: 150 Years of the Experts Advice to Women.* Garden City, N.Y.: Anchor Books, 1979.
64. Eitzen, S. Sport and social status in American public secondary education. *Rev. Sport Leisure* 1:139–155, 1976.
65. Felshin, J. The social anomaly of women in sports. *Physical Educator* 30:122–124, 1973.
66. Felshin, J. The fullcourt press for women in athletics. In B. Hoepner (ed.). *Women's Athletics: Coping With Controversy,* Washington, D.C.: American Association for Health, Physical Education, and Recreation, 1974, pp.
67. Felshin, J. The social view. In E.W. Gerber, J. Felshin, P. Berlin, and W. Wyrick (eds.). *The American Woman in Sport.* Reading, Mass.: Addison-Wesley, 1974, pp.177–279.
68. Felshin, J. The triple option . . . . for women in sport. *Quest* 21:36–40, 1974.
69. Felshin, J. Sport styles and social modes. *J. Health Phys. Educ. Recreat. Dance* 46:31–34, 1975.
70. Feltz, D. Athletics in the status system of female adolescents. *Rev. Sport Leisure* 3:98–108, 1978.
71. Fishwick, L., and S. Greendorfer. Socialization revisited: A critique of the sport-related research. *Quest* 39:1–8, 1987.
72. Gerber, E.W., J. Felshin, P. Berlin, and W. Wyrick. *The American Woman in Sport.* Reading, Mass.: Addison-Wesley, 1974.
73. Grabiner, V. Come out slugging. *Quest* 2:52–57, 1976.
74. Grant, C.H.B. The gender gap in sport: From Olympic to intercollegiate level. *Arena Rev.* 8:31–48, 1984.
75. Green, T.S., C.A. Oglesby, A. Alexander, and N. Franke. *The Black Woman in Sport.*

Reston, Va.: American Alliance for Health, Physical Education, Recreation, and Dance, 1981.

76. Greenberg, R.J. AIAW vs. NCAA: The takeover and implications. *J. Nat. Assoc. Women Deans, Administrators, Counselors* 47:29–36, 1984.

77. Greendorfer, S. Role of socializing agents in female sport involvement. *Res. Q.* 48:304–310, 1977.

78. Greendorfer, S. Socialization into sport. In C.A. Oglesby (ed.). *Women and Sport: From Myth to Reality.* Philadelphia: Lea & Febiger, 1978, pp. 115–140.

79. Greendorfer, S. Differences in childhood socialization influences of women involved in sport and women not involved in sport. In M. Krotee (ed.). *The Dimensions of Sport Sociology.* West Point, N.Y.: Leisure Press, 1979, pp. 59–72.

80. Greendorfer, S. Shaping the female athlete: The impact of the family. In M. Boutilier and L. SanGiovanni (eds.). *The Sporting Woman.* Champaign, Ill.: Human Kinetics Press, 1983, pp. 135–155.

81. Greendorfer, S. Gender bias in theoretical perspectives: The case of female socialization into sport. *Psychol. Women Q.* in press.

82. Greendorfer, S.L., and E.M. Blinde. "Retirement" from intercollegiate sport: Theoretical and empirical considerations. *Sociol. Sport J.* 2:101–110, 1985.

83. Greendorfer, S., and M. Ewing. Race and gender differences in children's socialization into sport. *Res. Q. Exerc. Sport* 52:301–310, 1981.

84. Greendorfer, S.L., and J.H. Lewko. Role of family members in sport socialization of children. *Res. Q.* 49:146–152, 1978.

85. Griffin, P.S. What's a nice girl like you doing in a profession like this? *Quest* 19:96–101, 1973.

86. Gruneau, R. *Class, Sport, and Social Development.* Amherst: University of Massachusetts Press, 1983.

87. Hall, M.A. A "feminine woman" and an "athletic woman" as viewed by participants and non-participants in sports. *Br. J. Phys. Educ.* 3:43–46, 1972.

88. Hall, M.A. The sociological perspective of females in sport. In M. Adrian and J. Brame (eds.). *DGWS Research Reports Women in Sports,* Vol 3. Washington, D.C.: American Alliance for Health, Physical Education, and Recreation, 1977, pp. 37–50.

89. Hall, M.A. *Sport and Gender: A Feminist Perspective on the Sociology of Sport.* CAHPER Sociology of Sport Monograph Series Ottawa: Canadian Assocation for Health, Physical Education, and Recreation, 1978.

90. Hall, M.A. Intellectual sexism in physical education. *Quest* 31:172–186, 1979.

91. Hall, M.A. Women and the Lawrentian wrestle. *Can. Woman Studies* 1:39–41, 1979.

92. Hall, M.A. Sport, sex roles and sex identity. The CRIAW Papers/Les Documents de L'CRIAF. Ottawa: Canadian Research Institute for the Advancement of Women, 1981.

93. Hall, M.A. Towards a feminist analysis of gender inequality in sport. In N. Theberge and P. Donnelly (eds.). *Sport and the Sociological Imagination.* Fort Worth: Texas Christian University Press, 1983, pp. 82–103.

94. Hall, M.A. Feminist prospects for sociology of sport. *Arena Rev.* 8:1–10, 1984.

95. Hall, M.A. Knowledge and gender: Epistemological questions in the social analysis of sport. *Sociol. Sport J.* 2:25–42, 1985.

96. Hall, M.A. How should we theorize sport in a capitalist partriarchy? *Int. Rev. Sociol. Sport* 20:109–115, 1985.

97. Halsey, E.C. *Women in Physical Education.* New York: Putnam, 1961.

98. Hanks, M. Race, sex, athletics and education achievement. *Social Sci. Q.* 60:482–496, 1979.

99. Harding, C. (ed.). Women in sport issue, Arena Rev. 1:1977.

100. Hargreaves, J. "Playing like gentlemen while behaving like ladies": Contradictory features of the formative years of women's sport. *Br. J. Sports History* 2:40–52, 1985.

101. Hargreaves, J.A. Where's the virtue? Where's the grace? A discussion of the social production of gender relations in and through sport. *Theory, Culture Society* 3:109–119, 1986.

102. Harres, B. Attitudes of students toward women's athletic competition. *Res. Q.* 39:278–284, 1968.

103. Harris, D. The social self and the competitive self of the female athlete. Paper presented at the Third International Symposium on the Sociology of Sport, Waterloo, 1971.

104. Harris, D. (ed.). *Women and Sport: A National Research Conference.* University Park: Pennsylvania State University Press, 1972.

105. Harris, D. Psychosocial dimensions. *J. Health Phys. Educ. Recreat.* 46:32–36, 1977.

106. Harris, D. Femininity and athleticism: Conflict or consonance. In D. Sabo and R. Runfola (eds.). *Jock: Sports and Male Identity.* Englewood Cliffs, N.J.: Prentice-Hall, 1980, pp. 222–239.

107. Harris, J. Hermeneutics and sport research: Understanding cultural interpretations. In S. Greendorfer and A. Yiannakis (eds.). *Sociology of Sport: Diverse Perspectives.* West Point, N.Y.: Leisure Press, 1981, pp. 15–22.

108. Hart, B., C. Hasbrook, and S. Mathes. An examination of the reduction in the number of female interscholastic coaches. *Res. Q.* 57:68–77, 1986.

109. Hart, M. Sport: Women sit in the back of the bus. *Psychol. Today.* 1971.

110. Hart, M. On being female in sport. In M. Hart (ed.). *Sports in the Sociocultural Process.* Dubuque: William C. Brown, 1972, pp. 291–301.

111. Hart, M. Stigma or prestige: The All American choice. In M. Hart (ed.). *Sport in the Sociocultural Process,* 2nd ed. Dubuque: William C. Brown, 1976, pp. 176–182.

112. Hartsock, N. The feminist standpoint: Developing the ground for a specifically feminist historical materialism. In S. Harding and M.B. Hintikka (eds.). *Discovering Reality.* Boston: Reidel, 1983, pp. 283–310.

113. Hartsock, N. *Money, Sex and Power.* Boston: Northeastern University Press, 1985.

114. Hasbrook, C.A. The theoretical notion of reciprocity and childhood socialization into sport. In A. Dunleavy, A.W. Miracle, and C.R. Ress (eds.). *Studies in the Sociology of Sport.* Fort Worth: Texas Christian University Press, 1982, pp. 139–151.

115. Hauge, A. The influence of the family on sport participation. In D. Harris (ed.). *DGWS Research Reports Women in Sports,* Vol. 2. Washington, D.C.: American Association for Health, Physical Education, and Recreation, 1973, pp. 17–26.

116. Heide, W.S. Feminism for a sporting future. In C.A. Oglesby (ed.). *Women and Sport: From Myth to Reality.* Philadelphia: Lea & Febiger, 1978, pp. 195–202.

117. Helling, M. Women's rights in athletes. In B. Hoepner (ed.). *Women's Athletics: Coping with Controversy.* Washington, D.C.: American Association for Health, Physical Education, and Recreation, 1974, pp. 20–205.

118. Hilliard, D. Media images of male and female professional athletes: An interpretive analysis of magazine articles. *Sociol. Sport J.* 1:251–262, 1984.

119. Hock, P. School for sexism. In *Rip Off the Big Game.* New York: Anchor Doubleday, 1972.

120. Hoepner, B. (ed.). *Women's Athletics Coping with Controversy.* Washington, D.C.: American Association for Health, Physical Education, and Recreation, 1974.

121. Hoffman, A. *About Face: Towards a Positive Image of Women in Sport.* Ontario: The Ontario Status of Women Council, Ontario Secretariat for Social Development, and The Ontario Ministry of Culture and Recreation, 1976.

122. Holmen, M.G., and B.L. Parkhouse. Trends in the selection of coaches for female athletes: A demographic inquiry. *Res. Q. Exerc. Sport* 52:9–18, 1981.
123. Houzer, S. Black women in athletics. *Physical Educator* 31:208–209, 1974.
124. Hull, G.T., P.B. Scott, and B. Smith (eds.). *But Some of Us Are Brave: Black Women's Studies.* Old Westbury, N.Y.: Feminist Press, 1982.
125. Ingham, A., J. Loy, and J. Berryman. Socialization, dialectics and sport. In D. Harris (ed.). *Women and Sport: A National Research Conference.* University Park: Pennsylvania State University, 1972, pp. 235–276.
126. Jagger, A.M., and P.S. Rothenberg Press (eds.). *Feminist Frameworks: Alternative Theoretical Accounts of the Relations Between Women and Men,* 2nd ed. New York: McGraw-Hill, 1984.
127. Jensen, J. Women's collegiate athletics: Incidents in the struggle for influence and control. In R. Lapchick (ed.). *Fractured Focus: Sport as a Reflection of Society.* Lexington, Mass.: Lexington Books, 1986, pp. 151–161.
128. Kane, J. Psychological aspects of sport with special reference to the female. In D. Harris (ed.). *Women and Sport: A National Research Conference.* University Park: Pennsylvania State University, 1972, pp. 19–34.
129. Kane, M.J. The influence of level of sport participation and sex-role orientation on female professionalization of attitudes toward play. *J. Sport Psychol.* 4:290–294, 1982.
130. Katner, R.M. *Men and Women of the Corporation.* New York: Basic Books, 1977.
131. Kennard, J.A. History of physical education. *Signs* 2:835–842, 1976.
132. Kenyon, G.S., and B.M. McPherson. Becoming involved in physical activity and sport: A process of socialization. In G.L. Rarick (ed.). *Physical Growth and Development.* New York: Academic Press, 1973, pp. 303–332.
133. Kidd, D. Getting physical: Compulsory heterosexuality and sport. *Can. Woman Studies* 4:62–65, 1983.
134. Kiger, G., and D. Lorentzen. The relative effects of gender, race and sport on university academic performance. *Sociol. Sport J.* 3:160–167, 1986.
135. Knoppers, A. Gender and the coaching profession. *Quest* 39:9–22, 1987.
136. Knoppers, A., and J. Scheuteman. Winning is not the only thing. *Sociol. Sport J.* 3:43–56, 1986.
137. Landers, D. Pscyhological femininity and the prospective female physical educator. *Res. Q.* 41:164–170, 1970.
138. Landers, D.M., D.L. Feltz, G.E. Obermeier, and T.R. Brouse. Socialization via interscholastic athletics: Its effects on educational attainment. *Res. Q.* 49:475–483, 1978.
139. Lee, M. The case for and against intercollegiate athletics for women and the situation as it stands today. *Am. Phys. Educ. Rev.* 29:13–19, 1924.
140. Lee, M. The case for and against intercollegiate athletics for women and the situation since 1923. *Res. Q.* 2:93–127, 1931.
141. Lenskyj, H. *Out of Bounds: Women, Sport and Sexuality.* Toronto: Women's Press, 1986.
142. Lever, J. Sex differences in the games children play. *Social Problems* 23:479–488, 1976.
143. Lever, J. Sex differences in the complexity of children's play. *Am. Sociol Rev.* 43:471–483, 1978.
144. Liu, X. Career mobility patterns of NCAA Division I coaches of women's basketball teams. Master's thesis, University of Iowa, Iowa City, 1987.
145. Lopiano, D.A. A political analysis of the possibility of impact alternatives for the accomplishment of feminist objectives within American intercollegiate sport. *Arena Rev.* 8:46–91, 1984.
146. Loy, J., S. Birrell, and D. Rose. Attitudes held toward agonic activities as a function of selected social issues. *Quest* 26:81–93, 1976.

147. Loy, J., G. Kenyon, and B. McPherson (eds.). *Sport, Culture and Society* 2nd ed. Philadelphia: Lea & Febiger, 1981.
148. Loy, J., and J. McElvogue. Racial segregation in American sport. *Int. Rev. Sport Sociol.* 5:5–23, 1970.
149. Loy, J., B. McPherson, and G. Kenyon. *The Sociology of Sport as an Academic Specialty.* CAPHER Sociology of Sport Monograph Series. Ottawa: Canadian Association for Health, Physical Education, and Recreation 1978.
150. Loy, J., and G. Sage. Athletic personnel in the academic marketplace: A study of the interorganizational mobility patterns of college coaches. *Sociol. Work Occup.* 5:446–469, 1978.
151. MacKinnon, C. Feminism, Marxism, method and the state: An agenda for theory. *Signs* 7:515–544, 1982.
152. MacKinnon, C. Women, self-possession and sport. In *Feminism Unmodified: Discourses on Life and Law.* Cambridge, Mass.: Harvard University Press, 1987, pp. 117–124.
153. Malumphy, T. Personality of women athletes in intercollegiate competition. *Res. Q.* 39:484–490, 1968.
154. Malumphy, T. College women athletes: Questions and tentative answers. *Quest* 14:18–27, 1970.
155. Mathes, S. Body image and sex stereotyping. In C.A. Oglesby (ed.). *Women and Sport: From Myth to Reality.* Philadelphia: Lea & Febiger, 1978, pp. 59–72.
156. McGee, R. Comparisons of attitudes toward intensive competition for high school girls. *Res. Q.* 27:60–73, 1956.
157. McHugh, M.C., M.E. Duquin, and I. Frieze. Beliefs about success and failure: Attribution and the female athlete. In C.A. Oglesby (ed.). *Women and Sport: From Myth to Reality.* Philadelphia: Lea & Febiger, 1978, pp. 173–191.
158. McKay, J. Marxism as a way of seeing. *Sociol. Sport J.* 3:261–272, 1986.
159. Metheny, E. Relative values in athletics for girls. *J. Educ. Sociol.* 28:268–270, 1955.
160. Metheny, E. *Connotations of Movement in Sport and Dance.* Dubuque: William C. Brown, 1962.
161. Millman, M., and R.M. Kanter (eds.). *Feminist Perspectives on Social Life and Social Science.* Garden City, N.Y.: Anchor Books, 1975.
162. Mullins, N.C. *Theories and Theory Groups in Contemporary American Sociology.* New York: Harper & Row, 1973.
163. Murphy, M.D. The Involvement of blacks in women's athletics in member institutions of the AIAW. Ph.D. dissertation, University of Florida, 1980.
164. Mushier, C.L. Personality of selected women athletes. *Int. J. Sport Psychol.* 3:25–31, 1972.
165. Myes, A.M., and H. Lips. Participation in competitive amateur sports as a function of psychological androgyny. *Sex Roles* 4:571–578, 1978.
166. NCAA files statement regarding civil rights legislation. *NCAA News* 21:1,3, June 6, 1984.
167. Oglesby, C.A. (ed.). *Women and Sport: From Myth to Reality.* Philadelphia: Lea & Febiger, 1978.
168. Peiss, K. *Cheap Amusements: Working Women and Leisure in Turn of the Century New York.* Philadelphia: Temple University Press, 1986.
169. Peterson, S.L., J.C. Weber, and W.W. Trousdale. Personality traits of women in team sports vs. women in individual sports. *Res. Q.* 38:686–690, 1967.
170. Phillips, M. Women in sport: The impact of society. In D. Harris (ed.). *Division for Girls and Women's Sports Research Reports Women in Sports,* Vol 1. Washington, D.C.: American Association for Health, Physical Education, and Recreation, 1971, pp. 5–14.
171. Phillips, M. Sociological considerations of the female participant. In D. Harris (ed.).

Women and Sport: A National Research Conference. University Park: Pennsylvania State University, 1972, pp. 185–202.

172. Portz, E. Influence of birth order and sibling sex on sports participation. In D. Harris (ed.). *Women and Sport: A National Research Conference.* University Park: Pennsylvania State University, 1972, pp. 225–234.

173. Prendergast, S. Stoolball—the pursuit of vertigo? *Women's Studies Int. Q.* 1:15–26, 1978.

174. Prus, R. Career contingencies: Examining patterns of involvement. In N. Theberge and P. Donnelly (eds.). *Sport and the Sociological Imagination.* Fort Worth: Texas Christian University Press, 1984, pp. 297–317.

175. Purdy, D.A., D.S. Eitzen, and R. Hufnagel. Are athletes also students? The educational attainment of college athletes. *Social Problems* 29:439–448, 1982.

176. Purdy, D.A., D.S. Eitzen, and R. Hufnagel. Educational achievements of college athletes by gender. *West. Georgia College Studies Social Sci.* 24:19–32, 1985.

177. Rao, V.V.P., and S.J. Overman. Psychological well-being and body image: A comparison of black women athletes and non-athletes. *J. Sport Behavior* 9:79–91, 1086.

178. Rintala, J., and S. Birrell. Fair treatment for the active female: A content analysis of *Young Athlete* magazine. *Sociol. Sport J.* 1:231–250, 1984.

179. Rosenbrock, P. Conundrum: A decade of struggle and change as experienced by women administrators in Division 1A intercollegiate athletic programs. Ph.D. dissertation, University of Iowa, 1987.

180. Sabo, D.F., and R. Runfola (eds.). *Jock: Sports and Male Identity.* Englewood Cliffs, N.J.: Prentice-Hall, 1980.

181. Safrit, M.J. Women in research in physical education. *Quest* 31:158– 171, 1979.

182. Safrit, M.J. Women in research in physical education: A 1984 update. *Quest* 36:103–114, 1984.

183. Sage, G. Orientation toward sport of male and female intercollegiate athletics. *J. Sport Psychol.* 2:355–362, 1980.

184. Sage, G., and S. Loudermilk. The female athlete and role conflict. *Res. Q.* 50:88–96, 1979.

185. Schriver, A. Competition: NSWA faces the issue. *J. Health Phys. Educ.* 20:451–472, 1949.

186. Scott, J. The masculine obsession in sport. In B. Hoepner (ed.). *Women's Athletics: Coping with Controversy.* Washington, D.C.: American Association for Health, Physical Education, and Recreation, 1974, pp. 83–88.

187. Scott, M.G. Competition for women in American colleges and universities. *Res. Q.* 16:49–71, 1945.

188. Seha, A. The administrative enforcement of Title IX in intercollegiate athletics. *Law and Inequality: A Journal of Theory and Practice* 2:121–326, 1984.

189. Sheard, K., and E. Dunning. The rugby football club as a type of male preserve: Some sociological notes, *Int. Rev. Sport Sociol.* 5:5– 24, 1973.

190. Sherif, C. Females and the competitive process. In D. Harris (ed.). *Women and Sport: A National Research Conference,* University Park: Pennsylvania State University, 1972, pp. 115–139.

191. Slatton, B. AIAW: The greening of American athletics. In J. Frey (ed.). *The Governance of Intercollegiate Athletics,* West Point, N.Y.: Leisure Press, 1982, pp. 144–154.

192. Smith, D.E. Women's perspective as a radical critique of sociology. *Sociol. Ing.* 44:7–13, 1974.

193. Snyder, E., and J. Kivlin. Women athletes and aspects of psychological well-being and body image. *Res. Q.* 46:191–199, 1975.

194. Snyder, E., J. Kivlin, and E. Spreitzer. The female athlete: Analyses of objective and subjective role conflict. In D. Landers (ed.). *Psychology of Sport and Motor Behavior,* University Park: Pennsylvania State University Press, 1975, pp. 165–180.

195. Snyder, E., and E. Spreitzer. Correlates of sport participation among adolescent girls. *Res. Q.* 47:804–809, 1976.

196. Snyder, E., and E. Spreitzer. Participation in sport as related to educational expectations among high school girls. *Sociol. Educ.* 50:47–55, 1977.

197. Snyder, E., and E. Spreitzer. Socialization comparisons of adolescent female athletes and musicians. *Res. Q.* 49:342–350, 1978.

198. Spears, B. The emergence of women in sport. In B. Hoepner (ed.) *Women's Athletics: Coping with Controversy.* Washington D.C.: American Association for Health, Physical Education, and Recreation, 1974, pp. 26–42.

199. Spears, B. Prologue: The myth. In C.A. Oglesby (ed.). *Women in Sport: From Myth to Reality.* Philadelphia: Lea & Febiger, 1978, pp. 3–15.

200. Spence, J., and R. Helmreich. On assessing "androgyny." *Sex Roles* 5:721–738, 1979.

201. Spreitzer, E., and E. Snyder. Socialization into sport: An exploratory path analysis. *Res. Q.* 47:238–245, 1976.

202. Statement of policies and procedures for competition in girls and women's sport. *J. Health Phys. Educ.* 28:57–58, 1957.

203. Statement of policies for competition in girls and women's sports. *J. Health Phys. Educ.* 34:31–33, 1963.

204. Sumption, D. Recent trends in sports for women. In *Sports for Women.* New York: Prentice-Hall, 1940, pp. 1–15.

205. Swanson, R. From glide to stride: Significant events in a century of American women's sport. In B. Hoepner (ed.). *Women's Athletics: Coping with Controversy.* Washington, D.C.: American Association for Health, Physical Education, and Recreation, 1974, pp. 43–53.

206. Theberge, N. On the need for a more adequate theory of sport participation. *Sociol. Sport. J.* 1:26–33, 1978.

207. Theberge, N. A critique of critiques: Radical and feminist writings on sport. *Social Forces* 60:341–353, 1981.

208. Theberge, N. Feminism and sport: Linking the two through a new organiztion. *Can. Woman Studies* 4:79–81, 1983.

209. Theberge, N. Joining social theory to social action: Some Marxist principles. *Arena Rev.* 8:21–30, 1984.

210. Theberge, N. Sport and feminism in North America. *West Georgia College Studies Social Sci.* 24:41–54, 1985.

211. Theberge, N. Toward a feminist alternative to sport as a male preserve. *Quest* 10:193–202, 1985.

212. Theberge, N. Sport and women's empowerment. *Women's Studies Int. Forum* 10:387–393, 1987.

213. Theberge, N., and A. Cronk. Work routines in newspaper sports departments and the coverage of women's sports, *Sociol. Sport J.* 3:195–203, 1986.

214. Theberge, N., J. Curtis, and B. Brown. Sex differences in orientations towards games: Tests of the sports involvement hypothesis. In A.O. Dunleavy, A.W. Miracle, and C.R. Rees (ed.) *Studies in the Sociology of Sport.* Fort Worth: Texas Christian Press, 1982, pp. 285–308.

215. Tyler, S. Adolescent crisis: Sport participation for the female. In D. Harris (ed.). *Division for Girls and Women's Sports Research Reports Women in Sports,* Vol 2. Washington, D.C.: American Association for Health, Physical Education, and Recreation, 1973, pp. 27–33.

216. Ulrich, C. Women in sport. In W. Johnson (ed.). *Science and Medicine in Exercise and sports.* New York: Harper, 1960, pp. 508–516.
217. Vickers, J., M. Appleton, S. Inglis, J. Frowson, G. Bean, C. Savoy, and D. Knight. A comparative study of relative opportunities for women in the C.I.A.U. Report presented to the Canadian Interuniversity Athletic Union, Ottawa, 1982.
218. Webb, H. Professionalization of attitudes toward play among adolescents. In G. Kenyon (ed.). *Aspects of Contemporary Sport Sociology.* Proceedings of the CIC Sport Symposium, University of Wisconsin, 1969, pp. 161–178.
219. Weiss, P. *Sport: A Philosophic Inquiry.* Carbondale: Southern Illinois Press, 1969.
220. Welter, B. The cult of true womanhood: 1820–1860. *Am. Q.* 18:155–174, 1966.
221. Westkott, M., and J. Coakley. Women in sport: Modalities of feminist social change. *J. Sport Social Issues* 4:32–45, 1981.
222. Wheatley, E. Playing, partying, and the process of culture creation: A subcultural examination of a woman's rugby group. Paper presented at the North American Society for the Sociology of Sport Annual Meetings, Las Vegas, November 1986.
223. Whitson, D. Structure, agency and the sociology of sport debate. *Theory, Culture and Society* 3:99–107, 1986.
224. Williams, J.M. Personality characteristics of the successful female athlete. In W. Straub (ed.). *Sport Psychology: An analysis of Athlete Behavior.* Ithaca, N.Y.: Mouvement Publications, 1978, pp. 249–255.
225. Williams, R. *Marxism and Literature.* New York: Oxford University Press, 1985.
226. Willis, P.E. Performance and meanings: A sociological view of women in sport. Unpublished paper, Centre for Contemporary Cultural Studies, Birmingham, 1974.
227. Willis, P.E. Women in sport in ideology. In J. Hargreaves (ed.). *Sport, Culture and Ideology.* London: Routledge & Kegan Paul, 1982, pp. 117–135.
228. Women's Division, National Amateur Athletic Federation. *Women and Athletics.* New York: Barnes, 1930.
229. Women's programs list legislative priorities. *NCAA News* 21:1–2, June 6, 1984.
230. Wughalter, E. Ruffles and flounces: The apologetic in women's sport. *Frontiers* 3:11–13, 1977.
231. Youngen, L. Attitudes toward physical activity as a function of the approval motive of first-year college women. In D. Harris (ed.). *NAGWS Research Reports: Women in Sports,* Vol. 3. Washington, D.C.: American Association for Health, Physical Education, and Recreation, 1977, pp. 125–136.
232. Ziegler, S. Self perception of athletes and coaches. In D. Harris (ed.). *Women and Sport: A National Research Conference.* University Park: Pennsylvania State University, 1972, pp. 293–305.
233. Zoble, J. Femininity and achievement in sports. In D. Harris (ed.). *Women and Sport: A National Research Conference.* University Park: Pennsylvania State University, 1972, pp. 203–223.
234. Zoble, J. Femininity, achievement, and sports. In D. Harris (ed.). *DGWS Research Reports: Women in Sports,* Vol 2. Washington, D.C.: AAHPER, 1973, pp. 34–48.

15
Growth and Physical Performance Relative to the Timing of the Adolescent Spurt

GASTON BEUNEN, Ph.D.
ROBERT M. MALINA, Ph.D.

INTRODUCTION

Individual variation in the timing and tempo of the adolescent or pubescent growth spurt is well documented. "Timing" refers to when the spurt occurs, while "tempo" refers to the rate or speed at which the individual goes through the spurt. Cross-sectional treatment of changes in body size, body composition, and performance during adolescence, however, ordinarily present a smooth growth curve for most characteristics. As a result, the wide range of individual differences in the initiation and duration of the adolescent spurt is absorbed.

In order to appreciate fully individual differences in timing and tempo, a point of reference other than chronological age is necessary. Such indicators of biological maturity include skeletal age, age at appearance of secondary sex characteristics, and age at peak height velocity (PHV), the maximal rate of growth during the adolescent spurt. Although age at menarche is a widely used maturity indicator in studies of female adolescence, it is a rather late maturational event that occurs most often after PHV. Further, it does not have a corresponding maturity indicator in males. Age at PHV, on the other hand, is a maturity indicator that can be used in both sexes.

When adolescent growth or performance is expressed relative to the timing of PHV, i.e., as a biological parameter, rather than to chronological age, the time spread along the chronological age axis is reduced considerably. This concept was first realized by Boas [14] in 1892. Boas [15, 16] subsequently attempted to express growth relative to the timing of maximal growth in a serial study of about 1000 children in the early 1930s, but it was not possible to establish PHV with certainty [73].

Given the individuality of the adolescent growth spurt, this chapter considers adolescent changes in physical performance in the context of longitudinal data. More specifically, it addresses two questions. First, are there adolescent spurts in physical performance similar to those for stature and other body dimensions? Second, what is the timing of performance spurts relative to the timing of the adolescent spurts in stature and weight? In order to place changes in performance in the context of

503

adolescent growth, changes in body size and composition during the adolescent spurt are first considered. Finally, the concept of "adolescent awkwardness" is reviewed in the context of results of longitudinal studies of motor performance.

LONGITUDINAL STUDIES

There are basically two kinds of growth studies: cross-sectional and longitudinal. The mixed-longitudinal study includes components of each. The relative merits of longitudinal, mixed-longitudinal, and cross-sectional growth studies, and of the unique requirements for the statistical treatment of data assembled in each type of study, have been discussed at length by Tanner [84]. A comprehensive discussion of sampling and analytical problems in the treatment of longitudinal data is presented by Goldstein [40].

Longitudinal studies are characterized by repeated measurements on the same subjects at regular intervals over a period of time. In many longitudinal studies, children are measured at or around their birthdays during childhood and at half-year or 3 month intervals during adolescence. Sample sizes, however, are typically quite small in such studies, and sampling bias is a potential problem. On the other hand, some longitudinal studies have measured larger numbers of subjects at the same time of the year. Since ages vary at the time of measurement, these studies have more variability than those that see children at or near their birthdays.

Measurement frequency in a longitudinal study depends upon the characteristics monitored, on the velocity of changes that are occurring, and on measurement variability. Stature, the most commonly measured dimension in longitudinal studies, shows relatively small measurement variability compared to the increments that occur over 3-month intervals. For some motor performance tasks, on the other hand, changes that occur during adolescence are small and measurement variability is large [96]. Consequently, measurement frequency should be less for such tasks, and measurements at yearly intervals generally yield sufficient information to describe accurately changes that occur during adolescence.

Mixed-longitudinal studies include a multiple longitudinal component, which some suggest is a more efficient design to study human growth [77, 95]. In the mixed-longitudinal design, several cohorts of children of different birth years are followed for several years with overlapping age intervals. This design has the advantage of covering the growth span, i.e., approximately 18 to 20 years, in a shorter period of time, and permits, under certain assumptions, the determination of cohort and time-of-measurement effects. A unique concern of longitudinal studies is the separation of changes associated with growth from those associated with time-of-measurement effects. The latter are temporary effects, primarily in stature, weight, and fatness, that reflect seasonal fluctuations, changes in nutritional state, short-term illnesses, and variation in instruments, methods, and observers. Although proper design and quality control can minimize such effects, it is difficult to be certain of their presence or absence.

Physical performance measurements present an additional problem for longitudinal studies. Performance on some items can be affected by testing or learning effects. When a test is repeatedly administered over time, some learning will occur. For example, in the Leuven Growth Study of Belgian Boys [68], boys who were the same age and from the same birth cohort, and measured at the same time of the year, but who differed in the number of times that they had taken the performance tests in the longitudinal study, differed in their average performance. Those who had already taken the tests several times attained better performances in four of seven motor tasks [8]. Motivation is an additional factor in testing or learning effects. Changes in the willingness to perform a motor task can influence performance and, in turn, the increment between observation periods.

Although longitudinal, mixed-longitudinal, and cross-sectional studies of growth and performance have relative strengths and limitations, the different kinds of studies are complementary rather than competitive. The approach selected depends on the specific question(s) under study.

One of the main advantages of the longitudinal design is that it permits the analysis of individual growth patterns, i.e., serial data for individuals. Of special interest is the velocity of growth at different ages and changes in velocity. Adolescence is characterized by an increase in growth velocity, i.e., an acceleration, which indicates the initiation of a growth spurt.

QUANTIFYING THE TIME AND MAGNITUDE OF ADOLESCENT SPURTS

Several methods are available for the calculation of velocities and, in turn, the timing and magnitude of adolescent growth spurts. They have been applied primarily to stature, although they can be applied to other dimensions and to physical performance variables.

The oldest method is the simple analysis of increments, i.e., changes between two observation periods. The analysis of increments has the disadvantage that the continuity of the growth process is overlooked by simply connecting the increments by a straight line. In addition, several methodological inconsistencies are introduced, e.g., two measurement errors are involved in computing each increment, and successive increments are negatively related [94].

A second approach to the analysis of serial growth data for individuals is graphic [11, 88, 99]. Attained statures at each age or observation period are plotted and a smoothed curve is fitted graphically through the points. Statures at specific ages are then read off the graph, and velocities are calculated and plotted. A smooth curve is fitted through the plotted velocities to yield the velocity curve for the individual. Parameters of the adolescent spurt, i.e., age and size at take-off, velocity at take-off, age at maximal velocity, and maximal velocity, are then read off the curves.

A third approach is the fitting of preselected mathematical equations (growth functions) to serial data for individuals. Several models are presently available [72, 73]. Logistic and Gompertz functions were used initially to describe the adolescent spurt [28, 61], while single, double and triple logistic models [17, 18, 60, 87] and a modified logistic model [71, 72] were subsequently used. Many of these functions require either a measure of final level, e.g., adult stature, or an estimate of the take-off point or initiation of the adolescent spurt. In addition, the models vary in the way they fit the data, i.e., in goodness of fit. A disadvantage of these approaches is that only normal growth curves may be described. Finally, the parameters of the mathematically fitted growth curves may not always be interpretable in a biologically meaningful manner.

A fourth approach to analyzing longitudinal growth data is the fitting of smoothing polynomials. Applications of this approach include, e.g., the use of cubic splines [54], moving polynomials [94], and nonparametric kernel estimations [38]. Since polynomials may be considered as a good approximation of each possible growth function, these methods have the advantage that no preselected growth model is necessary. They do have, however, the disadvantage that a high measurement frequency is necessary.

The graphic, mathematical fitting, and smoothing polynomial approaches provide a good description of the human growth curve for stature during adolescence and of the main parameters of the curve. These include the age at take-off or initiation of the spurt, age at maximal velocity, age at attainment of adult values, attained sizes at each of these ages, and velocities at each point. Several of these procedures have been applied to maximal aerobic power and to motor performance, primarily to identify the timing of adolescent spurts relative to the spurts in stature or body weight. These are discussed in more detail later in this chapter.

In order to reduce the time spread across the chronological age axis in studies of adolescent growth, PHV is used as the point of reference, and years before and after PHV are used as the time axis. In this procedure, individual children are classified by years before and after their own PHV, regardless of the age at which PHV occurs. When data for many individuals are grouped in this manner, the resulting curve is called a "mean-constant curve" [88]. The curve is obtained by plotting all individual curves relative to PHV, independent of chronological age, and then averaging the attained stature or velocity at each time point before or after PHV. When mathematical functions are used, the mean-constant curve is obtained by fitting a function to the measurements of each individual, estimating the constants for each individual, and then averaging the constants to yield the curve.

Since Shuttleworth [81] first applied the method of plotting growth curves against a biological parameter rather than chronological age, it has become common practice to express attained growth and velocities of various body dimensions on a time axis relative to the timing of PHV. This procedure has also been applied to maximal aerobic power and to motor performance. Age at PHV is determined with one of the procedures described above. Then the attained levels and velocities for each performance item are calculated and averaged at time points before and after the age at PHV. The same can be done for the timing of peak velocity of other measurements during the adolescent spurt, e.g., age at peak weight velocity or age at peak strength velocity.

ADOLESCENT PARAMETERS FOR STATURE

Several parameters of the adolescent growth spurt in stature for several samples of North American and European children are summarized in Table 1. The double logistic estimates [91] for the four major longitudinal studies of American children (the Berkeley Growth Study in California, the Child Research Council in Denver, the Fels Research Institute in Yellow Springs, Ohio, and the Harvard School of Public Health in Boston) are not included in the table. The double logistic model provides a poor fit to stature velocity and gives an early age at take-off and estimated age at PHV [31, 43]. Nevertheless, the results with the double logistic model indicate no differences in the timing of take-off and PHV, and in PHV, among the four United States samples [91].

Variation in the estimates of parameters of the adolescent growth spurt in stature is related, in part, to the different models and procedures used to derive them. When the same model is applied to different samples, however, the variation is considerably less. Allowing for methodological differences, the data show a reasonable degree of uniformity among samples of North American and European children. The uniformity is of interest given the period of time over which the longitudinal observations have been made. The studies of U.S. children in Berkeley and Denver were begun in the late 1920s. Many of the European studies were begun in the mid-1950s, while others were done in the 1960s and 1970s.

Several features should be noted in the values presented in Table 1. The first is the sex difference. Girls are advanced, on the average, about 2 years in the timing of the initiation of the spurt and age at PHV. In

508 | *Beunen, Malina*

TABLE 1
*Means and Standard Deviations (Medians as Indicated) for Age at Initiation of the Spurt, Age at PHV, and PHV in
North American and European Children*

Sample and Reference	Method	Girls							Boys						
		N	Age at Initiation (years)		Age at PHV (years)		PHV ($\text{cm} \cdot \text{yr}^{-1}$)		N	Age at Initiation (years)		Age at PHV (years)		PHV ($\text{cm} \cdot \text{yr}^{-1}$)	
			M	SD	M	SD	M	SD		M	SD	M	SD	M	SD
North American															
Colorado [28]	Gompertz	24			11.4	0.9	9.1	1.2	24			13.4	0.9	9.6	0.9
California [17]	Triple logistic	70			11.6	0.9			66			13.7	1.1		
Massachusetts [102]	Preece-Baines I	332	8.7	1.6	11.6	1.2	7.8	1.7							
Quebec [29]	Graphic	46			12.0	1.1									
Saskatchewan [64]	Preece-Baines I	22	9.0	1.0	11.8	0.7	8.0	1.2	75	11.1	1.0	14.3	1.0	9.4	1.5
European															
Belgium, Brussels [43]	Preece-Baines I	35	8.5	0.9	11.6	1.0	7.4	1.0							
	Single logistic	35	9.9	1.1	11.4	1.0	7.8	1.1							
	Graphic	35	9.9	1.1	11.7	1.0	7.8	0.9							
Belgium, national [6]	Nonsmoothed polynomials								432			14.2	1.0	9.2	1.6
England, Harpenden [88]	Graphic	41	10.3	0.9	12.1	0.9	9.0	1.0	49	12.1	0.9	14.1	0.9	10.3	1.5
England, Harpenden [87]	Single logistic	35	9.0	0.7	11.9	0.9	8.1	0.8	55	10.7	0.9	13.9	0.8	8.8	1.1
England, Harpenden [71]	Preece-Baines I	23	8.7	0.6	11.9	0.7	7.5	0.8	35	10.3	0.9	14.2	0.9	8.2	1.2
England, Harpenden and London [72]	Preece-Baines I	38			11.9	0.7	7.5	0.7	61			13.9	1.0	8.5	1.1

Location	Method	N							N						
England, London [22]	Preece-Baines I	42 746/695			12.2 12.2	1.1	8.0	1.1	50 653/539	11.0	1.3	13.9 14.1	1.0	9.6	1.2
England, Newcastle upon Tyne [12]	Graphic								68			13.8	0.9	9.7	1.1
France, Paris [74, 75]	Graphic	80	9.3	1.1	12.0	0.9	8.4	0.9							
Italy, Carrara, Tuscany [61]	Gompertz	121			10.2*	0.8	8.6	1.4							
Netherlands, Leiden [97]	Logistic	121			10.5	0.8	8.4	1.2	81			14.4			
	Graphic, half-year increments														
Netherlands, Amsterdam [48]	Moving polynomials	131/82			12.6†		6.7†		102/96			14.0†		9.6†	
Poland, Wrocław [9, 10]	Graphic	234	9.7	1.1	11.7	0.9	8.3	1.2	111	11.8	1.2	13.9	1.1	9.8	1.4
Sweden, urban [55]	Mid-year velocities	357/330			11.9	0.9			373/354			14.1	1.1		
Sweden, Stockholm [89, 90]	Three-month moving increments	90	10.0	1.3	12.0	1.0	8.6	1.1	122	12.1	1.2	14.1	1.1	9.9	1.1
Sweden, Umeå [37]	Midpoint‡	83			11.7	1.1	8.0	1.3				13.9	0.8	9.0	1.1
Switzerland, Zurich [54]	Splines	110	9.6	1.1	12.2	1.0	7.1	1.0	112	11.0	1.2	13.9	0.9	8.3	0.8
Switzerland, Zurich [38]	Kernel estimations	45	9.7	1.0	12.2	0.8	7.0	1.0	45	10.9	1.1	13.9			
	Preece-Baines 3	45	9.0	0.7	12.1	0.8	7.1	1.1	45	10.6	0.8	14.0	0.9	8.7	1.0

*This sample is composed largely of early-maturing girls; hence, the estimates are somewhat earlier (see text for more detail).

†Medians. The sample of girls in this study excludes early maturers; hence, the estimated median age at PHV is somewhat later and the velocity somewhat lower (see text for more detail).

‡Midpoint between the two consecutive height measurements during which maximum growth was noted.

contrast, the magnitude of the growth spurt, PHV, is greater in males. Second, the standard deviations around the mean ages are about 1 year in most studies. The larger standard deviations in the study of Zacharias and Rand [102] reflect the procedures used to collect stature data for such a large sample. The data were obtained, in part, from questionnaires and school records.

The estimates for two samples of girls in Table 1 need special mention. The study of Dutch adolescents by Kemper et al. [48] began when the subjects were 12 years of age. One-third of the girls had already passed their PHV before the start of the study. Thus, the reported median age at PHV is skewed upward, 12.6 years, and the estimated PHV is low, 6.7 cm $\cdot$ yr^{-1}. On the other hand, the sample of Italian girls reported by Marubini et al. [61] is limited largely to early-maturing girls who attained menarche, on the average, 0.6 year earlier than the general population of Carrara. Thus, estimated ages at PHV are quite low, 10.2 and 10.5 years with the Gompertz and logistic functions, respectively. Nevertheless, part of the earliness is probably population variation. Girls in southern Europe tend to attain menarche at earlier average ages than those in northern and northwestern Europe [27], and the earliness probably also applies to the growth spurt. Children from the latter areas comprise many of the samples in Table 1.

The values presented in Table 1 are sample estimates, and there is considerable variation within samples. For example, in 112 boys of the Zurich study, estimates for individuals boys range from 7.8 to 13.5 years for age at take-off of the spurt, from 12.0 to 15.8 years for age at PHV, and from 6.7 to 12.4 cm $\cdot$ yr^{-1} for PHV. Corresponding data for 110 Swiss girls are 6.6 to 12.9 years for age at initiation of the spurt, 9.3 to 15.0 years for age at PHV, and 5.0 to 10.1 cm $\cdot$ yr^{-1} for PHV [54]. Similar ranges of individual values are apparent in other studies as well.

Age at PHV and PHV are negatively correlated, the coefficients ranging from moderately high (-0.75) to almost zero (-0.02) [6, 12, 22, 28, 54, 55, 61, 87]. Thus, there is a tendency for children who experience an early growth spurt to have a somewhat higher PHV, and vice versa. There is, however, no relationship between age at PHV and adult stature; the correlations approach zero (-0.17 to $+0.05$) [22, 54, 87]. On the other hand, correlations between age at PHV and size at PHV are low but positive (0.13 to 0.33) [22, 54, 87], which suggests a tendency for youngsters who attain PHV at an earlier age to be somewhat taller at that age.

ADOLESCENT PARAMETERS IN OTHER DIMENSIONS

Maximum growth in body weight during adolescence, i.e., age at peak weight velocity (PWV), generally occurs after PHV, and standard deviations are about 1 year (Table 2). Although the data are not as extensive as for stature, PWV is, on the average, greater in boys than in girls. Among boys, the differences between mean ages at PHV and PWV range from 0.2 to 0.4 year, while among girls they vary between 0.3 and 0.9 year. The difference is related, in part, to sex differences in body composition. The adolescent weight spurt in boys includes principally gains in stature (skeletal tissue) and muscle mass, while fat mass is relatively stable at the time of PHV. Girls, on the other hand, experience a slightly less intense spurt in stature, a less dramatic increase in muscle mass, but a continuous rise in fat mass at this time (changes in body composition during the adolescent spurt are discussed later in this section).

Mean ages at peak velocity (PV) and PV for two segment lengths and two skeletal breadths for several longitudinal samples are summarized in Table 3. Age at PHV is included in the table as a reference point. The standard deviations around the means are of the same magnitude as those for stature, and as expected, there are sex differences. Differential timing of the growth spurt in each dimension relative to stature is apparent. PV for leg length occurs earlier than that for stature, while PV for sitting height or trunk length occurs after that for stature. Thus, rapid growth of the lower extremities is characteristic in the early part of the adolescent spurt.

In the samples of British and Polish boys, PV in bicristal breadth occurs, on average, quite close to that for stature, while PV for biacromial breadth occurs quite close to that for sitting height or trunk length. In girls, the available data are more variable, and the reason for the discrepancy between the studies is not clear. PVs for the two skeletal breadths do not differ in girls, but PV of biacromial breadth in boys is considerably greater than that for bicristal breadth. This variation in PV contributes to the sexual dimorphism in relative shoulder and hip breadths that occurs at this time.

In the Leuven Growth Study of Belgian Boys [6], distance and velocity curves for 12 anthropometric dimensions that showed an adolescent spurt were aligned on PHV and PWV (Table 4). Maximum velocities for leg length, bicondylar breadth of the femur, and two lower limb circumferences precede PHV, while maximum velocities for sitting height, and skeletal breadths and circumferences of the trunk and upper extremities, occur after PHV. In contrast, no dimensions show a growth spurt after PWV; rather, all dimensions experience their spurts prior to or coincident with PWV. Of those spurts that occur coincident with PWV, two are skeletal breadths of the trunk. The timing of adolescent spurts in limb circumferences is, to some extent, confounded by loss of subcutaneous fat on the extremities during male adolescence (see below).

Correlations between ages at PV and PV for sitting height, estimated leg length, and biacromial and bicristal breadths are generally lower

TABLE 2
Means and Standard Deviations for Estimated Ages at PWV and PWV for Several Samples of North American and European Children. Mean Ages at PHV Are Included for Comparison

Sample and Reference	Method	Girls						Boys					
		N	Age at PWV (years) M	SD	PWV (kg·yr⁻¹) M	SD	Age at PHV (years) M	N	Age at PWV (years) M	SD	PWV (kg·yr⁻¹) M	SD	Age at PHV (years) M
North American:													
Massachusetts [102, 103]	Preece-Baines I	207	12.5	1.2	6.6	2.0	11.6	75	14.5	1.1	8.7	2.3	14.3
Saskatchewan [64]	Preece-Baines I	22	12.1	0.7	6.8	1.2	11.8						
European:													
Belgium, national [6]	Nonsmoothed polynomials							429	14.6	1.2	8.8	2.3	14.2
England, Harpenden [88]	Graphic	33	12.9	1.0	8.8	1.5	12.1	46	14.3	0.9	9.8	2.0	14.1
Poland, Wrocław [9, 100]	Graphic	234	12.4	1.1			11.7	111	14.2	1.1			13.9
Sweden, urban [55]	Mid-year velocities	338	12.5	1.1	7.3	1.8	11.9	339	14.3	1.1	9.1	2.0	14.1

TABLE 3

Means and Standard Deviations for Estimated Ages at PV and PV in Several Samples of European Children. Mean Ages at PHV Are Included for Comparison

Sample and Reference	Method	N	Age at PHV (years) M	Leg Length*				Sitting Height†				Biacromial Breadth				Bicristal Breadth			
				Age at PV (years) M	SD	PV (cm·yr⁻¹) M	SD	Age at PV (years) M	SD	PV (cm·yr⁻¹) M	SD	Age at PV (years) M	SD	PV (cm·yr⁻¹) M	SD	Age at PV (years) M	SD	PV (cm·yr⁻¹) M	SD
Girls																			
England, Harpenden [87]	Logistic	35	11.9	11.6	0.9	4.3	0.6	12.2	1.0	4.0	0.5	12.2	1.1	1.7	0.3	12.3	1.0	1.5	0.3
England, London [22]	Preece-Baines I	38	12.2					12.7											
Poland, Wrocław [100]	Graphic	232/236	11.7	11.2	1.0			12.2	1.1			11.6	0.9			11.4	0.9		
Boys																			
Belgium, national [6]	Nonsmoothed polynomials	424/427	14.2	14.0	0.9	5.0	1.4	14.3	1.0	5.3	1.2								
England, Harpenden [87]	Logistic	55	13.9	13.6	0.8	4.3	0.7	14.3	0.9	4.5	0.7	14.2	0.9	2.2	0.3	14.0	1.0	1.4	0.3
England, London [22]	Preece-Baines I	51	13.9					14.1											
Poland, Wrocław [10, 100]	Graphic	175/177	14.0	13.6	1.1			14.4	1.1			14.3	1.1			14.1	1.1		

*Leg length is estimated as stature minus sitting height, with the exception of the Polish study, in which it is symphyseal height.
†Sitting height in the Polish study is measured as sitting height of cervicale.

TABLE 4

Timing of Maximum Observed Velocities of Anthropometric Dimensions Relative to PHV and PWV, and Median Maximal Velocities Aligned on PHV or PWV Whichever Yielded the Maximum Value. Data from the Leuven Growth Study of Belgian Boys [6]*

Dimension	PHV			PWV			Median Maximal Velocity
	Precedes	Coincides	Follows	Precedes	Coincides	Follows	
Height		—		X			8.9 cm · yr^{-1}
Weight			X		—		7.9 kg · yr^{-1}
Sitting height			X	X			4.4 cm · yr^{-1}
Leg length	X			X			4.3 cm · yr^{-1}
Biacromial breadth			X		X		2.3 cm · yr^{-1}
Chest breadth			X		X		1.7 cm · yr^{-1}
Biepicondylar breadth, humerus			X	X			3.1 mm · yr^{-1}
Bicondylar breadth, femur	X			X			3.0 mm · yr^{-1}
Chest circumference, inspiration			X	X			5.2 cm · yr^{-1}
Flexed arm circumference			X		X		2.0 cm · yr^{-1}
Thigh circumference	X				X		3.0 cm · yr^{-1}
Calf circumference	X			X			1.7 cm · yr^{-1}

*The table should be read as follows: X indicates whether the maximum observed velocities for each dimension precede, coincide with, or follow either PHV or PWV.

than those for stature [87]. All the correlations are negative, as are those for stature, with the exception for bicristal breadth. On the other hand, correlations between ages at PV for stature, weight, estimated leg length, and sitting height are moderate to high [6, 9, 10, 87, 88], while those between peak velocities for these dimensions, though positive, range from moderate to low [6, 87, 88].

Data relating changes in body composition to the timing of the adolescent growth spurt are not extensive. Densitometric estimates of fat-free mass (FFM) in a longitudinal sample of 40 Czechoslovak boys show an adolescent spurt coincident with PHV [69]. Fat mass, on the other hand, shows only small changes during the spurt. During the interval of PHV, boys gain about 7.5 kg of FFM per year and about 0.8 kg of fat mass per year. Although fat mass increases at this time, relative fatness, i.e., fat mass as a percentage of body weight, declines by about -0.4% per year during the interval of PHV. This, of course, reflects the marked increase in FFM, so that fat mass represents a relatively smaller percentage of body weight during the male adolescent spurt.

Corresponding longitudinal data for changes in the body composition of girls during the adolescent spurt are not available. When densitometric estimates of FFM and fat mass for cross-sectional samples of adolescents are collated and viewed for the years just before and after PHV, i.e., about 11 to 13 years in girls and 13 to 15 years in boys, changes in body composition at the time of the growth spurt can be approximated. The estimated annual increases in FFM are 3.5 kg · yr^{-1} for girls and 7.2 kg · yr^{-1} for boys. Corresponding estimates for changes in absolute fat mass at this time are 0.7 kg · yr^{-1} in boys and 1.4 kg · yr^{-1} in girls, but estimates for relative fatness are $+0.9\%$ in girls and -0.5% in boys [58]. The estimates for boys based on data collated from the literature are quite similar to those for the longitudinal sample of Czechoslovak boys [69] described earlier, i.e., a gain of about 7.5 kg of FFM per year and 0.8 kg of fat mass per year at PHV, but a decline in relative fatness of about -0.4% per year at PHV.

FFM and fat mass are gross estimates, which do not differentiate among regions of the body and among tissues, i.e., muscle and bone, or subcutaneous from deep fat. Radiographic measurements of tissue widths on the arm and calf provide some insight into regional tissue variation, and the trends are not entirely consistent with the gross estimates (Figure 1). For example, PV of arm and calf muscle widths occur after PHV in both sexes. In arm muscle, PV occurs about 3 to 4 months after PHV in boys and about 6 months after PHV in girls. For the calf, peak gain in muscle tissue occurs at PHV in boys, with no clear peak in girls. Gain in calf muscle appears to be more or less constant from 1 year or so before PHV to about 1.5 years after PHV in girls. Boys have a spurt in

FIGURE 1

Half-yearly gains in widths of muscle and fat tissue on the arm and calf aligned on PHV in children of the Harpenden Growth Study. (Modified from Tanner, J.M., P.C.R. Hughes, and R.H. Whitehouse. Radiographically determined widths of bone, muscle, and fat in the upper arm and calf from age 3–18 years. Ann. Human Biol. *8:495–517, 1981.)*

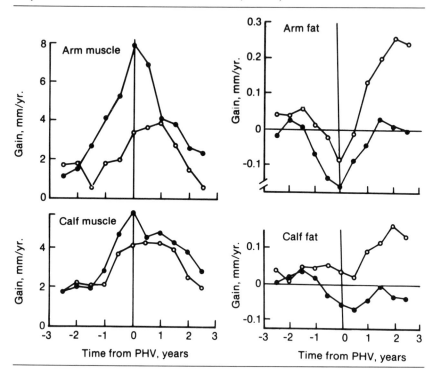

arm muscle that is approximately twice the magnitude of that for girls, while the peak in calf muscle is only slightly greater in boys.

Changes in subcutaneous fat on the arm and calf show an interesting pattern relative to PHV (Figure 1). Both boys and girls show negative velocities, i.e., a fat loss, on the arm coincident with PHV, but the loss in boys is greater than in girls. It appears that gains in the width of fat tissue on the arm begin to decline about 1 year before PHV, reach their lowest point coincident with PHV, and then rise systematically after PHV in both sexes. The increase in fatness after PHV is greater in girls than in boys. In the calf, on the other hand, girls show no loss of subcutaneous fat. Rather, the rate of fat accumulation slows down at PHV, reaches its lowest point about 6 months after PHV, and then rises sharply. Boys begin to lose fat on the calf during the year before PHV, and the loss,

FIGURE 2

Median half-yearly velocities of skinfold thicknesses aligned on PHV in Belgian boys. (Drawn from data reported by Beunen et al. [6].)

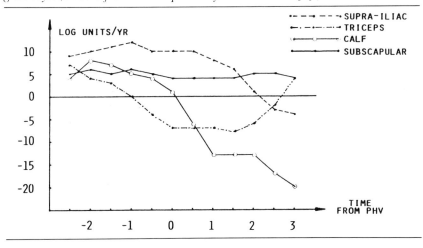

i.e., negative velocity, continues to about 6 months after PHV. The velocities for fat, however, tend to remain negative in boys for almost 3 years after PHV.

Regional variation in subcutaneous fatness is more apparent when changes in skinfold thicknesses measured on the trunk and extremities are related to PHV (Figure 2). Three of the four skinfolds show an increase in fat prior to PHV, the so-called preadolescent fat wave. Subsequently, changes in extremity and trunk skinfolds vary. Trends for the triceps and calf skinfolds in Belgian boys are quite similar to those for radiographic measurements of arm and calf fat widths in British children (Figure 1). Velocities of the triceps skinfold are positive until 1 year before PHV and then become negative, reaching a maximum negative velocity about 1.5 years after PHV. Velocities subsequently increase and eventually become positive. In contrast, velocities of the calf skinfold, though declining prior to PHV, approach zero at PHV and then become negative, reaching a maximum negative velocity about 3 years after PHV. It should be noted that arm fat widths on radiographs are the sums of anterior plus posterior fat widths, while calf fat widths are the sums of lateral and medial fat widths. Further, there is variation in the distribution of subcutaneous fat within each extremity during adolescence [59].

In contrast to skinfolds on the extremities, the two trunk skinfolds show different trends relative to PHV. Velocities for the subscapular skinfold remain positive through the stature spurt and do not vary relative to PHV. Velocities for the suprailiac skinfold peak about 1 year before PHV and then decline around the time of PHV. The velocities for this lower trunk skinfold, though declining, are still positive at PHV but become negative about 2 years after PHV (Figure 2).

Corresponding data for the triceps skinfold in small samples (about 29 of each sex) of Ohio adolescents [25] are generally similar to those for radiographic fat widths in British children (Figure 1) and the triceps skinfold in Belgian boys (Figure 2). However, in contrast to the Belgian data for the subscapular skinfold, increments for Ohio boys are negative just before and after PHV. They are also negative just after PHV in Ohio girls.

There is thus variation in subcutaneous fat in different areas of the body relative to PHV. This, in turn, is indicative of the significant changes that occur in the distribution of subcutaneous fat during adolescence [59].

MAXIMAL AEROBIC POWER

In a recent review of the developmental aspects of maximal aerobic power ($\dot{V}O_2$max), Krahenbuhl et al. [53] plotted mean values from 68 studies of clinically normal, untrained children and youths relative to chronological age ($N = 5793$ males and 3508 females). Between 6 and 16 years of age, growth in $\dot{V}O_2$max in boys is best described by a second-degree polynomial. Absolute $\dot{V}O_2$max increases from about $1.0 \cdot \text{l-min}^{-1}$ at 6 years of age to about $3.2 \text{ l} \cdot \text{min}^{-1}$ at 16 years. Average $\dot{V}O_2$max in girls is best described by a third-degree polynomial with a maximum value of almost $2.0 \text{ l} \cdot \text{min}^{-1}$ at about 14 years of age. Subsequently, $\dot{V}O_2$max declines with age in girls. Between 6 and 12 years of age, $\dot{V}O_2$max in boys and girls corresponds quite closely, but at 14 years of age a difference of approximately 25% is apparent. The relative difference between boys and girls exceeds 50% by 16 years of age.

When $\dot{V}O_2$max is expressed relative to body weight, mean values for boys remain constant at about $53 \text{ ml} \cdot \text{kg}^{-1} \cdot \text{min}^{-1}$ between 6 and 16 years. On the other hand, relative $\dot{V}O_2$max gradually decreases with age in girls from $52.0 \text{ ml} \cdot \text{kg}^{-1} \cdot \text{min}^{-1}$ at 6 years to $40.5 \text{ ml} \cdot \text{kg}^{-1} \cdot \text{min}^{-1}$ at 16 years. The most commonly offered explanation for the discrepancy in relative $\dot{V}O_2$max between boys and girls is the greater accumulation of fat in the latter. Expressing $\dot{V}O_2$max relative to FFM may provide a better indicator of the sex difference, but estimates of FFM based on skinfolds have significant error. Thus, in practice, relative maximal aerobic power is most commonly expressed relative to body weight.

The comprehensive review of Krahenbuhl et al. [53] indicates only

TABLE 5

Overview of Longitudinal and Mixed-Longitudinal Studies of Maximal Aerobic Power in Adolescents

Sample and Reference	Age Range	Sex	Mode*	N	Frequency of Measurements
Canada,		Boys	T	83	Annual for 10 years
Saskatchewan [21]	8–16				
[65]	7–17	Boys	T	25	Annual for 10 years
[64]	8–16	Boys	T	75	Annual for 10 years
[64]	8–16	Girls	T	22	Annual for 10 years
Canada, Ontario		Boys	B	62	Annual for 4 years
[26]	10–15				
Belgium, Leuven		Boys	B	21	Annual
[93]	11–13				
Czechoslovakia,		Boys	T	39	Annual
Prague [82]	11–18				
Czechoslovakia,		Boys	B	34/93†	Annual for 4 years
Brno [70]	12–15				
Germany,		Boys	B	26	Annual
Fredeburg [76]	12–18				
[76]	12–18	Girls	B	22	Annual
Netherlands,		Boys	T	102	Annual for 4 years
Amsterdam [50]	12–17				
[50]	12–17	Girls	T	131	Annual for 4 years
[51]		Boys	T	93	Annual for 4 years
	12–23				after 5-year interval
[51]		Girls	T	107	Annual for 4 years
	12–23				after 5-year interval
Netherlands,		Boys	B	17	Annual for 7 years
Nijmegen [13]	11–18				
Norway, Lom [1]	8–15	Boys	B	30	Annual
[76]	8–15	Girls	B	34	Annual
Japan, Nagoya [52]	9–18	Boys	T	7/43/6‡	Annual for 5–6 years

*T = treadmill, B = bicycle ergometer.
†34 controls, 93 athletes.
‡7 active, 43 nonactive, 6 highly trained runners.

five longitudinal studies of boys and one of girls. Features of these longitudinal studies and of several others are summarized in Table 5. Several of the studies relate individual distance and velocity curves for $\dot{V}o_2$max to the age at PHV [21, 50, 52, 64, 65, 76]. Although $\dot{V}o_2$max is measured on an annual basis in all studies, several studies cover only a relatively short period of time, so that estimates of the age at PHV are not as precise as desired. In the study of German children [76], for example, the subjects were followed longitudinally between 12 and 15 years of age, and median ages at PHV were 13.9 and 14.6 years in girls and boys, respectively. These ages are late compared to those for other European populations (see Table 1). In addition, several studies report only increments, and do not use smoothing techniques or graphic or algebraic fitting procedures. As discussed earlier, increments have a disadvantage, since the continuity of the developmental process is ignored and methodological inconsistencies may be introduced.

Only the data (stature, weight, $\dot{V}O_2$max) from the Saskatchewan Growth Study are analyzed with curve-fitting techniques. The initial analysis [21] utilized a graphic smoothing procedure, while the more recent analyses [64, 65] utilized the Preece-Baines modified logistic model. When such a model is fitted to $\dot{V}O_2$max or, for that matter, to any other variable, a necessary prerequisite is that the distance (performance level or size attained) curve should be similar in shape to the growth curve for stature [72].

The other longitudinal studies that relate $\dot{V}O_2$max to PHV have only four or five annual observations, so that the mathematical models presently used for fitting individual curves are not suitable. These models require a greater number of longitudinal observations. To overcome this problem, second-degree moving polynomials were used to estimate the age at PHV in the Dutch adolescents [50].

Given the preceding as background, several trends in changes in $\dot{V}O_2$max relative to the timing of the adolescent growth spurt are suggested. First, the maximal increase in $\dot{V}O_2$max occurs in the year of PHV in Canadian boys and girls [64]. Estimated velocities for $\dot{V}O_2$max are 0.412 l · min^{-1} · yr^{-1} at PHV in boys and 0.284 l · min^{-1} · yr^{-1} at PHV in girls. It appears that the maximal increase in $\dot{V}O_2$max occurs near PHV in Dutch boys but about 1 year before PHV in Dutch girls. Maximal velocities, however, are not reported [50]. Given the age range of the Dutch sample of girls (see Table 1), the relationship between $\dot{V}O_2$max and PHV in girls may not be accurate and needs to be considered with caution. The study of German and Norwegian adolescents reports only annual increments in $\dot{V}O_2$max [76]. Since the increments for individual children are not smoothed, they vary considerably from year to year, so that their relevance to PHV is limited. Although not quantified, striking increases in $\dot{V}O_2$max are closely related to PHV in many boys in the Japanese longitudinal study [52]. Another longitudinal study of Canadian boys [26] considers oxygen uptake interpolated to a heart rate of 155 b · min^{-1} · min^{-1} relative to PHV. The largest increase in $\dot{V}O_2$ (l · min^{-1}) at this heart rate occurs, on the average, in the year prior to PHV.

Allowing for the methodological variation among studies, the evidence appears to suggest an adolescent growth spurt in $\dot{V}O_2$max in boys. The spurt reaches a maximum gain near the time of PHV. On the other hand, the data are not sufficient to offer a generalization for girls.

Second, absolute $\dot{V}O_2$max begins to increase about 5 or 6 years before PHV in boys and continues to increase throughout the growth spurt in stature. This trend is reasonably consistent in Canadian [64], Dutch [50],

German, and Norwegian [76] boys. The trend for $\dot{V}O_2$ (l · min^{-1}) at this heart rate (155 b · min^{-1}) in the independent sample of Canadian boys [26] is similar, although it covers a shorter time span. $\dot{V}O_2$ (l · min^{-1}) at this heart rate (155 b · min^{-1}) begins to increase 2 years before PHV and continues to increase through 2 years after PHV.

Absolute $\dot{V}O_2$max also begins to increase several years prior to PHV in Canadian [64], Dutch [50], and Norwegian [76] girls and continues to increase for several years after PHV. In contrast to these three longitudinal samples, absolute $\dot{V}O_2$max does not change relative to PHV in German girls [76].

Third, trends for relative $\dot{V}O_2$max (ml · kg^{-1} · min^{-1}) are more variable. Relative $\dot{V}O_2$max tends to decline a year or so prior to PHV and continues to decline several years after PHV in Canadian [64] and German [76] boys and girls. In Norwegian adolescents [76], on the other hand, relative $\dot{V}O_2$max appears to increase prior to PHV in boys and girls, and then begins to decline at about PHV in girls and continues throughout the remainder of the growth spurt. Among boys, changes in relative $\dot{V}O_2$max after PHV are variable. (Relative $\dot{V}O_2$max data are not available for the Dutch adolescents [50].)

STRENGTH AND MOTOR PERFORMANCE

Cross-sectional analyses of a variety of strength measurements suggest several trends. Muscular strength, whether expressed as individual strength measurements or as a composite, increases linearly with chronological age from early childhood through approximately 13 or 14 years of age in boys and is then followed by a marked acceleration through the late teenage period into the early or mid-twenties. In girls, on the other hand, strength improves linearly with age through about 15 years of age, with no clear evidence of an adolescent spurt [2, 57]. The increase in strength during childhood and adolescence is more than that predicted from growth in stature [3, 4, 23].

The marked acceleration in strength development during male adolescence magnifies the relatively small preadolescent sex difference, so that after 16 years of age, few girls perform as well as boys (in mean values) in strength tests [47]. The sex difference in strength is more marked in the upper extremity and the trunk than in the lower extremity, even after adjusting for size differences between boys and girls [2].

Cross-sectional analyses of motor performance indicate similar trends. Performances in a variety of motor tasks also improve, on the average, from childhood through adolescence in boys, with some suggestion of a spurt in power tasks such as the vertical jump and the distance throw. The performances of girls, on the other hand, improve only to about 13 or 14 years of age, with little subsequent improvement [19, 35, 42].

Some evidence suggests that the plateau in performances of adolescent girls on speed and explosive strength tasks has shifted to a slightly older age in more recent studies [42]. During adolescence, the performances of boys exceed those of girls, on the average, and the differences become larger with increasing age. An exception is flexibility, usually measured with the sit and reach test, in which girls show greater flexibility at virtually all ages [42, 63].

Longitudinal studies of strength and motor performance during adolescence are fewer in number than those of maximal aerobic power. One of the earliest longitudinal studies to include measurements of strength and motor performance was the Adolescent Growth Study of children in Oakland, California, in the 1930s. Espenschade [33] considered the motor performance of 80 boys and 85 girls, who were followed at semi-annual intervals for a period of 3.5 years between 1934 and 1938. Seven motor items were included: a dash, an agility run, the standing long jump, the vertical jump, distance and accuracy throws, and the Brace test. In addition to age- and sex-associated variation, performance was related to skeletal age, the timing of menarche in girls, and the stage of pubescent development in boys (based on growth velocity and changes in penis and pubic hair development). In general, motor performance is negatively related to biological maturity status in girls but positively related to biological maturity status in boys. Unfortunately, the data are not related to the timing of the adolescent spurt.

Jones [47] reported data on four static strength measurements in 93 boys and 90 girls in the Adolescent Growth Study. Right and left grip, and pushing and pulling strength, were measured at semiannual intervals from 11 to 17 years of age. Age-, sex-, and maturity-associated variation are considered, but changes in strength during adolescence are not related to variation in the timing of the adolescent growth spurt. However, these strength data were subsequently considered relative to the timing of the adolescent growth spurt by Stolz and Stolz [83] for boys and by Faust [36] for girls. The results of these analyses are discussed in more detail later in this section.

The Medford Boys' Growth Study of the University of Oregon, which began in 1956, considered several measurements of strength and motor performance in two longitudinal cohorts of boys from 7 to 18 years of age [24]. Unfortunately, most of the longitudinal data in this study are reported in a cross-sectional manner. A variety of strength and motor performance tests are included in the study of young male Czechoslovak athletes and nonathletes 12 to 15 years of age, but only mean age changes and increments are reported [20, 70]. The Motor Performance Study of Michigan State University was begun in 1967 and still continues [19]. The study includes semiannual measurements of a variety of growth and performance variables, but the older children are not far enough along into adolescence for a meaningful analysis of variation in performance relative to the growth spurt.

Thus, although a number of longitudinal studies of strength and motor performance during adolescence have been conducted, the data are ordinarily presented in a cross-sectional manner and are not considered relative to variation in the timing of the growth spurt. Such analyses are available only for several samples and for relatively few strength and motor performance variables. These studies include the Adolescent Growth Study in Oakland, California [36, 83], the Saskatchewan Growth Study in Canada [23, 32], the study of the Growth, Health and Fitness of Teenagers in Amsterdam [49], and the Leuven Growth Study of Belgian Boys [6].

Data relating performance to the timing of the adolescent spurt are most extensive for static strength measured by various techniques. Using a composite strength score based on the sum of right and left grip, and pushing and pulling strength, Stolz and Stolz [83] report a peak in strength development of Oakland boys that occurs, on the average, about 14 months after PHV and 9 months after PWV. About 12% of the boys show a peak before PHV, while the peak in strength development occurs after PHV in more than 77% of the boys. In contrast, Faust [36] reports considerable variability in the timing of adolescent strength development in Oakland girls. Using the same procedures as Stolz and Stolz [83], she found that peak strength development precedes PHV in about 40%, coincides with PHV in about 11%, and follows PHV in about 49% of the girls. Although the apex in strength development in about one-half of the girls is apparent after PHV, many girls experience a decrease in strength after PHV. This trend suggests the possibility that high semiannual increments in strength may be, in part, a function of poor performance on the immediately preceding observation. Given the role of motivation in strength testing, this may be a significant factor.

Data from the longitudinal studies of Canadian [23], Dutch [49], and Belgian [6] boys are consistent with the observations of Stolz and Stolz [83]. Results for Canadian boys are summarized in Figure 3, while those for Dutch and Belgian boys are summarized in Figure 4. In the sample of 99 Canadian boys, upper body strength (the average of shoulder extension, wrist extension and flexion, elbow extension and flexion) and lower body strength (average of hip flexion and knee extension) reach a peak 1 year after PHV. The maximum velocity for lower body strength is 9.8 kg · yr^{-1}, while that for upper body strength is 7.4 kg · yr^{-1}. When strength increments are expressed as a percentage of the level of strength attained, the relative increase is greater for upper body strength than for lower body strength.

The data for Dutch and Belgian adolescents are based on the arm

FIGURE 3

Mean yearly velocities of upper and lower body static strength aligned on PHV in boys from the Saskatchewan Growth Study. (Drawn from data reported by Carron and Bailey [23].)

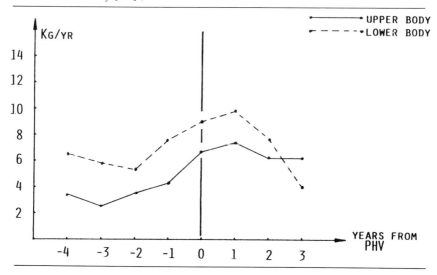

pull test, a measure of static strength of the upper extremity. The yearly velocities for 96 Dutch boys and half-yearly velocities for 219 Belgian boys are generally similar in both studies. The spurt in arm strength begins about 1.5 years before PHV and reaches a peak about 0.5 year after PHV. The spurt thus lasts for about 2 years, and then the velocities gradually decline. The maximum velocity of strength development is virtually identical in Dutch and Belgian boys, about 12 kg · yr^{-1}. The estimated velocity of strength development in Belgian boys is about 30% of the attained level of strength at the time of the peak, which indicates the marked increase in static strength that occurs during male adolescence. Further, none of 219 boys have a negative velocity at this time.

Although the preceding relates strength development to PHV, maximal gains in strength are actually more coincident with PWV in Belgian boys, which is consistent with the observations for Oakland [83] and Canadian [23] boys. The Dutch data are not considered relative to PWV.

The marked increase in upper extremity strength during male adolescence becomes more apparent when strength velocities are related to the timing of static strength PV. When so aligned for the Belgian boys, PV for arm pull strength reaches 15 kg · yr^{-1}. This observation suggests that the time-spreading effect in peaks for strength development in

FIGURE 4

Velocities of arm pull static strength aligned on PHV in Belgian boys (median half-yearly velocities) and Dutch boys and girls (mean yearly velocities). (Data for Belgian boys are drawn from data reported by Beunen et al. [6]; those for Dutch adolescents are redrawn after Kemper and Verschuur [49].)

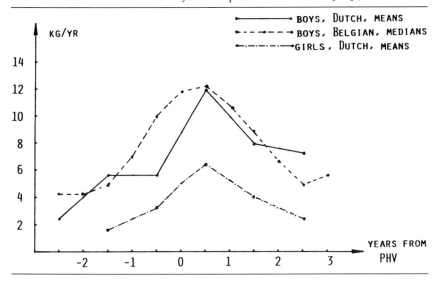

individual boys is not completely removed by aligning strength velocities on PHV [6]. Similar results are apparent for radiographic measurements of arm and calf muscle widths. PVs for arm and calf muscle widths are greater when aligned on the respective peak muscle velocities than when aligned on PHV [86].

Arm pull data for 82 Dutch girls are also shown in Figure 4. Peak strength development in girls is about one-half of that in boys. Mean velocities increase from 1.5 years before PHV and peak at 6.4 kg · yr^{-1} 0.5 year after PHV. The velocities then decline. The timing of the apex in strength development appears to be the same in Dutch boys and girls, which is in contrast to the data for Oakland boys and girls [36, 83]. Among Oakland girls, maximal strength development does not closely correspond to the growth spurt in stature, and a significant percentage of girls experience peak strength gains prior to PHV. Corresponding information is not available for Dutch girls.

The standing long jump and bent arm hang are, respectively, measures of explosive strength and functional strength or muscular endurance. In the 106 boys of the Saskatchewan Growth Study, maximum increments for explosive and functional strength occur during the year of PHV [32]. The maximum increments are about 15 cm · yr^{-1} in the

FIGURE 5

Median half-yearly velocities for functional strength (bent arm hang) and explosive strength (vertical jump) aligned on PHV in Belgian boys. (Drawn from data reported by Beunen et al. [6].)

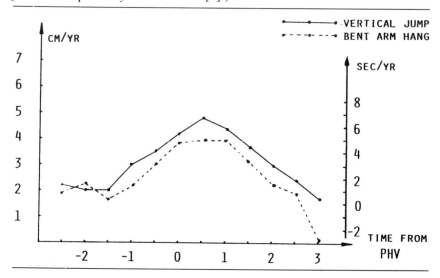

standing long jump and about 9 sec · yr^{-1} in the bent arm hang. The velocity curves for these two performance tasks are qualitatively similar to that for stature. In contrast, performance in bent knee sit-ups, a measure of trunk strength or abdominal muscular endurance, shows no clear peak. Although the highest increment occurs 1 year before PHV, the increments 3 years before and 3 years after PHV are only slightly less than the greatest increment.

Results from the Leuven Growth Study of Belgian Boys [6] are not entirely consistent with those for Canadian boys. In addition to static strength, which was discussed above, semiannual velocities were calculated with nonsmoothed polynomials for six motor performance items and subsequently aligned on PHV, PWV, or peak static strength (arm pull) velocity (PSV). The motor tests included the vertical jump (explosive strength), bent arm hang (functional strength or muscular endurance), leg lifts (trunk strength or abdominal muscular endurance), shuttle run (running speed), plate tapping (speed of limb movement), and sit and reach (flexibility of the lower back and hip).

The velocity curves for the vertical jump and bent arm hang (Figure 5) are similar to that for arm pull strength (Figure 4). Maximum increments in these two tasks follow PHV and PWV and are more coincident with PSV. Maximum velocities are about 5 cm · yr^{-1} for the vertical jump and about 5 sec · yr^{-1} for the bent arm hang. The timing of adolescent spurts in the vertical jump and bent arm hang is different from that observed in Canadian boys [32]. The standing long jump was used as a measure of explosive strength in the latter sample, and this may underlie some of the variation. However, the variation probably reflects analytical differences. Semiannual velocities were calculated for the Belgian sample, thus providing a more precise definition of the timing of maximum velocities. Annual velocities were used in the Canadian sample. Nevertheless, the results of the two studies indicate definite adolescent spurts in explosive strength, as measured in jumping tasks, and functional strength, as measured in the bent arm hang. The velocities for the explosive and functional strength tasks are positive before and after the adolescent growth spurt, which indicates that performance in these tasks improves, on the average, during this period.

Performance in the leg lift test does not show a clear adolescent spurt in the Belgian boys. The semiannual velocities fluctuate between zero and one leg lifts per year. This observation is generally consistent with the study of Canadian boys, in whom annual velocities for performance in the bent knee sit-up test are quite similar 3 years before, 1 year before, and 3 years after PHV [32]. These results suggest that there is no clear adolescent spurt in trunk strength or abdominal muscular endurance, as measured by leg lifts and bent knee sit-ups.

In contrast to static, explosive, and functional strength, it appears that the two speed tasks, the shuttle run and plate tapping, reach maximal velocities about 1.5 years prior to PHV (Figure 6). After the peak, velocities for the two speed tasks decline gradually throughout the adolescent spurt. Nevertheless, no negative median velocities are apparent, which indicates that speed of performance improves, on the average, during the male adolescent spurt.

Lower back and hip flexibility, as measured in the sit and reach test, shows only a small increase in velocity, 0 to about 2 cm · yr^{-1}, just before PHV, and then declines to 0.9 cm · yr^{-1} 3 years after PHV. If there is a spurt in flexibility, it probably occurs somewhat before PHV. The data, however, are not sufficiently definitive.

Thus, strength and motor performance show adolescent spurts in boys. Peak gains in several strength tasks occur, on the average, after PHV and PWV. They are more coincident with PWV. An exception, of course, is functional strength of the trunk, which does not appear to show an adolescent spurt. The adolescent spurt in muscle tissue also occurs after PHV and is more coincident with PWV. Thus, muscle tissue apparently increases first in mass and then in strength during male adolescence. This suggests changes in the metabolic and contractile features of muscle tissue as adolescence progresses and/or, perhaps, neuromuscular maturation affecting the volitional demonstration of

FIGURE 6

Median half-yearly velocities for running speed (shuttle run) and speed of limb movement (plate tapping) aligned on PHV in Belgian boys. (Drawn from data reported by Beunen et al. [6].)

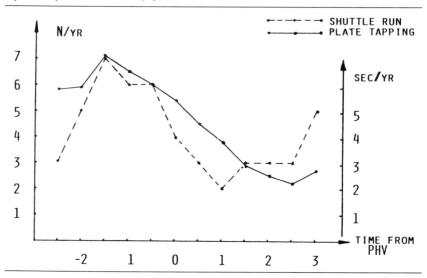

strength. In contrast to strength, speed and flexibility items apparently reach maximum velocities prior to PHV, and probably are more coincident with the adolescent spurt in leg length. There may be more optimal strength–lever arm relationships at this time, which might affect performance in running tasks. However, longitudinal analyses of biomechanical features of performance are necessary before such an inference can be accepted.

Corresponding longitudinal data on the strength and motor performance of girls during the adolescent spurt are lacking, and the available data for static strength are not consistent in two studies. A composite strength score shows considerable variation relative to the timing of the growth spurt in stature in Oakland girls, while the arm pull indicates a spurt after PHV in Dutch girls. Although information on the motor performance of girls relative to the timing of the adolescent spurt is lacking, cross-sectional analyses of longitudinal data do not suggest adolescent spurts in the motor performance of girls. For example, Espenschade [33] related the motor performance of the Oakland girls to the time before or after menarche, which occurs, on the average, after PHV. There is no tendency for performance to peak before, at, or after menarche; rather, performance levels are generally stable across time.

THE CONCEPT OF ADOLESCENT AWKWARDNESS

The literature on general development during adolescence commonly suggests the possibility of a temporary disruption of motor coordination during the growth spurt. The terms "adolescent awkwardness" or "overgrown, clumsy age" are often used to describe this tendency. As early as 1922, for example, Homburger [45] described this awkward period, but it is not clear whether his description was based on systematic observations or on accounts from his clinical practice as a psychiatrist. Ungerer [92], however, notes that Homburger's observations [45, 46] were based not only on psychiatric patients but also on normal adolescents.

Since this early description, the concept of adolescent awkwardness has persisted in the German literature [62, 66, 67, 104] and in literature elsewhere in the world [41, 80, 85]. Tanner [85], for example, indicates a possible period during the growth spurt, lasting no more than 6 months, when there may be temporary problems with balance that may affect performance in certain tasks and thus give the impression of awkwardness or clumsiness. Tanner relates this period to the time when trunk length has increased relative to length of the legs prior to the attainment of "full size and strength" of the muscles.

One of the earliest attempts to address this concept was that of Dimock [30]. In a sample of 200 boys measured annually for 3 years between 12 and 16 years of age, Dimock observed improved performances on the Brace test (a series of stunt items defined as measuring coordination, agility, and control) over the 3 years, but at every age, prepubescent boys (based on pubic hair as the criterion) had higher scores than pubescent and postpubescent boys. Thus, there did not appear to be a temporary decline in the performance of adolescent boys; rather, there was maturity-associated variation within chronological age groups. Espenschade [33, 34] subsequently demonstrated similar results with the Brace test in a longitudinal sample of adolescent boys, but not in girls. Performance levels of girls in the Brace test showed little change and even a decline in some items after 14 years of age.

In contrast to these early longitudinal studies, which do not suggest a period of temporary motor instability, other data [5, 39, 44, 79, 98] suggest a plateau or decline in tasks requiring balance and manual control at the time of the growth spurt. These data, however, are derived from cross-sectional studies or from longitudinal data analyzed in a cross-sectional manner. In short-term longitudinal studies that followed children for 2 to 2.5 years between 11 and 17 years of age, however, Schnabel [78] and Winter [101] report periods of no improvement or temporary disturbance in the running and jumping performances of adolescent boys, and no change or decline in the performances of girls.

It thus appears that if a period of temporary awkwardness exists, it occurs primarily in males. However, the longitudinal studies relating strength and motor performance to the timing of the growth spurt, which were discussed in the preceding section, indicate generally positive velocities for strength and motor tasks during the growth spurt in stature. There does not appear to be a period of a boy "outgrowing his strength" or of "adolescent awkwardness." These observations, of course, are based upon means and medians, so that there is the possiblity that individual boys may experience temporary problems with strength and performance during the adolescent spurt. Thus, two questions arise. First, are there children who demonstrate negative velocities in strength and motor performance during the growth spurt? Second, do these children have unique growth and performance characterisitics?

These questions were addressed in a longitudinal subsample of the Leuven Growth Study of Belgian Boys [6, 68]. A decline, i.e., a negative velocity, in a performance task in the year of PHV was accepted as an operational definition of a boy who experiences performance problems during the growth spurt. The time of PHV could be identified for 446 boys in the total Leuven sample, and annual increments were calculated for the performance tasks during the period of PHV. Boys who showed a negative velocity in a motor item at PHV were designated as "decliners," while the others were designated as "improvers."

The number and percentage of boys showing negative velocities for seven performance items at the time of PHV are given in Table 6. Only 6 boys (1.4%) present negative velocities in the arm pull (static strength) during the interval of PHV, while 7.0% and 9.5% show, respectively, negative velocities for plate tapping (speed of limb movement) and the vertical jump (explosive strength) at the time of PHV. In contrast, 18.7 to 33.5% of the boys have negative velocities in the other motor tasks at the time of PHV. Thus, a significant number of boys experience a decline in performance on four of the seven tasks during the interval of PHV.

Subsequently, the growth and performance characteristics of the decliners were considered relative to those who improved in performance during the interval of PHV. This was done for all the motor tasks except the arm pull, in which only a negligible percentage of boys did not improve during the spurt. The decliners and improvers were compared on several anthropometric dimensions at the beginning of the PHV interval and at an average age of 18 years (young adulthood). They were also compared on the levels of motor performance attained at the time of PHV, ages at PHV, and PHV. In addition, degree of sport participation over the duration of the study, as well as various sociocultural characteristics (e.g., occupational and educational status of the father, degree of urbanization of residence, and number of siblings), were compared.

TABLE 6

Number and Percentage of Boys Showing a Negative Velocity in Several Motor Performance Tasks During the Interval of PHV*

Motor Task	Total Number Observed	Boys with Negative Velocities	
		Number	Percentage
Static strength arm pull	444	6	1.4
Explosive strength— vertical jump	446	31	7.0
Functional strength— bent arm hang	446	136	30.5
Trunk strength— leg lifts	444	116	26.1
Speed of limb movement— plate tapping	441	42	9.5
Running speed— shuttle run	445	149	33.5
Flexibility— sit and reach	444	83	18.7

*Calculated from data of the Leuven Growth Study of Belgian Boys [6, 68].

The first significant finding in the analysis is that boys who show negative velocities in performance during PHV (decliners) have a significantly higher performance level in that specific ability at the beginning of the interval than those who improve in performance during PHV (Table 7). The only exception is the sit and reach test of flexibility.

Mean somatic and motor characteristics of decliners and improvers at the beginning of the PHV interval are summarized in Table 8. Boys who

TABLE 7

Means and Standard Deviations for Motor Abilities at the Beginning of the Interval of PHV for Boys Who Declined and Who Improved in Motor Performance During the Interval of PHV

Motor Tasks†	Decliners*		Improvers*		t-test
	M	SD	M	SD	
Vertical jump, cm	39.9	6.0	35.5	5.8	‡
Bent arm hang, sec	27.0	16.2	16.8	12.9	‡
Leg lifts, number/20 sec	16.3	2.4	14.0	2.8	‡
Plate tapping, number/20 sec	87.6	9.3	81.0	9.2	‡
Shuttle run, sec	21.7	1.5	22.8	1.6	‡
Sit and reach, cm	20.8	5.0	19.9	6.2	

*"Decliners" and "improvers" refer to boys who had, respectively, negative and positive velocities for the specific motor task during the interval of peak height velocity.
†Since there were so few decliners in the arm pull, this test is not included in the table.
‡Significant difference between the means $\alpha = 0.05$.

decline and improve in the vertical jump, leg lifts, and sit and reach during the interval of PHV do not differ significantly in other motor performance measurements at the beginning of the PHV interval (lower part of Table 8). However, boys who decline in the bent arm hang at PHV have significantly better performances in leg lifts and the shuttle run at the beginning of the PHV interval, while boys who decline in plate tapping at PHV have significantly higher performance levels in the vertical jump, leg lifts, shuttle run, and flexibility at the beginning of the PHV interval. Finally, boys who decline in the shuttle run at PHV perform significantly better in the bent arm hang at the beginning of the PHV interval. Thus, prior to PHV, boys who decline in performance during the interval of PHV have, in general, the same or better levels of strength and motor performance than those who improve in performance during the interval of PHV.

Comparisons of the anthropometric characteristics of decliners and improvers at the beginning of the PHV interval also suggest several trends (upper part of Table 8). Decliners and improvers in the vertical jump, plate tapping, shuttle run, and the sit and reach at PHV do not differ in any anthropometric dimensions at the beginning of the PHV interval. However, boys who decline in plate tapping and the sit and reach at PHV have significantly later mean ages at PHV than those who improve in these tasks at PHV. Estimated peak height velocities of boys who decline and improve in performance at PHV also do not differ. On the other hand, decliners in the bent arm hang and leg lifts at PHV tend to be significantly smaller than improvers in most anthropometric dimensions at the beginning of the PHV interval.

Decliners and improvers in performance at PHV do not significantly differ, on the average, in strength and motor performance at 18 years of age (young adulthood). They also do not differ in anthropometric characteristics, except that decliners in bent arm hang, shuttle run, and plate tapping performance tend to be smaller in several dimensions at 18 years of age. Thus, boys who decline in bent arm hanging performance, a measure of the functional strength of the upper extremities, are smaller in anthropometric dimensions both at the beginning of the PHV interval (Table 8) and in young adulthood. Otherwise, there are no consistent trends in anthropometric dimensions at the beginning of the PHV interval and in young adulthood in boys who decline in the performance of other tasks at the interval of PHV.

Finally, boys who decline in performance do not differ from those who improve in performance at the time of PHV in level of physical activity, as measured by an index of sports participation during the interval of the study. The two groups also do not differ in the socio-cultural characteristics of their families.

The concept of adolescent awkwardness is obviously complex. Some

TABLE 8
Mean Somatic Characteristics and Motor Performances at the Beginning of the Interval of PHV in Boys Who Declined and Improved in Performance of Specific Tasks During the Interval of PHV*

Dimension/Test	Vertical Jump		Bent Arm Hang		Leg Lifts		Plate Tapping		Shuttle Run		Sit and Reach	
	Decl.	Impr.	Decl.	Impr.	Decl.	Impr.	Decl.	Impr.	Decl.	Impr.	Decl.	Impr.
Height, cm	—	—	156.5	159.1	—	—	—	—	—	—	—	—
Weight, kg	—	—	44.6	48.2	45.6	47.6	—	—	—	—	—	—
Sitting height, cm	—	—	—	—	—	—	—	—	—	—	—	—
Leg length, cm	—	—	75.9	77.6	76.4	77.3	—	—	—	—	—	—
Biacromial breadth, cm	—	—	33.6	34.3	23.3	23.8	—	—	—	—	—	—
Flexed arm circumference, cm	—	—	23.1	23.9	—	—	—	—	—	—	—	—
Sum of skinfolds, log	—	—	488.2	517.0	497.7	511.2	—	—	—	—	—	—
Age at PHV, yr.	—	—	—	—	—	—	14.8	14.2	—	—	14.5	14.2
PHV, cm · yr^{-1}	—	—	—	—	—	—	—	—	—	—	—	—
Arm pull, kg	39.9	35.5	—	—	—	—	—	—	—	—	—	—
Vertical jump, cm	—	—	27.0	16.8	—	—	37.9	35.6	—	—	—	—
Bent arm hang, sec	—	—	15.1	14.4	—	—	15.6	14.5	22.1	18.9	—	—
Leg lifts, number	—	—	—	—	16.3	14.0	87.6	81.0	—	—	—	—
Plate tapping, number	—	—	—	—	—	—	21.9	22.5	—	—	—	—
Shuttle run, sec	—	—	22.2	22.5	—	—	14.8	14.2	21.7	22.8	—	—
Sit and reach, cm	—	—	—	—	—	—	14.8	14.2	—	—	14.5	14.2

*Means are reported only when a significant difference between decliners and improvers is observed (*t*-test, $\alpha = 0.05$).

boys do in fact decline in some performance items, but not all, during the adolescent growth spurt in stature. The percentages of those who decline vary from 1.4 to 33.5%. The highest percentages of decliners occur in tasks that require the boy to act against his own body weight, i.e., the bent arm hang (30.5%), leg lift (26.1%), and shuttle run (33.5%). In contrast, the percentage of boys who decline in the vertical jump during the interval of PHV is smaller (7.0%). The vertical jump, of course, is an explosive task, while the other tasks require the maintenance of body weight in one position (bent arm hang) or repetitive movements of the body (shuttle run) or parts of the body (leg lifts).

There is the possibility that the number of boys identified as decliners includes a number of false decliners due to the measurement error associated with motor tasks. However, this is probably offset by a number of false improvers for the same reason. There is no reason to believe that there is a systematic shift toward more or less decliners and improvers. Further, it should be noted that even the smallest decline in performance during the interval of PHV was classified as a decline.

Boys who decline in performance during the interval of PHV generally attain the same or better levels of motor performance at the beginning of the PHV interval than those who improve during the interval of PHV, while the two groups do not differ in motor performance at young adulthood. The decline in performance during the interval of PHV is thus temporary and does not influence young adult performance.

Since boys who decline in performance at the time of PHV are generally better performers, why do they decline in performance at this time? There are no consistent differences in the timing of PHV in the decliners and improvers with the exception of plate tapping and sit and reach. Hence, the size and strength advantages associated with early maturation and the corresponding disadvantages associated with late maturation in boys [47], or with temporary disproportion of leg and trunk lengths relative to overall body size, do not appear to be significant factors. The two groups also do not differ in the magnitude of PHV, which suggests that a decline or improvement in performance is not associated with larger or smaller rates of growth during the stature spurt. The two groups do not, in general, differ in anthropometric characteristics at the beginning of the PHV interval, with the exception of smaller dimensions in boys who decline in the bent arm hang and leg lifts. Since these two tasks require the boy to act against his body weight, it is somewhat surprising that those who improve in performance on these tasks during PHV are, on the average, heavier and fatter. Weight and fatness generally exert a negative influence on performances in which the body must be supported or moved [7, 56]. Decliners and improvers also do not differ in sports participation and social background.

Thus, a factor or factors that account for the decline in the performance of some boys during the interval of PHV is not immediately apparent. Variation in motivation or changing attitudes toward performance may be related factors, but they are difficult to specify and quantify. Change in body image during the period of maximal growth is an additional factor that may influence the motivation to perform or performance per se.

In summary, some boys decline in motor performance during the growth spurt. Those who show a decline in performance at the time of PHV are generally good performers at the beginning of the PHV interval. The decline in performance does not occur in all motor tasks, i.e., it is not a general trend, and is temporary. Obviously, these trends apply only to the motor tasks considered in this analysis. Nevertheless, the individuality of adolescent changes in growth and performance must be recognized and appreciated.

REFERENCES

1. Andersen, K.L., V. Seliger, J. Rutenfranz, and J. Skrobak-Kaczynski. Physical performance capacity of children in Norway. Part IV. The rate of growth in maximal aerobic power and the influence of improved physical education on children in a rural community. Population parameters in a rural community. *Eur. J. Appl. Physiol.* 35:49–58, 1976.
2. Asmussen, E. Muscular performance. In K. Rodahl and S.M. Horvath (eds.), *Muscle as a Tissue.* New York: McGraw-Hill, 1962, pp. 161–175.
3. Asmussen, E. Growth in muscular strength and power. In G.L. Rarick, (ed.), *Physical Activity: Human Growth and Development.* New York: Academic Press, 1973, pp. 60–79.
4. Asmussen, E., and Kr. Heebøll-Nielson. A dimensional analysis of performance and growth in boys. *J. Appl. Physiol.* 7:593–603, 1955.
5. Bachman, J.C. Motor learning and performance as related to age and sex in two measures of balance coordination. *Res. Q.* 32:123–137, 1961.
6. Beunen, G., R.M. Malina, M.A. Van't Hof, J. Simons, M. Ostyn, R. Renson, and D. Van Gerven. *Adolescent Growth and Motor Performance: A Longitudinal Study of Belgian Boys.* Champaign, Ill.: Human Kinetics Publishers, 1988.
7. Beunen, G., M. Ostyn, R. Renson, J. Simons, and D. Van Gerven. Anthropometric correlates of strength and motor performance in Belgian boys 12 through 18 years of age. In J. Borms, R. Hauspie, A. Sand, C. Susanne and M. Hebbelinck, (eds.). *Human Growth and Development.* New York: Plenum Press, 1984, pp. 503–509.
8. Beunen, G., J. Simons, M. Ostyn, R. Renson, and D. Van Gerven. Learning effects in repeated measurements designs. In K. Berg and B.O. Eriksson (eds.) *Children and Exercise,* Vol. IX. Baltimore: University Park Press, 1980, pp. 41–48.
9. Bielicki, T. Interrelationships between various measures of maturation rate in girls during adolescence. *Stud. Phys. Anthropol.* 1:51–64, 1975.
10. Bielicki, T., J. Koniarek, and R.M. Malina. Interrelationships among certain measures of growth and maturation rate in boys during adolescence. *Ann. Hum. Biol.* 11:201–210, 1984.
11. Bielicki, T., and Z. Welon. The sequence of growth velocity peaks of principal body dimensions in girls. *Mat. Prace Antropol.* 86:3–10, 1973.
12. Billewicz, W.Z., H.M. Fellowes, and A.M. Thomson. Pubertal changes in boys and girls in Newcastle upon Tyne. *Ann. Hum. Biol.* 8:211–219, 1981.
13. Binkhorst, R.A., M.C. de Jong-van de Kar, and A.C.A. Vissers. Growth and aerobic

power of boys aged 11–19 years. In J. Ilmarinen and I. Välimäki (eds.), *Children and Sports*. Berlin: Springer-Verlag, 1984, pp. 99–105.

14. Boas, F. The growth of children. *Science* 19:256–257, 281–282, and 20:351–352, 1892.
15. Boas, F. Studies in growth. I. *Hum. Biol.* 4:307–350, 1932.
16. Boas, F. Studies in growth. II. *Hum. Biol.* 5:429–444, 1933.
17. Bock, R.D., and D. Thissen. Statistical problems of fitting individual growth curves. In F.E. Johnston, A.F. Roche, and C. Susanne (eds.), *Physical Growth and Maturation. Methodologies and Factors*. New York: Plenum Press, 1980, pp. 265–290.
18. Bock, R.D., and D. Thissen. Fitting multi-component models for growth in stature. *Proc. 9th Int. Biometric Conf.* 1:431–442, 1976.
19. Branta, C., J. Haubenstricker, and V. Seefeldt. Age changes in motor skills during childhood and adolescence. In R.L. Terjung (ed.), *Exercise and Sport Sciences Reviews*. Lexington, Mass.: Collamore Press, 1984, pp. 467–520.
20. Buzek, V., and V. Drazil. The development of performance capacity. In Z. Placheta, (ed.), *Youth and Physical Activity*. Brno: J.E. Purkyne University, 1980, pp. 231–245.
21. Cameron, N., R.L. Mirwald, and D.A. Bailey. Standards for the assessment of normal absolute maximal aerobic power. In M. Ostyn, G. Beunen, and J. Simons (eds.), *Kinanthropometry*, Vol. II. Baltimore: University Park Press, 1980, pp. 349–359.
22. Cameron, N., J.M. Tanner, and R.H. Whitehouse. A longitudinal analysis of the growth of limb segments in adolescence. *Ann. Hum. Biol.* 9:211–220, 1982.
23. Carron, A.V., and D.A. Bailey. Strength development in boys from 10 through 16 years. *Monogr. Soc. Res. Child Dev.* 39 (serial no. 157), 1974.
24. Clarke, H.H. *Physical and Motor Tests in the Medford Boys' Growth Study*. Englewood Cliffs, N.J.: Prentice-Hall, 1971.
25. Cronk, C.E., D. Mukherjee, and A.F. Roche. Changes in triceps and subscapular skinfold thickness during adolescence. *Hum. Biol.* 55:707–721, 1983.
26. Cunningham, D.A., D.H. Paterson, C.J.R. Blimkie, and P. Donner. Development of cardiorespiratory function in circumpubertal boys: A longitudinal study. *J. Appl. Physiol.* 56:302–307, 1984.
27. Danker-Hopfe, H. Menarcheal age in Europe. *Yrbk. Phys. Anthropol.* 29:81–112, 1986.
28. Deming, J. Application of the Gompertz curve to the observed pattern of growth in length of 48 individual boys and girls during the adolescent cycle of growth. *Hum. Biol.* 29:83–122, 1957.
29. Demirjian, A., P.H. Buschang, R. Tanguay, and D.K. Patterson. Interrelationships among measures of somatic, skeletal, dental, and sexual maturity. *Am. J. Orthod.* 88:433–438, 1985.
30. Dimock, H.S. A research in adolescence. I. Pubescence and physical growth. *Child Dev.* 6:177–195, 1935.
31. El Lozy, M. A critical analysis of the double and triple logistic growth curves. *Ann. Hum. Biol.* 5:389–394, 1978.
32. Ellis, J.D., A.V. Carron, and D.A. Bailey. Physical performance in boys from 10 through 16 years. *Hum. Biol.* 47:263–281, 1975.
33. Espenschade, A. Motor performance in adolescence including the study of relationships with measures of physical growth and maturity. *Monogr. Soc. Res. Child Dev.* 5 (serial no. 24), 1940.
34. Espenschade, A. Development of motor coordination in boys and girls. *Res. Q.* 18:30–44, 1947.
35. Espenschade, A. Motor development. In W.R. Johnson (ed.), *Science and Medicine of Exercise and Sport*, New York: Harper & Row, 1960, pp. 419–439.
36. Faust, M.S. Somatic development of adolescent girls. *Monogr. Soc. Res. Child Dev.* 42 (serial no. 169), 1977.

37. Filipsson, R., and K. Hall. Correlation between dental maturity, height and sexual maturation in normal girls. *Ann. Hum. Biol.* 3:205–210, 1976.
38. Gasser, Th., W. Köhler, H.-G. Müller, A. Kneip, R. Largo, L. Molinari, and A. Prader. Velocity acceleration of height growth using kernel estimation. *Ann. Hum. Biol.* 11:397–411, 1984.
39. Goetzinger, C.P. A reevaluation of the Heath railwalking test. *J. Educ. Res.* 54:187–191, 1961.
40. Goldstein, H. *The Design and Analysis of Longitudinal Studies.* London: Academic Press, 1979.
41. Gorkin, M.J. Die Fragen der Physiologie des Jugendsports im Lichte der Lehre Pawlovs von der höheren Neventätigkeit. *Theor. Prax. Körperk.* 6:51–58, 1953.
42. Haubenstricker, J., and V. Seefeldt. Acquisition of motor skills during childhood. In V. Seefeldt (ed.), *Physical Activity and Well-Being.* Reston, Va.: American Alliance for Health, Physical Education, Recreation and Dance, 1986, pp. 41–102.
43. Hauspie, R.C., A. Wachholder, G. Baron, F. Contraine, C. Susanne, and H. Graffar. A comparative study of the fit of four different functions to longitudinal data of growth in height of Belgian girls. *Ann. Hum. Biol.* 7:347–358, 1980.
44. Heath, S.R. The rail walking test: Preliminary maturational norms for boys and girls. *Motor Skills Res. Exchange* 1:34–36, 1949.
45. Homburger, A. Über die Entwicklung der menschlichen Motorik und ihrer Beziehung zu den Bewegungsstörungen der Schizophrenen. *Z. Neurol. Psychiatr.* 78:561–570, 1922.
46. Homburger, A. Zur Gestaltung der normalen menschlichen Motorik und ihrer Beurteilung. *Z. Neurol. Psychiatr.* 85:274–314, 1923.
47. Jones, H.E. *Motor Performance and Growth: A Developmental Study of Static Dynamometric Strength.* Berkeley: University of California Press, 1949.
48. Kemper, H.C.G., L. Storm-van Essen, and R. Verschuur. Height, weight and height velocity. In H.C.G. Kemper (ed.), *Growth, Health and Fitness of Teenagers.* Basel: Karger, 1985, pp. 66–80.
49. Kemper, H.C.G., and R. Verschuur. Motor performance fitness tests. In H.C.G. Kemper (ed.), *Growth, Health and Fitness of Teenagers.* Basel: Karger, 1985, pp. 96–106.
50. Kemper, H.C.G., and R. Verschuur. Maximal aerobic power. In H.C.G. Kemper (ed.), *Growth, Health and Fitness of Teenagers.* Basel: Karger, 1985, pp. 107–126.
51. Kemper, H.C.G., R. Verschuur, L. Storm-van Essen, and R. van Aalst. Longitudinal study of maximal aerobic power in boys and girls from 12 to 23 years of age. In J. Rutenfranz, R. Mocellin and F. Klimt (eds.), *Children and Exercise*, Vol. XII. Champaign, Ill.: Human Kinetics Publishers, 1986, pp. 203–211.
52. Kobayashi, K., K. Kitamura, M. Muira, H. Sodeyama, Y. Murase, M. Miyashita, and H. Matsui. Aerobic power as related to body growth and training in Japanese boys: A longitudinal study. *J. Appl. Physiol.* 44:666–672, 1978.
53. Krahenbuhl, G.S., J.S. Skinner, and W.M. Kohrt. Developmental aspects of maximal aerobic power in children. In R.L. Terjung (ed.), *Exercise and Sport Sciences Reviews.* New York: Macmillian Co., 1985, pp. 503–538.
54. Largo, R.H., Th. Gasser, A. Prader, W. Stuetzle, and P.J. Huber. Analysis of the adolescent growth spurt using smoothing spline functions. *Ann. Hum. Biol.* 5:421–434, 1978.
55. Lindgren G. Growth of schoolchildren with early, average and late ages of peak height velocity. *Ann. Hum. Bio.* 5:253–267, 1978.
56. Malina, R.M. Anthropometric correlates of strength and motor performance. In J.H. Wilmore and J.F. Keogh (eds.), *Exercise and Sport Sciences Reviews.* New York: Academic Press, 1975, pp. 249–274.

57. Malina R.M. Growth of muscle tissue and muscle mass. In F. Falkner and J.M. Tanner (eds.), *Human Growth. Volume 2. Postnatal Growth, Neurobiology.* New York: Plenum Press, 1986, pp. 77–99.

58. Malina, R.M., and C. Bouchard. *Growth and Physical Activity.* Champaign, Ill.: Human Kinetics Publishers (in press).

59. Malina, R.M., and C. Bouchard. Subcutaneous fat distribution during growth. In C. Bouchard and F.E. Johnston (eds.), *Fat Distribution During Growth and Health Outcomes.* New York: Alan R. Liss (in press).

60. Marubini, E. Mathematical handling of long-term longitudinal data. In F. Falkner and J.M. Tanner (eds.), *Human Growth, Volume 1: Principles and Prenatal Growth.* New York: Plenum Press, 1978, pp. 209–225.

61. Marubini, E., L.F. Resele, and G. Barghini. A comparative fitting of the Gompertz and logistic functions to longitudinal height data during adolescence in girls. *Hum. Biol.* 43:237–252, 1971.

62. Meinel, K. *Bewegungslehre. Versuch einer Theorie der sportlichen Bewegung unter pädagogischen Aspekt.* Berlin: Volk und Wissen, 1971.

63. Merni, F., M. Balloni, S. Bargellini, and G. Menegatti. Differences in males and females in joint movement range during growth. In J. Borms, M. Hebbelinck, and A. Venerando (eds.), *The Female Athlete. A Socio-Psychological and Kinanthropometric Approach.* Basel: Karger, 1981, pp. 168–175.

64. Mirwald, R.L., and D.A. Bailey. *Maximal Aerobic Power.* London, Ontario: Sport Dynamics, 1986.

65. Mirwald, R.L., D.A. Bailey, N. Cameron, and R.L. Rasmussen. Longitudinal comparison of aerobic power in active and inactive boys ages 7 to 17 years. *Ann. Hum. Biol.* 8:405–414, 1981.

66. Möckelmann, H. *Leibeserziehung und jugendliche Entwicklung.* Schorndorf: Hofman, 1952.

67. Neuhaus, W. *Kinderpsychologie von Standpunkt der Entwicklung.* Flensburg: Flensburger Zeitungsverlag, 1948.

68. Ostyn, M., J. Simons, G. Beunen, R. Renson, and D. Van Gerven (eds.), *Somatic and Motor Development of Belgian Secondary Schoolboys.* Leuven: Leuven University Press, 1980.

69. Pařizkova, J. Growth and growth velocity of lean body mass and fat in adolescent boys. *Pediatr. Res.* 10:647–650, 1976.

70. Placheta, Z. Physical fitness development. In Z. Placheta (ed.), *Youth and Physical Activity.* Brno: J.E. Purkyne University, 1980, pp. 119–155.

71. Preece, M.A., and M.J. Baines. A new family of mathematical models describing the human growth curve. *Ann. Hum. Biol.* 5:1–24, 1978.

72. Preece, M.A., and I. Heinrich. Mathematical modelling of individual growth curves. *Br. Med. Bull.* 37:247–252, 1981.

73. Roche, A.F. Progress in the analysis of serial data during the century since Bowditch and future expectations. *Hum. Biol. 58:831–850, 1986.*

74. Roy, M.P. Evolution clinique de la puberté du garçon. *Compte Rendu de la XI Reunion des Equipes Chargees des Etudes sur la Croissance et le Developpement de l'Enfant Normal.* Paris: Centre International de l'Enfance, 1971, pp. 185–190.

75. Roy, M.P., M. Sempe, E. Orssaud, and G. Pedron. Evolution clinique de la puberté de la fille. *Arch. Franc. Pediatr.* 29:155–168, 1972.

76. Rutenfranz, F., K.L. Andersen, V. Seliger, J. Ilmarinen, F. Klimmer, H. Kylian, M. Rutenfranz, and M. Ruppel. Maximal aerobic power affected by maturation and body growth during childhood and adolescence. *Eur. J. Pediatr.* 139:106–112, 1982.

77. Schaie, K.W. A general model for the study of developmental problems. *Psychol. Bull.* 64:92–107, 1965.

78. Schnabel, G. Zur Bewegungskoordination in der Pubessenz. *Theor. Prax. Körperk.* 11–12:1070–1079, 1961.

79. Seashore, H.G. The development of a beam walking test and its use in measuring development of balance in children. *Res. Q.* 18:246–259, 1947.

80. Shields, C.E. Physical activity in the young. *Am Fam. Physician* 33:155–162, 1986.

81. Shuttleworth, F.K. Sexual maturation and the physical growth of girls aged six to nineteen. *Monogr. Soc. Res. Child Dev.* 2 (serial no. 12), 1937.

82. Šprynarova, S. Longitudinal study of the influence of different physical activity programs on functional capacity of the boys from 11 to 18 years. *Acta Paediatr. Belg.* 28 (suppl.):204–213, 1974.

83. Stolz, H.R., and L.M. Stolz. *Somatic Development of Adolescent Boys.* New York: Macmillan Co., 1951.

84. Tanner, J.M. Some notes on the reporting of growth data. *Hum. Biol.* 23:93–159, 1951.

85. Tanner, J.M. *Foetus into Man.* Cambridge, Mass.: Harvard University Press, 1978.

86. Tanner, J.M., P.C.R. Hughes, and R.H. Whitehouse. Radiographically determined widths of bone, muscle and fat in the upper arm and calf from age 3–18 years. *Ann. Hum. Biol.* 8:495–517, 1981.

87. Tanner, J.M., R.H. Whitehouse, E. Marubini, and L.F. Resele. The adolescent growth spurt of boys and girls of the Harpenden growth study. *Ann. Hum. Biol.* 3:109–126, 1976.

88. Tanner, J.M., R.H. Whitehouse, and M. Takaishi. Standards from birth to maturity for height, weight, height velocity and weight velocity. *Arch. Dis. Child.* 41:454–471, 613–635, 1966.

89. Taranger, J., and U. Hägg. The timing and duration of adolescent growth. *Acta Odontol. Scand.* 38:57–67, 1980.

90. Taranger, J., I. Engström, H. Lichtenstein, and I. Svennberg-Redegren. Somatic pubertal development. *Acta Paediatr. Scand.* 258(suppl.):121–135, 1976.

91. Thissen, D., R.D. Bock, H. Wainer, and A.F. Roche. Individual growth in stature: A comparison of four growth studies in the U.S.A. *Ann. Hum. Biol.* 3:529–542, 1976.

92. Ungerer, D. *Leistungs- und Belastungsfähigkeit im Kindes- und Jugendlater.* Schorndorf: Hofmann, 1967.

93. Vanden Eynde, B., J. Ghesquiere, D. Van Gerven, M. Vuylsteke-Wauters, and H. Vande Perre. Follow-up study of physical fitness of boys aged 10–14 years. In J. Ilmarinen and I. Valimaki (eds.), *Children and Sport.* Berlin: Springer-Verlag, 1984, pp. 111–118.

94. Van't Hof, M.A., M. Roede, and C. Kowalski. Estimation of growth velocities from individual longitudinal data. *Growth* 40:217–240, 1976.

95. Van't Hof, M.A., M. Roede, and C. Kowalski. A mixed longitudinal data analysis model. *Hum. Biol.* 49:165–179, 1977.

96. Van't Hof, M.A., J. Simons, and G. Beunen. Data quality evaluation and data processing. In M. Ostyn, J. Simons, G. Beunen, R. Renson, and D. Van Gerven (eds.), *Somatic and Motor Development of Belgian Secondary Schoolboys. Norms and Standards.* Leuven: Leuven University Press, 1980, pp. 45–48.

97. Wafelbakker, F. Adolescent growth spurt in relation to age and maturation: A longitudinal study. *Compte Rendu de la X Reunion des Equipes Chargees des Etudes sur la Croissance et le Developpement de l'Enfant Normal,* Tome II. Paris: Centre International de l'Enfance, 1970, pp. 33–38.

98. Wallon, H., E. Evart-Chmielinski, and R. Sauterey. Equilibre statique, equilibre en mouvement: Double lateralisation (entre 5 et 15 ans). *Enfance* 11: 1–29, 1958.

99. Welon, Z., and T. Bielicki. The adolescent growth spurt and the "critical body weight" hypothesis. *Mat. Prace Antropol.* 86:27–34, 1973.

100. Welon, Z., and T. Bielicki. The timing of adolescent growth spurts in eight body dimensions in boys and girls of the Wrocław Growth Study. *Stud. Phys. Anthropol.* 5:75–79, 1979.

101. Winter, R. Zur Entwicklung der Laufbewegungen bei Knaben und Mädchen in Schulalter. *Theor. Prax. Körperk.* 13:754–758, 1964.

102. Zacharias, L., and W.M. Rand. Adolescent growth in height and its relation to menarche in contemporary American girls. *Ann. Hum. Biol.* 10:209–222, 1983.

103. Zacharias, L., and W.M. Rand. Adolescent growth in weight and its relation to menarche in contemporary American girls. *Ann. Hum. Biol.* 13:369–386, 1986.

104. Zeller, W. *Konstitution und Entwicklung.* Göttingen: Verlaf fur Psychologie, 1964.

Index

541